THE
CHURCH CATALOGUE

OF this Catalogue not more than One Hundred and Fifty Copies have been printed on Holland hand-made paper, this being No............................

A CATALOGUE OF
BOOKS

CONSISTING OF
ENGLISH LITERATURE AND MISCELLANEA
INCLUDING MANY ORIGINAL EDITIONS OF

SHAKESPEARE

FORMING A PART OF
THE LIBRARY OF E. D. CHURCH

COMPILED AND ANNOTATED
BY
GEORGE WATSON COLE

VOLUME II
L-Z

Martino Publishing
Mansfield Centre, CT
2004

Martino Publishing
P.O. Box 373,
Mansfield Centre, CT 06250 USA

web-site: www.martinopublishing.com

ISBN 1-57898-475-0

© 2004 Martino Publishing

All rights reserved. No new contribution to this publication may
be reproduced, stored in a retrieval system, or transmitted, in any form or
by any means, electronic, mechanical, photocopying, recording, or otherwise,
without the prior permission of the Publisher.

Library of Congress Cataloging-in-Publication Data

Cole, George Watson, 1850-1939.
    A catalogue of books consisting of English literature and
miscellanea, including many original editions of Shakespeare:
forming a part of the library of E.D. Church / compiled and
annotated by George Watson Cole.
    p. cm.
Originally published: New York: Dodd, Mead & Co., 1909.
Contents: v. 1. A-K--v. 2 L-Z.
ISBN 1-57898-475-0 (cloth)
  1. Church, Elihu Dwight, 1835-1908--Library--Catalogs. 2. English
literature-First editions--Bibliography-Catalogs. 3. Shakespeare,
William, 1564-1616-Bibliography-Catalogs. 4. Private libraries-New
York (State)--New York--Catalogs. 5. Early printed books--
Bibliography--Catalogs. 6. English literature--Bibliography--
Catalogs. 7. Incunabula--Bibliography--Catalogs. 8. Rare books-
Bibliography--Catalogs. I. Church, Elihu Dwight, 1835-1908. II.
Title

Z997.C56C382004
011'.42-dc22   2003066537

Printed in the United States of America On 100% Acid-Free Paper

A CATALOGUE OF
BOOKS
CONSISTING OF
ENGLISH LITERATURE AND MISCELLANEA
INCLUDING MANY ORIGINAL EDITIONS OF
SHAKESPEARE
FORMING A PART OF
THE LIBRARY OF E. D. CHURCH

COMPILED AND ANNOTATED
BY
GEORGE WATSON COLE

VOLUME II
L–Z

NEW YORK
DODD, MEAD AND COMPANY
1909

THE UNIVERSITY PRESS, CAMBRIDGE, U.S.A.

ENGLISH LITERATURE
AND
MISCELLANEA

ENGLISH LITERATURE
AND
MISCELLANEA

LAMB, CHARLES (*b.* 1775, *d.* 1834). Bowles, Lamb, Coleridge, and others.

[SELECTED SONNETS FROM VARIOUS AUTHORS. Bristol, *privately printed*, 1796.] [417]

Small octavo.

COLLATION BY SIGNATURES: *A*, B, each 4 leaves; total 8 numbered leaves. Leaf B 2 has a signature-mark.

COLLATION BY PAGINATION: [editor's note, first page as reproduced; *See* No. 417], pp. [1]–2;—[28 numbered sonnets, 4 of them by Lamb], pp. 3–16.

CONDITION: Size of leaf, 6 13/16 × 4 7/16 inches. Bound with the Third Edition of Bowles's *Sonnets*, in the original boards, calf back. With inscription in ink on the recto of the front fly-leaf (which is torn): | *C. Lloyd Jr.* | ; and at the top of p. [1] of the pamphlet is written | *Charles Lloyd Jr* |. Sonnets III. and IV. (p. 4) contain corrections in Lloyd's handwriting.

REFERENCES.

Thomson, *Bibliography of the Writings of Charles and Mary Lamb* (1908), p. 5, No. IV.; South Kensington Museum, *Catalogue of the Dyce Collection*, 1 (1875): 111, No. 1298.

The excessively rare pamphlet of Coleridge's and Lamb's *Sonnets* here described was privately printed by Coleridge in 1796.

In a letter of his to Thomas Poole, dated November 7, 1796, which is printed in full in E. Hartley Coleridge's edition of his grandfather's *Letters*, 1 (1895): 176–178, he says:

"I amused myself the other day (having some *paper* at the printer's which I could employ no other way) in selecting twenty-eight sonnets, to bind up with Bowles's. I charge sixpence for them, and have sent you five to dispose of. I have only printed two hundred, as my paper held out to no more; and dispose of them privately, just enough to pay the printing. The essay which I have written at the beginning I like."

In a letter to John Thelwall, dated December 17, 1796, and also printed in the same volume (pp. 193–207), he says:

"I have sent you . . . a sheet of sonnets collected by me for the use of a few friends, who paid the printing."

No. 417   *Charles Lamb*   1796

In Coleridge's *Poetical and Dramatic Works*, 2 (1878): 377–379, it is stated: "This introduction [at p. 75 of Coleridge's Poems of 1797] originally appeared as the Preface to a privately-printed pamphlet of sixteen pages (1796), containing a selection of twenty-eight Sonnets from various Authors, made ' for the purpose of binding them up with the Sonnets of the Rev. W. L. Bowles.' . . . The selection . . . contains three Sonnets of Bowles, . . . and last, but not least, four of Charles Lamb, and four of Coleridge's own, which it will be worth while to particularize. . . .

"The copy in question of this singularly interesting pamphlet is bound up, according to Coleridge's intention, at the end of a copy of the fourth edition of Bowles's *Sonnets and other Poems* published at Bath in 1796. Thelwall, . . . to whose wife this copy was given, has written in the margins a number of sarcastic and disparaging remarks on poor Mr. Bowles's verses."

"This volume is now in the Dyce Collection at the South Kensington Museum."

Two of the sonnets by Lamb have a direct bearing upon his first love episode, the first beginning, "Was it some sweet device of faery land," which for the first time here appears in print, and the second beginning with the line, "When last I roved these winding wood-walks green." They refer to "a fair-hair'd maid" named "Anna" (Ann Simmons), who lived in a "little Cottage," with whom "in happier days" he had "held free converse," days, however, that "ne'er must come again."

This little collection of sonnets is chiefly remarkable as reflecting the diction and the graceful melancholy of Bowles, whose sonnets had in a singular degree influenced and inspired both Lamb and Coleridge. A full description of the pamphlet and of the changes which were made in subsequent issues of Lamb's and Coleridge's contributions to it, is given in the edition of Coleridge's *Letters* referred to above, footnote on p. 206, Vol. 1, where it is stated that "of this selection of sonnets, . . . the sole surviving copy is now in the Dyce Collection of the South Kensington Museum. On the fly-leaf, in Coleridge's handwriting, is a 'presentation note' to Mrs. Thelwall." And see also: Coleridge's *Poetical Works* (4 vols., 1877–1880), Vol. 2, pp. 377–379, also his *Poetical Works* (1893), pp. 542–544.

The copy here described bears Lloyd's autograph. Lloyd was living with Coleridge at the time it was printed. Two of Lloyd's sonnets in the pamphlet contain corrections in his handwriting, which were followed in the 1797 version of these Sonnets. It is bound with a copy of the third edition of Bowles's Sonnets (1794), which also bears Lloyd's autograph. The water-mark in the pamphlet is "1794." The introduction has been reprinted in full in Campbell's edition of Coleridge's *Poetical Works* (Macmillan, 1907), Appendix K, No. 4, pp. 542–544.

Charles Lamb, at the age of seven years, was admitted to Christ's Hospital (the Bluecoat School), where he remained seven years. He there attained considerable skill in his studies, especially in the reading of Latin, and also took an excellent stand in Greek. There too he formed a friendship with Coleridge, which was destined to continue until the last years of his life. Early in 1792 he was appointed to a clerkship in the India House and remained a member of its staff for the next thirty years. The

Charles Lloyd Jr. [signature]

I HAVE selected the following SONNETS from various Authors for the purpose of binding them up with the Sonnets of the Rev. W. L. BOWLES.

The composition of the Sonnet has been regulated by Boileau in his Art of Poetry, and since Boileau, by William Preston, in the elegant preface to his Amatory Poems: the rules, which they would establish, are founded on the practice of Petrarch. I have never yet been able to discover either sense, nature, or poetic fancy in Petrarch's poems; they appear to me all one cold glitter of heavy conceits and metaphysical abstractions. However, Petrarch, although not the inventor of the Sonnet, was the first who made it popular; and *his* countrymen have taken his poems as the model. Charlotte Smith and Bowles are they who first made the Sonnet popular among the present English: I am justified therefore by analogy in deducing its laws from *their* compositons.

The Sonnet then is a small poem, in which some lonely feeling is developed. It is limited to a *particular* number of lines, in order that the reader's mind having expected the close at the place in which he finds it, may rest satisfied; and that so the poem may acquire, as it were, a *Totality*,—in plainer phrase, may become a *Whole*. It is confined to fourteen lines, because as some particular number is necessary, and that particular number must be a small one, it may as well be fourteen as any other number. When no reason can be adduced against a thing, Custom is a sufficient reason for it. Perhaps, if the Sonnet were comprized in less than fourteen lines, it would become a serious Epigram; if it extended to more, it would encroach on the province of the Elegy. On this however we lay no stress. Poems, in which no lonely feeling is developed, are not Sonnets because the Author has chosen to write them in fourteen lines: they should rather be entitled Odes, or Songs, or Inscriptions. The greater part of Warton's Sonnets are severe and masterly likenesses of the style of the Greek επιγραμματα.

In a Sonnet then we require a developement of some lonely feeling, by whatever cause it may have been excited; but those Sonnets appear to me the most exquisite, in which moral Sentiments, Affections, or Feelings, are deduced from, and associated with, the scenery of Nature. Such compositions generate a habit of thought highly favourable to delicacy of character. They create a sweet and indissoluble union between the intellectual and the material world. Easily remembered from their briefness, and interesting alike to the eye and the affections, these are the poems which we can " lay up in our heart, and our foul," and repeat them " when we walk by the way, and when we lie down and when we rise up." Hence, the Sonnets of BOWLES derive their marked superiority over all other Sonnets; hence they domesticate with the heart, and become, as it were, a part of our identity.

A

No. 417. FIRST PAGE OF SELECTED SONNETS; BY BOWLES, LAMB, COLERIDGE, AND OTHERS; [1796].

Lamb family being poor were obliged to live upon his earnings and those of his sister Mary, who did needlework. Owing to overwork the latter became temporarily insane, and on September 22, 1796, took the life of her mother. Being found of unsound mind, she was placed in the custody of her brother, who continued to watch over her for the remainder of his life. Lamb himself was not entirely free from mental derangement, having spent six weeks during the winter of 1795/6 in an asylum at Hoxton, perhaps owing to his unsuccessful love episode with Ann Simmons.

Lamb's first appearance in print took place in the *Morning Chronicle* for December 29, 1794, with a sonnet, beginning "As when a child on some long winter's night." This and three other sonnets from his pen were included by Coleridge in his *Poems*, published in April, 1796, and were the first of Lamb's works to appear in any book. In July of the same year another sonnet, beginning "We were two pretty Babes, the youngest she," was printed in the *Monthly Magazine*. In October or early in November Coleridge privately printed a collection of twenty-eight sonnets (our present number). Among these were four by Lamb, three of which had already appeared in Coleridge's volume; the fourth begins 'When last I rov'd these winding wood-walks green." In 1796 appeared a handsome folio, Charles Lloyd's *Poems on the Death of Priscilla Farmer* (our next number), in which was included Lamb's poem in blank verse "The Grandam," probably written in 1792, when his grandmother died. In 1796 also appeared *Original Letters, &c. of Sir John Falstaff* (our No. 419), by Lamb's old schoolmate James White, and with possible hints and corrections by Lamb himself. In 1797 Coleridge issued the second edition of his *Poems*, in which he included eight sonnets by Lamb, who for the first time had the satisfaction of seeing his name on a title-page.

In the summer of 1797 Lamb visited Coleridge at Nether Stowey, and the next year a small volume of *Blank Verse* (our No. 422) by Lamb and Lloyd was published. The same year he issued *A Tale of Rosamund Gray and Old Blind Margaret* (our No. 420). Soon after this he began to add to his scanty income by writing for the newspapers. In 1802 he published *John Woodvil* (our No. 423), a blank verse play of the period of the Restoration. For some time he dreamed of dramatic successes, but these dreams were never to be realized, his last effort taking shape in the unsuccessful farce *Mr. H. or Beware a Bad Name* (our No. 433). In 1805 he was introduced to William Godwin, the publisher of children's books, for whom he agreed to write the *Tales from Shakespeare* (our No. 444), which was published in 1807; Lamb writing the tragedies and Mary the comedies. This was Lamb's first serious success, and brought him into prominence. Among other works prepared for Godwin were: *The Adventures of Ulysses* (our No. 427); *Prince Dorus* (our No. 428); *Beauty and the Beast* (our No. 431); and *Mrs. Leicester's School* (our No. 445), in which he was assisted by his sister Mary. A more important work by Lamb, *Specimens of English Dramatic Poetry*, appeared in 1808, which stamped him as a literary critic of the highest order.

In 1819 occurred an interesting incident in Lamb's life, when, on July 20, he proposed marriage to Fanny Kelly, an actress. The original letters (our No. 436) which passed between them on that occasion form one of the most interesting items of the present collection. A collection of 31 of Lamb's letters (our No. 437) to Edward Moxon, the publisher and the husband of Emma Isola, Lamb's adopted daughter, are also an important feature of the present collection.

All this time Lamb had been ripening for the production of those marvelous and unparalleled essays which stamp him as the foremost critic of his age. From 1820 to 1822 he wrote for the *London Magazine* the series of essays which were collected in book form in 1823 under the title *Elia* (our No. 438). He continued to contribute to the same periodical, with occasional papers to others, until 1833, when he published a second volume, *The Last Essays of Elia* (our No. 443), with the production of which his literary career may be said to have closed.

Numbering among his early friends, Coleridge, Southey, and Wordsworth, and among his later ones, Procter, Talfourd, Hood, Leigh Hunt, Hazlitt, and others, his life-long devotion to his unfortunate sister, his unfailing loyalty to his friends, and even his eccentricities and foibles, combined to make him one of the best known and best loved figures in the literature of his period.

LAMB, CHARLES. Lloyd, Charles. (*b.* 1775, *d.* 1839.)

POEMS ON THE DEATH OF PRISCILLA FARMER. BRISTOL, *N. Biggs*, 1796. [418]

Folio. First Edition.

COLLATION BY SIGNATURES: 14 numbered leaves, without signature-marks.

COLLATION BY PAGINATION: [title, as reproduced; *See* No. 418], p. [1];—[blank], p. [2];—[sonnet by Coleridge], p. 3;—[blank], p. [4];—| DEDICATORY LINES | TO THE | *AUTHOR'S BROTHER.*|, pp. 5–6;—[poems], pp. 7–24;—| *The following beautiful fragment was written by CHARLES LAMB,* | *of the India-House.*——*Its subject being the same with that of my* | *Poems, I was solicitous to have it printed with them: and I am* | *indebted to a Friend of the Author's for the permission.*| The Grandam. |, pp. 25–27; — | THE END. |, p. 27;—[blank], p. [28]. Page 23 is wrongly numbered 22.

CONDITION: Size of leaf, 15 x 10¾ inches. In the original marbled paper wrappers, uncut edges; in red crushed levant morocco portfolio, lettered on front cover:| POEMS | ON | THE DEATH | OF | PRISCILLA FARMER | BY | CHARLES LLOYD | AND | CHARLES LAMB. | BRISTOL 1796. |; green silk doublure, green silk covers; by Root & Son.

REFERENCES.

Thomson, *Bibliography* (1908), p. 6, No. v.; Livingston, *Bibliography* (1903), p. 11; Coleridge, *Poetical Works* (New Globe Poets; 1907), p. 583, *note* 99.

This copy has on the first fly-leaf the following autograph inscription, in the author's handwriting: | *Charles Lloyd* | *To his* | *affectionate Daughter* | *Agatha Lloyd June 11 1823* | .

The poems by Lloyd are preceded by an original sonnet by Coleridge, and are followed by Lamb's beautiful poem "The Grandam," written on the death of his grandmother, Mary Field. Coleridge's *Poems*, published in April, 1796, contains

POEMS

ON

The Death

OF

PRISCILLA FARMER,

BY HER GRANDSON

CHARLES LLOYD.

DEATH! THOU HAST VISITED THAT PLEASANT PLACE,
WHERE IN THIS HARD WORLD I HAVE HAPPIEST BEEN.

BOWLES.

BRISTOL:
PRINTED BY N. BIGGS,
And Sold by JAMES PHILLIPS, George-Yard, Lombard-Street, LONDON.

1796.

1796   *Charles Lloyd*   No. 418

four sonnets written by Charles Lamb from 1794 to 1796. "The Grandam" was probably written in 1792, the year of his grandmother's death, and if so is Lamb's earliest known literary production.

Coleridge's sonnet to Charles Lloyd was "first published in a magnificent folio pamphlet — '*Poems on the Death of Priscilla Farmer*, by her Grandson, Charles Lloyd. Bristol: Printed by N. Biggs, and sold by James Phillips, George Yard, Lombard Street, London. 1796.' It reappeared with the reprint of this set of Sonnets in the joint volume of 1797; again, in Lloyd's *Nugæ Canoræ*, 1819; and not afterwards printed until in *P. and D. W.* 1877–81, p. 217. The folio pamphlet (pp. 27) contained also Lamb's 'The Grandam'; and it is to this that Lamb is alluding in his letter to Coleridge of December 10, 1796 (misprinted '1797' in all the editions of his *Letters*): 'I cannot but smile to see my Granny so gayly deck'd forth.'"

[LAMB, CHARLES.]   [White, James.]   (*b.* 1775, *d.* 1820.)

ORIGINAL LETTERS, &c. OF SIR JOHN FALSTAFF. LONDON, *for the Author, by G. G. and J. Robinsons, etc.*, 1796.   [419]

Small duodecimo. First Edition.
COLLATION BY SIGNATURES: A, 12 leaves (the first blank and lacking); B to F, each 12 leaves; G, 2 leaves; total 74 numbered leaves.
COLLATION BY PAGINATION: [1 blank leaf], pp. [i.]–[ii.];—[title, as reproduced; See No. 419], p. [iii.];—[blank], p. [iv.];—| DEDICATYONE. | To Mafter Samuel Irelaunde. | [signed] | Thy fellow-labourer in the mynes of | antiquitie, and moste humble fer-|vante to commande, | ******. |, pp. [v.]–ix.;—[blank], p. [x.];—[preface], pp. [xi.]–xxiv.;—| ERRATUM. | . . . |, p. xxiv.;—[text, with heading] | ORIGINAL LETTERS.|, pp. [1]–123;—| FINIS. |, p. 123;—[blank], p. [124].

PLATE: Stipple engraving, with inscription: | *W. Leney Delin*! *et Sculp*! | I must dance, caper in the Air | like a Tun of Molafs'—only my | ascension will be heavier, in regard | I must rise without a crane, | Master Brook.—— | *Falstaff's Letters.* |; facing the title-page.
CONDITION: Size of leaf, 6 5/16 × 3¾ inches. Bound in calf, lettered on the back : | SHAKSPEAR | FALSTAFF'S | LETTERS. | LONDON | 1796 |.

REFERENCES.

Thomson, *Bibliography* (1908), p. 4, No. III.; Livingston, *Bibliography* (1903), pp. 16–20.

This work was originally issued in paper-covered boards, uncut edges, probably with a title-label.

James White, the author of the work, was a schoolmate of Lamb's, who may have assisted him in writing it. Lamb refers to the work in his correspondence, but makes no claim to taking any part in it. The strongest evidence that he did so is found in a letter by Southey to Moxon, written in February, 1836, more than a year after Lamb's death, in which, speaking of White, he says: "He and Lamb were joint authors of the '*Original Letters of Falstaff*.'"

Original Letters, &c.

OF

SIR JOHN FALSTAFF

AND

HIS FRIENDS;

NOW FIRST MADE PUBLIC BY A GENTLEMAN,
A DESCENDANT OF

DAME QUICKLY,

FROM

GENUINE MANUSCRIPTS

WHICH HAVE BEEN IN THE POSSESSION
OF THE

QUICKLY FAMILY

NEAR FOUR HUNDRED YEARS.

LONDON:
PRINTED FOR THE AUTHOR;
AND PUBLISHED BY
MESSRS. G. G. AND J. ROBINSONS, PATERNOSTER-ROW;
J. DEBRETT, PICCADILLY; AND MURRAY AND
HIGHLEY, NO. 32, FLEET-STREET.
1796.

No. 419. TITLE-PAGE OF WHITE'S ORIGINAL LETTERS, &C. OF SIR JOHN FALSTAFF; 1ST EDITION; 1796.

LAMB, CHARLES.

A TALE OF ROSAMUND GRAY. BIRMINGHAM, *Thomas Pearson*, 1798.
[420]

Foolscap octavo. First Edition.
COLLATION BY SIGNATURES: A to H, each 8 leaves; I, 4 leaves (the last blank and lacking); total 68 numbered leaves.

COLLATION BY PAGINATION: [title, as reproduced; *See* No. 420], p. [1];— [blank], p. [2];— | THIS TALE | IS | INSCRIBED IN FRIENDSHIP | TO |

1798   Charles Lamb   No. 420

A TALE

OF

ROSAMUND GRAY

AND

OLD BLIND MARGARET.

BY

CHARLES LAMB.

𝔅𝔦𝔯𝔪𝔦𝔫𝔤𝔥𝔞𝔪,
PRINTED BY THOMAS PEARSON.

1798.

No. 420. Title-page of Lamb's Tale of Rosamund Gray;
1st Edition; 1798.

MARMADUKE THOMPSON,| OF | *PEMBROKE HALL,*| CAMBRIDGE.|, p. [3];—[blank], p. [4];—[text, with heading]| A TALE | OF | ROSAMUND GRAY | AND | OLD BLIND MARGARET.|, pp. [5]-134;—| THE END.|, p. 134;—[1 blank leaf], [1 4].

CONDITION: Size of leaf, 6⅛ × 3¹³⁄₁₆ inches. Bound in old half calf; in red morocco solander case.

REFERENCES.

Thomson, *Bibliography* (1908), p. 11, No. IX.; Livingston, *Bibliography* (1903), pp. 35-40; Locker-Lampson, *Catalogue* (1886), p. 160.

On the recto of the first fly-leaf is written in ink: " *Joseph Cottle to Geo: E. Kiddell, Bristol, 1800.*" This book, Lamb's first work in imaginative literature, which for mere pathos far surpasses anything he wrote afterward, seems to have been published in the summer of 1798, as it is mentioned in the list of new publications in the *Monthly Magazine* for September, 1798. It was the first book of which he was the sole author, and his first printed prose work.

"Leigh Hunt, in 1819, sent a copy of the book to Shelley, then in Italy. In acknowledging it, Shelley wrote:

"'What a lovely thing is his "Rosamund Gray"! How much knowledge of the sweetest and deepest part of our nature in it! When I think of such a mind as Lamb's, when I see how unnoticed remain things of such exquisite and complete perfection, what should I hope for myself, if I had not higher objects in view than fame?'"

Charles Lloyd, who was comparatively wealthy, lived at Birmingham, where this work was printed. In this edition the title-page is an integral part of the first sheet. This title-page was almost immediately canceled and one with a London imprint (our next number) substituted for it. The book is rare with either imprint.

LAMB, CHARLES.

A TALE OF ROSAMUND GRAY. LONDON, *for Lee and Hurst*, 1798.

[421]

Foolscap octavo. Second Edition.

COLLATION BY SIGNATURES: A, 8 leaves (of leaf A only the stub remains, to which have been attached two leaves, the recto of the first bearing the title, the verso and the second leaf blank); B to H, each 8 leaves; I, 4 leaves (the last blank and genuine); total 69 leaves.

COLLATION BY PAGINATION: [title, as reproduced; *See* No. 421], p. [1];— [blank], p. [2];—[1 blank leaf];— | THIS TALE | IS | INSCRIBED IN FRIENDSHIP | TO | MARMADUKE THOMPSON, | OF | *PEMBROKE HALL,* | CAMBRIDGE. |, p. [3];—[blank], p. [4];—[text, with heading] | A TALE | OF | ROSAMUND GRAY | AND | OLD BLIND MARGARET. |, pp. [5]–134; — | THE END. |, p. 134;—[1 blank leaf], [1 4].

CONDITION: Size of leaf, 6⅝ × 4¼ inches. In the original blue blank paper wrappers, uncut edges; in brown morocco solander case.

REFERENCES.

Thomson, *Bibliography* (1908), p. 11, No. IX.; Livingston, *Bibliography* (1903), pp. 35–40; Lowndes, 3 (1869): 1300.

"The only copy seen in the original binding has the reprinted London title-page. It is in blue paper covers, edges untrimmed. The book was bound up with two blank fly-leaves at front and back. A piece of blue paper was then put around the back of the book and pasted down upon the outer of each of the two fly-leaves, front and back. Size of untrimmed leaf, 6⁹⁄₁₆ by 4⅛ inches. Rare in any shape, but especially so when uncut. Only two uncut copies are known, of which one only is in the original binding."— LIVINGSTON.

This is the same work as the Birmingham edition (our previous number), except that the title-page has been cut out and one with the London imprint substituted for it. The new title-page is printed on one of two leaves, the first evidently being intended

A TALE

OF

ROSAMUND GRAY

AND

Old Blind Margaret.

BY CHARLES LAMB.

LONDON,
PRINTED FOR LEE AND HURST,
NO. 32, PATER-NOSTER ROW.

1798.

No. 421. Title-page of Lamb's Tale of Rosamund Gray; 2d Edition; 1798.

as an additional fly-leaf, but in this copy it has been folded so as to follow instead of precede the title-page. It is printed upon the same kind of paper as that with the Birmingham imprint. The London imprint appears to have been an afterthought, and was doubtless inserted in copies designed for that market.

"The 'Monthly Review,' in a notice in its issue for August, 1800, about two years after publication, said in part: 'Mr. Lamb has here proved himself skilful in touching the nicest feelings of the heart and in affording great pleasure to the imagination.'"

No. 422   *Charles Lamb*   1798

BLANK VERSE,

BY

CHARLES LLOYD

AND

CHARLES LAMB.

LONDON:
PRINTED BY T. BENSLEY,
FOR JOHN AND ARTHUR ARCH, N.º 23, GRACE-CHURCH STREET.

1798.

No. 422.   Title-page of Lamb and Lloyd's Blank Verse; 1st Edition; 1798.

LAMB, CHARLES, *and* **LLOYD, CHARLES.**   (*b.* 1775, *d.* 1839.)

BLANK VERSE.   London, *by T. Bensley, for John and Arthur Arch,* 1798.

[422]

Foolscap octavo.   First Edition.

Collation by Signatures: [A] to F, each 8 leaves; total 48 numbered leaves.

Collation by Pagination: [title, as reproduced; *See* No. 422], p. [1]; — [blank], p. [2]; — [half-title] | BLANK VERSE, | by | *CHARLES LLOYD.* | [quotation] |, p. [3]; — [blank], p. [4]; — | to | ROBERT SOUTHEY. | [signed] | | C. LLOYD. | [dated] | London, | February 26, 1798. |, p. [5]; — [blank], p. [6]; — [text in numerous parts, the first with heading] | TO ******. |, pp. [7]–72; — [half-title] | BLANK VERSE, | by | *CHARLES LAMB.* |, p. [73]; — [blank], p. [74]; — [7 poems, the first with heading] | TO CHARLES LLOYD. |, pp. [75]–95; — [index], p. [96].

English Literature   [562]   Church Catalogue

CONDITION: Size of leaf, 6¹¹⁄₁₆ × 4¼ inches. Bound in the original boards, uncut edges; with paper title-label, lettered: | Lloyd | and | Lamb's | Blank | Verse. |.

REFERENCES.

Thomson, *Bibliography* (1908), p. 10, No. VIII.; Livingston, *Bibliography* (1903), pp. 31–34.

This volume contains twenty pieces, of which thirteen are by Lloyd and seven by Lamb. Most of the poems have the date of writing affixed. The volume must have been published early in the spring of 1798.

LAMB, CHARLES.

JOHN WOODVIL, A TRAGEDY. *Robinson*, 1802. LONDON, *by T. Plummer, for G. and J.*
[423]

Foolscap octavo. First Edition.

COLLATION BY SIGNATURES: [A], 2 leaves; B to I, each 8 leaves; total 66 leaves.

COLLATION BY PAGINATION: [title, as reproduced; *See* No. 423], recto of [A];—[blank], verso of [A] to recto of [A 2];—[list of characters, with heading] | JOHN WOODVIL, | *A TRAGEDY.* |, verso of [A 2];—[text], pp. [1]–104;— | END OF JOHN WOODVIL, A TRAGEDY. | [conventional tail-piece] |, p. 104;— | *BALAD.* | FROM THE GERMAN. |, p. 105; — | HELEN. |, pp. 106–107;—[blank], p. [108];—[half-title] | *CURIOUS FRAGMENTS,* | ETC. |, p. [109];— [blank], p. [110];—[text, with heading] | CURIOUS FRAGMENTS | *Extracted from a common-place book, which | belonged to Robert Burton, the famous Author | of The Anatomy of Melancholy.* |, pp. 111–128;— | FINIS. |', p. 128.

CONDITION: Size of leaf, 6½ × 4¹⁄₁₆ inches. Bound in olive green crushed levant morocco, gilt top, other edges uncut; by Bedford.

REFERENCES.

Thomson, *Bibliography* (1908), p. 18, No. xv.; Livingston, *Bibliography* (1903), pp. 47–52.

A presentation copy from Lamb to Edward Moxon.

This work was originally issued in paper-covered boards, uncut edges, apparently without a title-label.

It is Lamb's first play, and was written during the early part of 1799, as is shown by frequent references to it in his letters for that year. He first intended to call it "Pride's Cure," and several copies were circulated in manuscript, in 1799 to 1800, it being submitted to Coleridge, Southey, Wordsworth, and Manning. Two copies were sent to John Kemble, manager of Drury Lane Theatre, who declined it, and it was never acted. The play ends on p. 104. The rest of the volume is filled with selections, among them a little poem, "Helen," by Mary Lamb, which fills pp. 106–107, and is apparently her first appearance in print. The "Curious Fragments," though purporting to be from a commonplace book which belonged to Robert Burton, the famous author of the *Anatomy of Melancholy*, are really by Lamb himself, the idea having been suggested by the Ireland Shakespeare forgeries.

No. 423   *Charles Lamb*   1802

JOHN WOODVIL

A TRAGEDY.

BY

C. LAMB.

TO WHICH ARE ADDED,

FRAGMENTS OF BURTON,

THE AUTHOR OF

THE ANATOMY OF MELANCHOLY.

London:

PRINTED BY T. PLUMMER, SEETHING-LANE;
FOR G. AND J. ROBINSON, PATERNOSTER-ROW.

1802.

No. 423.   TITLE-PAGE OF LAMB'S JOHN WOODVIL;
1ST EDITION; 1802.

[LAMB, CHARLES.]

THE KING AND QUEEN OF HEARTS. LONDON, *for Thos. Hodgkins*, 1805.   [424]

Small quarto. First Edition.
COLLATION BY SIGNATURES: 4 sheets of 4 leaves each, without signature-marks; total 16 unnumbered leaves.

COLLATION BY PAGINATION: [blank], p. [1]; — [title, as reproduced; *See* No. 424 *a*], p. [2]; — [text, without heading, the first and third leaves of each sheet

No. 424 a. Title-page of Lamb's King and Queen of Hearts; 1st Edition; 1805.

printed on the versos only, and the second and fourth on the rectos only], pp. [3]–[32].

ILLUSTRATIONS : 15 copperplate engravings (including the vignette on the title-page), one at the head of each page of text, except p. [3].

CONDITION : Size of leaf, 5 9/16 × 3 7/8 inches. In the original pink paper wrappers, the front wrapper with title as reproduced (*See* No. 424 *b*); the back with the following advertisement : | AT | *HODGKINS'S* | Juvenile Library, | HANWAY-STREET, | (OPPOSITE SOHO-SQUARE) | OXFORD-STREET, | *ARE JUST PUBLISHED* | A VARIETY OF | INTERESTING LITTLE BOOKS, | Adorned with | BEAUTIFUL COPPER PLATES | FOR THE USE OF CHILDREN, | ALL OF WHICH MAY BE HAD OF EVERY BOOKSELLER. | ; enclosed in the same type-ornament border as the front wrapper ; in red

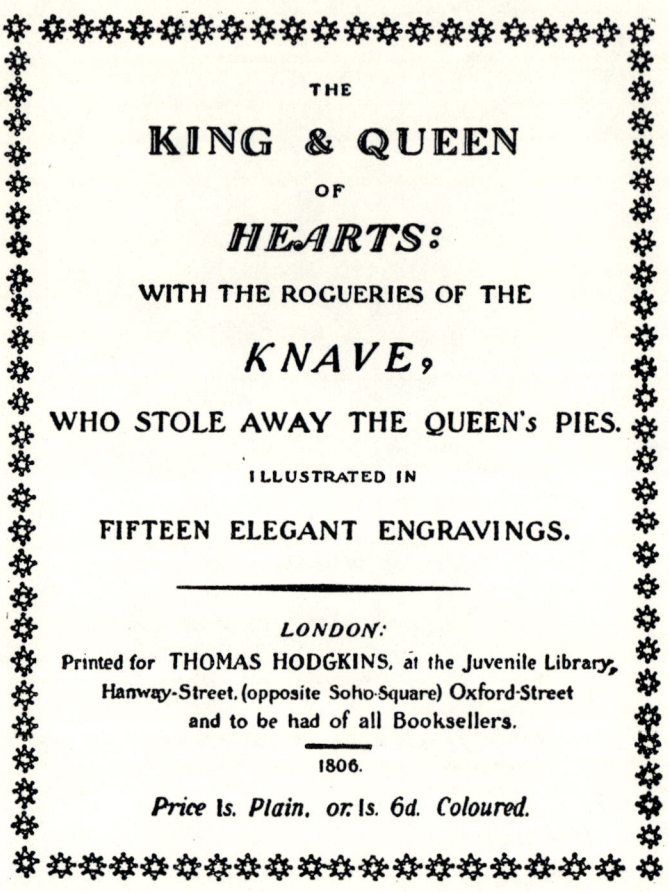

No. 424 *b*.   Title on wrapper of Lamb's King and Queen of Hearts; 1st Edition; 1806.

straight-grained morocco solander case. A portion of the inner title and vignette is lacking.

References.

Thomson, *Bibliography* (1908), p. 22, No. xviii.; Livingston, *Bibliography* *of the First Editions in Book Form of the Writings of Charles and Mary Lamb* (1903), pp. 53–59; Livingston, *Some Notes on Three of Lamb's Juveniles,* in *The Bibliographer,* 1 (1902): 215–220; *Book-Prices Current,* 16 (1902): 514, No. 5178.

This work was issued in pink paper, now faded to a dull light brown. The sixteen leaves were first slipped into a blank sheet, the fly-leaves. They were then stabbed from side to side and stitched; the printed pink paper wrapper was then put round the whole and pasted down on the two blank leaves. It was issued, apparently, with plain and colored plates, "though the only copy seen has the plates uncolored."

Of this work four editions are known, all having the title-page dated 1805, but with differently dated wrappers, viz.: 1806, 1808, 1809, and 1818. The copy here described is the only one known which has the earliest date. Of the 1809 edition only a single copy is known, that in the library of Mr. F. R. Halsey, New York. This has not the blank fly-leaves, but has the wrapper pasted to the blank pages of the first and last leaves. Though having the name of Thomas Hodgkins as publisher, it was probably issued by William Godwin, and must have been one of his first publications.

That Lamb is the author of this adaptation of the old rhyme of "The King and Queen of Hearts" is proved by the holograph letter by Charles Lamb to Wordsworth, dated February 1, 1806. Lamb was at that time sending a parcel of books to Wordsworth, in which was a copy of his new book. He acknowledges the authorship of the work in the following terms: ". . . *a Paraphrase on the King & Queen of Hearts, of which I being the author beg Mr. Johnny Wordsworth's acceptance & opinion. Liberal Criticism, as G. Dyer declares, I am always ready to attend to! — And that's all, I believe.*" The original of this long letter, which has been reprinted by Lucas (6 : 332–335), is written upon both sides of two foolscap leaves, and addressed, | Mr. Wordsworth | Grasmere | near Kendal | Westmoreland |, accompanies the book here described. Owing to the indistinctness of the original, the title-page of this work (No. 424 *b*) is reproduced from a drawing.

LAMB, CHARLES. Jolly, Jonathan, *pseudonym*.

THE CARE-KILLER. LONDON, [1807]. [425]

Small duodecimo. First Edition.

COLLATION BY SIGNATURES: [A], 4 leaves; B to E, each 6 leaves; total 28 leaves.

COLLATION BY PAGINATION: [blank], recto of [A];—[engraving, with inscription] | MARGATE FLY. | [at top and] | BOW. WOW. WOW. | [at bottom], verso of [A];—[title, as reproduced; *See* No. 425], p. [i.];—[imprint], p. [ii.];—[preface, dated] | *January* 28, 1807. |, pp. [iii.]– iv.;—[text, with heading] | THE CARE-KILLER. |, pp. [5]–54.

CONDITION: Size of leaf, 5⁷⁄₁₀ x 3⁵⁄₁₀ inches. Bound in green cloth, sprinkled edges; in red straight-grained morocco solander case. Leaves stabbed throughout.

REFERENCES.

Thomson, *Bibliography* (1908), p. 28, No. XXI.; Livingston, *Bibliography* (1903), pp. 73–74, 126.

This work is of interest because of the first appearance in print, on pp. 9–10, of Charles Lamb's *Prologue to Mr. H———*, a farce written by him and performed one night only (December 10, 1806) at Drury Lane Theatre, and then withdrawn.

The text of Lamb's play, but without the prologue, was first published in Phila-

No. 425   *Charles Lamb*   1807

THE

CARE-KILLER;

OR,

A HAPPY KNACK

OF

SPENDING AN EVENING

Without Company;

BEING A VALUABLE COLLECTION OF

PLEASING TALES,

Whimsical Anecdotes, Original Witticisms,

𝔅rilliant 𝔉lashes,

AND

GOOD THINGS.

Collected, Selected, and Nothing of Importance Neglected

By JONATHAN JOLLY, Esq.

Fellow of the Royal Society of Attic Wits.

———

LONDON.

Sold by J. COXHEAD, 420, Strand; J. GOODWIN, 14,
Brook-Street, Holborn; T. KAYGILL, 32,
Windmill-Street, Tottenham-Court-Road;
and T. BROOM, 154, Drury-Lane
opposite Long-Acre

Price Sixpence.

NO. 425.   TITLE-PAGE OF JOLLY'S CARE-KILLER; 1ST EDITION; [1807].

delphia in 1813 (our No. 433), and again in 1825. The prologue and the play were printed together for the first time in Vol. 2 of the collected edition of Lamb's *Works* in 1818 (our No. 435).

     In a letter to Thomas Manning dated December 5, 1806, Lamb writes: "The title is *Mr. H.*, no more. How simple, how taking! A great H. sprawling over the play-bill and attracting eyes at every corner. The story is a coxcomb appearing at Bath, vastly rich — all the ladies dying for him — all bursting to know who he is; but he goes by no other name than Mr. H. . . . When his true name comes out, 'Hogsflesh,' all the women shun him, avoid him, and not one can be found to change their name for him."

1807 — Henry Siddons — No. 426

TIME'S A TELL-TALE:

A COMEDY,

IN FIVE ACTS,

AS PERFORMED AT THE

THEATRE-ROYAL, DRURY-LANE.

Ὣ δὲ μεγαλήτορα θυμὸν,
Ἴσχων ἐν στήθεσσι· φιλοφροσύνη γὰρ ἀμείνων.   HOM. IL.

By HENRY SIDDONS.

LONDON:
PRINTED FOR LONGMAN, HURST, REES, AND ORME,
PATERNOSTER-ROW.

1807.

No. 426. Title-page of Siddons' Time's a Tell-Tale; 1st Edition; 1807.

LAMB, CHARLES. Siddons, Henry. (*b.* 1774, *d.* 1815.)

TIME'S A TELL-TALE. LONDON, *for Longman, Hurst, etc.*, 1807. [426]

Octavo. First Edition.
COLLATION BY SIGNATURES: [A], 4 leaves; B to E, each 8 leaves; F, 4 leaves; total 40 leaves.
COLLATION BY PAGINATION: [half-title], p. [i.];—[imprint], p. [ii.];—[title, as reproduced; *See* No. 426], p. [iii.];—[blank], p. [iv.];—|TO THE READER.| [signed]| *H. SIDDONS.*|, pp. [v.]-vi.; —[prologue], p. [vii.];—|DRAMATIS PERSONÆ.|, p. [viii.];—[text], pp. [1]-67;—[blank], p. [68];—|EPILOGUE

TO TIME'S A TELL-TALE.| *Written by* C. LAMB, Esq.|, pp. [69]-[70];—[publishers' advertisements], pp. [71]-[72].
CONDITION: Size of leaf, 8 13/16 × 5 3/4 inches. In the original blank blue paper wrappers, uncut edges.

REFERENCES.

Thomson, *Bibliography* (1908), p. 29, No. XXII.; Livingston, *Bibliography* (1903), pp. 71-72.

On the half-title appears, in Lamb's handwriting, the following inscription: | M^{rs} E Wilson | *from her grateful* | *Friend* | *the Authour* | .

The epilogue to this play, written by Charles Lamb, does not appear to have been reprinted during his lifetime.

Henry Siddons, the author of the play, was the son of Mrs. Sarah Siddons, England's greatest tragic actress, who inspired Lamb to write his first sonnet. Her son, though himself an actor, never acquired the fame of his mother or of his wife, Harriet Siddons.

LAMB, CHARLES.

THE ADVENTURES OF ULYSSES. LONDON, *by T. Davison, for the Juvenile Library*, 1808. [427]

Duodecimo. First Edition.
COLLATION BY SIGNATURES: 1 leaf, without signature-mark; [A], 2 leaves; B to I, each 12 leaves; K, 6 leaves; total 105 numbered leaves.
COLLATION BY PAGINATION: [title, as reproduced; *See* No. 427], p. [i.];—[blank], p. [ii.];—[preface and contents], pp. [iii.]-vi.;—[text, with heading]|THE | ADVENTURES OF ULYSSES|, pp. [1]-203;—| THE END. |[publisher's advertisements], pp. 203-[204].
PLATES: 2 plates, as follows:
[1]| FRONTISPIECE. |[vignette, inscribed]| ULYSSES *obliges* CIRCE *to restore*| *his Companions to their Shapes*| *Printed by H. Corbould.* p. 34. *Engraved by C. Heath.*|

Publifhed at Skinner Street June 6 1808. |; facing the engraved title-page.
[2] Engraved title, with imprint :| LONDON | *Published at the Juvenile Library,*| *41 Skinner Street.*| .
CONDITION: Size of leaf, 7 7/16 × 4 5/16 inches. Bound in green crushed levant morocco, gilt top, other edges uncut; by Rivière.

REFERENCES.

Thomson, *Bibliography* (1908), p. 31, No. XXIV.; Hoe, *Catalogue*, 2 (1905): 141; Livingston, *Bibliography* (1903), pp. 79-83; South Kensington Museum, *Catalogue of the Dyce Collection*, 2 (1875): 6, No. 5622; Lowndes, 3 (1869): 1300.

THE

ADVENTURES

OF

ULYSSES.

BY CHARLES LAMB.

LONDON:
Printed by T. Davison, Whitefriars,
FOR THE JUVENILE LIBRARY, NO. 41, SKINNER-
STREET, SNOW-HILL.

1808.

NO. 427.   TITLE-PAGE OF LAMB'S ADVENTURES OF ULYSSES;
1ST EDITION; 1808.

"Issued in paper-covered boards, edges untrimmed, with label, 'Adventures of Ulysses.' . . . Perhaps also issued bound in sheep, as uncut copies are rarely met with."

The success of the *Tales from Shakespear* (our No. 444), which appeared the year before, induced Lamb to prepare this volume, which was intended to be an introduction to the reading of *Telemachus*, and was prepared from Chapman's translation of the *Odyssey*, of which he was very fond. The manuscript was submitted to Godwin, who may have suggested its preparation. He criticised it mildly, and suggested that some passages be modified. Lamb did not take kindly to the criticism. He made one change, but as to the others wrote: "I only say that I will not consent to alter such passages, which I know to be some of the best in the book. . . . As to a friend I say, Don't plague yourself and me with nonsensical objections. I assure you I will not alter one more word."

PRINCE DORUS:

OR,

FLATTERY PUT OUT OF COUNTENANCE.

A POETICAL VERSION OF AN ANCIENT TALE.

ILLUSTRATED WITH A SERIES OF ELEGANT ENGRAVINGS.

―――

LONDON:
PRINTED FOR M. J. GODWIN,
AT THE JUVENILE LIBRARY, NO. 41, SKINNER STREET;
AND TO BE HAD OF ALL BOOKSELLERS AND TOYMEN IN THE
UNITED KINGDOM.

1811.

No. 428. Title-page of Lamb's Prince Dorus; 1st Edition, 1st (?) Issue; 1811.

―――

[LAMB, CHARLES.]

PRINCE DORUS. London, *for M. J. Godwin*, 1811. [428]

Sixteenmo. First Edition, First (?) Issue.

COLLATION BY SIGNATURES: B, 16 numbered leaves.

COLLATION BY PAGINATION: [title, as reproduced; *See* No. 428], p. [1];—[imprint], p. [2];—[text, with heading] |

PRINCE DORUS. |, pp. [3]–31;—| THE END. | [imprint] |, p. 31;—[blank], p. [32].

PLATES: 9 colored plates, as follows:
[1] | *The Enchanted Cat.* |; facing p. [3].
[2] | *Minon Asleep.* |; facing p. 6.

[3] | *The Transformation.*|; facing p. 7.
[4] | *Prince Dorus and his Maids.*|; facing p. 8.
[5] | *Claribel Carried off.*|; facing p. 19.
[6] | *Visit to the Beneficent Fairy.* | ; facing p. 21.
[7] | *Prince Dorus Offended.*|; facing p. 23.
[8] | *Truth brought Home.* | ; facing p. 29.
[9] | *Self-Knowledge obtains its Reward.*|; facing p. 30.

CONDITION: Size of leaf, 4$\frac{15}{16}$ × 4$\frac{1}{16}$ inches. Bound in brown crushed levant morocco, gilt top; by Rivière; in red straight-grained morocco solander case. With the original blue paper wrappers bound in, the front wrapper with a cut of Prince Dorus and the fairy (as reproduced by Livingston in the works cited below), the back wrapper blank.

REFERENCES.

Thomson, *Bibliography* (1908), p. 36, No. XXVII.; Livingston, *Bibliography* (1903), pp. 106–111; Livingston, *Some Notes on Three of Lamb's Juveniles*, in *The Bibliographer*, 1 (1902) : 219–226.

Of the two issues of *Prince Dorus* it is impossible to say with certainty which is the earlier.

"Issued with at least two varieties of paper covers. Copies of what seem to be the earlier issue are bound in blue-gray paper covers, with a cut of Prince Dorus and the old fairy . . . on the first page, the fourth cover-page being blank. The other form has a cover of yellow paper, the first page printed from types somewhat similar to the title-page, but enclosed in a key border. The fourth cover-page has the cut of Prince Dorus as used on the first page of the other variety. Size of trimmed copies, about 5 by 4¼ inches. Issued with plates plain and colored. The first edition is excessively rare in any shape." — LIVINGSTON.

There is no direct proof that this little book is by Lamb. That it was written by him is shown by an entry in the diary of Henry Crabb Robinson, dated May 15, 1811, in which he states that during a very pleasant call on the Lambs, Charles "read his version of the story of Prince Dorus, the Long-Nosed King." The plates, nine in number, are said to have been designed by Miss Flaxman, a sister of the sculptor.

[LAMB, CHARLES.]

PRINCE DORUS. LONDON, *for M. J. Godwin*, 1811. [429]

Sixteenmo. First Edition, Second (?) Issue.

COLLATION BY SIGNATURES: B, 16 numbered leaves.

COLLATION BY PAGINATION: Identically the same as in No. 428.

PLATES: Identically the same as in No. 428, except that they are not colored, and they face the title-page and pp. 6, 8, 10, 19, 21, 23, 30, and 31.

CONDITION: Size of leaf, 5 × 4¼ inches. In the original yellow stiff paper wrappers, the front wrapper with title as reproduced (*See* No. 429); the back wrapper with a cut of Prince Dorus and the fairy, the same as in No. 428; in a red morocco slip case.

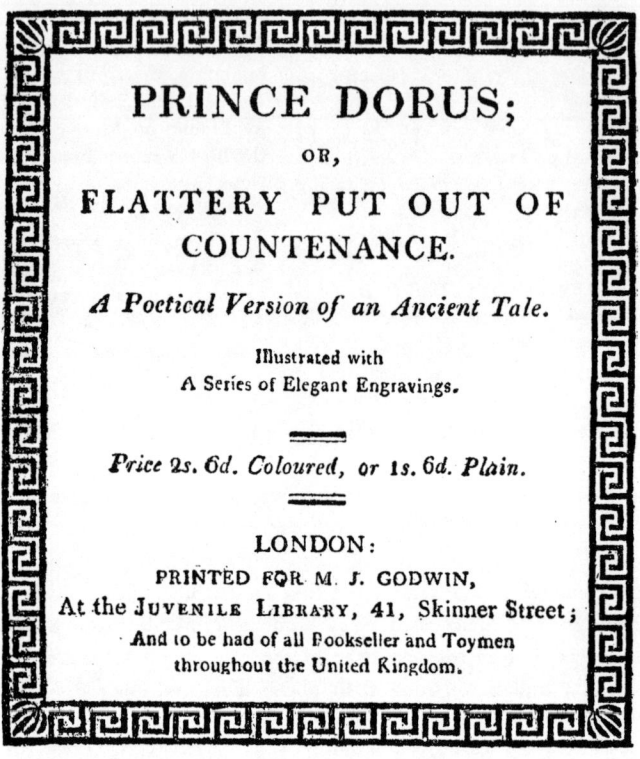

No. 429. Title on wrapper of Lamb's Prince Dorus; 1st Edition, 2d (?) Issue; 1811.

[LAMB, CHARLES.]

PRINCE DORUS. London, *for M. J. Godwin*, 1818.   [430]

Sixteenmo. Second Edition.
COLLATION BY SIGNATURES: B, 16 numbered leaves.
COLLATION BY PAGINATION: [title, as reproduced; *See* No. 430], p. [1]; — [imprint], p. [2]; — [text, with heading] | PRINCE DORUS. |, pp. [3]-31; — | THE END. | [imprint] |, p. 31; — [blank], p. [32].
PLATES: 9 colored plates, identically the same as in No. 428, but facing pp. 5, 6, 7, 10, 19, 21, 23, 29, and the title-page.
CONDITION: Size of leaf, 5 × 4⁵⁄₁₀ inches. In the original stiff paper wrappers, the front wrapper with title: | PRINCE DORUS; | OR, | FLATTERY PUT OUT OF | COUNTENANCE. | *A Poetical Version of an Ancient Tale.* | ILLUSTRATED WITH | A SERIES OF ELEGANT ENGRAVINGS. | *Price* 1s. 6d. *Coloured, or* 1s. *Plain.* | LONDON: |

PRINTED FOR M. J. GODWIN, | At the JUVE-
NILE LIBRARY, 41, Skinner-Street; | And
to be had of all Booksellers and Toymen |
throughout the United Kingdom. | ; the
whole enclosed by a Grecian fret or key
border; the back wrapper with publishers'
advertisements, with heading : | *Picture Books
for the Amusement of Children.* | 1*s.* plain, or
1*s.* 6*d.* coloured. |, in border same as the
front wrapper; in red straight-grained morocco solander case.

REFERENCES.

Thomson, *Bibliography* (1908), p.
36, No. XXVII.; Livingston, *Bibliography*
(1903), pp. 106–111.

PRINCE DORUS:

OR,

FLATTERY PUT OUT OF COUNTENANCE.

A POETICAL VERSION OF AN ANCIENT TALE.

ILLUSTRATED WITH A SERIES OF ELEGANT ENGRAVINGS.

LONDON:

PRINTED FOR M. J. GODWIN,
At the Juvenile Library, No. 41, Skinner-Street;
AND TO BE HAD OF ALL BOOKSELLERS AND TOYMEN IN THE
UNITED KINGDOM.

1818.

NO. 430.   TITLE-PAGE OF LAMB'S *PRINCE DORUS*; 2D EDITION; 1818.

Issued in light yellow-brown paper wrappers.

This edition is a very close reprint of that of 1811, but the type was reset, as is shown by the following differences, those of the edition here described being in parentheses: p. [3], heading, "PRINCE DORUS," the letters being almost three sixteenths of an inch in height (one eighth of an inch in height); p. 9, second line from the bottom ends, "gone," ("gone"); p. 13, second line from the bottom, "To keep th' unwelcome" ("To keep the unwelcome"); p. 26, second line ends "breeding;" ("breeding,"); p. 28, second line ends "nose;" ("Nose;").

For other juvenile books written by Charles Lamb, assisted in some cases by his sister, see *The King and Queen of Hearts, Tales from Shakespear, The Adventures of Ulysses, Mrs. Leicester's School, Poetry for Children*, and *Beauty and the Beast.*

No. 431   *Charles Lamb*   1813

[LAMB, CHARLES.]

BEAUTY AND THE BEAST.   London, *for M. J. Godwin*, [1813].
[431]

Sixteenmo. The "Surprise" Edition.
COLLATION BY SIGNATURES: [A], 1 leaf; B, 16 leaves; total 17 leaves. Leaf B 6 has a signature-mark.
COLLATION BY PAGINATION: [title, as reproduced; *See* No. 431], recto of [A];—[blank], verso of [A];—[text, with heading]|BEAUTY AND THE BEAST.|, pp. [1]-32;—| THE END. |[imprint]|, p. 32.
PLATES: 8 plates, as follows:
[1] | *Beauty in her Prosperous State.* |; facing p. [1].
[2] | *Beauty in a State of Adversity.* |; facing p. 2.
[3] | *The Rose Gather'd* |; facing p. 11.
[4] | *Beauty in the Enchanted Palace.* |; facing p. 16.
[5] | *Beauty Visits her Library.* |; facing p. 19.
[6] | *Beauty entertained with Invisible Music.* |; facing p. 21.
[7] | *The Absence of Beauty Lamented.* |; facing p. 28.
[8] | *The Enchantment Diſsolved.* |; facing p. 29.

Also a folding sheet of engraved music, 2 pages, with title | *Beauty's Song.* |; the first stanza on the verso of the first sheet, the second stanza on the recto of the second sheet; between p. 2 and plate [2].
CONDITION: Size of leaf, 5½⁄₁₀ × 4¼ inches. Bound in the original boards, with black leather back; with title on the front cover similar to the title-page, but with the date | 1813. | in the imprint; enclosed by a type-ornament rosette border. The back cover has a woodcut with inscription, | "GO, BE A BEAST! | HOMER. |. The folding sheet of music is backed with paper. In a red straight-grained morocco solander case.

REFERENCES.

Thomson, *Bibliography of the Writings of Charles and Mary Lamb* (1908), p. 38, No. XXVIII.; Livingston, *Bibliography of the First Editions in Book Form of the Writings of Charles and Mary Lamb* (1903), pp. 112–122 (also xi.–xiii.); Livingston, *Some Notes on Three of Lamb's Juveniles*, in *The Bibliographer*, 1 (1902): 226–230.

This volume was issued in stiff boards lettered along the back, with the plates plain and colored. It is not positively known that Lamb is the author of this work. It is known, however, that Godwin, the publisher, early in 1811 was seeking to have Wordsworth versify the old story of *Beauty and the Beast*. On Wordsworth's refusal to undertake it, as beneath his talents, it is probable that Godwin applied to Lamb, with whom he was on the best of terms. The fact that this work was published in uniform style with *Prince Dorus*, which we know to be by Lamb, lends plausibility to this theory.

Several editions of *Beauty and the Beast* were printed within a few years, the type being set at least twice and published in three varieties of covers, all similar in make-up and all apparently original. There are differences in the set-up of the two editions, but nothing which indicates the priority of either. They may be called the "Surprise" and "Surprize" editions, and may be distinguished by the following differences:

Page	7, line	11,	surprise,	surprize,
"	11, "	9,	pull'd—	pull'd—
"	12, "	7,	lord,	Lord,
"	17, "	4,	journey'd	journied
"	18, "	2,	lay,—	lay.—
"	18, "	11,	Father's	father's
"	18, "	11,	Heaven!	heaven!
"	20, "	4,	Sire."	sire."
"	23, "	11,	pass'd	past
"	23, "	12,	marked	mark'd
"	25, "	9,	agree,	agree

Mr. Livingston, in his excellent bibliography of Charles and Mary Lamb, gives three facsimile pages and notes further points of difference, to which the reader is referred.

A later edition, dated 1825, has "Second Edition" on the title-page.

Beauty
AND
THE BEAST:
OR,
A ROUGH OUTSIDE WITH A GENTLE HEART.

A Poetical Version of an Ancient Tale.

ILLUSTRATED WITH

A SERIES OF ENGRAVINGS,

And Beauty's Song at her Spinning Wheel,

Set to Music by Mr. WHITAKER.

LONDON:
PRINTED FOR M. J. GODWIN,
AT THE JUVENILE LIBRARY, 41, SKINNER STREET;
And to be had of all Booksellers and Toymen throughout the United Kingdom.

Price 5s. 6d. coloured; or 3s. 6d. plain.

NO. 431. TITLE-PAGE OF LAMB'S BEAUTY AND THE BEAST; THE "SURPRISE" EDITION; [1813].

BEAUTY
AND
THE BEAST:
OR
A ROUGH OUTSIDE WITH GENTLE HEART

A Poetical Version of an Ancient Tale

ILLUSTRATED WITH A
SERIES OF ELEGANT ENGRAVINGS

And Beauty's Song at Her Spinning Wheel,
Set to Music by Mr Whitaker

LONDON:
PRINTED FOR M. J. GODWIN,
AT THE JUVENILE LIBRARY, 41, SKINNER STREET;
And to be had of all Booksellers and Toymen
throughout the United Kingdom.

Price 5s. 6d coloured: or 3s. 6d plain.

No. 432 a. Title-page of Lamb's Beauty and the Beast; the "Surprize" Edition; [1813].

[LAMB, CHARLES.]

BEAUTY AND THE BEAST. LONDON, *for M. J. Godwin,* [1813]. [432]

Sixteenmo. The "Surprize" Edition.
COLLATION BY SIGNATURES: [A], 1 leaf; B, 16 leaves; total 17 leaves. Leaf B 6 has no signature-mark.
COLLATION BY PAGINATION: [title, as reproduced; *See* No. 432 *a*], recto of [A];—[blank], verso of [A];—[text, with heading] | BEAUTY AND THE BEAST. |, pp. [1]–32;—| THE END. | [imprint] |, p. 32.
PLATES: Identically the same as in No. 431, except that they are colored, and No. [1] faces p. 5; No. [2] faces p. 4.
Also a folding sheet of music, printed on both recto and verso; between plates [1] and [2].
CONDITION: Size of leaf, 5 1/10 × 4 1/4 inches. Bound in the original boards, with title on the front cover similar to the title-page, but enclosed by a Greek fret border, as reproduced (*See* No. 432 *b*); in a red straight-grained morocco solander case.

1813   *Charles Lamb*   No. 432

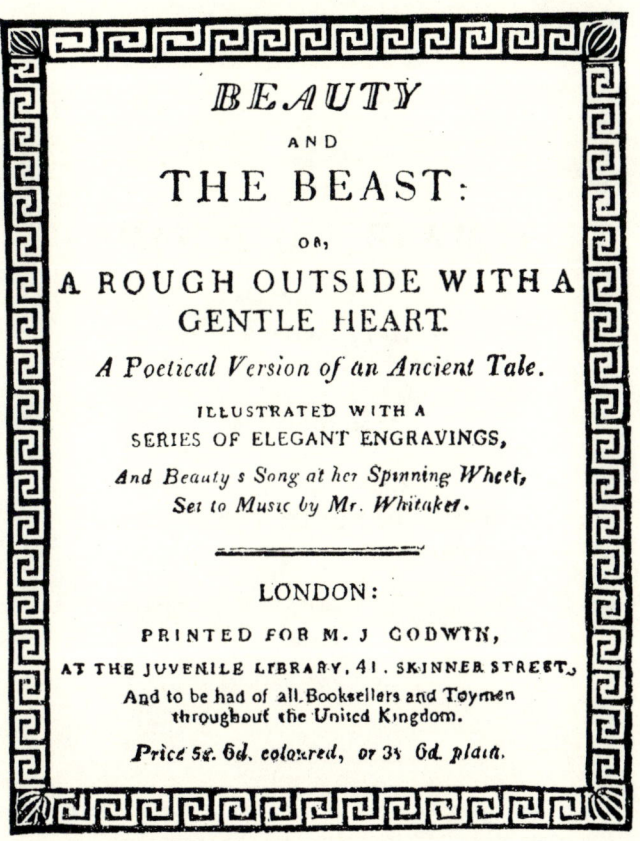

No. 432 *b*.   Title on front cover of Lamb's Beauty and the Beast; the "Surprize" Edition; [1813].

[LAMB, CHARLES.]

MR. H. OR BEWARE A BAD NAME.   Philadelphia, *M. Carey*, 1813.

[433]

Small twelvemo.   First Edition.

Collation by Signatures: A, B, C, each 6 leaves; total 18 numbered leaves.

Collation by Pagination: [title, as reproduced; *See* No. 433], p. [1];—| DRAMATIS PERSONÆ.|, p. [2];— [text, with heading]| MR. H.|, pp. [3]-36.

Condition: Size of leaf, 6⅛ × 3⅞ inches. Bound in red crushed levant morocco, edges uncut and unopened; by the Club Bindery, 1900.

References.

Thomson, *Bibliography* (1908), p. 43, No. xxxiii.; Livingston, *Bibliography* (1903), pp. 126–129.

No. 433   *Charles Lamb*   1813

MR. H.

OR

BEWARE A BAD NAME.

A FARCE IN TWO ACTS:

As performed at the

PHILADELPHIA THEATRE

PHILADELPHIA:

PUBLISHED BY M. CAREY, 122 MARKET STREET,
A. Fagan, Printer.
1813.

No. 433. Title-page of Lamb's Mr. H.; 1st Edition; 1813.

    The edition here described is the First. This play was reprinted at Philadelphia in 1825, but neither of these editions includes the Prologue, which first appeared without the play in *The Care-Killer* (our No. 425), and with the play in Vol. 2 of Lamb's *Works* in 1818 (our No. 435).
    This farce was written in the winter of 1805 and carried by Mary Lamb to Mr. Wroughton, at the Drury Lane Theatre, toward the end of February. On the 11th of June Lamb received word of its acceptance, and his anticipations ran high. Though he had nothing of the dramatic instinct, it had been his ambition to attain success as a playwright. The play was produced December 10, 1806, with Robert William Elliston in the title rôle. The prologue went well and the play itself seemed in a fair

way to succeed until the mystery of the name was revealed. When the name "Hogs-flesh" was announced a storm of hisses arose and the farce was hopelessly damned. It was not printed in England until it appeared in Lamb's *Works* in 1818.

It was played in New York in 1807, and was again put on the boards with great success in Philadelphia in 1812, Mrs. Jefferson, the mother of the famous Joseph Jefferson, being in the cast of characters. The play was revived in 1885 by the Dramatic Students' Society and presented at a Gaiety matinee on the 27th of October.

DEBTOR AND CREDITOR:

A COMEDY,

IN FIVE ACTS,

AS PERFORMED AT

The Theatre Royal, Covent Garden.

By JAMES KENNEY, Esq.

LONDON:

PRINTED FOR JOHN MILLER, 25, BOW STREET, COVENT GARDEN.

1814.

Price Three Shillings.

No. 434. Title-page of Kenney's Debtor and Creditor; 1st Edition; 1814.

No. 434   *Charles Lamb*   1814

LAMB, CHARLES. Kenney, James. (*b.* 1780, *d.* 1849.)

DEBTOR AND CREDITOR: A COMEDY. London, *for John Miller*, 1814.   **[434]**

Octavo. First Edition.

COLLATION BY SIGNATURES: [A], 2 leaves; B to N, each 4 leaves; 1 leaf, without signature-mark; total 51 leaves.

COLLATION BY PAGINATION: [title, as reproduced; *See* No. 434], recto of [A];— [imprint], verso of [A];— | PROLOGUE. | BY A LADY. | *Spoken by Mr. Terry.* |, recto of [A 2];— | DRAMATIS PERSONÆ. |, verso of [A 2];— [text], pp. [1]-95;— | EPILOGUE. | BY C. LAMB. | *Spoken by Mr. Liston and Mr. Emery in character.* |, pp. [96]-98.

CONDITION: Size of leaf, 8 13/16 × 5 7/16 inches. Bound in half calf, gilt top, other edges uncut.

REFERENCES.

Thomson, *Bibliography* (1908), p. 49, No. XXXVII.; Livingston, *Bibliography* (1903), pp. 130-131.

The epilogue to this play, as seen by the collation, was written by Lamb. He makes no reference to it in any of his published letters.

LAMB, CHARLES.

THE WORKS OF CHARLES LAMB. London, *for C. and J. Ollier*, 1818. 2 vols., foolscap octavo, viz.:   **[435]**

VOL. 1.

COLLATION BY SIGNATURES: [A], 6 leaves; B to T, each 8 leaves; U, 2 leaves; total 152 numbered leaves.

COLLATION BY PAGINATION: [title, as reproduced; *See* No. 435], p. [i.];—[imprint], p. [ii.];—[contents], pp. [iii.]-iv.; — | DEDICATION. | TO | S. T. COLERIDGE, ESQ. | [signed] | My dear Coleridge, | Your's, | With unabated esteem, | C. LAMB. |, pp. [v.]-ix.;—[blank], p.[x.];— [half-title] | POEMS. |, p. [xi.];—[blank], p. [xii.];—[poems], pp. [1]-53;—[blank], p. [54];—[sonnets, with half-title], pp. [55]-78;—[*John Woodvil*, with half-title], pp. [79]-164;—[*The Witch*, with half-title], pp. [165]-170;—[*Curious Fragments*, with half-title], pp. [171]-185;—[blank], p. [186];—[*Rosamund, Gray*, with half-title], pp. [187]-263; —[blank], p. [264];—[*Recollections of Christ's Hospital*, with half-title], pp. [265]-291;—[imprint], p. [292].

VOL. 2.

COLLATION BY SIGNATURES: [A], 4 leaves (the first blank and genuine); B to R, each 8 leaves; S, 4 leaves (the last blank and genuine); total 136 leaves.

COLLATION BY PAGINATION: [1 blank leaf], [A];—[title, same as in Vol. 1, except volume-number], recto of [A 2];— [imprint], verso of [A 2];—[contents], recto of [A 3];—[blank], verso of [A 3]; —[half-title] | ESSAYS. |, recto of [A 4]; —[dedication, in verse, with heading] | TO | MARTIN CHARLES BURNEY, ESQ. |, verso of [A 4];—[text], pp. [1]-136;— [half-title] | LETTERS, | UNDER ASSUMED SIGNATURES, PUBLISHED IN | *THE REFLECTOR.* |, p. [137];—[blank], p.[138]; —[text], pp. [139]-212;—[half-title] | MR. H——, | *A FARCE, IN TWO ACTS*,

THE
WORKS
OF
CHARLES LAMB.

IN TWO VOLUMES.

VOL. I.

LONDON:
PRINTED FOR C. AND J. OLLIER,
VERE-STREET, BOND-STREET.

1818.

No. 435. Title-page of the Works of Charles Lamb; 1st Collected Edition; 1818.

| As it was performed at Drury-Lane Theatre, | *December* 1806. |, p. [213]; — [text], pp. [214]-259; —[imprint], p. [260]; — [publishers' advertisements], pp. [261]-[262]; —[1 blank leaf], [s 4].

Condition: Size of leaf, 6⅞ × 4¼ inches. Bound in the original boards, uncut edges; with paper title-label, lettered: | WORKS | OF | C. LAMB. | VOL. I [-II.] | 12*s* |. In Vol. I the binder has placed leaf [A 8], the half-title of the Poems, before the title-page.

REFERENCES.

Thomson, *Bibliography* (1908), p. 52, No. xli.; Livingston, *Bibliography* (1903), pp. 135–140; South Kensington Museum, *Catalogue of the Dyce Collection,* 2 (1875): 5, No. 5615.

No. 435   *Charles Lamb*   1818

It should be noted that the name of the place in the imprint of the copy here described is printed in italic capitals, "*LONDON:*" instead of old English, "𝔏𝔬𝔫𝔡𝔬𝔫:" as in the copy recorded by Mr. Livingston, p. 136; the rest of the title-page being printed from the same setting of type in both.

This is the First Collected Edition of Lamb's works. Mr. Livingston, in his *Bibliography of the First Editions in Book Form of the Writings of Charles and Mary Lamb Published Prior to Charles Lamb's Death in 1834*, gives a list of the contents of these volumes, with the books or periodicals in which each article first appeared. Fourteen pieces are here printed for the first time, or if previously printed, their sources have not yet been determined.

LAMB, CHARLES, and KELLY, FRANCES MARIA. (b. 1790, d. 1882.)

AUTOGRAPH LETTERS. 1819.   [436]

Lamb's letter (3 pages, quarto) to Miss Frances Maria Kelly, dated "*20 July 1819*":

"... I am not so foolish as not to know that I am a most unworthy match for such a one as you, but you have for years been a principal object in my mind. ... Can you quit these shadows of existence, & come & be a reality to us? ... As plainly & frankly as I have seen you give or refuse afsent in some feigned scene, so frankly do me the justice to answer me. It is impofsible I should feel injured or aggrieved by your telling me at once, that the proposal does not suit you. ..."

Miss Kelly's reply (2 pages, small octavo) to the above, dated "*Henrietta Street July 20th 1819*"; signed "*F. M. Kelly*":

"An early & deeply rooted attachment has fixed my heart on one from whom no worldly prospect can ever induce me to withdraw it; but while I thus frankly & decidedly decline your proposal, believe me, I am not insensible to the high honour which the preference of such a mind as yours confers upon me. ..."

Lamb's reply (1 page, small octavo) to the above declination, dated "*July 20th 1819*":

"Your injunctions shall be obeyed to a tittle. ... You will be good friends with us, will you not? let what has past 'break no bones' between us. ..."

CONDITION: Inlaid to quarto size and enclosed in crimson corded moiré silk flap case, the whole enclosed in a red straight-grained morocco solander case, lettered on the back: | LAMB'S | MARRIAGE | PROPOSAL | 1819 |; and on the side, | ORIGINAL AUTOGRAPH LETTERS | BETWEEN CHARLES LAMB AND MISS KELLY | CONTAINING PROPOSAL OF MARRIAGE | AND HER REPLY JULY 20 1819 |.

An account of this romantic incident in Lamb's career, with the correspondence in full, may be found in E. V. Lucas's *Life of Charles Lamb* (New York, 1905), Vol. 2, pp. 17–25, and also in his edition of *The Works of Charles and Mary Lamb*, Vol. 6 (1905), pp. 527–530, letters 236, 237. Though it was vaguely known from statements made in two or three places that Lamb had proposed marriage to Miss Kelly, the correspondence between them upon this subject was first made public by the late John Hollingshead in *Harper's Monthly Magazine*, Vol. 107 (September,

1903), pp. 516–519. It is no exaggeration to say that the publication of this correspondence is the most interesting event connected with Lamb that has taken place since the publication of Talfourd's *Final Memorials of Charles Lamb,* in 1848.

Miss Fanny Kelly was probably introduced to Lamb by the Kenneys. She was a woman of character, integrity, and talent, and was imbued with a real and cultivated love of her art. Among the whole Kemble company at Drury Lane Theatre she was the only woman with whom Lord Byron considered it worth while to talk. She caused him so far to forget the shyness incident to his lameness that he walked across the historic greenroom of Drury Lane for the first time. Acquainted with a sympathetic woman like this there is little wonder that Lamb dreamed of her as a household companion who would bring sunshine into his home and be congenial to his literary tastes. With this in mind he made her a written offer of marriage, the first and last letter of the kind which ever came from his pen. But his dream was never to be realized. Neither of them ever married. Lamb died at Edmonton in 1834, in his sixtieth year, and Miss Kelly lived to be ninety-two years of age, dying in 1882.

LAMB, CHARLES.

AUTOGRAPH LETTERS TO MR. MOXON. 1821–1833. [437]

A collection of 31 autograph letters, all but the first addressed to his friend and publisher Moxon.

[1] To Miss Humphreys. London, Jan. 27, 1821. 1 page, quarto, with address. In this playful letter the writer announces the return of Emma to Cambridge. *I wish I could cure her,* says he, *of making dog's ears in books.* [Lucas, p. 549, No. 253.]

[2] To Mr. Moxon. Enfield, [July 17, 1827]. 1 page, quarto, with address. Emma must not go to Vauxhall with a single gentleman, but if any of the Hood family go she may go. Lamb invites Moxon to meet the Hoods. [Lucas, p. 734, No. 399.]

[3] To Mr. Moxon. Enfield, [Dec. 22, 1827]. 1 page, octavo, with address. The Lambs are doing well. The writer asks Moxon to come on Sunday week and sends a message to the Hoods. He also extends thanks for books offered and asks him to call on Mrs. Lovekin and Miss James. [Lucas, p. 765, No. 421.]

[4] To Mr. Moxon. [Feb. 18, 1828.] 1 page, small octavo, with address. The writer thanks Moxon for books, gives Hone's address, and invites Moxon and the Hoods. *Emma is very proud of her Valentine.* Mary has *a damn'd consignment of Novels in MS. from Malta: which I wish the Mediterranean had in its guts.* [Lucas, p. 768, No. 428.]

[5] To Mr. Moxon. [March 19, 1828.] 1 page, quarto, with address. Lamb is firmly determined *to have nothing to do with " Forget me nots,"* as he is absolutely pledged to Hood. [Lucas, p. 772, No. 431.]

[6] To Mr. Moxon. [January (?), 1828.] 1 page, quarto, with address. The writer has been very nervous, and sends excuses to the Hoods. The "Keepsake" returned by Mrs. Hazlitt. He is very sorry Hone's book should be given up. *The night was damnable & the morning is not too blefs-able.* The letter closes with remembrance to the Hoods, *with a malicious congratulation on their friend Rice's advancemt.* [Lucas, p. 767, No. 427.]

[7] To Mr. Moxon. Enfield, [Sept. 22, 1829]. 1 page, quarto, with address. This letter contains a request for the *Gar-*

rick *Papers* or *Ann of Gierstien.* Lamb is fearful Mary will not be able to enjoy any reading aloud, as she has had a relapse *into the saddest low spirits.* He is almost in despair, Mary's case seems so hopeless. He asks if Moxon has done any sonnets for him to overlook. *I do not want Mr. Jameson or Lady Morgan.* [Lucas, p. 815, No. 469.]

[8] To Mr. Moxon. [April 10, 1833?] 1 page, quarto. The writer praises some of Moxon's sonnets, two of which *may show their faces in any Annual unblushing. . . . You are destin'd to shine in Sonnets, I tell you.* He concludes by inviting Moxon for Sunday. [Lucas, p. 906, No. 549.]

[9] To Mr. Moxon. Enfield, [May 12, 1830]. 1 page, small octavo, with address. Lamb had dined with Rogers at Cary's. *I made Rogers laugh about your Nightingale Sonnet, not having heard one.* [Lucas, p. 851, No. 492.]

[10] To Mr. Moxon. [July 14, 1831.] 3 pages, quarto, with address. A long letter. *He* [Wordsworth] *& I used to dispute about Hell Eternities, I taking the affirmative. I love to puzzle atheists, and — parsons.* The writer had been to the Treasury about a pension for Coleridge; and speaks of Gilman's *insolent letter* in the *Times.* He says "C." is in *leading strings,* and closes his letter with the remark that Kenny *has just touch'd £100. . . . Your Brother fool, C. L.* [Lucas, p. 874, No. 510.]

[11] To Mr. Moxon. [Feb. 3, 1831.] 3 pages, foolscap, with address. This letter speaks of George Dyer and his libel of Rogers, and the writer expresses his contrition when it is quoted by Barker in his *Parriana. G. was born I verily think without original sin, but chooses to have a conscience, as every Christian Gentleman should have. His dear old face is insusceptible of the twist they call a sneer. His apology is like a dirty pocket handkerchief muck'd with tears of some indigent Magdalen.* Wordsworth, Emma, and Allsop are mentioned. [Lucas, p. 866, No. 506.]

[12] To Mr. Moxon. [Aug. 5, 1831.] 1 page, foolscap, with address. *Hunt is a fool. . . . Tis a poem I envy — that & Montgomery's Last Man. . . . S—— is a coxcomb. W—— is a —— & a great Poet.* [Lucas, p. 878, No. 512.]

[13] To Mr. Moxon. [Sept. 5, 1831.] 1 page, quarto, with address. Lamb thanks his friend for money received, and expresses pleasure at Moxon's intention to revisit Enfield. [Lucas, p. 879, No. 513.]

[14] To Mr. Moxon. Enfield, Oct. 24, [1831]. 3 pages, foolscap, with address. A long letter respecting some money transactions, very friendly. *P. S. the 2^d vol. Elia is delightful (-ly bound, I mean).* [Lucas, p. 880, No. 515.]

[15] To Mr. Moxon. [Dec. 15, 1831.] 1 page, quarto, with address. Business matter. "H." and "S." *Nothing with my name will sell, a blast is upon it. . . . Being praised, & being bought, are different things to a Book. Fancy books sell from fashion, not from the number of their real likers.* [Lucas, p. 882, No. 516.]

[16] To Mr. Moxon. [Jan. 3, 1833.] 1 page, foolscap, with address. A facetious letter, in which Rickman, Blackwood, and Emma are mentioned. [Lucas, p. 895, No. 531.]

[17] To Mr. Moxon. [1832.] 1 page, foolscap, with address. The writer sends ten shillings to a poor poet, and asks for Southey's *Devils Visit,* also *Hogarth which is complete, Noble's I think.* [Lucas, p. 891, No. 526.]

[18] To Mr. Moxon. [Jan. 24, 1833.] 1 page, quarto, with address. *Dear ~~Murray~~! Moxon, I mean ——.* Congratulates him on going to Dover Street. *I hope you liked my Cervantes Article which I sent yesterday.* [Lucas, p. 896, No. 535.]

[19] To Mr. Moxon. [March 30, 1833.] 1 page, octavo, with address. *Emma and we are delighted with the Sonnets, and she with her nice Walton.* The writer accidentally burned his leg and scarce can hobble across the room. [Lucas, p. 904, No. 546.]

[20] To Mr. Moxon. [April 25, 1833.] ½ page, foolscap, with address.

1821-33   Charles Lamb   No. 437

My dear Emma and Edward Moxon,

Accept my sincere congratulations, and imagine more good wishes than my weak nerves will let me put into good set words. The dreary blank of unanswered questions, which I ventured to ask in vain, was cleared up on the wedding-day by Mrs W— taking a glass of wine, and, with a total change of countenance, begged leave to drink Mr and Mrs Moxon's health. — It restored me, from that moment, as if by an electrical stroke, to the entire possession of my senses. — I never felt so calm and quiet, after a similar illness as I do now. I feel as if all tears were wiped from my eyes, and all care from my heart.

             Mary Lamb

Dears again.

Your letter interrupted a seventh game at Piequet which we were having, after walking to Wright's, & purchasing a Shoes. We pass our time in cards, walks, & reading. We attack Tasso soon   Wednesd

            CL

Never was such a calm, or such a recovery 'Tis her own words, undictated

---

No. 437a.   Facsimile of No. [26], Charles and Mary Lamb's Letter to Mr. Moxon; [1833?].
Reduced; original 8 11/16 × 7 5/16 inches.

No. 437 Charles Lamb 1821–33

The Buffams. *As our damn'd Times is a day after the fair, I am setting off to Enfield Highway to see in a morning paper (alas! the Publicans) how the play ran.* [Lucas, p. 908, No. 552.]

[21] To Mr. Moxon. [April 27, 1833.] 1 page, quarto, with address. *A sick child, ... sleeping ... next me with a pasteboard partition between, killed my sleep. The little bastard is gone. My bed-fellows are Cough and cramp, we sleep 3 in a bed. ... I do sadly want those 2 last Hogarths.* [Lucas, p. 908, No. 553.]

[22] To Mr. Moxon. [Edmonton, July 14, 1833.] 1 page, quarto, with address. *The Hogarths are* delicate. *Dined with C. V. Le Grice at Johnny Gilpin's.* [Lucas, p. 914, No. 560.]

[23] To Mr. Moxon. [July 28, 1833.] ½ page, foolscap, with address. The writer asks what can be done *to recover M B to a state of respectability.* [Referred to, but not printed, by Lucas, p. 915, No. 561, note.]

[24] To Mr. Moxon. [December, 1830?] ¾ page, foolscap, with address. Respecting literary matters. Mary is mending, but not equal to seeing Southey or Wordsworth. *I think the Devil may come out without prefaces.* He speaks of his will. [Lucas, p. 862, No. 503.]

[25] To Mr. Moxon. Edmonton, July 24, [1833]. 3 pages, narrow octavo, with address. A very funny letter about Emma's *gingerbread watch*; full of playful banter. [Lucas, p. 915, No. 561.]

[26] To Mr. and Mrs. Moxon. [July 31, 1833?] 2 pages, quarto (the first as reproduced; *See* No. 437 *a*). A most affectionate letter announcing Mary's recovery. On the reverse a letter from her corroborating it. Very touching. [Lucas, p. 916, No. 562.]

[27] To Mr. Moxon. [Edmonton, Sept. 26, 1833.] 1 page, quarto (as reproduced; *See* No. 437 *b*), with address. [Lucas, p. 918, No. 564.]

[28] To Mr. Moxon. [Edmonton, Oct. 17, 1833.] 3 pages, quarto, with address. The writer sadly wants books, and asks for *Shirley. We are poor devils, that's the truth of it. ... I sincerely hope the pastoral air of Dover St. will recruit dear Harriet.* Ryle always had *an old head on young shoulders — I fear I shall always have the opposite.* He hopes to go to see them soon, but cannot leave Mary and she is not quite equal to it. [Lucas, p. 919, No. 565.]

[29] To Mr. Moxon. [Edmonton, December, 1833.] *Let Dilke know that I shall not want the books. Mary is going off to be ill again. ... Convey this to Forster.* This letter is lacking, having been given to Augustine Birrell September 13, 1888, who has here given an autograph account of the transfer.

[30] To Mr. Moxon. [1833.] 3 pages, quarto. Mentions Taylor, Hessy, and Bilk, and speaks of copyright. *Proctor has acted a friendly part—when did he otherwise? ... Oblige me by sending a copy of Elia to Coleridge & B. Barton, & enquire ... how I can send one ... to Walter Savage Landor.* [Lucas, p. 900, No. 541.]

[31] To Mr. Moxon. [August, 1831.] 2 pages, small octavo. This letter deals with matters literary. *The Atheneum has been hoax'd with some exquisite poetry that was 2 or 3 month's ago in Hone's Book.* [Lucas, p. 877, No. 511.]

[32] To Mr. Moxon. [1833.] 1 page, quarto. Respecting some rascal whom he covers with mock abuse. *Amen. Maledicatur in extremis.* [Lucas, p. 904, No. 547.]

Thirty of the above letters are reprinted in Vol. 7 of *The Works of Charles and Mary Lamb*, edited by E. V. Lucas (London, 1905), the reference to page and number being given with each description.

PLATES: Inserted in this volume are 2 portraits, as follows:

Preceding the letters is a stippled portrait of Lamb, on India paper, inlaid to size, with facsimile signature. | *Painted & Engraved by H. Meyer.* | Published by Fisher, Son & Cº. Caxton, London, March 1, 1828. |

Following the letters is the Maclise portrait, inlaid to size, with facsimile signature, followed by : | THE AUTHOR OF "ELIA". | *Published by James Fraser, 215, Regent Street, London.* |.

CONDITION: Mounted in a folio volume

1821-33   Charles Lamb   No. 437

Thursday

We shall be most happy to see Emma, dear to every body. Mary's spirits are much better, and she longs to see again our twelve years' friend. You shall afternoon sip with me a bottle of superexcellent Port, after deducting a dinner-glass for them. We rejoyce to have E. come, the <u>first visit</u>, without Miss ——, who, I trust, will yet behave well; but she might perplex Mary with questions. — Pindar sadly wants Preface & notes. Pray, E., get to Snow Hill before 12, for we dine before 2. We will make it 2. By mistake I gave you Miss Betham's Letter, with the exquisite verses, which pray return to me; or if it be an improved copy, give me the other, & Albumize mine, keeping the signature. It is too pretty a family portrait, not for you to cherish

Your loving friends.

C Lamb
M Lamb

No. 437 *b*.   Facsimile of No. [27], Charles and Mary Lamb's Letter to Mr. Moxon; [1833].
Reduced; original 7⅛ x 6 9/10 inches.

bound in green crushed levant morocco, gilt edges; by Bedford; lettered: | CHARLES | LAMB | MSS. | LETTERS | 1821– |.

Reference.
Locker-Lampson, *Catalogue* (1886), p. 209.

The Locker-Lampson collection, with ex-libris.
A most interesting collection. There are many pathetic references to his sister,

sometimes grief at her illness, sometimes joy at her recovery. Coleridge, Wordsworth, Southey, Hood, and others are frequently mentioned.

On the recto of the first fly-leaf, tipped in, is a manuscript, as follows : *" Thirty two letters of Charles Lamb, all but the first addressed to his Friend & publisher, Moxon.*

" Moxon married his Adopted Daughter Emma Isola, the daughter of an Italian Professor. [Signed] *F. L."*

The twenty-ninth letter has been removed, and in its place is a note by Augustine Birrell, dated September 13, 1888, giving an account of its disposition.

[LAMB, CHARLES.]

ELIA. ESSAYS. LONDON, *for Taylor and Hessey,* 1823.   [438]

Post octavo. First Edition, First Issue.

COLLATION BY SIGNATURES : [A], 2 leaves; B to Y, each 8 leaves; Z, 6 leaves; total 176 leaves.

COLLATION BY PAGINATION : [title, as reproduced; *See* No. 438], recto of [A];—[blank], verso of [A];—[contents], recto and verso of [A 2];—[text in numerous essays, the first with heading]|THE SOUTH-SEA HOUSE.|, pp. [1]-341;—[imprint], p. [342];—[publishers' advertisements], pp. [343]-[348].

CONDITION : Size of leaf, 7⅝ × 4¾ inches. Bound in light polished calf, gilt top, other edges uncut; by Bedford.

REFERENCES.

Thomson, *Bibliography of the Writings of Charles and Mary Lamb* (1908), p. 78, No. LVIII.; Livingston, *Bibliography of the First Editions in Book Form of the Writings of Charles and Mary Lamb* (1903), pp. 149-155; Locker-Lampson, *Catalogue* (1886), p. 160.

The Tennyson-Locker Lampson copy, with the ex-libris of each.

Inserted in this copy is an autograph letter by Charles Lamb, as follows :

*" Dear Sir, We are both so poorly that we have been obliged to put off a party that was to have met here this eveng. I do not feel strong enough to venture on your dinner party on Sunday, but will see you both very soon. Pray take this excuse from Yours most respectf*ʸ*, C Lamb. Our kindest loves to Ellen & mother. I am glad you like my verses."*

This is the First Collected Edition of the *Essays*, which was issued in paper-covered boards, uncut edges, with title-label lettered: | Elia. | —— | 9*s.* 6*d.* | .

The twenty-eight essays included in this edition had, with a single exception, previously appeared in the *London Magazine* from August, 1820, to October, 1822; the exception being " Valentine's Day," which had appeared in *The Indicator* for February 14, 1821.

There is a Second Issue of this edition, which may be accounted for as follows : Soon after its appearance the publishers opened another place of business, and wishing to have its address appear on the title-page, the imprint was changed to read: | LONDON: | PRINTED FOR TAYLOR AND HESSEY, | 33, FLEET-STREET. | AND 13, WATERLOO-PLACE. | 1823. | . A copy with this imprint, which we have

E L I A.

ESSAYS WHICH HAVE APPEARED UNDER THAT SIGNATURE
IN THE
LONDON MAGAZINE.

LONDON:
PRINTED FOR TAYLOR AND HESSEY,
FLEET-STREET.
1823.

No. 438. TITLE-PAGE OF LAMB'S ELIA; 1ST EDITION, 1ST ISSUE; 1823.

examined, has also a half-title, | ELIA. | on page [i.], and on its verso the imprint, | LONDON : | PRINTED BY THOMAS DAVISON, WHITEFRIARS. | . This half-title is followed by the title-page, with the form of the imprint just described. The Second Issue, therefore, has three preliminary leaves instead of two, as in the First Issue; the place occupied by the title-page of the First Issue being taken by the half-title and title, both of which are printed upon a quarter of a sheet of paper.

Lamb wrote a dedication, which is given by Livingston; but, on second thought, he decided to have it omitted; for, as he said : " The Essays want no Preface : they are *all Preface*. A Preface is nothing but a talk with the reader ; and they do nothing else. Pray omit it." The name " Elia " was in fact the name of a fellow clerk with Lamb in the South Sea House.

E L I A.

ESSAYS

WHICH HAVE APPEARED UNDER THAT SIGNATURE

IN THE

LONDON MAGAZINE.

PHILADELPHIA:
CAREY, LEA, AND CAREY—CHESNUT STREET.
MIFFLIN AND PARRY, PRINTERS.

1828.

No. 439.   Title-page of Lamb's Elia; 1828.

[LAMB, CHARLES.]

ELIA. ESSAYS. PHILADELPHIA, *Carey, Lea, and Carey*, 1828. [439]

Small duodecimo.

COLLATION BY SIGNATURES: [A], 2 leaves; B to Z, Aa, BB, each 6 leaves; total 146 numbered leaves. Leaf BB 2 (really BB 3) has no signature-mark.

COLLATION BY PAGINATION: [title, as reproduced; *See* No. 439], p. [1];—[blank], p. [2];—[contents], p. [3];—[blank], p. [4];—[text in numerous essays, the first with heading]|THE SOUTH-SEA HOUSE.|, pp. [5]-292.

CONDITION: Size of leaf, 6⅞ × 4¹⁄₁₀ inches. Bound in the original yellow boards, uncut edges; with paper title-label lettered | ELIA. | ; lettered on the sides, | *ELIA.* | ; in green straight-grained morocco solander case.

REFERENCE.

Livingston, *Bibliography of the First Editions in Book Form of the Writings of Charles and Mary Lamb* (1903), p. 153.

The Foote copy, with ex-libris.

This copy is in the original boards, as issued. It is a reprint of the London edition (our previous number), and contains nothing not to be found in that volume.

[LAMB, CHARLES.]

ELIA. ESSAYS. SECOND SERIES. PHILADELPHIA, *Carey, Lea and Carey*, 1828. [440]

Duodecimo. First Edition.

COLLATION BY SIGNATURES: [1], 2 leaves; 2 to 20, each 6 leaves; total 116 leaves.

COLLATION BY PAGINATION: [title, as reproduced; *See* No. 440], p. [1];—[blank], p. [2];—[contents], p. [3];—[blank], p. [4];—[sonnet, with heading] | TO ELIA. | [signed] | BERNARD BARTON. |, p. [5];—[text in numerous essays, the first with heading] | REJOICINGS UPON | THE | NEW YEAR'S COMING OF AGE. |, pp. [6]-230;—[publishers' advertisements], pp. [231]-[232].

CONDITION: Size of leaf, 7⁸⁄₁₀ × 4⅛ inches. Bound in the original yellow boards, uncut edges; with paper title-label lettered | ELIA. | *Second Series.* | ; lettered on the sides, | *ELIA.* | SECOND SERIES. | ; in green straight-grained morocco solander case.

REFERENCES.

Thomson, *Bibliography* (1908), p. 95, No. LXVII.; Livingston, *Bibliography* (1903), pp. 156–160; Ainger, in *The Athenæum*, June 7, 1890, pp. 736, 737.

This copy is in the original boards, as issued. It is an unauthorized collection, the actual Second Series not being published in England until 1833, and then with the title *The Last Essays of Elia* (our No. 443).

It is made up of a selection of twenty-five articles from the *London Magazine* and other publications, and includes several essays by different writers. Of these, twelve appear in the authorized edition of the *Essays*, and four were taken from the second volume of the 1818 edition of Lamb's works.

No. 440   *Charles Lamb*   1828

ELIA.

ESSAYS

WHICH HAVE APPEARED UNDER THAT SIGNATURE

IN THE

LONDON MAGAZINE.

———◆———

SECOND SERIES.

———◆———

PHILADELPHIA:

CAREY, LEA AND CAREY—CHESNUT STREET.

J. R. A. SKERRETT, PRINTER.

1828.

No. 440.   Title-page of Lamb's Elia, Second Series; 1st Edition; 1828.

The following pieces, some of which were not written by Lamb, are of course not to be found in his *Last Essays of Elia*: "To Elia" [a sonnet by Bernard Barton]; "Reflections in the Pillory"; "Twelfth Night, or What You Will" [said to be by Bryan Waller Procter, "Barry Cornwall"]; "A Vision of Horns"; "The Nuns and Ale of Caverswell" [said to be by Allan Cunningham]; "Valentine's Day" [said to be by Bryan Waller Procter]; "Letter to an Old Gentleman whose Education has been Neglected"; "Guy Faux"; "Confessions of a Drunkard"; "The Old Actors"; and "The Gentle Giantess."

1828   Charles Lamb   No. 440

The last essay, "A Character of the Late Elia," here occurs as it originally appeared in the *London Magazine*. When inserted in the *Last Essays of Elia* it was very much condensed, and the title changed to "Preface. By a Friend of the Late Elia."

The four pieces which had previously been printed in the second volume of Lamb's works, 1818, were: "On the Danger of Confounding Moral with Personal Deformity"; "On the Melancholy of Tailors"; "On the Inconveniences Resulting from being Hanged"; and "On Burial Societies; and the Character of an Undertaker."

ALBUM VERSES,

WITH A FEW OTHERS,

BY CHARLES LAMB.

LONDON:
EDWARD MOXON, 64, NEW BOND STREET.
1830.

No. 441.   Title-page of Lamb's Album Verses; 1st Edition; 1830.

No. 441   *Charles Lamb*   1830

LAMB, CHARLES.

ALBUM VERSES. LONDON, *Edward Moxon*, 1830.   [441]

Post octavo. First Edition.
COLLATION BY SIGNATURES: [A], 4 leaves; B to K, each 8 leaves; L, 4 leaves; total 80 leaves.
COLLATION BY PAGINATION: [title, as reproduced; See No. 441], p. [i.]; — [imprint], p. [ii.]; — | DEDICATION. | To the Publisher. |[signed]| I am, Dear Moxon, | Your Friend and sincere Well-wisher, | CHARLES LAMB. | [dated] | *Enfield*, *1st June*, 1830. |, pp. [iii.]–iv.; — [contents], pp. [v.]–vii.; —[blank], p. [viii.];— | Album Verses. |, pp. [1]–150; —[publishers' advertisement], p. [151]; —[blank], p. [152].
CONDITION: Size of leaf, 7 9/16 × 4 9/16 inches. Bound in boards, uncut edges.

REFERENCES.

Thomson, *Bibliography* (1908), p. 103, No. LXXVI.; Livingston, *Bibliography* (1903), pp. 169–174.

This work, which appeared about the end of June, was originally issued in paper-covered boards, with uncut edges and paper title-label lettered: | Album | Verses. | By C. Lamb. | Price 7s. | .

This is one of the first volumes with Moxon's imprint, and was probably prepared at his suggestion. The "Album Verses," only nine in number, make up but a small part of the book. Several of the pieces — the two sonnets "Work" and "Leisure," "The Christening," "Going or Gone," "The Wife's Trial," and "Pindaric Ode to the Treadmill" — had previously appeared in other publications.

[LAMB, CHARLES.]

SATAN IN SEARCH OF A WIFE. LONDON, *Edward Moxon*, 1831.
[442]

Small duodecimo. First Edition.
COLLATION BY SIGNATURES: B, C, D, each 6 leaves; total 18 numbered leaves. Leaf D has no signature-mark.
COLLATION BY PAGINATION: [title, as reproduced; See No. 442], p. [1]; —[imprint], p. [2]; —[dedication], p. [3]; — [blank], p. [4]; —[text in 2 parts, the first with heading]| Satan | IN SEARCH OF A WIFE, | &c. | PART THE FIRST. |, pp. [5]–20; —[text of the second part, with heading]| SATAN IN SEARCH OF A WIFE. | The Second Part; | CONTAINING | THE COURTSHIP, AND THE WEDDING. |, pp. [21]–36.
PLATES: 4 plates, facing the title-page and pp. 8, [21], and 32; also 2 vignettes, on the title-page and p. 36; all by G. W. Bonner from designs by Isaac Robert Cruikshank.
CONDITION: Size of leaf, 6 × 3 13/16 inches. Bound in red crushed levant morocco, gilt top; by Stikeman. With the original pink paper wrappers bound in, the first with title similar to the title-page, surrounded by a double-rule border, with corner ornaments, with | Bradbury and Evans, Bouverie Street. | below; publisher's advertisement on the back wrapper.

REFERENCES.

Thomson, *Bibliography* (1908), p. 112, No. LXXXIV.; Livingston, *Bibliography* (1903), pp. 182–184.

𝔖𝔞𝔱𝔞𝔫 𝔦𝔫 𝔖𝔢𝔞𝔯𝔠𝔥 𝔬𝔣 𝔞 𝔚𝔦𝔣𝔢;

WITH THE WHOLE PROCESS OF

HIS COURTSHIP AND MARRIAGE,

AND WHO DANCED AT THE WEDDING

BY

AN EYE WITNESS.

London:
EDWARD MOXON, 64, NEW BOND STREET.
M.DCCC.XXXI.

No. 442.   TITLE-PAGE OF LAMB'S SATAN IN SEARCH OF A WIFE;
1ST EDITION; 1831.

The Foote copy, with ex-libris.
The first page of the wrapper is printed from the same setting of type as the title-page, but varies slightly.   There is a semicolon instead of a comma at the end of the third line; the short line above the vignette is omitted; and the words "PRICE ONE SHILLING." are added below the date.   The advertisement on the back cover reads: | JUST PUBLISHED, | BY E. MOXON, 64, NEW BOND STREET. | , etc.
The book, although it was published anonymously, was advertised as "by the Author of Elia."

No. 443   *Charles Lamb*   1833

THE LAST ESSAYS

of

ELIA.

BEING

A SEQUEL TO ESSAYS PUBLISHED UNDER
THAT NAME.

———•———

LONDON:
EDWARD MOXON, DOVER STREET.
1833.

No. 443.   TITLE-PAGE OF LAMB'S LAST ESSAYS OF ELIA; 1ST EDITION; 1833.

[LAMB, CHARLES.]

THE LAST ESSAYS OF ELIA. LONDON, *Edward Moxon*, 1833.   [443]

    Large duodecimo. First Edition.
    COLLATION BY SIGNATURES: [A], 6 leaves; B to N, each 12 leaves; total 150 leaves. Leaves E 3 [E 5], L 3 [L 5], and N 3 [N 5] have no signature-marks.
    COLLATION BY PAGINATION: [half-title], p. [i.];—[blank], p. [ii.];—[title, as reproduced; *See* No. 443], p. [iii.];—[imprint], p. [iv.];—| PREFACE.| BY A FRIEND OF THE LATE ELIA.|, pp. [v.]–x.;—[contents], pp. [xi.]–xii.;—[text in numerous essays, the first with heading]| BLAKESMOOR IN H——SHIRE.|, pp. [1]–283 ;—[imprint], p. [284];—

[publisher's advertisements], pp. [285]–[288].

CONDITION: Size of leaf, 7⅞ × 4⅞ inches. Bound in light polished calf, gilt top, other edges uncut; by Bedford.

REFERENCES.

Thomson, *Bibliography* (1908), p. 116, No. LXXXIX.; Livingston, *Bibliography* (1903), pp. 185, 189; Locker-Lampson, *Catalogue* (1886), p. 160.

The Locker-Lampson copy, with ex-libris.

Though the First Series was printed in octavo, and this in duodecimo, they are almost identical in size, the latter being about one fourth of an inch the taller of the two. This work was issued in paper-covered boards, uncut edges, with title-label.

"The 'Preface by a Friend of the Late Elia' is, of course, by Lamb himself. It seems, as Ainger remarks, to have been originally intended to be published as a conclusion to the first series of Elia Essays. It first appeared in the 'London Magazine' for January, 1823, as 'A Character of the Late Elia, by a Friend.' It is here considerably condensed. As already noted, the essay as originally printed is found at the end of the Philadelphia volume of 1828. . . .

"It seems that Taylor, formerly of Taylor and Hessey, publishers of the 'London Magazine,' claimed some rights in this second series of Essays, and sued Moxon, or Lamb and Moxon jointly, at law." — LIVINGSTON.

The following pieces were not included in the unauthorized series published in Philadelphia in 1828: "Stage Illusion," "To the Shade of Elliston," "Ellistoniana," "The Convalescent," "Sanity of True Genius," "The Superannuated Man," "The Genteel Style in Writing," "The Tombs in the Abbey," "Some Sonnets of Sir Philip Sydney," "Newspapers Thirty-five Years Ago," "Barrenness of the Imaginative Faculty in the Productions of Modern Art," "The Wedding," "A Death-bed," and "Popular Fallacies" (numbered from I. to XVI.).

LAMB, CHARLES and [MARY ANN]. (*b.* 1764, *d.* 1847.)

TALES FROM SHAKESPEAR. LONDON, *for Thomas Hodgkins*, 1807. 2 vols., duodecimo, viz.:

VOL. 1.

COLLATION BY SIGNATURES: [A], 6 leaves; B to K, each 12 leaves; L, 10 leaves; total 124 numbered leaves.

COLLATION BY PAGINATION: [title, as reproduced; *See* No. 444], p. [i.]; — [blank], p. [ii.]; — [preface], pp. [iii.]–ix.; — [blank], p. [x.]; — | CONTENTS | OF

| THE FIRST VOLUME. |, p. [xi.]; — [blank], p. [xii.]; — [text, with heading] | TALES FROM SHAKESPEAR. |, pp. [1]–235; — [blank], p. [236].

PLATES: 10 copperplates; facing the title-page and pp. [22], [43], [63], [86], [116], [140], [164], [188], and [215].

VOL. 2.

COLLATION BY SIGNATURES: 2 leaves, without signature-marks; A, 2 leaves; B to L, each 12 leaves; M, 10 leaves; total 134 leaves.

COLLATION BY PAGINATION: [title, same as in Vol. 1, except volume-number], p. [i.]; — [imprint], p. [ii.]; — | CONTENTS | OF | *THE SECOND VOLUME.* |, p. [iii.];

No. 444   *Charles Lamb*   1807

TALES

FROM

SHAKESPEAR.

DESIGNED

FOR THE USE OF YOUNG PERSONS.

—

By CHARLES LAMB.

—

EMBELLISHED WITH COPPER-PLATES.

———

IN TWO VOLUMES.
VOL. I.

———

LONDON:

PRINTED FOR THOMAS HODGKINS, AT THE JUVENILE LIBRARY, HANWAY-STREET (OPPOSITE SOHO-SQUARE), OXFORD-STREET; AND TO BE HAD OF ALL BOOKSELLERS.

—

1807.

No. 444. Title-page of Charles and Mary Lamb's Tales from Shakespear; 1st Edition; 1807.

—[blank], p. [iv.];—[text], pp. [1]–261; —[publisher's advertisements], pp. [262]–[264].

PLATES: 10 copperplates; facing the title-page and pp. 25, 45, 73, [97], [121], [145], [177], 207, and [231]. The plates facing pp. 25, 45, 73, and 206 should face pp. [24], [44], [70], and [206].

CONDITION: Size of leaf, 7⅜ × 4⁷⁄₁₆ inches. Bound in the original boards, uncut edges, with paper title-label on Vol. 2, lettered: | *Shakespear* | TALES | VOL. II. | 8s. | ; in brown crushed levant morocco solander case.

REFERENCES.

Thomson, *Bibliography* (1908), p. 24, No. XIX.; Livingston, *Bibliography* (1903), pp. 61–67; Locker-Lampson, *Catalogue* (1886), p. 160.

Inside of the front cover of Vol. 2 is written in ink, | *Louisa Ellis* | *January 1810* | ; and on the recto of the fly-leaf, | *Miss Ellis gave this* | *book to Miss Braddick* | *Thames Ditton* ᵗʰ⁄₁₄ *July* | *1816* | .

In some copies of Vol. 1, perhaps a later issue, p. [236] has the imprint, | T. Davison, Printer, | Whitefriars. | . Some copies have two additional leaves of advertisements at the end; but these are of a later date than the book, as the address of the *Juvenile Library* is given as " 41 Skinner-Street " ; besides, uncut copies show that sheet L consists of ten leaves only, sewed in the centre.

Of these *Tales* from Shakespeare's plays, written for young readers, especially girls, Mary Lamb wrote fourteen and Charles six, though he probably assisted in the others. Those written by him are: *King Lear, Macbeth, Timon of Athens, Romeo and Juliet, Hamlet,* and *Othello.* They were written during 1805 and 1806, apparently at the suggestion of William Godwin.

The plates, by William Blake from drawings by William Mulready, were engraved two on a copper, and the impressions separated with scissors. Each has the title engraved at the foot of the plate, and the page-number just above the plate in the right-hand corner. These plates give an added charm to the work.

The book was a commercial success, a Second Edition being called for in 1809 and a Third in 1810.

Some of the *Tales* were advertised by Godwin to be issued separately in " eight single numbers, each number being adorned with three plates, beautifully colored; price sixpence. The remainder will speedily follow."

[LAMB, CHARLES *and* MARY ANN.]

MRS. LEICESTER'S SCHOOL. LONDON, *for M. J. Godwin,* 1809. [445]

Duodecimo. First Edition.

COLLATION BY SIGNATURES: [A], 2 leaves; B to H, each 12 leaves; I, 6 leaves; total 92 leaves.

COLLATION BY PAGINATION: [title, as reproduced; *See* No. 445], recto of [A]; —[imprint], verso of [A]; —[contents], recto of [A 2]; —[blank], verso of [A 2]; — | MRS. | LEICESTER'S SCHOOL. | DEDICATION. | TO | THE YOUNG LADIES AT AMWELL SCHOOL. | [signed] | *Your faithful historiographer,* | *as well as true friend,* | *M. B.* | , pp. [i.]–viii. ; —[text in 10 parts, the first with heading] | I. | ELIZABETH VILLIERS. | , pp. [9]–179; —[publisher's advertisement], p. [180].

PLATE: Steel engraving, with inscription | FRONTISPIECE | across the top, and | *W. Hopwood, del. J. Hopwood, sculp.* | *In this manner, the epitaph on my mother's* | *tomb being my primer and my spelling-book,* | *I learned to read.* — *Page 9.* | below; facing the title-page.

CONDITION: Size of leaf, 7⅝ x 4⅝ inches. Bound in the original boards, uncut edges; with paper title-label lettered: | MRS. LEICESTER'S | SCHOOL. | ; in green crushed levant morocco solander case. With | *1825.* | *Miss Lake* | written in ink on the recto of the first fly-leaf. This copy does not contain the two leaves of advertisements, pp. [181–184] said to occur in some copies.

No. 445   *Charles Lamb*   1809

MRS. LEICESTER'S SCHOOL:

OR,

THE HISTORY

OF

SEVERAL YOUNG LADIES,

RELATED BY THEMSELVES.

𝕷𝖔𝖓𝖉𝖔𝖓:

PRINTED FOR M. J. GODWIN, AT THE JUVENILE
LIBRARY, NO. 41, SKINNER-STREET.

1809.

No. 445.   Title-page of Charles and Mary Lamb's Mrs. Leicester's School; 1st Edition; 1809.

REFERENCES.   No. xxv.; Livingston, *Bibliography* (1903),
Thomson, *Bibliography* (1908), p. 32,   pp. 84–87.

This edition was probably issued late in 1808, though dated 1809. A Second Edition, also dated 1809, was published probably, about June 1st. Some copies are said to have two leaves of advertisements, "New Books for Children," etc., pp. [181–184]; with imprint, "T. Davison, Printer, Whitefriars." at the bottom of p. [184].

English Literature   [602]   Church Catalogue

Mrs. Leicester's School contains ten stories supposed to be related by as many girls, pupils in a school at Amwell. The dedication is signed "M. B.," as one of the teachers of the school, who states that she has written these stories from notes taken at the time they were told.

Of these tales, three, "The Witch Aunt," "First Time of going to Church," and "The Sea Voyage," were written by Charles Lamb, the other seven being by his sister Mary, as shown in Lamb's letter to Bernard Barton written in 1824.

This book is no doubt one of those written at Godwin's suggestion.

[LAMB, CHARLES and MARY ANN.]

POETRY FOR CHILDREN. LONDON, *for M. J. Godwin,* 1809. 2 vols., small duodecimo, viz.: [446]

VOL. I.

COLLATION BY SIGNATURES: [A], 2 leaves; B to I, each 6 leaves; K, 4 leaves; total 54 numbered leaves.

COLLATION BY PAGINATION: [title, as reproduced; *See* No. 446], p. [i.]; — [imprint], p. [ii.]; — | CONTENTS | OF THE | FIRST VOLUME. |, pp. [iii.]-iv.; —[text, with heading] | POETRY | FOR | CHILDREN. |, pp. [1]-103; — [publisher's advertisement], p. [104].

PLATES: 1 plate, with inscription | FRONTISPIECE. | *VOL I.* | across the top, and | *Keep on your own side, do, Grey Pate!* | *p. 29.* | below; facing the title-page.

VOL. 2.

COLLATION BY SIGNATURES: [A], B, each 2 leaves; C to K, each 6 leaves; L, 2 leaves; total 54 numbered leaves.

COLLATION BY PAGINATION: [title, same as in Vol. 1, except volume-number], p. [i.]; — [imprint], p. [ii.]; — | CONTENTS | OF THE | SECOND VOLUME. |, pp. [iii.]-iv.; —[text], pp. [1]-104.

PLATE: 1 plate, with inscription | FRONTISPIECE. | *VOL. II.* | across the top, and | —— *He fear'd the little bird,* | *That singing in the air he heard,* | *Was telling his transgreſsion.* | *p. 7.* | below; facing the title-page.

CONDITION: Size of leaf, 5½ × 3⁷⁄₁₆ inches. Bound in marbled calf, gilt borders, marbled edges. The plate in Vol. 2 lacks part of the inscription at the bottom.

REFERENCES.

Thomson, *Bibliography* (1908), p. 33, No. XXVI.; Livingston, *Bibliography* (1903), pp. 88-102.

The Foote copy, with ex-libris.

Tipped in is a note by the Leadenhall Press: "*These are the two volumes of Lamb's 'Poetry for Children' from which the facsimile edition was copied.*"

These poems were issued in paper-covered boards, with leather backs lettered lengthwise: "Leicester's | Poetry." The paper has the watermark "1808." This work is the joint production of Charles and Mary Lamb, but just the share of each in it is difficult to determine. The book seems to have been published about the end of June. Only three of the pieces are included in the collected edition of Charles Lamb's

POETRY

FOR

CHILDREN,

ENTIRELY ORIGINAL.

BY THE AUTHOR OF
"MRS. LEICESTER'S SCHOOL."

IN TWO VOLUMES.

VOL I.

LONDON:
PRINTED FOR M. J. GODWIN,
AT THE JUVENILE LIBRARY, NO. 41, SKINNER STREET.

1809.

No. 446. TITLE-PAGE OF CHARLES AND MARY LAMB'S POETRY FOR CHILDREN; 1ST EDITION; 1809.

works published in 1818. Mr. Livingston gives a list of the contents of each volume with the name of the writer of each piece as far as known, and marks with an asterisk (*) the twenty-two pieces which were included in *The First Book of Poetry for the Use of Schools* edited by W. F. Mylius, and published by Godwin in November, 1810.

POETRY

FOR

CHILDREN,

ENTIRELY ORIGINAL.

BY THE AUTHOR OF
"MRS. LIECESTER'S SCHOOL."

BOSTON:

PUBLISHED BY WEST AND RICHARDSON,
AND EDWARD COTTON.

1812.

No. 447. TITLE-PAGE OF CHARLES AND MARY LAMB'S POETRY FOR CHILDREN; 1812.

[LAMB, CHARLES and MARY ANN.]

POETRY FOR CHILDREN. BOSTON, *West and Richardson, and Edward Cotton,* 1812. [447]

Twentyfourmo.
COLLATION BY SIGNATURES: [A], 4 leaves; B to M, each 6 leaves; N, 2 leaves; total 72 numbered leaves.
COLLATION BY PAGINATION: [title, as reproduced; *See* No. 447], p. [i.]; — [imprint], p. [ii.]; — [contents], pp. [iii.] – vi.; — [text, with heading] | POETRY | FOR | CHILDREN. |, pp. [7] – 144.

CONDITION: Size of leaf, 5%₁₆ × 3⁷⁄₁₆ inches. In the original boards, leather back.

REFERENCES.

Thomson, *Bibliography* (1908), p. 35; Livingston, *Bibliography of the First Editions of Charles and Mary Lamb* (1903), p. 99.

This is an American reprint of our preceding number. It includes but eighty-one of the eighty-four pieces contained in the First Edition.

Only a year and a half before Lamb's death, when sending some of his books to Mrs. Norris, he writes: "The first volume printed here is not to be had for love or money, not even an American edition of it, and the second volume, American also, to suit with it. It is much the same as the London one."

[LAMB, JOHN, Senior.] (b. ——, d. 1799.)

POETICAL PIECES ON SEVERAL OCCASIONS. LONDON, *for P. Shatwell*, [*c*. 1770]. [448]

Quarto. First Edition.

COLLATION BY SIGNATURES: [A], 2 leaves; B to K, each 4 leaves; L, 2 leaves; total 40 leaves. Leaves C 2, D 2, H 2, and K 2 have no signature-marks.

COLLATION BY PAGINATION: [title, as reproduced; *See* No. 448], recto of [A]; —[blank], verso of [A];—| *To the* Forty-nine *Members of the* Friendly | Society *for the* Benefit *of their* Widows, | *of which I have the honour of making the* | *Number Fifty*. | [signed] | I am, Gentlemen, | Your obedient humble Servant, | *A Brother Member*. |, recto of [A 2];—[blank], verso of [A 2];—[text, with heading] | POEMS, &c. |, pp. [1]–76.

CONDITION: Size of leaf, 9½ x 6¾ inches. Bound in dark green crushed levant morocco, gilt edges; by the Club Bindery, 1904. The leaves are stabbed on the inner margins throughout.

REFERENCES.

Thomson, *Bibliography* (1908), p. 137; Livingston, *Bibliography* (1903), pp. 199–203.

This volume of poems was written by John Lamb, the father of Charles and Mary Lamb. The text in this copy has been corrected with a pen in several places.

The date when this volume was published has never been accurately determined, but has been indefinitely given as "between the years 1760 and 1780." Mr. Livingston judges from circumstances connected with the poem the "Letter from a Child to his Grandmother," ending,

"And then the Lord will ever bleſſ
Your Grandſon dear,
John L — b the Leſſ."

and from the lines,

"For favours to my ſon and wife,
I ſhall love you whilſo I've life,
Your clyſters, potions, help'd to ſave,
Our infant lambkin from the grave."

in the "Letter to a Friend in the Country," that it was printed between 1765 and 1770.

"Charles Lamb, in the 'Elia' Essay 'The Old Benchers of the Inner Temple,' describes his father under the name of Lovel. Among other accomplishments, he says that Lovel 'possessed a fine turn for humourous poetry — next to Swift and Prior.'"

POETICAL PIECES

ON SEVERAL OCCASIONS.

Let such teach others, who themselves excel,
And censure freely *who have written well.*

POPE.

LONDON:

Printed for P. SHATWELL, opposite Adelphi, Strand.

No. 448. TITLE-PAGE OF JOHN LAMB'S POETICAL PIECES;
1ST EDITION; [c. 1770].
Reduced; original 7¼ × 4⅞ inches.

No. 449   *Charles James Lever*   1839

[LEVER, CHARLES JAMES.] (*b.* 1806, *d.* 1872.)

THE CONFESSIONS OF HARRY LORREQUER. DUBLIN, *William Curry, Jun. and Company, etc.,* 1839.   [449]

Octavo. First Edition.
COLLATION BY SIGNATURES: *a*, 8 leaves (placed between [A2] and [A3]); [A] to X, each 8 leaves; Y, 4 leaves; total 180 numbered leaves.
COLLATION BY PAGINATION: [title] | THE | CONFESSIONS | OF | HARRY LORREQUER. | WITH NUMEROUS ILLUSTRATIONS | BY | Phiz. | [quotation] | DUBLIN | WILLIAM CURRY, JUN. AND COMPANY. | WILLIAM S. ORR, AND CO. LONDON. | FRASER AND CRAWFORD, EDINBURGH. | MDCCCXXXIX. |, p. [i.]; — [imprint], p. [ii.]; — [introduction], pp. [3] – 4; — [dedication, preface, contents, and list of plates], pp. [iii.] – [xvii.]; — [blank], p. [xviii.]; — [text], pp. [5] – 344.
PLATES: Engraved title-page and 21 plates, as called for in the list of plates; seven of them incorrectly placed by the binder.
CONDITION: Size of leaf, 8 13/16 × 5 9/16 inches. Bound from the original parts, in light brown crushed levant morocco, gilt top, other edges uncut; by Zaehnsdorf. With pink wrappers and advertising pages on yellow and white paper, in all 36 leaves, bound in at the end. Nos. 1 – 11 (9 and 10 are missing, but two impressions of No. 8 are numbered 9 and 10 in ink) have 4, 4, 4, 2, 2, 8, 2, 2, 2, 2, and 4 leaves respectively. Published in 11 numbered monthly parts, from February, 1839, to March, 1840, in pink wrappers, at one shilling each, with pictorial title designed by "Phiz": | CONFESSIONS | OF | HARRY | LORREQUER | ILLUSTRATED BY PHIZ | WILLIAM CURRY, JUN. AND COMPANY, DUBLIN. | WILLIAM S. ORR AND COMPANY, LONDON. | BRADBURY AND EVANS,]   FRASER AND CRAWFORD, EDINBURGH.   [PRINTERS, WHITEFRIARS. |; the printer's imprint on some wrappers varying slightly from that here given.
REFERENCES.
Slater, *Early Editions* (1894), p. 169, No. 1; Thomson (D. C.), *Life and Labours of Hablôt Knight Browne,* "*Phiz*" (1884), p. 153.

Lever, who derived his talent for story-telling from his father, an English architect, was graduated from Trinity College, Dublin, in 1827, and received his degree of Bachelor of Medicine from the same institution in 1831. He inherited a considerable fortune, but his lack of economy and his heavy losses at cards soon reduced him to a very embarrassing condition. To better his circumstances he turned his attention to literature, and in February, 1837, the first installment of *Harry Lorrequer* (our present number) appeared in the *Dublin University Magazine.* When his position seemed assured, he left Ireland in 1840 and went to Brussels, where he continued to write with great activity. *Charles O'Malley,* the most popular of all his works (our No. 450), appeared in the *Dublin Magazine* in 1840, and *Jack Hinton, the Guardsman* (our No. 451) in 1843. These novels, without art and almost devoid of literary form, display Lever's best qualities: a superabundance of animal spirits and rollicking glee, accompanied by a copious and effective anecdote and a vigorous delineation of character, as reflected from his own experience. In 1842 he returned to Dublin, to become the editor of the *Dublin University Magazine.* During his incumbency one of his most characteristic novels, *Tom Burke of "Ours"* (our No. 451), appeared in its columns. This was followed in 1844 by *Arthur O' Leary* (our No. 452). The next year he resigned his editorship, and again went to the continent, where after wandering through Germany and Italy, he finally settled at Florence in August, 1847. He there wrote a number of his novels, in which he may be said to have reached his culmination as a novelist.

In 1857 he was appointed British consul at Spezzia, an appointment which, but for his enforced residence there, might have been considered a sinecure. While there he wrote *Sir Brook Fossbrooke* (our No. 476), which of all his novels was his own favorite. In 1867 he received the appointment to the consulship of Trieste. The insalubrious climate proved fatal to his wife, who soon sickened and died. Lever then becoming despondent fell into bad habits, and at length, gradually failing in health, died June 1, 1872.

"His earliest and most popular writings can hardly rank as literature, though their vigour and gaiety, and the excellent anecdotes and spirited songs with which they are interspersed, will always render them attractive. He is almost destitute of invention or imagination, his personages are generally transcripts from the life, and his incidents stories told at second-hand. At a later period in his career he awoke in some measure to the claims of art, and exhibited more proficiency as a writer, with less damage to his character as a humorist, than might have been expected. The transition is marked by 'Roland Cashel' [our No. 460], but in 'Glencore' [our No. 466] he first deliberately attempted analysis of character. His readers lamented the disappearance of his rollicking spendthrifts and daredevil heroes, but his later works exhibit fewer traces of exhaustion and decay than is usual with veteran writers."

[LEVER, CHARLES JAMES.]

CHARLES O'MALLEY. DUBLIN, *William Curry, Jun. and Company, etc.*, 1841. 2 vols., octavo, viz.: [450]

VOL. I.

COLLATION BY SIGNATURES: 2 leaves, without signature-marks (the first blank and lacking); [*a*], 4 leaves; *b*, 2 leaves; B to Y, each 8 leaves; z, 6 leaves; total 182 leaves.

COLLATION BY PAGINATION: [1 blank leaf];—[title]|CHARLES O'MALLEY, | THE IRISH DRAGOON. | EDITED BY | HARRY LORREQUER, | WITH ILLUSTRATIONS BY | Phiz. | IN TWO VOLUMES. | VOL. I.|DUBLIN|WILLIAM CURRY, JUN. AND COMPANY. | FRASER AND CRAWFORD, EDINBURGH. | W. S. ORR AND COMPANY, LONDON. | MDCCCXLI. |, recto of second leaf;—[imprint], verso of second leaf;—[dedication, contents, and list of plates], pp. [i.]-[xi.];—[blank], p. [xii.]; —[preface], pp. [1]-2;—[text], pp. [3]-348. Page vii. is wrongly numbered vi.

PLATES: Engraved title-page and 21 plates, as called for in the list of plates; many incorrectly placed by the binder.

No. 450   *Charles James Lever*   1841

VOL. 2.

COLLATION BY SIGNATURES: [A], 4 leaves; B to Y, each 8 leaves; total 172 numbered leaves.

COLLATION BY PAGINATION: [title, same as in Vol. 1, except volume-number], p. [i.];—[imprint], p. [ii.];—[contents and list of plates], pp. [iii.]–[viii.];—[text], pp. [1]–332;—| L'ENVOI. |, pp. 333–336.

PLATES: Engraved title-page and 21 plates, as called for in the list of plates; five of them incorrectly placed by the binder.

CONDITION: Size of leaf, 8¾ × 5⁹⁄₁₆ inches. Bound from the original parts, in light brown crushed levant morocco, gilt tops, other edges uncut; by Zaehnsdorf. With pink wrappers and advertising pages on white paper, in all 46 leaves, bound in at the end, as follows: Vol. 1, Nos. 1–11, 2, 2, 2, 2, 2, 2, 2, 2, 2, and 6 leaves respectively; Vol. 2, Nos. 12–22, each 2 leaves. Published in 22 numbered monthly parts (the last a double number), from April, 1840, to December, 1841, in pink (Slater says "white") wrappers, at one shilling each, with pictorial title designed by "Phiz": | CHARLES | O'MALLEY | THE | IRISH DRAGOON | BY | HARRY LORREQUER" | ILLUSTRATED BY | "PHIZ" | WILLIAM CURRY, JUN. AND COMPANY, DUBLIN. | WILLIAM S. ORR AND COMPANY, LONDON. | FRASER AND CRAWFORD, EDINBURGH. | JOHN S. FOLDS, | Printer,] [5, Bachelor's-walk, | Dublin. | ; the imprint on some wrappers varying slightly from that here given.

REFERENCES.

Slater, *Early Editions* (1894), p. 169, No. 2; Thomson, *Life and Labours of Hablôt Knight Browne "Phiz"* (1884), p. 154.

This is the First Edition.

On the inside of the wrapper of No. 7 appears the following note: "Owing to an accident, the Plates of CHARLES O'MALLEY, No. 7, were not finished in time for Publication, but Four will be given next Month. *Sackville-street, Dublin, Sept. 25th, 1840.*"

On the inside of the wrapper of No. 9: "An accident again obliges us to publish without Plates, but they shall appear with No. 10. *Dublin. Nov. 25th, 1840.*"

On the inside of the wrapper of No. 11: "TO THE PUBLIC: THE present number completes the first volume of CHARLES O'MALLEY, and contains the plates wanting in the previous one. . . .

"A fire in the printing office in Dublin, has consumed a considerable portion of the Manuscript, but the author hopes he may be able to avoid the necessity of claiming one month's indulgence from his readers, as at first appeared necessary. *Dublin. 25th January, 1841.*"

On the inside of the wrapper of No. 20 the two volumes of *Charles O'Malley* were announced to appear on the 30th November [1841]. "Nos. XXI. and XXII., completing the work, price 2s., will be ready at the same time."

The work was afterward published in two volumes, in pictorial cloth, with the same etchings as in the parts.

When Lever was asked where he obtained the material for his soldier stories he replied, "For what is in 'O'Malley' I am mainly indebted to Napier; for the rest, to 'Les Victoires et Conquêtes de l'Armée Française.'"

LEVER, CHARLES JAMES.

OUR MESS. Dublin, *William Curry, Jun. and Company, etc.*, 1843–1844. 3 vols., octavo, viz.: [451]

Vol. 1. *Jack Hinton, the Guardsman.* 1843.

Collation by Signatures: [A], 8 leaves (the first blank and lacking); B to Z, 2A, 2B, each 8 leaves; 2C, 6 leaves; total 206 leaves. With subsidiary signature-marks, as follows: MESS, NO. I.—VOL. I. to MESS, VOL. I.—NO. XIII. (this being the order of the last); about two sheets to a number.

Collation by Pagination: [1 blank leaf], [A];—[half-title] | OUR MESS. | JACK HINTON, THE GUARDSMAN. |, recto of [A 2];—[blank], verso of [A 2];—[title] | OUR MESS. | EDITED BY | CHARLES LEVER. | (Harry Lorrequer.) | VOL. I. | JACK HINTON, THE GUARDSMAN. | WITH | A PORTRAIT OF THE AUTHOR | AND NUMEROUS ILLUSTRATIONS ON WOOD AND STEEL, | BY | Phiz. | DUBLIN | WILLIAM CURRY, JUN. AND COMPANY | WILLIAM S. ORR AND CO. LONDON. | FRASER AND CO. EDINBURGH. | MDCCCXLIII. |, p. [i.];—[imprint], p. [ii.];—[dedication, contents, and list of illustrations], pp. [iii.]–[xi.];—[blank], p. [xii.];—[poem], p. [1];—[blank], p. [2];—[notice], pp. [3]–4;—[text], pp. [5]–394;—| Envoy. |, pp. 395–396.

Plates: 1 portrait and 26 plates, as called for in the list of illustrations; many incorrectly placed by the binder; also 9 woodcuts in the text, as called for in the list of illustrations.

Vol. 2. *Tom Burke of "Ours,"* Vol. 1. 1844.

Collation by Signatures: [A], 6 leaves (the first blank and lacking); B to Z, 2 A, each 8 leaves; 2 B, 2 leaves; total 192 numbered leaves. With subsidiary signature-marks, as follows: MESS, NO. XIV.—VOL. II. to MESS, NO. XXV.—VOL. II.; about two sheets to a number.

Collation by Pagination: [1 blank leaf], pp. [i.]–[ii.];—[title] | TOM BURKE | OF "OURS." | BY | CHARLES LEVER. | (Harry Lorrequer.) | WITH NUMEROUS ILLUSTRATIONS ON STEEL, | BY | H. K. BROWNE. | IN TWO VOLUMES. | VOL. I. | DUBLIN | WILLIAM CURRY JUN. AND COMPANY. | WILLIAM S. ORR AND CO. LONDON. | FRASER AND CO. EDINBURGH. | 1844. |, p. [iii.];—[imprint], p. [iv.];—[dedication, contents, and list of illustrations], pp. [v.]–[xii.];—[poem], p. [1];—[blank], p. [2];—[prefatory epistle], p. [3];—[blank], p. [4];—[text], pp. [5]–372. Page 316 has no page-number.

Plates: 24 plates, as called for in the list of illustrations; many incorrectly placed by the binder.

Vol. 3. *Tom Burke of "Ours,"* Vol. 2. 1844.

Collation by Signatures: [A], 4 leaves; B to T, each 8 leaves; U, 4 leaves; total 152 leaves. With subsidiary signature-marks, as follows: MESS, NO. XXVI.—VOL. III. to MESS, NO. XXXIV.—VOL. III.; about two sheets to a number.

Collation by Pagination: [title, same as in Vol. 1, except volume-number], p. [i.];—[imprint], p. [ii.];—[contents and list of illustrations], pp. [iii.]–[vii.];—[blank], p. [viii.];—[text], pp. [1]–293;—| A Parting Word. |, p. 294;—[publishers' advertisements], pp. [295]–[296]. Page vi. is wrongly numbered x.

PLATES: 20 plates, as called for in the list of illustrations; many incorrectly placed by the binder.

CONDITION: Size of leaf, 8 13/16 × 5½ inches. Bound from the original parts, in light brown crushed levant morocco, gilt tops, other edges uncut; by Zaehnsdorf. With the front pink wrappers only, in all 32 leaves, bound in at the end, as follows: Vol. 1, Nos. I.–XIII., 12 leaves; Vol. 2, Nos. XIV.–XXV., 11 leaves; Vol. 3, Nos. XXVI.–35, 9 leaves. Published in 35 numbered monthly parts (Nos. XIII., XXV., and 35 being double numbers), from January, 1842, to December, 1844, in pink, sometimes white, wrappers, at one shilling each, with pictorial title designed by "Phiz": | OUR MESS | JACK HINTON [TOM BURKE | OF "OURS." | No. *1.*–22], | EDITED BY | "HARRY LORREQUER" | ILLUSTRATED BY PHIZ | WILLIAM CURRY, JUN. AND CO., SACKVILLE-STREET, DUBLIN. | W. S. ORR AND COMPANY, PATERNOSTER-ROW, LONDON. | SOLD BY ALL BOOKSELLERS. |. The leaves are stabbed throughout in the inner margins of all the volumes.

REFERENCES.

Slater, *Early Editions* (1894), p. 170, No. 3; Thomson, *Life of Hablôt Knight Browne* (1884), p. 154.

This is the First Edition.

There are two distinct stories in *Our Mess*, viz., *Jack Hinton, the Guardsman*, and *Tom Burke of "Ours."* Notwithstanding this, the whole was issued as one work in thirty-five monthly parts. It was afterward published in three volumes, in cloth, with all the etchings and woodcuts, as follows: Vol. 1, *Jack Hinton;* Vols. 2 and 3, *Tom Burke of "Ours."* The latter story is regarded by many as Lever's best work. It is especially valuable for its portrayal of the enthusiasm excited by Napoleon I., and of the life of the Irish exiles in Paris.

[LEVER, CHARLES JAMES.]

ARTHUR O'LEARY. LONDON, *Henry Colburn*, 1844. 3 vols., post octavo, viz.: [452]

VOL. 1.

COLLATION BY SIGNATURES: [A], 2 leaves; B to T, each 8 leaves; U, 2 leaves (the last blank and lacking); total 148 leaves.

COLLATION BY PAGINATION: [title] | ARTHUR O'LEARY: | HIS WANDERINGS AND PONDERINGS | IN | MANY LANDS. | EDITED BY | HIS FRIEND, HARRY LORREQUER, | AND | *ILLUSTRATED BY GEORGE CRUIKSHANK.* | IN THREE VOLUMES. | VOL. I. | LONDON: | HENRY COLBURN, PUBLISHER, | GREAT MARLBOROUGH STREET. | 1844. |, recto of [A]; —[imprint], verso of [A]; —[list of illustrations], recto of [A 2]; —[blank], verso of [A 2]; —[preface], pp. [1]–26; —[text], pp. 27–290; —[1 blank leaf], [U 2]. Page 140 is wrongly numbered 40.

PLATES: 4 etchings, one a portrait of Arthur O'Leary, as called for in the list of illustrations.

VOL. 2.

COLLATION BY SIGNATURES: [A], 2 leaves (the first blank and lacking); B to X, each 8 leaves; total 162 leaves.

COLLATION BY PAGINATION: [1 blank leaf], [A]; —[title, same as in Vol. 1, except volume-number], recto of [A 2]; —[imprint], verso of [A 2]; —[text], pp. [1]–320.

PLATES: 3 etchings, as called for in the list of illustrations in Vol. 1.

VOL. 3.

COLLATION BY SIGNATURES: [A], 2 leaves (the first blank and lacking); B to X, each 8 leaves; Y, 4 leaves; total 166 leaves.

COLLATION BY PAGINATION: [1 blank leaf], [A];—[title, same as in Vol. 1, except volume-number], recto of [A 2];— [imprint], verso of [A 2];—[text], pp. [1]- 327;—[note], p. 328. Page 236 is wrongly numbered 36.

PLATES: 3 etchings, as called for in the list of illustrations in Vol. 1.

CONDITION: Size of leaf, 7⅝ × 4¾ inches. Bound in light brown crushed levant morocco, gilt tops, other edges uncut; by Zaehnsdorf.

REFERENCES.

Slater, *Early Editions* (1894), p. 171, No. 4; Reid, *Descriptive Catalogue of the Works of George Cruikshank*, 1 (1871):170, Nos. 2277–2286; p. 330, No. 4982.

This is the First Edition of the work here described.

[LEVER, CHARLES JAMES.]

NUTS AND NUTCRACKERS. LONDON, *Wm. S. Orr and Co., etc.*, 1845.

[453]

Sixteenmo. First Edition.

COLLATION BY SIGNATURES: [A], 4 leaves; B to P, each 8 leaves; Q, 4 leaves; total 120 numbered leaves.

COLLATION BY PAGINATION: [half-title], p. [i.];—[blank], p. [ii.];—[title] | NUTS AND NUTCRACKERS. | [quotations] | ILLUSTRATED BY "PHIZ." | LONDON: | WM. S. ORR AND CO., PATERNOSTER ROW; | WILLIAM CURRY, JUN., AND CO., DUBLIN. | MDCCCXLV. |, p. [iii.];—[imprint], p. [iv.];—[contents and preface], pp. [v.]- viii.;—[text], pp. [1]-232.

PLATES: 6 plates, drawn by "Phiz," as follows:

[1] Frontispiece, without title; facing the title-page.
[2] | The Man of Genius. |; facing p. 8.
[3] | Legal Functionaries. |; facing p. 22.
[4] | Gentlemen Jocks. |; facing p. [119].
[5] | "This is a Rembrant." |; facing p. 134.
[6] | Honorable Members. |; facing p. 185.

There are also 52 woodcuts, viz., 20 initials, 7 head-pieces, 14 tail-pieces, and 11 illustrations in the text.

CONDITION: Size of leaf, 5¹⁵⁄₁₆ × 3¹⁵⁄₁₆ inches. Bound in light brown crushed levant morocco, gilt edges; by Zaehnsdorf. With the original red cloth front cover and back, each with a title and design in gilt, mounted and bound in at the end.

REFERENCE.

Slater, *Early Editions* (1894), p. 172, No. 7.

A few copies of this book were dated 1844. It was originally issued in red cloth, with pictorial designs on the front and back by "Phiz."

The Second Edition also bears the date 1845, and like the First contains six full-page etchings and a number of woodcuts in the text by "Phiz."

The Third Edition, in small octavo, appeared in 1857.

LEVER, CHARLES JAMES.

THE O'DONOGHUE. DUBLIN, *William Curry, Jun. and Company, etc.,* 1845. [454]

Octavo. First Edition.

COLLATION BY SIGNATURES: [A], 6 leaves; B to Z, 2A, 2B, 2C, each 8 leaves; 2D, 6 leaves (the last blank and lacking); total 212 numbered leaves.

COLLATION BY PAGINATION: [half-title], p. [i.]; — [blank], p. [ii.]; — [title] | THE O'DONOGHUE; | A | TALE OF IRELAND | FIFTY YEARS AGO. | BY CHARLES LEVER, ESQ. | [2 lines] | WITH ILLUSTRATIONS BY H. K. BROWNE. | DUBLIN | WILLIAM CURRY, JUN. AND COMPANY. | WILLIAM S. ORR AND CO. LONDON. | FRASER AND CO. EDINBURGH. | 1845. |, p. [iii.]; — [imprint], p. [iv.]; — [dedication, contents, and list of illustrations], pp. [v.]– [xii.]; — [text], pp. [1]–410; — [1 blank leaf], [2 D 6].

PLATES: 26 plates, as called for in the list of illustrations; many incorrectly placed by the binder.

CONDITION: Size of leaf, 8⅜ x 5⁹⁄₁₆ inches. Bound from the original parts, in light brown crushed levant morocco, gilt top, other edges uncut; by Zaehnsdorf. With pink wrappers and advertising pages on pink and white paper, in all 25 leaves, bound in at the end: Nos. I.–XIII., 4, 2, 2 (1 slip), 2, 2, 2, 2, 2, 2, 2, and 3 leaves respectively. Published in 13 numbered monthly parts (Nos. X. and XII. being double numbers), from January to November, 1845, in pink, sometimes white wrappers, at one shilling each, with pictorial title designed by "Phiz": | THE O'DONOGHUE | A TALE OF IRELAND | *Fifty Years Ago.* | BY | HARRY LORREQUER. | WILLIAM CURRY, JUN. AND CO., SACKVILLE-STREET, DUBLIN. | WILLIAM S. ORR AND CO., 2, AMEN-CORNER, LONDON. |.

REFERENCES.

Slater, *Early Editions* (1894), p. 172, No. 8; Thomson, *Life and Labours of Hablôt Knight Browne "Phiz"* (1884), p. 160.

" Dr. Fitzpatrick tells the amusing story of a mistake which occurred with the title of one of 'The O'Donoghue' illustrations. 'Phiz' wrote to Lever to explain how the lengthy and ridiculous title came to appear, saying: —

"'As to myself, when I saw it I was convulsed with laughter. I do not know whether to attribute the mistake to the carelessness, stupidity, inebriety, or the practical joking peculiarities of the writing engraver. I think it is a compound. Orr [the publisher] sent to me for a title to the plate, and as I was rather at a loss to name the child I wrote on a slip of paper thus: — 1 "Mark recognises an old acquaintance," or simply 2 "The Glen," or, (addressing Orr) anything else you like, my little dears — meaning that Orr might give a better if he could, and behold the writing engraver makes a Chinese copy of the whole.'"

The title on the etching is engraved in two lines across the plate: *"Mark recognised by an old acquaintance, or The Glen — anything you please my little dear."*

This romance owes its existence to a holiday spent by the author in the district of Killarney. Lever took its name from that of an eccentric old Irish peasant, Tim O'Donoghue, whom he met in the wild valley of Glenflesk. O'Donoghue, though in comfortable circumstances, did not scruple to ask alms, showing his rags as proof of his poverty.

LEVER, CHARLES JAMES.

ST. PATRICK'S EVE. LONDON, *Chapman and Hall*, 1845. [455]

Small quarto. First Edition.

COLLATION BY SIGNATURES: [A], 2 leaves; B, C, each 4 leaves; D, 8 leaves; E, F, each 10 leaves; G, 9 leaves; H, 12 leaves; I, 5 leaves; K, 6 leaves; L to O, each 8 leaves; P, 2 leaves; total 104 leaves.

COLLATION BY PAGINATION: [title] | ST. | PATRICK'S | EVE. | BY | CHARLES LEVER. | ILLUSTRATED BY PHIZ. | LONDON: | CHAPMAN AND HALL, 186 STRAND. | MDCCCXLV. | [engraved title-page, imprint only in type], recto of [A]; — [imprint], verso of [A]; — [dedication], recto of [A2]; — [blank], verso of [A2]; — [text in 3 parts, the first with engraved heading] | THE FIRST ERA. |, pp. [1]-203; — [imprint], p. [204].

PLATES: Engraved title-page, designed by "Phiz," and 4 plates, as follows:

[1] Frontispiece, without title; facing the title-page.
[2] | *The Rescue.* | ; facing p. 24.
[3] | *The Cholera Hut.* | ; facing p. 82.
[4] | *The Ambuscade.* | ; facing p. 186.

Each plate also carries the name of the publishers: *London: Chapman and Hall, 186, Strand.*

There are also 12 woodcuts — 3 head-pieces and 9 illustrations in the text.

CONDITION: Size of leaf, 6½ × 4⅞ inches. Bound in light brown crushed levant morocco, gilt edges; by Zaehnsdorf. With the original fancy green cloth front cover and back, each with title and designs in gilt, mounted and bound in at the end.

REFERENCE.

Slater, *Early Editions* (1894), p. 171, No. 6.

On the completion of *The O'Donoghue* Lever wrote this short novel, which he dedicated to his children. His relations with his publishers at that time being none too pleasant, Mr. Pearce, his friend, took the manuscript to London and read the greater part of the story to the Brothers Chapman, of Chapman & Hall, who promptly purchased it.

[LEVER, CHARLES JAMES.]

TALES OF THE TRAINS. LONDON, *Wm. S. Orr & Co., etc.*, 1845. [456]

Small octavo. First Edition.

COLLATION BY SIGNATURES: [A], 4 leaves; B, 8 leaves; C, 6 leaves; D to G, each 8 leaves; H, 4 leaves; I, 8 leaves; K, 4 leaves; L, 8 leaves; M, 6 leaves; total 80 numbered leaves.

COLLATION BY PAGINATION: [title] | TALES OF THE TRAINS: | BEING | Some Chapters of Railroad Romance. | BY TILBURY TRAMP, | QUEEN'S MESSENGER. | [quotation] | LONDON: | W^{M.} S. ORR & Co., PATERNOSTER ROW; | AND W^{M.} CURRY & Co., DUBLIN. | MDCCCXLV. |, p. [i.]; — [imprint], p. [ii.]; — [introduction], pp. [iii.]-viii.; — [text in 5 tales, with engraved heading to each], pp. [5]-156.

ILLUSTRATIONS: 15 woodcuts, designed by "Phiz" and engraved by E. Evans, viz.: 5 head-pieces, 3 tail-pieces, and 7 illustrations in the text.

CONDITION: Size of leaf, 6 × 4 3/16 inches. Bound in light brown crushed levant morocco, gilt edges; by Zaehnsdorf. With the original red cloth front cover and back, each with title and designs in gilt, mounted and bound in at the end.

REFERENCE.

Slater, *Early Editions* (1894), p. 171, No. 5.

LEVER, CHARLES JAMES.

THE KNIGHT OF GWYNNE. London, *Chapman and Hall*, 1847. [457]

Octavo. First Edition.

COLLATION BY SIGNATURES: [A], 6 leaves; B to Z, 2 A to 2 R, each 8 leaves; 2 S, 2 leaves; total 320 numbered leaves.

COLLATION BY PAGINATION: [half-title], p. [i.];—[blank], p. [ii.];—[title] | THE | KNIGHT OF GWYNNE; | A Tale of the Time of the Union. | BY CHARLES LEVER, | . . . | WITH ILLUSTRATIONS BY "PHIZ." | LONDON: | CHAPMAN AND HALL, 186, STRAND. | MDCCCXLVII. |, p. [iii.];—[imprint], p. [iv.];—[dedication, contents, and list of plates], pp. [v.]–[xi.];—[blank], p. [xii.];—[text], pp. [1]–628.

PLATES: Engraved title-page and 39 plates, as called for in the list of plates; five of them incorrectly placed by the binder.

CONDITION: Size of leaf, 8¾ x 5½ inches. Bound from the original parts, in light brown crushed levant morocco, gilt top, other edges uncut; by Zaehnsdorf.

With pink wrappers and advertising pages on white paper, in all 58 leaves, bound in at the end of the volume: Nos. I.–XX., 2, 2, 8, 2, 2, 2, 2, 10, 2, 2, 2, 2, 2, 6, 2, 2, 2, and 4 leaves respectively. Published in 20 numbered monthly parts (the last a double number), from January, 1846, to July, 1847, in pink wrappers, at one shilling each, with pictorial title designed by "Phiz": | THE KNIGHT | OF | GWYNNE | A TALE | OF THE TIME OF THE UNION | BY | CHARLES LEVER | ILLUSTRATED BY PHIZ. | LONDON: CHAPMAN AND HALL, 186, STRAND. | J. MENZIES, EDINBURGH; J. CUMMING, DUBLIN. |; the imprint on some wrappers varying slightly from that here given.

REFERENCES.

Slater, *Early Editions* (1894), p. 173, No. 9; Thomson, *Life of Hablôt Knight Browne* (1884), p. 160.

In the last number is an advertising leaf, verso blank, announcing that "THE KNIGHT OF GWYNNE, complete in One Volume, will be ready for delivery on the 20th instant." This announcement is dated July 1, 1847.

[LEVER, CHARLES JAMES.]

DIARY AND NOTES OF HORACE TEMPLETON. London, *Chapman and Hall*, 1848. 2 vols., post octavo, viz.: [458]

VOL. I.

COLLATION BY SIGNATURES: [A], 2 leaves; B to U, each 8 leaves; X, 2 leaves; total 156 leaves.

COLLATION BY PAGINATION: [half-title], recto of [A];—[editor's notice of a German translation, and imprint], verso of [A];—[title] | DIARY AND NOTES | OF | HORACE TEMPLETON, ESQ. | LATE SECRETARY OF LEGATION AT ——. | IN TWO VOLUMES. | VOL. I. | LONDON: | CHAPMAN AND HALL, 186 STRAND. | 1848. |, recto of [A2];—[blank], verso of [A2];—[text], pp. [1]–308.

VOL. 2.

COLLATION BY SIGNATURES: [A], 2 leaves; B to S, each 8 leaves; T, 4 leaves; total 142 leaves.

COLLATION BY PAGINATION: [half-title], recto of [A]; — [imprint], verso of [A]; — [title, same as in Vol. 1, except volume-number], recto of [A2]; — [blank], verso of [A2]; — [text], pp. [1]–280.

CONDITION: Size of leaf, 7⅝ × 4¾ inches. Bound in light brown crushed levant morocco, gilt tops, other edges uncut; by Zaehnsdorf.

REFERENCE.

Slater, *Early Editions* (1894), p. 173, No. 10.

This is the First Edition of the work here described.

[LEVER, CHARLES JAMES.]

CONFESSIONS OF CON. CREGAN. LONDON, *Wm. S. Orr and Co.*, [1850]. 2 vols., post octavo, viz.: [459]

VOL. 1.

COLLATION BY SIGNATURES: [A], 4 leaves; B to Y, each 8 leaves; total 172 numbered leaves.

COLLATION BY PAGINATION: [title] | CONFESSIONS | OF | CON. CREGAN: | THE IRISH GIL BLAS. | With Illustrations on Wood and Steel. | BY HABLOT K. BROWN. | VOL. I. | LONDON: | WM. S. ORR AND CO., AMEN-CORNER, | PATERNOSTER-ROW. |, p. [i.]; — [imprint], p. [ii.]; — [preface, contents, and list of illustrations], pp. [iii.]–viii.; — [text], pp. [1]–336.

PLATES: Engraved title-page and 13 plates, as called for in the list of illustrations; also 30 woodcuts, viz., 22 head-pieces and 8 tail-pieces.

VOL. 2.

COLLATION BY SIGNATURES: [A], 4 leaves; B to I, each 8 leaves; K, 6 leaves; L to U, each 8 leaves; X, 4 leaves; total 158 numbered leaves.

COLLATION BY PAGINATION: [half-title], p. [i.]; — [blank], p. [ii.]; — [title, same as in Vol. 1, except volume-number], p. [iii.]; — [imprint], p. [iv.]; — [contents and list of illustrations], pp. [v.]–viii.; — [text], pp. [1]–305; — [blank], p. [306]; — [publishers' announcement], pp. [i.]–ii.

PLATES: Engraved title-page and 14 plates, as called for in the list of illustrations (the frontispiece is lacking); also 14 woodcut head-pieces.

CONDITION: Size of leaf, 7½ × 4⅞ inches. Bound from the original parts, in light brown crushed levant morocco, gilt tops, other edges uncut; by Zaehnsdorf. With green wrappers and advertising pages on white paper, numbering in all 60 leaves, bound in at the end, as follows: Vol. 1, Nos. I.–VII., 6, 6, 6, 6, 6, 4, and 8 leaves respectively; Vol. 2, Nos. VIII.–XIV., 4, 2, 4, 2, 2, and 4 leaves respectively. Published in 14 monthly parts (the last a double number), in green wrappers, at one shilling each, with pictorial title designed by "Phiz": | CON | CREGAN | THE IRISH | GIL BLAS. | LONDON | W. S. ORR & C° | TYLER AND REED, PRINTERS,] [BOLT-COURT, FLEET-STREET. |; the printer's imprint on some wrappers varying slightly from that here given.

REFERENCES.
Slater, *Early Editions* (1894), p. 174, No. 12; Thomson, *Life of Hablôt Knight Browne* (1884), p. 165.

This is the First Edition.

Though published anonymously, this book is usually considered to have been written by Lever. Originally issued in parts, it was afterward published in two volumes, in pictorial cloth designed by "Phiz."

LEVER, CHARLES JAMES.

ROLAND CASHEL. LONDON, *Chapman and Hall*, 1850. [460]

Octavo. First Edition.

COLLATION BY SIGNATURES: [A], 4 leaves; B to Z, 2A to 2R, each 8 leaves; 2S, 2 leaves; total 318 numbered leaves.

COLLATION BY PAGINATION: [half-title], p. [i.];—[blank], p. [ii.];—[title]|ROLAND CASHEL.|BY|CHARLES LEVER,|[2 lines]|WITH ILLUSTRATIONS BY PHIZ.|LONDON:|CHAPMAN AND HALL, 186, STRAND.|MDCCCL.|, p. [iii.];—[imprint], p. [iv.];—[dedication and list of plates], pp. [v.]-viii.;—[text], pp. [1]-627;—[imprint], p. [628].

PLATES: Engraved title-page and 39 plates, as called for in the list of plates; three of them incorrectly placed by the binder.

CONDITION: Size of leaf, 8 13/16 × 5 5/8 inches. Bound from the original parts, in light brown crushed levant morocco, gilt top, other edges uncut; by Zaehnsdorf. With wrappers and advertising pages on pink, blue, and white paper, in all 75 leaves, bound in at the end. Nos. I.–XX. (No. III. is lacking), 8, 4, 2, 2, 3, 2, 11, 4 (and duplicate front wrapper), 3, 8 (back wrapper lacking), 4, 3 (back wrapper lacking), 2, 2, 2, 2, 6, and 6 leaves respectively. Published in 20 monthly numbered parts (the last a double number), from May, 1848, to November, 1849, in pink wrappers, at one shilling each, with pictorial title designed by "Phiz":| ROLAND | CASHEL | BY | CHARLES LEVER.| ILLUSTRATED | BY PHIZ.| LONDON: CHAPMAN AND HALL, 186, STRAND.| J. MENZIES, EDINBURGH; J. M'GLASHAN, DUBLIN. | C. WHITING,] [1848–]1849 [BEAUFORT HOUSE.|; the imprint on some wrappers varying slightly from that here given.

REFERENCES.

Slater, *Early Editions* (1894), p. 174, No. 11; Thomson, *Life of Hablôt Knight Browne* (1884), p. 165.

This work, originally issued in parts, was afterward published in one volume, in pictorial cloth.

"Occasionally an edition in one, or sometimes two volumes, dated 1851, is described as the first. This is not correct, for unless the book is dated 1850 in Roman figures, it does not belong to the first issue."

Writing to Alexander Spencer, from Florence, August 19, 1848, Lever says: "I hope you continue to like 'Roland Cashel.' Has anyone detected Archbishop Whately as my Dean of Drumcondra? The whole *dramatis personæ* are portraits." He also informs him in another letter, April 17, 1849, that by the burning of a mail-boat, "I (with my accustomed luck) lost a whole number of 'Roland Cashel' —twelve days' work, of which I have, of course, not a note or memorandum."

LEVER, CHARLES JAMES.

THE DALTONS. LONDON, *Chapman and Hall*, 1852. 2 vols., octavo, viz.:

VOL. 1.

COLLATION BY SIGNATURES: [A], 4 leaves; B to Z, 2A, 2B, each 8 leaves; total 196 numbered leaves.
COLLATION BY PAGINATION: [half-title], p. [i.]; —[blank], p. [ii.]; —[title] | THE DALTONS | OR | THREE ROADS IN LIFE. | BY | CHARLES LEVER | . . . | WITH ILLUSTRATIONS BY PHIZ. | IN TWO VOLUMES.

| VOL. I. | LONDON: | CHAPMAN AND HALL, 193, PICCADILLY. | 1852. |, p. [iii.]; —[blank], p. [iv.]; —[dedication, contents, and list of plates], pp. [v.]-[viii.]; —[text], pp. [1]-384.

PLATES: Engraved title-page and 25 plates, as called for in the list of plates; nine of them incorrectly placed by the binder.

VOL. 2.

COLLATION BY SIGNATURES: [A], 4 leaves; B to Z, each 8 leaves; 2A, 4 leaves; total 184 numbered leaves.
COLLATION BY PAGINATION: [half-title], p. [i.]; —[blank], p. [ii.]; —[title, same as in Vol. 1, except volume-number], p. [iii.]; —[blank], p. [iv.]; —[contents and list of plates], pp. [v.]-[vii.]; —[blank], p. [viii.]; —[text], pp. [1]-357; — | ENVOY. |, pp. 358-360.

PLATES: 22 plates, as called for in the list of plates; eight of them incorrectly placed by the binder.

CONDITION: Size of leaf, 8¾ × 5⅝ inches. Bound from the original parts, in light brown crushed levant morocco, gilt tops, other edges uncut; by Zaehnsdorf. With wrappers and advertising pages on pink and white paper, in all 47 leaves, bound in at the end, viz.: Vol. 1, Nos. I.–XI., 2, 2, 3, 2, 3, 2, 2, 2, 3, 2, and 2 leaves respectively; Vol. 2, Nos. XII.–XXIV., 2 (1 slip), 2, 2, 2, 2, 2, 2, 2 (1 slip), 2 (1 slip), 2, 2, and 2 leaves respectively. Published in 24 monthly parts (the last a double number), from May, 1850, to April, 1852, in pink wrappers, at one shilling each, with pictorial title designed by "Phiz": | THE | DALTONS | O 3 R [or 3] | ROADS IN LIFE | BY | CHARLES LEVER. | ILLUSTRATED | BY PHIZ. | LONDON: CHAPMAN AND HALL, 193, PICCADILLY | (LATE 186, STRAND). | J. MENZIES, EDINBURGH; J. M'GLASHAN, DUBLIN. | C. WHITING,] 1851. [BEAUFORT HOUSE.]; the imprint on some wrappers varying from that here given.

REFERENCES.

Slater, *Early Editions* (1894), p. 175, No. 13; Thomson, *Life of Hablôt Knight Browne* (1884), p. 165.

This is the First Edition.

The Daltons, originally issued in parts, was afterward published in two volumes. Proof impressions of the plates were separately issued in a portfolio.

In *The Daltons*, possibly Lever's most ambitious work, were embodied some of the ideas he had expected to use in "Corrig O'Neill," a novel which he had abandoned in 1845. In a letter to Spencer, February 26, 1850, he says, "I am now cudgelling my brains about a new story for Chapman, to be called 'The Daltons, or, Three Roads in Life,' in which I have attempted — God knows with what chance of success! — the quiet homely narrative style of German romance-writers.

LEVER, CHARLES JAMES.

THE DODD FAMILY ABROAD. LONDON, *Chapman and Hall*, 1854. [462]

Octavo. First Edition.

COLLATION BY SIGNATURES: [A] to z, 2 A to 2 R, each 8 leaves; total 320 numbered leaves.

COLLATION BY PAGINATION: [half-title], p. [i.];—[blank], p. [ii.];—[title]|THE|DODD FAMILY ABROAD.|BY|CHARLES LEVER,|[2 lines]|WITH ILLUSTRATIONS BY PHIZ.|LONDON:|CHAPMAN AND HALL, 193, PICCADILLY.|MDCCCLIV.|, p. [iii.];—[blank], p. [iv.];—[dedication, preface, contents, and list of plates], pp. [v.]-[xvi.];—[text], pp. [1]-624.

PLATES: Engraved title-page and 39 plates, as called for in the list of plates. The plate facing p. 616 should face p. 617.

CONDITION: Size of leaf, 8 13/16 × 5 11/16 inches. Bound from the original parts, in light brown crushed levant morocco, gilt top, other edges uncut; by Zaehnsdorf. With wrappers and advertising pages on pink, white, and yellow paper, in all 62 leaves, bound in at the end as follows: Nos. I.–XX., 6, 2, 2, 8, 2, 2, 2, 2, 3, 2, 2, 4, 3, 3, 3, 4, 4, 4, and 4 leaves respectively. Published in 20 monthly parts (the last a double number), from September, 1852, to April, 1854, in pink or white wrappers, at one shilling each, with title designed by "Phiz": | THE | DODD | FAMILY | ABROAD. | BY | CHARLES LEVER | LONDON : CHAPMAN AND HALL, 193, PICCADILLY.|J. MENZIES, EDINBURGH; J. M'GLASHAN, DUBLIN.|C. WHITING,] 1852[-1854]. [BEAUFORT HOUSE.|.

REFERENCE.

Slater, *Early Editions* (1894), p. 175, No. 14.

[LEVER, CHARLES JAMES.]

MAURICE TIERNAY. LONDON, *Thomas Hodgson*, [1855]. [463]

Small octavo. First Edition.

COLLATION BY SIGNATURES: 2 leaves, without signature-marks; [1] to 31, each 8 leaves; 2 leaves, without signature-marks; total 252 leaves.

COLLATION BY PAGINATION: [blank], p. [i.];—[publisher's advertisement], pp. [ii.]-[iii.];—[blank], p. [iv.];—[half-title], p. [1];—[blank], p. [2];—[title]|MAURICE TIERNAY,|THE|SOLDIER OF FORTUNE.|[3 lines]|LONDON:|THOMAS HODGSON, 13, PATERNOSTER ROW.|, p. [3];—[imprint]|LONDON: PRINTED BY WOODFALL AND KINDER,|ANGEL COURT, SKINNER STREET.|, p. [4];—[preface], p. [5];—[blank], p. [6];—[text], pp. [7]-495;—[blank], p. [496];—[publisher's notice], p. [497];—[publisher's advertisement], pp. [498]-[499];—[blank], p. [500].

CONDITION: Size of leaf, 6½ × 3⅞ inches. Bound in light brown crushed levant morocco, gilt top, other edges uncut; by Zaehnsdorf. With the green paper covers of the original board binding, two sides and back, bound in at the end, with title: | THE | PARLOUR | LIBRARY | MAURICE TIERNAY,| THE | SOLDIER OF FORTUNE. | TWO SHILLINGS.|LONDON: THOMAS HODGSON.|13, Paternoster Row.|.

REFERENCE.

Slater, *Early Editions* (1894), p. 176, No. 15.

[LEVER, CHARLES JAMES.]

SIR JASPER CAREW. LONDON, *Thomas Hodgson*, [1855]. [464]

Foolscap octavo. First Edition.

COLLATION BY SIGNATURES: 2 leaves, without signature-marks; [1] to 30, each 8 leaves; 2 leaves, without signature-marks; total 244 leaves.

COLLATION BY PAGINATION: [blank], recto of first leaf;—[publisher's advertisement], verso of first leaf to recto of second leaf;—[blank], verso of second leaf;—[half-title], p. [i.];—[blank], p. [ii.];—[title]|SIR JASPER CAREW,|HIS|LIFE AND EXPERIENCES.|[2 lines]||LONDON:|THOMAS HODGSON, 13, PATERNOSTER ROW.|, p. [iii.];—[imprint], p. [iv.];—[dedication and preface], pp. [v.]–viii.;—[text], pp. [9]–480; —[blank], p. [481];—[publisher's advertisements], pp. [482]–[483];—[blank], p. [484].

CONDITION: Size of leaf, 6$\frac{7}{16}$ × 3$\frac{7}{8}$ inches. Bound in light brown crushed levant morocco, gilt top; by Zaehnsdorf. With the paper cover of the original board binding, two sides and back, with designs in colors, bound in at the end, with title: |SIR|JASPER CAREW.|HODGSON LONDON.|*J. KING, LITH.*|; and on back:|PARLOUR|LIBRARY.|SIR|JASPER|CAREW.|25|.

REFERENCE.

Slater, *Early Editions* (1894), p. 176, No. 16.

LEVER, CHARLES JAMES.

THE MARTINS OF CRO' MARTIN. LONDON, *Chapman and Hall*, 1856. 1 vol. in 2. [465]

Octavo. First Edition.

COLLATION BY SIGNATURES: 1 leaf, without signature-mark; [a], 4 leaves; b, 2 leaves; B to Z, 2 A to 2 R, each 8 leaves; 2 S, 1 leaf (the companion leaf to this is probably the half-title); total 320 numbered leaves.

COLLATION BY PAGINATION: [half-title], p. [i.];—[blank], p. [ii.];—[title]|THE|MARTINS OF CRO' MARTIN|BY|CHARLES LEVER,|[2 lines]|WITH ILLUSTRATIONS BY "PHIZ."|LONDON:|CHAPMAN AND HALL, 193, PICCADILLY.|MDCCCLVI.|, p. [iii.];—[blank], p. [iv.];—[dedication, preface, contents, and list of plates], pp. [v.]–[xiv.];—[text], pp. [1]–625;—[imprint], p. [626].

PLATES: Engraved title-page and 39 plates, as called for in the list of plates; many incorrectly placed by the binder.

CONDITION: Size of leaf, 8¾ × 5⅝ inches. Bound from the original parts, in light brown crushed levant morocco, gilt tops, other edges uncut; by Zaehnsdorf. With pink wrappers and advertising pages on pink and white paper, in all 63 leaves, bound in at the end, as follows: Vol. 1, Nos. I–X., 5, 6, 6, 2, 2, 8, 4, 3, 4, and 4 leaves respectively; Vol. 2, Nos. XI.–XX., 2, 2, 3, 2, 2, 2, 2, 2, and 2 leaves respectively. Published in 20 numbered monthly parts (the last a double number), from December, 1854, to June, 1856, in pink, sometimes white, wrappers, at one shilling each, with pictorial title designed by "Phiz":|THE|MARTINS|OF|CRO' MARTIN|BY|CHARLES LEVER|LONDON: CHAPMAN AND HALL, 193, PICCADILLY.|MENZIES, EDINBURGH; MURRAY & SON, GLASGOW; J. M'GLASHAN, DUBLIN.|C. WHITING,] 1854. [BEAUFORT HOUSE.|. The binder has placed the half-title as the first leaf in the second volume.

REFERENCES.

Slater, *Early Editions* (1894), p. 176, No. 17; Thomson, *Life of Hablôt Knight Browne* (1884), p. 166.

On the completion of this novel it was published in one volume, octavo. In it we have a fine picture of life in the west of Ireland in the time of an epidemic which made fearful ravages in the wilds of Clare.

LEVER, CHARLES JAMES.

THE FORTUNES OF GLENCORE. London, *Chapman and Hall*, 1857. 3 vols., crown octavo, viz.: [466]

VOL. 1.

COLLATION BY SIGNATURES: [*a*], 2 leaves (the first blank and lacking); *b*, 4 leaves; B to U, each 8 leaves; total 158 numbered leaves.

COLLATION BY PAGINATION: [1 blank leaf], [*a*]; — [title] | THE | FORTUNES OF GLENCORE. | BY | CHARLES LEVER. | IN THREE VOLUMES. | VOL. I. | LONDON : | CHAPMAN AND HALL, 193, PICCADILLY. | MDCCCLVII. |, p. [i.]; — [blank], p. [ii.]; — [dedication and preface], pp. [iii.] – x.; — [text], pp. [1] – 303; — [blank], p. [304].

VOL. 2.

COLLATION BY SIGNATURES: [A], 2 leaves (the first blank and lacking); B to T, each 8 leaves; U, 4 leaves; total 150 leaves.

COLLATION BY PAGINATION: [1 blank leaf], [A]; — [title, same as in Vol. 1, except volume-number], recto of [A2]; — [blank], verso of [A2]; — [text], pp. [1] – 296.

VOL. 3.

COLLATION BY SIGNATURES: [A], 2 leaves (the first blank and lacking); B to U, each 8 leaves; X, 4 leaves; total 158 leaves.

COLLATION BY PAGINATION: [1 blank leaf], [A]; — [title, same as in Vol. 1, except volume-number], recto of [A2]; — [blank], verso of [A2]; — [text], pp. [1] – 311; — [imprint], p. [312].

CONDITION: Size of leaf, 7⅝ × 4⅞ inches. Bound in light brown crushed levant morocco, gilt tops, other edges uncut; by Zaehnsdorf.

REFERENCE.

Slater, *Early Editions* (1894), p. 177, No. 18.

This, the First Edition of this work, was originally published in green cloth.

LEVER, CHARLES JAMES.

DAVENPORT DUNN. London, *Chapman and Hall*, 1859. [467]

Octavo. First Edition.

COLLATION BY SIGNATURES: [A], 4 leaves; B to Z, 2A to 2X, each 8 leaves; 2Y, 4 leaves; total 352 numbered leaves. Leaf 2M is wrongly marked M.

COLLATION BY PAGINATION: [title] | DAVENPORT DUNN | A MAN OF OUR DAY | BY | CHARLES LEVER, | [2 lines] | WITH ILLUSTRATIONS BY "PHIZ." | LONDON : | CHAPMAN AND HALL, 193, PICCADILLY. | MDCCCLIX. |, p. [i.]; — [blank], p. [ii.];

—[dedication, contents, and list of plates], pp. [iii.]–[viii.];—[text], pp. [1]–695; —[blank], p. [696].

PLATES: Engraved title-page and 43 plates, as called for in the list of plates; five of them incorrectly placed by the binder.

CONDITION: Size of leaf, 8 11/16 x 5 5/8 inches. Bound from the original parts, in light brown crushed levant morocco, gilt top, other edges uncut; by Zaehnsdorf. With wrappers on pink paper and advertising pages on pink, white, and green paper, in all 93 leaves, bound in at the end, as follows: Nos. I.–XXII., 6, 5, 4, 4, 5 (2 slips), 4, 6, 4, 4, 4, 5, 6, 4, 4, 4, 4, 4, 4, 4, 4, and 4 leaves respectively. Published in 22 monthly parts (the last a double number), from July, 1857, to April, 1859, in pink wrappers, at one shilling each, with pictorial title designed by "Phiz": | DAVENPORT | DUNN. | OR | THE MAN OF THE DAY. | BY | CHARLES LEVER. | LONDON: CHAPMAN AND HALL, 193, PICCADILLY. | J. MENZIES, EDINBURGH; MURRAY & SON, GLASGOW; M'GLASHAN & GILL, DUBLIN. | C. WHITING,] 1857. [BEAUFORT HOUSE.] ; the printer's imprint on some wrappers varying slightly from that here given.

REFERENCES.

Slater, *Early Editions* (1894), p. 177, No. 19; Thomson, *Life of Hablôt Knight Browne* (1884), p. 169.

This book, one of Lever's best, is said to be founded on the leading incidents in the career of John Sadler, a Junior Lord of the Admiralty.

LEVER, CHARLES JAMES.

ONE OF THEM. LONDON, *Chapman and Hall*, 1861. [468]

Octavo. First Edition.

COLLATION BY SIGNATURES: [A], 4 leaves; B to Z, 2 A to 2 G, each 8 leaves; 2 H, 4 leaves; total 240 numbered leaves.

COLLATION BY PAGINATION: [title]| ONE OF THEM | BY | CHARLES LEVER, | [2 lines] | WITH ILLUSTRATIONS BY PHIZ. | LONDON: | CHAPMAN AND HALL, 193, PICCADILLY. | MDCCCLXI. | [*The right of Translation is reserved.*]|, p. [i.];— [blank], p. [ii.];—[dedication, contents, and list of plates], pp. [iii.]–[viii.];— [preface], pp. [1]–2;—[text], pp. [3]– 471;—[imprint], p. [472].

PLATES: Engraved title-page and 29 plates, as called for in the list of plates; many incorrectly placed by the binder.

CONDITION: Size of leaf, 8 3/4 x 5 1/2 inches. Bound from the original parts, in light brown crushed levant morocco, gilt top, other edges uncut; by Zaehnsdorf. With wrappers and advertising pages on pink, white, and various colored papers, in all 67 leaves and 4 slips, bound in at the end, as follows: Nos. I.–XV., 8, 5 (2 slips), 6, 2, 2, 8, 5, 6 (1 slip), 4 (1 slip), 6, 5, 2, 6, and 2 leaves respectively. Published in 15 numbered monthly parts (the last a double number), from December, 1859, to January, 1861, in pink or white wrappers, at one shilling each, with pictorial title designed by "Phiz": | ONE | OF | THEM | BY | CHARLES LEVER | LONDON: CHAPMAN AND HALL, 193, PICCADILLY. | J. MENZIES, EDINBURGH; MURRAY & SON, GLASGOW; M'GLASHAN & GILL, DUBLIN. | C. WHITING,] *The right of Translation is reserved.* [BEAUFORT HOUSE.|.

REFERENCES.

Slater, *Early Editions* (1894), p. 177, No. 20; Thomson, *Life of Hablôt Knight Browne* (1884), p. 169.

LEVER, CHARLES JAMES.

BARRINGTON. LONDON, *Chapman and Hall*, 1863. [469]

Octavo. First Edition.
COLLATION BY SIGNATURES: [A], b, each 2 leaves; B to Z, 2 A, 2 B, 2 C, each 8 leaves; 2 D, 4 leaves; 2 E, 2 leaves; total 210 numbered leaves.
COLLATION BY PAGINATION: [title] | BARRINGTON. | BY | CHARLES LEVER, | [2 lines] | WITH ILLUSTRATIONS BY PHIZ. | LONDON : | CHAPMAN AND HALL, 193, PICCADILLY. | 1863. | [*The right of Translation is reserved.*] |, p. [i.]; —[blank], p. [ii.]; —[dedication, contents, and list of illustrations], pp. [iii.]-[vii.]; —[blank], p. [viii.]; —[text], pp. [1]-411; —[imprint], p. [412].
PLATES: Engraved title-page (not included in the list of illustrations) and 25 plates, as called for in the list of illustrations; eight of them incorrectly placed by the binder.
CONDITION: Size of leaf, 8¾ x 5⁹⁄₁₆ inches. Bound from the original parts, in light brown crushed levant morocco, gilt top, other edges uncut; by Zaehnsdorf. With pink wrappers and advertising pages on pink and white paper, in all 62 leaves, bound in at the end, as follows: Nos. I.-XIII., 5 (1 slip), 4 (2 slips), 5, 4, 8, 4, 6, 4, 8, 8, 6 (1 slip), and 4 leaves respectively. Published in 13 numbered monthly parts (the last a double number), from February, 1862, to January, 1863, in pink wrappers, at one shilling each, with pictorial title designed by "Phiz": | BARRINGTON | BY | CHARLES LEVER, | AUTHOR OF "HARRY LORREQUER," "CHARLES O'MALLEY," &c. | ILLUSTRATED by H. K. BROWNE | LONDON: CHAPMAN AND HALL, 193, PICCADILLY. | J. MENZIES, EDINBURGH; MURRAY & SON, GLASGOW; M'GLASHAN & GILL, DUBLIN. | C. WHITING,] *The right of Translation is reserved*. [BEAUFORT HOUSE. |. The binder has wrongly placed the preliminary leaves, as follows: title-page, table of contents, list of illustrations, and dedication.

REFERENCES.

Slater, *Early Editions* (1894), p. 178, No. 21; Thomson, *Life of Hablôt Knight Browne* (1884), p. 170.

Though dated 1863, this work was really published at the close of the preceding year. The story is interesting, being, it is said, partly the history of Lever's own son.

LEVER, CHARLES JAMES.

A DAY'S RIDE. LONDON, *Chapman and Hall*, 1863. 2 vols., crown octavo, viz.: [470]

VOL. I.

COLLATION BY SIGNATURES: [A], 2 leaves (the first blank and lacking); B to X, each 8 leaves; total 162 leaves.
COLLATION BY PAGINATION: [1 blank leaf], [A]; —[title] | A DAY'S RIDE: | A LIFE'S ROMANCE. | BY | CHARLES LEVER, | [2 lines] | IN TWO VOLUMES. | VOL. I. | Second Edition. | LONDON: | CHAPMAN AND HALL, 193, PICCADILLY. | 1863. |, recto of [A 2]; —[blank], verso of [A 2]; —[text], pp. [1]-318; —[blank], p. [319]; —[publishers' announcement], p. [320].

VOL. 2.

COLLATION BY SIGNATURES: [A], 2 leaves (the first blank and lacking); B to X, each 8 leaves; Y, 4 leaves; total 166 leaves.

COLLATION BY PAGINATION: [1 blank leaf], [A];—[title, same as in Vol. 1, except volume-number], recto of [A 2];—[blank], verso of [A 2];—[text], pp. [1]-327;—[blank], p. [328].

CONDITION: Size of leaf, 7⅝ × 4⅞ inches. Bound in light brown crushed levant morocco, gilt tops, other edges uncut; by Zaehnsdorf.

REFERENCE.

Slater, *Early Editions* (1894), p. 178, No. 22.

This story first appeared in *All the Year Round*, and was subsequently issued in two volumes. Though the words "Second Edition," appear on the title-page this is usually considered to be the First Edition. The first illustrated edition appeared in 1864. Of this story, which relates the adventures of a half-shrewd, half-foolish day-dreamer, Lever did not hold a very high opinion.

[LEVER, CHARLES JAMES.]

CORNELIUS O'DOWD. EDINBURGH AND LONDON, *William Blackwood and Sons*, 1864. 3 vols., crown octavo, viz.: [471]

VOL. 1. 1864.

COLLATION BY SIGNATURES: 6 leaves, without signature-marks; A to S, each 8 leaves; T, 4 leaves; U, 2 leaves; 10 quired leaves, without signature-marks; total 166 numbered leaves.

COLLATION BY PAGINATION: [half-title], p. [i.];—[blank], p. [ii.];—[title] | CORNELIUS O'DOWD | UPON | MEN AND WOMEN | AND | OTHER THINGS

IN GENERAL | [quotation] | WILLIAM BLACKWOOD AND SONS | EDINBURGH AND LONDON | MDCCCLXIV | *The Right of Translation is reserved.* |, p. [iii.];—[publishers' notice], p. [iv.];—[dedication, preface, and contents], pp. [v.]-xii.;—[text], pp. [1]-299;—[blank], p. [300];—[publishers' catalogue], pp. [1]-[20].

VOL. 2. 1865.

COLLATION BY SIGNATURES: 4 leaves, without signature-marks; A to U, each 8 leaves; X, 2 leaves (the last blank and lacking); total 166 numbered leaves.

COLLATION BY PAGINATION: [half-title], p. [i.];—[blank], p. [ii.];—[title,

same as in Vol. 1, except series-number and date], p. [iii.];—[publishers' notice], p. [iv.];—[dedication and contents], pp. [v.]-viii. [wrongly numbered xii.];—[text], pp. [1]-322;—[1 blank leaf], [X 2].

VOL. 3. 1865.

COLLATION BY SIGNATURES: 4 leaves, without signature-marks; A to S, each 8 leaves; 12 quired leaves, without signature-marks; total 160 numbered leaves.

COLLATION BY PAGINATION: [half-

title], p. [i.];—[blank], p. [ii.];—[title, same as in Vol. 1, except series-number and date], p. [iii.];—[publishers' notice], p. [iv.];—[dedication and contents], pp. [v.]-viii.;—[text], pp. [1]-287;—[blank],

No. 471   *Charles James Lever*   1864

p. [288]; — [publishers' advertisement], pp. [1]-[4]; — [publishers' catalogue], pp. [1]-[20].

CONDITION: Size of leaf, 7½ × 5⅟₁₆ inches. Bound in light brown crushed levant morocco, gilt tops; by Zaehnsdorf. With the original green cloth front cover and back, each with title, mounted and bound in at the end of each volume.

REFERENCE.

Slater, *Early Editions* (1894), p. 178, No. 23.

This is the First Edition of *Cornelius O'Dowd*, which was originally published in *Blackwood's Magazine*.

LEVER, CHARLES JAMES.

LUTTRELL OF ARRAN. LONDON, *Chapman and Hall*, 1865.   [472]

Octavo. First Edition.

COLLATION BY SIGNATURES: [A], 4 leaves; B to Z, 2A to 2I, each 8 leaves; 2K, 4 leaves; total 256 numbered leaves.

COLLATION BY PAGINATION: [title] | LUTTRELL OF ARRAN | BY | CHARLES LEVER, | ... | WITH ILLUSTRATIONS BY "PHIZ." | LONDON : | CHAPMAN AND HALL, 193, PICCADILLY. | MDCCCLXV. | *The Right of Translation is reserved.* |, p. [i.]; — [blank], p. [ii.]; — [dedication, contents, and list of illustrations], pp. [iii.]-[viii.]; — [text], pp. [1]-503; — [imprint], p. [504].

PLATES: Engraved title-page (not included in the list of illustrations) and 31 plates, as called for in the list of illustrations; three of them incorrectly placed by the binder.

CONDITION: Size of leaf, 8¾ × 5⅝ inches. Bound in light brown crushed levant morocco, gilt top, other edges uncut; by Zaehnsdorf. With pink wrappers and advertising pages on pink, white, and blue paper, in all 102 leaves, bound in at the end, as follows: Nos. I.–XVI, 6 (2 slips), 9 (1 slip), 5, 7, 7 (1 slip), 10, 10, 4 (1 slip), 6, 5 (1 slip), 8, 7, 8 (1 slip), 4, and 6 (2 slips) leaves respectively. Published in 16 numbered monthly parts (the last a double number), from December, 1864, to February, 1865, in pink wrappers, at one shilling each, with pictorial title designed by "Phiz": | LUTTRELL | OF | ARRAN. | BY | CHARLES LEVER | LONDON : | CHAPMAN AND HALL, 193, PICCADILLY. | J. MENZIES, EDINBURGH; MURRAY & SON, GLASGOW; M'GLASHAN & GILL, DUBLIN. | C. WHITING,] *The right of Translation is reserved.* [BEAUFORT HOUSE. |.

REFERENCES.

Slater, *Early Editions* (1894), p. 179, No. 24; Thomson, *Life of Hablôt Knight Browne* (1884), p. 170.

LEVER, CHARLES JAMES.

A RENT IN A CLOUD. LONDON, *Chapman and Hall*, [1865].   [473]

Foolscap octavo. First Edition.

COLLATION BY SIGNATURES: 4 leaves, without signature-marks (the first blank and lacking); 1 to 15, each 8 leaves; 2 leaves, without signature-marks (the last blank and lacking); total 126 leaves.

COLLATION BY PAGINATION: [1 blank leaf]; — [half-title], p. [i.]; — [blank], p.

1865   *Charles James Lever*   No. 473

[ii.];—[title]||A RENT IN A CLOUD. | BY | CHARLES LEVER, | [2 lines] | LONDON: | CHAPMAN AND HALL, 193, PICCADILLY. | [*The right of translation is reserved*]|, p. [iii.];—[blank], p. [iv.];—[contents], p. [v.];—[blank], p. [vi.];—[text], pp. [1]–242.

CONDITION: Size of leaf, 6⁷⁄₁₆ × 4½ inches. Bound in light brown crushed levant morocco, gilt edges; by Zaehnsdorf.

REFERENCE.

Slater, *Early Editions* (1894), p. 179, No. 25.

This work was originally published in green cloth. Though included in the collected edition of Lever's works, it is believed to have been written by his daughter.

[LEVER, CHARLES JAMES.]

TONY BUTLER. EDINBURGH AND LONDON, *William Blackwood and Sons*, 1865. 3 vols., crown octavo, viz.:   [474]

VOL. 1.

COLLATION BY SIGNATURES: 2 leaves, without signature-marks; A to U, each 8 leaves; X, 2 leaves (the last blank and lacking); total 164 leaves.

COLLATION BY PAGINATION: [half-title], p. [i.];—[publishers' notice], p. [ii.];—[title]|TONY BUTLER| IN THREE VOLUMES | VOL. I. | WILLIAM BLACKWOOD AND SONS | EDINBURGH AND LONDON | MDCCCLXV. | *The Right of Translation is reserved* |, p. [iii.];—[blank], p. [iv.];—[text], pp. [1]–322.

VOL. 2.

COLLATION BY SIGNATURES: 2 leaves, without signature-marks (the first lacking); A to U, each 8 leaves; X, 2 leaves; total 164 leaves.

COLLATION BY PAGINATION: [1 leaf, probably a half-title], pp. [i.]–[ii.];—[title, same as in Vol. 1, except volume-number], p. [iii.];—[blank], p. [iv.];—[text], pp. [1]–324.

VOL. 3.

COLLATION BY SIGNATURES: 2 leaves, without signature-marks (the first lacking); A to U, each 8 leaves; X, 2 leaves (the last blank and lacking); total 164 leaves.

COLLATION BY PAGINATION: [1 leaf, probably a half-title], pp. [i.]–[ii.];—[title, same as in Vol. 1, except volume-number], p. [iii.];—[blank], p. [iv.];—[text], pp. [1]–322;—[1 blank leaf], [X 2].

CONDITION: Size of leaf, 7⅝ × 4⅞ inches. Bound in light brown crushed levant morocco, gilt tops, other edges uncut; by Zaehnsdorf.

REFERENCES.

Downey, *Charles Lever, His Life in his Letters*, 2 (1906): 97; Slater, *Early Editions* (1894), p. 179, No. 26.

This, the First Edition, originally appeared as a serial in *Blackwood's Magazine*, after which it was published in three volumes, post octavo, in green cloth.

Tony Butler was published anonymously, and Lever was "sorely put out" by its poor reception, it being as he said "as good trash as the other trash vendors are selling."

LEVER, CHARLES JAMES.

GERALD FITZGERALD. New York, *Harper & Brothers*, [1866?].   [475]

Octavo. First Edition.
COLLATION BY SIGNATURES: [A] to K, each 8 leaves; total 80 leaves.
COLLATION BY PAGINATION: [publishers' advertisement], pp. [1]-[2];—[title] | GERALD FITZGERALD, | "THE CHEVALIER." | BY CHARLES LEVER, | [3 lines] | NEW YORK: | HARPER & BROTHERS, PUBLISHERS, | FRANKLIN SQUARE. |, p. [3];—[publishers' advertisement], p. [4];—[text, in double columns], pp. [5]-150;—[publishers' advertisement], pp. [1]-[10].
CONDITION: Size of leaf, 9⅛ x 5¹³⁄₁₆ inches. Bound in half brown crushed levant morocco, gilt top; by Macdonald. With the original brown paper wrappers bound in at the end, with title: | No. 210, 211. | LIBRARY OF SELECT NOVELS. | GERALD FITZGERALD, | "THE CHEVALIER." | BY CHARLES LEVER, | [4 lines] | NEW YORK: | HARPER & BROTHERS, PUBLISHERS, | FRANKLIN SQUARE. Complete 50 Cents. [with slip pasted over this line reading: "Price 40 Cents."] | ALL THE WORKS IN THIS SERIES ARE | Unabridged and Unaltered. |; the whole enclosed by a type-ornament border.

Slater, in his *Early Editions*, does not include *Gerald Fitzgerald* among the list of Lever's works.

LEVER, CHARLES JAMES.

SIR BROOK FOSSBROOKE. Edinburgh and London, *William Blackwood and Sons*, 1866. 3 vols., crown octavo, viz.:   [476]

VOL. 1.

COLLATION BY SIGNATURES: 4 leaves, without signature-marks (the first blank and lacking); A to U, each 8 leaves; X, 2 leaves; total 166 leaves.
COLLATION BY PAGINATION: [1 blank leaf];—[half-title], p. [i.];—[publishers' notice], p. [ii.];—[title] | SIR BROOK FOSSBROOKE | BY | CHARLES LEVER | IN THREE VOLUMES | VOL. I. | WILLIAM BLACKWOOD AND SONS | EDINBURGH AND LONDON | MDCCCLXVI | *The Right of Translation is reserved* |, p. [iii.];—[blank], p. [iv.];—[dedication], p. [v.];—[blank], p. [vi.];—[text], pp. [1]-324.

VOL. 2.

COLLATION BY SIGNATURES: 2 leaves, without signature-marks; A to U, each 8 leaves; X, 4 leaves; total 166 leaves.
COLLATION BY PAGINATION: [half-title], p. [i.];—[publishers' notice], p. [ii.];—[title, same as in Vol. 1, except volume-number], p. [iii.];—[blank], p. [iv.];—[text], pp. [1]-328.

VOL. 3.

COLLATION BY SIGNATURES: 2 leaves, without signature-marks; A to U, each 8 leaves; X, 2 leaves; 12 leaves, without signature-marks; total 176 leaves.
COLLATION BY PAGINATION: [half-title], p. [i.];—[publishers' notice], p. [ii.];—[title, same as in Vol. 1, except volume-number], p. [iii.];—[blank], p.

[iv.]; — [text], pp. [1]-324; — [publishers' advertisements], pp. [1]-4; — [publishers' catalogue], pp. [1]-[20].

CONDITION: Size of leaf, 7⅝ × 4⅞ inches. Bound in light brown crushed levant morocco, gilt tops, other edges uncut; by Zaehnsdorf.

REFERENCE.

Slater, *Early Editions* (1894), p. 180, No. 27.

This is the First Edition of *Sir Brook Fossbrooke*, which first appeared as a serial in *Blackwood's Magazine*, and was then issued in three volumes, post octavo, in blue cloth.

Baron Lendrick, in this story, was one of Lever's favorite characters. It was a study of Sergeant Lefroy, afterwards Lord Chief-Justice of Ireland. Lever is said to have been the only man who could make Lefroy laugh.

LEVER, CHARLES JAMES.

THE BRAMLEIGHS OF BISHOP'S FOLLY. LONDON, *Smith, Elder and Co.*, 1868. 3 vols., crown octavo, viz.: [477]

VOL. 1.

COLLATION BY SIGNATURES: *a*, 4 leaves (the first with signature-mark, otherwise blank); 1 to 21, each 8 leaves; 22, 2 leaves; total 174 numbered leaves.

COLLATION BY PAGINATION: [1 leaf, with signature-mark in the lower right-hand corner of the recto, otherwise blank], pp. [i.]-[ii.]; —[title] | THE | BRAMLEIGHS OF BISHOP'S FOLLY. | BY | CHARLES LEVER. | *IN THREE VOLUMES.* | VOL. I. | LONDON : | SMITH, ELDER AND CO., 65, CORNHILL. | 1868. |, p. [iii.]; —[publishers' notice], p. [iv.]; —[dedication and contents], pp. [v.]-viii.; —[text], pp. [1]-339; —[imprint], p. [340].

VOL. 2.

COLLATION BY SIGNATURES: 2 leaves, without signature-marks; 23 to 44, each 8 leaves; 45, 2 leaves; total 180 numbered leaves.

COLLATION BY PAGINATION: [title, same as in Vol. 1, except volume-number], p. [i.]; —[publishers' notice], p. [ii.]; —[contents], pp. [iii.]-iv.; —[text], pp. [1]-356.

VOL. 3.

COLLATION BY SIGNATURES: 2 leaves, without signature-marks; 46 to 67, each 8 leaves (the last blank and lacking); total 178 numbered leaves.

COLLATION BY PAGINATION: [title, same as in Vol. 1, except volume-number], p. [i.]; —[publishers' notice], p. [ii.]; —[contents], pp. [iii.]-iv.; —[text], pp. [1]-350; —[1 blank leaf], [67₈].

CONDITION: Size of leaf, 7 7/16 × 4⅝ inches. Bound in light brown crushed levant morocco, gilt tops, other edges uncut; by Zaehnsdorf.

REFERENCE.

Slater, *Early Editions* (1894), p. 180, No. 28.

This, the First Edition of this work, was originally issued in red cloth.

[LEVER, CHARLES JAMES.]

PAUL GOSSLETT'S CONFESSIONS. London, *Virtue & Co., etc.*, 1868. [478]

Post octavo. First Edition.
COLLATION BY SIGNATURES: [A], 2 leaves; B to K, each 8 leaves; L, 4 leaves; 2 leaves, without signature-marks; total 80 leaves.

COLLATION BY PAGINATION: [title] | PAUL GOSSLETT'S | CONFESSIONS | IN | LOVE, LAW, AND THE CIVIL SERVICE. | *With an Illustration by Marcus Stone.* | LONDON: | VIRTUE & CO., 26, IVY LANE. | NEW YORK: VIRTUE AND YORSTON. | 1868. |, recto of [A]; — [publishers' notice], verso of [A]; — [contents], recto of [A2]; — [blank], verso of [A2]; — [text], pp. [1]–152; — [publishers' advertisements], pp. [153]–[156].

PLATE: Engraved frontispiece by Marcus Stone, containing three scenes and title.

CONDITION: Size of leaf, 7¹⁰⁄₁₆ × 4¹¹⁄₁₆ inches. Bound in light brown crushed levant morocco, gilt top, other edges uncut; by Zaehnsdorf. With the original blue pictorial cloth covers and back, with titles on each and a vignette on the front cover, all in gilt, mounted and bound in at the end.

REFERENCE.

Slater, *Early Editions* (1894), p. 180, No. 29.

This work is divided into three parts, as follows: "My First Mission under F. O.," pp. [1]–50; "Confession the Second. As to Love.", pp. [51]–98; and "Confession the Last. As to Law.", pp. [99]–152.

LEVER, CHARLES JAMES.

THAT BOY OF NORCOTT'S. London, *Smith, Elder & Co.*, 1869. [479]

Octavo. First Edition.
COLLATION BY SIGNATURES: *a*, 4 leaves; 1 to 17, each 8 leaves; 18, 2 leaves; total 142 leaves.

COLLATION BY PAGINATION: [half-title], p. [i.]; — [blank], p. [ii.]; — [title] | THAT BOY OF NORCOTT'S. | BY | CHARLES LEVER. WITH FIVE ILLUSTRATIONS. | LONDON: | SMITH, ELDER & CO., 15, WATERLOO PLACE. | 1869. | [*The right of Translation is reserved.*] |, p. [iii.]; — [blank], p. [iv.]; — [dedication and contents], pp. [v.]–viii.; — [text], pp. [1]–274; — [publishers' advertisements], pp. [275]–[276].

PLATES: 5 plates; facing the title-page and pp. 7, 131, 198, and 259.

CONDITION: Size of leaf, 8³⁄₁₆ × 5⁵⁄₁₆ inches. Bound in light brown crushed levant morocco, gilt top, other edges uncut; by Zaehnsdorf.

REFERENCE.

Slater, *Early Editions* (1894), p. 181, No. 30.

This work originally appeared as a serial in the pages of *The Cornhill Magazine*, after which it was published in book form in green cloth, lettered in gilt on the front cover, with illustrations by Swain.

LEVER, CHARLES JAMES.

LORD KILGOBBIN. London, Smith, Elder & Co., 1872. 3 vols., crown octavo, viz.: [480]

VOL. 1.

COLLATION BY SIGNATURES: 4 leaves, without signature-marks; 1 to 18, each 8 leaves; 19, 4 leaves (the last blank and lacking); total 152 numbered leaves.

COLLATION BY PAGINATION: [half-title], p. [i.];—[blank], p. [ii.];—[title]|LORD KILGOBBIN : | A Tale of Ireland in our Own Time. | BY | CHARLES LEVER, LL.D., |[3 lines]| IN THREE VOLUMES. VOL. I. | LONDON : | SMITH, ELDER & CO., 15, WATERLOO PLACE. | 1872. |[THE RIGHT OF TRANSLATION IS RESERVED.] |, p. [iii.];—[blank], p. [iv.]; —[dedication and contents], pp. [v.]-viii.; —[text], pp. [1]-293;—[imprint], p. [294];—[1 blank leaf], [194].

VOL. 2.

COLLATION BY SIGNATURES: 2 leaves, without signature-marks; 20 to 37, each 8 leaves; total 146 numbered leaves.

COLLATION BY PAGINATION: [title, same as in Vol. 1, except volume-number], p. [i.];—[blank], p. [ii.];—[contents], pp. [iii.]-iv.;—[text], pp. [1]-288.

VOL. 3.

COLLATION BY SIGNATURES: 2 leaves, without signature-marks; 38 to 53, each 8 leaves; 54, 2 leaves; total 132 leaves.

COLLATION BY PAGINATION: [title, same as in Vol. 1, except volume-number], p. [i.];—[blank], p. [ii.];—[contents], pp. [iii.]-iv.;—[text], pp. [1]-258;—[imprint], p. [259];—[blank], p. [260].

CONDITION: Size of leaf, $7\frac{5}{16} \times 4\frac{7}{8}$ inches. Bound in light brown crushed levant morocco, gilt top, other edges uncut; by Zaehnsdorf.

REFERENCE.

Slater, *Early Editions* (1894), p. 181, No. 31.

This, the First Edition of *Lord Kilgobbin*, was originally issued in green cloth. It was the last work written by Lever, who died at Trieste the same year. "In finishing it," its author said, "I have also finished my own career as a story-writer."

LOVELACE, RICHARD. (b. 1618, d. 1658.)

LUCASTA. London, *Tho. Harper*, 1649. [481]

Small octavo. First Edition.

COLLATION BY SIGNATURES: a, 8 leaves; A, 4 leaves (the last blank and lacking); B to L, each 8 leaves; M, 4 leaves (the last blank and lacking); total 96 leaves.

COLLATION BY PAGINATION: [rubricated title, as reproduced; See No. 481], recto of [a];—[blank], verso of [a];— | THE DEDICATION. | *To the Right Honourable,* | *my Lady* | ANNE LOVELACE. | [signed] | *RICHARD LOVELACE.* |, recto and verso of a 2;—[complimentary verses in English, Latin, and Greek, by numerous writers, the first with heading] | *To my beſt Brother on his Poems,* | *called* LUCASTA. | [signed] | Francis Lovelace *Col.* |,

No. 481 *Richard Lovelace* 1649

LUCASTA:
EPODES, ODES, SONNETS, SONGS, &c.
TO WHICH IS ADDED
ARAMANTHA,
A
PASTORALL.
BY
RICHARD LOVELACE,
Esq.

LONDON,
Printed by THO. HARPER, and are to be sold by THO. EVVSTER, at the GUN, in Ivie Lane. 1649.

No. 481.   TITLE-PAGE OF LOVELACE'S LUCASTA; 1ST EDITION; 1649.

recto of *a* 3 to verso of *A* 3; — [1 blank leaf, lacking but substituted], [A 4]; — [poems, the first with heading] | Song. | Set by Mr. *Henry Lawes*. | To LUCASTA, | *Going beyond the Seas.* |, pp. 1–164; — | FINIS. |, p. 164; — | *A Table of the* CONTENTS. |, pp. [165]–[166]; — [1 blank leaf], [M 4]. Page 127 is wrongly numbered 137; and p. 151 has no page-number.

PLATES: 2 plates engraved on copper, by W. Faithorne, from designs by P. Lilly; the first facing the title-page; the second, a title-page, with inscription: | LUCASTA | BY 137; and | *R: L:* | *Esq*^r |.

CONDITION: Size of leaf, 5⁹⁄₁₆ × 3⁵⁄₁₆ inches. Bound in red crushed levant morocco, gilt edges; by Bedford.

OTHER COPIES.

Dyce Collection; Devonshire; Huth; Morgan; and White Libraries.

REFERENCES.

Nicoll and Seccombe, *A History of English Literature*, 1 (1907): 369; Grolier Club, *Wither to Prior*, 2 (1905): 141, No. 528; Hoe, *Catalogue*, 3 (1903): 85; Locker-Lampson, *Catalogue* (1886), p. 70; Huth, *Catalogue*, 3 (1880): 869; Lowndes, 3 (1869): 1403; Hazlitt, *Collections and Notes* (1876), p. 266; same, *Hand-Book* (1867), p. 355; *Bibliotheca Anglo-Poetica* (1815), p. 193, No. 424.

The *Lucaſta, Poſthume Poems* (our next number), which was published in 1659, after Lovelace's death, by his kinsman, Dudley Posthumus-Lovelace, is not a reprint of the work here described but a distinct work. It contains other poems by Lovelace, to which are appended elegies to his memory by several of his friends. It has as a frontispiece a portrait by Hollar. Facsimiles of the portrait and engraved title-page of the edition here described, and the portrait of the 1659 edition, are given in the Grolier Club's *Wither to Prior*, 2: 150, 166.

The title *Lucasta* was derived from the "lady of his love," Miss Lucy Sacheverell, whom Lovelace used to call *Lux Casta*.

"Lovelace's immortality rests upon two short lyrics in *Lucasta*, 'Tell me not (sweet) I am unkind,' and *To Althea from Prison*, containing the famous couplet, 'Stone walls do not a prison make, Nor iron bars a cage.' In the whole garden of Caroline lyric poetry these are perhaps (if we except a blossom or two of Wither's, such as 'Shall I, wasting in despair?') the most perfect flowers."

Richard Lovelace, the Cavalier poet, was thrown into prison in April, 1642, for a short time, for delivering a petition to the House of Commons praying that the king might be restored to his rights. During his confinement he wrote the poem containing the celebrated line, "Stone walls do not a prison make." Imprisoned again in 1648 after his return to England, he occupied his time in preparing for the press his *Lucasta*, which contains all the poet's best productions. The portrait, probably of Lucy Sacheverell sitting under a tree, sometimes found facing p. 145, is supposed to be that of Lucasta, whom Wood identifies with a certain Lucy Sacheverell who, "upon a stray report that Lovelace was dead of his wound received at Dunkirk, soon after married."

LOVELACE, RICHARD.

LUCASTA. POSTHUME POEMS. London, *by William Godbid for Clement Darby*, 1659. [482]

Small octavo. Second Edition.

COLLATION BY SIGNATURES: [A], 2 leaves; B to H, each 8 leaves; I, 6 leaves; total 64 leaves. The following leaves have no signature-marks: B 2, B 3, B 4, C 2, C 4, D 3, G 3, G 4, H 2, H 3, H 4, and I 3. The first two leaves were doubtless imposed with sheet I.

COLLATION BY PAGINATION: [title, as reproduced; See No. 482], recto of [A]; —[blank], verso of [A]; —|[type-ornament head-piece]| THE DEDICATION. | To the Right Honorable | *John Lovelace* | Eſquire. | [signed] | SIR, | Your moſt obedient | Servant and Kinſman | *Dudley Poſthumus-Lovelace.*|, pp. 1–[2]; —|

No. 482   *Richard Lovelace*   1659

LUCASTA.

Posthume
POEMS

O F

Richard Lovelace Eſq:

Thoſe Honours come too late,
That on our Aſhes waite.
                Mart. lib. 1. Epig. 26.

LONDON.

Printed by *William Godbid* for
Clement Darby.
1 6 5 9.

No. 482. Title-page of Lovelace's Lucasta. Posthume Poems;
2d Edition; 1659.

[type-ornament head-piece] | POEMS. | To *LVCASTA.* |, pp. [1]–107 ; — [copper-plate frontispiece, representing cupids holding a mantle, with title] | *ELEGIES* | sacred | to ỹ memory | of | *R: Louelace* | *Eſq*ʳ: | [signed] | *P. Lilly Inu : W. Faithorne ſcu. Paris* |, p. [108]; — | [title] | ELEGIES | SACRED | To the Memory of the | AUTHOR : | By ſeveral of his Friends. | Collected and Publiſhed | BY | *D. P. L.* | *Nunquam ego te vitâ frater amabilior* | *Adſpiciam poſthac ; at certè ſemper amabo.* | *Catullus.* | *London,* Printed 1660. |, p. [109]; — [blank], p. [110]; — [elegies, the first with heading] | [type-ornament head-piece] | ELEGIES. | *To the Memory* *of my Worthy | Friend, Coll.* Richard Lovelace.|, pp. 1 [wrongly numbered 101] to 14.

PLATE: Portrait bust of Lovelace supported on a vase, with laurel wreath above the head; inscription on vase,| LVCASTA | POSTHVME POEMS | OF | R. L. *Arm.*|; and below the plate :| *In memoriam fratris defideratifsimi; delin: Fran: Louelace, A | Wenceflaus Hollar Bohem, fculp:* 1662 |.

CONDITION: Size of leaf, 5 11/16 × 3¾ inches. Bound in red crushed levant morocco, gilt edges; by Bedford. The portrait is extended on all margins.

OTHER COPIES.

Trinity College, Cambridge; Dyce Collection; Boston Public; and White Libraries.

REFERENCES.

Grolier Club, *Wither to Prior*, 2 (1905): 141, No. 529; Hoe, *Catalogue*, 3 (1903): 85; Locker-Lampson, *Catalogue* (1886), p. 71; also *Appendix to Catalogue* (1900), p. 23; Lowndes, 3 (1869): 1403; Hazlitt, *Hand-Book* (1867), p. 355; *Bibliotheca Grenvilliana*, 2 (1842): 414; *Bibliotheca Anglo-Poetica* (1815), p. 194, No. 425.

The Locker-Lampson copy, with ex-libris.

The frontispiece to the second part of this volume is the same engraved title-page that appeared in the 1649 edition, with the inscription on the mantle changed.

The authors of the Elegies are Charles Cotton, James Howell, Eldred Revett, Symon Ognell, T. Lovelace, and Dudley Posthumus-Lovelace.

Of this edition W. Carew Hazlitt, who published a new edition with a life and notes in 1864, says: "The text of the old copy, however, is very corrupt, and in a literary respect, it is entirely worthless."

[MALORY, Sir THOMAS.] (*fl.* 1470.)

THE MOST ANCIENT AND FAMOVS HISTORY OF THE RENOWNED PRINCE ARTHVR KING OF BRITAINE. LONDON, by *William Stansby, for Iacob Bloome*, 1634.   3 parts in 1 vol., small quarto, viz.:

[483]

PART I.

COLLATION BY SIGNATURES: ¶, ⁂, A to H, each 4 leaves; I, 8 leaves; K to Z, Aa to Ii, each 4 leaves; total 140 unnumbered leaves.

COLLATION BY PAGINATION: [blank], recto of [¶];—[woodcut of King Arthur and his Round Table, with 5 lines of letterpress above and 3 below], verso of [¶];—[title, as reproduced; *See* No. 483], recto of [¶2];—[blank], verso of [¶2];—| [type-ornament head-piece] | ⁂ A Preface, or Aduertisement to the| *Reader, for the better illuftration and* | vnderftanding of this famous| HISTORIE. |, recto of ¶3 to verso of [¶4];—|[type-ornament head-piece]

| The Prologue.|, recto of ⁂ to verso of ⁂2;—|[type-ornament head-piece]| The Preface of *William Caxton,* | *To the Chriftian Reader.*|, recto and verso of [⁂3];—|THE CONTENTS AND | Chapters of the firft | PART.|, recto of [⁂4] to verso of [A 4];—[text, with heading] | *THE* | HISTORIE OF THE MOST | Noble and worthy Prince KING | *ARTHVR*, | Sometime King of Great BRITAINE, now | called *England, which Treateth of his Noble* | A&ts and feates of Armes and Chiualrie, and | *of his Noble Knights of the Round*| TABLE.|, recto of B to verso of [Ii 4];—| FINIS.|, verso of [Ii 4].

Part 2.

COLLATION BY SIGNATURES: 2 leaves, without signature-marks; ¶, 4 leaves; (a), 1 leaf; A to Z, Aa to Qq, each 4 leaves; Rr, 1 leaf; total 164 unnumbered leaves. Leaf ¶ is marked A ¶; Y 3 has no signature-mark; and Aa 3, Bb 3, Ff 3, Ii 3, Ll 3, and Mm 3 have no signature-marks.

COLLATION BY PAGINATION: [blank], recto of first leaf; —[woodcut, same as in Part 1], verso of first leaf; —[title, same as in Part 1, except that after line 7 is added a line as follows] | The second Part. | , recto of second leaf; —[blank], verso of second leaf; — | THE CONTENTS AND | Chapters of the second. | PART. | , recto of ¶ [marked A ¶] to verso of (a); —[text, with heading] | [type-ornament head-piece] | THE | MOST ANCIENT AND | FAMOVS HISTORIE OF | THE RENOWNED | PRINCE | ARTHVR King of | Britaine. | *The fecond Part.* | , recto of A to verso of Rr; — | FINIS. | , verso of Rr.

Part 3.

COLLATION BY SIGNATURES: ¶, ¶ (repeated), A to Z, Aa to Pp, each 4 leaves; total 160 unnumbered leaves.

COLLATION BY PAGINATION: [blank], recto of [¶]; —[woodcut, same as in Part 1], verso of [¶]; —[title, same as in Part 1, except that after line 7 is added a line as follows] | The third Part. | , recto of [¶ 2]; —[blank], verso of [¶ 2]; — | [type-ornament head-piece] | THE CONTENTS AND | Chapters of the third. | PART. | , recto of ¶ 3 to verso of [the repeated ¶ 4]; —[text, with heading] | [type-ornament head-piece] | THE | MOST ANCIENT AND | FAMOVS HISTORIE OF | THE RENOWNED | PRINCE | ARTHVR King of | Britaine. | *The third Part.* | , recto of A to recto of [Pp 4]; — | FINIS. | , recto of [Pp 4]; —[blank], verso of [Pp 4].

CONDITION: Size of leaf, 7⅞ × 5¼ inches. Bound in brown calf, with blind tooled diagonal fillet lines or rulings, floral decoration in gilt on covers, gilt edges; by Roger Payne; in brown straight-grained morocco solander case lettered on the back: | HISTORY | OF | KING ARTHUR | 1634 | BOUND BY | ROGER PAYNE | .

OTHER COPIES.

Capell Collection; Crawford; Huth; Boston Public; and Lenox Libraries.

REFERENCES.

Nicoll and Seccombe, 1 (1907): 35, 36, 37; Grolier Club, *Wither to Prior*, 2 (1905): 144, No. 532; Hoe, *Catalogue*, 3 (1903): 104 (a description of the only perfect copy of the *editio princeps*, printed by Caxton in 1485); Huth, *Catalogue*, 1 (1880): 53; Hazlitt, *Collections and Notes* (1876), p. 13; Hazlitt, *Hand-Book* (1867), p. 14; Collier, *Rarest Books*, 1 (1866): 40; *Bibliotheca Grenvilliana*, 1 (1842): 47.

This work is printed in black-letter.

"Concerning Sir Thomas Malory practically nothing is known. The work, which is mainly translated from French romances, was finished between March 4, 1469, and March 4, 1470. Of the first edition, printed by Caxton in 1485, only one perfect copy is known, the Hoe copy. It was reprinted by Wynkyn de Worde in 1498 and 1529, by William Copland in 1557, and by Thomas East about 1585. The edition described above is the last of the early editions."

"Malory's *Morte d'Arthur*, completed in 1470, was the last important work finished before the introduction of printing, and our knowledge of it depends wholly upon the printed text, for no manuscript of it is known to be extant. . . . The popu-

1634   *Sir Thomas Malory*   No. 483

THE MOST
ANCIENT AND
FAMOVS HISTORY
OF THE RENOWNED
PRINCE
ARTHVR
King of *Britaine*,

Wherein is declared his Life and Death, with all his glorious Battailes against the Saxons, Saracens and Pagans, which (for the honour of his Country) he most worthily atchieued.

As also, all the *Noble Acts*, and *Heroicke* Deeds of his Valiant KNIGHTS of the ROVND TABLE.

Newly refined, and published for the delight, and profit of the READER.

LONDON,
Printed by *William Stansby*,
for *Iacob Bloome*, 1634.

No. 483. TITLE-PAGE OF MALORY'S MOST ANCIENT AND FAMOUS HISTORY OF THE RENOWNED PRINCE ARTHUR; 1634.

larity of the romances of chivalry which Caxton had translated from the French may very possibly have been the stimulus which prompted Malory to undertake the work in the closing years of his life. But Malory's *Morte d'Arthur* is much more than a translation; it is, in fact, a welding together from different fabrics of the main sources which go to forming the Arthurian cycle. By the perfect adaptation of his treatment to the subject, Malory succeeded in handing down the romance, with unimpaired freshness, from mediæval to modern literature. In both form and style the compilation compares very favourably with the *Cent Nouvelles* and other French *recueils* of the period. . . .

"Only by those readers whose poetic instinct is stimulated by the surpassing colour and imagery of the detail can the *Morte d'Arthur* be assimilated with a genuine sense of enjoyment. To the romantic poets in a special degree the *Morte d'Arthur* has been an inexhaustible fountain of allegory and of poetic inspiration. It was freely used by Spenser for his *Faerie Queene*, by Tennyson for his *Idylls of the King*, by Swinburne for his *Tristram of Lyonesse*, and by Matthew Arnold for his *Tristam and Iseult*; while in the present day it has formed the staple of the quaintly perfumed romances of Maurice Hewlett."

MARSTON, JOHN. (*b.* c. 1575, *d.* 1634.)

WORKES, BEING TRAGEDIES AND COMEDIES, COLLECTED INTO ONE VOLUME. LONDON, *for William Sheares*, 1633.   [484]

Small octavo. First Edition, First Issue. COLLATION BY SIGNATURES: A, 4 leaves (the first blank and lacking); 1 leaf, inserted, without signature-mark; B to Z, Aa to Dd, each 8 leaves (the last three blank and genuine); total 213 unnumbered leaves. Leaf N 3 is wrongly marked M 3; and X 4 has no signature-mark.

COLLATION BY PAGINATION: [1 blank leaf], [A]; — [title, as reproduced; *See* No. 484], recto of [A 2]; — [blank], verso of [A 2]; — [inserted title] | THE | WORKES | OF | Mr. IOHN MARSTON, | Being | Tragedies and Comedies, | Collected into one | Volume. | [conventional ornament] | LONDON, | Printed for WILLIAM SHEARES, | at the Harrowe in *Britaines* | *Burſſe*. 1633. |, recto of inserted leaf; — [blank], verso of inserted leaf; — | [type-ornament head-piece] | TO THE RIGHT | HONOVRABLE, THE | Lady ELIZABETH CARIE, | Viſcounteſſe FAVVKLAND. | [signed] | Your truly devoted, | WILLIAM SHEARES. |, recto of A 3 to verso of A 4; — [play in 2 parts introduction to the first part with heading] | [type-ornament head-piece] | THE HISTORY OF | ANTONIO and MELLIDA. | *The firſt Part.* | INDVCTION. |, recto of B to recto of B 3; — | The Prologue. |, verso of B 3; — [text of the first part, without heading], recto of B 4 to recto of [E 6]; — | FINIS. | EPILOGVS. | [10 lines] |, recto of [E 6]; — [blank], verso of [E 6].

| ANTONIO'S | REVENGE. | The Second Part of the Hi- | ſtorie of ANTONIO and | MELLIDA. | As it hath beene ſundrie times | Acted by the Children of | PAVLS. | [conventional ornament] | LONDON, | Printed for WILLIAM SHEARES. | 1633. |, recto of [E 7]; — [blank], verso of [E 7]; — | [type-ornament head-piece] | ANTONIOS | REVENGE. | The Hiſtory of ANTONIO | and MELLIDA. | *The ſecond Part.* | The PRO-

1633   *John Marston*   **No. 484**

LOGVE. | , recto and verso of [E 8] ; — [text, without heading], recto of F to verso of [I 7] ; — | FINIS. | , verso of [I 7].

| THE | WONDER | OF VVOMEN : | OR, | THE TRAGEDIE OF | SOPHONISBA. | As it hath been fundry times acted | at the Blacke Fryers. | [conventional ornament] | LONDON, | Printed for WILLIAM SHEARES. | 1633. | , recto of [I 8] ; — [blank], verso of [I 8] ; — | [type-ornament head-piece] | TO THE GENERALL | READER. | , recto of K ; — | [type-ornament head-piece] | Argumentum. | , verso of K ; — | [type-ornament head-piece] | THE TRAGEDIE | of *Sophonisba.* | PROLOGVS. | , recto and verso of K 2 ; — [text, without heading], recto of K 3 to recto of N 3 [wrongly marked M 3] ; — | EPILOGVS. | [16 lines] | FINIS. | , verso of N 3.

| VVHAT | YOV VVILL. | A | COMEDIE. | [conventional ornament] | LONDON, | Printed for WILLIAM SHEARES. | 1633. | , recto of [N 4] ; — [blank], verso of [N 4] ; — | [type-ornament head-piece] | WHAT YOV | VVILL. | *Induction.* | , recto of [N 5] to verso of [N 6] ; — | Prologue. | , recto of [N 7] ; — [text, with heading] | [type-ornament head-piece] | VVHAT YOV | VVILL. | , verso of [N 7] to verso of [R 5] ; — | FINIS. | , verso of [R 5].

| PARASITASTER, | OR, | THE FAVVNE. | As it hath been divers times | Prefented at the Black Fryers, | by the Children of the Queens | *Majefties Revells.* | [conventional ornament] | LONDON, | Printed for WILLIAM SHEARES. | 1633. | , recto of [R 6] ; — [blank], verso of [R 6] ; — | [type-ornament head-piece] | *To my equall Reader.* | , recto and verso of [R 7] ; — | Prologus. | , recto of [R 8] ; — | [conventional head-piece] | Interlocutores. | , verso of [R 8] ; — [text, with heading] | [type-ornament head-piece] | THE FAVVNE. | , recto of S to verso of Z ; — | Epilogus. | [20 lines] | FINIS. | , verso of Z.

| THE | DVTCH | COVRTEZAN. | As it hath been divers times | Prefented at the Black Fryers, | by the Children of the Queenes | *Majefties Revells.* | [conventional ornament] | LONDON, | Printed for WILLIAM SHEARES. | 1633. | , recto of [Z 2] ; — [blank], verso of [Z 2] ; — | Prologue. | , recto of Z 3 ; — | *Dramatis perfonæ.* | , verso of Z 3 ; — [text, with heading] | [type-ornament head-piece] | THE | DVTCH COVR- | TEZAN. | , recto of Z 4 to verso of [Dd 5] ; — | FINIS. | , verso of [Dd 5] ; — [3 blank leaves], [Dd 6] to [Dd 8].

CONDITION : Size of leaf, $5\frac{9}{16}$ × $3\frac{11}{16}$ inches. Bound in old limp vellum, with circuit fore edges and leather tie strings; in red crushed levant morocco solander case. Leaf [E 7] has been placed after [E 8] by the binder.

OTHER COPIES.

British Museum ; Dyce Collection ; Ellesmere and Boston Public Libraries.

REFERENCES.

Lowndes, 3 (1869) : 1487 ; Hazlitt, *Hand-Book* (1867), p. 379.

In this copy has been inserted an impression of the title-page, *The Workes of Mr. Iohn Marfton*, etc., which belongs to the Second Issue.

    The copy here described contains the dedication by the publisher to Lady Elizabeth Carie, Viscountess Faulkland, which is often lacking. Lowndes gives the reason for the change of title, as follows : " This volume contains Antonio and Mellida, Antonio's Revenge, Parifitaster, Wonder of Women, What you will, and The Dutch Courtezan. It was issued twice in the same year, the titles differing ; for ' The Puritans and Prynne ' had brought so great an odium on the Stage, and everything connected with it, that the very name of Tragedy or Comedy was offensive ; and Sheares, the publisher, found it a bad speculation to offer it under the obnoxious title, so changed it to ' Workes, being Tragedies and Comedies collected into one Volume.' "

> # TRAGEDIES
> ### AND
> # COMEDIES
> ### COLLECTED INTO
> ### ONE VOLVME.
>
> Viz.
> 1. *Antonio and Mellida.*
> 2. *Antonio's Revenge.*
> 3. *The Tragedie of Sophonisba.*
> 4. *What you Will.*
> 5. *The Fawne.*
> 6. *The Dutch Courtezan.*
>
>
>
> LONDON,
> Printed by *A. M* for *William Sheares,*
> at the Harrow in *Britaines Burſſe.*
> 1 6 3 3.

NO. 484. TITLE-PAGE OF MARSTON'S TRAGEDIES AND COMEDIES;
1ST EDITION, 1ST ISSUE; 1633.

There are copies of both issues in the British Museum, and of the Second Issue only in the Huth and Hoe libraries.

"Drake, in his account of the writers of Shakespeare's time," says Corser, "observes of Marston, that ' all his dramas give evidence of great wealth and vigour of description, of much felicity in expression, and of much passionate eloquence; nor are his characters raw or indistinct sketches, but highly coloured and well supported.' "

MILTON, JOHN. (*b.* 1608, *d.* 1674.) Autograph Signature.

COLLECTANEA EX HISTORIJS, DE ORIGINE ET FUNDATIONE OMNIVM FERÈ MONASTICORVM ORDINVM; PER IOHANNEM CRECCELIUM. Francofvrti, IoH. Th. de Brÿ, 1614. [485]

Small quarto.
Collation by Signatures:):(, 4 leaves;):( ):(, 2 leaves; A to Z, Aa, Bb, each 4 leaves; Cc, 2 leaves; total 108 leaves.
Collation by Pagination: [title, as reproduced; *See* No. 485], recto of [ ):( ]; —[blank], verso of [ ):( ]; —[epistle dedicatory], recto of):(2 to recto of [ ):( ):(2]; —[blank], verso of [ ):( ):(2]; —[text], pp. 1–203; —[blank], p. [204].
Plates: 11 plates, each containing 9 ecclesiastical costumes; bound in at the end.

Condition: Size of leaf, 7¾ × 6 inches. Bound in modern vellum, red edges.

References.

Locker-Lampson, *Catalogue* (1886), p. 210; Masson (D.), *Specimens of Milton's Signature* (in his edition of *The Poetical Works of John Milton*, Vol. 1; 1890), pp. 69–74; Sotheby, *Autograph Signatures of Milton* (in his *Ramblings in the Elucidation of the Autograph* [*Handwriting*] *of Milton*; 1861), pp. 124–129.

The Locker-Lampson copy, with ex-libris.
This book, which may have been in Milton's library, is now of interest solely because of his autograph at the top of the title-page. *See* reproduction.

[MILTON, JOHN.]

A MASKE [COMUS] PRESENTED AT LUDLOW CASTLE, 1634. London, *for Humphrey Robinſon,* 1637. [486]

Small quarto. First Edition.
Collation by Signatures: A, 2 leaves; B to E, each 4 leaves; F, 2 leaves; total 20 leaves. Leaf B 3 is wrongly marked A 3.
Collation by Pagination: [title, as reproduced; *See* No. 486], recto of [A]; —[blank], verso of [A]; —|[type-ornament head-piece]| TO THE RIGHT | HONORABLE,| IOHN *Lord Vicount* BRACLY, | Son and heire apparent to the Earle | *of Bridgewater, &c.*|[signed]| Your faithfull, and moſt |*humble Servant,*| H. Lavves.|, recto and verso of A 2; —[text, with heading] | [conventional head-piece] | A MASKE | PERFORMED BEFORE | the Præſident of Wales | at *Ludlow,* 1634.|, pp. 1–35; — | *The principall*

perſons in this Maske; . . . |[2 lines]| *The End.*|, p. 35; —[blank], p. [36].
Condition: Size of leaf, 7⁹⁄₁₀ × 5¼ inches. Bound in maroon crushed levant morocco, gilt edges; by Zaehnsdorf.

Other Copies.

Capell Collection; Dyce Collection; Forster Collection; Huth; Boston Public; Lenox; Morgan; and White Libraries.

References.

Grolier Club, *Wither to Prior,* 2 (1905): 162, No. 554; Livingston, *Introduction* to facsimile reprint (1903), pp. 5–7; Locker-Lampson, *Catalogue* (1886), p. 81; Lenox Library, *Works of Milton* (1881), p. 3, No. 1; Huth, *Catalogue,* 3 (1880): 968;

pr 3 6. John Milton 1633. 21 October

S. GREGORIVS

S. HIERONIMVS

GERMANICUS ORDO ALBAT

RHODIUS ORDO ATRATUS

S. AVGVSTINVS

S. AMBROSIVS

COLLECTANEA
Ex Historijs,
De
ORIGINE ET FUNDATIONE
Omnium ferè Monasticorum Ordinum in specie: Simulq; de
FVNDATIONE ET DONATIONE
Cathedralium ac Collegiatarum Ecclesiarum cum suis Canonicatibus: vero usu et abusu talium bonorum, tam apud quosdam reformatæ quàm Papisticæ Religionis Canonicos et Vicarios,
Per IOHANNEM CRECCELIUM, olim Monachum Augustinianum; nunc verò Præconem Verbi divini.
Quibus illustrandi et delectandi gratiâ, accesserunt variorum ac diversorum Ordinum, Ecclesiæ Papisticæ variæ ac diversæ Imagines, habitum et mores, tam Virorum quam Feminarũ Cænobitarum referentes, æri eleganter incisæ

Per IoH. Th. de Brÿ
in Cujus Icono-Biblio-polio
prostat
FRANCOFVRTI
Anno
MDC XIV.

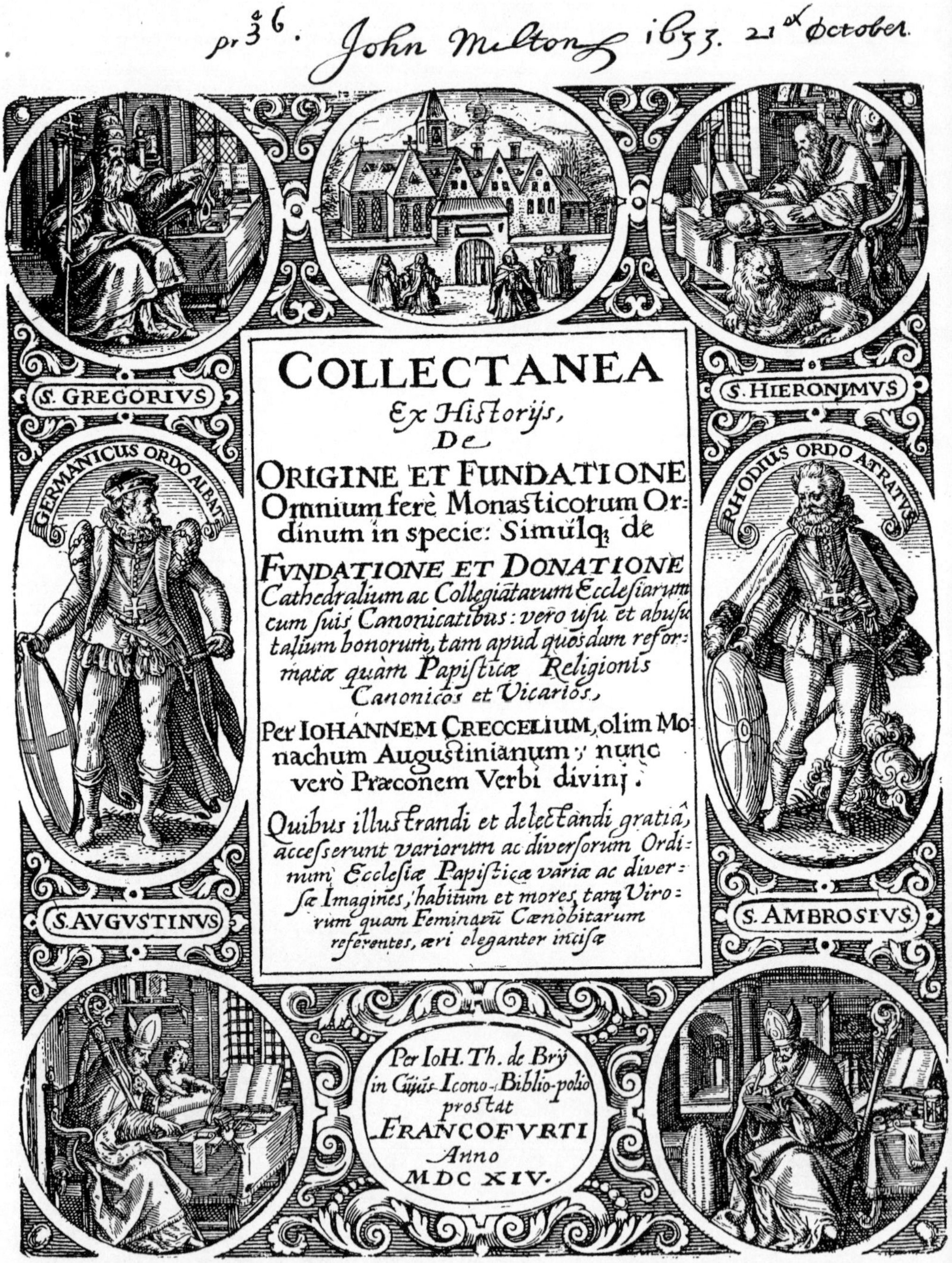

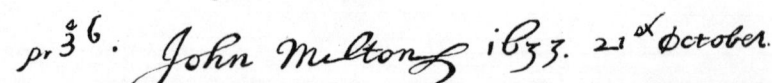

No. 485. Title-page of Creccelius' Collectanea; with Milton's Autograph; 1614.

Lowndes, 3 (1869) : 1562 ; Hazlitt, *Hand-Book* (1867), p. 396; Brunet, 3 (1862) : 1731 ; Sotheby, *Ramblings in the Elucida-tion of the Autograph of Milton* (1861), pp. 60–62; Masson, *Life of Milton*, I (1859) : 573, 586.

This is the first work of Milton's separately printed, and the First Edition of *Comus*, the rarest of his poems. The name *Comus* was not given to it by Milton, but first appears in an edition printed after his death.

This *Maske* or poem, which was written at the request of Henry Lawes, by whom the music was composed, was performed in the great hall or council-chamber of Ludlow Castle on Michaelmas night, September 29, 1634, to celebrate Lord Bridgewater's assumption of the Lord Presidency of the Welsh Marches.

The plot of the poem is based on a legend for which Oldys is the earliest known authority, to the effect that Lord Brackley, Mr. Thomas Egerton, and their sister Lady Alice, while on their way to Ludlow Castle were benighted in Haywood Forest. Of the six speaking parts four are known to have been taken by Lawes, Lady Alice, and her brothers.

Of the poem itself there are three distinct versions: that in the edition here described; one in the original manuscript in Milton's handwriting, in Trinity College, Cambridge; and the third in a manuscript copy in the Bridgewater Library. "Much as Milton wrote afterwards," says Masson, "he never wrote anything more beautiful, more perfect than *Comus*." The work was published by Lawes in consequence of the numerous requests for copies which he had received. In the dedication he says: "*Although not openly acknowledg'd by the Author, yet it is a legitimate off-spring, so lovely, and so much desired, that the often copying of it hath tir'd my pen to give my severall friends satisfaction, and brought me to a necessitie of producing it to the publick view.*"

The copy here described was reproduced in facsimile, with an introduction by Luther S. Livingston, by Dodd, Mead & Company, New York, in 1903. Sotheby has given a facsimile of the first page of the autograph manuscript in Trinity College Library at Cambridge. There is also a manuscript copy in the Earl of Ellesmere's library, at Bridgewater House.

John Milton evinced rare poetic talent at a very early age. As a boy he received instruction in music from his father and was a skillful organist. Passionately fond of study, he first attended St. Paul's School, and later matriculated at Christ College, Cambridge, in 1625, from which he was graduated M.A., July 3, 1632. He was proficient in Latin, Greek, French, and Italian, knew some Hebrew, and was well read in English literature. While in college he carried on a correspondence with several of his friends in Latin prose and verse. He also wrote some English poems, and in his sonnet to Shakespeare, written in 1630 and printed in the Second Folio edition of Shakespeare's plays (our No. 625), he made his first appearance in English literature. He had been educated with a view to taking holy orders, but later studied law, which he soon abandoned to devote himself to literature.

After his graduation he settled with his father at Horton, in Buckinghamshire, where he remained for six years, devoting himself to study and the composition of several of his shorter poems. During this period, probably in 1632, he wrote the exquisite companion pieces *L'Allegro* and *Il Penseroso*. In 1634 he wrote *Comus* (the present number), which was performed as a mask at Ludlow Castle. It was published the same year, but without Milton's name. In November, 1637, he wrote his matchless pastoral monody *Lycidas* (our No. 487), his contribution to a collection of obituary verses published to commemorate the death of his college friend Edward King. These four absolutely perfect poems were the fruit of this youthful period — poems which, had he written no others, would have entitled him to a place in the front rank among English poets.

In April, 1638, Milton found himself in a position to gratify a desire which he had long entertained of visiting Italy. Provided with excellent letters of introduction he was everywhere received with distinction. During his journey he met Grotius and Galileo, and at a magnificent concert given by Cardinal Barberini heard the celebrated singer Leonora Baroni, to whom he inscribed three Latin epigrams. This tour formed one of the chief pleasures of his memory through all his subsequent life. He returned to England at the end of July, 1639, and settled in London, where he began to teach his two nephews, John and Edward Phillips. Other pupils being added, Milton at length found himself at the head of a private school. At the same time he was busy with plans for future poems. His attention, however, was soon diverted from poetry to theological disputes, in which he took an active part and wrote several pamphlets. In May, 1643, he was married, and about three months later, having been deserted by his wife, he published his celebrated pamphlet *The Doctrine and Discipline of Divorce*. The reconciliation between Milton and his wife in 1645 put an end to his personal interest in this subject. His pamphlet had been published without a license. The Stationers' Company, owing to the prevalent practice of publishing books without their permission, applied to the House of Commons for an ordinance requiring all publications to be licensed. Complaint having been made against Milton for having violated this ordinance he was led to write his *Areopagitica* (our No. 490), which was published in 1644. This work, not only because of its subject but on account of its eloquent arguments for the liberty of the press, still ranks as the most popular, if not the greatest, of all his prose writings. The first collected edition of his *Poems* (our No. 491) appeared the following year.

Immediately after the death of Charles I., in 1649, appeared *The Tenure of Kings and Magistrates* (our No. 493), in which Milton defends the conduct of the Court ordering the king's execution. Upon the invitation of the new Council of State, Milton became its Latin Secretary. While holding this position he published several political pamphlets in support of the Commonwealth. His eyesight had been gradually failing him for ten years, and about May, 1652, he became totally blind. At the Restoration Milton concealed himself, but no serious charges being made against him, he afterward resumed his usual habits of life. About this time he met with serious financial losses, and shortly after his third marriage, in 1663, moved to a house in Artillery Walk, in Bunhill Fields. Here he continued to live during the remainder of

1637   *John Milton*   No. 486

A MASKE
PRESENTED
At Ludlow Castle,
1 6 3 4 :
On *Michaelmaſſe night*, *before the*
RIGHT HONORABLE,

IOHN *Earle of Bridgewater*, *Vicount* BRACKLY,
Lord *Præſident of* WALES, And one of
His MAIESTIES moſt honorable
Privie Counſell.

Eheu quid volui miſero mihi ! floribus auſtrum
Perditus ————

LONDON,
Printed for HVMPHREY ROBINSON,
at the ſigne of the *Three Pidgeons* in
Pauls Church-yard. 1 6 3 7.

No. 486. TITLE-PAGE OF MILTON'S MASKE PRESENTED AT LUDLOW CASTLE,
1634; 1ST EDITION; 1637.

CHURCH CATALOGUE   [645]   ENGLISH LITERATURE

his life, except for a short interval during the Great Plague, when he retired to a cottage, which still exists, at Chalfont St. Giles, near Beaconsfield, in Buckinghamshire.

As a youth he had resolved to write a great poem. This resolution began to take shape in 1642, when, it is said, he wrote the speech of Satan, the beginning of the Fourth Book of *Paradise Lost* (our No. 494). It was not until 1658, however, that he settled down to the serious composition of this work. It was dictated in "parcels of ten, twenty, and thirty verses at a time" as the inspiration came upon him. Early in 1667 it was completed, and on April 27 he signed a contract with Samuel Symons for its publication. This precious document, by which Milton received during his lifetime the sum of £10, is now in the British Museum and has recently been reproduced in facsimile. The last of his poems, *Paradise Regained* and *Samson Agonistes*, appeared in 1671. The latter poem is in part a personification of the author himself. In 1669 he published *Accedence Commenc't Grammar* (our No. 497), a Latin grammar, probably compiled from notes made while he was teaching that language. He died November 8, 1674, and was buried in the church of St. Giles, Cripplegate.

MILTON, JOHN, and others.

JUSTA EDOVARDO KING NAVFRAGO, AB AMICIS MŒRENTIBVS, AMORIS & μνείας χάειν. CANTABRIGIÆ, *Thomam Buck, & Rogerum Daniel*, 1638. [487]

Small quarto.

COLLATION BY SIGNATURES: A to D, each 4 leaves; E, 6 leaves; F, G, H, each 4 leaves; I, 2 leaves; total 36 leaves. Leaf G 3 has no signature-mark.

COLLATION BY PAGINATION: [title, as reproduced; *See* No. 487], recto of [A]; — [blank], verso of [A]; — [biographical sketch of Edward King], recto of [A 2]; — [blank], verso of [A 2]; — [dedication, in Latin verse, to King, beginning] | [type-ornament head-piece] | HÆc, Edovarde, Jufta Tibi folvunt dolor, | , recto of A 3 to verso of [A 4]; — [text, several short poems in Latin and Greek, by various authors, the first with heading] | In obitum eruditifsimi viri | EDVARDI KING, | *C. C. Socii, in mari Hibernico* | *fubmerfi.* | , pp. 1–36; — [title, enclosed by heavy mourning borders, as follows] | Obfequies to | the memorie | of | Mr EDWARD | KING, | *Anno Dom.* | 1638. | [type-ornament] | Printed by *Th.* Buck, and R. Daniel, | printers to the Vniverfitie of | Cambridge. 1638. | , recto of [F]; — [blank], verso of [F]; — [text, numerous verses in English, by various authors, the first with heading] | [type-ornament head-piece] | ¶ Obfequies to the memorie of | Mr *Edward King.* | , pp. 1–20; — | Lycidas. | [signed] | J. M. | , pp. 20–25; — [blank], p. [26].

CONDITION: Size of leaf, 7⅛ × 5⅜ inches. Bound in brown crushed levant morocco, gilt edges, with red moire doublure and facing fly-leaves; by Clarke & Bedford. The leaves are stabbed on the inner margins throughout the book.

OTHER COPIES.

Dyce Collection; Huth; Lenox; Halsey; Hoe; and White Libraries.

REFERENCES.

Grolier Club, *Wither to Prior*, 2 (1905): 164, No. 555; Hoe, *Catalogue*, 3 (1903): 165; Masson, *Poetical Works of John Mil-*

JUSTA
EDOVARDO KING
naufrago,
ab
Amicis mœrentibus,
amoris
&
μνείας χάειν.

Si rectè calculum ponas, ubique naufragium est.
Pet. Arb.

CANTABRIGIÆ:
Apud *Thomam Buck*, & *Rogerum Daniel*, celeberrimæ
Academiæ typographos. 1638.

No. 487. TITLE-PAGE OF JUSTA EDOVARDO KING NAVFRAGO; 1638.

ton, 1 (1890) : 187; Locker-Lampson, *Catalogue* (1886), p. 81; Lenox Library, *Works of Milton* (1881), p. 4, No. 11; Huth, *Catalogue*, 3 (1880) : 969; Lowndes, *Bibliographer's Manual*, 3 (1869) : 1563; Hazlitt, *Hand-Book* (1867), p. 318; Sotheby, *Ramblings in the Elucidation of the Autograph of Milton* (1861), p. 62.

Edward King, a fellow student of Milton's at Christ Church College, Cambridge, was drowned with several other passengers in crossing from Chester Bay to Dublin on the Irish Sea in 1637. This volume of memorial verses written by his sorrowing friends contains, in the first part, nineteen Latin and three Greek poems, and in the second part, thirteen English poems, of which the last, entitled "Lycidas," pp. 20–25, Milton's contribution to the volume is signed with his initials, "J. M.". The original draft, in Milton's own handwriting, is among the Milton manuscripts at Trinity College, Cambridge. Sotheby in his interesting work has given a facsimile reproduction of the first page of this precious manuscript.

MILTON, JOHN.

THE REASON OF CHVRCH-GOVERNEMENT URG'D AGAINST PRELATY. London, *by E. G. for Iohn Rothwell,* 1641. [488]

Small quarto.

COLLATION BY SIGNATURES: 1 leaf, without signature-mark; A to H, each 4 leaves; [I], 1 leaf; total 34 leaves. Leaves C 3 and H 3 have no signature-marks.

COLLATION BY PAGINATION: [title, as reproduced; *See* No. 488], recto of first leaf; — [blank], verso of first leaf; — [text, including preface, with heading] | [type-ornament head-piece] | The Reaſon of Church-government | urg'd againſt PRELATY.|, pp. 1–32 [wrongly numbered 44]; —|[type-ornament head-piece]|The ſecond Book.|, pp. 33–59;— |The Concluſion.|, pp. 59–65;— | *The end.*|, p. 65;— [errata, with heading] | [type-ornament rule]| Faults eſcap't in Printing are here corrected.| [3 lines] | [type-ornament rule]|, p. [66]. Page 14 is numbered on the inner corner instead of the outer; 17 is wrongly numbered 25; 20 is 28; 21 is 29; 24 is 32; 32 is 44; and 45 is 55.

CONDITION: Size of leaf, 7¼ × 5 5⁄16 inches. Bound in dark green crushed levant morocco, gilt edges; by the Club Bindery, 1899. Many leaves are uncut at the bottom but closely trimmed at the top; the first word of the title-page and the page-number and head-line on p. 48 are cut into.

OTHER COPIES.

Trinity College, Cambridge; Lenox; and White Libraries.

REFERENCES.

Grolier Club, *Wither to Prior,* 2 (1903): 167, No. 559; Lenox Library, *Works of Milton* (1881), p. 14, No. 95.

MILTON, JOHN. [Hall, Joseph, *Bishop of Norwich.*] (*b.* 1574, *d.* 1656.)

A SHORT ANSWER TO THE TEDIOVS VINDICATION OF SMECTYMNVVS. London, *for Nathaniel Butter,* 1641. [489]

Small quarto.

COLLATION BY SIGNATURES: A, a, B to O, each 4 leaves; total 60 leaves.

COLLATION BY PAGINATION: [title, as reproduced; *See* No. 489], recto of [A]; —[blank], verso of [A];— |[conventional head-piece] | TO | The moſt High Court | OF | PARLIAMENT.|, recto and verso

1641 — John Milton — No. 488

THE REASON OF Church-governement
Urg'd againſt
PRELATY
By Mr. *John Milton.*

In two Books.

LONDON,
Printed by *E. G.* for *John Rothwell*, and are to be ſold
at the Sunne in *Pauls* Church-yard. 1641.

No. 488. Title-page of Milton's Reason of Chvrch-governement Urg'd against Prelaty; 1641.

No. 489   *John Milton*   1641

A SHORT ANSWER
TO THE
Tedious Vindication
OF
SMECTYMNVVS.

BY
The *AVTHOR* of the
Humble Remonstrance.

LONDON,
Printed for NATHANIEL BUTTER in *Pauls*
Church-yard at the pyde-Bull neare
Sᵗ. *Auſtins gate.* 1641.

No. 489. Title-page of Hall's Short Answer to the Tedious Vindication of Smectymnvvs; 1641.

of A 2 ; — | [type-ornament head-piece] | An ANSWER | TO | *A Calumniatory EPISTLE,* | Directed by way of PREFACE to | the Reader. |, recto of A 3 to verso of [a 4] ; — [text, with heading] | [type-ornament rule] | A Short | ANSWER | To the Tedious | VINDICATION | OF | SMEC-TYMNVVS. |, pp. 1–103 ; — | FINIS. |, p. 103 ; — [blank], p. [104]. Page 5 is wrongly numbered 23 ; and 8 is 22.

CONDITION : Size of leaf, 7⅜ × 5⅝ inches. Bound in dark green crushed levant morocco, gilt edges ; by the Club Bindery, 1899. The leaves are stabbed on the inner margins throughout the book.

OTHER COPIES.

Trinity College, Cambridge ; and Lenox Libraries.

REFERENCE.

Lenox Library, *Works of Milton* (1881), p. 24, No. 157.

Smectymnuus was a cryptic name adopted by several writers in a controversial work against episcopacy written in the middle of the seventeenth century, in answer to Bishop Hall — a controversy in which Milton took part. It is a sort of acrostic made up from the initials of the names of the authors: **S**tephen **M**arshall, **E**dmund **C**alamy, **T**homas **Y**oung, **M**atthew **N**ewcomen, and **VV**illiam Spurstowe.

MILTON, JOHN.

AREOPAGITICA ; A SPEECH ... FOR THE LIBERTY OF VN-LICENC'D PRINTING. LONDON, *Printed in the Yeare,* 1644.   [490]

Small quarto. First Edition.

COLLATION BY SIGNATURES : A to E, each 4 leaves ; F, 2 leaves (the last blank and lacking) ; total 22 leaves.

COLLATION BY PAGINATION : [title, as reproduced ; *See* No. 490], recto of [A] ; — [blank], verso of [A] ; — [text, with heading] | [type-ornament head-piece] | For the Liberty of unlicenc'd Printing. |, pp. 1–40 ; — | *The End.* |, p. 40 ; — [1 blank leaf], [F 2].

CONDITION : Size of leaf, 7 × 5⅜ inches.   Bound in green crushed levant morocco, gilt edges ; by the Club Bindery, 1899. The side-note on p. 8 is cut into.

OTHER COPIES.

Trinity College, Cambridge ; Lenox ; Halsey ; and White Libraries.

REFERENCES.

Grolier Club, *Wither to Prior,* 2 (1905) : 172, No. 569 ; Lenox Library, *Works of Milton* (1881), p. 16, No. 104 ; Hazlitt, *Collections and Notes* (1889), p. 68 ; Lowndes, 3 (1869) : 1565.

This work, by far the best known of any of Milton's prose writings, was published in November, 1644. It was a protest against an ordinance of Parliament passed the 14th of the preceding June, with which it was proposed to crush him. Milton had always condemned licensing regulations, both in theory and practice, by publishing several unlicensed tracts. Nor was Milton pleading his own cause alone, for we learn that he had been asked by a respectable constituency to be their spokesman and write this pamphlet.

Areopagitica is composed with more care and art than his other works, and is the best example he has given us of his ability as an advocate. Of all his prose works

AREOPAGITICA;
A
SPEECH
OF
Mr. JOHN MILTON
For the Liberty of Vnlicenc'd
PRINTING,
To the Parlament of England.

Τῶλάθερον δ' ἐκεῖνο, εἴ τις θέλει πόλει
Χρηστόν τι βούλευμ' εἰς μέσον φέρειν, ἔχων.
Καὶ ταῦθ' ὁ χρῄζων, λαμπρός ἐσθ', ὁ μὴ θέλων,
Σιγᾷ. τί τούτων ἔστιν ἰσαίτερον πόλει;

Euripid. Hicetid.

*This is true Liberty when free born men
Having to advise the public may speak free,
Which he who can, and will, deserv's high praise,
Who neither can nor will, may hold his peace;
What can be juster in a State then this?*

Euripid. Hicetid.

LONDON,
Printed in the Yeare, 1644.

No. 490. Title-page of Milton's Areopagitica; 1st Edition; 1644.

it is the only one read with pleasure to-day, and contains several passages that have become well known. Who is not familiar with "For Books are not abſolutely dead things, but doe contain a potencie of life in them to be as active as that ſoule was whoſe progeny they are"? or "As good almoſt kill a Man as kill a good Book; who kills a Man kills a reaſonable creature, Gods Image; but hee who deſtroyes a good Booke kills reaſon it ſelfe, kills the Image of God, as it were in the eye. Many a man lives a burden to the Earth; but a good Booke is the pretious life-blood of a maſter ſpirit, imbalm'd and treaſur'd up on purpoſe to a life beyond life."

This work was reprinted by the Grolier Club in 1890.

MILTON, JOHN.

POEMS, BOTH ENGLISH AND LATIN. LONDON, *by Ruth Raworth for Humphrey Moſeley*, 1645. 2 parts in one, small octavo, viz.: [491]

PART 1.

COLLATION BY SIGNATURES: a, 4 leaves; A to G, each 8 leaves; H, 4 leaves; total 64 leaves.

COLLATION BY PAGINATION: [blank], recto of [a]; — [portrait of Milton], verso of [a]; — [title, as reproduced; *See* No. 491], recto of [a2]; — [blank], verso of [a2]; — | [type-ornament head-piece] | THE | STATIONER | TO THE | READER. | [signed] | *Thine to command* | HUMPH. MOSELEY. |, recto of a 3 to verso of a 4; — [text, several verses in English and Italian, the first with heading] | [conventional head-piece] | On the morning of CHRISTS | Nativity. Compos'd 1629. |, pp. 1–65; — | [type-ornament rule] | E | [type-ornament rule] |, p. 65; — [blank], p. [66].

| A | MASK | Of the ſame | AUTHOR | PRESENTED | At *LVDLOW*-Caſtle, | 1634. | Before | The Earl of BRIDGEWATER | Then Preſident of WALES. | [conventional ornament] | Anno Dom. 1645. |, p. [67];

— [blank], p. [68]; — | [type-ornament rule] | To the Right Honourable, | JOHN Lord Vicount BRACLY, | Son and Heir apparent to the Earl | of *Bridgewater, &c.* | [signed] | *Your faithfull, and most* | *humble Servant* | H. LAWES. |, pp. 69–70; — | The Copy of a Letter Writt'n | By Sir HENRY WOOTTON, | To the Author, upon the | following Poem. | [signed] | *Henry Wootton.* |, pp. 71–73; — | [type-ornament rule] | The Perſons. |, p. 74; — [text, with heading] | [type-ornament head-piece] | A | MASK | PRESENTED | At LUDLOW-Caſtle, | 1634. *&c.* |, pp. 75–120; — | [type-ornament tail-piece] | *The End.* |, p. 120.

ILLUSTRATION: Portrait of Milton, in an oval frame containing a Latin inscription, ending, "ANNO ÆTATIS *ViGeſs : Pri :*"; with figures of the Muses *Melpomene, Erato, Urania,* and *Clio* in the corners; below, 4 lines of Greek and "*W. M. ſculp :*".

PART 2.

COLLATION BY SIGNATURES: A to E, each 8 leaves; F, 4 leaves; total 44 numbered leaves.

COLLATION BY PAGINATION: [title] | Joannis Miltoni | *LONDINENSIS* | POEMATA. | Quorum pleraque intra | Annum ætatis Vigeſimum | Conſcripſit. | *Nunc primum Edita.* | [conventional ornament] | *LONDINI,* | Typis R. R. Proſtant ad Inſignia Principis, | in Cœmeterio D. *Pauli,* apud Humphredum | *Moſeley.* 1645. |, p. [1]; — [blank], p. [2]; — [preface in Latin,

POEMS

OF

Mr. *John Milton*,

BOTH

ENGLISH and LATIN,
Compos'd at several times.

Printed by his true Copies.

The Songs were set in Musick by
Mr. HENRY LAWES Gentleman of
the KINGS Chappel, and one
of His MAIESTIES
Private Musick.

——— *Baccare frontem*
Cingite, ne vati noceat mala lingua futuro;
Virgil, Eclog. 7.

Printed and publish'd according to
ORDER.

LONDON,
Printed by *Ruth Raworth* for *Humphrey Moseley*,
and are to be sold at the signe of the Princes
Arms in *Pauls* Church-yard. 1645.

NO. 491. TITLE-PAGE OF MILTON'S POEMS, BOTH ENGLISH AND LATIN; 1645.

beginning] | [type-ornament head-piece] | HÆc quæ sequuntur de Autho- | re testimonia, . . . | , p. 3 ; — [odes, etc., to Milton], pp. 4–10 ; — [poems, the first with heading] | [type-ornament rule] | ELEGIARUM | Liber primus. | Elegia prima ad *Carolum Diodatum*. | , pp. 11–87 ; — | *FINIS.* | , p. 87 ; — [blank], p. [88].

1645 — John Milton — No. 491

Laid in is a portrait of Milton, after Marshall, in an oval frame containing a Latin inscription, ending, "ANNO ÆTATIS. 21."; with 4 lines of Greek below.

CONDITION: Size of leaf, 6¼ x 3¹⁵⁄₁₆ inches. Bound in brown crushed levant morocco, gilt edges; by Rivière. With many leaves uncut at the bottom, but all closely trimmed at the top.

OTHER COPIES.

Dyce Collection; Trinity College, Cambridge; Crawford; Devonshire; Ellesmere; Huth; Boston Public (2, contents differently arranged); Lenox; Halsey; Hoe; Morgan; and White Libraries.

REFERENCES.

Grolier Club, *Wither to Prior*, 2 (1905): 173, No. 572; Hoe, *Catalogue*, 3 (1903): 165; Locker-Lampson, *Catalogue* (1886), p. 82; Lenox Library, *Works of Milton* (1881), p. 11, No. 73; Huth, *Catalogue*, 3 (1880): 969; Masson, *Life of John Milton*, 3 (1873): 451, 459; Lowndes, 3 (1869): 1563; *Bibliotheca Anglo-Poetica* (1815), p. 210, No. 453.

In some copies the last line of the imprint reads: | Arms in S. *Pauls* Church-yard. 1645. |, instead of | Arms in *Pauls* Church-yard. 1645. |.

This is the First Collected Edition of Milton's poems, and contains all that he had written up to the time of its publication, with the exception of those "On the Death of a Fair Infant dying of a Cough," and "At a Vacation Exercise in the Colledge," both of which appeared in the Second Edition of the poems in 1673.

With the exception of "Lycidas," "Comus," and the epitaph on Shakespeare, all the pieces here printed appear for the first time.

The portrait by Marshall is the first engraved portrait of Milton ever published. The Greek inscription was intended by the poet as a satire on the engraver for representing him as of middle age. It has been translated into English, as follows:

> "Who that my real lineament has scanned
> Will not in this detect a bungler's hand?
> My friends, in doubt on whom his art was tried,
> The idiot limner's vain attempt deride."

Laid into the copy here described is a portrait, apparently a copy of Marshall's. It differs from the original in the following respects: (*a*) The portrait is in a smaller oval; (*b*) the inscription in the oval closes "ÆTATIS. 21." instead of "ÆTATIS viGeſs: Pri:"; (*c*) it lacks the figures of the four Muses in the corners; and (*d*) it lacks the words "*W. M. ſculp:*" below the Greek lines at the bottom.

Milton wrote the poems in this collection between his sixteenth and thirty-eighth years. "The order in which the poems are printed, within each division or class, is, as nearly as possible, the order in which they were written; the deviations being only such as proper editorial art required. To almost every juvenile piece, too, whether in English or in Latin, there is prefixed some indication of the exact date of its composition; and the title-page of the Latin Poems distinctly solicits attention to the fact that most of them were composed before the author was twenty. Even more remarkable than this care in the dating is the introduction into the volume of all the eulogiums which Milton had already received from private friends on account of the Poems, or of any portion of them." — MASSON.

[MILTON, JOHN.] Lawes, Henry (b. 1596, d. 1662) and William (b. ——, d. 1645).

CHOICE PSALMES PUT INTO MUSICK, FOR THREE VOICES. LONDON, by *James Young, for Humphrey Moseley, and Richard Wodenothe*, 1648. 4 vols., small quarto, viz.: [492]

VOL. 1. *Cantus Primus.*

COLLATION BY SIGNATURES: A, 3 leaves; a, 2 leaves; B to L, each 4 leaves; 1 leaf, without signature-mark, probably imposed as A 4; total 46 unnumbered leaves.

COLLATION BY PAGINATION: [title, as reproduced; *See* No. 492], recto of [A]; —[portrait of Charles I., with inscription] | *Carolus D: G: Rex Ang:* | *Sco: Fran: et Hiber:* | [1 staff of music] | Regi, Regis, &c. Regum Ar-ca-na cano. | Henricus Lawes | Regiæ Majestatis à sacra Musica. |, verso of [A]; — | [conventional headpiece] | TO HIS | Most Sacred Majestie, | CHARLES, | [4 lines] | [signed] | Your Majesties most humble, | most loyally devoted Subject and Servant, | HENRY LAWES. |, recto and verso of A 2; — | To the READER. | [signed] | Henry Lawes. |, recto and verso of [A 3]; —[4 poems, one by Milton, the first with heading] | [conventional headpiece] | To the Incomparable Brothers, M^r. *Henry*, | and M^r. *William Lawes* (Servants to His Majestie) | upon the setting of these Psalmes. |, recto of a to verso of [a 2]; —[music, with words], recto of B to recto of unmarked leaf; — | THE TABLE. |, verso of unmarked leaf; — | FINIS. |, verso of unmarked leaf.

VOL. 2. *Cantus Secundus.*

COLLATION BY SIGNATURES: A, 4 leaves; a, 2 leaves; M to X, each 4 leaves; total 46 unnumbered leaves.

COLLATION BY PAGINATION: [blank], recto of [A]; —[portrait of Charles I., with inscription] | *Carolus D: G: Rex Ang:* | *Sco: Fran: et Hiber:* |, verso of [A]; —[title, same as in Vol. 1], recto of [A 2]; — [portrait of Charles I., with inscription and music, same as in Vol. 1], verso of [A 2]; —[dedication, preface, and poems, same as in Vol. 1], recto of A 3 to verso of [a 2]; —[music, with words], recto of M to recto of [X 4]; — | THE TABLE. |, verso of [X 4]; — | FINIS. |, verso of [X 4].

VOL. 3. *Bassus.*

COLLATION BY SIGNATURES: A, 4 leaves (the first lacking); a, 2 leaves; Y, Z, Aa to Hh, each 4 leaves; total 46 unnumbered leaves.

COLLATION BY PAGINATION: [1 leaf], [A]; —[title, same as in Vol. 1], recto of [A 2]; —[portrait of Charles I., with inscription and music, same as in Vol. 1], verso of [A 2]; —[dedication, preface, and poems, same as in Vol. 1], recto of A 3 to verso of [a 2]; —[music, with words], recto of Y to verso of [Hh 4].

VOL. 4. *Thorough Base.*

COLLATION BY SIGNATURES: A, 4 leaves; a, 2 leaves; Ii to Oo, each 4 leaves; total 30 unnumbered leaves.

COLLATION BY PAGINATION: [title, same as in Vol. 1], recto of [A]; — | [1 staff of music] | Regi, Regis, &c. Regum Ar-ca-na cano. | Henricus Lawes | Regiæ Majestatis à sacra Musica. |, verso of [A]; —[blank], recto of [A 2]; —[portrait of Charles I., with inscription] | *Carolus D:*

CHOICE PSALMES PUT INTO MUSICK,

For Three Voices.

The moſt of which may properly enough be ſung by any three, with a Thorough Baſe.

Compos'd by

Henry and *William* } *Lawes*, Brothers; and Servants to His Majeſtie.

With divers Elegies, ſet in Muſick by ſev'rall Friends, upon the death of WILLIAM LAWES.

And at the end of the Thorough Baſe are added nine Canons of Three and Foure Voices, made by *William Lawes*.

LONDON,
Printed by *James Young*, for *Humphrey Moſeley*, at the Prince's Armes in S. *Pauls* Church-yard, and for *Richard Wodenothe*, at the Star under S. *Peters* Church in Corn-hill. 1648.

NO. 492. TITLE-PAGE OF LAWES' CHOICE PSALMES PUT INTO MUSICK; 1648.

No. 492   *John Milton*   1648

G : Rex Ang : | Sco : Fran : et Hiber : |, verso of [A 2]; — [dedication, preface, and poems, same as in Vol. 1], recto of A 3 to verso of [a 2]; — [music, with words], recto of Ii to recto of [Oo 4]; — | THE TABLE. |, verso of [Oo 4]; — | FINIS. |, verso of [Oo 4].

CONDITION : Size of leaf, 8 to 8½ × 6¼ to 6½ inches. Bound in boards, blue morocco back.

OTHER COPIES.

Huth ; and White Libraries.

REFERENCES.

Locker-Lampson, *Catalogue* (1886), p. 66 ; Lowndes, 3 (1869) : 1324 ; *Bibliotheca Anglo-Poetica* (1815), p. 194, No. 426.

The Locker-Lampson copy, with ex-libris.

This work is of interest to the Milton collector because it contains among other commendatory verses a short poem by Milton upon the setting of these Psalms, beginning :

        "H*Arry*, whofe tunefull and well meafur'd fong
        Firft taught our Englifh Mufic how to fpan
        Words with juft note and accent, . . ."

MILTON, JOHN.

THE TENURE OF KINGS AND MAGISTRATES. LONDON, *Matthew Simmons*, 1649.   [493]

Small quarto. First Edition.

COLLATION BY SIGNATURES : A to E, each 4 leaves ; F, 2 leaves ; total 22 leaves.

COLLATION BY PAGINATION : [title, as reproduced ; *See* No. 493], recto of [A]; — [blank], verso of [A]; — [text, with heading] | [type-ornament head-piece] | THE TENURE OF | KINGS | And MAGISTRATES. |, pp. 1–42 ; — | *The End*. |, p. 42.

CONDITION : Size of leaf, 7³⁄₁₀ × 5½ inches. Bound in dark green crushed levant morocco, gilt edges ; by the Club Bindery, 1899.

OTHER COPIES.

Edinburgh University ; Ellesmere ; Boston Public ; Lenox ; Halsey ; Hoe ; and White Libraries.

REFERENCES.

Grolier Club, *Wither to Prior*, 2 (1905) : 177, No. 575 ; Hoe, *Catalogue*, 5 (1905) : 336 ; Lenox Library, *Works of Milton* (1881), p. 16, No. 109 ; Masson, *Life of John Milton*, 4 (1877) : 64, 65 ; Lowndes, *Bibliographer's Manual of English Literature*, 3 (1869) : 1566.

A Second Edition containing additional matter was printed the same year ; A to H, each 4 leaves.

The main purpose of this pamphlet, so far as it is theoretical, is to inculcate Republican or Democratic principles. It was omitted from all editions of Milton's prose works until that of 1806, as its contents would have made its possession a treasonable offence after the Restoration.

"Milton was the first Englishman of mark, out of Parliament, that signified his unqualified adhesion to the Republic. This he did on the 13th of February, 1648–9, by publishing that pamphlet [*The Tenure of Kings*] on which we saw

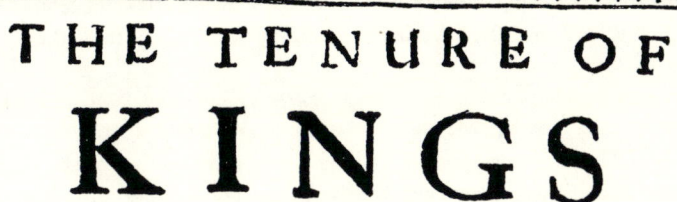

him engaged in his house in High Holborn during the King's trial. . . . This new pamphlet, like most of its predecessors, was unlicensed. It was published exactly a fortnight after the King's death, and exactly a week after the Republic had been declared. The *Eikon Basilike*, the supreme publication on the other side, had preceded it by four days.

"*The Tenure of Kings and Magistrates* is not equal, in richness or literary interest, to the best of Milton's previous pamphlets. It is, however, a strong, thoroughly Miltonic performance, falling with hammer-like force on the question discussed; and it must have been welcomed by the founders of the Commonwealth in their first hour of difficulty."

MILTON, JOHN.

PARADISE LOST. A POEM WRITTEN IN TEN BOOKS. London, 1667.

[494]

Small quarto. First Edition, with the First Title-page.

COLLATION BY SIGNATURES: 2 leaves, without signature-marks (the first blank and genuine); A to Z, Aa to Tt, each 4 leaves; Vv, 2 leaves; total 172 unnumbered leaves.

COLLATION BY PAGINATION: [1 blank leaf];—[title, as reproduced; *See* No. 494], recto of second leaf;—[blank], verso of second leaf;—[text in 10 books, with heading] | [type-ornament head-piece] | PARADISE | LOST. |, recto of A to verso of [Vv 2];—| THE END. |, verso of [Vv 2]. Errors in the numbering of the lines: Book 2, line 360 is wrongly numbered 366; 459 is 460; 721 is 720. Book 3, line 530 is 5 0; 600 to 609 are omitted in the numbering; 741 is 740; 751 is 750. Book 4, line 661 is 660; 671 is 670; 681 is 680; 759 is omitted in the numbering; 810 is 381. Book 5, line 510 is 150. Book 7, line 99 is 100. Book 9, line 230 is 2go; 240 has no number; 248 is 250; 258 is 260; 268 is 270; 510 is 570. Book 10, line 181 is 180; 881 is 880; 1079 is 1080; and 1110 is 1100.

CONDITION: Size of leaf, 7$\frac{3}{16}$ × 5$\frac{3}{8}$ inches. Bound in red crushed levant morocco, gilt edges; by Bedford. Several leaves are uncut on the lower edges.

OTHER COPIES.

Capell Collection; Crawford; Ellesmere; Huth; Lenox; Chew; Halsey; Hoe; Morgan; and White Libraries; and Library of Congress.

REFERENCES.

Williamson, *Early Editions of Milton's Works*, in *Milton Tercentenary* (Cambridge, 1908), pp. 92–120; Grolier Club, *Wither to Prior*, 2 (1903): 187, No. 599; Baxter, *Milton's "Paradise Lost,"* in *The Bibliographer*, 2 (1903): 73–91, 140; Hoe, *Catalogue*, 3 (1903) : 169; Masson, *Poetical Works of John Milton*, 2 (1890) : 12–14; Lenox Library, *Works of Milton* (1881), p. 5, No. 15; Huth, *Catalogue*, 3 (1880) : 970; Masson, *Life of John Milton*, 6 (1880) : 516–518, 621–629; Corser, *Collectanea Anglo-Poetica*, Part 8 (Chetham Society, Vol. CII., 1878), p. 410; Lowndes, 3 (1869) : 1557–1558; Hazlitt, *Hand-Book* (1867), p. 396; Sotheby, *Ramblings in the Elucidation of the Autograph of Milton* (1861), pp. 81–84, 196; *Bibliotheca Grenvilliana*, 2 (1842) : 465.

The Locker-Lampson copy, with ex-libris.

Of the First Edition of *Paradise Lost* 1300 copies were printed, and it was offered for sale probably toward the end of August, 1667. Appearing as it did during the troublesome times following the Restoration, and soon after the Great Plague and Great Fire of London, it did not meet with a ready sale. Whether for reasons of policy or of business is not known, but copies of this edition are known to have been issued with six distinct title-pages, in which variations are to be found in the name of the writer, in the names of the booksellers, and in the dates of imprint, as follows:

(1) Of the First Title-page a reproduction is given with the copy here described. The facsimile of this title-page in the *Milton Tercentenary* (p. 94) is inaccurate. The first line should end with a period, and "Printed" be followed by a comma.

(2) The Second Title-page differs from our reproduction only in the sixth line, which reads | By *john milton*. | instead of | By *JOHN MILTON*. |. This title-page has been reproduced in the Grolier Club's *Wither to Prior* (2:187); *The Bibliographer* (2:77); and the *Milton Tercentenary* (1908), p. 95.

(3) The Third Title-page reads: | Paradife loft. | A | POEM | IN | TEN BOOKS | The Author *J. M.* | Licenfed and Entred according | to Order. | *LONDON* | Printed, and are to be fold by *Peter Parker* | under *Creed* Church neer *Aldgate* ; And by | *Robert Boulter* at the *Turks Head* in *Bifhopfgate-ftreet* ; | And *Matthias Walker*, under St. *Dunftons* Church | in *Fleet-ftreet*, 1668. |. This title-page has been reproduced in *The Bibliographer* (2:80) and the *Milton Tercentenary* (1908), p. 96. Of this title-page there is a copy in the Lenox Library.

Mr. Hoe has a copy which differs from it only in the fifth line, which reads | TEN BOOKS. |, the space between the two words being slightly reduced and a period inserted at the end. A facsimile of this title-page is given in the Grolier Club's *Wither to Prior* (2:190, No. 601).

(4) Of the Fourth Title-page a reproduction is given with our No. 495.

(5) Of the Fifth Title-page a reproduction is given with our No. 496.

(6) The Sixth Title-page reads: | Paradife loft. | A | POEM | IN | TEN BOOKS | The Author | *JOHN MILTON*. | *london,* | Printed by *S. Simmons,* and are to be fold by | *T. Helder,* at the *Angel* in *Little Brittain,* | 1669. |. This title-page has been reproduced in the Grolier Club's *Wither to Prior* (2:192, No. 604); *The Bibliographer* (2:85); and the *Milton Tercentenary* (1908), p. 101.

Lowndes describes two other title-pages, and to these Masson and Sotheby add still another, making nine in all. They have been followed by Baxter and Dr. Williamson. We are informed by the latter that Dr. Masson told him that there was a copy of the three-star title-page, so called, in a private collection in Scotland, but he refused to say by whom it was owned. Since then Dr. Masson has died and his secret with him. Information regarding another of the title-pages has been promised, but has not yet come to hand. Mr. Marshall C. Lefferts, a prominent New York collector of Milton's works, has for many years been searching diligently in the public and private libraries of this country and Europe for copies containing these alleged title-pages. In his search he has also enlisted the assistance of many booksellers. His efforts have proved unsuccessful, and he confidently believes that no such title-pages exist, but that the descriptions of them rest wholly upon the inaccurate or confused descriptions of the six given above. In view of this uncertainty and

Paradise lost.

A
POEM
Written in
TEN BOOKS
By *JOHN MILTON.*

Licensed and Entred according to Order.

LONDON
Printed, and are to be sold by *Peter Parker* under *Creed* Church neer *Aldgate*; And by *Robert Boulter* at the *Turks Head* in *Bishopsgate-street*; And *Matthias Walker,* under St. *Dunstons* Church in Fleet-street, 1667.

No. 494. Title-page of Milton's Paradise Lost; 1st Edition, 1st Title-page; 1667.

because they have not been definitely located nor their existence conclusively demonstrated by facsimile reproductions, they have not been enumerated in the above list.

Paradise Lost as originally issued with the First Title-page seems to have had no preliminary matter, the text of the poem beginning on the second leaf. With the Fourth Title-page there appear to have been issued for the first time seven leaves, containing: (*a*) "The Printer to the Reader," 4 lines; followed by (*b*) "The Argument," 11 pages; (*c*) "The Verse," 2 pages; and (*d*) "Errata," 1 page. The "Address to the Reader" not being altogether grammatical in form, was changed, increasing it to six instead of four lines. The preliminary leaves with this six-line note are found with the Fifth Title-page, and sometimes with the Fourth. With the Sixth Title-page these leaves were reprinted, "The Printer to the Reader" being omitted. This reprint may still further be distinguished by the erratum in the list of "Errata," where "Lib. 6. V. 215." is made to read "Lib. 2. V. 215." The presumable order and arrangement of the different issues or editions, as they originally appeared, therefore seems to have been as follows:

(1) The First Title-page, followed immediately by the poem; there being no preliminary matter.

(2) The Second Title-page, followed immediately by the poem as in (1).

(3) The Third Title-page, followed immediately by the poem as in (1).

(4) The Fourth Title-page, with the preliminary leaves containing the four-line note "The Printer to the Reader," but *sometimes* with those containing the six-line note "The Printer to the Reader."

(5) The Fifth Title-page, with the six-line note "The Printer to the Reader."

(6) The Sixth Title-page, with the reprinted preliminary leaves, in which "The Printer to the Reader," is omitted.

The numerous differences which appear in the body of the work are probably due to the corrections made from time to time as the work was passing through the press, and it is possible that some of the sheets were actually reprinted. As the sheets containing the corrections were mixed with the uncorrected ones before or during the binding, these differences are of little or no value in determining the priority of the issue of the copy in which they are found. The list of "Errata," doubtless compiled by Milton himself, first appeared after the work had been printed. Of the changes there called for but one appears to have caught the printer's eye, that in Book 3, line 751 (last line but one), in which the word "with" has been changed to "in." It thus appears that the compiler of the "Errata" must have made up his list from a copy containing the uncorrected line.

The delinquencies of the printer are to be observed: (1) in mistakes made in numbering the lines of the poem; (2) in faulty punctuation; (3) in errors of spelling; (4) in inconsistencies of capitalization; (5) in errors in the catchwords; and (6) in miscellaneous errors and variations.

(1) A list of the errors in line numberings found in each of the copies here described is given with their collations. In some of the 26 copies examined, line 731 of Book 3 is wrongly numbered 740; 741 is 750; 751 is 760. Book 4, line

90 is 80; 100 is 90; 110 is 100. Book 9, line 824 is 820; 834 is 830; 844 is 840; 854 is 850; 864 is 860; 874 is 870; 944 is renumbered 940; 954 is 950; 964 is 960; 974 is 970; 984 is 980; 994 is 990; 1004 is 1000; and 1010 is 0110. The line numbers are printed in a ruled space outside of the text, but do not always align with it. When out of alignment they are assigned to the nearest line.

(2) The following variations in punctuation occur in different copies, those employed in the Second Edition being with a single exception placed in parentheses: Book 3, line 663, "accoftes." ("accoftes;"); Book 4, line 88, "groane:" ("groane;"); Book 4, line 720, "ftood," ("ftood."), Second Edition, "ftood"; Book 5, line 301, "Raies, to" ("Raies to"); Book 5, line 608, "Lord," ("Lord:"); Book 5, line 710, "within," ("within"); Book 5, line 743, "Morning" ("Morning,"); Book 8, line 1101, "renown'd;" ("renown'd,"); Book 9, line 982, "mifery." ("mifery,"); Book 10, line 139, "linkt," ("linkt;"); Book 10, line 904, "few," ("few;"). All the above varieties we have seen in the First Edition except "ftood." and "renown'd;", for which we take R. H. Shepherd's assertion in the Pickering reprint. In Book 4, line 720, the comma after "ftood" appears much worn and indistinct, gradually wearing down to what seems to be a period; and in Book 10, line 904, the upper part of what is described as a semicolon after "few" looks in most cases much like a blur.

(3) The following misprints and other variations occur in different copies, the corrected forms used in the Second Edition being placed in parentheses: Book 2, line 1009, "Havook" ("Havock"); Book 3, line 97, "me"("mee"); Book 5, line 827, "our" ("one"); Book 9, line 1078, "fupply" ("fupplie"); and Book 10, line 32, "pray let me," ("pray, let mee"). When Milton wished to be emphatic he used the form "mee" instead of "me".

(4) The following variations occur in the use of capitals, the forms used in the Second Edition being placed in parentheses. Book 4, line 83, "Spirits" ("fpirits"); Book 4, line 91, "fupream" ("Supream"); Book 5, line 287, "bands" ("Bands"); Book 10, line 76, "doom" ("Doom"); Book 10, line 101, "warriours" ("Warriours").

(5) The catchwords are not always followed by the same word on the next page. On leaf [B 4], verso, "with" is followed by "Turns"; [I 4], verso, "Their" by "Thir"; [M 4], verso, "Happy;" by "Happie,"; [R 4], recto, "Had" by "Hath"; Bb, recto, "Created," by "Created"; [Pp 3], recto, "Depar-" by "Departure".

(6) In but one copy (one of the ten at the Lenox Library) have we found the head-line on the recto of leaf K 2 to read "Book 2," all other copies reading correctly "Book 3." In six copies only (three in the Lenox Library, two belonging to Mr. Morgan, and that of the Grolier Club) have we found the first word of line 616 of Book 5 printed to align with the other verses; in all other cases it has been indented, and it is so printed in the Second Edition.

The original or printer's manuscript of Book 1 of *Paradise Lost* is now in the library of Mr. J. Pierpont Morgan.

MILTON, JOHN.

PARADISE LOST. A POEM IN TEN BOOKS. LONDON, S. Simmons, 1668. [495]

Small quarto. First Edition, with the Fourth Title-page.

COLLATION BY SIGNATURES : A, a, A to Z, Aa to Tt, each 4 leaves ; Vv, 2 leaves ; total 178 unnumbered leaves.

COLLATION BY PAGINATION : [title, as reproduced ; See No. 495], recto of [A] ; — [blank], verso of [A] ; — | *The Printer to the Reader.* | [5 lines] | [signed] | *S. Simmons* |, recto of *A 2* ; — | [type-ornament rule] | THE | ARGUMENT : |, recto of *A 2* to recto of [a 3] ; — | THE VERSE. |, verso of [a 3] to recto of [a 4] ; — | [type-ornament rule] | *ERRATA.* | [14 lines] | [type-ornament rule] |, verso of [a 4] ; — [text in 10 books, with heading] | [type-ornament head-piece] | PARADISE | LOST. |, recto of A to verso of [Vv 2] ; — | *THE END.* |, verso of [Vv 2]. The errors in the numbering of the lines agree with our No. 494, except that in Book 2 line 981 is wrongly numbered 980 ; 991 is 990 ; 1001 is 1000 ; 1011 is 1010 ; 1021 is 1020 ; 1031 is 1030 ; 1041 is 1040. Book 3, line 50 is 60 ; 60 is 70 ; 70 is 80 ; 80 has no number ; in Book 4, lines 660, 670, 680, and 810 are correctly numbered ; and in Book 5, line 510 is correctly numbered.

CONDITION : Size of leaf, 6⅞ x 5¼ inches. Bound in dark blue crushed levant morocco, gilt edges ; by Bedford. Before the title-page has been inserted a copy of the First Title-page.

OTHER COPIES.

Trinity College, Cambridge ; Boston Public ; Lenox (3) ; Grolier Club ; Hoe (2) ; and Morgan Libraries.

REFERENCES.

Grolier Club, *Wither to Prior,* 2 (1903) : 191, No. 602 ; Baxter, *Milton's " Paradise Lost,"* in *The Bibliographer,* 2 (1903) : 79, 81 ; Lenox Library, *Works of Milton* (1881), p. 6, No. 19 ; Huth, *Catalogue,* 3 (1880) : 970 ; Lowndes, 3 (1869) : 1557.

MILTON, JOHN.

PARADISE LOST. A POEM IN TEN BOOKS. LONDON, S. Simmons, 1669. [496]

Small quarto. First Edition, with the Fifth Title-page.

COLLATION BY SIGNATURES : A, a, A to Z, Aa to Tt, each 4 leaves ; Vv, 2 leaves ; total 178 unnumbered leaves.

COLLATION BY PAGINATION : [title, as reproduced ; See No. 496], recto of [A] ; — [blank], verso of [A] ; — | *The Printer to the Reader.* | [5 lines] | [signed] | *S. Simmons.* |, recto of *A 2* ; — | [type-ornament rule] | THE | ARGUMENT : |, recto of *A 2* to recto of [a 3] ; — | THE VERSE. |, verso of [a 3] to recto of [a 4] ; — | [type-ornament rule] | *ERRATA.* | [14 lines] | [type-ornament rule] |, verso of [a 4] ; — [text in 10 books, with heading] | [type-ornament head-piece] | PARADISE | LOST. |, recto of A to verso of [Vv 2] ; — | *THE END.* |, verso of [Vv 2]. The errors in the numbering of the lines agree with those in our No. 494, except that in Book 4 lines 660, 670, 680, and 810 are correctly numbered, and in Book 5, line 510 is correctly numbered.

CONDITION : Size of leaf, 7⅛ x 5¼ inches. Bound in red crushed levant morocco, gilt edges ; by Bedford.

OTHER COPIES.

Capell Collection ; Dyce Collection ; Devonshire ; Lenox (4) ; Chew ; Hoe ; and Morgan Libraries.

Paradise lost.

A POEM IN TEN BOOKS.

The Author
JOHN MILTON.

LONDON,
Printed by *S. Simmons*, and to be sold by *S. Thomson* at the *Bishops-Head* in *Duck-lane*, *H. Mortlack* at the *White Hart* in *Westminster* Hall, *M. Walker* under *St. Dunstans* Church in *Fleet street*, and *R. Boulter* at the *Turks-Head* in *Bishopsgate* street, 1668.

1669 John Milton No. 496

REFERENCES.
Grolier Club, *Wither to Prior*, 2 (1905): 193, No. 603; Baxter, Milton's "Paradise Lost," in *The Bibliographer*, 2 (1903): 82, 84; Lenox Library, *Works of Milton* (1881), p. 6, No. 21; Lowndes, 3 (1869): 1558.

The Second Edition of *Paradise Lost* appeared in 1674, the year of Milton's death. It is in small octavo, some copies containing Dolle's portrait, reduced in 1671 from the Faithorne engraving. Two sets of commendatory verses, one in Latin by Samuel Barrow, the other in English by Andrew Marvell, precede the poem. "The Argument" is divided, that portion appropriate to each book being printed before its text. The pages are numbered, but the numbering of the lines, which had occasioned much trouble in the First Edition, was omitted.

The poem was divided into twelve books instead of ten. No change occurs in the first six books.

Book 7 is divided into two, the seventh ending at line 640:

"Aught, not furpaffing human meafure, fay."

Book 8 begins with line 641,

"To whom thus *Adam* gratefully repli'd."

which has been amplified to read:

"The Angel ended, and in *Adams* Eare
So Charming left his voice, that he a while
Thought him ftill fpeaking, ftill ftood fixt to hear;
Then as new wak't thus gratefully repli'd."

Book 8 became Book 9, and Book 9 became Book 10.
Book 10 is divided into Books 11 and 12. Book 11 ends with line 896:

"Both Heav'n and Earth, wherein the juft fhall dwell."

Book 12 begins with five new lines followed by line 897, as follows:

"As one who in his journey bates at Noone,
Though bent on fpeed, fo heer the Archangel pauf'd
Betwixt the world deftroy'd and world reftor'd,
If *Adam* aught perhaps might interpofe;
Then with tranfition fweet new Speech refumes.
Thus thou haft feen one World begin and end;".

A few additions were also made to the poem. Lines 636–638 of Book 5,

"They eat, they drink, and with refection fweet
Are fill'd, before th' all bounteous King, who
With copious hand, rejoycing in thir joy."

Paradise lost.

A POEM IN TEN BOOKS.

The Author
JOHN MILTON.

LONDON,
Printed by *S. Simmons*, and are to be sold by
T. Helder at the Angel in *Little Brittain.*
1669.

No. 496. Title-page of Milton's Paradise Lost; 1st Edition, 5th Title-page; 1669.

are amplified (p. 135) to read:

> "They eate, they drink, and in communion fweet
> Quaff immortalitie and joy, fecure
> Of furfet where full meafure onely bounds
> Excefs, before th' all bounteous King, who fhowr'd
> With copious hand, rejoycing in thir joy."

Between lines 484 and 485 of Book 10,

> "Inteftin Stone and Ulcer, Colic pangs,
> Dropfies, and Afthma's, and Joint-racking Rheums."

were added three lines (p. 300), enumerating other ills:

> "Dæmoniac Phrenzie, moaping Melancholie
> And Moon-ftruck madnefs, pining Atrophie,
> Marafmus and wide-wafting Peftilence,"

Lines 547 and 548 of Book 10,

> "Which I muft keep till my appointed day
> Of rendring up. *Michael* to him repli'd."

were changed to read:

> "Which I muft keep till my appointed day
> Of rendring up, and patiently attend
> My diffolution. *Michael* repli'd,"

MILTON, JOHN.

ACCEDENCE COMMENC'T GRAMMAR. London, *for* S. S., 1669.

[497]

Small duodecimo. First Edition.

COLLATION BY SIGNATURES: A, B, C, each 12 leaves (the last blank and lacking); total 36 leaves.

COLLATION BY PAGINATION: [title, as reproduced; *See* No. 497], recto of [A]; —[blank], verso of [A]; —| TO THE | READER. | [signed] | J. M. |, recto and verso of A 2; —[text, with heading] | [2 type-ornament rules] | ACCEDENCE | Commenc't | GRAMMAR. |, pp. 1–65; —| FINIS. | ERRATA. | [6 lines] |, p. 65; —[blank], p. [66]; —[1 blank leaf], [C 12].

CONDITION: Size of leaf, 5⅝ x 3¼ inches. Bound in olive green crushed levant morocco, gilt edges; by Rivière.

OTHER COPIES.

Trinity College, Cambridge; Lenox; and White Libraries.

REFERENCES.

Grolier Club, *Wither to Prior*, 2 (1905): 195, No. 608; Hazlitt, *Collections and Notes* (1887), p. 161; Lenox Library, *Works of Milton* (1881), p. 20, No. 130; Lowndes, 3 (1869): 1566.

> **ACCEDENCE**
> **Commenc't**
> **GRAMMAR,**
> Supply'd with sufficient
> **RULES,**
> For the use of such (Younger
> or Elder) as are desirous, with-
> out more trouble than
> needs to attain the
> *LATIN TONGUE;*
> The Elder sort especially, with
> little Teaching, and their
> own Industry.
>
> *By* JOHN MILTON.
>
> *LONDON*, Printed for *S. S.* and are
> to be sold by *John Starkey* at the Miter in *Fleet-
> street*, near *Temple-bar.* 1 6 6 9.

No. 497. Title-page of Milton's Accedence Commenc't Grammar; 1st Edition; 1669.

Some copies of this work have the initials "J. M." instead of the full name of the author on the title-page, which is printed from a different setting of the type.

It was a favorite idea of Milton's that the Latin tongue could be far more quickly learned than by the ordinary school methods. This little Latin grammar was probably worked up from the manuscripts which had been lying by him since his pedagogical days. Dr. Johnson could find nothing remarkable in the book except that it afforded proof that Milton could descend to drudgery.

Mʳ John Miltons
CHARACTER
OF THE
𝕷ong 𝔓arliament
AND
Assembly of DIVINES.
In MDCXLI.

Omitted in his other Works, and never before Printed,
And very seasonable for these times.

LONDON:
Printed for *Henry Brome*, at the *Gun* at the West-
end of St. *Pauls*. 1 6 8 1.

MILTON, JOHN.

CHARACTER OF THE LONG PARLIAMENT. LONDON, *for Henry Brome*, 1681. [498]

Small quarto.

COLLATION BY SIGNATURES: A, B, each 4 leaves; total 8 leaves.

COLLATION BY PAGINATION: [title, as reproduced; *See* No. 498], recto of [A]; —[blank], verso of [A]; — | TO THE | READER. |, recto and verso of A 2; — [text, with heading] | Mr. *JOHN MILTONS* Character | OF THE | Long Parliament | In 1641. |, pp. 1-11; — | *FINIS.* |, p. 11; —[blank], p. [·12].

CONDITION: Size of leaf, 6^{15}/$_{16}$ × 5^{7}/$_{16}$ inches. Bound in green crushed levant morocco, gilt edges; by the Club Bindery, 1899.

OTHER COPIES.

There is also a copy in the Earl of Ellesmere's Library.

REFERENCES.

Grolier Club, *Wither to Prior*, 2 (1905): 198, No. 612; Hazlitt, *Collections and Notes* (1882), p. 397; Masson, *Life of Milton*, 6 (1880): 808-809; Lowndes, 3 (1869): 1566.

This pamphlet, which did not appear until seven years after Milton's death, seems, from the address "To the Reader," to have been a portion of his *History of Britain*, omitted from that work, perhaps having been struck out by the licenser. It is now always inserted immediately after the first paragraph of the third book, and forms eleven paragraphs of the text from that point onward. These paragraphs in modern editions are usually found within brackets, to indicate that they did not appear in the original edition as published in 1670.

"It may be a question, however," says Masson; "whether they ought to have been adopted into the *History* at all and ought not now to be turned out. They are an attack upon the memory of the Long Parliament and the Westminster Assembly; and, though the part of the attack that concerns the Westminster Assembly corresponds closely enough, in parts of the wording, with what Milton had written in his wrath, more than once, against the Presbyterian Divines, or indeed against Divines generally, the part about the Long Parliament seems positively renegade from his previous testimonies of reverence for the persons and acts of that body, and from all that we now remember as historically Miltonic. . . .

"It is not the mere irrelevancy of the diatribe to the context in which it is imbedded that ought to make us sceptical. . . . The doctrine that pervades the whole diatribe, for example, the very 'point' that starts Milton on his supposed 'digression,' is the natural unfitness of the British genius and temper, as proved in all ages, for real liberty or any high political undertaking; and no one can read the sarcastic language in which this doctrine is asserted without remembering on the instant that extraordinary passage in the *Areopagitica* of 1644 in which Milton had asserted the dead opposite, declaring it, on the evidence of all British history, to be God's established manner, when He had any great new design in hand for the whole world, invariably to move it first among His own Englishmen."

A MYRROVR FOR MAGISTRATES. LONDON, *Thomas Marſhe*, 1563.

[499]

Small quarto. Second Edition. Printed in black-letter.

COLLATION BY SIGNATURES: ¶, A, each 4 leaves; B to N, each 8 leaves; O to U, each 4 leaves; X, Y, Z, Aa, Bb, each 8 leaves; Cc, 4 leaves; total 176 leaves. Leaf H vii. is wrongly marked H ii.; L i. is K i.; and N i. is B i. Some of the signature-marks are lacking in nearly every sheet.

COLLATION BY PAGINATION: [title, as reproduced; *See* No. 499], recto of [¶ i.]; — [blank], verso of [¶ i.]; — | Love and live. | ¶ *TO THE NOBILITIE AND* | *all other in office, God graunt wiſedome* | *and all thinges nedefull for the* | *preſeruacion of theyr* | *Eſtates. Amen.* | [signed] | *Yours moſt humble* | *VVilliam Baldwin.* |, recto of ¶ ii. to recto of [¶ iiii.]; — [blank], verso of [¶ iiii.]; — [preface, with heading] | ¶ *A Briefe memoriall* | *OF SVNDRYE VN-FORTV-* | *nate Engliſhmen.* | ¶ *VVillyam Baldwin to* | *the Reader.* |, recto of A i. to recto of A ii.; — [blank], verso of A ii.; — [text of Part 1, in numerous unnumbered chapters, the first with heading] | ¶ *The fall of Robert Treſilian chiefe Iuſtice of* | *England, and other his felowes, for miſ-* | *conſtruing the lawes, and expoun-* | *ding them to ſerue the Prin-* | *ces affections.* |, recto of folio i. to recto of folio lxxv. [wrongly numbered xxxv.]; — [blank], verso of folio lxxv.; — [introduction to the second part, with heading] | ¶ *The* ſeconde | *PARTE OF THE* | *Mirrour for* Ma- | *giſtrates.* | *Wylliam Baldwyn* | *to the Reader.* |, recto of folio [lxxvi.] to verso of folio lxxvii. [wrongly numbered lxxxxvi.]; — [text in verse, in numerous unnumbered chapters, the first with heading] | *How Sir Anthony VVudvile Lorde Ri-* | *vers and Skales, Gouernour of prince* | *Edward, was with his Neuew Lord* | *Richard Gray and other cauſeles* | *impriſoned, and cruelly* | *murdered.* |, recto of folio lxxviii. [wrongly numbered lxxxviii.] to verso of folio clxviii. [wrongly numbered clx.]; — | ¶ *The contes and Table of the firſt* | *parte of this Booke.* |, recto of folio [clxix.]; — | ¶ *The contentes of the* | *ſecond parte.* |, verso of folio [clxix.]; — | *Faultes eſcaped in the Print-* ing. |, recto and verso of folio [clxx.]. The numbering of the folios is extremely irregular, an erroneous number being the rule rather than the exception.

CONDITION: Size of leaf, $7\frac{1}{16} \times 5\frac{5}{16}$ inches. Bound in green straight-grained morocco, gilt edges; by Rivière; in green morocco slip case.

OTHER COPIES.

Capell Collection; and Huth Library.

REFERENCES.

Nicoll and Seccombe, 1 (1907): 97; Grolier Club, *Langland to Wither* (1893), pp. 150–156, Nos. 174–179; Huth, *Catalogue*, 3 (1880): 975; Corser, *Collectanea Anglo-Poetica*, Part 8 (Chetham Society, Vol. CII.; 1878), p. 421; Lowndes, 3 (1869): 1571; Hazlitt, *Hand-Book* (1867), p. 396; *Bibliotheca Grenvilliana*, 2 (1842): 466; *Bibliotheca Anglo-Poetica* (1815), p. 202, No. 438.

The George Steevens copy, with his autograph on the back of the title-page. In this copy the last line of the first stanza of Sackville's "Induction" reads:

"The tapets torne, and euery tree downe blowen."

In some copies this line reads:

"The tapets torne, and euery blome downe blowen."

This is the Second Edition of the first published portion of one of the most brilliant works of English poetry produced in the interval between Surrey and Spenser. It is

No. 499   *A Myrrour for Magistrates*   1563

divided into two parts, the first of which contains the nineteen legends or tragedies of the First Edition; in the second part are eight new ones, the one by Sackville being preceded by his celebrated "Induction." His contributions far surpass in excellence those of the other writers.

The First Edition, published in 1559, was a bookseller's plan for a poetical sequel to Lydgate's popular *Fall of Prynces*. "Its main purpose was didactic; moralising such incidents of English history as illustrate the fall from high estate, the humiliation of the strong, and the fickleness of Fortune." Sackville, the originator of the plan, became so immersed in public affairs that he was unable to complete the work, and it was turned over to William Baldwin. Jasper Heywood in the preface to his *Second Tragedie of Seneca* mentions Baldwin and his work, which had then recently appeared, as follows:

> "There heare thou ſhalt a great reporte
> of Baldwyn's worthie name,
> Whoſe Myrrour doth of Magiſtrates
> proclayme eternall fame."

The First Edition contained nineteen historical tragedies narrated by six poets — Sackville, Baldwin, Ferrers, Churchyard, Phaer, and Skelton. Of these Haslewood, in his edition of 1815, attributes twelve to the pen of Baldwin. The Second Edition, published in 1563, is that here described. The Third Edition appeared in 1571. Though this was the first portion of the work to be published, it was afterward known in the collected edition, for reasons which will presently be given, as the *Third* or *Last Part*.

The Fourth Edition of the book here described was published in 1574, under the title *The Laſt parte of the Mirour for Magiſtrates*, because in this year Higgins issued the first edition of his portion, which chronologically took precedence of Baldwin's earlier book. Under this latter title it was reprinted in 1575 and 1578.

"It was intended," says Hazlitt, "that this book should have been published four years before in folio, and a portion of it was actually set up in type, when the authorities suppressed it. The title page, however, has come down to us by some accident, bound up at the end of a few copies of Lydgate's *Falls of Princes*, and runs as follows: — A Memorial of suche Princes, as since the tyme of King Richard the seconde, haue been vnfortunate in the Realme of England. Londini In aedibus Iohannis waylandi, cum priuilegio per septennium. At the back of this is printed 'The copy of the quenes Maiesties letters Patentes [1558.].'"

This work covers the same ground as several of Shakespeare's historical tragedies, and perhaps exercised more influence on English poetry, and contributed more to the advancement of English metrical literature, than any other work of its day. It familiarized the people of England with its history, as recorded by her ancient chroniclers, and is written in verse which called forth the admiration of Sir Philip Sidney.

In 1574 appeared a new series consisting of sixteen legends composed by John Higgins, which, because the subjects related to an earlier period than those in Baldwin's work, he called *The Firſt parte of The Mirour for Magiſtrates*; and it was

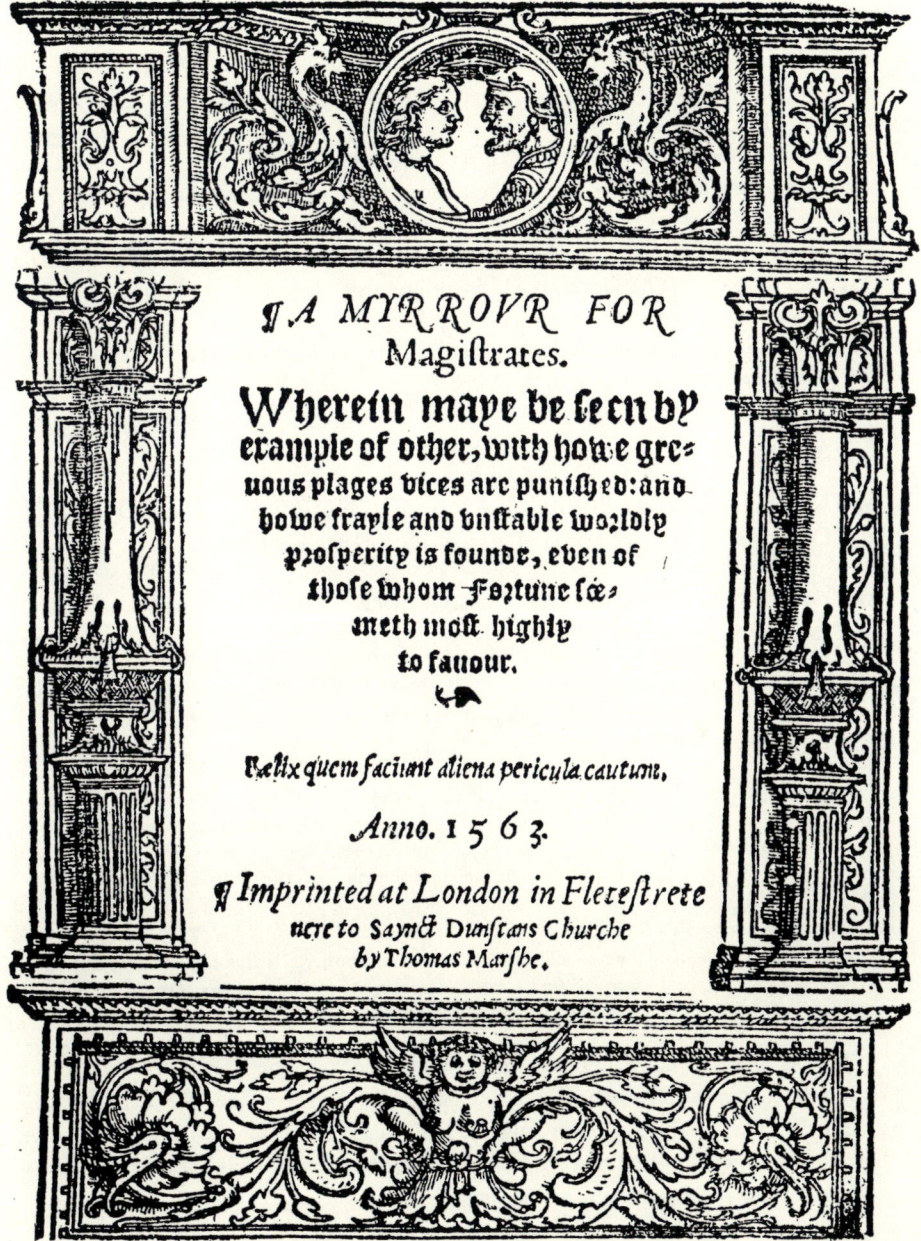

No. 499. Title-page of A Myrrovr for Magistrates; 2d Edition; 1563.

thus that Baldwin's publication came to be called *The Laſte Parte*. Higgins' part was reprinted in 1575 and again in 1578.

In 1578 Thomas Blener Hasset, or Blenerhasset, published a volume containing twelve legends, all written by himself, entitled *The Seconde part of the Mirrour for Magiſtrates*. This covered chronologically the interval between Higgins' *Firſt Parte* and Baldwin's *Laſte Parte*.

In 1587 the three parts were first published together, the whole containing seventy-four legends, twenty-four of the twenty-seven new legends having been written by Higgins. This was followed in 1610 by an edition by Richard Niccols. In this edition the preliminary matter and prose inductions were omitted, the volume containing, according to "The Contents," ninety-one legends, and in addition "A Winter Night's Vision," and an original poem, "England's Eliza," written by the editor. The edition of 1619 is identical with that of 1610, but with a new title, *The Falles of Vnfortunate Princes*.

MÜNCHHAUSEN, *Baron* KARL FRIEDRICH HIERONYMUS VON. (*b.* 1720, *d.* 1797.) Raspe, Rudolph Erich. (*b.* 1737, *d.* 1794.)

BARON MUNCHAUSEN'S NARRATIVE OF HIS MARVELLOUS TRAVELS. OXFORD, *for the Editor,* 1786. [500]

Duodecimo. Second Edition.

COLLATION BY SIGNATURES: [A], 4 leaves; B to E, each 6 leaves (the last blank and genuine); total 28 leaves.

COLLATION BY PAGINATION: [half-title], recto of [A]; — [blank], verso of [A]; — [title, as reproduced; *See* No. 500], recto of [A 2]; — | ††† *The Baron is ſuppoſed to relate theſe | extraordinary Adventures over his Bottle, | when ſurrounded by his Friends.* |, verso of [A 2]; — [preface], pp. [i.]–iv.; — [text, with heading] | BARON MUNCHAUSEN's |

NARRATIVE, &c. |, pp. [5]–49; — [blank], p. [50]; — [1 blank leaf], [E 6].

CONDITION: Size of leaf, 7¼ × 4 5/16 inches. In the original plain blue paper wrappers (the front wrapper missing). With the autograph of | George Birch | on the recto and verso of the half-title.

REFERENCES.

Allibone, *Dictionary of English Literature*, 2 (1881): 1741–1743; Lowndes, 3 (1869): 1629.

This is the Second Edition in English of a book famous for its strict adherence to veracity! and is said to have been intended as a satire on the Memoirs of Baron de Tott. It was published anonymously, and has been attributed to several writers; but is now generally admitted to have been written by Rudolph Erich Raspe, the author of several other works in English.

Allibone, who gives a very full account (2: 1743) of Raspe, fixes the date of the First Edition as 1785. He says that a new edition, probably the one here described, was called for the next year, and was followed in less than a month by a Third, with important additions and engravings, to make it more attractive. The

1786 *Karl Friedrich Hieronymus von Münchhausen* No. 500

BARON MUNCHAUSEN's
NARRATIVE
OF HIS
MARVELLOUS TRAVELS
AND
CAMPAIGNS
IN
RUSSIA.

HUMBLY DEDICATED AND RECOMMENDED

TO

COUNTRY GENTLEMEN;

AND, IF THEY PLEASE,

TO BE REPEATED AS THEIR OWN, AFTER A HUNT AT HORSE RACES, IN WATERING-PLACES, AND OTHER SUCH POLITE ASSEMBLIES; ROUND THE BOTTLE AND FIRE-SIDE.

OXFORD:

Printed for the EDITOR, and fold by the Bookfellers there and at Cambridge, alfo in London by the Bookfellers of Piccadilly, the Royal Exchange, and M. SMITH, at No. 46, in Fleet-ftreet.—And in Dublin by P. BYRNE, No. 108, Grafton-ftreet.

MDCCLXXXVI.

No. 500. TITLE-PAGE OF BARON MÜNCHHAUSEN'S NARRATIVE OF HIS MARVELLOUS TRAVELS; 2D EDITION; 1786.

imprint of this edition, as given by Allibone, differs from the one here described. The First Edition seems to have disappeared, no copy of it being known.

"The second advertisement, dated 'London, April 20, 1786,' and speaking of the first as 'a little pamphlet,' holds the same tone about the Baron, declaring him to be 'a man of great honour;' and the third, which followed in less than a month, under date of 'May 18, 1786,' speaks of the additions to the volume as so important that 'it may fairly be considered a new work.' After all, however, in this form it is a very small book; but it has proved large enough to make its way to immortality."

No. 500   *Karl Friedrich Hieronymus von Münchhausen*   1786

"There lived, in the latter half of the eighteenth century, at Bodenweder, in the Electorate of Hanover, a certain Baron Friederich von Munchausen, who had been in the Russian service against the Turks, but who was then established on his own estates near the Weser, and much addicted to the chase, to good cheer, and to story-telling of the most extravagant sort. He was connected with the old family of which Baron Munchausen — who was minister to George II. for Hanover and induced that monarch to found the University of Göttingen — was the most eminent member, so that, from his respectable connexions, social qualities, and free hospitality, the Baron of Bodenweder was tolerated, if not respected, by the nobility and gentry of his neighborhood. He died in 1797. Among the persons who often visited him was Rudolph Erich Raspe, a man of learning, who was for some time connected with the library at Göttingen, and afterwards, in 1767, became a Professor in Cassel, and Keeper of a curious collection of antique gems and medals belonging to the Elector of Hesse." Having stolen and sold some gems, Raspe fled to England, where he looked to authorship for support. Falling into extreme poverty he became an employee in a German coffee-house. Here, remembering the stories he had heard at Baron Munchausen's hospitable table, he wrote the work here described.

"Soon after the appearance of Munchausen's Travels in England, the little book was naturally carried to Germany and became known in the kingdom of Hanover. Gottfried August Bürger, author of the famous ballad of 'Lenore,' was then living at Göttingen, almost as poor as Raspe, and quite as unprincipled. He, too, was a personal acquaintance of Munchausen's, — had enjoyed his riotous hospitality and had heard his wild stories. As a promising literary adventure, he translated the little book of Raspe, and made additions to it from the stores of his own memory, so that it was published in 1787 and 1788 in two editions, or perhaps only with a changed title-page, at Göttingen, not very far from where Munchausen lived, and where his habits and stories were perfectly well known. But this was more than the fox-hunting baron could submit to. He therefore took legal proceedings against Bürger and against the bookselling house who were his publishers, and so thoroughly alarmed them that the imprint of 'London' instead of 'Göttingen' was put on the copies that had not been sold, and subsequently, as the matter was still further pressed, the remainder of the edition was destroyed, and the suit stopped by the full submission of the offending parties. . . .

"The 'miserable book,' however, has since gone its way over the world triumphantly, little regarding law or truth. It has been translated into many languages; printed and reprinted in all forms; altered and enlarged; and, although generally injured by the changes it has undergone, it has never been absolutely spoiled by any of them. It would be difficult to find a dozen books of amusement in modern times, that have been so attractive to all classes of society in all civilized countries; the peculiar delight of children, and yet not neglected by the mature and the cultivated; affording materials for the gayest frolics in the arts, and happy illustrations for the wit of orators, poets, and statesmen."

1811 *Karl Friedrich Hieronymus von Münchhausen* No. 501

MÜNCHHAUSEN, Baron KARL FRIEDRICH HIERONYMUS VON. Raspe, Rudolph Erich.

SURPRISING ADVENTURES OF THE RENOWNED BARON MUNCHAUSEN. London, *for Thomas Tegg*, 1811. [501]

Duodecimo.

COLLATION BY SIGNATURES: [A], 6 leaves; B to G, each 12 leaves; total 78 leaves. Leaf C 6 has no signature-mark; and G 4 is wrongly marked G 5.

COLLATION BY PAGINATION: [half-title], recto of [A]; —[blank], verso of [A]; —[title] | SURPRISING | ADVENTURES | OF THE RENOWNED | BARON MUNCHAUSEN, | CONTAINING | Singular Travels, | CAMPAIGNS, VOYAGES, AND ADVENTURES. | ALSO, AN ACCOUNT OF | *A VOYAGE TO THE MOON AND DOG STAR.* | EMBELLISHED WITH NUMEROUS ENGRAVINGS. | London: | PRINTED FOR THOMAS TEGG, | No. 111, | OPPOSITE BOW CHURCH, CHEAPSIDE. | 1811. |, recto of [A 2]; —[imprint], verso of [A 2]; —[contents], pp. [i.]–viii.; —[text], pp. [1]–144. Page iv. is wrongly numbered vi.; and p. 62 has no page-number.

PLATES: Folding frontispiece and 8 plates, by Rowlandson, as follows:

Frontispiece, representing the Baron's extraordinary flight on the back of an eagle, with inscription: | *Rowlandson. Del. Frontispiece* |.

[1] | *The Baron arrives at Ceylon, combats and conquers two extraordinary opponents*. Chap. 1 |; facing p. [1].

[2] | *The Baron proves himself a good shot*. Chapt. 2 |; facing p. 7.

[3] | *Presented with a famous horse by Count Przzobosky, with which he performs many extraordinary feats*. Chap. 5 |; facing p. 15.

[4] | *Bathes in the Mediterranean is swallowed by a Fish from which he is extricated by dancing a hornpipe*. Chapt. 7 |; facing p. 25.

[5] | *The Baron Jumps into the Sea with a Turkish piece of Ordnance*. Chapter 9 |; facing p. 34.

[6] | *The Ship driven by a Whirlwind a thousand leagues above the surface of the water*. Chapt 11 |; facing p. 42.

[7] | *Lose their Compaſs, their ship slips between the teeth of a fish unknown in this part of the world*. Cha. 12 |; facing p. 49.

[8] | *The Baron croſses the Thames, without the aſsistance of a bridge ship boat or balloon, or even his own will*. Chap 25 |; facing p. 142.

CONDITION: Size of leaf, 6⅝ × 4 1/16 inches. Bound in half tan colored morocco, gilt top.

REFERENCE.

Grego, *Rowlandson, The Caricaturist*, 2 (1880): 175.

MUSSET, PAUL EDME DE. (*b.* 1804, *d.* 1880.)

LE DERNIER ABBÉ. Paris, *A. Ferroud*, 1891. [502]

Octavo. One of 210 copies printed on vellum paper.

COLLATION BY SIGNATURES: [*a*], *b*, 1 to 8, each 4 leaves; 2 leaves, without signature-marks (the last blank and genuine); total 42 leaves.

COLLATION BY PAGINATION: [half-title], p. [i.]; —[edition notice], p. [ii.]; —[rubricated title] | PAUL DE MUSSET | LE | DERNIER ABBÉ | ILLUSTRÉ DE DIX-NEUF COMPOSITIONS | PAR | AD. LALAUZE | PRÉFACE PAR ANATOLE FRANCE

No. 502 — Paul Edme de Musset — 1891

| [vignette] | PARIS | LIBRAIRIE DES AMATEURS | A. FERROUD, LIBRAIRE-ÉDITEUR | 192, BOULEVARD SAINT-GERMAIN, 192 | 1891 |, p. [iii.]; — [blank], p. [iv.]; — | PRÉFACE | [signed] | ANATOLE FRANCE. |, pp. [v.]–XVI.; — [text, without heading], pp. 1–64; — [colophon] | IMPRIMÉ | PAR | GEORGES CHAMEROT | 19, rue des Saints-Pères, 19 | PARIS |, p. [65]; — [blank], p. [66]; — [1 blank leaf].

ILLUSTRATIONS: 19 etchings, as follows: title-page vignette, 7 head-pieces, 4 illustrations in the text, and 7 tail-pieces; each one is also separately printed "avec des remarques qui sont elles-mêmes de véritables compositions représentant des scènes du livre."

CONDITION: Size of leaf, 9⁹⁄₁₀ × 6¼ inches. Bound in blue crushed levant morocco, with elaborately tooled and inlaid panels, red crushed levant morocco doublure with richly tooled gilt border, marbled end papers with outer light blue brocade linings, gilt on rough edges; by Raparlier; in slip case. With the original wrappers and prospectus (4 pp.) bound in.

NASH or NASHE, THOMAS. (b. 1567, d. 1601.)

NASHES LENTEN STUFFE. LONDON, for N. L. and C. B., 1599. [503]

Small quarto. Printed with side-notes.

COLLATION BY SIGNATURES: A to K, each 4 leaves; L, 2 leaves; total 42 leaves.

COLLATION BY PAGINATION: [title, as reproduced; See No. 503], recto of [A]; — [blank], verso of [A]; — | [conventional head-piece] | To his worthie good patron, Lu- | ſtie Humfrey, . . . | [8 lines] | [signed] | Th. Naſhe. |, recto of A 2 to verso of A 3; — | To his Readers, hee cares not | what they be. |, recto and verso of [A 4]; — [text, with heading] | [conventional head-piece] | THE PRAISE OF | the red herring. |, pp. 1–75; — | FINIS. |, p. 75; — [blank], p. 76.

CONDITION: Size of leaf, 6⅝ × 5⅛ inches. Bound in red morocco, gilt edges.

OTHER COPIES.

Trinity College, Cambridge; Ellesmere; Huth; and White Libraries.

REFERENCES.

Nicoll and Seccombe, 1 (1907): 302; Grolier Club, *Langland to Wither* (1903), p. 166, No. 190; Locker-Lampson, *Catalogue* (1886), p. 85; Huth, *Catalogue*, 3 (1880): 1019; Lowndes, 3 (1869): 1652; Hazlitt, *Hand-Book* (1867), p. 414; Collier, *Rarest Books*, 3 (1866): 15.

The Locker-Lampson copy, with ex-libris.

"Nash being a native of Lowestoft, on one occasion paid a visit to Yarmouth, and having obtained a loan of money there, he endeavored, as he admits in this tract, to make a due return by praising the herring, the great source of that town's prosperity."

"Greene, Dekker, and Nash were three curious types who anticipated Murger's *Vie de Bohème* in a metropolis hardly sufficiently developed to welcome such precocious children. Their lot collectively was dramatic job-work, pamphlets, poems, novels, the bottle, loose women, Henslowe (the well-known impresario who commissioned plays from the jobbers), the Clink, literary squabbles, and premature decline and death. Nash was perhaps the gayest and most good-humoured; Greene the most fluent and the biggest liar; Dekker the most perceptive and the most poetic — he rivalled Breton in the delicacy with which he could tune a stave or vamp a

1599   *Thomas Nash*   No. 503

NASHES
Lenten Stuffe,

Containing,

The Description and firſt Procreation and Increaſe of the towne of Great Yarmouth in Norffolke:

With a new Play neuer played before, of the praiſe of the RED HERRING.

Fitte of all Clearkes of Noblemens Kitchins to be read: and not vnneceſſary by all Seruing men that haue ſhort boord-wages, to be remembred.

Famam peto per vndas.

LONDON
Printed for N. L. and C. B. and are to be ſold at the weſt end of Paules.
1599.

No. 503.   Title-page of Nash's Lenten Stuffe; 1599.

lament in a minor key. But Nash also could lilt a pretty song, and, gross borrower from Latin, French, and Italian though he seems, he was the most original prose writer of his age, full of artistic theories as to the use of adjectives and the divinity of Aretino, Rabelais, Sidney, Marlowe, and 'heavenly' Spenser, a connoisseur of metaphors and expletives and a bigoted devotee of the *mot propre*.

"The work of Nash, with its numerous eccentricities of style, subject, and point of view, serves as a convenient link between the novelists and the satirical essayists, who literally swarmed in London during the late and post-Elizabethan periods."

NEWTON, THOMAS, *translator.* (*b.* c. 1542, *d.* 1607.) **Seneca, Lucius Annæus.** (*b.* 4 B.C., *d.* 65 A.D.)

SENECA HIS TENNE TRAGEDIES, TRANSLATED INTO ENGLYSH. LONDON, *Thomas Marſh*, 1581. [504]

Small quarto.

COLLATION BY SIGNATURES: [A], 4 leaves (the first blank and lacking); B to Z, Aa to Ee, each 8 leaves; Ff, 4 leaves (the last blank and lacking); total 224 leaves. Roman numerals and Arabic figures are used indiscriminately in the signature-marks.

COLLATION BY PAGINATION: [1 blank leaf], [A]; —[title, as reproduced; *See* No. 504], recto of [A 2]; —[blank], verso of [A 2]; —| TO THE RIGHT VVOR-|SHIPFVL, SIR THOMAS HEN-|NEAGE KNIGHT, TREASVRER OF | *HER MAIESTIES CHAMBER :*| *Thomas Newton wisheth all abundaunce*| of Felicitie, and Spirituall bene-|dictions in Chriſte. | [signed]| Your Wor-ſhippes moſt humble, | *Thomas Newton.* | [dated]| From Butley in Cheſſhyre the *24. of Aprill.* | *1581.* |, recto of A 3 to recto of [A 4]; —| THE NAMES OF | *THE TRAGEDIES OF* | *SENECA,* AND | *by whom each of* | them was tran-| ſlated. |, verso of [A 4]; —| The Argument | of this Tragedy. |, recto of folio 1;—[text in 5 acts, the first with heading]| THE FIRST | ACTE. |, recto of folio 1 to verso of folio 20; —| HERE ENDETH THE FIRST| Tragedye of *Seneca,* called *Her-*| *cules furens, tranſ-*|*lated into En-*| gliſhe by Iaſper Heywood ſtu-|dente in Oxenforde. |, verso of folio 20.

|THE SECOND| TRAGEDIE OF SENECA ENTITV-| tuled Thyeſtes, faythfully Engliſhed | by Iaſper Heywood Felow | of Alſolne Colledge in | Oxenfoꝛde. |, recto of folio 21; —| *The Argument of this Tragedie.* |, recto of folio 21;—[text, with heading] | THIESTES OF SENECA | THE FIRST ACTE. |, verso of folio 21 to verso of folio 39; —| FINIS. | [conventional tail-piece] |, verso of folio 39.

| THE THYRD TRA-|GEDY OF L. ANNAEVS | *Seneca:* entituled *Thebais*, tranſ-| lated out of Latin into En-| gliſhe, by | *Thomas Newton.* | *1581.* |, recto of folio 40; —| *The Argument.* |, recto and verso of folio 40; —[text in 4 acts, the first with heading] | THE FIRTE | ACTE. |, recto of folio 41 to verso of folio 54; —| FINIS. |, verso of folio 54.

| THE FOVRTH, AND MOST | *RVTH-FVL TRAGEDY OF L. AN-*| *NAEVS SENECA, EN-*| tituled HIPPOLYTVS, tran-| ſlated into Engliſhe, by | *Ihon Studley.* |, recto of folio 55; —| *The Argument.* |, recto and verso of folio 55; —[text in 5 acts, the first with heading] | THE FIRSTE | ACTE. |, recto of folio 56 to recto of folio 75; —| FINIS. |, recto of folio 75.

| OEDIPVS. | THE FIFTH TRAGEDY | OF SENECA, ENGLISHED | The yeare of our Lord | M. D. LX. | BY | ALEXANDER NEVYLE. |, verso of folio 75; —| [type-ornament rule] | TO THE RIGHT HONORA-| BLE, MAISTER

1581 **Thomas Newton, translator** **No. 504**

DOCTOR | WOTTON : ONE OF THE | *Queenes Maiesties priuy Coun-* | sayle : Alexander Neuyle wish- | eth Helth, vvith encrease of | Honor. | [signed] | *All your Honours to commaund.* | *Alexander Neuile.* | , verso of folio 75 to verso of folio 76 ; — | [type-ornament rule] | 🙛 THE PREFACE TO | the Reader. | [signed] | A. Neuile. | , verso of folio 76 to verso of folio 77 ; — | [type-ornament rule] | The Speakers names. | , recto of folio 78 ; — [text in 5 acts, the first with heading] | THE FIRST | ACTE. | , recto of folio 78 to verso of folio 94 ; — | FINIS. | , verso of folio 94.

| *THE SIXTE* | TRAGEDIE OF THE MOST GRAVE | & prudẽt Author LVCIVS ANNÆVS SENECA, | entituled *TROAS*, vvith diuers and | sundrye Additions to the same, | by IASPER HEY- | VVOOD. | , recto of folio 95 ; — | *To the Reader.* | , recto of folio 95 to recto of folio 96 ; — | The Argument. | , verso of folio 96 to verso of folio 97 ; — | [type-ornament rule] | The Speakers names. | , recto of folio 98 ; — [text in 5 acts, the first with heading] | THE FIRST | ACTE. | , recto of folio 98 to verso of folio 118 ; — | FINIS. | , verso of folio 118.

| *THE* | *SEVENTH TRAGEDYE OF* | L. ANNAEVS SENECA, | Entituled MEDEA : Translated | out of Latin into Englishe, by | IOHN STVDLEY. | , recto of folio 119 ; — | *The Argument.* | *To the Tragedy, by the* | Translator. | , recto of folio 119 ; — | [type-ornament rule] | The Speakers names. | , verso of folio 119 ; — [text in 5 acts, the first with heading] | THE FIRST | ACTE. | , verso of folio 119 to verso of folio 139 ; — | FINIS. | , verso of folio 139.

| *THE* | *EYGHTH TRAGEDYE OF* | L. ANNAEVS SENECA, | Entituled AGAMEMNON : Transla- | ted out of Latin into Englishe, | by | IOHN STVDLEY. | , recto of folio 140 ; — | *The Argument.* | , recto and verso of folio 140 ; — | [conventional ornament] | [type-ornament rule] | The Speakers names. | , verso of folio 140 ; — [text in 5 acts, the first with heading] | THE FIRST | ACTE. | , recto of folio 141 to verso of folio 160 ; — | FINIS. | , verso of folio 160.

| THE NINTHE | Tragedy of Lucius Annæus Seneca, called Octauia. | Translated out of Latine in- | to Englishe by | T. N. | , recto of folio 161 ; — | The Argument. | , recto of folio 161 ; — [text in 4 acts, the first with heading] | THE FIRST | SCENE. | The Speakers names. | , verso of folio 161 to verso of folio 186 ; — | FINIS. | , verso of folio 186.

| *THE* | *TENTH TRAGEDY OF* | L. ANNAE. SENECA, En- | tituled HERCVLES OETÆVS : | Translated out of Latin into | Englishe by I. S. | , recto of folio 187 ; — | *The Argument.* | , recto and verso of folio 187 ; — | FINIS. | , verso of folio 187 ; — | [type-ornament rule] | The Speakers names. | , recto of folio 188 ; — [text in 5 acts, the first with heading] | [type-ornament rule] | THE FIRST | ACTE. | , recto of folio 188 to verso of folio 217 ; — | FINIS. | [Latin quotation, 2 lines] | [colophon] | IMPRINTED | *AT LONDON IN FLETSTREATE* | *Neare vnto Sainct Dunstons church* | by Thomas Marshe. | 1581. | , verso of folio 217 ; — [1 blank leaf], [Ff 4]. The numbers 64 and 65 are repeated in numbering the folios ; 85 is wrongly numbered 81 ; and 123 is 124. Several of the folio-numbers are followed by periods, i.e. " 67." etc.

CONDITION : Size of leaf, 7 7/16 × 5 5/16 inches. Bound in red crushed levant morocco, gilt edges ; by Bedford.

OTHER COPIES.

Devonshire ; Huth ; Boston Public ; Morgan ; and White Libraries.

REFERENCES.

Greg, *List of English Plays* (Bibliographical Society ; 1900), p. 92 ; Grolier Club, *Langland to Wither* (1893), p. 168, No. 191 ; Corser, *Collectanea Anglo-Poetica*, Part 10 (Chetham Society, Vol. CVIII. ; 1880), p. 231 ; Huth, *Catalogue*, 4 (1880) : 1326 ; Lowndes, 4 (1869) : 2241 ; Hazlitt, *Hand-Book* (1867), p. 543, No. 10 ; Dibdin, *Typographical Antiquities*, 4 (1819) : 529 ; *Bibliotheca Anglo-Poetica* (1815), p. 315, No. 662.

No. 504. Title-page of Newton's Seneca His Tenne Tragedies, Translated into Englysh; 1581.

1581   *Thomas Newton, translator*   No. 504

Nine of the ten tragedies here given had previously appeared in separate editions. Copies of seven of these are in the British Museum. They were here collected into one volume by Thomas Newton, the translator of one of them, *The Thebais*, and were published under his editorship.

Jasper Heywood the younger, son of John Heywood, the author of *The Spider and the Flie* (our No. 393), was the translator of three, viz.: *Troas* (London, "by Richard Tottyll," 1559, and "by Thomas Powell, for George Bucke," c. 1560), *Hercules Furens* (London, "by Henrye Sutton," 1561), and *Thyestes* (London, "Thomas Berthelettes," 1560). Alexander Neville translated *Œdipus* (London, "Thomas Colwell," 1563). John Studley translated *Hippolytus* (no separate edition known), *Medea* (London, "Thomas Colwell," 1566), *Agamemnon* (London, "Thomas Colwell," 1666), and *Hercules Oetæus* (no separate edition known). Thomas Nuce translated *Octavia* (London, "Henry Denham," n. d.). Thomas Newton translated *Thebais*, which here appears for the first time.

As the first collected edition of the English translation of the tragedies of Seneca, this work is of considerable importance, and merits the attention of every admirer of the ancient classical drama. All of the translations except Nuce's *Octavia* are written in Alexandrine measure.

[PARKER, HENRY.]   (*b.* ——, *d.* 1470.)

DIVES AND PAUPER.   LONDON, *Richarde Pynſon*, 1493.   [505]

Small folio. First Edition. Printed in black-letter.

COLLATION BY SIGNATURES: a, 6 leaves (the first blank and lacking); b, 6 leaves; a (repeated), 8 leaves (the first blank and lacking); b (repeated), c to v, A to I, each 8 leaves; total 244 unnumbered leaves. Leaf a ii. (repeated) is marked ii. a; c i. is c ii.; c ii. is c iii.; c iii. is c iiii.; and c iiii. is c v.

COLLATION BY PAGINATION: [1 blank leaf], [a i.]; —[contents], recto of a ii. to verso of [b vi.]; —[1 blank leaf], [a]; —[text in 10 Precepts, the first with heading] | ¶ Of holy pouertie. | The firſte chaptre. |, recto of a ii. to verso of [I vii.]; —[colophon, as reproduced; *See* No. 505 *a*], verso of [I vii.]; —[blank], recto of [I viii.]; —[Pynson's device, as reproduced; *See* No. 505 *b*], verso of [I viii.].

CONDITION: Size of leaf, 10⅞ × 7⅛ inches. Bound in brown crushed levant morocco, paneled, with elaborate blind tooling, gilt edges; by Bedford; in slip case.

OTHER COPIES.

Devonshire; Huth; Lenox; Halsey; and Morgan Libraries.

REFERENCES.

Quaritch, *Catalogue of the Monuments of the Early Printers* (1888), p. 3923, No. 37941; also *General Catalogue*, 1 (1887): 739, No. 7990; also 4:2125, No. 21873; 6:3923, No. 37941; British Museum, *Catalogue of Books to 1640*, 1 (1884): 484; Huth, *Catalogue*, 4(1880):1093; Lowndes, 2 (1869):652; Graesse, 2 (1861):411; Dibdin, *Typographical Antiquities*, 2 (1812): 401.

Printed in double columns, with thirty-six and thirty-seven lines to the full page.

The present very fine and genuine copy is quite perfect and of great rarity. The capital letter D on leaf a ii. is the only ornamented initial letter in the book. Dibdin has described this very rare work, giving a specimen of the type, but it is to be remarked that neither of the copies he describes — one probably Mr. Heber's, the other Lord Spencer's — appears to have contained the leaf bearing Pynson's device, and both were therefore imperfect.

This is the first work from Pynson's press. It has no title-page, but this copy contains the final leaf with his device, the existence of which has been questioned by some and even positively denied by others. The different books begin as follows, and have the following head-lines :

"Of holy Pouertie" begins on leaf a ii., marked ii. a ; "The firſte pꝛecepte," on leaf b i.; "The ſecounde pꝛecepte," on leaf h i.; "The thridde pꝛecepte," on leaf [i viii.] ; "The fourthe pꝛecepte," on leaf [l viii.] ; "The fyfte pꝛecepte," on leaf [o vi.]; "The ſyxte pꝛecepte," on leaf r iiii. ; "The ſeuenth pꝛecepte," on the verso of leaf [v viii.]; "The eight pꝛecepte," on the verso of leaf D iiii.; "The nynthe pꝛecepte," on the verso of leaf F iiii.; and "The tenthe pꝛecepte," on the verso of leaf H iii. There are errors in many of the head-lines.

"The author of this curious work was Henry Parker, of Doncaster, a Carmelite. He preached against the pomp of the priesthood, and reproved the prelates for their wealth and their modes of living, which he contrasted with the utter poverty of Christ. He was compelled to do public penance and ask pardon for his scandalous statements; but the winged words had gone forth, and Pynson printed them in 1493 with the title of 'Dives and Pauper.'

"The book is full of curious and suggestive matter, historical allusions, and racy proverbial phrases."

No. 505 *a*. Colophon of Parker's Dives and Pauper ; 1st Edition ; 1493.

No. 505 *b*. Pynson's Device in Parker's Dives and Pauper ; 1st Edition ; 1493.

PAULUS DE SANCTA MARIA.

DIALOGUS QUI VOCATUR SCRUTINIUM SCRIPTURARUM.
MANTUE, *Johannem Schallus*, 1475. [506]

Small folio. Printed in black-letter.
COLLATION BY SIGNATURES: [a] to m, each 10 and 8 leaves, alternately; n, 10 leaves; o, p, q, r, each 8 leaves (the last blank and lacking); A to K, each 10 and 8 leaves, alternately; L, 10 leaves (the last blank and genuine); M, N, each 10 leaves; total 270 unnumbered leaves. Leaf L 2 is wrongly marked L 3.
COLLATION BY PAGINATION: [text, with heading as reproduced; *See* No. 506*a*], recto of [a] to verso of [r 7]; — [colophon] |. Prima Pars Scrutinij huius fcripturarum. | fiue Capiftri Judeo4 finit. Sequitur | Secunda et ultima.|, verso of [r 7]; — [1 blank leaf], [r 8]; — [table of contents, beginning]| INcipit Secunda pars tractatus de Scru | tinio fcripturarum. . . . |, recto of A; — [text in 6 chapters, the first with heading]| Capitulũ Primũ In quo ponũtur a difcipulo quedã ar/ | gumetatõnes contra ea que dicta funt de deitat expī. . . . | . . . |, recto of A to recto of [L 9]; — [colophon in verse] | [6 lines] | Hoc opus impreffit rerum fcrutinia Schallus | Johannes docto? artis Apollinee. |. Anno domini Millefimo | quadringentefimofep/ | tuagefimoquinto. |, recto of [L 9]; — [blank], verso of [L 9]; — [1 blank leaf], [L 10]; — [translation, in Latin, of the Arabic letter of Rabbi Samuel to Rabbi Isaac, introduction, table of contents, and text], recto of M to verso of [N 9]; — [colophon, as reproduced; *See* No. 506*b*], recto of [N 10]; — [blank], verso of [N 10].

CONDITION: Size of leaf, 11 11/16 × 8⅛ inches. Bound in boards, vellum back. With initial letters, crudely illuminated in red and blue, at the beginning of Parts I. and II.

OTHER COPIES.

Lenox; and Morgan Libraries.

REFERENCES.

Quaritch, *Catalogue and Monuments of the Early Printers* (1888), p. 3846, No. 37629; Graesse, 5 (1864): 174; Brunet, 4 (1863): 451; Hain, *Repertorium Bibliographicum*, 3 (1831): 358, No. 10765.

This volume curiously illustrates the growth of the modern use of signature-marks. Signature-marks b to g are printed on the lower outer margins of the page; for example, e 2 is one and three-sixteenths inches to the right and one and eleven-sixteenths inches

No. 506*a*. HEADING OF THE FIRST PAGE OF THE DIALOGUS OF PAULUS DE SANCTA MARIA; 1475.

below the letterpress of the page, which is about the average position of these marks. From h onward the signature-marks are set close up to the lower outer corners of the printed matter, as in modern books.

> Nota ꝙ iste libellus uidetur fuisse occultatꝰ per iudeos ultra ducentos annos ⁊ triginta. quod connicitur ex hoc. quia cū iste doctor Samuel scriberet Rabbi ysaac. solum dixit fluxisse mille annos a tempe quo p Titum expugnan/tē sanctam ciuitatē iudei sūt dispersi. ⁊ ideo uidetur ꝙ sta tim post illos mille annos captiuitatis ⁊ dispersiois iude/orum. iste liber fuerit conscriptus. Sed iudei uidentes ꝙ p tot euidentia testimonia prophetarū. ipsorū errores ɔuin cerentur. istum librū tanto tempe ut dictū est occultaue/rūt. ne p catholicos fideles ipsoꝝ errores possent argui per contenta in hoc libello. Qui translatus est sub annis dñi. M.cc.xxxix. Et cum diligenti emenda per me Johannem Schallus artiū doctorē Mantue impressus. sub annis pre/fati domī nostri Jhesu xpi. M.cccc.lxxv. regnante ibidem felicissime Jllustrissimo uño Dño Lodouico de Gonzaga Marchione Secundo.

No. 506b. COLOPHON OF THE DIALOGUS OF PAULUS DE SANCTA MARIA; 1475.

PEMBROKE, MARY (SIDNEY) HERBERT, Countess of. (b. 1561, d. 1621.)

THE TRAGEDIE OF ANTONIE. DOONE INTO ENGLISH. LONDON, *for William Ponſonby*, 1595. [507]

Small octavo. Second Edition. Printed with type-ornament head- and tail-pieces on each page of text and of the colophon.

COLLATION BY SIGNATURES: A to G, each 8 leaves (the last, probably blank, lacking); total 56 unnumbered leaves.

COLLATION BY PAGINATION: [title, as reproduced; *See* No. 507], recto of [A]; — [woodcut], verso of [A]; — | [conventional head-piece] | ¶ The Argument. |, recto of *A* 2 [wrongly marked *A* 3] to recto of [A 3]; — | [type-ornament head-piece] | ¶ *The Actors.* |, verso of [A 3]; — [text], recto of [A 4] to recto of [G 7]; — | *At Ramsbury. 26. of Nouember.* | 1590. | [type-ornament tail-piece] |, recto of [G 7]; — [colophon] | [type-ornament head-piece] | *Printed at London by P. S.* | for William Ponſonby. 1595. | [type-ornament tail-piece] |, verso of [G 7]; — [1 leaf, probably blank], [G 8].

CONDITION: Size of leaf, 5¹³⁄₁₆ × 3¾₆ inches. Bound in red morocco, gilt edges; by C. Smith.

1595 Mary Herbert, Countess of Pembroke No. 507

THE TRAGEDIE OF Antonie.

Doone into English by the Countesse of *Pembroke*

Imprinted at London for *William* Ponsonby 1595.

No. 507. Title-page of the Countess of Pembroke's Tragedie of Antonie; 2d Edition; 1595.

OTHER COPIES.
British Museum; Bodleian; Edinburgh University; Devonshire; Halsey; and White Libraries.

REFERENCES.
Greg, *List of English Plays* (Bibliographical Society; 1900), p. 111; Hazlitt, *Manual of Old English Plays* (1892), p. 15; Locker-Lampson, *Catalogue* (1886), p. 57; Lowndes, 2 (1869): 865; Hazlitt, *Hand-Book to the Popular, Poetical, and Dramatic Literature of Great Britain* (1867), pp. 220, 403; *Bibliotheca Anglo-Poetica* (1815), p. 264, No. 544.

The Jolley-Locker Lampson copy, with ex-libris of each. With autograph of Thomas Jolley on the front fly-leaf.

This is the first separate edition of the English translation of Robert Garnier's *Marc Antoine*. It had previously appeared in 1592, at the end of the Countess of Pembroke's translation of De Mornay's *Discourse of Life and Death*, and is dated "Ramsbury, 26th of November, 1590."

No. 507   *Mary Herbert, Countess of Pembroke*   1595

"Mary Herbert, Countess of Pembroke, the translator of this little volume, was sister of the famous Sir Philip Sydney, to whom that great genius dedicated his well known romance called the Arcadia, in consequence, it almost invariably bears the appellation of the Countess of Pembroke's Arcadia. This alone was sufficient to immortalize her memory, but her merits required no borrowed honours, being themselves entitled to the highest praise. She was not only a lover of the Muses, but gave great encouragement to polite literature."

PEMBROKE, WILLIAM HERBERT, *third Earl (of the second creation) of.* (*b.* 1580, *d.* 1630.)

POEMS. LONDON, *Matthew Inman*, 1660.   [508]

Small octavo. First Edition. Thick-paper copy.

COLLATION BY SIGNATURES: [A], 4 leaves (the second lacking); B to H, each 8 leaves; I, 4 leaves (the last blank and genuine); total 64 leaves.

COLLATION BY PAGINATION: [title, as reproduced; *See* No. 508], recto of [A]; —[blank], verso of [A]; —["To the Reader," lacking], leaf [A 2]; — | [conventional head-piece] | To the Right Honorable | CRISTIANA, | COUNTESS of *DEVONSHIRE,* | *DOWAGER.* | [signed] | *MADAM,* | Your moſt humble and o- | bedient Servant, | JOHN DONNE. | , recto of [A 3] to recto of [A 4]; —[blank], verso of [A 4]; —[poems, the first with heading] | [conventional head-piece] | EARLE OF | PEMBROKE, | Lord Steward: | SON-NET. | , pp. 1–118; —[1 blank leaf], [I 4]. Page 66 is wrongly numbered 96.

CONDITION: Size of leaf, 6⁹⁄₁₆ x 4⁵⁄₁₆ inches. Bound in old red morocco, gilt edges.

OTHER COPIES.

British Museum; Devonshire; Ellesmere; Huth; Hoe; and White Libraries.

REFERENCES.

Hoe, *Catalogue*, 5 (1905): 363; Grolier Club, *Wither to Prior*, 2 (1905): 80, 82, No. 440; Huth, *Catalogue*, 4 (1880): 1121; Lowndes, 4 (1869): 1820; Hazlitt, *Hand-Book* (1867), p. 452; Collier, *Rarest Books*, 3 (1866): 178; *Bibliotheca Grenvilliana*, 2 (1842): 531; *Bibliotheca Anglo-Poetica* (1815), p. 264, No. 545.

The Horace Walpole copy, with ex-libris.

Some copies were printed on fine paper for presentation only. The copy here described was ruled throughout by hand in red ink before the book was bound.

The authorship of most of the poems is indicated by the initial P or R at the head of those written respectively by the Earl of Pembroke or Sir Benjamin Rudyerd. Besides these the volume contains poems by Sir Walter Raleigh, Sir Edward Dyer, Carew, William Strode, and others. Among them is the celebrated epitaph on the Countess of Pembroke, beginning

"Underneath this ſable Herſe,
Lyes the ſubjeƈt of all Verſe."

"The first six lines of this epitaph are commonly attributed to Ben Jonson. The whole poem was first published in Osborne's 'Traditional Memoirs on the Reign

POEMS,

Written by the
RIGHT HONORABLE
WILLIAM
EARL OF
PEMBROKE,

Lord Steward of his Maiesties Houshold.

WHEREOF
Many of which are answered by way of Repartee,

BY

Sr BENJAMIN RUDDIER,
KNIGHT.

With several Distinct
POEMS,
Written by them Occasionally, and Apart.

LONDON,
Printed by *Matthew Inman*, and are to be sold by
James Magnes, in *Russel-street*, near the *Piazza*,
in *Covent-Garden*, 1660.

of King James', 1658, and afterwards in the present volume. In 1756 Peter Whalley printed the first six lines in his edition of Ben Jonson's works, and since then they have been generally considered to belong to Jonson. Considerable evidence tending to prove that it was written by William Browne is given in the 'Poems of William Browne of Tavistock', edited by Gordon Goodwin, 1894 (Vol. II, p. 350).''

This First Edition of the Earl of Pembroke's poems was edited by John Donne the younger, "at the request of Christiana Countess of Devonshire the Platonick Mistress of the author : She was sister to the Sir Ed. Bruce, who was killed in the remarkable duel with Sackville afterwards Earl of Dorset." In the dedication the editor "states that the poems had been preserved by the Countess of Devonshire, who had employed him to edit them, while in his address 'To The Reader' [lacking in the copy here described] he states that he obtained them from Henry Lawes and Nicholas Laniere, who had set some of them to music."

In 1817 the work was reprinted, some portions being suppressed, under the editorship of Sir S. E. Brydges.

Collier says : " In some copies certain leaves are cancelled, and the paging is therefore irregular."

PHAER, THOMAS (*b.* ——, *d.* 1560), *and* **TWYNE, THOMAS** (*b.* 1543, *d.* 1613), *translators.* **Virgilius Maro, Publius.** (*b.* 70 B.C., *d.* 19 B.C.)

THE XIII. BOOKES OF ÆNEIDOS. LONDON, *by William How, for Abraham Veale,* 1584. [509]

Small quarto. First Edition.
COLLATION BY SIGNATURES : 4 leaves, without signature-marks ; A to V, each 8 leaves ; X, 4 leaves (the last blank and lacking); total 168 unnumbered leaves. Leaves A v., C v., and V v. have no signature-marks.
COLLATION BY PAGINATION : [title, as reproduced ; *See* No. 509], recto of first leaf ; — [blank], verso of first leaf ; — | *TO THE RIGHT WORSHIP-*| *full* Maifter *Robert Sackeuill Efquire,* | moft worthie Sonne and heire apparant to the Right | honorable *Syr Thomas Sackeuill* Knight, | Lorde Buckehurft. | [signed] | *Your Worſhips moſt bounden, and willing* : | Thomas Twyne. | [dated] | . . . At my houfe in *Lewis,* | this firſt of Ianuarie. 1584. | , recto of second leaf to recto of third leaf ; — | To the gentle and courteous | *Readers.* | , verso of third leaf ; — | *VIRGILS LIFE, SET FORTH* | *as it is fuppofed, by* Aelius Donatus, | and done into Englifh. | , recto of fourth leaf to verso of [A vii.] ; — [contents, with heading] | [type-ornament head-piece] | *THE ARGVMENTES OF* | *the thirteene bookes of Aeneidos,* | expreffed in verfe. | , verso of [A vii.] ; — | *A GENERALL SVM* | *whereof all the xij. Bookes of* | Aeneidos do entreate. | , recto and verso of [A viii.] ; — [text in 12 books, the first with heading] | [type-ornament head-piece] | THE FIRST BOOKE OF | *the Æneidos of Virgill.* | , recto of B to recto of V ; — | ☙ *Maifter Phaers* Conclufion to his in- | terpretation of the Æneidos of Virgill, | by

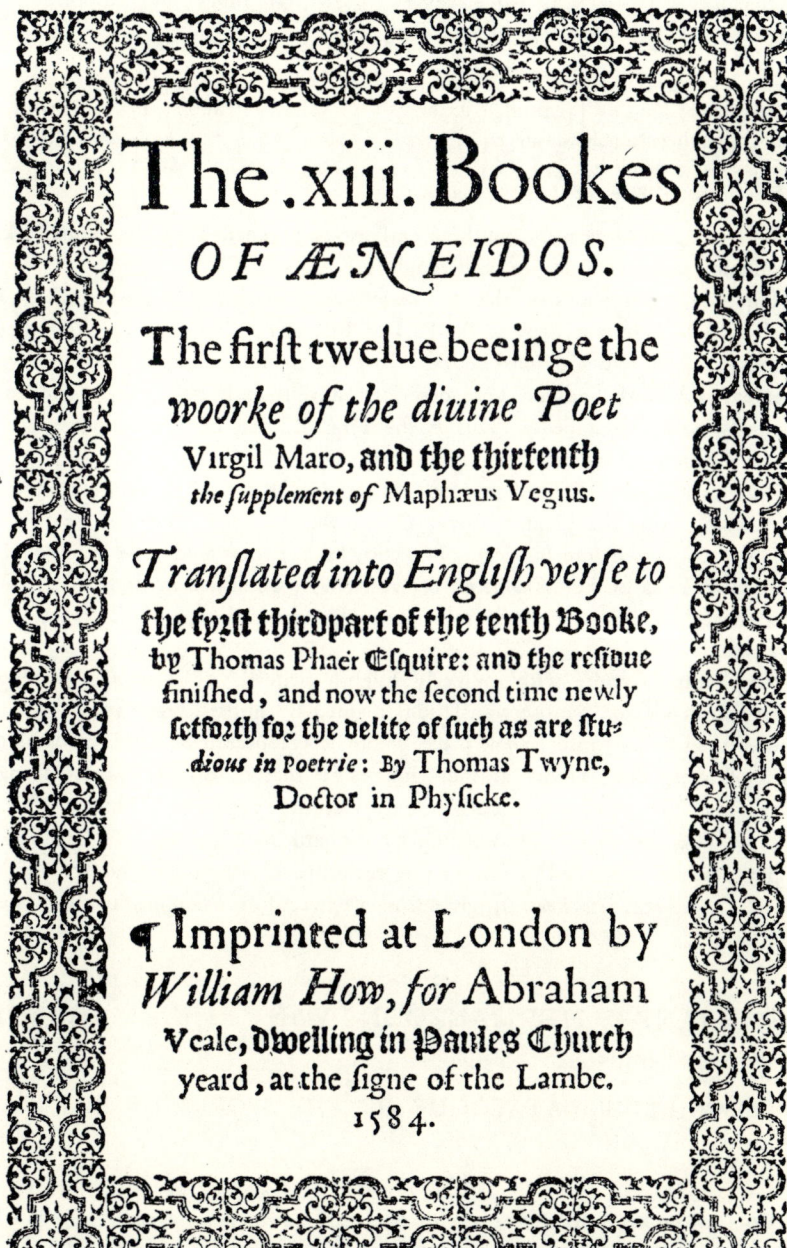

No. 509. Title-page of Phaer and Twyne's translation of Virgil's Æneid; 1st edition; 1584.

No. 509   *Thomas Phaer and Thomas Twyne*   1584

him conuerted into english verſe. | , verso of V to recto of V ij. ; — [text, with heading] | [type-ornament head-piece] | THE *THIR-TENTH* BOOKE | *of Æneidos, ſupplyed by* Maphæus | Vegius Laudenſis. | , verso of V ij. to verso of X iij. ; — | [editor's colophon, 3 lines] | [conventional tail-piece] | , verso of X iij. ; — [1 blank leaf], [X 4] .

CONDITION: Size of leaf, 7⅞ × 5¹¹⁄₁₆ inches. Bound in brown crushed levant morocco, gilt edges ; by Bedford.

REFERENCES.

Huth, *Catalogue*, 5 (1880): 1538 ; Lowndes, 5 (1869): 2783 ; Hazlitt, *Hand-Book* (1867), p. 632, No. 8 *a* ; Collier, *Rarest Books*, 3 (1866): 189.

This is a fine large copy, with several leaves untouched by the binder's knife at the bottom, and several leaves with rough fore-edges.

The first seven books of this translation were originally published in 1558, of which edition there is a copy in the Earl of Ellesmere's library. In 1562 they were republished, with two additional books. In 1573 the translation of all the twelve books appeared, and in the edition here described a thirteenth book, the Supplement of Maphæus, was first added. This is the First Edition of the complete work, the Second Edition of which was published in 1596.

Thomas Phaer, an Oxford student and barrister-at-law of Lincoln's Inn, and also a physician, wrote the poem "Owen Glendower" in the *Myrrour for Magiſtrates* (our No. 499). Before his death, in 1560, he had translated nine books and a part of the tenth book of the *Æneid*, all of which were published in the edition of 1562. After Phaer's death the work was taken up and finished by Twyne, a fellow physician.

Virgil was a favorite with the early English writers. The *Æneid* first appeared in English in Caxton's prose translation, printed by himself, in 1490. An interval of more than half a century took place before it reappeared in three metrical translations following one another at short intervals: that of Bishop Gawin Douglas, in 1553 (our No. 371) ; the Earl of Surrey's, in 1557 ; and Thomas Phaer's, in 1558. The next metrical translation, by Richard Stanyhurst, of the first four books (1583), is justly regarded as one of the curiosities of English literature. Corser, in his *Collectanea Anglo-Poetica*, gives some extracts as examples of its "excessive absurdity."

REMBRANDT HERMANZOON VAN RIJN. (*b.* 1607, *d.* 1669.)
Daulby, Daniel.

A DESCRIPTIVE CATALOGUE OF THE WORKS OF REMBRANDT.
LIVERPOOL, J. M'CREERY, 1796.   [510]

Post octavo.

COLLATION BY SIGNATURES: 2 leaves, without signature-marks ; a, b, c, each 4 leaves ; A to X, each 8 leaves ; Y, 4 leaves ; 1 leaf, without signature-mark ; total 187 leaves. Leaf T has no signature-mark.

COLLATION BY PAGINATION: [half-title], recto of first leaf ; — [blank], verso of first leaf ; — [title] | A | DESCRIPTIVE CATALOGUE | OF THE | *WORKS* | OF | REMBRANDT, | AND OF HIS | SCHOLARS, | *BOL, LIVENS, and VAN*

1796   *Rembrandt Hermanzoon van Rijn*   No. 510

VLIET, | COMPILED FROM | THE ORIGINAL ETCHINGS, | AND FROM | THE CATALOGUES | OF DE BURGY, GERSAINT, HELLE AND GLOMY, | MARCUS, AND YVER. | *BY DANIEL DAULBY.* | LIVERPOOL, | PRINTED BY J. M'CREERY, | AND SOLD BY J. EDWARDS, PALL MALL, AND CADELL AND | DAVIES, IN THE STRAND, LONDON. | 1796. |, recto of second leaf; — [blank], verso of second leaf; — | OBSERVATIONS | ON THE | WORKS OF REMBRANDT. |, pp. [i.]-xxii.; — [tabulated list of etchings], p. [xxiii.]; — [blank], p. [xxiv.]; — [text], pp. [1]-234; — [1 blank leaf, unnumbered]; — [supplement, with half-title], pp. [235]-259; — [blank], p. [260]; — [prints after Rembrandt, with half-title], pp. [261]-285; — [blank], p. [286]; — [imitations, with half-title], pp. [287]-295; — [blank], p. [296]; — [works of Rembrandt's scholars, with half-title], pp. [297]-331; — [blank], p. [332]; — [appendix, with half-title], pp. [333]-339; — [blank], p. [340]; — [index], pp. [341]-[342] — [errata], p. [343]; — [blank], p. [344].

PLATE: Portrait of Rembrandt; stipple; engraved by Chapman, after Rembrandt; facing the title-page.

EXTRA-ILLUSTRATED.

Inserted in this work are 21 etchings, 14 of which are by Rembrandt.

[22] A Portrait of Rembrandt; size, 4¾ × 4⅛ inches; signed, "*Rembrandt f. 1633*," in reverse, at bottom; facing p. 10.

[28] A Portrait of Rembrandt; partially in an oval; size, 4⅛ × 3½ inches; unsigned; facing p. 14.

[67] The Tribute to Cæsar; size, 2⅞ × 4 inches; unsigned; facing p. 44.

[72] Jesus and the Samaritan Woman at the Well; an upright; size, 4⁹⁄₁₆ × 3¾ inches; signed, "*Rembrandt f. 1639*" in the upper right-hand corner; facing p. 47.

[117] The Rat-killer; size, 5⁵⁄₁₆ × 4¾ inches; signed, "*Rt. 1632*" (the 3 and 2 reversed), at bottom; facing p. 86.

[132] An Old Man with a Boy; size, 4⅝ × 3³⁄₁₆ inches; signed, "*Rembrandt. f.*" in reverse, in the lower right-hand corner; facing p. 94.

[140] Another Polander; size, 3 × 2⅛ inches; signed, "*Rt. 1630*" at bottom; facing p. 95.

[144] An Old Man with a Bushy Beard; size, 4³⁄₁₆ × 3 inches; signed, "*Rt*" in reverse, in the upper right-hand corner; facing p. 99.

[168] A Beggar with his Mouth Open; size, 4⁹⁄₁₆ × 2¾ inches; signed, "*Rt. 1630*," at bottom; facing p. 112.

[200] Six's Bridge; size, 2¹¹⁄₁₆ × 8½ inches; signed, "*Rembrandt f. 1645*," in the lower right-hand corner; facing p. 133.

[225] Rembrandt's Father's Mill; size, 5¾ × 8⁹⁄₁₆ inches; signed, "*Rembrandt delin 1641*" in the lower left-hand corner; "*1758 — F. Vinares fecit excud*" in the lower right-hand corner; facing p. 146.

[246] Janus Silvius; size, 6⁷⁄₁₆ × 5⁷⁄₁₆ inches; unsigned; facing p. 156.

[240] Bust of an Old Man with a Long Beard; size, 4½ × 3¹⁵⁄₁₆ inches; signed, "*Rembrand, pinx*," in the lower left-hand corner, and "*Hertel, excud*," in the lower right-hand corner; "*N° 95.*" in the centre; facing p. 156.

[266] Oriental Head; size, 5¹¹⁄₁₆ × 3¾ inches; signed, "*Rembrandt Venetiis fecit*," in reverse, in the upper left-hand corner; facing p. [179].

[366] The Portrait of an Old Man, with a Frizled Beard; size, 3¹⁵⁄₁₆ × 3⅜ inches; signed, "*Rembrandt | 1631*," in the upper left-hand corner; facing p. [179].

[268] The Bust of an Old Man with a Large Beard; size, 6⅛ × 4⁹⁄₁₆ inches; unsigned; facing p. 180.

[268] The Bust of an Old Man with a Large Beard; size, 4 × 4⅛ inches; signed, "*Rmbrandt*," in the upper right-hand portion; facing p. 181.

[119] An Old Man's Head with a White Beard; size, 4⁹⁄₁₆ × 4 inches; mezzotint; signed, "*Rembrandt Pinx*ᵗ" in the lower left-hand corner, and "*Richᵈ Houston Fecit*" in the lower right-hand corner; facing p. 274.

[120] An Old Woman's Head; size, 4⅜ × 3⅞ inches; mezzotint; signed, "*Rem-*

No. 510　　*Rembrandt Hermanzoon van Rijn*　　1796

*brandt Pinx*ᵗ" in the lower left-hand corner, and "*Rich. Houston Fecit.*" in the lower right-hand corner; facing p. [275].

Also 2 unidentified plates, loosely inserted, as follows:

[1] Portrait, bust with whiskers and moustache, mouth open, profile view facing to left; cap with feather at top, ruffle around neck; shading in cross-hatching in lower left-hand portion; size, 4⁵⁄₁₆ × 3⅜ inches; signed, "*Remb*ᵗ *f.*" in the right-hand centre margin.

[2] Group; 5 busts: three bearded men and woman with child in arms; man in centre playing upon musical instrument, two horns of which extend above his head; size, 2⁹⁄₁₆ × 3⅞ inches; unsigned.

CONDITION: Size of leaf, 7¹⁵⁄₁₆ × 5 inches. Bound in red crushed levant morocco, gilt edges; by Bain. Text interleaved with plate paper throughout. Bound with this volume is an auction *Catalogue of a . . . Collection of the Etchings by Rembrandt*, 1835.

The main interest of this copy is in its extra-illustrations, fourteen of which are etchings by Rembrandt, who has been styled "the greatest etcher that ever lived."

[ROBINSON, THOMAS.] (*fl.* 1622.)

THE ANATOMIE OF THE ENGLISH NVNNERY AT LISBON IN PORTVGALL. [LONDON], *for Philemon Stephens & Christopher Meredith,* 1630.　　　　　　　　　　　　　　　　　　　　　　　　　　　　　　　[511]

Small quarto. Third Edition.

COLLATION BY SIGNATURES: A to E, each 4 leaves; total 20 leaves.

COLLATION BY PAGINATION: [blank], recto of [A]; — | *The explanation of the Picture in the Title.* |, verso of [A]; — [title, as reproduced; *See* No. 511], recto of [A 2]; — [blank], verso of [A 2]; — | [type-ornament head-piece] | TO THE RIGHT | VVORSHIPFVLL, | Mr. *Thomas Gurlin,* Maior of the no leſſe | ancient then loyall and wel-gouerned Towne | of *Kings-Lynne* in *Norfolke,* and his Wor- | ſhipfull Brethren, the Aldermen of | the ſame, &c. | [signed] | *Your Worſhips dutifull debtor,* | THOMAS ROBINSON. |, recto of A 3 to recto of [A 4]; — | [type-ornament head-piece] | To the indifferent Reader.

| [signed] | T. R. |, verso of [A 4]; — [text, with heading] | [conventional head-piece] | THE | ANATOMIE OF | THE ENGLISH | NVNNERY, AT LISBON | IN PORTVGALL. |, pp. 1–31; — | FINIS. |, p. 31; — [blank], p. [32].

CONDITION: Size of leaf, 7 × 5⁵⁄₁₆ inches. Bound in red crushed levant morocco, gilt edges; by Rivière.

OTHER COPIES.

Trinity College, Cambridge; and Ellesmere Libraries.

REFERENCES.

Lowndes, 4 (1869): 2111; Hazlitt, *Hand-Book* (1867), p. 517; Collier, *Rarest Books,* 3 (1866): 335.

The First Edition of this curious work appeared in 1622. In the next edition, published in 1623, a copy of which is owned by Mr. W. A. White, of Brooklyn, is an engraved title-page, in one of the compartments of which is a full-length portrait of Robinson, the author, in miniature. "The writer exhibits a strong Protestant bias, and his evidence cannot be accepted quite literally."

"The work is of no authority, but it has a passage containing an unquoted notice of two remarkable publications, — Shakspeare's 'Venus and Adonis,' and 'Peele's

No. 511. Title-page of Robinson's Anatomie of the English Nvnnerie at Lisbon; 3d Edition; 1630.

Jests,' — both of which the author accuses the confessor of the nunnery of reading. Shakspeare's exquisite poem is spoken of as an 'idle pamphlet.'"

"And when he is merrily difpofed, (as that is not feldom) then muft his darling *Kate Knightly* play him a merry fit, & fifter *Mary Brooke*, or fome other of his late-come Wags muft fing him one bawdy fong or other to digeft his meat. The after fupper it is vfuall for him to reade a little of *Venus and Adonis*, the Iefts of *George Peele*, or fome fuch fcurrilous Book: for there are few idle Pamphlets printed in *Englād* which he hath not in the houfe."

ROGERS, SAMUEL. (*b.* 1763, *d.* 1855.)

THE PLEASURES OF MEMORY. London, *for* T. Cadell and W. Davies, 1803. [512]

Small octavo.

COLLATION BY SIGNATURES: [A], 4 leaves (the first blank and lacking); B to M, each 8 leaves; N, 6 leaves; total 98 leaves.

COLLATION BY PAGINATION: [1 blank leaf], [A]; — [title] | THE | PLEASURES | OF | MEMORY, | WITH OTHER | POEMS. | BY SAMUEL ROGERS, ESQ. | *A NEW EDITION.* | London : | PRINTED FOR T. CADELL AND W. DAVIES, | IN THE STRAND, | BY T. BENSLEY, BOLT-COURT, FLEET-STREET. | 1803. |, recto of [A 2]; — [blank], verso of [A 2]; — [introduction, in verse, without heading], recto and verso of [A 3]; — [contents], recto and verso of [A 4]; — [half-title], p. [1]; — [blank], p. [2]; — [text in 2 parts, with half-title to each], pp. 3–90; — [other poems, the first with half-title], pp. 91–187; — [imprint], p. [188].

ILLUSTRATIONS: 15 head- and tail-pieces, engraved on copper by Heath, from designs by Stothard.

CONDITION: Size of leaf, 6¼ × 3¹³⁄₁₆ inches. Bound in half blue crushed levant morocco, gilt edges; by Matthews.

REFERENCES.

Locker-Lampson, *Catalogue* (1886), p. 170; Lowndes, 4 (1869): 2118.

This poem was reprinted many times. The First Edition appeared in 1792; the Fifth, or first illustrated edition, was published the following year, with four illustrations on copper by Stothard. In 1801 appeared a new edition with fifteen head- and tail-pieces by Heath, after Stothard, and the year after, another edition with the same number. The copy here described appears to be the third edition containing this series of illustrations. Copies of the 1793, 1801, and 1802 editions were in the Locker-Lampson library.

Samuel Rogers, the banker-poet, began contributing to *The Gentleman's Magazine* in 1781. He first achieved popularity in 1792 by the publication of *The Pleasures of Memory*, the work here described. Having retired from business on the death of his father in 1793, he became intimate with the most eminent men of his day. Visiting Paris he there cultivated his tastes as an art connoisseur. He attained a high position among men of letters, many of whom were indebted to his influence or personal generosity. In 1850 he received the offer of the laureateship, which he declined.

ROGERS, SAMUEL.

ITALY, A POEM. London, *for T. Cadell, Jennings and Chaplin, and E. Moxon*, 1830. [513]

Post octavo. First Edition, First Issue. COLLATION BY SIGNATURES: [A] to Z, [AA] to NN, each 4 leaves; OO, 2 leaves; total 146 numbered leaves. Leaves Q and AA have no signature-marks.

COLLATION BY PAGINATION: [title] | ITALY, | A POEM. | BY | SAMUEL ROGERS. | LONDON: | PRINTED FOR T. CADELL, STRAND; JENNINGS AND CHAPLIN, | 62, CHEAPSIDE; AND E. MOXON, 64, NEW BOND-STREET. | 1830. |, p. [i.]; — [imprint], p. [ii.]; — [preface and contents], pp. [iii.] – vii.; — [blank], p. [viii.]; — [text], pp. [1] – 236; — [notes], pp. [237] – 284.

ILLUSTRATIONS: 55 unsigned engravings in the text, after designs by Turner and Stothard.

CONDITION: Size of leaf, 7⅞ x 5¼ inches. Bound in olive morocco, gilt gauffered edges; by Clarke & Bedford.

REFERENCES.

Nicoll and Seccombe, 3 (1907): 906; Locker-Lampson, *Catalogue* (1886), p. 171; Lowndes, 4 (1869): 2118.

The Slade-Locker Lampson copy with the latter's ex-libris.

A presentation copy, with inscription, "*Frederick Locker from his friend Felix Slade 1864.*"

Inserted in this copy is a letter from the author to | *Edward Moxon Esq.* | *Dover St.* | *London* |, as follows:

"*Dear M*^r *Moxon*

If an opportunity occurs, you will oblige me very much by making another trial for the Copper-plate of my Portrait — but take no trouble about it. Many thanks for your kind letter. [Signed] *Yours very truly S. Rogers.* [Dated] *Strathfield Saye, Nov*^r *27, 1840.*"

This is the First Issue of the First Edition, containing the earliest impressions of Finden's exquisite engravings from pictures by Turner and Stothard. It is distinguished by having the engraving of Petrarch's house with balcony and distant view of the mountains as a head-piece to the poem "Arquà" on p. 88, and the tomb of Petrarch as a tail-piece on p. 91. These engravings are incorrectly placed, their positions having been reversed. This work was reissued several times.

Rogers, a rich poet-banker and idolized poet of *The Edinburgh* and *Quarterly*, was celebrated for his breakfast-parties. His house in St. James's Place was celebrated as a resort of many eminent literary and public men, among whom were Scott, Byron, Moore, Wordsworth, Southey, and Coleridge. His *Table Talk* survives his *Poems*, and promises to become a classic of its kind.

"His poems, the Akensidean *Pleasures of Memory* (1793), and the metrical tale of *Jacqueline*, or the dilettante poem on *Italy*, which a romantic footboy of Byron's might have written, . . . are almost negligible, if we omit one or two little pastels — the mantle of Shenstone — such as 'Mine be a cot beside the hill,' which is truly delightful and deserves its place in *The Golden Treasury*."

No. 514   *Samuel Rogers*   1834

ROGERS, SAMUEL.

POEMS.   LONDON, *for T. Cadell and E. Moxon,* 1834.   [514]

Post octavo.

COLLATION BY SIGNATURES: [A], 4 leaves (the first lacking); B to Z, AA to PP, each 4 leaves; total 152 numbered leaves. Leaves X and HH have no signature-marks.

COLLATION BY PAGINATION: [half-title], p. [i.]; — [imprint], p. [ii.]; — [title] | POEMS | BY | SAMUEL ROGERS. | LONDON : | PRINTED FOR T. CADELL, STRAND; AND E. MOXON, | DOVER-STREET. | 1834. |, p. [iii.]; — [blank], p. [iv.]; — [poem, dated 1793], p. [v.]; — [blank], p. [vi.]; — [contents], pp. [vii.]–viii.; — [text in several sections, each with its own notes, the first with half-title], pp. [1]–295; — [engraving], p. [296].

ILLUSTRATIONS: 72 copper-plate engravings (proofs, every plate so marked) in the text, after designs by Turner, Stothard, and others.

CONDITION: Size of leaf, 7⅞ × 5¼ inches. Bound in olive morocco, gilt gauffred edges; by Clarke & Bedford.

REFERENCES.

Locker-Lampson, *Catalogue* (1886), p. 171; Lowndes, 4 (1869): 2117.

The Slade-Locker Lampson copy, with the latter's ex-libris and a presentation inscription from Felix Slade to Frederick Locker-Lampson.

This copy lacks the half-title, and leaf X has no signature-mark, though it appears in some copies.

Inserted is an autograph letter by Samuel Rogers, the author, addressed to | M*r* Moxon | Dover Street | London |, as follows:

"Dec*r* 9, 1833.

" My dear Sir

May I beg the favor of you, when you look in upon the Copper-plate printers, to see that they are printing according to their patterns? Gad and Keningale are working p. *180* by night as well as by day. So also are Reynolds and Allen working a plate by night. When *6000* are struck off, they are to print by night no longer, as night-work is more expensive than day-work. When you have anything to communicate, pray write by post. I will come up, if I am wanted at any time. [Signed] *Yours very sincerely Sam'l Rogers.* [Dated] *Brighton. Marine Parade. N° 14.*

" It would be right, I think, to send *100* copies to Cadell a day or two before the day of publication. Indeed as he supplies, I believe, his namesake at Edinburgh, he should be enabled perhaps to supply him sooner, if he asks for it. To-night I hope will compleat the number of *6000* — that is of *5000* copies, independent of the proofs. The printers may then proceed leisurely. [Dated] *Dec*r *12*."

Tipped in is a double leaf, apparently two half-titles. On the recto of the first, in ink, in Rogers' handwriting: | *Poems* | *By* | *Samuel Rogers.* | *Vol. II* | *London.* | *Printed for &c* | *1834.* |. On the recto of the second leaf: " *Italy.*"

Inserted at the end is also an autograph letter from Felix Slade, as follows:

"*Walcot Place, Lambeth, S.*
26th Sept. 1864.

"My dear Locker

It will be, I flatter myself, agreeable to you to receive, as it is a great pleasure to me to offer, the accompanying two volumes containing Roger's Italy & poems, as a memorial of the regard of yours ever truly, [signed] *Felix Slade.* Frederick Locker Esq."

The First Edition, published in 1812, was followed by others in 1814, 1816, 1822, 1824, etc. The tardy success of this work occasioned among other epigrams Lady Blessington's *mot* that "it would have been dished were it not for the plates."

ROWLANDSON, THOMAS, *illustrator.* (*b.* 1756, *d.* 1827.) Stevens, George Alexander. (*b.* 1710, *d.* 1784.)

A LECTURE ON HEADS. LONDON, *for Vernor, Hood, and Sharpe, etc.,* 1808. [515]

Duodecimo.

COLLATION BY SIGNATURES: 2 leaves, without signature-marks (the first blank and lacking); A to I, each 6 leaves; total 56 leaves.

COLLATION BY PAGINATION: [1 blank leaf]; — [half-title], recto of second leaf; — [blank], verso of second leaf; — [title] | A | LECTURE ON HEADS, | BY | GEO. ALEX. STEVENS, | with | ADDITIONS, | As delivered by | MR. CHARLES LEE LEWES. | To which is added, | AN ESSAY ON SATIRE. | [vignette] | Embellished with | TWENTY-FIVE HUMOUROUS CHARACTERISTIC PRINTS, | *From Drawings by G. M. Woodward, Esq.* | LONDON: | PRINTED FOR VERNOR, HOOD, AND SHARPE; CUTHELL | AND MARTIN; J. WALKER; OTRIDGE AND SON; AND | LONGMAN, HURST, REES, AND ORME; | *By W. Wilson, Printer, St. John's* Square. | 1808. |, p. [i.]; — [blank], p. [ii.]; — [half-title], p. [iii.]; — [publishers' advertisement], p. [iv.]; — [address to the public], pp. [v.]-vii. ; — [prologue], pp. [viii.]-ix.; — [additional lines to the prologue], p. [x.]; — [index], pp. [xi.]-[xii.]; — [directions for placing the prints], p. [xii.]; — [text], pp. [1]-96.

PLATES: Folding frontispiece in colors, and 24 plates, as called for in the directions to the binder.

CONDITION: Size of leaf, 6 7/16 x 4 inches. Bound in blue polished calf, gilt top, other edges uncut; by Ringer. The binder has transposed the plates of "The Crying Philosopher" and "The Laughing Philosopher."

REFERENCE.

Grego, *Rowlandson the Caricaturist,* 2 (1880): 117-119.

"George Stevens, the originator of the 'Lecture on Heads,' was a very indifferent actor, but a man of humorous parts, and in himself was considered, by his contemporaries, most entertaining company. The idea of the lecture was given him by a country carpenter, who made the character-blocks which formed the subjects of illustration. It proved an extraordinary success in the hands of the originator. He carried it about England, through the States of America, and, on his return, to Ireland; and managed to net some ten thousand pounds by this lucky venture. After he retired more than one actor attempted it, with poor results. Lewis was the most successful of Stevens's imitators, and he had made such arrangements with the author as entitled the latter to a royalty for the use of his 'Lecture on Heads.' It probably derived its principal charm from the style of its delivery. Read in cold blood, its brilliancy and point are by no means startling."

Thomas Rowlandson, the artist and caricaturist, learned to draw before he could write, and at ten years of age had already filled his exercise-books with caricatures of his teachers and schoolmates. He studied at the Royal Academy, which he left when about sixteen and went to Paris, where he continued his studies, at the same time becoming an adept in French. After two years he returned to England, and resumed his studies at the Academy, showing such proficiency in his art that it became the fashion to pit him against the favorite of the life school, John Hamilton Mortimer. After two years, during which he seems to have visited Paris again, he returned to London and established himself as a portrait-painter, contributing regularly to the Academy and exhibiting both portraits and landscapes. He appears to have frequently visited Flanders, Holland, and Germany, where he filled his sketch-books with studies.

Among his associates were several caricaturists, Gillray, Wigstead, and Bunbury. By 1781 his own tendency to caricature had become pronounced, and in 1784 he produced "Vauxhall Gardens," a typical example of his skill. This was followed by other works of a similar character.

During his later years he devoted much of his attention to book illustration. For Ackermann's *Poetical Magazine*, established in 1809, he furnished two plates monthly, illustrating *The Schoolmaster's Tour*, the metrical text of which was supplied by William Combe, who was then living in the King's Bench Prison. The success of this combined effort, published when completed as *The Tour of Doctor Syntax, in Search of the Picturesque* (our No. 516), led to its two sequels, *The Second Tour of Doctor Syntax, in Search of Consolation* (our No. 521) in 1820, and *The Third Tour of Doctor Syntax, in Search of a Wife* (our No. 522) in 1822. They each passed through many editions, and in 1823 Ackermann published a pocket edition of the three Tours in sixteenmo, with the plates reëngraved and reduced in size. Combe also furnished the text for Rowlandson's plates of the *History of Johnny Quæ Genus, the Foundling of the Late Doctor Syntax* (our No. 524), *The English Dance of Death* (our No. 518), and *The Dance of Life* (our No. 520).

The success of Rowlandson and Combe's works led to the publication of numerous imitations of the Doctor Syntax *Tours*, among which may be named: *Doctor Syntax in Paris* (our No. 525); *The Tour of Doctor Syntax through London* (our No. 526); and *The Tour of Doctor Prosody, in Search of the Antique and Picturesque* (our No. 527).

Rowlandson also furnished illustrations for Stevens' *Lectures on Heads* (the present number), Goldsmith's *Vicar of Wakefield* (our No. 385), and Englebach's *Naples and the Campagna Felice* (our No. 517).

The extraordinary facility and fertility of Rowlandson's work may be observed in his power of managing crowds, his eye for the picturesque, and the grace and accuracy of his feminine figures, many of which are exceedingly beautiful. Several of his female portraits have been mistaken for sketches by Gainsborough or Morland, showing that if he had confined himself to this branch of his art he would have proved a serious competitor for the honors bestowed upon Reynolds, Romney, Gainsborough, and other painters of their class. "With every qualification to ensure success, Rowlandson, as his story indicates, deliberately threw away the serious chances of life, to settle down as the delineator of the transitory impressions of the hour."

ROWLANDSON, THOMAS, *illustrator.* Combe, William. (*b.* 1741, *d.* 1823.)

THE TOUR OF DOCTOR SYNTAX, IN SEARCH OF THE PICTURESQUE. LONDON, *R. Ackermann*, 1812. [516]

Octavo. First Edition.

COLLATION BY SIGNATURES: A, 2 leaves; B to Z, Aa to Nn, each 4 leaves (the last blank and lacking); total 142 leaves.

COLLATION BY PAGINATION: [engraved title, verso blank; inserted as a plate] | *THE TOUR | of | DOCTOR SYNTAX, | In Search of the | PICTURESQUE.* [in a colored vignette] | *A Poem.* | [quotation] | *Pub. 1st May 1812,* at R. Ackermann's Repository of Arts *101 Strand, London.* | ; —[advertisement], pp. [i.]–iii.; —[imprint], p. [iv.]; —[text, in verse, chapters 1–26], pp. [1]–275; —[blank], p. [276]; — | *Directions to the Binder for Placing the Plates.* |, p. [277]; —[blank], p. [278]; —[1 blank leaf], [Nn 4].

PLATES: Frontispiece, title-page, and 29 plates, all designed and etched by Rowlandson, and colored by hand; published May 1, 1812, at R. Ackermann's Repository of Arts, 101 Strand; all as called for in the directions to the binder.

CONDITION: Size of leaf, $8\tfrac{13}{16}$ x $5\tfrac{5}{8}$ inches. Bound in light polished calf, yellow edges; by Tout.

REFERENCES.

Slater, *Early Editions* (1894), p. 72, No. 2; Grego, *Rowlandson the Caricaturist,* 2 (1880): 247–250, also p. 317; Lowndes, 5 (1869): 2564.

There are many later editions of this book, a Fourth and Fifth appearing in 1813, and a Ninth in 1819. They contain the same plates, but the impressions are much inferior, the plates having been several times reëtched.

This poem was first published in the *Poetical Magazine* under the title *The Schoolmaster's Tour.* It was then separately published with the title changed, as here described. For this volume the old subjects were reëngraved by Rowlandson, with the outlines somewhat less bold and three new subjects added: the frontispiece, the vignette on the title-page, and plate 27, The Doctor's Dream of the Battle of the Books, not included in the work on its original publication. In the introduction the relative position of the artist and the writer of the poem is explained. Combe says: "I undertook to give metrical Illustrations of the prints with which Mr. ACKERMANN decorated the *Poetical Magazine,* a work published by him in *Monthly*

Numbers, for the reception of original compositions. . . . An Etching or a Drawing was accordingly sent to me every month, and I composed a certain proportion of pages in verse, in which, of course, the subject of the design was included: the rest depended upon what my imagination could furnish. — When the first print was sent to me, I did not know what would be the subject of the second; and in this manner, in a great measure, the Artist continued designing, and I continued writing, every month for two years, 'till a work, containing near ten thousand Lines was produced: the Artist and the Writer having no personal communication with, or knowledge of each other."

The popularity of the work was so great that several editions followed, and translations appeared in French and German.

"Numerous imitations, less legitimate than the foreign translations, . . . also appeared in this country [England], such as *The Tour of Doctor Syntax through London; Doctor Syntax in Paris, in Search of the Grotesque; Doctor Prosody; Sentimental Tour through Margate and Hastings by Doctor Comparative, Junr.*; and *Doctor Syntax's Life of Napoleon*, which is possibly due to Combe's pen, and derives a strong additional interest from the illustrations, which are fair examples of George Cruikshank's handiwork. A parody, in verse, entitled *The Adventures of Doctor Comicus, by a modern Syntax*, was also issued, with coloured imitations of Rowlandson's designs."

William Combe went to Eton, where he was the contemporary of Lord Lyttelton, Fox, and Beckford. Going from there to Oxford, he gave himself up to a life of dissipation and left without taking a degree. After some years spent in France and Italy, he returned to London and took up the profession of the law. His princely style of living won for him the sobriquet of "Count Combe." Later becoming embarrassed by debt, he is said to have been successively a common soldier, a waiter at Swansea, a teacher of elocution, a cook at Douai College, and a private in the French army. In 1771 he returned to London, where he engaged in authorship as a profession and became a voluminous writer. His works are for the most part now forgotten. As early as 1780 he had been obliged to live within the "rules" of the King's Bench or debtor's prison. Thus he lived for over forty years, and does not seem to have greatly cared to change his condition.

His best known works were written to illustrate the plates of Rowlandson the caricaturist. The first of these was *The Schoolmaster's Tour* (1812), which made the fortune of Ackermann's *New Poetical Magazine*. On its completion it was published in an independent volume as *The Tour of Doctor Syntax, in Search of the Picturesque* (our present number). This was followed in 1820 and 1822 by the *Second* and *Third Tours of Doctor Syntax* (our Nos. 521 and 522). Combe's practice was "regularly to pin up the sketch against a screen of his apartment in the King's Bench and write off his verses as the printer wanted them. . . . It is doubtful whether Syntax would ever have attained much popularity without Rowlandson." The success of Doctor Syntax led to a further collaboration between Rowlandson and Combe, resulting in *The Dance of Death* (our No. 518), *The Dance of Life* (our No. 520), and other works. In *The Dance of Death* are to be found some of the best specimens of Combe's versification.

ROWLANDSON, THOMAS, *illustrator.*   Englebach, Lewis.

NAPLES AND THE CAMPAGNA FELICE.   LONDON, *R. Ackermann*, 1815.

[517]

Royal octavo.

COLLATION BY SIGNATURES: [A], 2 leaves; B to Z, AA to ZZ, AAA to EEE, fff, each 4 leaves; ggg, 2 leaves; total 208 leaves.

COLLATION BY PAGINATION: [title]| NAPLES | AND THE | CAMPAGNA FELICE. | IN A | SERIES OF LETTERS, | ADDRESSED | TO A FRIEND IN ENGLAND, | IN 1802. | London : | PUBLISHED BY R. ACKERMANN, 101, STRAND. | 1815. |, p. [1]; —[imprint], p. [2]; —[preface], pp. [3]–4; —[text], pp. [1]–400; — [index], recto of fff to verso of ggg ; — [list of plates for the binder], recto of [ggg 2]; —[blank], verso of [ggg 2].

PLATES: 15 colored engravings, by Thomas Rowlandson; and 3 maps; as called for in the directions to the binder.

CONDITION: Size of leaf, 9⅞ × 6⅛ inches. Bound in publisher's brown cloth, gilt top, other edges uncut.

REFERENCE.

Grego, *Rowlandson the Caricaturist*, 2 (1880): 267, 301–308.

This work was first published as *Letters from Italy* in Ackermann's *Repository of Arts* from 1809 to 1815, and then issued in book form with the title given above.

ROWLANDSON, THOMAS, *illustrator.*   [Combe, William.]

THE ENGLISH DANCE OF DEATH.   LONDON, *R. Ackermann*, 1815–1816.

2 vols., royal octavo, viz.:

[518]

VOL. I. 1815.

COLLATION BY SIGNATURES: a, A to Z, AA to OO, each 4 leaves; [PP], 2 leaves; total 154 leaves.

COLLATION BY PAGINATION: [title]| THE | English Dance of Death, | FROM THE DESIGNS OF | THOMAS ROWLANDSON, | WITH | METRICAL ILLUSTRATIONS, | BY THE AUTHOR OF | "*DOCTOR SYNTAX.*" | [quotation] | VOL. I. | London : | PRINTED BY J. DIGGENS, ST. ANN'S LANE; | Published at R. ACKERMANN'S Repository of Arts, 101, Strand; | AND TO BE HAD OF | All the Book and Print-sellers in the United Kingdom. | 1815. |, p. [i.]; — [blank], p. [ii.]; —[advertisement], pp. [iii.]–vii.; —[blank], p. [viii.]; —[text, in verse], pp. [1]–295; —[imprint], p. [296]; —[index to plates], pp. [297]–[300].

PLATES: 36 colored plates, as called for in the index to plates ; also frontispiece and engraved title-page. The plates in this volume are dated, from April 1, 1814, to March 1, 1815. The engraved title-page, Vol. 1 only in this copy, has the imprint | LONDON, *Published March 1, 1816, by R. Ackermann, 101, Strand.* | .

No. 518   *Thomas Rowlandson*   1815–16

VOL. 2. 1816.

COLLATION BY SIGNATURES: 1 leaf, without signature-mark; A to Z, AA to PP, each 4 leaves; total 153 leaves.

COLLATION BY PAGINATION: [title, same as in Vol. 1, except volume-number and date of imprint], p. [i.];—[blank], p. [ii.];—[text, in verse], pp. [1]–299;—[blank], p. [300];—[index to plates], pp. [301]–[304].

PLATES: 36 colored plates, as called for in the index. The plates in this volume are dated from April 1, 1815, to March 1, 1816.

CONDITION: Size of leaf, 10⅛ × 6¼ inches. Bound in the original boards, uncut edges; with green paper title-labels, lettered: | THE | ENGLISH | DANCE | OF | Death. | 73 | *Coloured Engravings* | IN TWO VOLS. | VOL. I. [–II.] | *Price, in Boards*, | £3. 3s. |.

REFERENCES.

Slater, *Early Editions* (1894), p. 74, No. 5; Grego, *Rowlandson the Caricaturist*, 2 (1880): 317–355.

This series was begun in 1814 and finished in 1816, and was issued by Ackermann in twenty-four monthly parts with paper wrappers, uncut edges, like the *Tour of Doctor Syntax* and its successive works.

These are Rowlandson's famous series of illustrations on the *Dance of Death*, a subject which, in spite of its grimness, is quite suited to the artistic humor. It secured great praise during the designer's lifetime, and "in point of execution the set leaves nothing to be desired; in regard to picturesque action and easy grouping, the illustrations will bear comparison with any of the artist's works. As in the well-known series by Holbein, Della Bella, &c., Death appears at the most unexpected and inopportune moments, with that stern and ghastly reminder of the futility of human pleasures, successes, and pursuits, of which the most playful satirists have never been able to lose sight. . . .

"Both artist and author seem to have appreciated the resources of their subject so thoroughly, and have worked out its grotesque spirit with such appropriateness, that the *Dance of Death* must remain a fitting monument of their genius. A large circulation could hardly be anticipated for a work conceived in this realistically fearful vein. Rowlandson has drawn the various episodes which his invention suggested with a completeness of detail rarely found in his later designs. . . . Combe has worked with a vigour worthy of the occasion; and for wit, point, and felicity we are inclined to believe the versification to the *Dance of Death* surpasses all his other contributions to literature in this branch. The entire series may be accepted as a work of higher character, in all respects, than its popular predecessors, the better recognised *Tours of Doctor Syntax;* and it is superior, beyond comparison, to the works which followed it."

Under "The Miser's End," on p. 119, Vol. 2, occur these lines:

> "— If none form'd Libraries for show,
> Nor wish'd to make each Book a Beau;
> If Learning never was profuse,
> Nor e'er bought volumes but for use,
> Morocco, with its gawdy airs,
> Would be confin'd to Shoes and Chairs."

ROWLANDSON, THOMAS, *illustrator.* "Quiz," *pseudonym.*

THE GRAND MASTER OR ADVENTURES OF QUI HI? IN HINDOSTAN. LONDON, *Thomas Tegg*, 1816. [519]

Royal octavo.

COLLATION BY SIGNATURES : 1 leaf, without signature-mark ; A, 4 leaves ; B, 8 leaves ; C, 7 leaves ; D, E, each 8 leaves ; F, 9 leaves ; G to Q, each 8 leaves ; R, 4 leaves ; S, 2 leaves ; total 131 numbered leaves.

COLLATION BY PAGINATION : [engraved title] | The | GRAND MASTER | *or Adventures of* | QUI HI? | in | *HINDOSTAN.* | A | *Hudibrastic Poem* | *in* | Eight Cantos | *by* | QUIZ. | *Illustrated with Engravings* | by | ROWLANDSON. | London. | *Printed by Thomas Tegg,* | No. 111, Cheapside. | 1816. |, p. [i.] ; — [blank], p. [ii.] ; — [preface, in verse], pp. [iii.]–viii. ; — [invocation to Butler], pp. [ix.]–x. ; — [text, in verse], pp. [1]–252. A slip of errata, with heading | ERRATA. | [13 lines] | is inserted at the end. The numbers 31 and 32 are omitted and 73 and 74 are repeated in the pagination ; and p. 167 is wrongly numbered 16.

PLATES : 28 plates, engraved by Rowlandson, as follows :

[1] Folding plate, | A NEW MAP OF INDIA FROM THE LATEST AUTHORITY. | ; facing the title-page.

[2] Engraved title, as above ; p. [i.].

[3] | A SCENE IN THE CHANNEL. | ; facing p. 16.

[4] | THE MODERN IDOL JAGGERNAUT. | ; facing p. 46.

[5] | MISERIES OF THE FIRST OF THE MONTH. | ; facing p. 52.

[6] | THE BURNING SYSTEM ILLUSTRATED. | ; facing p. 54.

[7] | MISSIONARY INFLUENCE OR HOW TO MAKE CONVERTS. | ; facing p. 68.

[8] | AN EXTRAORDINARY ECLIPSE. | ; facing p. 72.

[9] | LABOUR IN VAIN OR HIS REVERENCE CONFOUNDED. | ; facing p. 82.

[10] | HINDOO PREJUDICES. | ; facing p. 92.

[11] | JOHN BULL CONVERTING THE INDIANS. | ; facing p. 124.

[12] | MORE INCANTATIONS OR A JOURNEY TO THE INTERIOR. | ; facing p. 128.

[13] | MISERIES IN INDIA. | ; facing p. 140.

[14] | THE BEAR & RAGGED STAFF. | ; facing p. 178.

[15] | HINDOO INCANTATIONS A VIEW IN ELEPHANTA. | ; facing p. 194.

[16] | PHANTASMAGORIA A VIEW IN ELEPHANTA. | ; facing p. 196.

[17] | THE MODERN PHAETON OR THE HUGELY IN DANGER. | ; facing p. 198.

[18] | QUI HI ARRIVES AT THE BUNDER-HEAD. | ; facing p. 206.

[19] | QUI HI IN THE BOMBAY TAVERN. | ; facing p. 208.

[20] | PAYS A NOCTURNAL VISIT TO DUNGAREE. | ; facing p. 214.

[21] | ATTENDS GENERAL KOIR WIGS LEVEE. | ; facing p. 220.

[22] | QUI HI'S INTRODUCTION & COOL RECEPTION. | ; facing p. 224.

[23] | QUI HI SHEWS OFF AT THE BOBBERY HUNT. | ; facing p. 228.

[24] | QUI HI AT BOBBERY HALL. | ; facing p. 230.

[25] | ALL ALIVE IN THE CHOKEE. | ; facing p. 236.

[26] | LAST VISIT FROM THE DOCTORS ASSISTANT. | ; facing p. 242.

[27] | QUI HI'S LAST MARCH TO PADREE BURROWS'S GO DOWN. | ; facing p. 250.

[28] | *STRANGE FIGURES NEAR THE CAVE OF ELEPHANTA*—1814. | ; facing p. 252.

Each plate bears the publisher's imprint, | London, Published by T. Tegg. No. 111, Cheapside, Oct. 1 [– Nov. 1] *1815*. | .

CONDITION : Size of leaf, 10 × 6⅛ inches. Bound in boards, uncut edges.

REFERENCE.

Grego, *Rowlandson the Caricaturist*, 2 (1880) : 299–301.

The object of this work seems to have been to hold up the Governor-General, the Marquis of Hastings, to opprobrium, but whether justly or not the present generation is in no position to judge.

ROWLANDSON, THOMAS, *illustrator*. [Combe, William.]

THE DANCE OF LIFE. LONDON, *R. Ackermann*, 1817. [520]

Royal octavo.

COLLATION BY SIGNATURES: 2 leaves, without signature-marks; a, 2 leaves; A to z, AA to NN, each 4 leaves (the last blank and lacking); total 148 leaves.

COLLATION BY PAGINATION: [title] | THE | Dance of Life, | A POEM, | BY THE AUTHOR OF | " *DOCTOR SYNTAX*; " | ILLUSTRATED WITH | COLOURED ENGRAVINGS, | BY | THOMAS ROWLANDSON. | [quotation] | London: | PUBLISHED BY R. ACKERMANN, | REPOSITORY OF ARTS, 101, STRAND. | 1817. |, recto of first leaf; — [blank], verso of first leaf; — [publisher's advertisement], recto of second leaf; — [blank], verso of second leaf; — [author's advertisement],

pp. [i.] – ii.; — [index to plates], pp. [i.] – ii.; — [text, in verse], pp. [1] – 285; — [blank], p. [286]; — [1 blank leaf], [NN 4].

PLATES: 26 colored plates, including frontispiece and engraved title; as called for in the index to plates.

CONDITION: Size of leaf, 9¹¹⁄₁₆ × 6³⁄₁₆ inches. Bound in publisher's brown cloth, gilt top, other edges uncut.

REFERENCES.

Slater, *Early Editions* (1894), p. 74, No. 6; Lowndes, 5 (1869): 2564; Grego, *Rowlandson the Caricaturist*, 2 (1880): 359 – 361.

This work was first published in eight monthly parts, in paper wrappers, uncut edges, after which it was "presented to the Public in an accumulated Volume," in which form Slater says it was published in boards.

In the frontispiece, a panoramic scroll giving the other illustrations in miniature, "Father Time, with his accessories of scythe, hourglass, and globe, is acting as showman and pointing out the subjects of the work to a group of spectators, whose faces and attitudes are expressive of the admiration and interest which the pictorial history is exciting.

ROWLANDSON, THOMAS, *illustrator*. [Combe, William.]

THE SECOND TOUR OF DOCTOR SYNTAX, IN SEARCH OF CONSOLATION. LONDON, *R. Ackermann*, 1820. [521]

Octavo.

COLLATION BY SIGNATURES: [A], 2 leaves; B to Z, Aa to Nn, each 4 leaves; total 142 leaves.

COLLATION BY PAGINATION: [title] | THE | SECOND TOUR | OF | DOCTOR SYNTAX, | In Search of Consolation; | A POEM. | VOLUME SECOND. | [quotation] | PUBLISHED BY R. ACKERMANN, | AT THE REPOSITORY OF ARTS, 101, STRAND, LONDON: | AND TO BE HAD OF ALL THE BOOKSELLERS IN THE | UNITED KINGDOM. | 1820. |, recto of [A]; — [imprint], verso of [A]; — [introduction], recto and verso of [A 2]; — [text, cantos 27-33], pp. [1] – 277; — [blank], p. [278]; — | *Directions to the Binder for placing the Plates.* |, p. [279]; — [blank], p. [280].

PLATES: 24 aquatint engravings, by Rowlandson, as called for in the directions to the binder.

CONDITION: Size of leaf, 8⅞ x 5⅝ inches. Bound in light polished calf, yellow edges; by Tout.

REFERENCES.

Slater, *Early Editions* (1894), p. 72, No. 2; Lowndes, *Bibliographer's Manual*, 5 (1869) : 2564; Grego, *Rowlandson the Caricaturist*, 2 (1880) : 250.

The words "VOLUME SECOND" on the title-page and the numbering of the cantos show that it was the publisher's plan to connect the Second Tour with the first (our No. 516), but the volume-number was dropped in the Third Tour (our next number), though the cantos were still numbered continuously.

This part of Doctor Syntax's Tour was issued in eight monthly parts, with paper wrappers, uncut edges, and when completed, in 1820, was published in book form, uniform with the first volume.

In order to give Doctor Syntax an opportunity to continue his eccentric tours, his termagant wife, who figures in the First Tour, is decently buried in the first canto of the present work, and he proceeds to new adventures.

ROWLANDSON, THOMAS, *illustrator.* **[Combe, William.]**

THE THIRD TOUR OF DOCTOR SYNTAX, IN SEARCH OF A WIFE. LONDON, *R. Ackermann*, [1822]. [522]

Octavo.

COLLATION BY SIGNATURES: [A], 2 leaves; B to Z, Aa to Nn, each 4 leaves; total 142 leaves.

COLLATION BY PAGINATION: [engraved title, verso blank, inserted as a plate] | THE | THIRD TOUR | OF | DOCTOR SYNTAX, | In Search of a Wife, | A POEM. | [aquatint vignette] | [quotation] | LONDON. | *Published at R.* ACKERMANN'S *REPOSITORY of ARTS, 101, Strand.* | ; — [preface], recto of [A]; — [imprint], verso of [A]; — | *Directions to the Binder for placing the Plates.* |, recto of [A 2]; — [blank], verso of [A 2]; — [text, cantos 34–38], pp. [1]–279; — [blank], p. [280].

PLATES: 24 aquatint engravings, by Rowlandson, as called for in the directions to the binder; also 2 vignettes, on the title-page and p. 279 respectively.

CONDITION: Size of leaf, 8¹³⁄₁₆ x 5⁹⁄₁₆ inches. Bound in light polished calf, yellow edges; by Tout.

REFERENCES.

Slater, *Early Editions* (1894), p. 72; Grego, *Rowlandson the Caricaturist*, 2 (1880) : 250–252; Lowndes, 5 (1869) : 2564.

The Third and final Tour was originally issued in eight monthly parts, with paper wrappers, uncut edges, and when completed it was published in collected form, in 1822. This tour ends with the death and burial of the hero. Its popularity, like that of the Second Tour, was sufficient to carry it through several editions, though neither was as successful as the First of the series. The illustrations are quite equal in spirit, invention, and execution to those in the First and Second Tours. In 1823 Ackermann issued a "miniature edition" of the three series in sixteenmo, instead of royal octavo, for which the plates were reëngraved one third of the original size.

ROWLANDSON, THOMAS, *illustrator.*

JOURNAL OF SENTIMENTAL TRAVELS IN THE SOUTHERN PROVINCES OF FRANCE. London, *R. Ackermann*, 1821. [523]

Octavo.

COLLATION BY SIGNATURES: 2 leaves, without signature-marks; B to Z, Aa to Oo, each 4 leaves; Pp, 2 leaves; total 148 leaves.

COLLATION BY PAGINATION: [title] | JOURNAL | OF | Sentimental Travels | IN THE | SOUTHERN PROVINCES | OF | FRANCE, | *SHORTLY BEFORE THE REVOLUTION*; | EMBELLISHED WITH | SEVENTEEN COLOURED ENGRAVINGS, | FROM DESIGNS BY | T. ROWLANDSON, ESQ. | [quotation] | *LONDON:* | PUBLISHED BY R. ACKERMANN, 101, STRAND; | AND MAY BE HAD | OF ALL THE BOOKSELLERS IN THE UNITED KINGDOM. | 1821. |, recto of first leaf; — [imprint], verso of first leaf; — | ADDRESS. |, pp. [i.]–ii.; — [text], pp. [1]–291; — [directions to the binder], p. [292].

PLATES: 18 colored plates, designed by Rowlandson, as called for in the directions to the binder.

CONDITION: Size of leaf, 9⅝ × 6³⁄₁₆ inches. Bound in half brown crushed levant morocco, gilt top, other edges uncut. Many leaves uncut on lower edges, several plates mounted on guards; the leaves about ¼ inch taller than the plates.

REFERENCE.

Grego, *Rowlandson the Caricaturist*, 2 (1880): 368–370.

" ' We travellers are in very hard circumstances. If we say nothing but what has been said before us, we are dull, and have observed nothing. If we tell any thing new, we are laughed at as fabulous and romantic.' *Lady M. W. Montagu's Letters.*"
— *Quotation on the title-page.*

ROWLANDSON, THOMAS, *illustrator.* [Combe, William.]

THE HISTORY OF JOHNNY QUÆ GENUS. London, *R. Ackermann*, 1822. [524]

Octavo.

COLLATION BY SIGNATURES: [A], 2 leaves; B to Z, Aa to Ll, each 4 leaves; Mm, 2 leaves; total 136 leaves.

COLLATION BY PAGINATION: [title] | THE | HISTORY | OF | JOHNNY QUÆ GENUS, | THE | LITTLE FOUNDLING | OF THE LATE | DOCTOR SYNTAX: | A Poem, | BY THE AUTHOR OF THE THREE TOURS. | [quotation] | *LONDON:* | PUBLISHED BY R. ACKERMANN, | AT THE REPOSITORY OF ARTS, 101, STRAND, LONDON: | AND TO BE HAD OF ALL THE BOOKSELLERS IN THE | UNITED KINGDOM. | 1822. |, recto of [A]; — [imprint], verso of [A]; — [introduction], recto and verso of [A 2]; — [text], pp. [1]–267; — | *Directions to the Binder for placing the Plates.* |, p. [268]. The numbers 249–256 are repeated and 257–264 are omitted in the pagination.

PLATES: 24 aquatint engravings, by Rowlandson, as called for in the directions to the binder.

CONDITION: Size of leaf, 9⅛ × 5⅝ inches. Bound in light polished calf, gilt top; by Rivière.

REFERENCES.

Slater, *Early Editions* (1894), p. 75, No. 7; Lowndes, *Bibliographer's Manual*, 5 (1869): 2564; Grego, *Rowlandson the Caricaturist*, 2 (1880): 371–373.

This work was originally published in boards.

The introduction gives the following account of its origin:

"THE Favour which has been bestowed on the different TOURS OF DOCTOR SYNTAX, has encouraged the Writer of them to give a HISTORY OF THE FOUNDLING, who has been thought an interesting Object in the latter of those Volumes; and it is written in the same style and manner, with a view to connect it with them. . . .

"The Idea of an English GIL BLAS predominated through the whole of this Volume; which must be considered as fortunate in no common degree, if its readers, in the course of their perusal, should be disposed to acknowledge even a remote Similitude to the incomparable Work of Le Sage."

ROWLANDSON, THOMAS, *imitated.* Combe, William, *imitated.*

DR. SYNTAX IN PARIS. LONDON, *for W. Wright,* 1820. [525]

Octavo.

COLLATION BY SIGNATURES: a, B to Z, 2A to 2S, each 4 leaves (the last blank and lacking); total 164 numbered leaves.

COLLATION BY PAGINATION: [engraved title] | DOCTOR SYNTAX | IN | Paris | OR A | TOUR | *in search of the* | GROTESQUE [in colored vignette] | *A HUMOROUS & SATIRICAL POEM.* | [quotations] | LONDON: *Printed for W. WRIGHT, 46, Fleet Street, 1820.* |, p. [i.]; —[blank], p. [ii.]; —| ADVERTISEMENT, EPISODE, AND FINALE. | TRIA JUNCTA IN UNO. |, pp. [iii.]–viii.; —[text, in verse], pp. [1]–318; —[1 blank leaf], [2s4].

PLATES: 17 aquatint engravings, including that on the title-page, 6 of which are signed | *Williams del. et fc.* |, as follows:

[1] | DOCTOR SYNTAX | *READING HIS TOUR* |; facing the title-page.

[2] Engraved title-page, with colored vignette.

[3] | DOCTOR SYNTAX | *EMBARKING AT DOVER* |; facing p. [1].

[4] | DOCTOR SYNTAX | *LANDING AT CALAIS* |; facing p. 14.

[5] | DOCTOR SYNTAX | *ON THE ROAD TO PARIS* |; facing p. 45.

[6] | DOCTOR SYNTAX | *ARRIVES AT PARIS* |; facing p. 56.

[7] | DOCTOR SYNTAX | *AT THE DECROTEURS OR SHOE-BLACK'S* |; facing p. 61.

[8] | DOCTOR SYNTAX | *AND THE FEMALE TONSOR* |; facing p. 84.

[9] | DOCTOR SYNTAX | *AT THE OPERA* |; facing p. 112.

[10] | DOCTOR SYNTAX | *LOOKING AT LODGINGS* |; facing p. 128.

[11] | DOCTOR SYNTAX | *CHATTING WITH THE BAR MAID—CAFÉ DES MILLE COLONNES* |; facing p. 137.

[12] | DOCTOR SYNTAX | *CONDUCTED TO THE PREFECTURE ON A CHARGE OF LIBERALISM* |; facing p. 183.

[13] | DOCTOR SYNTAX | *PRODUCING HIS CERTIFICATE OF MARRIAGE TO HIS HOSTESS* |; facing p. 207.

[14] | DOCTOR SYNTAX | *AND HIS WIFE DESCENDING THE RUSSIAN MOUNTAINS* |; facing p. 210.

[15] | DOCTOR SYNTAX | *ALARMED BY A DOMICILIARY VISIT* |; facing p. 262.

[16] | DOCTOR SYNTAX | *AND HIS WIFE INSPECTING THE CATACOMBS* |; facing p. 309.

[17] | DOCTOR SYNTAX | *AND HIS WIFE MAKING AN EXPERIMENT IN PNEUMATICS* |; facing p. 312.

CONDITION: Size of leaf, $8^{15}/_{16} \times 5^{11}/_{16}$ inches. Bound in half brown crushed levant morocco, gilt top. Plate [14] is closely clipped on the outer margin and the inscription is cut into.

REFERENCES.

Slater, *Early Editions* (1894), p. 75; Grego, *Rowlandson the Caricaturist*, 2 (1880): 249.

This work is written and illustrated in imitation of the style of Doctor Syntax's Tours by William Combe and Thomas Rowlandson. Despite this fact, it is of importance, and difficult to procure.

ROWLANDSON, THOMAS, *imitated*. Combe, William, *imitated*.

THE TOUR OF DOCTOR SYNTAX THROUGH LONDON. London, J. *Johnston*, 1820. [526]

Royal octavo.

COLLATION BY SIGNATURES: 1 leaf, without signature-mark; [A], 2 leaves; B to Z, AA to SS, each 4 leaves; total 163 leaves.

COLLATION BY PAGINATION: [engraved title] | *THE TOUR | of |* DOCTOR SYNTAX | *THROUGH LONDON, | or the | Pleasures and Miseries | of the |* Metropolis. | *A Poem |* [vignette] | By | DOCTOR | SYNTAX | London | *Published by J. JOHNSTON, Cheapside |* 1820. |, p. [i.]; — [blank], p. [ii.]; — [preface and list of plates], pp. [iii.]–[v.]; — [blank], p. [vi.]; — [text, in verse], pp. [1]–319; — [blank], p. [320].

PLATES: 19 aquatint engravings, as called for in the list of plates.

CONDITION: Size of leaf, 10 × 6¼ inches. In the 8 original parts, as published, in gray paper wrappers, with title:

| PART I. [– VIII.] PRICE 2s. 6d. | DOCTOR SYNTAX | IN | LONDON; | OR, THE | Pleasures and Miseries | OF THE | METROPOLIS. | A Poem. | BY DOCTOR SYNTAX. | TO THE PUBLIC. | [8 lines] | LONDON: | PUBLISHED BY J. JOHNSTON, CHEAPSIDE; | SHERWOOD, NEELY AND JONES, PATERNOSTER ROW; SIMPKIN AND | MARSHALL, STATIONER'S COURT; AND WILLIAM CLARKE, ROYAL | EXCHANGE; R. MILLIKIN, DUBLIN; AND SOLD BY ALL BOOKSELLERS. | W. Shackell, Printer, Johnson's-court, Fleet-street, London. |; enclosed by a fret border. Parts I. and III. are of the "Second Edition." There is an advertising slip in each of Parts II. and V.

REFERENCE.

Slater, *Early Editions* (1894), p. 75.

The work is written and illustrated in imitation of Doctor Syntax's Tours.

ROWLANDSON, THOMAS, *imitated*. Combe, William, *imitated*.

THE TOUR OF DOCTOR PROSODY, IN SEARCH OF THE ANTIQUE AND PICTURESQUE. London, *Matthew Iley, etc.*, 1821. [527]

Royal octavo.

COLLATION BY SIGNATURES: [A], 2 leaves; B to Z, 2 A to 2 I, each 4 leaves; 2 K, 2 leaves; total 128 leaves. Leaf 1 is wrongly marked H; and Y is X.

COLLATION BY PAGINATION: [title] | THE | TOUR | OF | DOCTOR PROSODY, | IN SEARCH OF | The Antique and Picturesque, | THROUGH | SCOTLAND, THE HEBRIDES, THE ORKNEY AND

SHETLAND ISLES; | ILLUSTRATED BY TWENTY HUMOUROUS PLATES. | [quotation] | LONDON: MATTHEW ILEY, SOMERSET STREET. | EDINBURGH: BELL AND BRADFUTE, AND W. BLACKWOOD. | GLASGOW: W. TURNBULL. | MDCCCXXI. |, recto of [A]; —[imprint], verso of [A]; —| ADVERTISEMENT TO THE READER. |, recto of [A 2]; —[blank], verso of [A 2]; —[text, in verse], pp. [1]- 243; —[blank], p. [244]; —[notes], pp. [245]-251; —[blank], p. [252].

PLATES: 20 colored engravings, as follows:

[1] | *D:* *Prosody arrives in the Vicinity of Edinburgh.* |; facing the title-page.

[2] | DOCTOR PROSODY | *ENTERTAINED AFTER THE MANNER OF THE ANCIENTS* |; facing p. 44.

[3] | DOCTOR PROSODY | *DISCOVERS A CURIOUS RELIC OF ANTIQUITY* |; facing p. 59.

[4] | DOCTOR PROSODY | *VISITS THE SCOTTISH REGALIA* |; facing p. 77.

[5] | DOCTOR PROSODY | *TRIES HIS FRIENDS AT THE FALLS OF CLYDE* |; facing p. 89.

[6] | DOCTOR PROSODY | *DOING PENNANCE ON DRUNKEN ISLAND—LOCH LOMMOND* |; facing p. 102.

[7] | DOCTOR PROSODY | *PARADING ON LOCHLEVEN, IS CHALLENGED TO NAME HIS CHIEF* |; facing p. 109.

[8] | DOCTOR PROSODY | *TAKEN FOR A POACHER IN THE NEIGHBOURHOOD OF STIRLING* |; facing p. 113.

[9] | DOCTOR PROSODY'S | *DISASTER IN OSSIAN'S HALL, DUNKELD* |; facing p. 120.

[10] | DOCTOR PROSODY | *REPROVES THE AUDACITY OF A HIGHLAND HOST* |; facing p. 136.

[11] | DOCTOR PROSODY | *IN PERIL AT CORRYVRECKAN.* |; facing p. 150.

[12] | DOCTOR PROSODY | *VISITS A CHIEFTAIN OF THE ISLE OF MULL* |; facing p. 153.

[13] | DOCTOR PROSODY | *CLEARS UP THE ANTIQUITIES OF JONA* [corrected in ink to *IONA*] |; facing p. 163.

[14] | DOCTOR PROSODY | *PROVES THE INCONVENIENCE OF A TIMID COMPANION AT STAFFA.* |; facing p. 171.

[15] | DOCTOR PROSODY | *FISHING FOR PEARLS IN THE ISLE OF SKY.* |; facing p. 188.

[16] | DOCTOR FACTOBEND'S | *RECANTATION IN THE BIRD BASKET, S.T KILDD.* |; facing p. 203.

[17] | DOCTOR PROSODY | *MEETS A HIGHLAND WEDDING ON THE CALIDONION CANAL.* |; facing p. 206.

[18] | DOCTOR PROSODY | *ATTACKED BY SOLAND FOWL, IN THE ORKNEYS.* |; facing p. 226.

[19] | DOCTOR PROSODY | *AND THE SMUGLERS IN THE SHETLANDS* |; facing p. 234.

[20] | DOCTOR PROSODY | *CORRECTING HIS PROOF IN A PRINTING OFFICE.* |; facing p. 242.

Plate [1] is unsigned; plates [2]-[10], [12], and [13] are drawn and engraved by C. Williams; plates [11] and [14]-[20] are drawn and engraved by W. Read; all except the frontispiece bear the imprint | *Publish'd by M. Iley, 1, Somerset Str.t Portman Square.* | .

CONDITION: Size of leaf, 10⅛ x 6½ inches. Bound in boards, uncut edges.

REFERENCE.

Slater, *Early Editions* (1894), p. 75.

This work is written and illustrated in imitation of Doctor Syntax's Tours.
Dr. Paul Prosody, D.D., announces the object of his journey (p. 5), as follows:

> "Patron and counsellors, I've come
> To a resolve to leave my home;
> My purpose is to travel North,
> And glean whatever may be worth
> The notice and the approbation
> Of all the sçavans of the nation."

ROWLANDSON, THOMAS, *imitated.* [Egan, Pierce.] (*b.* 1772, *d.* 1849.)

REAL LIFE IN LONDON. London, *for Jones & Co.*, 1821. 2 vols., octavo, viz.:

[528]

VOL. 1.

COLLATION BY SIGNATURES: [A], 4 leaves; b, 4 leaves (inserted between A and A 2); B to Z, 2 A to 2 Z, 3 A to 3 Z, 4 A to 4 N, each 4 leaves; total 332 numbered leaves.

COLLATION BY PAGINATION: [title] | REAL | LIFE IN LONDON; | OR, THE | RAMBLES AND ADVENTURES | OF | BOB TALLYHO, ESQ. | AND HIS COUSIN, | THE HON. TOM DASHALL, | THROUGH THE | METROPOLIS; | EXHIBITING A LIVING PICTURE OF FASHIONABLE | CHARACTERS, MANNERS, AND AMUSEMENTS | IN | HIGH AND LOW LIFE. | BY AN AMATEUR. | [vignette] | EMBELLISHED AND ILLUSTRATED | With a Series of Coloured Prints, | DESIGNED AND ENGRAVED BY MESSRS. ALKEN, DIGHTON, | BROOKE, ROWLANDSON, &c. | London: | PRINTED FOR JONES & CO. | OXFORD ARMS PASSAGE, WARWICK LANE. | 1821. |, p. [1]; — [imprint], p. [2]; — [contents], pp. [iii.]–x.; — | *Directions to the Binder.* |, p. x.; — [text], pp. [3]–656.

PLATES: 19 colored plates, including frontispiece and engraved title; as called for in the directions to the binder.

Inserted, as an extra-illustration, is | TOM & BOB *Catching a Charley Napping.* | *London Pub.^d by Jones & Co May 21st 1822.* |; facing p. 230.

VOL. 2.

COLLATION BY SIGNATURES: [A], 4 leaves; b, 4 leaves (inserted between A and A 2); B to Z, 2 A to 2 Z, 3 A to 3 Z, 4 A to 4 O, each 4 leaves; 4 P, 2 leaves; 1 leaf, without signature-mark; total 339 leaves. Leaf Q has no signature-mark.

COLLATION BY PAGINATION: [title, similar to that in Vol. 1, but without vignette and date], p. [1]; — [blank], p. [2]; — [contents], pp. [i.]–viii.; — [text], pp. [3]–[668]; — [remainder of contents], p. [ix.]; — | *Directions to the Binder* |, p. [ix.]; — [advertisement of books], p. [x.].

PLATES: 13 colored plates, including frontispiece and engraved title; as called for in the directions to the binder.

Inserted, as an extra-illustration, is a colored engraving, | St GEORGE'S DAY, PRESENTATION AT THE LEVEE. |; facing p. 421.

CONDITION: Size of leaf, 8½ × 5⁷⁄₁₆ inches. Bound in half brown crushed levant morocco, gilt tops.

REFERENCE.

Slater, *Early Editions* (1894), p. 118, No. 3.

Slater says: "It is very doubtful whether this work, which is clearly an imitation of the 'Life in London,' was written by Egan, but as it is . . . usually attributed to him, I have included it in the list." It was originally issued in parts, in pink pictorial wrappers, and on completion was published in book form in pictorial boards. A few copies were printed on large paper. The plates, some of which are by Alken and some by Read, are after the style of Rowlandson. Later editions appeared in 1822–1823, and in 1829–1830.

1828 *Sir Charles D'Oyly* No. 529

ROWLANDSON, THOMAS, *imitated.* [D'OYLY, SIR CHARLES.] (*b.* 1781, *d.* 1845.)

TOM RAW, THE GRIFFIN. LONDON, *for R. Ackermann,* 1828.   [529]

Octavo.

COLLATION BY SIGNATURES: [a], 2 leaves; b, 4 leaves; B to Y, each 8 leaves; total 174 leaves. Leaf E has no signature-mark.

COLLATION BY PAGINATION: [half-title], recto of [a]; — [imprint], verso of [a]; — [title] | TOM RAW, THE GRIFFIN: | A BURLESQUE POEM, | IN TWELVE CANTOS: | ILLUSTRATED BY | TWENTY-FIVE ENGRAVINGS, | DESCRIPTIVE OF | THE ADVENTURES OF A CADET | IN THE EAST INDIA COMPANY'S SERVICE, | FROM THE PERIOD OF HIS QUITTING ENGLAND TO HIS OBTAINING | A STAFF SITUATION IN INDIA. | BY A CIVILIAN AND AN OFFICER | ON THE BENGAL ESTABLISHMENT. | LONDON: | PRINTED FOR R. ACKERMANN, | 96, STRAND. | M.DCCC.XXVIII. |, p. [i.]; — [blank], p. [ii.]; — [preface and index to the plates], pp. [iii.]-[ix.]; — [blank], p. [x.]; — [text in 12 cantos], pp. [1]-325; — [blank], p. [326]; — [publisher's advertisements], pp. [1]-[10].

PLATES: 25 engravings, colored by hand, as called for in the list of plates. The plate facing p. 254 should face p. 256.

CONDITION: Size of leaf, 9⅝ x 6 inches. Bound in half calf, gilt top.

REFERENCE.

Dictionary of National Biography, 15 (1888): 418.

Though this burlesque poem was published anonymously, it was written by Sir Charles D'Oyly, seventh baronet, an East-Indian civilian and artist. The plates and text are descriptive of the adventures of a cadet in the East India Company's service, and are more meritorious from an artistic than a literary point of view.

The whole is in the style of the Rowlandson and Combe works.

[SCOTT, *Sir* WALTER.] (*b.* 1771, *d.* 1832.)

WAVERLEY; OR, 'TIS SIXTY YEARS SINCE. EDINBURGH, *by James Ballantyne and Co. for Archibald Constable and Co., etc.,* 1814. 3 vols., duodecimo, viz.:   [530]

VOL. 1.

COLLATION BY SIGNATURES: 2 leaves, without signature-marks; [A] to P, each 12 leaves; total 182 leaves.

COLLATION BY PAGINATION: [half-title], p. [i.]; — [blank], p. [ii.]; — [title, as reproduced; *See* No. 530], p. [iii.]; — [blank], p. [iv.]; — [half-title], p. [1]; — [blank], p. [2]; — [text in 23 chapters], pp. [3]-358; — [imprint] | EDINBURGH: | Printed by James Ballantyne & Co. |, p. [359]; — [blank], p. [360].

VOL. 2.

COLLATION BY SIGNATURES: 2 leaves, without signature-marks; A to P, each 12 leaves; Q, 6 leaves; total 188 leaves.

COLLATION BY PAGINATION: [half-title], p. [i.]; — [blank], p. [ii.]; — [title, same as in Vol. 1, except volume-number],

No. 530   Sir Walter Scott   1814

p.[iii.];—[blank], p.[iv.];—[half-title], p.[1];—[blank], p.[2];—[text in 24 chapters], pp.[3]-370;—[imprint, same as in Vol. 1], p.[371];—[blank], p.[372].

VOL. 3.

COLLATION BY SIGNATURES: 2 leaves, without signature-marks; A to P, each 12 leaves; Q, 6 leaves; total 188 leaves.

COLLATION BY PAGINATION: [half-title], p.[i.];—[blank], p.[ii.];—[title, same as in Vol. 1, except volume-number], p.[iii.];—[blank], p.[iv.];—[half-title], p.[1];—[blank], p.[2];—[text in 24 chapters], pp.[3]-371;—[dedication]| THESE VOLUMES | BEING RESPECTFULLY INSCRIBED | TO | OUR SCOTTISH ADDISON, | HENRY MACKENZIE, | BY | AN UNKNOWN ADMIRER | OF | HIS GENIUS.|, p. 371;—[imprint, same as in Vol. 1], p. 371;—[blank], p.[372].

CONDITION: Size of leaf, 7½ × 4½ inches. Bound in the original boards, dark drab backs, gray sides, with paper title-labels lettered: | WAVERLEY; | OR, | 'Tis Sixty Years Since.| VOL. 1. [– III.] | ; edges uncut; in green crushed levant morocco solander cases.

REFERENCES.

Locker-Lampson, *Appendix to Catalogue* (1900), p. 86; Lockhart, *Life of Scott*, 4 (Second Edition; 1839): 394-396; also 10:272. See also Allibone, *Critical Dictionary of English Literature*, 2 (1881): 1971-1974, and Lowndes, *Bibliographer's Manual*, 4 (1869): 2224-2227, for complete lists of Scott's works in prose and verse.

This, the First Edition of the romance which gave its name to the long series which followed it, was published July 7, 1814.

The original leaf containing pp. 7 and 8 of Vol. 1 appears to have been cancelled and is replaced by another tipped to the stub of the original leaf.

Vol. 1 ends with the chapter entitled | *Waverley continues at Glennaquoich.*| ; Vol. 2, with that entitled | *The Conflict.*| ; and Vol. 3, with | *A Postscript, which should have been a Preface.*|, the latter closing with the dedication as given above. Vol. 2, p. 136, line 1, second word is "our" instead of "your."

The First Edition consisted of 1000 copies. So great was its popularity that three more editions were called for before the end of the year. The First Edition was sold within five weeks; the Second Edition, of 2000 copies, appeared before the end of August; the Third Edition, of 1000 copies, was published in October; and a Fourth, of a like number, appeared in November. These were followed by the Fifth Edition, of 1000 copies, January, 1815; the Sixth Edition, of 1500 copies, June, 1816; the Seventh Edition, of 2000 copies, October, 1817; and the Eighth Edition, of 2000 copies, April, 1821. Fragments of the original manuscript of *Waverley* are now in the library of Mr. J. Pierpont Morgan.

We are indebted to the courtesy of Mr. P. A. Valentine and of Mr. F. R. Halsey, both of New York City, for the privilege of collating their sets of the Waverley Novels, both being bound in the original boards, as issued.

For brief historical synopses of the novels which follow we are indebted to the *Class List of English Prose Fiction*, Sixth Edition, April, 1877, prepared for the Boston Public Library under the editorship of its librarian and superintendent, Dr. Justin Winsor.

This picture of the life and manners of Scotland (1745) at the time when the old feudal feeling and the Covenanters' fanaticism had not wholly died out, though their equivalents had long since disappeared in the southern country, accompanies the historical events of the rebellion of the Chevalier Charles Edward, the battle of Prestonpans, the "race to Derby," and the Pretender's court in Holyrood Castle, Edinburgh.

Sir Walter Scott, a descendant of an old border family, was the son of a writer to the Signet, of Edinburgh. Owing to an illness, he was sent at an early age to live with his grandfather. He there recovered his health, but was left with a permanent lameness. From his grandmother, the neighboring old women, and others he learned many songs and legends of the old moss-troopers and of his border ancestors. After being taken to Bath for a year to try the waters for his lameness, he returned to his father's house in Edinburgh, in 1778. Soon after this he was sent to the high school, but failed to distinguish himself there as a scholar, though he became a fair Latinist and won praise for his poetical renderings of Horace and Virgil. Among his schoolmates he gained a great reputation for his out-of-the-way information and talent as a storyteller. In 1783 he began attending classes at college. He learned enough Italian to read Tasso and Ariosto in the original, acquired some Spanish, and read through several old French romances.

In 1786 he was apprenticed to his father as a writer to the Signet, and was called to the bar in 1792. His ample leisure was employed in scouring the country in search of ballads and other relics of antiquity. In December, 1799, he was appointed sheriff-deputy of Selkirkshire, and in 1806 obtained a reversion of the office of clerk of sessions, but did not enter into the full enjoyment of its salary until after the death of the incumbent, Mr. Home, in 1812. Though the duties of the latter position demanded three or four hours of fatiguing labor daily during six out of the twelve months that the court was in session, yet much leisure for literary pursuits was left to him.

His first publication, a metrical translation, or rather, imitation, of two ballads by Bürger, "The Chase" and "William and Helen," appeared in a small volume in October, 1796. This was followed three years later by a translation of Goethe's *Götz von Berlichingen*. Scott's first original poems, "Glenfinlas," "The Eve of St. John," and "The Gray Brother," were published in Lewis's *Tales of Wonder* in 1801. These Scott justly calls his "first serious attempts in verse." His next important undertaking was the publication of his collection of ballads entitled *Minstrelsy of the Scottish Border*, the first two volumes of which appeared in 1802, the third and last in 1803. A little later Scott wrote many reviews, mostly of poetical publications, and did much editorial work; but his critical articles, labors in biography, and annotations he looked upon as merely a relaxation from original composition.

The first of his long poems, *The Lay of the Last Minstrel*, begun in 1803, was not published until January, 1805. Much to the author's astonishment, it became widely popular, and its success decided for him that literature was thenceforth to be the main calling of his life.

Soon after the appearance of this poem he began a prose romance, *Waverley*, which being unfavorably criticised by a friend, was laid aside and was not completed until several years later. It was at about this time also that Scott associated himself with Ballantyne, an old schoolmate, as silent partner in the publishing business — a business connection which, owing to Ballantyne's mismanagement, caused him much anxiety and trouble, especially in 1813, and again in 1826 when it resulted in his financial ruin.

In 1808 *Marmion* appeared. In the composition of this poem Scott had taken unusual care, having kept it in his hands about a year and a half before giving it to the printer. Its triumphant success at once placed its author at the head of living poets. In 1810 he published *The Lady of the Lake*. This was followed in 1811 by *The Vision of Don Roderick*; by *Rokeby* in 1812; *The Bridal of Triermain* in 1813; and *The Lord of the Isles* in 1815. These poems, abounding in delightful descriptions of local scenes and stirring accounts of the principal events of Scottish history, were extremely popular, and the appearance of each new poem from Scott's pen was an event to which his readers looked forward with ever increasing eagerness.

In 1813 the popularity of Scott's poetry had somewhat declined, owing to the appearance of several poems by his younger rival Lord Byron. Scott thereupon, having accidentally come across the manuscript of the romance which he had written and laid aside several years before, took it up and completed it in four weeks in the summer of 1814. This work, *Waverley* (our present number), a story illustrative of Scottish life and character, was published anonymously in July, 1814, during the same week as his edition of Swift's *Works* in nineteen volumes. It met with instant favor, and several editions were called for within a few months. Scott lost no time in taking advantage of its success, and at once began work upon *Guy Mannering* (our next number), which also appeared anonymously the following year. None of Scott's intimate friends ever had the slightest doubt of his being the author of *Waverley*, and Jeffrey, the editor of the *Edinburgh Review*, who had known him from his youth, was at no pains to conceal his conviction of its authorship.

His third story, *The Antiquary* (our No. 532), appeared in 1816. From this time on romance followed romance in rapid succession, among the most important being *The Heart of Midlothian* (in our No. 535), in 1818; *The Bride of Lammermoor* (in our No. 536), in 1819; *Ivanhoe* (our No. 538), in 1820; *Kenilworth* (our No. 540), in 1821; and *Quentin Durward* (our No. 544), in 1823. Scott was now at the zenith of his fame as a novelist.

In 1811 he had purchased Abbotsford, upon the Tweed. This property he had greatly enlarged by the purchase of adjoining land. The next year he began building a mansion which in the course of a few years he so enlarged and furnished in accordance with his antiquarian and artistic tastes that it became one of the show places and literary shrines of Scotland. Here he kept open house and entertained in such a fine old feudal fashion that Abbotsford was seldom without guests.

In 1826, through Ballantyne's failure, Scott was brought face to face with financial ruin. Then began one of the most pathetic struggles recorded in the annals of literary history. Scott, who had lost his wife in the early part of the year and was himself in

WAVERLEY;

OR,

'TIS SIXTY YEARS SINCE.

IN THREE VOLUMES.

Under which King, Bezonian? speak, or die!
Henry IV. Part II.

VOL. I.

EDINBURGH:

Printed by James Ballantyne and Co.

FOR ARCHIBALD CONSTABLE AND CO. EDINBURGH; AND
LONGMAN, HURST, REES, ORME, AND BROWN,
LONDON.

1814.

No. 530. TITLE-PAGE OF VOL. I OF SCOTT'S WAVERLEY;
1ST EDITION; 1814.

broken health, having developed symptoms of apoplexy, heroically set to work to cancel by the labors of his pen the enormous sum of £130,000, an indebtedness for which he was morally blameless. *Woodstock* (our No. 548) was the first of the novels published after the failure. His *Life of Napoleon Buonaparte* in nine volumes and *Chronicles of the Canongate*, first series (our No. 549), appeared the next year. Between

January, 1826, and January, 1828, he had earned nearly £40,000 for the benefit of his creditors. Other works followed, among them *Anne of Geierstein* (our No. 551), in 1829. But the terrific labor was too much for his endurance.

In November, 1830, he had a slight touch of apoplexy, and a distinct stroke of paralysis the following April. Still he continued to write, and by the autumn of 1831 had finished *Count Robert of Paris* and *Castle Dangerous* (in our No. 553). With these two romances the long series of the Waverley Novels was brought to a close.

In September, Scott, by the advice of his physicians, left Abbotsford and was taken on a cruise about the Mediterranean, which lasted for the greater part of a year. Feeling that the end was near, he insisted on being carried across Europe that he might die at his beloved Abbotsford. There he expired, September 21, 1832, and five days later was buried at Dryburgh Abbey.

[SCOTT, Sir WALTER.]

GUY MANNERING. EDINBURGH, *by James Ballantyne and Co. for Longman, Hurst, Rees, Orme, and Brown, etc.,* 1815. 3 vols., duodecimo, viz.: [531]

VOL. 1.

COLLATION BY SIGNATURES: 2 leaves, without signature-marks; A to O, each 12 leaves; P, 4 leaves (the last blank and genuine); total 174 leaves.
COLLATION BY PAGINATION: [half-title], p. [i.]; — [blank], p. [ii.]; — [title] | GUY MANNERING; | OR, | *THE ASTROLOGER.* | BY THE AUTHOR OF "WAVERLEY." | 'Tis said that words and signs have power |[3 lines] | *Lay of the Last Minstrel.* | IN THREE VOLUMES.

| VOL. I. | EDINBURGH: | *Printed by James Ballantyne and Co.* | FOR LONGMAN, HURST, REES, ORME, AND BROWN, | LONDON; AND ARCHIBALD CONSTABLE AND CO. | EDINBURGH. | 1815. |, p. [iii.]; — [blank], p. [iv.]; — [half-title], p. [1]; — [blank], p. [2]; — [text in 21 chapters], pp. [3]–341; — [imprint] | EDINBURGH: | Printed by James Ballantyne & Co. |, p. 341; — [blank], p. [342]; — [1 blank leaf], [P 4].

VOL. 2.

COLLATION BY SIGNATURES: 2 leaves, without signature-marks; A to O, each 12 leaves; P, 6 leaves; total 176 leaves.
COLLATION BY PAGINATION: [half-title], p. [i.]; — [blank], p. [ii.]; — [title, same as in Vol. 1, except volume-number], p. [iii.]; — [blank], p. [iv.]; — [half-title], p. [1]; — [blank], p. [2]; — [text in 17 chapters], pp. [3]–346; — [imprint, same as in Vol. 1], p. [347]; — [blank], p. [348]. Page 292 is wrongly numbered 92, but is correctly numbered in the Halsey copy.

VOL. 3.

COLLATION BY SIGNATURES: 2 leaves, without signature-marks; A to P, each 12 leaves; total 182 leaves.
COLLATION BY PAGINATION: [half-title], p. [i.]; — [blank], p. [ii.]; — [title, same as in Vol. 1, except volume-number], p. [iii.]; — [blank], p. [iv.]; — [half-title], p. [1]; — [blank], p. [2]; — [text in 19

chapters], pp. [3]–358; — | ERRATA. | [4 lines] |, p. [359]; — [imprint, same as in Vol. 1], p. [359]; — [blank], p. [360].

CONDITION: Size of leaf, 6¹³⁄₁₆ × 4⅛ inches. Bound in green crushed levant morocco, gilt tops; by Rivière. Page 23, Vol. 2, is mended on the inner margin, a few letters lacking.

REFERENCES.

Locker-Lampson, *Appendix to Catalogue* (1900), p. 86; Lockhart, *Life of Scott*, 5 (Second Edition; 1839): 35, 36.

This, the First Edition of this work, was originally published in boards, with drab backs and blue sides, uncut edges, and with title-labels lettered: | GUY MANNERING; | OR | *The Astrologer*. | IN THREE VOLUMES. | VOL. I. [–III.]|.

In both the Valentine and Halsey copies, sheet P, 2 leaves, of Vol. 1, is followed by one leaf without signature-mark tipped to [P 2].

Guy Mannering, published February 24, 1815, was, as Scott was often heard to say, "the work of six weeks at a Christmas." The First Edition, which consisted of 2000 copies, was sold the day after its publication, and within three months a Second and a Third impression followed, making 5000 copies more. It was received with eager curiosity, and pronounced by acclamation fully worthy of sharing honors with *Waverley*. Before the appearance of the first collected edition of the novels the sale of this romance reached nearly 10,000 copies.

This tale gives a picture of the southern coast of Scotland and its manners in the eighteenth century (1750–70), with the life of smugglers and gypsies — Meg Merrilies being of the last — and with the portrait of a devoted old family tutor in Dominie Sampson. Guy Mannering himself has been said to greatly resemble Scott in his traits of a high-minded gentleman.

The original manuscript of *Guy Mannering* is in the library of Mr. J. Pierpont Morgan.

[SCOTT, *Sir* WALTER.]

THE ANTIQUARY. EDINBURGH, *by James Ballantyne and Co. for Archibald Constable and Co., etc.*, 1816. 3 vols., duodecimo, viz.: [532]

VOL. I.

COLLATION BY SIGNATURES: 2 leaves, without signature-marks (the first, a half-title, lacking); a, 2 leaves; A to O, each 12 leaves; total 172 numbered leaves.

COLLATION BY PAGINATION: [half-title], pp. [i.]–[ii.]; — [title] | THE | ANTIQUARY. | BY THE | AUTHOR OF "WAVERLEY" AND "GUY MANNERING." | [quotation, 8 lines] | IN THREE VOLUMES. | VOL. I. | EDINBURGH: | *Printed by James Ballantyne and Co.* | FOR ARCHIBALD CONSTABLE AND CO. EDINBURGH; AND | LONGMAN, HURST, REES, ORME, AND BROWN, | LONDON. | 1816. |, p. [iii.]; — [blank], p. [iv.]; — | ADVERTISEMENT. |, pp. [v.]–viii.; — [half-title], p. [1]; — [blank], p. [2]; — [text in 15 chapters], pp. [3]–336; — [imprint] | EDINBURGH: | Printed by James Ballantyne and Co. |, p. 336.

VOL. 2.

COLLATION BY SIGNATURES: 2 leaves, without signature-marks (the first, a half-title, lacking); A to O, each 12 leaves; P, 6 leaves; total 176 leaves.

COLLATION BY PAGINATION: [half-title], pp. [i.]–[ii.]; — [title, same as in Vol. 1, except volume-number], p. [iii.]; — [blank], p. [iv.]; — [half-title], p. [1]; — [blank], p. [2]; — [text in 14 chapters], pp. [3]–348; — [imprint, same as in Vol. 1], p. 348.

VOL. 3.

COLLATION BY SIGNATURES: 2 leaves, without signature-marks (the first, a half-title, lacking); A to O, each 12 leaves; P, 6 leaves; Q, 12 leaves; total 188 leaves.

COLLATION BY PAGINATION: [half-title], pp. [i.]–[ii.]; — [title, same as in Vol. 1, except volume-number], p. [iii.]; — [blank], p. [iv.]; — [half-title], p. [1]; — [blank], p. [2]; — [text in 16 chapters], pp. [3]–355; — [blank], p. [356]; — [glossary of "the Scottish words requiring explanation in the Novels of Waverley, Guy Mannering, and the Antiquary," with heading] | GLOSSARY. |, pp. [357]–372.

CONDITION: Size of leaf, 7 7/10 × 4 1/2 inches. Bound in green crushed levant morocco, gilt tops, other edges uncut; by Rivière. Page 89 of Vol. 1 is mended on the lower margin, a few letters lacking.

REFERENCES.

Locker-Lampson, *Appendix to Catalogue* (1900), p. 90; Locker-Lampson, *Catalogue* (1886), p. 172; Lockhart, *Life of Scott*, 5 (Second Edition; 1839): 142.

This, the First Edition of this work, was originally published in boards, with light drab backs and blue sides, uncut edges, with title-labels lettered: | THE | ANTIQUARY. | IN THREE VOLS. | VOL. I. [–III.] | .

In the Valentine copy, but not in the Halsey copy, is a publisher's advertisement, dated "Feb., 1816," between the paste-down and first fly-leaf of Vol. 1.

The Antiquary appeared early in May, 1816; 6000 copies of it were sold the first six days after its publication. It thus had a larger immediate sale than any of its predecessors. On May 16th Scott wrote to his friend Morritt that it was again on the press. After a little pause it attained a popularity not inferior to that of *Guy Mannering*.

"It may be worth noting," says Lockhart, "that it was in correcting the proof-sheets of this novel that Scott first took to equipping his chapters with mottoes of his own fabrication. On one occasion he happened to ask John Ballantyne, who was sitting by him, to hunt for a particular passage in Beaumont and Fletcher. John did as he was bid, but did not succeed in discovering the lines. 'Hang it, Johnnie,' cried Scott, 'I believe I can make a motto sooner than you will find one.' He did so accordingly; and from that hour, whenever memory failed to suggest an appropriate epigraph, he had recourse to the inexhaustible mines of 'old play' or 'old ballad,' to which we owe some of the most exquisite verses that ever flowed from his pen."

This picture of Scotch manners during the last ten years of the eighteenth century (1798) has little to connect it with public events, except an episode of the alarm felt along the coast through the fear of a French invasion. The chief characters of interest are Jonathan Oldbuck, the Laird of Monkbarns, and Edie Ochiltree, a Scottish mendicant of the privileged Blue Gown order.

1816   *Sir Walter Scott*   No. 533

[SCOTT, Sir WALTER.]

TALES OF MY LANDLORD, [FIRST SERIES]. EDINBURGH, *for William Blackwood, etc.*, 1816. 4 vols., duodecimo, viz. :   [533]

VOL. 1.

COLLATION BY SIGNATURES : 2 leaves, without signature-marks ; A to P, each 12 leaves ; Q, 2 leaves ; total 184 leaves.

COLLATION BY PAGINATION : [half-title] | TALES OF MY LANDLORD. |, p. [i.] ; —[quotation from *Don Quixote*, 6 lines in Spanish ; the same in English, 7 lines, Jarvis's translation], p. [ii.] ; —[title] | TALES OF MY LANDLORD, | COLLECTED AND ARRANGED | BY | JEDEDIAH CLEISHBOTHAM, | SCHOOLMASTER AND PARISH-CLERK OF GANDERCLEUGH. | Hear, Land o' Cakes and brither Scots, | [5 lines] | BURNS. | IN FOUR VOLUMES. | VOL. I. | EDINBURGH : | PRINTED FOR WILLIAM BLACKWOOD, PRINCE'S STREET : | AND JOHN MURRAY, ALBEMARLE STREET, LONDON. | 1816. |, p. [iii.] ; —[imprint] | *Edinburgh, Printed by James Ballantyne and Co.* |, p. [iv.] ; — | TO | HIS LOVING COUNTRYMEN, | [6 lines] | THESE TALES, | [3 lines] | ARE RESPECTFULLY INSCRIBED, | BY THEIR FRIEND AND LIEGE FELLOW-SUBJECT, | JEDEDIAH CLEISHBOTHAM., | p. [1] ; —[blank], p. [2] ; —[introduction, with heading] | TALES OF MY LANDRLOD ; | COLLECTED AND REPORTED BY | JEDEDIAH CLEISHBOTHAM, | PARISH-CLERK AND SCHOOLMASTER OF GANDERCLEUGH. | INTRODUCTION. | [signed] | JEDEDIAH CLEISHBOTHAM. |, pp. [3]-21 ; —[blank], p. [22] ; —[half-title] | THE | BLACK DWARF. |, p. [23] ; —[blank], p. [24] ; —[text in 19 chapters, with heading] | TALE I. | THE | BLACK DWARF. |, pp. [25]-363 ; —[imprint] | [double rule] | EDINBURGH : | Printed by James Ballantyne & Co. |, p. 363 ; —[blank], p. [364].

VOL. 2.

COLLATION BY SIGNATURES : 2 leaves, without signature-marks (the first blank and lacking) ; A to O, each 12 leaves ; P, 2 leaves ; total 172 leaves.

COLLATION BY PAGINATION : [1 blank leaf] ; —[half-title], p. [i.] ; —[quotation], p. [ii.] ; —[title, same as in Vol. 1, except volume-number], p. [1] ; —[imprint], p. [2] ; —[text in 13 chapters, with heading] | TALE II. | OLD MORTALITY. |, pp. [3]-340 ; —[imprint, same as in Vol. 1, except that it has a single rule instead of a double rule above it], p. 340.

VOL. 3.

COLLATION BY SIGNATURES : 2 leaves, without signature-marks (the first blank and lacking) ; A to O, each 12 leaves ; P, 6 leaves ; 2 leaves, without signature-marks (the last blank and lacking) ; total 178 leaves.

COLLATION BY PAGINATION : [1 blank leaf] ; —[half-title], p. [i.] ; —[quotation], p. [ii.] ; —[title, same as in Vol. 1, except volume-number], p. [1] ; —[imprint], p. [2] ; —[text in 16 chapters, with heading] | TALE II.—CONTINUED. | OLD MORTALITY. |, pp. [3]-349 ; —[imprint, same as in Vol. 2], p. 349 ; —[blank], p. [350] ; —[1 blank leaf].

VOL. 4.

COLLATION BY SIGNATURES : 2 leaves, without signature-marks (the first blank and lacking) ; A to O, each 12 leaves ; P, 6 leaves ; total 176 leaves.

COLLATION BY PAGINATION : [1 blank leaf] ; —[half-title], p. [i.] ; —[quotation], p. [ii.] ; —[title, same as in Vol. 1, except volume-number], p. [1] ; —[imprint], p.

[2]; —[text in 15 chapters, with heading] | TALE II.— CONTINUED. | OLD MORTALITY. |, pp. [3]-335; — | CONCLUSION. |, pp. 336-345; — | PERORATION. | [signed] | JEDEDIAH CLEISHBOTHAM. | [dated] | *Gandercleugh, Nov.* 15, 1816. |, pp. [346]-347; — [imprint, same as in Vol. 2], p. 347; — [blank], p. [348].

CONDITION: Size of leaf, 7½ × 4⁷⁄₁₀ inches. Bound in green crushed levant morocco, gilt tops, other edges uncut; by Rivière.

REFERENCES.

Locker-Lampson, *Catalogue* (1886), p. 172; Lockhart, *Life of Scott*, 5 (Second Edition; 1839): 154-159.

This, the First Edition of the First Series of the *Tales of My Landlord*, contains *The Black Dwarf* and *Old Mortality*. It was published December 1, 1816, and was originally issued in boards, with drab backs and gray sides, uncut edges, and with title-labels lettered: | TALES | OF | MY LANDLORD. | IN FOUR VOLS. | VOL. I. [-IV.] | . The head-lines on the recto pages of Vol. 1 read: | THE BLACK DWARF. | ; of Vols. 2-4, | OLD MORTALITY. |. In less than six weeks after its publication two editions of 2000 copies each had been sold, and a third of 2000 was put to press. Writing to Morritt on January 30, 1817, Scott informs him that 6000 copies had been disposed of, and 3000 more "are pressing onward."

In these volumes the half-title and title-page are printed on companion leaves. Leaf [A], the companion-leaf of [A 12], appears to have been a blank leaf or a cancelled title-page which disappeared when the volumes were bound, as shown by stubs in both the Valentine and the Halsey copies.

Old Mortality was the author's first attempt to repeople the past by the power of imagination working on the material furnished by books, and the story is framed with a deeper skill than any of his preceding novels. Lockhart said that it had always appeared to him to be the *Marmion* of the Waverley Novels.

This is a tale of the West Country Covenanters and their defeats by and their victories over the royal troops under Claverhouse (1679-90), with the actions at Drumclog and Bothwell Bridge. It is a vivid picture of the passions and manners of the two parties in politics and Church while the Revolution of 1688 was impending. The friends of the Covenanters may claim that Balfour of Burley, their leader, is drawn in darker colors, and Claverhouse with more indulgence, than the records warrant. "Old Mortality," an aged religious wanderer, who cleans gravestones of their mosses, is represented as furnishing the material of the story.

The Black Dwarf. This short story uses for a prototype a dwarf whom the author had known, placing the incidents along the Midland Border, at a period (1708) when the Jacobites were planning a rising, which did not take shape in rebellion until the events portrayed in *Rob Roy*.

While the closing sheets of *The Black Dwarf* were passing through the press, Blackwood wrote to Ballantyne on what seemed to him the lame and impotent conclusion of the story, and proceeded to suggest what would, in his judgment, be a better unwinding of the plot, at the same time offering to bear the expense of cancelling and reprinting a number of sheets. This elicited from Scott his well-known "Black Hussars" letter, in which he wrote to Ballantyne: "Tell him and his coadjutor that I belong to the Black Hussars of Literature, who neither give nor receive criticism. I'll be cursed but this is the most impudent proposal that ever was made."

The original manuscript of *The Black Dwarf* and *Old Mortality* is in the library of Mr. J. Pierpont Morgan.

[SCOTT, *Sir* WALTER.]

ROB ROY. EDINBURGH, *by James Ballantyne and Co. for Archibald Constable and Co., etc.*, 1818. 3 vols., duodecimo, viz.: [534]

VOL. 1.

COLLATION BY SIGNATURES: 4 leaves, without signature-marks; A to N, each 12 leaves; O, 6 leaves (the last blank and lacking); total 166 leaves.
COLLATION BY PAGINATION: [half-title], p. [i.]; — [blank], p. [ii.]; — [title] | ROB ROY. | BY THE | AUTHOR OF "WAVERLEY," "GUY MANNERING," AND | "THE ANTIQUARY." | For why? Because the good old rule | Sufficeth them; the simple plan, | That they should take, who have the power, | And they should keep who can. | *Rob Roy's Grave.* — WORDSWORTH. | IN THREE VOLUMES. | VOL. I. | EDIN-
BURGH: | *Printed by James Ballantyne and Co.* | FOR ARCHIBALD CONSTABLE AND CO. EDINBURGH ; AND | LONGMAN, HURST, REES, ORME, AND BROWN, | LONDON. | 1818. |, p. [iii.]; — [blank], p. [iv.]; — | ADVERTISEMENT. |, pp. [v.] - viii.; — [half-title], p. [1]; — [blank], p. [2]; — [text in 13 chapters], pp. [3] - 321 ; — [imprint] | EDINBURGH | Printed by James Ballantyne & Co. |, p. 321 ; — [blank], p. [322] ; — [1 blank leaf], [O 6]. Page 25 is wrongly numbered 52 but is correctly numbered in the Halsey copy.

VOL. 2.

COLLATION BY SIGNATURES: 2 leaves, without signature-marks; A to N, each 12 leaves; O, 6 leaves; total 164 leaves.
COLLATION BY PAGINATION: [half-title], p. [i.]; — [blank], p. [ii.]; — [title, same as in Vol. 1, except volume-number], p. [iii.]; — [blank], p. [iv.]; — [half-title], p. [1]; — [blank], p. [2] ; — [text in 13 chapters], pp. [3] - 324 ; — [imprint, same as in Vol. 1, except that it is in larger type and has a colon after "Edinburgh"], p. 324.

VOL. 3.

COLLATION BY SIGNATURES: 2 leaves, without signature-marks; A to O, each 12 leaves; P, 6 leaves; total 176 leaves.
COLLATION BY PAGINATION: [half-title], p. [i.]; — [blank], p. [ii.]; — [title, same as in Vol. 1, except volume-number], p. [iii.]; — [blank], p. [iv.]; — [half-title], p. [1]; — [blank], p. [2]; — [text in 12 chapters], pp. [3] - 348 ; — [imprint, same as in Vol. 2], p. 348.

CONDITION: Size of leaf, 7⅝ x 4⅝ inches. Bound in green crushed levant morocco, gilt tops, other edges uncut; by Rivière.

REFERENCES.

Locker-Lampson, *Appendix to Catalogue* (1900), p. 87 ; Lockhart, *Life of Scott*, 5 (Second Edition ; 1839) : 267-270.

No. 534   *Sir Walter Scott*   1818

This is the First Edition of this novel. It was published December 31, 1817, in an edition of 10,000 copies, and within a fortnight a second impression of 3000 was called for. It was originally issued in boards, with drab backs and blue sides, uncut edges, and with title-labels lettered: | ROB ROY. | IN THREE VOLS. | VOL. I. [–III.] |.

Scott in a note to Ballantyne, which probably accompanied the last proof-sheet shortly before *Rob Roy* was published, says, "'Twas a tough job." Lightly and airily as the story reads, "the author had struggled almost throughout with the pains of cramp or the lassitude of opium."

Rob Roy contrasts the wild Highland life with that of the town (Glasgow), and shows the marauding exploits of Rob Roy, the outlawed MacGregor at the time of the first attempt to make head in rebellion for the Pretender (1715). Besides Rob Roy, much of whose historic career is told in the long introduction to this work afterward written for the collected edition of the novels, no actual characters of this era appear with any prominence; but the historic names of Argyle and Mar were borne by the opposing commanders of the forces. The serious interest of the plot rests in Rob Roy and Diana Vernon; and the comic in Baillie Nicol Jarvie and Andrew Fairservice.

[SCOTT, Sir WALTER.]

TALES OF MY LANDLORD, SECOND SERIES. EDINBURGH, *for Archibald Constable and Company*, 1818. 4 vols., duodecimo, viz.:   [535]

VOL. I.

COLLATION BY SIGNATURES: 2 leaves, without signature-marks; A to O, each 12 leaves (the last blank and lacking); total 170 leaves.
COLLATION BY PAGINATION: [half-title] | TALES OF MY LANDLORD, | Second Series. |, p. [i.]; — [publishers' advertisement] | *This day were published,* | IN ONE VOLUME, | CRIMINAL TRIALS, | ILLUSTRATIVE OF THE TALE ENTITLED "THE HEART | OF MID-LOTHIAN." | —— "A thousand heads, | A thousand hands, ten thousand tongues and voices | Employ'd at once in several acts of malice! | [4 lines] | BEN JONSON. |, p. [ii.]; — [imprint] | *Printed by James Ballantyne and Co.* |, p. [ii.]; — [title] | TALES OF MY LANDLORD, | Second Series, | COLLECTED AND ARRANGED | BY | JEDEDIAH CLEISHBOTHAM, | SCHOOLMASTER AND PARISH-CLERK OF GANDERCLEUGH. | Hear, Land o' Cakes and brither Scots, | [5 lines] | BURNS.

| IN FOUR VOLUMES. | VOL. I. | EDINBURGH : | PRINTED FOR ARCHIBALD CONSTABLE AND COMPANY. | 1818. |, p. [iii.]; — [quotation from *Don Quixote*, 6 lines in Spanish; 7 lines in English, Jarvis's translation], p. [iv.]; — [imprint] | *Printed by James Ballantyne and Co.* |, p. [iv.]; — [preface, with heading] | TO THE BEST OF PATRONS, | A PLEASED AND INDULGENT READER, | JEDEDIAH CLEISHBOTHAM | WISHES HEALTH, AND INCREASE, AND CONTENTMENT. | [signed] | J. C. | [dated] | GANDERCLEUGH, | *this 1st of April*, 1818. |, pp. [1]–10; — [half-title] | THE | HEART OF MID-LOTHIAN. |, p. [11]; — [blank], p. [12]; — [text in 11 chapters], pp. [13]–333; — [imprint] | EDINBURGH: | Printed by James Ballantyne & Co. |, p. 333; — [blank], p. [334]; — [1 blank leaf], [O 12].

Vol. 2.

COLLATION BY SIGNATURES: 2 leaves, without signature-marks; A to N, each 12 leaves; O, 6 leaves (the last blank and lacking); total 164 leaves.

COLLATION BY PAGINATION: [half-title of the series], p. [i.]; — [quotation and imprint], p. [ii.]; — [title, same as in Vol. 1, except volume-number], p. [iii.]; — [blank], p. [iv.]; — [half-title] | THE | HEART OF MID-LOTHIAN. |, p. [1]; — [blank], p. [2]; — [text in 13 chapters], pp. [3]–322; — [imprint, same as in Vol. 1], p. 322; — [1 blank leaf], [O 6].

Vol. 3.

COLLATION BY SIGNATURES: 2 leaves, without signature-marks; A to N, each 12 leaves; O, 6 leaves; P, 2 leaves; total 166 leaves.

COLLATION BY PAGINATION: [half-title of the series], p. [i.]; — [quotation and imprint], p. [ii.]; — [title, same as in Vol. 1, except volume-number], p. [iii.]; — [blank], p. [iv.]; — [half-title] | THE | HEART OF MID-LOTHIAN. |, p. [1]; — [blank], p. [2]; — [text in 12 chapters], pp. [3]–328; — [imprint, same as in Vol. 1], p. 328.

Vol. 4.

COLLATION BY SIGNATURES: 2 leaves, without signature-marks; A to P, each 12 leaves; Q, 6 leaves; R, 2 leaves; 6 leaves, without signature-marks; total 196 leaves.

COLLATION BY PAGINATION: [half-title of the series], p. [i.]; — [quotation and imprint], p. [ii.]; — [title, same as in Vol. 1, except volume-number], p. [iii.]; — [blank], p. [iv.]; — [half-title] | THE | HEART OF MID-LOTHIAN. |, p. [1]; — [blank], p. [2]; — [text in 14 chapters], pp. [3]–373; — | *L'Envoy*, by JEDEDIAH CLEISHBOTHAM. |, pp. 374–375; — [imprint] | EDINBURGH : | Printed by James Ballantyne and Co. |, p. 375; — [blank], p. [376]; — [publishers' advertisement, with heading] | *June*, 1818. | WORKS | PUBLISHED BY | ARCHIBALD CONSTABLE & CO. | *EDINBURGH*. |, pp. [1]–12.

CONDITION: Size of leaf, 7⁵⁄₁₆ × 4⅜ inches. Bound in green crushed levant morocco, gilt tops, other edges uncut; by Rivière.

REFERENCES.

Locker-Lampson, *Catalogue* (1886), p. 172; Lockhart, *Life of Scott*, 5 (Second Edition; 1839): 270, 315, 357, 362.

This, the First Edition of this work, was published in June, 1818. It was originally issued in boards, with drab backs and blue sides, uncut edges, and with title-labels lettered: | TALES | OF | MY LANDLORD, | 𝕾𝖊𝖈𝖔𝖓𝖉 𝕾𝖊𝖗𝖎𝖊𝖘. | IN FOUR VOLS. | VOL. I. [–IV.] | . The head-lines on the verso pages read, | TALES OF MY LANDLORD. | , and on the recto pages, | THE HEART OF MID-LOTHIAN. | .

The Halsey copy has four pages of Longmans' advertisements between the pastedown and the first fly-leaf of Vol. I.

This, the Second Series of the *Tales of my Landlord*, contains *The Heart of Midlothian*. This story, which it was originally intended should appear on the King's birthday, was received with unbounded enthusiasm. Never before had its author "seized such really noble features of the national character as were canonized in the person of his humble heroine." It had been Scott's intention to include two separate stories in this series of the *Tales*, but owing to the length of *The Heart of Midlothian* this was given up. The story thus deferred appeared the next year in the Third Series of the *Tales* (our next number) as *The Bride of Lammermoor*.

This novel, of which the scene is laid mostly in Edinburgh (1736–51), with an episode in London, opens with the famous Porteous Mob, which lynched an officer of that name for hanging smugglers. The story is otherwise a domestic one, with little dependence upon historical events, although some well known characters figure in it, like John, Duke of Argyle, and Queen Caroline, the wife of George II. The pathetic interest of the touching story is developed in the characters of Jeanie and Effie Deans; its mysterious element lies in the personage known in the opening as Madge Wildfire; and its grotesqueness in the Laird of Dumbiedikes. Its descriptions of the Edinburgh of the eighteenth century lend interest to the localities of the modern town.

[SCOTT, Sir WALTER.]

TALES OF MY LANDLORD, THIRD SERIES. EDINBURGH, *for Archibald Constable and Co.*, etc., 1819. 4 vols., duodecimo, viz. : [536]

VOL. 1.

COLLATION BY SIGNATURES: 2 leaves, without signature-marks; A to O, each 12 leaves (the last blank and lacking); total 170 leaves.

COLLATION BY PAGINATION: [half-title] | TALES OF MY LANDLORD, | Third Series. |, p. [i.]; — [quotation from *Don Quixote*, 6 lines in Spanish; the same in English, 7 lines, Jarvis's translation], p. [ii.]; — [imprint] | *Printed by James Ballantyne and Co.* |, p. [ii.]; — [title] | TALES OF MY LANDLORD, | Third Series, | COLLECTED AND ARRANGED | BY | JEDEDIAH CLEISHBOTHAM, | SCHOOLMASTER AND PARISH-CLERK OF GANDERCLEUGH. | Hear, Land o' Cakes and brither Scots, | [5 lines] | BURNS. | IN FOUR VOLUMES. | VOL. I. | EDINBURGH : | PRINTED FOR ARCHIBALD CONSTABLE AND CO. EDINBURGH ; | LONGMAN, HURST, REES, ORME, AND BROWN, PATERNOSTER-ROW ; | AND HURST, ROBINSON, AND CO. 90, CHEAPSIDE, LONDON. | 1819. |, p. [iii.]; — [blank], p. [iv.]; — [half-title] | THE | BRIDE OF LAMMERMOOR. |, p. [1]; — [blank], p. [2]; — [text in 12 chapters, with heading] | THE | BRIDE OF LAMMERMOOR. |, pp. [3]–333 ; — [imprint] | EDINBURGH : | Printed by James Ballantyne and Co. |, p. 333 ; — [blank], p. [334]; — [1 blank leaf], [O 12].

VOL. 2.

COLLATION BY SIGNATURES: 2 leaves, without signature-marks; A to N, each 12 leaves ; O, 6 leaves ; total 164 leaves.

COLLATION BY PAGINATION: [half-title of the series], p. [i.]; — [quotation and imprint], p. [ii.]; — [title, same as in Vol. 1, except volume-number], p. [iii.]; — [blank], p. [iv.]; — [half-title] | THE | BRIDE OF LAMMERMOOR. |, p. [1]; — [blank], p. [2]; — [text in 13 chapters], pp. [3]–324 ; — [imprint, in smaller type than that in Vol. 1] | EDINBURGH : | Printed by James Ballantyne & Co. |, p. 324.

1819   *Sir Walter Scott*   No. 536

VOL. 3.

COLLATION BY SIGNATURES: 2 leaves, without signature-marks; A to O, each 12 leaves (the last blank and genuine); total 170 leaves.

COLLATION BY PAGINATION: [half-title of the series], p. [i.]; — [publishers' advertisement, beginning] | *In November will be published*, | ILLUSTRATIONS | OF THE | NOVELS AND TALES | OF THE | AUTHOR OF WAVERLEY. | [3 lines] |, p. [ii.]; — [imprint], p. [ii.]; — [title, same as in Vol. 1, except volume-number], p. [iii.]; — [blank], p. [iv.]; — [half-title] | THE | BRIDE OF LAMMERMOOR. |, p. [1]; — [blank], p. [2]; — [text in 8 chapters], pp. [3]-131; — [blank], p. [132]; — [half-title] | A | LEGEND OF MONTROSE. |, p. [133]; — [blank], p. [134]; — | INTRODUCTION. |, pp. [135]-147; — [blank], p. [148]; — [text in 8 chapters], pp. [149]-333; — [imprint, same as in Vol. 2], p. 333; — [blank], p. [334]; — [1 blank leaf], [O 12].

VOL. 4.

COLLATION BY SIGNATURES: 2 leaves, without signature-marks; A to O, each 12 leaves (the last, probably blank, lacking); total 170 leaves.

COLLATION BY PAGINATION: [half-title of the series], p. [i.]; — [publishers' advertisement, beginning] | *This day were published*, | In One Octavo Volume, with Portraits, | MEMOIRS | OF | THE MOST RENOWNED | JAMES GRAHAM, | [8 lines] |, p. [ii.]; — [imprint], p. [ii.]; — [title, same as in Vol. 1, except volume-number], p. [iii.]; — [blank], p. [iv.]; — [half-title] | A | LEGEND OF MONTROSE. |, p. [1]; — [blank], p. [2]; — [text in 15 chapters], pp. [3]-330; — [imprint, same as in Vol. 1], p. 330; — [publishers' advertisement, with heading] | JUNE, 1819. | WORKS | PUBLISHED | BY ARCHIBALD CONSTABLE AND CO. | EDINBURGH. |, pp. [1]-4; — [1 leaf, probably blank], [O 12].

CONDITION: Size of leaf, $7\frac{5}{16}$ × $4\frac{3}{8}$ inches. Bound in green crushed levant morocco, gilt tops, other edges uncut; by Rivière.

REFERENCES.

Locker-Lampson, *Catalogue* (1886), p. 172; Lockhart, *Life of Scott*, 5 (Second Edition; 1839): 315; 6: 85, 87-88.

This is the First Edition of the Third Series of the *Tales of My Landlord*, which was published June 10, 1819. It was originally issued in boards, with drab backs and blue sides, uncut edges, and with title-labels lettered: | TALES | OF | MY LANDLORD, | Third Series. | IN FOUR VOLS. | VOL. I. [-IV.] |. The head-lines of Vols. 1 and 2 and pp. 4-131 of Vol. 3 read, | TALES OF MY LANDLORD. |, on the verso pages, and | THE BRIDE OF LAMMER-MOOR. |, etc., on the recto pages; those on the recto pages of pp. 137-333 of Vol. 3 and all of Vol. 4, | A LEGEND OF MONTROSE. |.

This edition contains numerous typographical errors, which arose from the author's inability to correct the proof-sheets. Scott dictated the story to his amanuensis while suffering from an illness which disabled him from performing the duties of his legal office, and on one occasion brought him near to death's door; even at the time of its publication his illness was of such a serious character that it was the general impression that this would be the last of his literary productions. He also dictated the *Legend of Montrose*, and almost the whole of *Ivanhoe*, his next great work.

The Bride of Lammermoor is one of the purest and most powerful tragedies that Scott ever penned. It is a story of a private family, and in no way refers to public events. It is placed at about the same period as *The Pirate* (1700).

The scene of the *Legend of Montrose* (1645–46) is laid near the Trossachs, and on the west coast of Scotland. The central historical event is the murder of Lord Kilpont in Montrose's camp by Ardvoirlich, who fled to the Covenanters. Montrose's career is traced from his escape to the Highlands, in disguise, to raise the Highlanders in King Charles's behalf, and the story carries him through much of his year's victorious career, in which he sought to save the English Royalists by forcing the withdrawal to their own territory of the army which the Covenanters had lent the Parliamentarians. The tragedy is enlivened by the humors of Captain Dalgetty, a soldier of fortune.

[SCOTT, Sir WALTER.]

THE ABBOT. EDINBURGH, *for Longman, Hurst, Rees, Orme, and Brown, etc.,* 1820. 3 vols., duodecimo, viz.: [537]

VOL. 1.

COLLATION BY SIGNATURES: 2 leaves, without signature-marks; a, 2 leaves; A to O, each 12 leaves; P, 6 leaves; total 178 leaves.

COLLATION BY PAGINATION: [half-title], recto of first leaf; — [imprint] | *Printed by James Ballantyne & Co. Edinburgh.* |, verso of first leaf; — [title] | THE | ABBOT. | BY THE AUTHOR OF "WAVERLEY." | IN THREE VOLUMES. | VOL. I. | EDINBURGH : | PRINTED FOR LONGMAN, HURST, REES, ORME, AND BROWN, | LONDON ; | AND FOR ARCHIBALD CONSTABLE AND COMPANY, | AND JOHN BALLANTYNE, EDINBURGH. | 1820. |, recto of second leaf; — [blank], verso of second leaf; — | INTRODUCTORY EPISTLE | FROM | THE AUTHOR OF "WAVERLEY," | TO | CAPTAIN CLUTTERBUCK, | OF HIS MAJESTY'S —— REGIMENT OF INFANTRY. |, pp. [i.]–iv.; — [half-title] | THE ABBOT; | BEING | THE SEQUEL | OF | THE MONASTERY. |, p. [1]; — [blank], p. [2]; — [text in 15 chapters], pp. [3]–348; — [imprint] | EDINBURGH : | Printed by James Ballantyne & Co. |, p. 348.

VOL. 2.

COLLATION BY SIGNATURES: 2 leaves, without signature-marks; A to O, each 12 leaves; P, 6 leaves; Q, 2 leaves; total 178 leaves.

COLLATION BY PAGINATION: [half-title], p. [i.]; — [imprint], p. [ii.]; — [title, same as in Vol. 1, except volume-number], p. [iii.]; — [blank], p. [iv.]; — [half-title], p. [1]; — [blank], p. [2]; — [text in 11 chapters], pp. [3]–351; — [imprint] | EDINBURGH : | Printed by James Ballantyne and Co. |, p. 351; — [blank], p. [352].

VOL. 3.

COLLATION BY SIGNATURES: 2 leaves, without signature-marks; A to P, each 12 leaves; Q, 6 leaves (the last, probably blank, lacking); total 188 leaves.

COLLATION BY PAGINATION: [half-title], p. [i.]; — [imprint], p. [ii.]; — [title, same as in Vol. 1, except volume-number], p. [iii.]; — [blank], p. [iv.]; — [half-title], p. [1]; — [blank], p. [2]; — [text in 11 chapters], pp. [3]–367; — [imprint, same as in Vol. 2], p. [368]; — [publishers' advertisement, with heading] | NEW EDI-

TIONS | OF WORKS BY THE SAME AUTHOR. |, p. [369] ; — [blank], p. [370] ; — [1 leaf, probably blank], [Q6].

CONDITION: Size of leaf, 7 5/16 × 4 3/8 inches. Bound in green crushed levant morocco, gilt tops, other edges uncut; by Rivière.

REFERENCE.

Lockhart, *Life of Scott*, 6 (Second Edition; 1839): 255, 257.

This, the First Edition of this work, appeared in September, 1820. It was originally issued in boards, with drab backs and blue sides, uncut edges, and with title-labels lettered: | THE | ABBOT. | BY | THE AUTHOR OF | WAVERLEY. | IN THREE VOLS. | VOL. I. [–III.] | .

The Valentine copy has four pages of publishers' advertisements, dated "September, 1820," inserted between the paste-down and the first fly-leaf of Vol. 1.

This novel, which is partly a continuation of *The Monastery*, includes an account of the imprisonment of Mary, Queen of Scots, in Lochleven Castle (1568), her escape from it, and the battle of Langside, which decided her future.

[SCOTT, Sir WALTER.]

IVANHOE. EDINBURGH, *for Archibald Constable and Co., etc.*, 1820. 3 vols., octavo, viz. :

[538]

VOL. 1.

COLLATION BY SIGNATURES: 4 leaves, without signature-marks (the first blank and lacking); A to X, each 8 leaves; Y, 2 leaves; total 174 leaves.

COLLATION BY PAGINATION: [1 blank leaf]; — [half-title], recto of second leaf; — [blank], verso of second leaf; — [title] | IVANHOE; | A ROMANCE. | BY "THE AUTHOR OF WAVERLEY," &c. | Now fitted the halter, now traversed the cart, | And often took leave, — but seem'd loth to depart! | PRIOR. | IN THREE VOLUMES. | VOL. I. | EDINBURGH : | PRINTED FOR ARCHIBALD CONSTABLE AND CO. EDINBURGH ; | AND HURST, ROBINSON, AND CO. 90, CHEAPSIDE, LONDON. | 1820. |, recto of third leaf; — [imprint] | *Printed by James Ballantyne and Co. Edinburgh.* |, verso of third leaf; — | ADVERTISEMENT. |, recto of fourth leaf; — [blank], verso of fourth leaf; — [half-title], p. [i.]; — [blank], p. [ii.]; — | DEDICATORY EPISTLE | TO | THE REV. DR. DRYASDUST, F. A. S | *Residing in the Castle-Gate, York.* | [signed] | Reverend, and very dear Sir, | Your most faithful humble Servant, | LAURENCE TEMPLETON. | [dated] | TOPPINGWOLD, NEAR EGREMONT, | CUMBERLAND, Nov. 17, 1817. |, pp. [iii.]–xxxiii.; — [blank], p. [xxxiv.]; — [text in 14 chapters], pp. [1]–298 ; — [imprint] | EDINBURGH : | Printed by James Ballantyne and Co. |, p. 298. The numbers 151–158 are repeated in the pagination.

VOL. 2.

COLLATION BY SIGNATURES: 2 leaves, without signature-marks; A to U, each 8 leaves; X, 4 leaves; total 166 leaves.

COLLATION BY PAGINATION: [half-title], p. [i.]; — [blank], p. [ii.]; — [title, same as in Vol. 1, except volume-number], p. [iii.]; — [imprint], p. [iv.]; — [half-title], p. [1]; — [blank], p. [2]; — [text in 16 chapters], pp. [3]–327; — [imprint, same as in Vol. 1, except that it is in smaller type], p. 327; — [blank], p. [328].

No. 538   *Sir Walter Scott*   1820

VOL. 3.

COLLATION BY SIGNATURES: 2 leaves, without signature-marks; A to Z, each 8 leaves; 2 A, 4 leaves; total 190 numbered leaves.

COLLATION BY PAGINATION: [half-title], p. [i.]; — [blank], p. [ii.]; — [title, same as in Vol. 1, except volume-number], p. [iii.]; — [imprint], p. [iv.]; — [half-title], p. [1]; — [blank], p. [2]; — [text in 14 chapters], pp. [3] - 371 ; — [imprint, same as in Vol. 2], p. 371 ; — [blank], p. [372]; — [publishers' advertisement, with heading] | WORKS | PUBLISHED | BY ARCHIBALD CONSTABLE, & Co. | EDINBURGH. |, pp. [1] - 3 ; — [blank], p. [4].

CONDITION: Size of leaf, 7⅝ × 4¾ inches. Bound in green crushed levant morocco, gilt tops, other edges uncut; by Rivière.

REFERENCES.

Locker-Lampson, *Appendix to Catalogue* (1900), p. 88; Lockhart, *Life of Scott*, 6 (Second Edition; 1839): 169, 174-179.

This, the First Edition of *Ivanhoe*, was published December 18, 1820, and was originally issued in drab boards, uncut edges, with title-labels lettered : | IVANHOE | BY | THE AUTHOR OF | WAVERLEY. | IN THREE VOLS. | VOL. I. [—III.] |.

It was first planned to give the impression that this work was by a new writer, by printing it in a size and manner unlike *Waverley* and its successors; but this idea was abandoned. It was therefore issued in post octavo, on finer paper and with much better presswork than had been hitherto employed, and the price raised from eight shillings to ten shillings, yet 12,000 copies were sold.

Ivanhoe was received with more clamorous delight than any of the Scotch novels had been. As a work of art it perhaps ranks as the first of all Scott's efforts, whether in prose or verse, and its publication marks the most brilliant epoch of Scott's history as the literary favorite of his contemporaries. Six years later, when in Paris, he attended a dramatic representation of *Ivanhoe* at the Odéon Theatre.

This novel was Scott's first attempt outside of Scottish history. It introduces Richard Cœur-de-Lion in disguise as a knight, and is an interesting study of a period in English history when the subjugated Saxons had not yet lost their characteristics under the rule of the Normans. Other well known characters are Friar Tuck, Robin Hood, Isaac of York, a representative of the Jews in England at the time, and his daughter Rebecca, the Jewish maiden.

The original manuscript of *Ivanhoe*, and some fragments of the same romance, also in Scott's handwriting, are in the library of Mr. J. Pierpont Morgan.

[SCOTT, Sir **WALTER**.]

THE MONASTERY. EDINBURGH, *for Longman, Hurst, Rees, Orme, and Brown, etc.*, 1820. 3 vols., duodecimo, viz.:   [539]

VOL. I.

COLLATION BY SIGNATURES: 2 leaves, without signature-marks; A to N, each 12 leaves; O, 6 leaves; P, 4 leaves; total 168 leaves. Sheet C is marked c.

COLLATION BY PAGINATION: [half-title], p. [i.]; — [imprint] | *Printed by James Ballantyne & Co. Edinburgh.* |, p. [ii.]; — [title] | THE | MONASTERY. | A RO-

MANCE. | BY THE AUTHOR OF "WAVER-
LEY." | IN THREE VOLUMES. | VOL. I. |
EDINBURGH : | PRINTED FOR LONGMAN,
HURST, REES, ORME, AND BROWN, | LON-
DON ; | AND FOR ARCHIBALD CONSTABLE
AND CO., | AND JOHN BALLANTYNE, BOOK-
SELLER TO THE KING, | EDINBURGH. | 1820. |,
p. [iii.]; — [blank], p. [iv.]; — | INTRO-
DUCTORY EPISTLE | FROM | CAP-
TAIN CLUTTERBUCK, | OF HIS
MAJESTY'S —— REGIMENT OF INFANTRY, |
TO | THE AUTHOR OF "WAVER-
LEY." |, pp. [1]-58; — | ANSWER | BY
| "THE AUTHOR OF WAVERLEY,"
| TO THE | FOREGOING LETTER | FROM | CAP-
TAIN CLUTTERBUCK. |, pp. [59]-
76; — [half-title], p. [77]; — [blank], p.
[78]; — [text in 11 chapters], pp. [79]-
331; — [imprint] | EDINBURGH : | Printed
by James Ballantyne & Co. |, p. 331; —
[blank], p. [332].

VOL. 2.

COLLATION BY SIGNATURES : 2 leaves,
without signature-marks ; A to O, each 12
leaves (the last blank and lacking) ; total
170 leaves.
COLLATION BY PAGINATION : [half-
title], p. [i.]; — [imprint], p. [ii.]; — [title,
same as in Vol. 1, except volume-number],
p. [iii.]; — [blank], p. [iv.]; — [half-title],
p. [1]; — [blank], p. [2]; — [text in 11
chapters], pp. [3]-333; — [imprint, in
smaller type than that in Vol. 1] | EDIN-
BURGH : | Printed by James Ballantyne and
Co. |, p. 333; — [blank], p. [334]; — [1
blank leaf], [O 12].

VOL. 3.

COLLATION BY SIGNATURES : 2 leaves,
without signature-marks ; A to O, each 12
leaves ; P, 6 leaves ; Q, 2 leaves ; total 178
leaves.
COLLATION BY PAGINATION : [half-
title], p. [i.]; — [imprint], p. [ii.]; — [title,
same as in Vol. 1, except volume-number],
p. [iii.]; — [blank], p. [iv.]; — [half-title],
p. [1]; — [blank], p. [2]; — [text in 12
chapters], pp. [3]-351; — [imprint, same
as in Vol. 2], p. 351; — [blank], p. [352].
CONDITION : Size of leaf, 7 7/10 × 4 5/8
inches. Bound in green crushed levant
morocco, gilt tops, other edges uncut ; by
Rivière.
REFERENCE.
Lockhart, *Life of Scott*, 6 (Second
Edition ; 1839) : 188, 199, 255–257.

This, the First Edition of this work, appeared at the beginning of March, 1820. It
was originally issued in boards, with drab backs and blue sides, uncut edges, and
title-labels lettered : | THE | MONASTERY | BY | THE AUTHOR OF | WAVERLEY. | IN
THREE VOLS. | VOL. I. [–III.] | . It was not printed in the post octavo size of *Ivan-
hoe*, but in duodecimo, like the earlier works of the series. In fact, a few sheets had
been printed before Scott agreed to have the words "By the Author of Waverley"
on its title-page. The different shapes of the two books (*Ivanhoe* and this) belonged
to an abortive scheme of passing off "Mr. Laurence Templeton" as a hitherto
unheard-of candidate for literary success.

In the Valentine, but not in the Halsey copy, between the paste-down and first
fly-leaf of Vol. 1 is inserted a slip advertising Dunlop's *History of Fiction*. The Halsey
copy has the genuine blank leaf at the end of Vol. 2.

This work was considered a failure, the first of the series on which any such sentence was pronounced. Its scenery is laid at Melrose Abbey. In the introduction
Scott points out his variations from the geography of the neighborhood. The ecclesi-

astical life of the Abbey is, however, at a different stage (1559–68), for its existence is threatened, and the story turns upon the contrast of two enthusiasts, one Catholic and the other Reformed, and upon the rivalries between the vassals of the Church and the lay barons.

The original manuscript of *The Monastery* is in the library of Mr. J. Pierpont Morgan.

[SCOTT, Sir WALTER.]

KENILWORTH. EDINBURGH, *for Archibald Constable and Co., and John Ballantyne, etc.*, 1821. 3 vols., octavo, viz. : [540]

VOL. 1.

COLLATION BY SIGNATURES : 2 leaves, without signature-marks ; A to U, each 8 leaves; total 162 leaves.
COLLATION BY PAGINATION : [half-title], p. [i.] ; — [blank], p. [ii.] ; — [title] | KENILWORTH ; | A ROMANCE. | BY THE AUTHOR OF "WAVERLEY," "IVANHOE," &c. | No scandal about Queen Elizabeth, I hope? | *The Critic*. | IN THREE VOLUMES. | VOL. I. | EDINBURGH : | PRINTED FOR ARCHIBALD CONSTABLE AND CO.; | AND JOHN BALLANTYNE, EDINBURGH ; | AND HURST, ROBINSON, AND CO., | LONDON. | 1821. | , p. [iii.] ; — [imprint] | *Printed by James Ballantyne and Co. Edinburgh.* | , p. [iv.] ; — [half-title], p. [1] ; — [blank], p. [2] ; — [text in 12 chapters], pp. [3]–320 ; — [imprint] | EDINBURGH : | Printed by James Ballantyne and Co. | , p. 320.

VOL. 2.

COLLATION BY SIGNATURES : 2 leaves, without signature-marks ; A to X, each 8 leaves ; Y, 2 leaves ; total 172 leaves.
COLLATION BY PAGINATION : [half-title], p. [i.] ; — [blank], p. [ii.] ; — [title, same as in Vol. 1, except volume-number], p. [iii.] ; — [imprint], p. [iv.] ; — [half-title], p. [1] ; — [blank], p. [2] ; — [text in 13 chapters], pp. [3]–339 ; — [imprint, in larger type than that in Vol. 1] | EDINBURGH : | Printed by James Ballantyne & Co. | , p. 339 ; — [blank], p. [340].

VOL. 3.

COLLATION BY SIGNATURES : 2 leaves, without signature-marks ; A to Y, each 8 leaves; total 178 leaves.
COLLATION BY PAGINATION : [half-title], p. [i.] ; — [blank], p. [ii.] ; — [title, same as in Vol. 1, except volume-number], p. [iii.] ; — [imprint], p. [iv.] ; — [half-title], p. [1] ; — [blank], p. [2] ; — [text in 16 chapters], pp. [3]–348 ; — [imprint, same as in Vol. 2, except that it is in smaller type], p. 348 ; — [publishers' advertisement, with heading] | WORKS, | PUBLISHED | BY ARCHIBALD CONSTABLE AND CO. | EDINBURGH. | , pp. [1]–[4].

CONDITION : Size of leaf, 7¹¹⁄₁₆ × 4¾ inches. Bound in green crushed levant morocco, gilt tops, other edges uncut ; by Rivière.

REFERENCE.

Lockhart, *Life of Scott*, 6 (Second Edition ; 1839) : 294.

This, the First Edition of this romance, was published in January, 1821, in the same form that had been adopted in *Ivanhoe*, a form which was adhered to with all the subsequent novels of the series. It was originally issued in boards, with drab backs and blue sides, uncut edges, and with title-labels lettered : | KENILWORTH. | BY | THE AUTHOR OF | WAVERLEY. | IN THREE VOLUMES. | VOL. I. [–III.] | .

In the Valentine copy, but not in the Halsey copy, are four numbered pages of publishers' advertisements, dated " February, 1821," between the paste-down and the first fly-leaf of Vol. 1.

" Kenilworth was one of the most successful of them all [Scott's novels] at the time of publication; and it continues, and, I doubt not, will ever continue to be placed in the very highest rank of prose fiction. The rich variety of character, and scenery, and incident in this novel, has never indeed been surpassed; nor, with the one exception of the Bride of Lammermoor, has Scott bequeathed us a deeper and more affecting tragedy than that of Amy Robsart."

In this story, as in others, Scott takes liberties with chronology. It turns upon the death of Amy Robsart, the Countess of Leicester, leaving the ambitious earl more at liberty to gain the favor of Queen Elizabeth, with a possibility of sharing her throne; and it exemplifies his flattery in the splendid reception accorded to the queen at his castle of Kenilworth.

[SCOTT, Sir WALTER.]

THE FORTUNES OF NIGEL.   EDINBURGH, *for Archibald Constable and Co.,* *etc.*, 1822.   3 vols., octavo, viz.:   [541]

VOL. 1.

COLLATION BY SIGNATURES: 2 leaves, without signature-marks; a, b, c, A to T, each 8 leaves; U, 4 leaves; [x], 2 leaves (the last blank and lacking); total 184 leaves.

COLLATION BY PAGINATION: [half-title], recto of first leaf; —[blank], verso of first leaf; —[title] | THE | FORTUNES OF NIGEL. | BY THE AUTHOR OF " WAVERLEY, | KENILWORTH," &c. | *Knifegrinder.* Story ? Lord bless you! I have none to tell, sir. | POETRY OF THE ANTI-JACOBIN. | IN THREE VOLUMES. | VOL. I. | EDINBURGH : | PRINTED FOR ARCHIBALD CONSTABLE AND CO. EDINBURGH ; | AND HURST, ROBINSON, AND CO., | LONDON. | 1822. |, recto of second leaf; —[imprint] | *Printed by James Ballantyne and Co. Edinburgh.* |, verso of second leaf; — | INTRODUCTORY EPISTLE. | CAPTAIN CLUTTERBUCK, TO THE | REV. DR DRYASDUST. |, pp. [i.]–xlviii.; —[half-title], p. [1]; —[blank], p. [2]; —[text in 11 chapters], pp. [3]–313; —[imprint] | EDINBURGH : | Printed by James Ballantyne & Co. |, p. 313; —[blank], p. [314]; —[1 blank leaf], [x2].

VOL. 2.

COLLATION BY SIGNATURES: 2 leaves, without signature-marks; A to X, each 8 leaves; total 170 leaves.

COLLATION BY PAGINATION: [half-title], p. [i.]; —[blank], p. [ii.]; —[title, same as in Vol. 1, except volume-number], p. [iii.]; —[imprint], p. [iv.]; —[half-title], p. [1]; —[blank], p. [2]; —[text in 13 chapters], pp. [3]–334; —[imprint, same as in Vol. 1], p. [335]; —[blank], p. [336].

VOL. 3.

COLLATION BY SIGNATURES: 2 leaves, without signature-marks; A to Y, each 8 leaves (the last blank and lacking); total 178 leaves.

COLLATION BY PAGINATION: [half-title], p. [i.]; —[blank], p. [ii.]; —[title, same as in Vol. 1, except volume-number], p. [iii.]; —[imprint], p. [iv.]; —[half-title], p. [1]; —[blank], p. [2]; —[text in 12 chapters], pp. [3]–349; —[imprint] | EDINBURGH: | Printed by James Ballantyne and Co. |, p. 349; —[blank], p. [350]; —[1 blank leaf], [Y 8].

CONDITION: Size of leaf, 7⅝ x 4¾ inches. Bound in green crushed levant morocco, gilt tops, other edges uncut; by Rivière.

REFERENCES.

Locker-Lampson, *Appendix to Catalogue* (1900), p. 88; Lockhart, *Life of Scott*, 6 (Second Edition; 1839): 414; 7: 19–21, 26.

This is the First Edition of this work, which was originally published in boards, with drab backs and blue sides, uncut edges, and with title-labels lettered: | THE | FORTUNES | OF | NIGEL. | BY | THE AUTHOR OF | WAVERLEY, | KENILWORTH, &C. | IN THREE VOLS. | VOL. I. [–III.] | .

The Valentine copy, but not the Halsey copy, has 12 numbered and 12 unnumbered pages of publishers' advertisements (Chapples, Pall Mall) at the end of each volume. In the Halsey copy only 6 numbered pages of Constable's advertisements are found in Vol. 3; these also appear in the Valentine copy.

This work was published May 30, 1822. Constable, writing from London the day after, says: "The Smack Ocean, by which the new work was shipped, arrived at the wharf on Sunday; the bales were got out by *one* on Monday morning, and before half-past ten o'clock 7000 copies had been dispersed from 90 Cheapside."

"I well remember the morning," says Lockhart, "that he began the Fortunes of Nigel. . . . While Terry and I were chatting, Scott came out, bareheaded, with a bunch of MS. in his hand, and said, 'well, lads, I've laid the keel of a new lugger this morning — here it is — be off to the water-side, and let me hear how you like it.' Terry took the papers, and walking up and down by the river, read to me the first chapter of Nigel."

"Nigel was," Lockhart also says, "considered as ranking in the first class of Scott's romances. Indeed, as a historical portraiture, his of James I. stands forth pre-eminent, and almost alone. . . . Hardly a single picturesque point of manners touched by Ben Jonson and his contemporaries but has been dovetailed into this story, and all so easily and naturally, as to form the most striking contrast to the historical romances of authors who *cram*, as the schoolboys phrase it, and then set to work oppressed and bewildered with their crude and undigested burden."

The hero of this volume (besides Nigel himself, the lover) is Heriot, the king's goldsmith of Edinburgh, who accompanied James VI. of Scotland to London when he became James I. of England, and the tale is an attempt by Scott to invest a man without the conventional attributes of heroism with importance. The tale, however, depicts the king in a masterly manner, and is one of Scott's most famous delineations. In his portrayal of London life (1620) Scott has shown his familiarity with the dramatists of the period, particularly in the wild existence of Alsatia or Whitefriars.

[SCOTT, Sir WALTER.]

PEVERIL OF THE PEAK. EDINBURGH, *for Archibald Constable and Co.*, etc., 1822. 4 vols., octavo, viz.: [542]

VOL. 1.

COLLATION BY SIGNATURES: 2 leaves, without signature-marks; a, b, A to T, each 8 leaves (the last blank and genuine); total 170 leaves.

COLLATION BY PAGINATION: [half-title], recto of first leaf;—[publishers' advertisement, beginning] | This day were published, in foolscap 8vo., | Price 7s. 6d. | MEMOIRS OF GEORGE HERIOT, | [3 lines] |, verso of first leaf;—[title] | PEVERIL OF THE PEAK. | BY THE AUTHOR OF "WAVERLEY, | KENILWORTH," &c. | "If my readers should at any time remark that I am particularly dull, they may be assured there is a design under it." —*British Essayist.* | IN FOUR VOLUMES. |

VOL. I. | EDINBURGH: | PRINTED FOR ARCHIBALD CONSTABLE AND CO. EDINBURGH; | AND HURST, ROBINSON, AND CO., | LONDON. | 1822. |, recto of second leaf;—[imprint] | *Printed by James Ballantyne and Co. Edinburgh.* |, verso of second leaf;— | PREFATORY LETTER, | FROM THE | REVEREND DOCTOR DRIASDUST OF YORK, | TO | CAPTAIN CLUTTERBUCK, RESIDING AT FAIRY- | LODGE, NEAR KENNAQUHAIR, N. B. |, pp. [i.]-xxxii.;—[half-title], p. [1]; —[blank], p. [2];—[text in 12 chapters], pp. [3]-302;—[imprint] | EDINBURGH: | Printed by James Ballantyne and Co. |, p. 302;—[1 blank leaf], [T 8].

VOL. 2.

COLLATION BY SIGNATURES: 2 leaves, without signature-marks; A to U, each 8 leaves; total 162 leaves.

COLLATION BY PAGINATION: [half-title], p. [i.];—[publishers' advertisement, beginning] | Just published, in foolscap 8vo., | Price 9s. | THE POETRY | CONTAINED IN THE NOVELS, TALES, AND ROMANCES OF | THE AUTHOR OF WAVERLEY, | *With Vignette Title-page.* |, p. [ii.];—[title, same as in Vol. 1, except volume-number], p. [iii.]; —[imprint], p. [iv.];—[half-title], p. [1]; —[blank], p. [2];—[text in 11 chapters], pp. [3]-319;—[imprint, same as in Vol. 1], p. 319;—[blank], p. [320].

VOL. 3.

COLLATION BY SIGNATURES: 2 leaves, without signature-marks; A to T, each 8 leaves; U, 4 leaves; X, 2 leaves; total 160 leaves.

COLLATION BY PAGINATION: [half-title], p. [i.];—[blank], p. [ii.];—[title, same as in Vol. 1, except volume-number], p. [iii.];—[imprint], p. [iv.];—[half-title], p. [1];—[blank], p. [2];—[text in 12 chapters], pp. [3]-315;—[imprint, same as in Vol. 1], p. 315;—[blank], p. [316]. A slip of errata, with heading and one line, is inserted after the title-page.

VOL. 4.

COLLATION BY SIGNATURES: 2 leaves, without signature-marks; A to U, each 8 leaves; total 162 leaves.

COLLATION BY PAGINATION: [half-title], p. [i.];—[blank], p. [ii.];—[title, same as in Vol. 1, except volume-number], p. [iii.];—[imprint], p. [iv.];—[half-title], p. [1];—[blank], p. [2];—[text in 13 chapters], pp. [3]-320;—[imprint, same as in Vol. 1], p. 320.

No. 542   *Sir Walter Scott*   1822

CONDITION: Size of leaf, 7⅝ × 4⅞ inches. Bound in green crushed levant morocco, gilt tops, other edges uncut; by Rivière.

REFERENCE.

Lockhart, *Life of Scott*, 7 (Second Edition; 1839): 117.

This is the First Edition of this work, which appeared in January, 1823. It was originally issued in boards, with dark drab backs and blue sides, uncut edges, and with title-labels lettered: | PEVERIL | OF | THE PEAK. | BY | THE AUTHOR OF | WAVERLEY | KENILWORTH, &c. | IN FOUR VOLS. | VOL. I. [–IV.] |.

In the Valentine copy, but not in Mr. Halsey's, the blank leaf at the end of Vol. 1 is used as a paste-down. Leaf U (pp. 305, 306) of Vol. 2 appears to have been cancelled, the original leaf having been torn out and the substituted leaf pasted to its stub. In the Halsey copy of Vol. 3 the errata slip is placed at the end of the volume.

The reception of this romance, says Lockhart, "was somewhat colder than that of its three immediate predecessors. The post-haste rapidity of the Novelist's execution was put to a severe trial, from his adoption of so wide a canvass as was presented by a period of twenty busy years, and filled by so very large and multifarious an assemblage of persons, not a few of them, as it were, struggling for prominence."

This novel, which opens just after the Restoration of Charles II., and extends in its action over a score of years (1660–80), describes the contrasts of society at that time, in the jovial Cavalier and the soberer Puritan, and the hero and heroine of this story evince these respective sympathies. The scene is laid partly in Derbyshire and partly in London, and for a while in the Isle of Man, where the Countess of Derby had judicially executed a Manxman for siding with the Parliamentarians in the late civil war, and is now pursued for this assumption of feudal right. The famous Popish plot of 1678–80 comes incidentally into the thread of the story, which is carried in one place to the metropolis, and presents a picture of the dissolute court of Charles II.

The original manuscript of *Peveril of the Peak* is in the library of Mr. J. Pierpont Morgan.

[SCOTT, Sir WALTER.]

THE PIRATE.   EDINBURGH, *for Archibald Constable and Co.*, etc., 1822.   3 vols., octavo, viz.:   [543]

VOL. 1.

COLLATION BY SIGNATURES: 2 leaves, without signature-marks; a, 4 leaves; A to U, each 8 leaves; X, 1 leaf; total 167 leaves. Leaf C is marked c.

COLLATION BY PAGINATION: [half-title], recto of first leaf; — [blank], verso of first leaf; — [title] | THE | PIRATE. | BY THE AUTHOR OF "WAVERLEY, | KENILWORTH," &c. | Nothing in him ——— | But doth suffer a sea-change. | *Tempest.* | IN THREE VOLUMES. | VOL. I. | EDINBURGH: | PRINTED FOR ARCHIBALD CONSTABLE AND CO.; | AND HURST, ROBINSON, AND CO., | LONDON. | 1822. |, recto of second leaf; — [imprint] | *Printed by James Ballantyne and Co. Edinburgh.* |, verso of second leaf; — | ADVERTISEMENT. |, pp. [i.]–vii.; — [blank], p. [viii.]; — [half-title], p. [1]; — [blank], p. [2]; — [text in 13 chapters], pp. [3]–322; — [imprint] | EDINBURGH: | Printed by James Ballantyne & Co. |, p. 322.

VOL. 2.

COLLATION BY SIGNATURES: 2 leaves, without signature-marks; A to U, each 8 leaves; X, 4 leaves; Y, 2 leaves; total 168 leaves.

COLLATION BY PAGINATION: [half-title], p. [i.]; — [blank], p. [ii.]; — [title, same as in Vol. 1, except volume-number], p. [iii.]; — [imprint, in smaller type than that in Vol. 1], p. [iv.]; — [half-title], p. [1]; — [blank], p. [2]; — [text in 14 chapters, with heading in larger type than that in Vol. 1], pp. [3]–332; — [imprint, same as in Vol. 1], p. 332.

VOL. 3.

COLLATION BY SIGNATURES: 2 leaves, without signature-marks; A to X, each 8 leaves; Y, 4 leaves; Z, 1 leaf; total 175 leaves.

COLLATION BY PAGINATION: [half-title], p. [i.]; — [blank], p. [ii.]; — [title, same as in Vol. 1, except volume-number], p. [iii.]; — [imprint, same as in Vol. 2], p. [iv.]; — [half-title], p. [1]; — [blank], p. [2]; — [text in 15 chapters, with heading same as in Vol. 2], pp. [3]–346; — [imprint, same as in Vol. 1], p. 346.

CONDITION: Size of leaf, 7 11/16 × 4 3/4 inches. Bound in green crushed levant morocco, gilt tops, other edges uncut; by Rivière.

REFERENCES.

Locker-Lampson, *Appendix to a Catalogue of the Printed Books, Manuscripts, Autograph Letters, etc., Collected since the Printing of the First Catalogue in 1886* (1900), p. 88. Lockhart, *Life of Scott*, 4 (Second Edition; 1839):275, *note*; 6:423.

This is the First Edition of *The Pirate*, which was published in the beginning of December, 1821. It was originally issued in boards, with dark drab backs and blue sides, uncut edges, and with title-labels lettered: | THE | PIRATE. | BY | THE AUTHOR OF | WAVERLEY, | KENILWORTH, &c. | IN THREE VOLS. | VOL. I. [–III.] | .

Mr. Halsey's copy has four pages of Longman's advertisements between the pastedown and first fly-leaf of Vol. 1.

This splendid romance, with the wild freshness of its atmosphere, the beautiful contrast of Minna and Brenda, and the exquisitely drawn character of Captain Cleveland, found the reception which it deserved.

The story has no historical basis, but is a picture of life in the Orkneys and northern parts of Scotland, about the beginning of the eighteenth century (1700), and is developed largely through the author's imagination from observation of what he saw in that region in 1814.

"The publication of the Pirate satisfied the natives of Orkney as to the authorship of the Waverley Novels. It was remarked by those who had accompanied Sir Walter Scott in his excursions in these Islands, that the vivid descriptions which the work contains were confined to those scenes which he visited."

Mr. Halsey possesses the corrected proof-sheets of Vols. 1 and 2 of *The Pirate*, in which considerable changes were made by the author. They came from the library of Mr. Cadell, Sir Walter Scott's publisher.

[SCOTT, Sir WALTER.]

QUENTIN DURWARD. EDINBURGH, *for Archibald Constable and Co., etc.*, 1823. 3 vols., crown octavo, viz.: [544]

VOL. I.

COLLATION BY SIGNATURES: 2 leaves, without signature-marks; a to d, A to R, each 8 leaves; 2 leaves, without signature-marks (the last blank and lacking); total 172 leaves.

COLLATION BY PAGINATION: [half-title], recto of first leaf; —[blank], verso of first leaf; —[title] | QUENTIN DUR-WARD. | BY THE AUTHOR OF "WAVERLEY, | PEVERIL OF THE PEAK," &c. | La guerre est ma patrie, | Mon harnois ma maison, | Et en toute saison | Combattre c'est ma vie. | IN THREE VOLUMES. | VOL. I. | EDIN-BURGH: | PRINTED FOR ARCHIBALD CONSTABLE AND CO. EDINBURGH; | AND HURST, ROBINSON, AND CO. | LONDON. | 1823. |, recto of second leaf; —[imprint] | *Printed by James Ballantyne and Co. Edinburgh.* |, verso of second leaf; —[introduction], pp. [i.]-lxiii.; —[blank], p. [lxiv.]; —[half-title], p. [1]; —[blank], p. [2]; —[text in 10 chapters], pp. [3]-273; —[imprint] | EDINBURGH: | Printed by James Ballantyne and Co. |, p. 273; —[blank], p. [274]; —[1 blank leaf].

VOL. 2.

COLLATION BY SIGNATURES: 2 leaves, without signature-marks; A to U, each 8 leaves; X, 4 leaves; Y, 2 leaves; total 168 leaves.

COLLATION BY PAGINATION: [half-title], p. [i.]; —[blank], p. [ii.]; —[title, same as in Vol. 1, except volume-number], p. [iii.]; —[imprint], p. [iv.]; —[half-title], p. [1]; —[blank], p. [2]; —[text in 13 chapters], pp. [3]-331; —[imprint, same as in Vol. 1], p. 331; —[blank], p. [332].

VOL. 3.

COLLATION BY SIGNATURES: 2 leaves, without signature-marks; A to Y, each 8 leaves; Z, 4 leaves; total 182 leaves.

COLLATION BY PAGINATION: [half-title], p. [i.]; —[blank], p. [ii.]; —[title, same as in Vol. 1, except volume-number], p. [iii.]; —[imprint], p. [iv.]; —[half-title], p. [1]; —[blank], p. [2]; —[text in 14 chapters], pp. [3]-360; —[imprint] | EDINBURGH: | Printed by James Ballantyne and Co. |, p. 360.

CONDITION: Size of leaf, 7⅝ × 4⅞ inches. Bound in green crushed levant morocco, gilt tops, other edges uncut; by Rivière.

REFERENCES.

Hoe, *Catalogue*, 3 (1905): 49; Locker-Lampson, *Appendix to Catalogue* (1900), p. 89; Lockhart, *Life of Scott*, 7 (Second Edition; 1839): 117, 161–163.

This is the First Edition of this novel, which was published June 20, 1823. It was originally issued in boards, with drab backs and blue sides, uncut edges, and with title-labels lettered: | QUENTIN | DURWARD. | BY | THE AUTHOR OF | WAVERLEY, | PEVERIL OF THE | PEAK, &c. | IN THREE VOLS. | VOL. I. [–III.] | .

While this work was being printed its name was kept secret, owing to an alarm which had arisen about one of Ballantyne's workmen playing foul and transmitting proof-sheets of *Peveril* to some American pirate. In the works previously issued the title of the story had been carried along in the head-lines. In this work the headlines were changed to give only the titles of the chapters: | CHAP. I. THE CONTRAST. |, etc., thus keeping the name of the book secret until the printing of the title-page.

"Surpassing as its popularity was eventually, Constable, who was in London at the time, wrote in cold terms of its immediate reception." It soon recovered from being "frost-bit," as Scott expressed it, and emerged into a most fervid and flourishing life. "In fact, the sensation which this novel, on its first appearance, created in Paris, was extremely similar to that which attended the original Waverley in Edinburgh, and Ivanhoe afterwards in London."

This novel was Scott's first attempt to make use of a continental theme. It depicts the period of the decay of chivalry in France under Louis XI. (1470), who, with Charles the Bold, is the leading hero. The French king is depicted with detestable characteristics, and his nature is closely analyzed in the introduction to the novel.

[SCOTT, Sir WALTER.]

REDGAUNTLET. EDINBURGH, *for Archibald Constable and Co., etc.*, 1824.
3 vols., octavo, viz. : [545]

VOL. 1.

COLLATION BY SIGNATURES: 2 leaves, without signature-marks; A to U, each 8 leaves; total 162 leaves.
COLLATION BY PAGINATION: [half-title], p. [i.]; —[blank], p. [ii.]; —[title] | REDGAUNTLET.| A TALE OF THE EIGHTEENTH CENTURY.| BY THE AUTHOR OF "WAVERLEY." | Master, go on; and I will follow thee, | To the last gasp, with truth and loyalty.| *As You Like it.* | IN THREE VOLUMES.| VOL. I.| EDINBURGH: | PRINTED FOR ARCHIBALD CONSTABLE AND CO. EDINBURGH; | AND HURST, ROBINSON, AND CO.| LONDON. | 1824.|, p. [iii.];—[imprint] | EDINBURGH: | PRINTED BY JAMES BALLANTYNE AND CO.|, p. [iv.]; —[half-title], p. [1]; —[blank], p. [2]; —[text in 13 chapters], pp. [3]-319; —[imprint] | EDINBURGH: | Printed by James Ballantyne and Co.|, p. 319;—[blank], p. [320].

VOL. 2.

COLLATION BY SIGNATURES: 2 leaves, without signature-marks; A to U, each 8 leaves; X, 4 leaves; total 166 leaves.
COLLATION BY PAGINATION: [half-title], p.[i.]; —[blank], p. [ii.]; —[title, same as in Vol. 1, except volume-number], p. [iii.]; —[imprint], p. [iv.]; —[half-title], p. [1]; —[blank], p. [2]; —[text in 13 chapters], pp. [3]-328; —[imprint, same as in Vol. 1], p. 328.

VOL. 3.

COLLATION BY SIGNATURES: 2 leaves, without signature-marks; A to X, each 8 leaves; total 170 leaves.
COLLATION BY PAGINATION: [half-title], p. [i.]; —[blank], p. [ii.]; —[title, same as in Vol. 1, except volume-number], p. [iii.]; —[imprint], p. [iv.]; —[half-title], p. [1]; —[blank], p. [2]; —[text in 10 chapters], pp. [3]-325; — | CONCLUSION, | BY DR DRYASDUST, | IN

A LETTER TO THE AUTHOR OF WAVERLEY. |, pp. 326–331; —[imprint, same as in Vol. 1], p. 331; —[blank], p. [332]; — [publishers' advertisement, with heading] | WORKS | *Published by* A. CONSTABLE & Co. *Edinburgh*; | *and* HURST, ROBINSON, & Co. *London*.|, pp. [333]–[336].

CONDITION: Size of leaf, 7¹¹⁄₁₆ × 4⅞ inches. Bound in green crushed levant morocco, gilt tops, other edges uncut; by Rivière.

REFERENCES.

Locker-Lampson, *Appendix to Catalogue* (1900), p. 89; Lockhart, *Life of Scott*, 7 (Second Edition; 1839): 213, 214.

This, the First Edition of *Redgauntlet*, was published in June, 1824. It was originally issued in boards, with drab backs and blue sides, uncut edges, and with title-labels lettered: | REDGAUNTLET. | BY | THE AUTHOR OF | WAVERLEY, | &c. | IN THREE VOLS. | VOL. I. [–III.]|. The head-lines read: | LATIMER TO FAIRFORD.|, etc.

"With posterity," says Lockhart, "assuredly this novel will yield in interest to none of the series; for it contains perhaps more of the author's personal experiences than any other of them, or even than all the rest put together."

This novel has less of historical interest than *Waverley*, to which it is in some sort a sequel, as it pertains to the last attempt of the Chevalier Charles Edward, when an old man, to head a Jacobite rising in the north (1770). The scene is laid in large part on both sides of Solway Frith and in the old town of Edinburgh. The introduction (written for a later edition), sketches the history of the Pretender from the rebellion of 1745–46, where *Waverley* leaves him, till he comes again on the scene in this novel.

"The re-introduction of the adventurous hero of 1745, in the dulness and dimness of advancing age and fortunes hopelessly blighted, . . . was a rash experiment, and could not fail to suggest many disagreeable and disadvantageous comparisons; yet," says Lockhart, "had there been no Waverley, I am persuaded the fallen and faded Ascanius of Redgauntlet would have been universally pronounced a masterpiece."

[SCOTT, Sir WALTER.]

ST RONAN'S WELL. EDINBURGH, *for Archibald Constable and Co., etc.,* 1824. 3 vols., octavo, viz.: [546]

VOL. I.

COLLATION BY SIGNATURES: 2 leaves, without signature-marks; A to T, each 8 leaves; U, 4 leaves (the last blank and genuine); total 158 leaves.

COLLATION BY PAGINATION: [half-title], p. [i.]; —[blank], p. [ii.]; —[title] | ST RONAN'S WELL. | BY THE AUTHOR OF "WAVERLEY, | QUENTIN DURWARD," &c. | A merry place, 'tis said, in days of yore; | But something ails it now — the place is cursed. | WORDSWORTH. | IN THREE VOLUMES. | VOL. I. | EDINBURGH: | PRINTED FOR ARCHIBALD CONSTABLE AND CO. EDINBURGH; | AND HURST, ROBINSON, AND CO. | LONDON. | 1824. |, p. [iii.]; — [imprint] | EDINBURGH: | PRINTED BY JAMES BALLANTYNE AND CO. |, p. [iv.]; — [half-title], p. [1]; —[blank], p. [2]; —[text in 13 chapters], pp. [3]–310; —[imprint] | EDINBURGH: | Printed by James Ballantyne & Co.|, p. 310; —[1 blank leaf], [U 4].

VOL. 2.

COLLATION BY SIGNATURES: 2 leaves, without signature-marks; A to U, each 8 leaves; X, 4 leaves (the last blank and lacking); total 166 leaves.

COLLATION BY PAGINATION: [half-title], p. [i.];—[blank], p. [ii.];—[title, same as in Vol. 1, except volume-number], p. [iii.];—[imprint], p. [iv.];—[half-title], p. [1];—[blank], p. [2];—[text in 13 chapters], pp. [3]–325;—[imprint, same as in Vol. 1], p. 325;—[blank], p. [326];—[1 blank leaf], [X 4].

VOL. 3.

COLLATION BY SIGNATURES: 2 leaves, without signature-marks; A to U, each 8 leaves; X, 4 leaves; total 166 leaves.

COLLATION BY PAGINATION: [half-title], p. [i.];—[blank], p. [ii.];—[title, same as in Vol. 1, except volume-number], p. [iii.];—[imprint], p. [iv.];—[half-title], p. [1];—[blank], p. [2];—[text in 13 chapters], pp. [3]–323;—[imprint, same as in Vol. 1], p. [324];—[publishers' advertisement, beginning]| IN THE PRESS, | *And speedily will be published,* | BY ARCHIBALD CONSTABLE AND CO. EDINBURGH, | AN ACCOUNT OF | THE SIEGE OF PTOLEMAIS, | [5 lines] |, p. [i.];—[publishers' advertisement, with heading]| WORKS, | PUBLISHED | BY ARCHIBALD CONSTABLE AND CO.| EDINBURGH.|, pp. [ii.]–[iv.].

CONDITION: Size of leaf, 7 11/16 × 4 7/8 inches. Bound in green crushed levant morocco, gilt tops, other edges uncut; by Rivière.

REFERENCES.

Hoe, *Catalogue*, 3 (1905): 49; Locker-Lampson, *Appendix to Catalogue* (1900), p. 89; Lockhart, *Life of Scott*, 7 (Second Edition; 1839): 206–209.

This, the First Edition of this work, was published about the middle of December, 1823. It was originally issued in boards, with drab backs and blue sides, uncut edges, and with title-labels lettered: | ST RONAN'S | WELL. | BY | THE AUTHOR OF | WAVERLEY, | QUENTIN DURWARD, | &C. | IN THREE VOLS. | VOL. I. [–III.] |. The head-lines read : | CHAP. I. AN OLD-WORLD LANDLADY. |, etc.

In England this novel, which is a tale of life at a Scotch watering-place in Scott's own day (1800), met with a lukewarm reception, which caused the booksellers to become somewhat dispirited.

"Scotch readers in general dissented stoutly from this judgment, alleging (as they might well do), that Meg Dods deserved a place by the side of Monkbarns, Bailie Jarvie, and Captain Dalgetty;—that no one who had lived in the author's own country, could hesitate to recognise vivid and happy portraitures in Touchwood, MacTurk, and the recluse minister of St Ronan's;—[and] that the descriptions of natural scenery might rank with any he had given."

At the end of this story, as originally written and printed, "Miss Mowbray's mock marriage had not halted at the profane ceremony of the church." Ballantyne took alarm at this ending, and objected so strongly that Scott "very reluctantly consented to cancel and re-write about twenty-four pages, which was enough to obliterate, to a certain extent, the dreaded scandal," and, as Scott always persisted, "to perplex and weaken the course of his narrative, and the dark effect of its catastrophe."

The original manuscript of *St. Ronan's Well* is in the library of Mr. J. Pierpont Morgan.

[SCOTT, Sir WALTER.]

TALES OF THE CRUSADERS. Edinburgh, *for Archibald Constable and Co.,* etc., 1825. 4 vols., octavo, viz.:

[547]

Vol. 1.

Collation by Signatures: 2 leaves, without signature-marks; a, 8 leaves; b, 4 leaves; c, 2 leaves; A to U, each 8 leaves; x, 4 leaves; total 180 leaves.

Collation by Pagination: [half-title]|TALES OF THE CRUSADERS.|, recto of first leaf;—[blank], verso of first leaf;—[title]|TALES | OF THE CRUSADERS.| BY THE AUTHOR OF "WAVERLEY,| QUENTIN DURWARD," &c.| IN FOUR VOLUMES.| VOL. I.| The Betrothed.| EDINBURGH: | PRINTED FOR ARCHIBALD CONSTABLE AND CO. EDINBURGH; | AND HURST, ROBINSON, AND CO. LONDON.| 1825.|, recto of second leaf;—[imprint] | EDINBURGH: | PRINTED BY JAMES BALLANTYNE AND CO.|, verso of second leaf;—[introduction], pp. [i.]–xxviii.;—[half-title] | TALES OF THE CRUSADERS. | TALE I.| The Betrothed.|, p. [1];—[blank], p. [2];—[text in 16 chapters], pp. [3]–327;—[imprint] | EDINBURGH: | Printed by James Ballantyne and Co.|, p. 327;—[blank], p. [328].

Vol. 2.

Collation by Signatures: 2 leaves, without signature-marks; A to Y, each 8 leaves; z, 2 leaves; total 180 leaves.

Collation by Pagination: [half-title], p. [i.];—[blank], p. [ii.];—[title, same as in Vol. 1, except volume-number], p. [iii.];—[imprint], p. [iv.];—[half-title] | TALES OF THE CRUSADERS. | TALE I.| The Betrothed.|, p. [1];—[blank], p. [2];—[text in 15 chapters, and "Conclusion"], pp. [3]–355;—[imprint] | EDINBURGH: | Printed by JAMES BALLANTYNE & Co.|, p. 355;—[blank], p. [356]. Page 91 is wrongly numbered 95, but is correctly numbered in the Halsey copy.

Vol. 3.

Collation by Signatures: 2 leaves, without signature-marks; A to U, each 8 leaves; x, 4 leaves (the last blank and lacking); total 166 leaves.

Collation by Pagination: [half-title], p. [i.];—[blank], p. [ii.];—[title] | [3 lines] | QUENTIN DURWARD, &c. | ... | VOL. III.| The Talisman.| [4 lines] |, p. [iii.];—[imprint], p. [iv.];—[half-title] | TALES OF THE CRUSADERS. | TALE II.| The Talisman.|, p. [1];—[blank], p. [2];—[text in 13 chapters], pp. [3]–325;—[imprint, in larger type than that in Vol. 1] | EDINBURGH: | Printed by James Ballantyne & Co.|, p. 325;—[blank], p. [326];—[1 blank leaf], [x 4].

Vol. 4.

Collation by Signatures: 2 leaves, without signature-marks; A to Z, each 8 leaves; total 186 leaves.

Collation by Pagination: [half-title], p. [i.];—[blank], p. [ii.];—[title, same as in Vol. 3, except volume-number], p. [iii.];—[imprint], p. [iv.];—[half-title, same as in Vol. 3], p. [1];—[blank],

p. [2]; — [text in 15 chapters], pp. [3]-364; — [imprint, same as in Vol. 3, except that it is in smaller type], p. 364; — [publishers' advertisement, with heading] | WORKS | JUST PUBLISHED BY | ARCHIBALD CONSTABLE & Co. | EDINBURGH, | AND | HURST, ROBINSON, & Co. LONDON. |, pp. [1]-4.

CONDITION: Size of leaf, 7$\frac{11}{16}$ × 4$\frac{7}{8}$ inches. Bound in green crushed levant morocco, gilt tops, other edges uncut; by Rivière.

REFERENCES.

Hoe, *Catalogue*, 3 (1905): 50; Lockhart, *Life of Scott*, 7 (Second Edition; 1839): 384-386.

This, the First Edition of these *Tales*, was published early in June, 1825, and was originally issued in drab boards, uncut edges, with title-labels lettered: | TALES | OF | THE CRUSADERS. | BY | THE AUTHOR OF | WAVERLEY, | &c. | IN FOUR VOLS. | VOL. I. [–II.] | 𝕿𝖍𝖊 𝕭𝖊𝖙𝖗𝖔𝖙𝖍𝖊𝖉. |. The title-labels of Vols. 3 and 4 are the same as those for Vols. 1 and 2, except the volume-numbers and title which read, | VOL. II. [–III.] | 𝕿𝖍𝖊 𝕿𝖆𝖑𝖎𝖘𝖒𝖆𝖓. |. The head-lines read, | TALES OF THE CRUSADERS. | on the verso pages, and | TALE I. THE BETROTHED. |, etc., on the recto pages.

Under this title first appeared the two stories *The Betrothed* and *The Talisman*. The story of *The Betrothed* found no favor with Ballantyne. Scott lost heart in it, and it became a serious question whether it should not be cancelled. All but a chapter or two having been printed off, the sheets were hung up, and in the meantime, Scott, roused by the spur of disappointment, began another story, *The Talisman*, which Ballantyne, as it approached its end, pronounced "such a masterpiece, that The Betrothed might venture abroad under its wing." The remaining chapters of the latter story were then written, and the two were published under the above title. Few of Scott's publications met with a more enthusiastic greeting than *The Talisman*, which hid the defects of its twin-story.

The Betrothed is a tale of warfare on the Welsh border at the time when the Third Crusade was in contemplation (1187), while efforts were being made to turn the warring propensities of the age against the infidel.

The Talisman is a story of the Third Crusade (1193). The scene is laid in Palestine, and the characters of Richard Cœur de Lion and Saladin, who both appear, are strongly contrasted. The personages are historical, but the action is chiefly fictitious.

[SCOTT, Sir WALTER.]

WOODSTOCK. EDINBURGH, *for Archibald Constable and Co., and Longman, Rees, etc.*, 1826. 3 vols., octavo, viz.: [548]

VOL. I.

COLLATION BY SIGNATURES: 8 leaves, without signature-marks; A to T, each 8 leaves; U, 4 leaves; X, 2 leaves; total 166 numbered leaves.

COLLATION BY PAGINATION: [half-title], p. [i.]; — [imprint] | EDINBURGH: | PRINTED BY JAMES BALLANTINE AND CO. |, p. [ii.]; — [title] | WOODSTOCK; | OR,

No. 548   *Sir Walter Scott*   **1826**

| THE CAVALIER. | A TALE | OF THE | YEAR SIXTEEN HUNDRED AND FIFTY-ONE. | BY THE AUTHOR OF "WAVERLEY, | TALES OF THE CRUSADERS," &c. | He was a very perfect gentle Knight. | CHAUCER. | IN THREE VOLUMES. | VOL. I. | EDINBURGH: | PRINTED FOR ARCHIBALD CONSTABLE AND CO. EDINBURGH; | AND LONGMAN, REES, ORME, BROWN, AND GREEN, | LONDON. | 1826. |, p. [iii.]; — [blank], p. [iv.]; — [preface], pp. [v.]–xvi. — [half-title], p. [1]; — [blank], p. [2]; — [text in 12 chapters], pp. [3]–315; — [imprint] | EDINBURGH: | PRINTED BY JAMES BALLANTYNE AND CO. |, p. 315; — [blank], p. [316].

VOL. 2.

COLLATION BY SIGNATURES: 2 leaves, without signature-marks; A to U, each 8 leaves; X, 4 leaves; Y, 2 leaves; total 168 leaves.

COLLATION BY PAGINATION: [half-title], p. [i.]; — [imprint, same as in Vol. 1, except that "Ballantyne" is spelled correctly], p. [ii.]; — [title, same as in Vol. 1, except volume-number], p. [iii.]; — [blank], p. [iv.]; — [half-title], p. [1]; — [blank], p. [2]; — [text in 12 chapters], pp. [3]–332; — [imprint, same as in Vol. 1], p. 332.

VOL. 3.

COLLATION BY SIGNATURES: 2 leaves, without signature-marks; A to Z, each 8 leaves; 2 A, 2 leaves (the last blank and lacking); total 188 leaves.

COLLATION BY PAGINATION: [half-title], p. [i.]; — [imprint, same as in Vol. 2], p. [ii.]; — [title, same as in Vol. 1, except volume-number], p. [iii.]; — [blank], p. [iv.]; — [half-title], p. [1]; — [blank], p. [2]; — [text in 14 chapters], pp. [3]–370; — [imprint] | EDINBURGH: | Printed by James Ballantyne & Co. |, p. 370; — [1 blank leaf], [2A 2].

CONDITION: Size of leaf, 7 11/16 × 4 7/8 inches. Bound in green crushed levant morocco, gilt tops, other edges uncut; by Rivière.

REFERENCES.

Lockhart, *Life of Scott*, 8 (Second Edition; 1839): 316, 350, 353–357.

This is the First Edition of *Woodstock*, which was published in June, 1826. It was originally issued in drab boards, uncut edges, with title-labels lettered: | WOODSTOCK. | BY | THE AUTHOR OF | WAVERLEY, | TALES OF | THE CRUSADERS, | &c. | IN THREE VOLS. | VOL. I. [–III.] | .

This was the first novel to appear after Scott's financial disaster. Its success was so great that the sum of £8000 was realized on it in a short time, much to the gratification of his creditors.

The principal actors in the story are Charles II. and Cromwell, and though as portraits they are inaccurately drawn, as imaginary characters they are admirable. The scene of the story is mostly at the old royal lodge of Woodstock, or what is now known as the domain of Blenheim, and the time extends from just after the battle of Worcester, when Charles II. as a fugitive found shelter there, to that monarch's restoration (1652–60). The machinery of the tale comes from some witchcraft tricks played by a crafty Royalist, which are explained at length in the introduction, written for a later edition.

The original manuscript of *Woodstock* is in the library of Mr. J. Pierpont Morgan.

SCOTT, Sir WALTER.

CHRONICLES OF THE CANONGATE. [FIRST SERIES.] EDINBURGH, for Cadell and Co., etc., 1827. 2 vols., octavo, viz.: [549]

VOL. 1.

COLLATION BY SIGNATURES: 2 leaves, without signature-marks; a, 8 leaves; b, 4 leaves; c, 2 leaves; A to Y, each 8 leaves; total 192 leaves.

COLLATION BY PAGINATION: [half-title], p. [i.]; — [blank], p. [ii.]; — [title] | CHRONICLES | OF | THE CANONGATE; | BY | THE AUTHOR OF "WAVERLEY," &c. | SIC ITUR AD ASTRA. | Motto of the Canongate Arms. | IN TWO VOLUMES. | VOL. I. | EDINBURGH: | PRINTED FOR CADELL AND CO., EDINBURGH; | AND SIMPKIN AND MARSHALL, LONDON. | 1827. | , p. [iii.]; — [imprint] | EDINBURGH: | PRINTED BY BALLANTYNE AND CO. | , p. [iv.]; — [introduction, signed] | WALTER SCOTT. | [dated] | ABBOTSFORD, October 1, 1827. | , pp. [i.] – xxviii.; — [text in 14 chapters], pp. [1]–351; — [imprint] | EDINBURGH: | PRINTED BY BALLANTYNE AND CO. | , p. 351; — [blank], p. [352].

VOL. 2.

COLLATION BY SIGNATURES: 2 leaves, without signature-marks; A to Z, 2 A, each 8 leaves (the last blank and lacking); total 194 leaves.

COLLATION BY PAGINATION: [half-title], p. [i.]; — [blank], p. [ii.]; — [title, same as in Vol. 1, except volume-number], p. [iii.]; — [imprint], p. [iv.]; — [text in 16 chapters], pp. [1]–374; — [ending] | ... If | my lucubrations give pleasure, I may again re- | quire the attention of the courteous reader; if | not, here end the | CHRONICLES OF THE CANONGATE. | EDINBURGH: | PRINTED BY BALLANTYNE & CO. | , p. 374; — [publishers' announcement, beginning] | *Nearly Ready for Publication,* | BY CADELL AND CO. EDINBURGH, | IN THREE VOLUMES, 18MO, | [2 lines] | TALES OF A GRANDFATHER; | , p. [1]; — | WORKS | PUBLISHED BY | CADELL AND CO. | 41, ST ANDREW SQUARE, EDINBURGH. | , pp. [2]–8; — [1 blank leaf], [2A 8].

CONDITION: Size of leaf, 7¹¹⁄₁₆ × 4⅞ inches. Bound in green crushed levant morocco, gilt tops, other edges uncut; by Rivière.

REFERENCE.

Lockhart, *Life of Scott*, 9 (Second Edition; 1839): 173.

This is the First Edition of the First Series of this work, which was originally published in boards, with dark drab backs and light blue sides, uncut edges, and with title-labels lettered: | CHRONICLES | OF THE | CANONGATE. | BY THE | AUTHOR OF | WAVERLEY, &c. | IN TWO VOLS. | VOL. I. [–II.] | . The work is printed without head-lines, the page-numbers occupying the centre of the page.

The First Series of the *Chronicles of the Canongate* was published early in November, 1827, and contains three short stories, as follows: *The Highland Widow* (1755), *The Two Drovers* (1765), and *The Surgeon's Daughter* (1750–70).

These *Chronicles* met with no great favor at the time of their publication, and Scott was a good deal discouraged by their reception.

At the end of Vol. 2 the publishers announce the *Tales of a Grandfather*, "humbly inscribed to Hugh Littlejohn, Esq." [i.e., John Hugh Lockhart, Scott's grandson], Abbotsford, October, 1827.

"This is a series of short stories, published after Scott had dropped his incognito, and in the introduction he makes the first printed acknowledgment of his authorship of the Waverley novels, with some details of their composition. The Chronicles themselves have pleasant prefatory matter representing an imaginary editor, Mr. Croftangry."

A considerable portion of the original manuscript of these *Tales* is in the library of Mr. J. Pierpont Morgan.

[SCOTT, *Sir* WALTER.]

CHRONICLES OF THE CANONGATE. SECOND SERIES. EDINBURGH, *for Cadell and Co., etc.*, 1828. 3 vols., octavo, viz.: [550]

VOL. 1.

COLLATION BY SIGNATURES: 2 leaves, without signature-marks; A to X, each 8 leaves; total 170 leaves.

COLLATION BY PAGINATION: [half-title]|CHRONICLES|OF|THE CANONGATE. | Second Series. |, p. [i.];— [blank], p. [ii.];—[title]|CHRONICLES | OF |THE CANONGATE. | Second Series.|BY|THE AUTHOR OF "WAVERLEY," &c.| SIC ITUR AD ASTRA. | *Motto of the Canongate Arms.*| IN THREE VOLUMES. | VOL. I.| EDINBURGH: PRINTED FOR CADELL AND CO., EDINBURGH; | AND SIMPKIN AND MARSHALL, LONDON.| 1828.|, p. [iii.];—[imprint]| EDINBURGH : | PRINTED BY BALLANTYNE AND CO.|, p. [iv.];— [half-title]|CHRONICLES | OF | THE CANONGATE.|, p. [1];—[blank], p. [2];—[text in 11 chapters, with heading]|CHRONICLES|OF|THE CANONGATE.| Second Series.|, pp. [3]-336; —[imprint]| EDINBURGH | PRINTED BY BALLANTYNE AND CO.|, p. 336.

VOL. 2.

COLLATION BY SIGNATURES: 2 leaves, without signature-marks; A to X, each 8 leaves; total 170 leaves.

COLLATION BY PAGINATION: [half-title of the series], p. [i.];—[blank], p. [ii.];—[title, same as in Vol. 1, except volume-number], p. [iii.];—[imprint], p. [iv.];—[half-title]| CHRONICLES|OF | THE CANONGATE.|, p. [1];— [blank], p. [2];—[text in 11 chapters], pp. [3]-336;—[imprint]| EDINBURGH : | PRINTED BY BALLANTYNE AND CO. |, p. 336.

VOL. 3.

COLLATION BY SIGNATURES: 2 leaves, without signature-marks; A to Y, each 8 leaves; 1 leaf, with signature-mark "VOL. III" (lacking); total 179 leaves.

COLLATION BY PAGINATION: [half-title of the series], p. [i.];—[blank], p. [ii.];—[title, same as in Vol. 1, except volume-number], p. [iii.];—[imprint], p.

1828   Sir Walter Scott   No. 550

[iv.];—[half-title] | CHRONICLES | OF | THE CANONGATE. |, p. [1]; —[blank], p. [2]; —[text in 13 chapters], pp. [3]-348; —[imprint, same as in Vol. 2], p. 348; —[publishers' announcement, with heading] | *Lately Published* | BY | CADELL AND CO. | 41, ST ANDREW SQUARE, EDINBURGH; AND | SIMPKIN AND MARSHALL, LONDON. |, pp. [1]-6.

CONDITION: Size of leaf, $7\frac{11}{16}$ × $4\frac{3}{4}$ inches. Bound in green crushed levant morocco, gilt tops, other edges uncut; by Rivière.

REFERENCES.

Hoe, *Catalogue*, 3 (1905): 51; Lockhart, *Life of Scott*, 9 (Second Edition; 1839): 182, 222-225.

This is the First Edition of the Second Series of the *Chronicles*. It was originally issued in boards, with light drab backs and blue sides (the Halsey copy entirely in drab boards), uncut edges, and with title-labels lettered: | CHRONICLES | OF THE | CANONGATE. | 𝔖𝔢𝔠𝔬𝔫𝔡 𝔖𝔢𝔯𝔦𝔢𝔰. | BY THE | AUTHOR OF | WAVERLEY, &C. | IN THREE VOLUMES. | VOL. I. [–III.] | .

The Halsey copy has four pages of publishers' advertisements inserted between the paste-down and the first fly-leaf of Vol. 1. In both the Valentine and Halsey copies the publishers' advertisements at the end of Vol. 3 consist of six numbered pages, pp. 5 and 6 being a single leaf with the signature-mark "VOL. III."

As in the First Series, the Second has no head-lines, and the page-numbers occupy the centre of the folio lines.

The Second Series of the *Chronicles of the Canongate* was published in April, 1828, and contains the story *Saint Valentine's Day; or, The Fair Maid of Perth*, now better known by its alternative title, *The Fair Maid of Perth* (1402). This series was written in compliance with the entreaties of the publishers. Scott first wrote the tales of *My Aunt Margaret's Mirror* (1700), *The Laird's Jock* (1600), and *The Tapestried Chamber* (1780); but at Ballantyne's entreaty they were omitted from the Second Series of Croftangry's *Chronicles*. Lockhart says that in Heath's *Keepsake* for 1828 appeared a long-forgotten juvenile drama, *The House of Aspen*, with *My Aunt Margaret's Mirror* and two other little tales, probably those just named.

The work was finished by the end of March, 1828, after which Sir Walter immediately went to London, where the last proof-sheets were sent to him. The scene is laid in the time of King Robert III. of Scotland (1402). It illustrates the wild mediæval manners, the wager of battle between leaders of the rival Highland clans, and the haughty power of the Douglas beside the throne.

Of the glee-maiden a careful critic has said, "Louise is a delightful sketch.—Nothing can be more exquisite than the manner in which her story is partly told, and partly hinted, or than the contrast between her natural and her professional character."

The manuscript of both series of the *Chronicles of the Canongate*, with the exception of some pages or portions which are missing, is now in the Drexel Institute at Philadelphia. On the fly-leaf is written: " *This, the original manuscript of Chronicles of the Canongate, first and second series, I received as a gift from Sir Walter Scott at Abbotsford on 9th April, 1831.* [Signed] *Rob Cadell, 1834.*"

No. 551　　　　　　*Sir Walter Scott*　　　　　　1829

[SCOTT, Sir WALTER.]

ANNE OF GEIERSTEIN. EDINBURGH, *for Cadell and Co., etc.*, 1829. 3 vols., Vol. 1 mixed octavo and duodecimo, Vols. 2 and 3 duodecimo, viz.:　　[551]

VOL. 1.

COLLATION BY SIGNATURES: 2 leaves, without signature-marks; A to M, each 8 leaves; N, O, Q, R, S, T, each 12 leaves; total 170 leaves.
COLLATION BY PAGINATION: [half-title], p. [i.];—[blank], p. [ii.];—[title] | ANNE OF GEIERSTEIN; | OR, | THE MAIDEN OF THE MIST. | BY | THE AUTHOR OF "WAVERLEY," &c. | What ! will the aspiring blood of Lancaster | Sink in the ground? | SHAKSPEARE. | IN THREE VOLUMES. | VOL. I. | EDINBURGH: | PRINTED FOR CADELL AND CO., EDINBURGH; | AND SIMPKIN AND MARSHALL, LONDON. | 1829. |, p. [iii.];—[imprint] | EDINBURGH: | PRINTED BY BALLANTYNE AND COMPANY, | PAUL'S WORK, CANONGATE. |, p. [iv.];—[half-title], p. [1];—[blank], p. [2];—[text in 11 chapters], pp. [3]-336;—[imprint] | EDINBURGH: | PRINTED BY BALLANTYNE AND COMPANY, | PAUL'S WORK, CANONGATE. |, p. 336.

VOL. 2.

COLLATION BY SIGNATURES: 2 leaves, without signature-marks; A to O, each 12 leaves; P, 6 leaves (the last, probably blank, lacking); total 176 leaves.
COLLATION BY PAGINATION: [half-title], p. [i.];—[blank], p. [ii.];—[title, same as in Vol. 1, except volume-number], p. [iii.];—[imprint], p. [iv.];—[half-title], p. [1];—[blank], p. [2];—[text in 11 chapters], pp. [3]-346;—[imprint, same as in Vol. 1], p. 346;—[1 leaf, probably blank], [P 6].

VOL. 3.

COLLATION BY SIGNATURES: 2 leaves, without signature-marks; A to Q, each 12 leaves; total 194 leaves.
COLLATION BY PAGINATION: [half-title], p. [i.];—[blank], p. [ii.];—[title, same as in Vol. 1, except volume-number], p. [iii.];—[imprint], p. [iv.];—[half-title], p. [1];—[blank], p. [2];—[text in 13 chapters], pp. [3]-381;—[imprint, same as in Vol. 1], p. 381;—[blank], p. [382];—[publishers' advertisement, with heading | *Works Published* | BY | CADELL AND COMPANY, | 41, ST ANDREW SQUARE, EDINBURGH; AND | SIMPKIN AND MARSHALL, LONDON. |, pp. [i.]-[ii.]. Page 342 is wrongly numbered 42, but is correctly numbered in the Valentine and Halsey copies.

CONDITION: Size of leaf, $7^{13}/_{16}$ × $4^{3}/_{4}$ inches. Bound in green crushed levant morocco, gilt tops, other edges uncut; by Rivière.

REFERENCE.

Lockhart, *Life of Scott*, 9 (Second Edition; 1839): 320-323.

This, the First Edition of this work, originally appeared about the middle of May, 1829, and was published in boards, with drab backs and blue sides, uncut edges, with title-labels lettered: | ANNE | OF GEIERSTEIN. | BY THE | AUTHOR OF | WAVERLEY, &c. | IN THREE VOLS. | VOL. I. [—III.] | .

There is no blank leaf at the end of Vol. 2 in either the Valentine or Halsey copy, leaf P having no companion-leaf.

This story, which may be almost called the last work of Scott's imaginative genius, turns on the union of the Swiss with Louis XI. of France against Charles the Bold (1474–77). Some of the same characters appear in *Quentin Durward*. The author has used historical events to suit the purposes of fiction, and has written about Swiss scenery without personal knowledge of it.

The original manuscript of *Anne of Geierstein* is in the library of Mr. J. Pierpont Morgan.

SCOTT, Sir WALTER.

LETTERS ON DEMONOLOGY AND WITCHCRAFT. London, *John Murray*, 1830. [552]

Pott octavo. First Edition.

COLLATION BY SIGNATURES: a, 7 leaves; A to Z, 2 A, 2 B, each 8 leaves; 1 leaf, without signature-mark, probably imposed as [a 8]; total 208 leaves. Leaf a 3 is wrongly marked a.

COLLATION BY PAGINATION: [half-title], recto of [a]; — [imprint] | EDINBURGH: | PRINTED BY BALLANTYNE AND COMPANY, | PAUL'S WORK, CANONGATE. |, verso of [a]; — [title] | LETTERS | ON | DEMONOLOGY AND WITCH-CRAFT, | ADDRESSED TO | J. G. LOCKHART, ESQ. | BY | SIR WALTER SCOTT, BART. | LONDON: | JOHN MURRAY, ALBEMARLE STREET. | MDCCCXXX. |, recto of [a 2]; — [blank], verso of [a 2]; — [contents], pp. [i.] ix.; — [blank], p. [x.]; — [text, with heading] | LETTERS | ON | DEMONOLOGY AND WITCHCRAFT. | To J. G. LOCKHART, ESQ. |, pp. [1] – 402; — [imprint] | EDINBURGH: | PRINTED BY BALLANTYNE AND COMPANY, | PAUL'S WORK, CANONGATE. |, p. 402.

EXTRA-ILLUSTRATED.

Inserted in this work are the following plates:

Engraved frontispiece, after a design by J. Skene; an inserted title-page, as follows: | TWELVE SKETCHES | ILLUSTRATIVE OF | SIR WALTER SCOTT'S | DEMONOLOGY AND WITCHCRAFT, | BY GEORGE CRUIKSHANK. | London : | PUBLISHED FOR THE ARTIST, | BY J. ROBINS AND CO. IVY LANE, PATERNOSTER ROW. | 1830. | ; and 12 numbered plates, designed, etched, signed, and dated | *Novr 1830* | by George Cruikshank, as follows :

1. | The "Corps de Ballet" | ; facing p. 20.
2. | The Spectre Skeleton | ; facing p. 32.
3. | The Goddefs Freya. | ; facing p. 111.
4. | Elfin tricks | ; facing p. 126.
5. | The Persecuted Butler | ; facing p. 127.
6. | Elfin arrow Manufactory | ; facing p. 162.
7. | Fairy Revenge | ; facing p. 181.
8. | Puck in Mischief | ; facing p. 182.
9. | "Black John" Chastising the Witches | ; facing p. 288.
10. | Witches Frolic | ; facing p. 312.
11. | "Tak aff the Ghaist!" | ; facing p. 387.
12. | The Ghost of Mrs Leckie | ; facing p. 393.

CONDITION: Size of leaf, 6¹/₁₆ × 3¾ inches. Bound in light polished calf, gilt top.

References.

Douglas, *Works of George Cruikshank* (1903), p. 35, No. 115; Marchmont, *The Three Cruikshanks* (1897), p. 105, No. 420; Reid, *Descriptive Catalogue of the Works of George Cruikshank*, 1 (1871): 128, Nos. 1471–1482; 321, No. 4881; Lockhart, *Life of Scott*, 9 (Second Edition; 1839): 349, 369–370.

In his diary, under date of June 27, 1830, Scott says: "Yesterday morning I worked as usual at proofs and copy of my infernal Demonology, a task to which my poverty and not my will consents." It was, however, not published until Christmas. This work, which contains many passages worthy of Scott at his best, was written for Murray's *Family Library*. It abounds with "little snatches of picturesque narrative and the like — in fact, transcripts of his own familiar fireside stories. The shrewdness with which evidence is sifted on legal cases attests [that Scott's] main reasoning faculty remained unshaken. But, on the whole, [it] can hardly be submitted to a strict ordeal of criticism."

George Cruikshank, in November, 1830, issued *Twelve Sketches Illustrative of Sir Walter Scott's Demonology and Witchcraft*, with printed title-page, in two editions, one of India proofs, each etching being accompanied by a duodecimo page of descriptive letterpress.

[SCOTT, Sir WALTER.]

TALES OF MY LANDLORD. FOURTH SERIES. EDINBURGH, *for Robert Cadell, etc.*, 1832. 4 vols., duodecimo, viz.: [553]

VOL. I.

COLLATION BY SIGNATURES: *a*, 12 leaves (the first blank and lacking); *b*, 12 leaves; 1 leaf, without signature-mark (inserted between [*b*11] and [*b*12]); A to N, each 12 leaves; O, 6 leaves; P, 4 leaves (the last blank and lacking); total 191 leaves.

COLLATION BY PAGINATION: [1 blank leaf], [*a*]; — [half-title] | TALES OF MY LANDLORD. | Fourth and Last Series. | , p. [i.]; — [blank], p. [ii.]; — [title] | TALES OF MY LANDLORD, | Fourth and Last Series, | COLLECTED AND ARRANGED | BY | JEDEDIAH CLEISHBOTHAM, | SCHOOLMASTER AND PARISH-CLERK OF GANDERCLEUGH. | The European with the Asian shore — | [5 lines] | *Don Juan.* | IN FOUR VOLUMES. | VOL. I. | PRINTED FOR ROBERT CADELL, EDINBURGH; | AND WHITTAKER AND CO., LONDON. | 1832. | , p. [iii.]; — [imprint] | EDINBURGH: | PRINTED BY BALLANTYNE AND COMPANY, | PAUL'S WORK, CANONGATE. | , p. [iv.]; — | INTRODUCTION. | JEDEDIAH CLEISHBOTHAM, M.A. | To the loving Reader wisheth health and | prosperity. | , pp. [v.]-xliii.; — [blank], p. [xliv.]; — | ERRATA. | VOL. I. | [2 lines] | , p. [xlv.]; — [blank], p. [xlvi.]; — [half-title] | TALES OF MY LANDLORD. | Fourth and Last Series. | , p. [xlvii.]; — [blank], p. [xlviii.]; — [half-title] | COUNT ROBERT OF PARIS. | , p. [1]; — [blank], p. [2]; — [text in 11 chapters], pp. [3]-329; — [imprint] | EDINBURGH: | PRINTED BY BALLANTYNE AND COMPANY, | PAUL'S WORK, CANONGATE. | , p. 329; — [blank], p. [330]; — [1 blank leaf], [P4].

VOL. 2.

COLLATION BY SIGNATURES: 2 leaves, without signature-marks; 1 leaf, without signature-mark (inserted between the two preceding leaves); A, 12 leaves; 1 leaf, without signature-mark (inserted between A and [A2]); B to N, each 12 leaves; O, 8 leaves; [P], 2 leaves (the last blank and lacking); total 170 leaves.

COLLATION BY PAGINATION: [half-title of the series], p. [i.]; — [blank], p. [ii.]; — [title, same as in Vol. 1, except volume-number], p. [iii.]; — [imprint], p. [iv.]; — | ERRATA. | VOL. II. | [3 lines] |, p. [v.]; — [blank], p. [vi.]; — [half-title of the series], p. [vii.]; — [blank], p. [viii.]; — [half-title] | COUNT ROBERT OF PARIS. |, p. [1]; — [blank], p. [2]; — [text in 13 chapters], pp. [3]-330; — [imprint, same as in Vol. 1, except that there is no rule above it], p. 330; — [1 blank leaf], [P2].

The binder, in this copy, has placed the leaves at the beginning of the volume in the following order: A, title-page, leaf of errata, half-title of the series, half-title of the tale, [A2], etc.

VOL. 3.

COLLATION BY SIGNATURES: 2 leaves, without signature-marks; A to O, each 12 leaves; P, 4 leaves (the last blank and lacking); total 174 leaves.

COLLATION BY PAGINATION: [half-title of the series], p. [i.]; — [blank], p. [ii.]; — [title, same as in Vol. 1, except volume-number], p. [iii.]; — [imprint], p. [iv.]; — [half-title of the series], p. [1]; — [blank], p. [2]; — [half-title] | COUNT ROBERT OF PARIS. |, p. [3]; — [blank], p. [4]; — [text in 10 chapters], pp. [5]-211; — | END OF COUNT ROBERT OF PARIS. |, p. 211; — [blank], p. [212]; — [half-title] | CASTLE DANGEROUS. | As I stood by yon roofless tower, | [7 lines] | ROBERT BURNS. |, p. [213]; — [blank], p. [214]; — [text in 6 chapters], pp. [215]-342; — [imprint, same as in Vol. 1], p. 342; — [1 blank leaf], [P4].

VOL. 4.

COLLATION BY SIGNATURES: 2 leaves, without signature-marks; A to N, each 12 leaves; O, 8 leaves; P, 2 leaves (the last blank and lacking); total 168 leaves.

COLLATION BY PAGINATION: [half-title of the series], p. [i.]; — [blank], p. [ii.]; — [title] | [6 lines] | As I stood by yon roofless tower, | [7 lines] | ROBERT BURNS. | IN FOUR VOLUMES. | VOL. IV. | [3 lines] |, p. [iii.]; — [imprint, same as in Vol. 1, except that it has no comma after "WORK"], p. [iv.]; — [half-title of the series], p. [1]; — [blank], p. [2]; — [half-title] | CASTLE DANGEROUS. |, p. [3]; — [blank], p. [4]; — [text in 13 chapters], pp. [5]-330; — [imprint, same as in Vol. 1, except that it has a period instead of a comma at the end of the second line], p. 330; — [1 blank leaf], [P2].

CONDITION: Size of leaf, 7 11/16 × 4 13/16 inches. Bound in green crushed levant morocco, gilt tops, other edges uncut; by Rivière.

REFERENCE.

Lockhart, *Life of Scott*, 10 (Second Edition; 1839): 10, 105, 118–119.

This is the First Edition of the Fourth and last Series of the *Tales of my Landlord*, which was published the last of November, 1831. It was originally issued in boards, with drab backs and blue sides, uncut edges, and with title-labels lettered: | TALES | OF | MY LANDLORD. | 𝔉𝔬𝔲𝔯𝔱𝔥 𝔖𝔢𝔯𝔦𝔢𝔰. | IN FOUR VOLS. | VOL. I. [–II.] | COUNT

ROBERT | OF PARIS. | The title-labels of Vols. 3 and 4 are the same as those for Vols. 1 and 2, except the volume-numbers and titles, which read: | VOL. III. | COUNT ROBERT | OF PARIS, | AND | CASTLE DANGEROUS. | ; and | VOL. IV. | CASTLE | DANGEROUS. |. The head-lines read | COUNT ROBERT OF PARIS. | in Vols. 1, 2, and part of Vol. 3, and | CASTLE DANGEROUS. | in the latter part of Vol. 3 and in Vol. 4.

In the Valentine and Halsey copies, [a 11] of Vol. 1 is on a single leaf, the leaf of errata is at the end of the volume, and P, 2 leaves, is followed by one leaf without signature-mark. In the Valentine copy the leaf of errata is placed before the last blank leaf, which is lacking in the Halsey copy. In Vol. 3 the verso of the half-title (p. 214) contains a long quotation from Burns; and there is no blank leaf at the end of the volume, the last leaf being pasted to leaf [P 2]. In Vol. 4 there is also no blank leaf at the end, leaf P being pasted to the preceding leaf.

The Fourth Series of the *Tales of my Landlord* contains the two stories *Count Robert of Paris* and *Castle Dangerous*. In the preface, dated October 15, 1831, written just before his trip to the continent for his health, Scott takes a touching leave of his readers; on the 21st of September in the following year he breathed his last.

The scene of *Count Robert of Paris* is laid in Constantinople at the time when the army of the Crusaders reached that city (1090) on their way to the Holy Land, and is a general history of the times of the First Crusade.

Castle Dangerous has its scene laid in Scotland in the time of Bruce (1306–1307), and pictures the efforts of Lord Douglas, "Black Douglas," one of Bruce's adherents, to advance the Scottish attempts to wrest Scotland from the rule of Edward of England. Considerable liberty is taken with historical events.

In the preface referred to, in the character of Jedediah Cleishbotham, Scott takes farewell of his readers as follows:

"It would ill become me, whose name has been spread abroad by those former collections, bearing this title of 'Tales of my Landlord,' . . . to suffer this, my youngest literary babe, and, probably, at the same time, the last child of mine old age, to pass into the world without some such modest apology for its defects, as it has been my custom to put forth on preceding occasions of the like nature. . . .

"The history of my first publications is sufficiently well known. Nor did I relinquish the purpose of concluding these 'Tales of my Landlord,' which had been so remarkably fortunate; but Death, which steals upon us all with an inaudible foot, cut short the ingenious young man to whose memory I composed that inscription, and erected, at my own charge, that monument which protects his remains, by the side of the river Gander, which he has contributed so much to render immortal, and in a place of his own selection, not very distant from the school under my care. . . .

"Under such circumstances, the last 'Remains' of Peter Pattison must even be accepted, as they were left in his desk; and I humbly retire in the hope that, such as they are, they may receive the indulgence of those who have ever been but too merciful to the productions of his pen, and in all respects to the courteous reader's obliged servant, J. C."

WILLIAM SHAKESPEARE.

William Shakespeare, the son of John Shakespeare and Mary Arden his wife, was born at Stratford, April 22 or 23, 1564. The house in which he was born is now under a deed of trust, converted into a public museum. Shakespeare received his education at the grammar-school in Stratford, his instruction being mainly confined to the Latin language and literature. Later, as shown by his writings, he acquired a knowledge of French. He was removed from school at an unusually early age, probably about 1577. When a little more than eighteen years of age he married Anne Hathaway of Shottery, a hamlet in the old parish of Stratford.

In 1585 he left Stratford, and the next year found him in London, where he soon secured employment in one of the theatres. His earliest reputation was made as an actor, but his work as a playwright soon eclipsed his histrionic fame. His early dramatic efforts appear to have been confined to revising or rewriting plays that had passed, by purchase or otherwise, into the possession of the theatre. From this the transition to original work was natural, and he was no doubt encouraged to it by the praise given to his work of revision.

The exact order in which his plays were written is based largely on conjecture. Of the thirty-seven plays now attributed to him but sixteen were published during his lifetime, the dates of publication rarely indicating the exact period of their composition. The order now generally accepted by Shakespearian scholars as determined by a variety of tests is as follows:

1. THE EPOCH OF HIS EARLY WORK, 1591–1593.

Love's Labour's Lost, 1591.
Two Gentlemen of Verona, 1591.
Comedy of Errors, 1592.
Romeo and Juliet, 1592.

Henry VI., 1592.
Richard III., 1593.
Richard II., 1593.
Titus Andronicus, 1593.

Intermediate Epoch of the Early Poems, 1593–1594.

Venus and Adonis, 1593.   Lucrece, 1594.
A Lover's Complaint, 1594.

2. THE EPOCH OF HIS MATURING ART — THE PERIOD OF HIS GREAT "COMEDIES" AND THE "HISTORIES," 1594–1601.

The Merchant of Venice, 1594.
King John, 1594.
A Midsummer Night's Dream, 1594–1595.
All's Well that Ends Well, 1595.
The Taming of the Shrew, 1595.
Henry IV., 1597.

The Merry Wives of Windsor, 1597.
Henry V., 1598.
Much Ado about Nothing, 1599.
As You Like It, 1599.
Twelfth Night, 1600.
Julius Cæsar, 1601.

The Later Poems, 1599–1601.

The Passionate Pilgrim, 1599.   The Phœnix and the Turtle, 1601.

3. THE EPOCH OF HIS MATURE ART — THE PERIOD OF THE GREAT PROBLEM PLAYS, 1602–1609.

Hamlet, 1602.
Troilus and Cressida, 1603.
Othello, 1604.
Measure for Measure, 1604.
Macbeth, 1606.

King Lear, 1607.
Timon of Athens, 1608.
Pericles, 1608.
Anthony and Cleopatra, 1608.
Coriolanus, 1609.

Intermediate Epoch of the Sonnets, 1608–1609.

4. THE EPOCH OF REPOSEFUL CONTEMPLATION, 1610–1611.

Cymbeline, 1610.   The Tempest, 1611.
        The Winter's Tale, 1611.

Plays completed by others after his Retirement.

Cardenio (lost), 1611.   Henry VIII., 1611.
        Two Noble Kinsmen, 1611.

Of Shakespeare's works his poems are the only ones which there is any reason to believe passed through the press with his sanction and under his own supervision. The plays were probably for the most part published surreptitiously, as it was not considered good policy by the theatrical management to have them given to the public in printed form.

AUTHORITIES. For sources of information regarding the different editions of Shakespeare's writings, the extensive list given in Bohn's edition of Lowndes' *Bibliographer's Manual* (London, 1869) is still an indispensable aid. Winsor's *Bibliography of the Original Quartos and Folios of Shakespeare* (Boston, 1876), written with special reference to copies in the United States, contains sixty-eight heliotype facsimiles of title-pages, which of themselves are great aids in the identification of different editions. The location of other copies, together with the records of change of ownership by public sales or otherwise, is also one of the important features. Greg's *List of English Plays Written before 1643* (Bibliographical Society, 1900) gives a full list of the folio and quarto editions for the period covered, and locates copies in the larger English libraries. William Carew Hazlitt's *Hand-Book to the Popular, Poetical, and Dramatic Literature of Great Britain* (London, 1867), his series of *Collections and Notes* (London, 1876, 1882, 1887, 1889, 1892, 1893, 1903), and his *Manual of Old English Plays* (London, 1892) contain descriptions of nearly all the early editions. The prefaces to the different volumes of Furness' *New Variorum Edition* (1871–1908), as well as those to *The Cambridge Shakespeare* edited by William Aldis Wright (First Edition, 1863–1866; Second Edition, Vol. 1, 1867, Vols. 2–9, 1891–1893; Third Edition, Vol. 1, 1891), contain much valuable bibliographical information. Concise lists are also to be found in H. R. Tedder's article on Shakespeare in the ninth edition of the *Encyclopædia Britannica* (1886), and Allibone's *Dictionary of English Literature* (1870).

The special catalogues of the British Museum, Boston Public, and Lenox Libraries record numerous editions, as do also the private catalogues of the Huth, Locker-Lampson, and Hoe libraries, while Sinker, in describing the Capell Collection in his *Library of Trinity College, Cambridge* (1891), gives a short list of the different editions in that famous collection.

The bibliographical history of the First Folio has been exhaustively treated by Sidney Lee in the introduction to his *Facsimile Reprint* (Oxford, 1902), in the *Census of Copies* which accompanies it, and in his "Notes and Additions to the Census of Copies of the Shakespeare First Folio," published in *The Library* for April, 1906. In *The Library* for July, 1903, appeared an interesting paper by Walter W. Greg on the bibliographical history of the First Folio, in which he differs somewhat from some conclusions reached by Mr. Lee. Mr. Greg in *The Library* for April and October, 1908, endeavors to show that certain quartos bearing the dates 1600 and 1608 were actually printed in 1619.

The last word relative to Shakespeare's poems is given in the introductions to Sidney Lee's *Facsimile Reprints* (Oxford, 1905), while Winsor's *Shakespeare's Poems, a Bibliography of the Early Editions*, which forms No. 11 of the *Bibliographical Contributions* of Harvard University (Cambridge, 1879), though now somewhat out of date, gives considerable interesting information. Several editions are described in the Grolier Club's *Catalogue of Original and Early Editions of English Writers from Langland to Wither* (New York, 1893).

COLLECTIONS. The largest collections of the early editions of Shakespeare's works, as is naturally to be expected, are in England. Among the most important of these are those in the Bodleian Library (the Malone Collection); the British Museum (the Garrick and George III. Collections); Trinity College, Cambridge (the Capell Collection); and the Duke of Devonshire's library. Less complete collections are to be found in the Victoria and Albert Museum at South Kensington (the Dyce Collection); the University of Edinburgh (the Halliwell-Phillipps Collection); the Earl of Ellesmere's library, the Egerton or Bridgewater Collection; the Alfred H. Huth library; the Christie-Miller library at Britwell Court, Maidenhead; and that of Captain George Lindsay Holford at Dorchester House, London. The quartos formerly owned by Frederick Locker-Lampson have been absorbed in the present collection, while those of Earl Howe were dispersed at Sotheby's in December, 1907.

The most important collections in this country are those in the Boston Public (the Barton Collection) and Lenox Libraries. There are several notable collections in private hands: among the most important, after the one here described, are those of Robert Hoe, J. Pierpont Morgan, and F. R. Halsey, of New York; William Augustus White and H. C. Folger, Jr., of Brooklyn, N. Y.; Marsden J. Perry, of Providence, Rhode Island; and H. H. Furness, of Wallingford, Pennsylvania.

In the notes appended to the descriptions of the various copies in the present collection, an attempt has been made to locate, as far as possible, copies in the above-named collections of all editions of Shakespeare's plays down to and including the year 1700. In order that this information might be as reliable as possible, check-lists were sent to all the institutions and private collectors just named, as well as to a few others, with a request that they would indicate such copies as might be in their possession. These requests have been most kindly complied with and the information asked for supplied in nearly every instance. Of the private collectors to whom check-lists were sent, two in England and two in this country have preferred not to make public the extent of their collections; copies in these, therefore, do not appear in our lists of other copies, except in cases where their possession is already a matter of public record. Our obligations to and thanks for the extent to which we are able to locate other copies are hereby acknowledged and extended to all who have been so kind as to furnish information for this purpose.

The table on the following page shows at a glance the relative importance of the largest of the collections above named, each being arranged by the showing it makes of editions printed before 1623.

The collection of works by and about Shakespeare here described is grouped in the following order, each group being arranged chronologically as issued, unless otherwise indicated:

1. Poems.
2. Separate plays — quarto editions (as in the First Folio; *See* p. 778).
3. Folio editions of the plays (*See* p. 881).
4. Supposititious or Spurious plays (*See* p. 916).
5. Shakespeariana (*See* p. 944).

SHAKESPEARE'S POEMS.

(1) *Venus and Adonis*, the first of Shakespeare's works to appear in print, was published by Richard Field, in 1593. Other editions followed in 1594, 1596, 1599, 1600 (?), 1602 (two issues), 1617, 1620, 1627, 1630, 1636, and 1675.

Of the First Edition (1593), "Imprinted by Richard Field," but a single copy is known, that in the Bodleian Library, which belonged to Edmund Malone, the famous Shakespeare commentator. This copy was reproduced in facsimile by Sidney Lee, with an exhaustive bibliographical introduction, in 1905; also by W. Griggs under the supervision of Dr. F. J. Furnivall in their series of *Shakspere-Quarto Facsimiles* [1886], No. 12; and in 1866 it was reproduced as No. 2 in a series of pen-and-ink lithograph facsimiles made by E. W. Ashbee, of which a small number of copies was issued to subscribers by J. O. Halliwell-Phillipps. Of the 50 copies printed, 31 of the best and clearest impressions were selected and the others destroyed. Sets were broken up, and a fire in 1874 in the storehouse in London where the unsold copies were stored further reduced the number, so that Mr. Halliwell-Phillipps, writing on February 13th of that year, expressed the opinion that not more than 15 complete sets were in existence. Winsor located four of them in this country, among which were those in the Furness and Lenox Libraries. The critical value of this work, however, has been completely superseded by the Griggs- and Praetorius-Furnivall photolithographic facsimiles.

SHAKESPEARE COLLECTIONS

CONTAINING FIFTEEN OR MORE EDITIONS PUBLISHED BEFORE 1623

LIBRARY OR COLLECTION	Before 1590	1590–99	1600–09	1610–19	1620–29	1630–39	1640–49	1650–59	1660–69	1670–79	1680–89	1690–99	1700	Different Editions	Before 1623	Duplicates	Total
Bodleian Library	2^5	21^4	36^5	21^1	5^1	21^5	1	3^2	6	15^3	12^5	10	3^2	156	83	33	189
British Museum	2	17^7	33^{15}	24^{13}	9^8	24^{12}	2^1	5^4	6^3	12^6	16^{10}	16^7	3^4	169	80	92	261
Capell Collection	3	14	28	17	9	18	2	4	3		1			99	67	—	99
Duke of Devonshire	1	14	29	15	3	6			2	6	8	4	2	90	61	—	90
E. Dwight Church	1	10	24	17^1	4	18	1	3	2		4			84	54	1	85
Alfred H. Huth	1	6	21	14	2	7	1		3	4	8	1		68	43	—	68
William Augustus White	1	7^1	18	12	4	16	1	4		9	16	9	3	100	40	1	101
Boston Public Library	1^1	1	12	13	5	20^1	1	3	6	10^6	12^1	12^1	2	98	30	10	108
Earl of Ellesmere		10	16	1	2	7		1	2	3	3		1	46	28	—	46
Lenox Library			10	10^6	3^3	19^3	1	3	4	3	3^1	2		58	21	13	71
Dyce Collection		2	8^2	7	7	10^3		1	3^1	7^3	3	1		49	20	9	58
Robert Hoe	1		9	9	2	8^1	1		2^3	5	10	7		54	19	4	58
Edinburgh University		2	6	4	4	17		4		1	3			41	15	—	41
Totals (including duplicates)	19	116	272	185	71	216	12	37	48	93	116	70	20	—	561	163	1275

The superior figures indicate the number of duplicates, i.e., "2^5" = 7 copies.
Unreported: The Britwell Library, Captain George L. Holford, H. C. Folger, Jr., and Marsden J. Perry.
It should be borne in mind that this table includes all editions of source plays, quarto and folio editions of Shakespeare's poems and plays, alterations of his plays, supposititious plays, and shakesperiana referred to or described in the pages which follow.

For the purposes of tabulation the undated editions are placed in the following columns: *Fair Em*, 1590–99; Preston's *Cambyses*, 1600–09; *Romeo and Juliet* and *Hamlet*, 1610–19; *Mucedorus*, 1620–29, and a second undated edition of *Mucedorus*, 1640–49. The *Whole Contention* (1619) is treated as three plays.
In the following pages, of the 241 editions (1562–1700) recorded, 1566 copies are located, 701 being of editions before 1623, and 62 are untraced.

No. 554　　　　　　　*William Shakespeare*　　　　　　　1594

Of the Second Edition (1594), "Imprinted by Richard Field," there are copies in the British Museum (Jolley-Grenville copy), Bodleian (Caldecott copy), and Huth (Daniel copy) Libraries. The first of these was reproduced in the Ashbee-Halliwell pen-and-ink *Facsimiles* (1867), No. 4.

Of the Third Edition (1596), "by R. F. [i. e. Richard Field] for Iohn Harifon," but two copies are known, those in the British Museum (Daniel copy) and Bodleian (Malone copy) Libraries.

Of the Fourth Edition (1599), "for William Leake," only a single copy is known (the Isham or Lamport Hall copy) now in the library of Mrs. Wakefield Christie-Miller at Britwell Court, Maidenhead, Berkshire, England.

Of the Fifth Edition (1600?) the only copy known is one in the Bodleian Library (Malone copy), with the title-page supplied in manuscript.

Of the Sixth Edition (1602), "for William Leake," there are two issues. Of the First, with the words "*vulgus, mihi*" on the title-page, there is a unique copy (Steevens-Bindley-Daniel copy) in the British Museum. Of the Second Issue, with the words "*vulgus: mihi*" (colon instead of comma), two copies are known, that in the Bodleian (Robert Burton copy) Library and that owned by the Earl of Macclesfield at Shirburn Castle, Oxfordshire, England.

Of the Seventh Edition (1617), "for W. B.," but a single copy is known, the Caldecott copy in the Bodleian Library.

Of the Eighth Edition (1620), "for I. P." (i. e. John Parker), but a single copy is known, that in the Capell Collection at Trinity College, Cambridge.

Of the Ninth Edition (1627), "by Iohn Wreittoun, Edinburgh," but two copies are known, one in the British Museum (Chalmers-Bright copy), the other (Griswold copy) in the library of Mr. Robert Hoe of New York, the latter being the only perfect copy known.

Of the Tenth Edition (1630), "by J. H. [i. e. John Haviland] and fold by Francis Coules," the Anthony à Wood copy in the Bodleian Library is the only one known.

Of the Eleventh Edition (1630?) but one copy is known, that in the Bodleian Library (Malone copy), which has the title-page supplied in manuscript.

Of the Twelfth Edition (1636), "by I. H., and are to be fold by Francis Coules," but two copies are known, that in the British Museum (Hibbert copy) and that in the library of Marsden J. Perry (Ives copy) of Providence, R. I.

Of the Thirteenth Edition (1675), "by Elizabeth Hodgkinfonne for F. Coles, T. Vere, J. Wright and J. Clark," the last edition known to have been produced in the seventeenth century, there are copies in the libraries of H. C. Folger, Jr., and W. A. White; and one in the Bodleian Library (Malone copy, mislaid), in which the title-page is lacking.

(2) *Lucrece* was the second of Shakespeare's works to appear in print. A full account of the different editions through which it passed will be found under our No. 554.

(3) *The Passionate Pilgrim* was the next volume of Shakespeare's poems to appear. This work is a collection of fourteen lyrical pieces, to which are appended

six pieces of the same character, which are introduced by a separate title, *Sonnets to Sundry notes of Musicke*. Of the twenty poems in this volume not more than five can confidently be ascribed to Shakespeare's pen. The First Edition appeared in 1599, and was followed by others in 1600 and 1612.

Of the First Edition (1599), "for W. Iaggard, and are to be fold by W. Leake," but two copies are known, that in the Capell Collection at Trinity College, Cambridge, and that (the Isham or Lamport Hall copy) in the Britwell Library. This latter copy was reproduced in facsimile by Sidney Lee, with an exhaustive bibliographical introduction, in 1905; and the Capell copy was reproduced in photo-lithography in the Griggs-Furnivall *Shakspere-Quarto Facsimiles* [1883], No. 10.

Of the Second Edition (1600) no copy is now traceable. "The poet Drummond of Hawthornden," says Sidney Lee, "noted that he read the book in 1606, possibly in a second edition."

Of "The Third Edition" (1612), "by W. Iaggard," but two copies are known, one in the Bodleian Library, the other owned by Mr. John E. T. Loveday of Williamscote, near Banbury, England. This edition was enlarged by the addition of Heywood's rendering of two of Ovid's *Epistles*.

(4) *The Phœnix and the Turtle*, a poem of thirteen four-line stanzas concluding with the "Threnos" of five three-line stanzas, first appeared in Chester's *Loves Martyr*, 1601 (our No. 558). Descriptions of the different quarto editions, with locations of copies, will be found under this and the other numbers to which reference is made in this list.

(5) Shakespeare's *Sonnets* appeared in 1609, and will be found fully described under our No. 559.

(6) The only collected edition of Shakespeare's *Poems* which appeared in the seventeenth century was published as a bookseller's venture, in 1640. There is a copy in the present collection (our No. 560).

SHAKESPEARE, WILLIAM. (*b.* 1564, *d.* 1616.)

LUCRECE. LONDON, *by Richard Field, for Iohn Harrifon*, 1594.   [554]

Small quarto. First Edition.

COLLATION BY SIGNATURES: A, 2 leaves; B to M, each 4 leaves; N, 2 leaves (the last blank and lacking); total 48 unnumbered leaves.

COLLATION BY PAGINATION: [title, as reproduced; *See* No. 554], recto of [A]; —[blank], verso of [A]; — | TO THE RIGHT | HONOVRABLE, HENRY | VVriothefley, Earle of Southhampton, | and Baron of Titchfield. | [signed] | Your Lordfhips in all duety. | William Shakefpeare. |, recto of A 2; — | THE ARGVMENT. |, verso of A 2; —[text, with heading] | [conventional head-piece] | THE RAPE OF | LVCRECE. |, recto of B to recto of N; — | FINIS. |, recto of N; —[blank], verso of N; —[1 blank leaf], [N 2].

CONDITION: Size of leaf, 6 11/16 x 5 inches. Bound in red morocco, gilt paneled sides, Grolier style (front cover lettered | SHAKESPEARE. | LVCRECE. | 1594. |), vellum fly-leaves, gilt edges; by Zaehnsdorf. With manuscript corrections of the text on the rectos of leaves B and D 4 and the verso of C 4.

OTHER COPIES.

British Museum (2; Bright, and Combe-Grenville copies); Bodleian (2; Malone, and Caldecott copies; with variant readings); Sion College, London (James copy); Devonshire (Kemble copy); Huth (Daniel copy); Holford; and W. A. White, Brooklyn (2; the Perkins copy, and a fragment) Libraries.

REFERENCES.

Lee, *Shakespeare's Lucrece, 1594* (Facsimile Edition; 1905), p. 39; Plomer, *Shakespeare Printers.* 1. Richard Field, in *The Bibliographer*, 2 (1903) : 182–184; Grolier Club, *Langland to Wither* (1893), p. 183, No. 209; British Museum, *Catalogue; Shakespeare* (1897), col. 140; Locker-Lampson, *Catalogue* (1886), p. 110; Huth, *Catalogue*, 4 (1880) : 1340; Winsor, *Shakespeare's Poems* (Harvard University, *Bibliographical Contributions*, No. 2; 1879), p. 5; Lowndes, 4 (1869) : 2305; Hazlitt, *Hand-Book* (1867), p. 545, No. 2a.

The Tite-Locker Lampson copy, with ex-libris of the latter and autograph of the former.

On the recto of the first fly-leaf of the copy here described is a note in manuscript, as follows : " *This is one of the rarest of the Shakespeare 4^{tos}. It is the first Edition & Lowndes says there is another in the Bodleian. This particular Copy was found in Devonshire bound up with other Tracts of the Period of no great Value & was presented to me by a Friend at Colhampton.* [Signed] *Willm Tite 1860.*"

There is also a slip laid in from a Quaritch *Catalogue*, No. 2750 : " Mr. Halliwell considers the Dedication to the Earl of Southampton as a precious relic, it being one of the only two letters of Shakespeare that have reached our time."

Plomer says: " There is evidence that the work was corrected while passing through the press, by whom we do not know, although naturally one inclines to the belief that the corrections were made by the poet himself."

Thus, in the third line of the fifth stanza, one copy reads,

"VVhat needeth then Apologies be made",

while in another we find,

"VVhat needeth then Appologie be made";

and again in the eighteenth stanza, we have in one reading,

" And euerie one to reſt themſelues betake,
Saue theeues, and cares, and troubled minds that wake.",

and in the other,

" And euerie one to reſte himſelfe betakes
Saue theeues, and cares, and troubled minds that wakes."

The copy here described follows the former of each of these readings.

Of this poem editions were published in 1594, 1598, 1600, 1607, 1616, 1624, 1632, and 1655.

The First Edition (1594) is that here described. It was reproduced in the Ashbee-Halliwell *Facsimiles* (1866), No. 3, and also (the British Museum copy) in the Praetorius-Furnivall *Shakspere-Quarto Facsimiles* [1886], No. 35.

Of the Second Edition (1598), "by P. S. [i.e. Peter Short], for Iohn Harriſon,"

1594   *William Shakespeare*   No. 554

LVCRECE.

LONDON.
Printed by Richard Field, for Iohn Harriſon, and are to be ſold at the ſigne of the white Greyhound in Paules Churh-yard. 1594.

No. 554.   Title-page of Shakespeare's Lucrece; 1st Edition; 1594.

Church Catalogue   [763]   English Literature

No. 554 *William Shakespeare* 1594

only a single copy is known, that in the Capell Collection at Trinity College, Cambridge.

Of the Third Edition (1600), "by I. H. for Iohn Harifon," only two copies are known, both in the Bodleian Library (the Farmer-Malone and an imperfect one).

Of the Fourth Edition (1607), "be N. O. [i.e., Nicholas Okes] for Iohn Harifon," but two copies are known, that in the Capell Collection and that in the library of the Earl of Ellesmere at Bridgewater House, London.

The Fifth Edition (1616) is that described in our next number.

The Sixth Edition (1624) is that described in our No. 556.

Of the Seventh Edition (1632), "by R. B. for Iohn Harrifon," there are copies in Corpus Christi College, Oxford (Rosewell copy), the Britwell (Steevens-Heber copy), Edinburgh University (Halliwell-Phillipps copy, imperfect and tentatively ascribed by him to the date 1610), and the Marsden J. Perry (Halliwell-Phillipps copy) Libraries, and one (the Mackenzie copy) untraced.

The Eighth Edition (1655) is that described in our No. 557.

Malone mentions editions of 1596 and 1602, but as no copies with either of these dates have as yet been located, notwithstanding the great pains taken by Mr. Sidney Lee to do so when preparing his facsimile reprint of the First Edition, these dates are probably due to a printer's error.

In 1646 a friend of Sir John Suckling's made a collection of his poems, letters, and plays, which was published under the general title *Fragmenta Aurea*. On p. 29 of these poems, says Winsor, " will be found '*a Supplement of an Imperfect Copy of verses of Mr.* Wil. Shakespears, *By the Author*.' These verses correspond in good part with the stanza [56, commencing with line 386] in Lucrece, beginning ' Her lily hand her rosy cheek lies under,' and the next following, at the end of which in the margin, ' Thus far Shakespear,' then two more stanzas by Suckling."

There is a copy of *Fragmenta Aurea* (1648) in the Harvard University Library.

SHAKESPEARE, WILLIAM.

LUCRECE. LONDON, *by T. S. for Roger Iackson*, 1616. [555]

Small octavo. Fifth Edition.

COLLATION BY SIGNATURES: A to D, each 8 leaves; total 32 unnumbered leaves. Leaf A 2 has no signature-mark.

COLLATION BY PAGINATION: [title, as reproduced; *See* No. 555], recto of [A]; — [blank], verso of [A];—|[type-ornament head-piece]| TO THE RIGHT HONOV-| rable, HENRY WRIOTHESLEY, | Earle of *South-hampton*, and | Baron of *Tichfield*.|[signed]| *Your Lordfhips in all duety*, | William Shakefpeare.| , recto of [A 2];—|[type-ornament head-piece]| The Argument.| , verso of [A 2] to recto of A 3 ;—|[type-ornament head-piece]| *The Contents.*| , verso of A 3 ;—[text, with heading]|[type-ornament head-piece]| THE RAPE OF | LVCRECE.| , recto of A 4 to recto of [D 8];—| *FINIS.*|[conventional tail-piece]| , recto of [D 8];— [blank], verso of [D 8].

CONDITION: Size of leaf, 5 1/16 × 3 3/8 inches. Bound in dark olive green polished morocco, gilt edges; by Rivière. Closely

1616   *William Shakespeare*   No. 555

THE
RAPE
OF
LVCRECE.

By
Mr. *William Shakeſpeare.*

Newly Reuiſed.

LONDON:
Printed by *T. S.* for *Roger Iackson*, and are
to be ſolde at his ſhop neere the Conduit

No. 555.   TITLE-PAGE OF SHAKESPEARE'S LUCRECE; 5TH EDITION; 1616.

trimmed on all the margins, with many head-lines, side-notes, signature-marks, catchwords, and last lines clipped, some completely cut away.

The lower line of the imprint on the title-page, | in Fleet-ſtreet. 1616. | , is completely cut off.

OTHER COPIES.

British Museum; Bodleian (Caldecott copy); and Lenox Libraries.

REFERENCES.

Lee, *Shakespeare's Lucrece* (Facsimile Edition; 1905), p. 47; British Museum, *Catalogue; Shakespeare* (1897), col. 140; Locker-Lampson, *Catalogue* (1886), p. 110; Lenox Library, *Works of Shakespeare* (1880), p. 9, No. 5; Winsor, *Shakespeare's Poems* (Harvard University, *Bibliographical Contributions*, No. 2; 1879), p. 6; Lowndes, 4 (1869): 2306; Hazlitt, *Hand-Book* (1867), p. 545, No. 2*e*.

The Ouvry-Locker Lampson copy, with ex-libris of each.

No. 556   *William Shakespeare*   1624

THE
RAPE
OF
LVCRECE.

By
Mr. William Shakespeare.

Newly Reuised.

LONDON.
Printed by *I. B.* for *Roger Iackson*, and are
to be fold at his fhop neere the Conduit
in Fleet-ftreet. 1 6 2 4.

No. 556.   Title-page of Shakespeare's Lucrece ; 6th Edition ; 1624.

SHAKESPEARE, WILLIAM.

LUCRECE.   London, *by I. B. for Roger Iackson,* 1624.   [556]

Small octavo.   Sixth Edition.
COLLATION BY SIGNATURES : A to D,
each 8 leaves ; total 32 unnumbered leaves.
Leaf A 4 is wrongly marked B 4 ; and A 2
and C 4 have no signature-marks.

COLLATION BY PAGINATION : [title, as
reproduced ; *See* No. 556], recto of [A] ;—
[blank], verso of [A] ;— | [type-ornament
head-piece] | TO THE RIGHT HONOV-
| rable, HENRY WRIOTHESLEY, | Earle of

South-hampton, and | Baron of *Tich-field.* | [signed] | *Your Lordſhips in all duty,* | VVilliam Shake-ſpeare. |, recto of [A 2]; — | [type-ornament head-piece] | The Argument |, verso of [A 2] to recto of A 3; — | [type-ornament head-piece] | *The Contents.* |, verso of A 3; — [text, with heading] | [type-ornament head-piece] | THE RAPE OF | LVCRECE. |, recto of A 4 [wrongly marked B 4] to recto of [D 8]; — | FINIS. | [conventional tail-piece] |, recto of [D 8]; — [blank], verso of [D 8].

CONDITION: Size of leaf, 5⁹⁄₁₆ × 3⅝ inches. Bound in green crushed levant morocco, gilt top; by Bradstreet. The title-page is skillfully mended in the lower portion, and the leaves are stabbed on the inner margins throughout.

OTHER COPIES.

British Museum (2; one the Jolley?-Grenville copy); Folger; Morgan (Luttrell-Ouvry-Locker Lampson-Van Antwerp copy); and Perry (Halliwell-Phillipps copy) Libraries.

REFERENCES.

Lee, *Shakespeare's Lucrece,* 1594 (Facsimile Edition; 1905), p. 48; British Museum, *Catalogue; Shakespeare* (1897), col. 140; Locker-Lampson, *Catalogue* (1886), p. 111; Winsor, *Shakespeare's Poems* (Harvard University, *Bibliographical Contributions,* No. 2; 1879), p. 6; Lowndes, 4 (1869): 2306; Hazlitt, *Hand-Book* (1867), p. 545, No. 2 *f.*

The Fenn-Frere-McKee copy, with ex-libris of the last.

This copy "formerly belonged to Sir John Fenn, being the same sold in London a few years since from which the woodcut and imprint had been cut out, which fragment after a century was found by W. Aldis Wright among Sir John Fenn's cuttings, and replaced. Used by the editors of the Cambridge edition of Shakespeare."

SHAKESPEARE, WILLIAM.

LUCRECE. LONDON, *by J. G. for John Stafford, and Will: Gilbertſon,* 1655.

[557]

Small octavo. Eighth Edition.

COLLATION BY SIGNATURES: A, 4 leaves (the first blank and lacking); B to F, each 8 leaves; G, 4 leaves; total 48 leaves. Leaf F 4 has no signature-mark.

COLLATION BY PAGINATION: [1 blank leaf], [A]; — [title, as reproduced; *See* No. 557 *a*], recto of [A 2]; — [blank], verso of [A 2]; — | [type-ornament head-piece] | To my eſteemed friend | Mr. NEHEMIAH MASSEY. | [signed] | *Your abſolute friend,* | JOHN QUARLES. |, recto and verso of A 3; — | [type-ornament rule] | The Argument. |, recto and verso of [A 4]; — [text, with heading] | [type-ornament head-piece] | THE | RAPE OF *LVCRECE.* |, pp. 1–71; — | FINIS. |, p. 71; — [blank], p. [72]. Page 12 is numbered 1z.

| TARQVIN | BANISHED | [*See* reproduction No. 557 *b*], recto of [F 5]; — [blank], verso of [F 5]; — | [type-ornament rule] | To the READER. |, recto and verso of [F 6]; — [text, with heading] | [type-ornament rule] | *TARQVIN* Baniſhed: | OR, | *The reward of Luſt.* |, pp. 1–12; — | FINIS. |, p. 12.

PLATE: Copperplate engraving, representing Lucrece stabbing herself in the presence of Collatine; with a head of Shakespeare, in oval, in the upper portion; and with inscription below: | *The Fates decree, that tis a mighty wrong* | *To Woemen Kinde, to have more Greife, then Tongue* | ; facing the title-page. This plate is mounted on a guard and is closely trimmed on all four edges (size, 5⁹⁄₁₆ × 3

No. 557   *William Shakespeare*   1655

The Rape of
LUCRECE,
Committed by
TARQUIN the Sixt;
AND
The remarkable judgments that befel him for it.
BY
The incomparable Master of our *English Poetry,*
WILL: SHAKESPEARE Gent.

Whereunto is annexed,
The Banishment of TARQUIN:
Or, *the Reward of Lust.*
By J. QUARLES.

LONDON.
Printed by *J. G.* for *John Stafford* in George-yard neer Fleet-bridge, and *Will: Gilbertson* at the Bible in Giltspur-street, 1655.

No. 557 *a*. TITLE-PAGE OF SHAKESPEARE'S LUCRECE; 8TH EDITION; 1655.

inches), and evidently lacks one or more lines of the inscription.

CONDITION: Size of leaf, 5 7/16 × 3 3/8 inches. Bound in old calf; in red morocco solander case. The text is clipped on the fore edges and also at the bottoms of pp. 19 and 51.

OTHER COPIES.

British Museum (3; two imperfect, and the Halliwell-Phillipps copy); Bodleian (Caldecott copy); Edinburgh University (imperfect); Britwell Library (2, both imperfect); Boston Public; Folger (Farmer?-Sewall copy); Morgan (Daniel-Asay-Irwin copy); and White Libraries.

TARQVIN
BANISHED:
OR,
THE REVVARD
Of Lust.

VVritten by *J. Q.*

Quicquid boni cum discretione feceris, virtus est; quicquid sine discretione gesseris, vitium est: virtus enim indiscreta pro vitio deputatur.

LONDON.
Printed by *J. G.* for *John Stafford* at Fleet-bridge, and *Will: Gilbertson* in Giltspur-street.
1655.

No. 557 *b*.   TITLE-PAGE OF QUARLES' TARQVIN BANISHED; 1655.

REFERENCES.

Lee, *Shakespeare's Lucrece, 1594* (Facsimile Edition; 1905), p. 52; British Museum, *Catalogue*; Shakespeare (1897), col. 140; Grolier Club, *Langland to Wither* (1893), p. 183, No. 210; Boston Public Library, *Catalogue*; Barton Collection (1880), p. 51, No. 741; Winsor, *Shakespeare's Poems* (Harvard University, *Bibliographical Contributions*, No. 2; 1879), p. 7; Lowndes, 4 (1869): 2306; Hazlitt, *Hand-Book* (1867), p. 546, No. 2 *h*; *Bibliotheca Anglo-Poetica* (1815), p. 302.

No. 557   *William Shakespeare*   1655

This copy seems to be identically the same as the one which was purchased at Sotheby's in 1850 by Sir William Tite, and was sold at his sale in 1874. It is carefully described in the Grolier Club's *Contributions to English Bibliography; Langland to Wither* (1893), p. 183.

This edition, though a late one, is valuable and interesting from the fact that it contains the third engraved portrait of Shakespeare. The first portrait was engraved by Droeshout for the First Folio (our No. 610) published in 1623, and the second, by Marshall, appeared in the first collected edition of his Poems in 1640 (our No. 560).

SHAKESPEARE, WILLIAM. Chester, Robert. (*b*. c. 1566, *d*. c. 1640.)

LOVES MARTYR: OR, ROSALINS COMPLAINT. LONDON, *for* E.R., 1601.   [558]

Small quarto.   First Edition.
COLLATION BY SIGNATURES: A, 4 leaves (the first blank and lacking); B to Z, Aa, each 4 leaves; Bb, 2 leaves; total 98 leaves. Leaves P4 and Q4 have signature-marks.

COLLATION BY PAGINATION: [1 blank leaf], [A]; — [title, as reproduced; See No. 558], recto of [A 2]; — [blank], verso of [A 2]; — | [type-ornament head-piece] | TO THE HONORA- | ble, and (of me before all other) | *honored Knight, Sir Iohn Salisburie,* | one of the Esquires of the bodie to the | *Queenes moſt excellent Maieſtie, Robert* | Cheſter wiſheth increaſe of vertue | *and honour.* | [signed] | *Yours in all ſeruice,* | RO. CHESTER. |, recto and verso of A 3; — | [type-ornament head-piece] | The Authors requeſt to | the Phœnix. |, recto of [A 4]; — | [type-ornament head-piece] | To the kind Reader. |, verso of [A 4]; — [several poems, the first with heading] | ROSALINS COM- | PLAINT, METAPHORI- | cally applied to Dame Nature at a Parlia- | *ment held (in the high Star-chamber) by the* | Gods, for the preſer- uation and increaſe of | *Earths beauteous Phœnix.* |, pp. 1–163; — [blank], p. [164].

| HEREAFTER | FOLLOW DI- VERSE | Poeticall Eſſaies on the former Sub- | ieƈt; viz: the *Turtle* and *Phœnix.* | Done by the beſt and chiefeſt of our | moderne writers, with their names ſub- | ſcribed to their particular workes: | *neuer before extant.* | And (now firſt) conſecrated by them all generally, | *to the loue and merite of the true-noble Knight,* | Sir Iohn Salisburie. | *Dignum laude virum Muſa vetat mori.* | [device with motto "ANCHORA SPEI."] | MDCI. |, p. [165]; — [blank], p. [166]; — | INVOCATIO, |, p. 167; — | To the worthily honor'd Knight | Sir Iohn Salisburie. |, p. 168; — [short poems], pp. 169–183; — [type-ornament tail-piece], p. 183; — [blank], p. [184]. Page 11 is wrongly numbered 5; 14 is 41; 63 is 59; 103 is 101; 120 is 112; 134 is 118; 135 is 119; and the numbers 141–144 are repeated in the pagination.

CONDITION: Size of leaf, 5⅝ × 4⁹⁄₁₀ inches. Bound in light brown morocco, leather hinges, gilt edges; by C. Lewis. Closely trimmed at top; many head-lines and a few page-numbers and side-notes cut into.

OTHER COPIES.

Britwell Library (Roxburghe-Sykes copy).

REFERENCES.

Lee, *Life of Shakespeare* (1898), p. 184, *note*; Locker-Lampson, *Catalogue*

LOVES MARTYR:
OR,
ROSALINS COMPLAINT·

Allegorically shadowing the truth of Loue,
in the constant Fate of the Phœnix
and Turtle.

A Poeme enterlaced with much varietie and raritie;
now first translated out of the venerable Italian Torquato
Cæliano, *by* Robert Chester.

With the true legend of famous King *Arthur*, the last of the nine
Worthies, being the first *Essay* of a new *Brytish* Poet: collected
out of diuerse Authenticall Records,

*To these are added some new compositions, of seuerall moderne Writers
whose names are subscribed to their seuerall workes, vpon the
first Subiect: viz.* the Phœnix *and*
Turtle.

Mar: ——— *Mutare dominum non potest liber notus.*

LONDON
Imprinted for E. R.

No. 558. Title-page of Chester's Loves Martyr; 1st Edition; 1601.

(1886), p. 15; Winsor, *Shakespeare's Poems* (Harvard University, *Bibliographical Contributions*, No. 2; 1879), p. 9; Hazlitt, *Collections and Notes* (1876), p. 84; Lowndes, 1 (1869): 433; Corser, *Collectanea Anglo-Poetica*, Part 4 (Chetham Society, Vol. LXXVII.; 1869), pp. 339, 349; Hazlitt, *Hand-Book* (1867), p. 99.

The Daniel-Tite-Locker Lampson copy, with ex-libris of the last.
Of this work there were two editions printed, the First in 1601, the Second in 1611.

The First Edition (1601) is that here described.

Of the Second Edition (1611), a reissue with a new title-page, *The Annals of Great Brittaine*, printed for Matthew Lownes, with the preliminary matter of the First Edition (two leaves after the title, containing the dedication, the author's request to the phœnix, and a short address to the reader) suppressed, the only known copy (the Lyte-Corser copy) is that in the British Museum.

On the recto of the first fly-leaf of the copy here described is written in ink: "*This volume is of the greatest rarity. A copy was sold many years ago, & was purchased, I think, by M. Miller for £68.0.0. The present is a very fine & perfect one. The date is not cut off, the* Title *never having had one. The date (1601) will be found at p. 165. . . . At Page 171* [really *172*] *is a poem ("Threnos") by Shakespeare. . . . George Daniel, Canonbury, 1838.*"

Laid into this copy is a catalogue slip from the Tite sale *Catalogue*, which, after quoting the above note, proceeds as follows:

"In confirmation of the excessive rarity of this volume see Mr. Halliwell's notes, that of 20 July, 1864, in which he writes, 'of extraordinary rarity, and immense literary interest, including the only contribution of Shakespeare to any other author's work;' and that of 25 July, 1864, in which he again writes to Sir W. Tite: 'I was so impressed with the excessive rarity and literary importance of Chester's Loves Martyr that I raised the commission for it on the morning of sale from £160. to £180. It sold for £138. Next to the Shakespeare quartos and Romeus and Juliet, it is the literary gem of the sale.'"

This is the only work by another author to which Shakespeare contributed. The poem "Threnos," says Corser, "is culled from 'The Passionate Pilgrim,' and is the xx. in that collection. It has been copied by Malone, in his *Supplement*."

In the "Diverſe Poeticall Eſſaies" are to be found eighteen stanzas by Shakespeare, pp. 170–172, subscribed with the poet's name in full, "*Wiłliam Shake-ſpeare*." This poem here appears for the first time.

SHAKESPEARE, WILLIAM.

SONNETS. London, *by G. Eld for T. T.*, 1609. [559]

Small quarto. First Edition.

COLLATION BY SIGNATURES: [A], 2 leaves; B to K, each 4 leaves; L, 2 leaves; total 40 unnumbered leaves. Leaves B4 and K4 have signature-marks.

COLLATION BY PAGINATION: [title, as reproduced; *See* No. 559*a*], recto of [A]; —[blank], verso of [A]; —[dedication, as reproduced; *See* No. 559*b*], recto of [A2]; —[blank], verso of [A2]; —[text, with heading] | [conventional head-piece] | Shake-speares, | sonnets. | , recto of B to recto of K; — | FINIS. | , recto of K; —[text, with heading] | A Louers complaint. | *B Y* | William Shake-speare. | , verso of K to verso of L2; — | FINIS. | [type-ornament tail-piece] |, verso of L2.

Condition: Size of leaf, 6⅞ × 5 inches at top, 4⅞ inches at bottom. Bound in brown morocco, gilt edges; with the monogram

SHAKE-SPEARES

SONNETS.

Neuer before Imprinted.

pretium — f — N. L. S^r.

Gloria virtutis merces.

George Steevens.

AT LONDON
By *G. Eld* for *T. T.* and are
to be folde by *Iohn Wright*, dwelling
at Chrift Church gate.
1609.

No. 559 a. TITLE-PAGE OF SHAKESPEARE'S SONNETS; 1ST EDITION; 1609.

of George Daniel within a small circle in the centre of the front cover; by Charles Lewis. The leaves are stabbed on the inner margins throughout. There are marginal marks in ink under the fourth line of many sonnets, and sonnet 129 has been crossed out.

OTHER COPIES.

Aspley imprint: British Museum (Inglis?-Grenville copy); Bodleian (Malone copy); Ellesmere (Bridgewater-Chalmers copy); and Halsey (Jolley-Utterson-Halliwell Phillipps-Tite-Locker Lampson copy) Libraries. Wright imprint: British Museum (Bright copy); Bodleian (Caldecott copy); Capell Collection (imperfect; Wright title-page supplied in manuscript); Rylands (Farmer-Spencer copy); and Huth (Bentinck-Halliwell Phillipps copy) Libraries. Still another copy, with title-page and dedication in facsimile, is owned by W. A. White, of Brooklyn, N. Y.

REFERENCES.

Lee, *Shakespeare's Sonnets, 1609* (Facsimile Edition; 1905), p. 64; British Museum, *Catalogue*; Shakespeare (1897), col. 148; Grolier Club, *Langland to Wither* (1893), p. 184, No. 211; Locker-Lampson, *Catalogue* (1886), p. 111 (Aspley imprint); Huth, *Catalogue*, 4 (1880): 1340; Winsor, *Shakespeare's Poems* (Harvard University, Bibliographical Contributions, No. 2; 1879), p. 8; Lowndes, 4 (1869): 2307; Hazlitt, *Hand-Book* (1867), p. 546, No. 4; *Bibliotheca Anglo-Poetica* (1815), p. 301.

The Luttrell-Steevens-Roxburghe-Daniel-Griswold copy.

The recto of the second fly-leaf has the following note, written in ink:

"*Shakespeare's Sonnets, 1609.*

"*Large, sound, beautiful, & perfect copy. Bound by Charles Lewis. 1829.*

"*The Copies of Shakespeare's Sonnets usually met with are stated in the imprint to be sold by William Aspley, without the mention of any place of business. The very curious variation in the imprint of the present copy was first commented upon by M*.^r *Collier, in his edition of Shakespeare, Vol. 8. p. 471, and, in a recent number of the Athenæum, he states it is so rare that not a single perfect copy exists in England.*

"*A copy with the* same imprint, *but dirty; with the top margins cut close, & with some of the head lines cut into the print, belonging to M*.^r *Halliwell, was sold by Mess.*^s *Sotheby & Wilkinson, June 14: 1858, to M*.^r *Lilly, for One Hundred & forty seven Guineas. . . .* [Signed] *George Daniel, Canonbury.*"

At the end of the seventeenth century the copy here described was purchased by Narcissus Luttrell for one shilling. It subsequently belonged to George Steevens and has his autograph on the title-page. It was sold in 1800 at the sale of his library for £3 19s. It was then acquired by the Duke of Roxburghe, at the sale of whose library in 1812 it brought £21 10s. It was again sold at Evans' salesrooms in a valuable collection of "Books of a Gentleman gone abroad," on January 25, 1830, for £29 10s. 6d., and was afterward acquired by George Daniel, whose monogram is stamped on the cover. At the sale of his library in 1864 it was sold for £225 15s., and afterward passed into the collection of Almon W. Griswold of New York, from whose possession it passed into the present collection. The title-page was reproduced in facsimile in the Grolier Club's *Langland to Wither* (1893), p. 185.

This volume contains 154 numbered sonnets, to which are appended "A Louers Complaint." The *Sonnets* were only once separately printed before 1640, when

TO.THE.ONLIE.BEGETTER.OF.
THESE.INSVING.SONNETS.
Mʳ. W. H. ALL.HAPPINESSE.
AND.THAT.ETERNITIE.
PROMISED.

BY.

OVR.EVER-LIVING.POET.

WISHETH.

THE.WELL-WISHING.
ADVENTVRER.IN.
SETTING.
FORTH.

T. T.

No. 559 *b*.   DEDICATION OF SHAKESPEARE'S SONNETS; 1ST EDITION; 1609.

they were incorporated in the collected edition of Shakespeare's Poems.   Of this edition (1609) there are two issues.

In one issue the imprint reads: | AT LONDON | By *G. Eld* for *T. T.* and are | to be folde by *William Aspley.* | 1609. | .   The Bodleian copy with this imprint was reproduced in facsimile by Sidney Lee in his Facsimile Edition in 1905.

In the other issue, that here described, the imprint reads as in our reproduction. The British Museum copy with this imprint was reproduced in the Praetorius-Furnivall *Shakspere-Quarto Facsimiles* [1886], No. 30.

"From Meres's 'Wits Treasury', 1598, it is known that although not printed until 1609, these 'sugred sonnets' were circulated by the author in manuscript 'among his private friends' certainly as early as 1598."

SHAKESPEARE, WILLIAM.

POEMS. LONDON, *Tho. Cotes, and are to be ſold by Iohn Benſon,* 1640. [560]

Small octavo. First Edition.

COLLATION BY SIGNATURES: *, 4 leaves; A to L, each 8 leaves; M, 4 leaves; total 96 unnumbered leaves. Leaf B 3 is wrongly marked B 5.

COLLATION BY PAGINATION: [title, as reproduced; *See* No. 560], recto of [*]; —[blank], verso of [*]; — | [type-ornament head-piece] | To the Reader. | [signed] | I. B. | , recto and verso of * 2 ; — | [type-ornament head-piece] | Vpon Maſter WILLIAM | SHAKESPEARE, the | *Deceaſed Authour, and his* | POEMS. | [signed] | *Leon. Digges.* | , recto of * 3 to recto of [* 4] ; — | [type-ornament head-piece] | Of M^r. *William Shakespeare.* | [signed] | *John Warren.* | , verso of [* 4] ; — [title, as reproduced, but without date and with the last line centred], recto of [A] ; — [blank], verso of [A] ; — | [type-ornament head-piece] | POEMS | BY | WILL. SHAKESPEARE | Gent. | , recto of A 2 to verso of L ; — | FINIS. | , verso of L ; — | [type-ornament rule] | An Addition of ſome Excellent | Poems, to thoſe precedent, of | Renowned *Shakeſpeare,* | By other Gentlemen. | , recto of L 2 to recto of [M 4] ; — | FINIS. | , recto of [M 4] ; — [blank], verso of [M 4].

PLATE : Portrait of Shakespeare, engraved by William Marshall after the portrait by Droeshout; with 8 lines of verse; signed | *W. M. ſculpſit.* | ; facing the title-page.

CONDITION: Size of leaf, 5 9/16 x 3 1/2 inches. Bound in cadet blue crushed levant morocco, gilt edges; by Rivière.

OTHER COPIES.

British Museum (2); Bodleian (Malone copy); Capell Collection; Shakespeare Memorial, Stratford; Huth; Hunterian Museum, Glasgow; Boston Public; Lenox; Chew; Winston H. Hagen; Halsey; Hoe; Morgan (Irwin copy); Valentine; White; Furness (Heber copy, imperfect); and Wrenn Libraries; also the Locker Lampson-Van Antwerp copy (untraced).

REFERENCES.

Lee, *Shakespeare's Sonnets, 1609* (Facsimile Edition; 1905), p. 69; Hoe, *Catalogue,* 4 (1904): 108; British Museum, *Catalogue;* Shakespeare (1897), col. 40; *The Cambridge Shakespeare,* 9 (1895): xvii., xviii.; Grolier Club, *Catalogue of Original and Early Editions of ſome of the Poetical and Proſe Works of Engliſh Writers from Langland to Wither* (1893), p. 184, No. 212; Locker-Lampson, *Catalogue* (1886), p. 111; Boston Public Library, *Catalogue;* Barton Collection (1880), p. 51, No. 743; Huth, *Catalogue,* 4 (1880): 1341; Lenox Library, *Works of Shakespeare* (1880), p. 10, No. 6; Winsor, *Shakespeare's Poems. A Bibliography of the Earlier Editions* (Harvard University, Bibliographical Contributions, No. 2; 1879), p. 8; Lowndes, 4 (1869): 2307; Hazlitt, *Hand-Book* (1867), p. 546, No. 5; *Bibliotheca Anglo-Poetica; or, A Descriptive Catalogue of a Rare and Rich Collection of Early English Poetry* (1815), p. 301.

This is the only collected edition of Shakespeare's poems that was published during the seventeenth century. The volume was a bookseller's compilation, and has little or no value as an authority in the settlement of questions regarding the correctness of the text. *Lucrece* and *Venus and Adonis* are omitted, but it contains some of the poems from *The Passionate Pilgrim* and *A Lover's Complaint.* It also contains some translations from Ovid and poems by Ben Jonson, Beaumont, Fletcher, and other writers of the period.

POEMS:

VVRITTEN
BY
WIL. SHAKE-SPEARE.
Gent.

Printed at *London* by *Tho. Cotes,* and are to be sold by *Iohn Benson,* dwelling in S*t*. *Dunstans* Church-yard. 1640.

No. 560.   Title-page of Shakespeare's Poems; 1st Edition; 1640.

"The order of the poems in this volume," says the editor of *The Cambridge Shakespeare,* "is very arbitrary, but it is followed in the editions by Gildon (1710), and Sewell (1725 and 1728), as well as those published by Ewing (1771) and by Evans (1775). In all these editions, Sonnets 18, 19, 43, 56, 75, 76, 96 and 126 are omitted, and Sonnets 138 and 144 are given in the form in which they appear in the 'Passionate Pilgrim.'"

SHAKESPEARE, WILLIAM. Etching Club.

SONGS OF SHAKESPEARE. LONDON, *by Gad & Keningale,* 1843. [561]

Folio. A collection of 19 plates, including title-page, proofs on India paper, containing songs (printed in red) from Shakespeare, with etchings by Horsley, Stonhouse, Bell, Webster, Knight, and others, 35 in all.

COLLATION: [rubricated title] | SONGS | OF | SHAKESPEARE, | ILLUSTRATED | BY | THE ETCHING CLUB. | LONDON. | MDCCCXLIII. | PRINTED BY GAD & KENINGALE. |, followed by 18 plates, as follows:

[1] | "MY LADY SWEET, ARISE." | CYMBELINE — ACT 2. SCENE 3. |.

[2] | ARIEL'S SONG. | TEMPEST — ACT 1. SCENE 2. |.

[3] | AUTOLYCUS' SONG. | WINTER'S TALE — ACT 4. SCENE 2 & 3. |.

[4] | "WHERE THE BEE SUCKS." | TEMPEST — ACT 5. SCENE 1. |.

[5] | DRINKING SONG. | OTHELLO — ACT 2. SCENE 3. |.

[6] | "UNDER THE GREENWOOD TREE." | AS YOU LIKE IT — ACT 2. SCENE 5. |.

[7] | THE SONG OF POOR BARBARA. | OTHELLO — ACT 4. SCENE 3. |.

[8] | THE FORESTER'S SONG. | AS YOU LIKE IT — ACT 4. SCENE 2. |.

[9] | YOUTH AND AGE. | THE PASSIONATE PILGRIM. |.

[10] | SLEEPEST, OR WAKEST THOU | KING LEAR — ACT 3. SCENE 6. |.

[11] | THE VINE. | SONG IN ANTONY AND CLEOPATRA — ACT 2. SCENE 7. |.

[12] | FAIRIES' SONG. | MIDSUMMER NIGHT'S DREAM — ACT 2. SCENE 3. |.

[13] | WHO IS SYLVIA? | TWO GENTLEMEN OF VERONA — ACT IV. SCENE II. |.

[14] | COME AWAY, COME AWAY, DEATH. | TWELFTH NIGHT; OR, WHAT YOU WILL — ACT 2. SCENE 4. |.

[15] | CALIBANS' SONG. | TEMPEST — ACT 2. SCENE 2. |.

[16] | BLOW, BLOW, THOU WINTER WIND. | AS YOU LIKE IT — ACT 2. SCENE 7. |.

[17] | BALTHAZARS' SONG. | MUCH ADO ABOUT NOTHING — ACT 2. SCENE 3. |.

[18] | WINTER SONG. | LOVE'S LABOUR LOST — ACT 5. SCENE 2. |.

CONDITION: Size of leaf, $14\tfrac{3}{4} \times 10\tfrac{7}{8}$ inches. Bound in lavender bevelled boards, lettered: | Songs | and | Ballads | of | Shakspeare. | on the front cover, and | The | Etching | Club. | on the back cover.

REFERENCES.

Boston Public Library, *Catalogue;* *Barton Collection* (1880), p. 51, No. 746; Lowndes, 6 (1869): 87.

This work was presented to subscribers of the Royal Polytechnic Union.

SHAKESPEARE'S PLAYS — QUARTO EDITIONS.

Of the plays contained in the First Folio, sixteen, or, if we include the First Part of the *Whole Contention* and the *True Tragedie* as the Second and Third Parts of *Henry VI.*, eighteen appeared, most of them in several editions, during Shakespeare's lifetime. Between his death and 1623, when the First Folio was published, *Othello* appeared for the first time, in 1622. All of these and *The Taming of the Shrew,* together with *The Sonnets* and *A Lover's Complaint,* were reprinted by Steevens in his *Twenty Plays* (1766). Even after the appearance of the First Folio numerous editions of the plays were published, so that before and including the year 1700 more than 190 different editions had been issued. In this number are, of course, included not only (*a*) the plays actually written by Shakespeare himself, but (*b*) those known as Source Plays; (*c*) those known as Players' Quartos, printed for stage purposes; and (*d*) Alterations or Adaptations of Shakespeare's plays by later writers. To these should also be added a number of Supposititious Plays, which, at one time or another, have been falsely ascribed to Shakespeare. An account of these latter plays will be found under our No. 621.

The thirty-six plays which appeared in the First Folio were in that volume divided into three groups: Comedies (14), Histories (10), and Tragedies (12); *Pericles* not being included until the Third Folio in 1664.

The separate editions of the plays, in the descriptions which follow, are arranged in the order in which they occur in the First Folio, as follows; those there printed for the first time being marked with an asterisk (*):

COMEDIES.

- *The Tempest.
- *The Two Gentlemen of Verona.
- The Merry Wives of Windsor.
- *Measure for Measure.
- *The Comedy of Errors.
- Much Ado about Nothing.
- Love's Labour's Lost.
- A Midsummer Night's Dream.
- The Merchant of Venice.
- *As You Like It.
- *The Taming of the Shrew.
- *All's Well that Ends Well.
- *Twelfth Night.
- *The Winter's Tale.

HISTORIES.

- *King John.
- Richard II.
- Henry IV., Part I.
- Henry IV., Part II.
- Henry V.
- *Henry VI., Part I.
- *Henry VI., Part II.
- *Henry VI., Part III.
- Richard III.
- *Henry VIII.

TRAGEDIES.

- Troilus and Cressida.
- *Coriolanus.
- Titus Andronicus.
- Romeo and Juliet.
- *Timon of Athens.
- *Julius Cæsar.
- *Macbeth.
- Hamlet.
- King Lear.
- Othello.
- *Anthony and Cleopatra.
- *Cymbeline.
- Pericles (Third Folio).

COMEDIES.

(1) *The Tempest* was printed for the first time in the First Folio.

This play as altered by John Dryden was published as *The Tempeſt, or The Enchanted Iſland* in 1670, 1674, 1676, 1690, and 1695. Dryden in his preface claims Sir William Davenant as a collaborator.

Of the First Edition (1670), "J. M. for Henry Herringman," there are copies in the British Museum, Bodleian, Trinity College (Cambridge), Devonshire,

Ellesmere, Dyce Collection, Huth, Harvard University, Boston Public (2), Hoe, White and Wrenn Libraries, and the Library of Congress.

Of the Second Edition (1674), "T. N. for Henry Herringman," there are copies in the Bodleian, Ellesmere, and Harvard University Libraries.

Of the Third Edition (1676), "J. Macock, for Henry Herringman," there are copies in the British Museum, Bodleian, Trinity College (Cambridge), Birmingham Free, Dyce Collection (3), Devonshire, Harvard University, Boston Public, Lenox, and White Libraries.

Of the Fourth Edition (1690), "J. M. for H. Herringman, fold by R. Bentley," there are copies in the British Museum, Bodleian, Trinity College (Dublin), Harvard University, Boston Public (2), Lenox, Hoe, and White Libraries, and the Library of Congress.

Of the Fifth Edition (1695), "by Tho. Warren, for Henry Herringman," there are copies in the Bodleian, Birmingham Free, Harvard University, Lenox, and White Libraries.

An edition of this play as altered by Thomas Duffet, and entitled *The Mock Tempeſt: Or The Enchanted Caſtle*, was published in 1675. Of this there are copies in the Harvard University and other libraries.

(2) *The Two Gentlemen of Verona* was first printed in the First Folio, and did not subsequently appear in a separate edition during the seventeenth century.

(3) *The Merry Wives of Windsor* was first published in the quarto edition of 1602 (our No. 562).

(4) *Measure for Measure* was first printed in the Folio of 1623.

This play as altered by Sir William Davenant was published as *The Law againſt Lovers* in his *Works* (pp. 272–329, second pagination), in 1673. This altered play is a mixture of the two plots of *Measure for Measure* and *Much Ado about Nothing*. There are copies of Davenant's *Works* in the British Museum, Bodleian, Trinity College and University Library (Cambridge), Dyce Collection, and Boston Public (2) Libraries, and the Library of Congress.

Of this play as altered by Charles Gildon and published as *Meaſure for Meaſure; or, Beauty the Beſt Advocate*, "for D. Brown, and R. Parker," in 1700, there are copies in the British Museum (3), Bodleian (2), Devonshire, Birmingham Free, Boston Public, and White Libraries.

(5) *The Comedy of Errors* was first printed in the Folio of 1623. It does not seem to have been issued separately during the seventeenth century.

(6) *Much Ado about Nothing* was published in but one quarto edition, that of 1600 (our No. 564).

(7) *Love's Labour's Lost* first appeared in the quarto edition of 1598 (our No. 565).

(8) Of *A Midsummer Night's Dream* two editions were printed in 1600, the Second of which is in the present collection (our No. 567).

(9) *The Merchant of Venice* also first appeared in two different editions in 1600, both of which are in the present collection (our Nos. 568 and 569).

(10) *As You Like It* was printed for the first time in the Folio of 1623. It does not seem to have been issued separately.

(11) *The Taming of the Shrew* first appeared in the First Folio. Of the reprint in quarto (1631) there is a copy in the present collection (our No. 571).

(12) *All's Well that Ends Well* appeared in print for the first time in the First Folio, and was not reprinted separately.

(13) *Twelfth Night; or, What You Will* is found for the first time in the Folio of 1623, and does not seem to have been issued separately.

(14) *The Winter's Tale* also first appeared in print in the First Folio. No separate edition appears to have been published.

HISTORIES.

(1) *King John* was printed for the first time in the Folio of 1623. No separate edition of this play was published.

The Source Play, *The Troublefome Raigne of King Iohn of England*, of which Shakespeare made use in the construction of his drama, first appeared in 1591, and was followed by other editions in 1611 and 1622. A copy of the Second Edition is in the present collection (our No. 572).

(2) *Richard II.* was first published in the quarto edition of 1597. A copy of the Second Edition (1598) is in the present collection (our No. 573).

(3) *Henry IV.*, Part I., was printed for the first time in the quarto edition of 1598. There is a copy of the Second Edition (1599) in the present collection (our No. 577).

(4) *Henry IV.*, Part II., appeared in but two quarto editions, both in 1600. Copies of each of these are in the present collection (our Nos. 581 and 582).

(5) *Henry V.* first appeared in the quarto edition of 1600 (our No. 583).

(6) *Henry VI.*, Part I., was printed for the first time in the Folio of 1623, and was not published separately.

This play as altered by John Crowne appeared as *Henry the Sixth, The Firſt Part. With the Murder of Humphrey Duke of Glocefter*, "for R. Bentley, and M. Magnes," in 1681. Of this edition there are copies in the British Museum (2), Bodleian Library (2), Dyce Collection, Devonshire, Huth, Harvard University, Hoe, and White Libraries.

(7) *Henry VI.*, Part II., originally appeared in 1594 as *The Firſt Part of the Contention betwixt the two famous Houfes of Yorke and Lancafter*. A copy of the Third Edition [1619], forming the First Part, leaves A–[H 4], of *The Whole Contention betweene the two Famous Houfes, Lancafter and Yorke*, is in the present collection (our No. 585).

(8) *Henry VI.*, Part III., first appeared in print as *The true Tragedie of Richard Duke of Yorke*, in 1595. The Second Edition (1600) is in the present collection (our No. 586).

(9) Of *Richard III.* no fewer than eight editions were published in quarto, the

first appearing in 1597. Of the Second Edition (1598) there is a copy in the present collection (our No. 588).

(10) *Henry VIII.* appeared in print for the first time in the Folio of 1623, and does not seem to have been separately reprinted.

TRAGEDIES

(1) *Troilus and Cressida* was first given to the public in the two quarto editions of 1609, one of which, the Second Edition, is in the present collection (our No. 593).

(2) *Coriolanus* was printed for the first time in the Folio of 1623.

An edition of this play, altered by Nahum Tate, was published in 1682, "by T. M. for Joseph Hindmarsh," under the title *The Ingratitude of a Common-Wealth: Or, the Fall of Caius Martius Coriolanus.* Of this edition there are copies in the British Museum (2), Bodleian, Harvard University, Devonshire, Huth, Boston Public, Hoe, White, and Wrenn Libraries.

(3) *Titus Andronicus* was first published in 1594. Though this edition was mentioned by Gerard Langbaine the younger in the latter part of the seventeenth century, no copy of it was known until one was discovered at Lund in Sweden in January, 1905. There is a copy of the Third Edition (1611) in the present collection (our No. 594).

(4) *Romeo and Juliet* was printed for the first time in the quarto edition of 1597. There is a copy of the Second Edition (1599) in the present collection (our No. 595).

(5) *Timon of Athens* was printed for the first time in the Folio of 1623. Shakespeare's text was not printed separately.

This play as altered by Thomas Shadwell was first published as *The History of Timon of Athens, the Man-Hater,* in 1678. Later editions appeared in [1680?], 1688, and 1696.

Of the First Edition (1678), "by J. M. for Henry Herringman," there are copies in the British Museum, Bodleian (2), Birmingham Free, Devonshire, Huth, Boston Public, Hoe, and White Libraries, and the Library of Congress.

Of the Second Edition (1680?), "H. Hills," there are copies in the British Museum and Boston Public (ascribed in the *Barton Catalogue* to 1700) Libraries.

Of the Third Edition (1688), "H. Herringman," there are copies in the British Museum, Harvard University, and Boston Public Libraries, and the Library of Congress.

Of the Fourth Edition (1696), "H. Herringman," there are copies in the British Museum, Boston Public, and White Libraries.

(6) *Julius Cæsar* was printed for the first time in the Folio of 1623. It was not separately printed until about 1680, when it appeared in an undated edition (our No. 599).

(7) *Macbeth* first appeared in the Folio of 1623.

The first separate edition of this play, reprinted from the First Folio with changes in the witch scenes, was printed "for William Cademan," in 1673. Of this edition there are copies in the British Museum, Bodleian, Birmingham Free, Dyce Collection, and Ellesmere Libraries.

The lines of this edition differing from the First Folio have been reprinted in Furness's *New Variorum Edition* (1903), pp. 507–543. That editor, to prevent confusion, cites this edition as Betterton's version.

This play as altered by Davenant was published in several editions: 1674 (two editions), 1687, and 1695.

Of the First Edition (1674), "for P. Chetwin," there are copies in the British Museum, Bodleian (2), Devonshire, Lenox, Hoe, and White Libraries.

Of the Second Edition (also 1674), "for A. Clark," there are copies in the Bodleian, Edinburgh University, Boston Public, and White Libraries.

Of the Third Edition (1687), "for Hen: Herringman fold by Jos. Knight and Fra. Saunders," there are copies in the British Museum, Bodleian, Birmingham Free, Trinity College (Dublin), White, and Wrenn (2) Libraries.

Of the Fourth Edition (1695), "for H. Herringman, and R. Bentley; and fold by R. Bentley, J. Tonfon, T. Bennet, and F. Sanders," there are copies in the British Museum (2), Bodleian, Trinity College (Cambridge), Forster Collection in the South Kensington Museum, Boston Public, and Hoe Libraries.

(8) *Hamlet* was first printed in the quarto edition of 1603. The Fourth Edition (1611) is in the present collection (our No. 600).

(9) *King Lear* first appeared in two quarto editions in 1608, the Second of which is in the present collection (our No. 603).

(10) *Othello* was first printed in the quarto edition of 1622. The Second Edition (1630) of this play is in the present collection (our No. 605).

(11) *Anthony and Cleopatra* was printed for the first time in the Folio of 1623.

This play as altered by Dryden was published in 1678 as *All for Love: or, The World well Loft*. Other editions followed in 1692 and 1696.

Of the First Edition (1678), "by Tho. Newcomb, for Henry Herringman," there are copies in the British Museum (2), Bodleian, Dyce Collection (2), Devonshire, Birmingham Free, Huth, Harvard University, Boston Public (3), Hoe, White, and Wrenn Libraries, and the Library of Congress.

Of the Second Edition (1692), "for H. Herringman, and Sold by R. Bently, J. Tonfon, F. Saunders, and T. Bennet," there are copies in the British Museum, Bodleian, Dyce Collection, Devonshire, Harvard University, and Hoe Libraries.

Of the Third Edition (1696), "H. Herringman," there are copies in the British Museum, Trinity College (Cambridge), Birmingham Free, Harvard University, and Boston Public Libraries.

Another but different play of the same name, by Sir Charles Sedley, founded on the same story, was published in 1677.

(12) *Cymbeline* first appeared in the Folio of 1623, and is the last play in that volume.

This play as altered by Thomas Durfey was printed "for R. Bentley and M.

Magnes," in 1682, as *The Injured Princes, or the Fatal Wager*. There are copies of this edition in the British Museum (2), Bodleian, Dyce Collection, Devonshire, Huth, and White Libraries.

(13) *Pericles* first appeared in two quarto editions in 1609, one of which, the Second Edition, is in the present collection (our No. 607).

SHAKESPEARE, WILLIAM.

THE MERRY WIVES OF WINDSOR. LONDON, *by T. C. for Arthur Iohnſon*, 1602. [562]

Small quarto. First Edition.

COLLATION BY SIGNATURES: A to G, each 4 leaves; total 28 unnumbered leaves.

COLLATION BY PAGINATION: [1 blank leaf, except that the recto has the signature-mark A];—[title, as reproduced; *See* No. 562], recto of [A 2];—[blank], verso of [A 2];—[text, with heading] | [conventional head-piece] | A pleaſant conceited Co-| medie, of Syr *Iohn Falſtaffe*, and the | merry Wiues of *VVindſor*.|, recto of A 3 to verso of [G 4]; — | *FINIS*.|, verso of [G 4].

CONDITION: Size of leaf, 6¾ × 4⅞ inches. Bound in red crushed levant morocco, gilt edges; by Bedford.

OTHER COPIES.

Bodleian (Malone copy); Capell Collection; Shakespeare Memorial, Stratford (two leaves only); Devonshire; and Huth (the Theobald-Steevens-Bindley-Heber-Daniel copy) Libraries.

REFERENCES.

The Cambridge Shakespeare, 1 (1902): 199; Greg, *List of English Plays* (Bibliographical Society; 1900), pp. 99, 100; Locker-Lampson, *Appendix to Catalogue* (1900), p. 27; Hazlitt, *Manual of Old English Plays* (1892), p. 156; Huth, *Catalogue*, 4 (1880): 1336; Winsor, *Bibliography* (1876), p. 48; Lowndes, 4 (1869): 2288; Hazlitt, *Hand-Book* (1867), p. 549, No. 17 a.

The Gaisford-Locker Lampson copy, with the ex-libris of the former.

Of this play several editions appeared, this being the First. Other editions were published in 1619 and 1630.

The First Edition (1602), that here described, was reproduced in the Ashbee-Halliwell *Facsimiles* (1866), No. 23, and also (the Devonshire copy and 4 pages from the Huth copy) in the Griggs-Furnivall *Shakspere-Quarto Facsimiles* [1881], No. 6.

The Second Edition (1619) is that described in our next number.

The Third Edition (1630), "printed by T. H., for R. Meighen," was reprinted from the First Folio. There are copies in the British Museum, Bodleian, Capell Collection, Edinburgh University, Ellesmere, Boston Public, and Lenox Libraries; also the Howe copy (untraced). This edition was reprinted by Steevens in his *Twenty Plays* (1766), Vol. 1.

The text of the First and Second Editions is an early sketch of that of the Third Edition. It differs so greatly from the received text that it has been reprinted in *The Cambridge Shakespeare* (9: 421–460).

A
Moſt pleaſaunt and
excellent conceited Co-
medie, of Syr *Iohn Falſtaffe*, and the
merrie Wiues of *Windſor*.

Entermixed with ſundrie
variable and pleaſing humors, of Syr *Hugh*
the Welch Knight, Iuſtice *Shallow*, and his
wiſe Couſin M. *Slender*.

With the ſwaggering vaine of Auncient
Piſtoll, and Corporall *Nym*.

By *William Shakeſpeare*.

As it hath bene diuers times Acted by the right Honorable
my Lord Chamberlaines ſeruants. Both before her
Maieſtie, and elſe-where.

LONDON
Printed by T. C. for Arthur Iohnſon, and are to be ſold at
his ſhop in Powles Church-yard, at the ſigne of the
Flower de Leuſe and the Crowne.
1 6 0 2.

No. 562. Title-page of Shakespeare's Merry Wives of Windsor;
1st Edition; 1602.

No. 562 *William Shakespeare* 1602

On the second fly-leaf of the copy here described is a note in pencil, as follows: "*This is the first sketch of this play, which was not printed entire until it appeared in the folio of 1623. The only other copies besides the present are in Bodleian, the Capel Collection & the Duke of Devonshire's & Mr. Huth's; this last had belonged to Wm Bindley, Heber and G. Daniel. See Huth Catalogue, Vol. V, Page 1337. See also Daniel sale Cat.*"

On a slip tipped in on the recto of the last fly-leaf is the following note: "*This 4to of the Merry Wives of Windsor (1602) was sold at Sotheby's on 30 Ap! 1890, in the coll. of Thos Gaisford, & fetched £385. An American bid up to £375 & lost it. Mr. Gaisford was present & he told me that this 4to & three others (1) Love's Labour lost 1st Edⁿ. (2) " Much Ado about Nothing" and "the London Prodigal" came to him the four plays bound together in an old paper cover. That excepting for a leaf in facsimile which he added to the last, they were in their present state. All he did was to get them bound by Bedford. Gaisford said they had been a century in the family from whom he had them.*

"*Daniel's copy sold in '64 fetched £346.10/. Considering the price such books sell for now this is not dearer than Daniel's.*"

SHAKESPEARE, WILLIAM.

THE MERRY WIVES OF WINDSOR. LONDON, *for Arthur Johnfon*, 1619.

[563]

Small quarto. Second Edition.
COLLATION BY SIGNATURES: A to G, each 4 leaves; total 28 unnumbered leaves.
COLLATION BY PAGINATION: [title, as reproduced; *See* No. 563], recto of [A]; —[blank], verso of [A];—[text, with heading] | [conventional head-piece] | A | Pleafant conceited Come- | die of Sir IOHN FALSTAFFE, | *and the merry wiues of VVindfor.* |, recto of A 2 to verso of [G 4]; — | FINIS. |, verso of [G 4].
CONDITION: Size of leaf, 7⅜₁₆ × 5⅜ inches. Bound in red straight-grained morocco, gilt edges; by Bedford.

OTHER COPIES.

British Museum (2, one the Garrick copy); Bodleian (Malone copy); Capell Collection; Dyce Collection; Shakespeare Memorial, Stratford (Van Antwerp copy); Devonshire; Huth; Boston Public; Perry (Gwynn copy); Lenox; Hoe; Morgan; Trowbridge; and White Libraries: also the Howe copy (untraced).

REFERENCES.

Hoe, *Catalogue*, 4 (1904): 102; Greg, *List of English Plays* (Bibliographical Society; 1900), p. 100; British Museum, *Catalogue*; *Shakespeare* (1897), col. 123; Locker-Lampson, *Catalogue* (1886), p. 104; Boston Public Library, *Catalogue*; *Barton Collection* (1880), p. 32, No. 469; Huth, *Catalogue*, 4 (1880) : 1336; Lenox Library, *Works of Shakespeare* (1880), p. 20, No. 96; Winsor, *Bibliography* (1876), p. 49; Lowndes, 4 (1869) : 2289; Hazlitt, *Hand-Book* (1867), p. 550, No. 17 *b*.

The Locker-Lampson copy, with ex-libris.
This edition was reproduced in the Ashbee-Halliwell *Facsimiles* (1866), No. 47. It was reprinted by Steevens in his *Twenty Plays* (1766), Vol. 1.

A Most pleasant and excellent conceited Comedy,
of Sir Iohn Falstaffe, and the merry VViues of VVindsor.

VVith the fwaggering vaine of Ancient *Piftoll*, and Corporall *Nym*.

Written by W. SHAKESPEARE.

Printed for *Arthur Johnſon*, 1619.

NO. 563.   TITLE-PAGE OF SHAKESPEARE'S MERRY WIVES OF WINDSOR;
2D EDITION; 1619.

"Mr. Knight says 'this play as it now stands appeared first in the folio *1623*. The copy in the folio contains nearly twice the number of lines that the 4to. contains. Except in one instance, the succession of scenes is the same, but the speeches of the several characters are greatly elaborated in the amended copy (or *folio*).'"

CHURCH CATALOGUE   [787]   ENGLISH LITERATURE

SHAKESPEARE, WILLIAM.

MUCH ADO ABOUT NOTHING. LONDON, *by V. S. for Andrew Wiſe, and William Aſpley*, 1600. [564]

Small quarto. First Edition.

COLLATION BY SIGNATURES: A to I, each 4 leaves; total 36 unnumbered leaves.

COLLATION BY PAGINATION: [title, as reproduced; *See* No. 564], recto of [A]; —[blank], verso of [A]; —[text, with heading, enclosed by conventional border] | Much adoe about | *Nothing.* |, recto of A 2 to verso of [I 4]; — | *FINIS.* | [two conventional tail-pieces] |, verso of [I 4].

CONDITION: Size of leaf, 7$\frac{11}{16}$ × 5⅜ inches. Bound in green straight-grained morocco, with George Daniel's monogram on the front cover, gilt edges.

OTHER COPIES.

British Museum (2, one imperfect); Bodleian (Malone copy); Capell Collection; Dyce Collection; Edinburgh University; Devonshire; Ellesmere; Huth; Boston Public (Steevens-Bright copy); and White (the Halliwell-Phillipps copy) Libraries.

REFERENCES.

Plomer, *Shakespeare Printers*. II. *Valentine Simmes*, in *The Bibliographer*, 2 (1903): 299; Greg, *List of English Plays* (Bibliographical Society; 1900), p. 99; Furness, *New Variorum Edition* (1899), p. xiii.; British Museum, *Catalogue*; *Shakespeare* (1897), col. 131; Hazlitt, *Manual of Old English Plays* (1892), p. 161; Locker-Lampson, *Catalogue* (1886), p. 104; Boston Public Library, *Catalogue*; *Barton Collection* (1880), p. 34, No. 505; Huth, *Catalogue*, 4 (1880): 1335; Winsor, *Bibliography* (1876), p. 52; Lowndes, 4 (1869): 2290; Hazlitt, *Hand-Book* (1867), p. 549, No. 15.

The Heber-Daniel-Lewis-Locker Lampson copy, with George Daniel's monogram on the front cover, and with the ex-libris of Lewis and of Locker-Lampson.

On the recto of the first fly-leaf of the copy here described is written: "*Of all my books this is one of the most valuable. F. L.*"

Laid into the copy here described is a slip from a catalogue, which reads: "A marvellous copy. We have no hesitation in saying that, in every respect, the present is by far the finest copy known of this edition, if not the finest copy of any early edition of Shakespeare's Dramas in existence." This is evidently a description of this identical copy.

Of this play but the single quarto edition here described was published.

The "V. S." in the imprint on the title-page stands for Valentine Simmes. The text is not divided into acts. As the play is not mentioned by Meres in his *Palladis Tamia* (our No. 637), in 1598, it was, in all probability, written after that date. From internal evidence it appears to have been written in 1599. It was reproduced in the Ashbee-Halliwell *Facsimiles* (1865), No. 14, also (the Devonshire copy) in the Praetorius-Furnivall *Shakspere-Quarto Facsimiles* (1886), No. 14. Steevens included it in his *Twenty Plays* (1766), Vol. I.

"The First Folio edition," says *The Cambridge Shakespeare* (2: ix.), "was obviously printed from a copy of the Quarto belonging to the library of the theatre, and cor-

Much adoe about Nothing.

As it hath been sundrie times publikely acted by the right honourable, the Lord Chamberlaine his seruants.

Written by William Shakespeare.

LONDON
Printed by V.S. for Andrew Wise, and
William Aspley.
1600.

rected for the purposes of the stage. Some stage directions of interest occur first in the Folio, but as regards the text, where the Folio differs from the Quarto it differs almost always for the worse. The alterations are due however to accident not design."

SHAKESPEARE, WILLIAM.

LOVE'S LABOUR'S LOST. LONDON, *by W. W. for Cutbert Burby*, 1598.

[565]

Small quarto. First Edition.

COLLATION BY SIGNATURES: A to I, each 4 leaves; K, 2 leaves; total 38 unnumbered leaves. The fourth leaf of each sheet has a signature-mark, except leaves [D4] and [F4].

COLLATION BY PAGINATION: [title, as reproduced; *See* No. 565], recto of [A]; —[blank], verso of [A]; —[text, with heading] | [type-ornament head-piece] | Enter Ferdinand K. of Nauar, Berovvne, | Longauill, and Dumaine. | , recto of A2 to verso of K2; — |FINIS.| [conventional tail-piece] | , verso of K2.

CONDITION: Size of leaf, 7¼ × 5⅛ inches. Bound in brown morocco, coats of arms on sides, gilt edges. Leaf A4 is in facsimile.

OTHER COPIES.

British Museum (Bindley-Heber-Daniel copy); Bodleian (Malone copy); Capell Collection; Edinburgh University (Drummond copy); Devonshire; Ellesmere; and White Libraries.

REFERENCES.

Furness, *New Variorum Edition* (1904), p. 324; *The Cambridge Shakespeare*, 2 (1902): ix.; Greg, *List of English Plays* (Bibliographical Society; 1900), p. 98; British Museum, *Catalogue*; *Shakespeare* (1897), col. 194; Locker-Lampson, *Catalogue* (1886), p. 104; Winsor, *Bibliography* (1876), p. 45; Lowndes, 4 (1869): 2285; Hazlitt, *Hand-Book* (1867), p. 548, No. 10.

This play was published twice in quarto, the first time in 1598 and the second in 1631. The First Edition (1598) is that here described. The Second Edition (1631) is that described in our next number.

The words "Newly corrected and augmented" on the title-page of the edition here described has led to the supposition that there may have been an earlier edition. On this point Furness says: "STAUNTON did not 'despair of the first draft, like the *Hamlet* of 1603, turning up some day.' Thus far, however, none has 'turned up' and we must do the best we can with the edition that has survived, making content with our fortune fit, merely with the remark, in passing, that if the Qto of 1598, with its lawless punctuation and abandoned spelling, be a 'corrected' copy, imagination halts before the conception of what in these regards, that lost Qto must have been, and we breathe a sigh of relief and of gratitude over the loss; and yet is this gratitude tempered; we cannot but remember the fertility of such a field and the proud sheaves the commentators would have brought home from it. Let us then regard the vanished treasure of an earlier Qto with one auspicious and one dropping eye."

This edition was reproduced in the Ashbee-Halliwell *Facsimiles* (1869), No. 8, and also (the Devonshire copy) in the Griggs-Furnivall *Shakspere-Quarto Facsimiles* [1880], No. 5. In 1766 Steevens was unable to find a copy from which to make a reprint.

1598   *William Shakespeare*   No. 565

A
PLEASANT
Conceited Comedie
CALLED,
Loues labors loft.

As it vvas prefented before her Highnes
this laft Chriftmas.

Newly corrected and augmented
By *W. Shakespere.*

Imprinted at London by *W.W.*
for *Cutbert Burby.*
1598.

No. 565.   Title-page of Shakespeare's Love's Labour's Lost;
1st Edition; 1598.

The text in the First Folio is a reprint of the first quarto edition, from which it differs only in being divided into acts. As usual, it is inferior to the original in accuracy.

SHAKESPEARE, WILLIAM.

LOVE'S LABOUR'S LOST. LONDON, *by W. S. for Iohn Smethwicke*, 1631.

[566]

Small quarto. Second Edition.

COLLATION BY SIGNATURES: A to I, each 4 leaves; K, 2 leaves; total 38 unnumbered leaves.

COLLATION BY PAGINATION: [title, as reproduced; *See* No. 566], recto of [A]; — [blank], verso of [A]; — [text, with heading] | [conventional head-piece] | Loues Labour's loft. |, recto of A 2 to recto of K 2; — | FINIS. |, recto of K 2; — [blank], verso of K 2.

CONDITION: Size of leaf, 7 1/16 × 5 3/8 inches. Bound in red crushed levant morocco, with coat of arms of Almon W. Griswold on the front cover, gilt edges; by Bedford. The leaves are stabbed on the inner margins throughout, indicating that the book was originally issued stitched, with or without wrappers.

OTHER COPIES.

British Museum (2); Bodleian; Capell Collection; Dyce Collection; Edinburgh University; Boston Public; Lenox; Hoe; Morgan; and White Libraries; also the Howe copy (untraced).

REFERENCES.

Furness, *New Variorum Edition* (1904), p. 323; Hoe, *Catalogue*, 4 (1904): 103; Greg, *List of English Plays* (Bibliographical Society; 1900), p. 98; British Museum, *Catalogue*; *Shakespeare* (1897), col. 104; Boston Public Library, *Catalogue*; *Barton Collection* (1880), p. 27, No. 383; Lenox Library, *Works of Shakespeare* (1880), p. 18, No. 78; Lowndes, 4 (1869): 2285; Hazlitt, *Hand-Book* (1867), p. 548, No. 10 *b*.

The Griswold copy.

This edition was reprinted by Steevens in *Twenty of the Plays of Shakefpeare, Being the whole Number printed in Quarto During his Life-time, or before the Reftoration* (1766), Vol. 1.

SHAKESPEARE, WILLIAM.

A MIDSUMMER NIGHT'S DREAM. LONDON, *Iames Roberts*, 1600.

[567]

Small quarto. Second Edition.

COLLATION BY SIGNATURES: A to H, each 4 leaves; total 32 unnumbered leaves. Leaf B 4 has a signature-mark.

COLLATION BY PAGINATION: [title, as reproduced; *See* No. 567], recto of [A]; — [blank], verso of [A]; — [text, with heading] | [type-ornament head-piece] | A |MIDSOMMER NIGHTS|DREAME.|, recto of A 2 to verso of [H 4]; — | FINIS. | [conventional tail-piece] |, verso of [H 4].

CONDITION: Size of leaf, 7 1/16 × 5 1/4 inches. Bound in red morocco, gilt edges; by Hayday.

OTHER COPIES.

British Museum (2); Bodleian (Malone copy); Capell Collection; Shakespeare Memorial, Stratford (Van Antwerp copy); Edinburgh University; Devonshire; Huth; Boston Public (Bright copy); Perry (Gwynne copy); Lenox; Halsey; Hoe; Morgan (Steevens?-Roxburghe-Hanrott-Asay-Irwin copy); and White Libraries; and the Library of Congress; also the Howe copy (untraced). Winsor locates a copy (the Capell copy) in the library of the Marquis of Bute.

1631   *William Shakespeare*   No. 566

Loues Labours loft.

A WITTIE AND
PLEASANT
COMEDIE,

As it was Acted by his Maiesties Seruants at
the Blacke-Friers *and the* Globe.

Written

By WILLIAM SHAKESPEARE.

LONDON,

Printed by *W.S.* for *Iohn Smethwicke,* and are to be
sold at his Shop in Saint *Dunstones* Church-
yard vnder the Diall.
1631.

No. 566. Title-page of Shakespeare's Love's Labour's Lost;
2d Edition; 1631.

No. 567　　　　　　　*William Shakespeare*　　　　　　　1600

REFERENCES.

Hoe, *Catalogue*, 4 (1904): 96; Greg, *List of English Plays* (Bibliographical Society; 1900), p. 99; British Museum, *Catalogue; Shakespeare* (1897), col. 127; Furness, *New Variorum Edition* (1895), pp. ix, 247; Locker-Lampson, *Catalogue* (1886), p. 105; Hazlitt, *Collections and Notes* (1882), p. 148; Boston Public Library, *Catalogue; Barton Collection* (1880), p. 33, No. 483; Huth, *Catalogue*, 4 (1880): 1335; Lenox Library, *Works of Shakespeare* (1880), p. 21, No. 100; Winsor, *Bibliography* (1876), p. 51; Lowndes, 4 (1869): 2289; Hazlitt, *Hand-Book* (1867), pp. 319, 549, No. 14 a.

The Holgate-Ives copy, with ex-libris of each.

Of this play two editions in quarto appeared the same year.

Of the First Edition (1600), "imprinted for Thomas Fisher," there are copies in the British Museum, Bodleian (Malone copy), Capell Collection (Theobald copy), Devonshire, Ellesmere, Huth, and Boston Public (Heber copy) Libraries. This edition was reproduced in the Ashbee-Halliwell *Facsimiles* (1864), No. 16, and also (the Devonshire and Huth copies, with extra leaves B — B 2 laid in at the end) in the Griggs-Furnivall *Shakspere-Quarto Facsimiles* (1880), No. 3.

The Second Edition (also 1600), that here described, was reproduced in the Ashbee-Halliwell *Facsimiles* (1865), No. 17, and also (the Devonshire copy) in the Griggs-Furnivall *Shakspere-Quarto Facsimiles* (1880), No. 4. It was reprinted by Steevens in his *Twenty Plays* (1766), Vol. 1.

Of the Second Edition Furness says: "The second place is properly allotted to it, because, apart from the plea that an unregistered edition ought not, in the absence of proof, to take precedence of one that is registered, it is little likely, so it seems to me, that Fisher would have applied for a license to print when another edition was already on the market; and he might have saved his registration fee. There are, however, two eminent critics (Halliwell and Fleay) who are inclined to give the priority to this unregistered quarto of Roberts."

"On comparing these two Quartos we find that they correspond page for page, though not line for line, except in the first five pages of sheet G. The printer's errors in Fisher's edition are corrected in that issued by Roberts, and from this circumstance, coupled with the facts that in the Roberts Quarto the 'Exits' are more frequently marked, and that it was not entered at Stationers' Hall, as Fisher's edition was, we infer that the Roberts Quarto was a pirated edition of Fisher's, probably for the use of the players. This may account for its having been followed by the First Folio. Fisher's edition, though carelessly printed, contains on the whole the best readings, and may have been taken from the author's manuscript."

An earlier edition of 1595 is mentioned by Chetwood, but "no copy," says Halliwell, writing in 1841, "either with this date or under this title has yet been discovered." Halliwell's statement, so far as it relates to the discovery of a copy of this alleged edition, still holds true.

The interlude of this play was altered by Robert Cox and separately printed in quarto, in 1661, "for F. Kirkman and H. Marſh," as *The Merry-conceited Humours of Bottom the Weaver*. There are copies in the British Museum (2), Dyce Collection, and Huth Library. In 1672 and again in 1673 it was included in the Second

A
Midſommer nights
dreame.

As it hath beene ſundry times publikely acted, by the Right Honourable, the Lord Chamberlaine his
ſeruants.

VVritten by VVilliam Shakeſpeare.

Printed by Iames Roberts, 1600.

No. 567.   Title-page of Shakespeare's Midsummer Night's Dream;
2d Edition; 1600.

Part of *The Wits, or, Sport upon Sport,* published by Francis Kirkman. Hazlitt says, "the author of the Second Part was Robert Cox." Of the 1672 edition there are copies in the British Museum (3) and Bodleian Libraries. Copies of the 1673 edition are in the British Museum, Bodleian (2), Boston Public (2), and Harvard University Libraries.

The Fairy-Queen: An Opera, founded upon this comedy by Dryden, was published in 1692 and again in 1693.

Of the First Edition (1692), "for Jacob Tonſon," there are copies in the British Museum (3), Huth, Boston Public, Harvard University, and White Libraries.

Of the Second Edition (1693), "for Jacob Tonſon," there are copies in the British Museum and White Libraries.

SHAKESPEARE, WILLIAM.

THE MERCHANT OF VENICE. [LONDON], *J. Roberts*, 1600. [568]

Small quarto. First Edition.

COLLATION BY SIGNATURES: A to K, each 4 leaves; total 40 unnumbered leaves. Leaf I 3 is marked *I* 3.

COLLATION BY PAGINATION: [title, as reproduced; *See* No. 568], recto of [A]; —[blank], verso of [A];—[text, with heading] | [conventional head-piece] | The Comical Hiſtory of the | Merchant of Venice. |, recto of A 2 to recto of [K 4]; — | *FINJS.* | [conventional tail-piece] |, recto of [K 4];—[blank], verso of [K 4].

CONDITION: Size of leaf, 7 9/16 x 5 1/4 inches. Bound in red crushed levant morocco, gilt edges; by Bedford.

OTHER COPIES.

British Museum (2); Bodleian (Malone copy); Capell Collection; Shakespeare Memorial, Stratford (2, one imperfect); Edinburgh University; Devonshire (Kemble copy); Huth; Boston Public; Perry (Gwynn copy); Lenox; Halsey; Hoe; F. K. Trowbridge; and Furness (Capell copy) Libraries; also the Howe copy (untraced).

REFERENCES.

Hoe, *Catalogue,* 4 (1904) : 97; *The Cambridge Shakespeare,* 2 (1902) : xi.; Greg, *List of English Plays* (Bibliographical Society; 1900), p. 98; British Museum, *Catalogue; Shakespeare* (1897), col. 115; Furness, *New Variorum Edition* (1888), p. 272; Locker-Lampson, *Catalogue* (1886), p. 105; Boston Public Librar*y, Catalogue;* Barton Collection (1880), p. 30, No. 439; Huth, *Catalogue,* 4 (1880) : 1335; Lenox Library, *Works of Shakespeare* (1880), p. 19, No. 88; Winsor, *Bibliography* (1876), p. 47; Lowndes, 4 (1869) : 2287; Hazlitt, *Hand-Book* (1867), p. 549, No. 16 a.

The Locker-Lampson copy.

Four editions of this play were printed, two in 1600, and one each in 1637 and 1652.

Of the First Edition (1600), that here described, Furness, who considers it superior to the Second, says: "This has been in recent times, by common consent, called THE FIRST QUARTO." It was reproduced in the Ashbee-Halliwell *Facsimiles* (1865), No. 19, and (the Devonshire copy) in the Griggs-Furnivall *Shakspere-*

1600   *William Shakespeare*   No. 568

THE
EXCELLENT
History of the Merchant of *Venice*.

With the extreme cruelty of *Shylocke* the Iew towards the saide Merchant, in cutting a iust pound of his flesh. And the obtaining of *Portia*, by the choyse of three Caskets.

Written by W. SHAKESPEARE.

Printed by *J. Roberts*, 1600.

No. 568.   TITLE-PAGE OF SHAKESPEARE'S MERCHANT OF VENICE;
1ST EDITION; 1600.

CHURCH CATALOGUE   [797]   ENGLISH LITERATURE

No. 568   *William Shakespeare*   1600

Quarto Facsimiles [1881], No. 7. It was reprinted by Steevens in his *Twenty Plays* (1766), Vol. 1.

The Second Edition (also 1600) is that described in our next number.

The Third Edition (1637) is that described in our No. 570.

The Fourth Edition (1652), "Printed for William Leake," is merely a reissue of the Third Edition with a new title-page. There are copies in the British Museum (2), Capell Collection, Edinburgh University, Lenox, and White Libraries; also the Howe copy (untraced).

The Folio of 1623 followed the text of the Second Edition (our next number), known as the "Heyes Quarto."

SHAKESPEARE, WILLIAM.

THE MERCHANT OF VENICE.   LONDON, *by I. R. for Thomas Heyes*, 1600.

[569]

Small quarto. Second Edition.

COLLATION BY SIGNATURES: A to I, each 4 leaves; K, 2 leaves; total 38 unnumbered leaves. Leaf E is marked *E.*; and I is *J.*

COLLATION BY PAGINATION: [title, as reproduced; *See* No. 569], recto of [A]; —[blank], verso of [A]; —[text, with heading] | [type-ornament head-piece] | The comicall Hiftory of the Mer- | chant of Venice. |, recto of A 2 to recto of [K 2]; — | FINIS. | [conventional tail-piece] |, recto of [K 2]; —[blank], verso of [K 2].

CONDITION: Size of leaf, 6 11/16 × 4 7/16 inches. Bound in red polished morocco, elaborately panelled sides, gilt edges; by Hayday. The head-line on the recto of leaf H 2 is entirely cut off.

OTHER COPIES.

British Museum (3); Bodleian (Malone copy); Capell Collection; Dyce Collection; Devonshire; Ellesmere; Huth; Boston Public (Heber copy); Lenox (Heber copy); and White (Lord Mostyn copy) Libraries. Winsor locates the Steevens copy in the library of the Marquis of Bute.

REFERENCES.

Greg, *List of English Plays* (Bibliographical Society; 1900), p. 99; British Museum, *Catalogue*; Shakespeare (1897), col. 116; Furness, *New Variorum Edition* (1888), p. 272; Locker-Lampson, *Catalogue* (1886), p. 105; Boston Public Library, *Catalogue*; Barton Collection (1880), p. 30, No. 438; Huth, *Catalogue*, 4 (1880): 1336; Lenox Library, *Works of Shakespeare* (1880), p. 19, No. 87; Winsor, *Bibliography* (1876), p. 46; Lowndes, 4 (1869): 2287; Hazlitt, *Hand-Book* (1867), p. 549, No. 16 *b*.

The Gardner-Lilly-Tite-Locker Lampson copy, with ex-libris of the last.

This edition was reproduced in the Ashbee-Halliwell *Facsimiles* (1870), No. 18, and also (the Devonshire copy) in the Praetorius-Furnivall *Shakspere-Quarto Facsimiles* (1887), No. 16.

Tipped in at the end of the copy here described is a facsimile of a black-letter ballad having a newspaper clipping pasted on its back endorsed in ink: "LIT! GAZETTE, 5 July 1856." The ballad is entitled "A new Song: Shewing the crueltie of *Gernutus* a Jew, who lending to a Merchant a hundred Crownes, would have a pound

The moſt excellent
Hiſtorie of the *Merchant of Venice*.

VVith the extreame crueltie of *Shylocke* the Iewe towards the ſayd Merchant, in cutting a iuſt pound of his fleſh: and the obtayning of *Portia* by the choyſe of three cheſts.

As it hath beene diuers times acted by the Lord Chamberlaine his Seruants.

Written by William Shakeſpeare.

AT LONDON,
Printed by *I. R.* for Thomas Heyes,
and are to be ſold in Paules Church-yard, at the
ſigne of the Greene Dragon.
1 6 0 0.

No. 569. Title-page of Shakespeare's Merchant of Venice; 2d Edition; 1600.

of his fleſh, becauſe he could not pay him at the day appointed, To the Tune of *Black and Yellow.*'' At the bottom: '' *Old Ballad, preserved in the Ashmolean Library, Oxford, supposed to have furnished Shakspeare with the suggestion of the plot of the Merchant of Venice.*''

SHAKESPEARE, WILLIAM.

THE MERCHANT OF VENICE. 1637.   LONDON, by M. P. for Laurence Hayes, [570]

Small quarto. Third Edition.
COLLATION BY SIGNATURES: A to I, each 4 leaves; total 36 unnumbered leaves.
COLLATION BY PAGINATION: [title, as reproduced; *See* No. 570], recto of [A]; — | [type-ornament head-piece] | *The Actors Names.* | [18 lines] | [type-ornament tail-piece] |, verso of [A]; — [text, with heading] | [type-ornament head-piece] | The Comicall History of the Mer- | chant of Venice. |, recto of A 2 to verso of [I 4]; — | FINIS. |, verso of [I 4].
CONDITION: Size of leaf, 6½ × 5¼ inches. Bound in green morocco, gilt edges; by Bedford.

OTHER COPIES.

British Museum; Bodleian (2); Capell Collection; Shakespeare Memorial, Stratford; Edinburgh University; Boston Public; Lenox; Hoe; and White Libraries.

REFERENCES.

Hoe, *Catalogue*, 4 (1904) : 97; Greg, *List of English Plays* (Bibliographical Society; 1900), p. 99; British Museum, *Catalogue*; *Shakespeare* (1897), col. 116; Furness, *New Variorum Edition* (1888), p. 273; Boston Public Library, *Catalogue*; *Barton Collection* (1880), p. 30, No. 440; Lenox Library, *Works of Shakespeare* (1880), p. 19, No. 89; Lowndes, 4 (1869) : 2287; Hazlitt, *Hand-Book to the Popular, Poetical, and Dramatic Literature of Great Britain, From the Invention of Printing to the Restoration* (1867), p. 549, No. 16 c.

Lenox Library duplicate copy, with stamp.
The running head-lines here, as in the First Edition, read: | *The Comicall Historie of* | *the Merchant of Venice.* | . This is a reprint of the Second Edition, and the first of Shakespeare's plays in which a list of "*The Actors Names*" is given.

SHAKESPEARE, WILLIAM.

THE TAMING OF THE SHREW. wicke, 1631.   LONDON, by W. S. for Iohn Smeth- [571]

Small quarto. First Separate Edition.
COLLATION BY SIGNATURES: A to I, each 4 leaves; total 36 unnumbered leaves. Leaf I 3 has no signature-mark.
COLLATION BY PAGINATION: [title, as reproduced; *See* No. 571], recto of [A]; — [blank], verso of [A]; — [text, with heading] | [type-ornament head-piece] | THE | Taming of the Shrew. |, recto of A 2 to verso of [I 4]; — | FINIS. |, verso of [I 4].
CONDITION: Size of leaf, 8 × 5⁷⁄₁₀ inches. Bound in red crushed levant morocco, dark blue crushed levant morocco doublure with dentelle border, marbled fly-leaves, gilt edges; by Motte.

OTHER COPIES.

British Museum (2); Bodleian (2); Capell Collection; Edinburgh University; Boston Public; Lenox; Morgan (Tite-Asay-Irwin copy); and White Libraries; also the Locker Lampson-Van Antwerp copy (untraced).

REFERENCES.

Greg, *List of English Plays* (Bibliographical Society; 1900), p. 102; British Museum, *Catalogue*; *Shakespeare* (1897),

The moſt excellent Hiſtorie of the Merchant of *VENICE.*

With the extreame crueltie of *Shylocke* the Iewe towards the ſaid Merchant, in cutting a juſt pound of his fleſh: and the obtaining of PORTIA by the choice *of three Cheſts.*

As it hath beene divers times acted by the Lord Chamberlaine his Servants.

Written by WILLIAM SHAKESPEARE.

LONDON,
Printed by M. P. for *Laurence Hayes,* and are to be ſold at his Shop on Fleetbridge. 1637.

No. 570. TITLE-PAGE OF SHAKESPEARE'S MERCHANT OF VENICE; 3D EDITION; 1637.

A WITTIE AND PLEASANT COMEDIE

Called

The Taming of the Shrew.

As it was acted by his Maiesties *Seruants at the* Blacke Friers and the Globe.

Written by Will. Shakespeare.

LONDON,

Printed by *W. S.* for *Iohn Smethwicke,* and are to be sold at his Shop in Saint *Dunstones* Churchyard vnder the Diall.
1631.

col. 150; *The Cambridge Shakespeare*, 3 (1894) : vii.; Hazlitt, *Manual of Old English Plays* (1892), p. 223; Locker-Lampson, *Catalogue* (1886), p. 105; Boston Public Library, *Catalogue*; Barton Collection (1880), p. 40, No. 615; Lenox Library, *Works of Shakespeare* (1880), p. 28, No. 158; Lowndes, 4 (1869) : 2298; Hazlitt, *Hand-Book* (1867), p. 551, No. 23.

A fine, tall copy; with many leaves absolutely untouched by the binder's knife on the lower and fore edges.

This play, which first appeared in the Folio of 1623, was for the first and only time separately published in the quarto edition here described. The Cambridge editor has no hesitancy in deciding that it was reprinted from the First Folio, notwithstanding Collier's dictum that it was printed long before 1623, perhaps as early as 1607 or 1609. It was reprinted by Steevens in his *Twenty Plays of Shakespeare, printed during his Life-time, or before the Restoration* (1766), Vol. 2.

The Taming of the Shrew is a revision of an old anonymous play, *A Pleaſant Conceited Hiſtorie, Called The Taming of a Shrew*, which first appeared in 1594 and was republished in 1596 and 1607.

Of the earliest of these editions (1594), "by Peter Short and are to be fold by Cutbert Burbie," the only known copy (Malone-Heber-Inglis) is in the Duke of Devonshire's Library. It was reproduced in the Praetorius-Furnivall *Shakspere-Quarto Facsimiles* (1886), No. 15.

Of the Second Edition (1596), "by P. S. and are to be fold by Cuthbert Burbie," there are copies in the British Museum and Ellesmere Libraries.

Of the Third Edition (1607), "by V. S. for Nicholas Ling," there are copies in the Bodleian, Devonshire (Steevens-Kemble copy), and Ellesmere Libraries.

This play as altered by John Lacy was published in quarto in 1698, by E. Whitlock, under the title *Sauny the Scott; or, the Taming of the Shrew*.

Of the First Edition of this play (1698) there are copies in the British Museum (2), Bodleian, Devonshire, Harvard University, Boston Public, Hoe, and White Libraries.

SHAKESPEARE, WILLIAM.   Source Play.

KING JOHN. THE TROUBLESOME RAIGNE OF JOHN KING OF ENGLAND. LONDON, *by Valentine Simmes for Iohn Helme*, 1611.   [572]

Small quarto.   Second Edition.

COLLATION BY SIGNATURES: A to L, each 4 leaves; M, 2 leaves (the last blank and lacking); total 46 unnumbered leaves.

COLLATION BY PAGINATION: [title, as reproduced; *See* No. 572], recto of [A]; —[blank], verso of [A]; —[text, with heading] | [type-ornament head-piece] | The troubleſome Raigne of | King Iohn. |, recto of A2 to recto of G3; — | [type-ornament head-piece] | To the Gentlemen Readers. | [15 lines] |, verso of G3; —[text of second part, with heading] | The ſecond part of | The troubleſome Raigne | of King Iohn. | *Containing* | *The entrance of* Lewis *the French Kings ſonne* : | *With the poyſoning of King* Iohn | *by a Monke.* |, recto of [G4] to verso of M; — | FINIS. |, verso of M; —[1 blank leaf], [M2].

CONDITION: Size of leaf, 7 x 5 11/16 inches.

Bound in red crushed levant morocco, gilt edges; by Bedford.

OTHER COPIES.

British Museum (3, one imperfect); Bodleian (Malone copy); Capell Collection; Devonshire; Huth; Boston Public (Loscombe-Halliwell Phillipps copy); Hoe; and White Libraries.

REFERENCES.

Hoe, *Catalogue*, 4 (1904): 99; Greg, *List of English Plays* (Bibliographical Society; 1900), p. 124; British Museum, *Catalogue*; *Shakespeare* (1897), col. 181; Hazlitt, *Manual of Old English Plays* (1892), p. 122; Locker-Lampson, *Catalogue* (1886), p. 111; Boston Public Library, *Catalogue*; *Barton Collection* (1880), p. 25, No. 346; Winsor, *Bibliography* (1876), p. 40; Lowndes, 4 (1869): 2283; Hazlitt, *Hand-Book* (1867), p. 302.

The Locker-Lampson copy, with ex-libris.

This is the Source Play of which Shakespeare made use in writing his play *King John*. Though divided into two parts it was published as one work, editions appearing in 1591, 1611, and 1622.

The First Edition (1591), "Imprinted for Sampſon Clarke," was published in two volumes, with a separate title-page and series of signature-marks for each. The only copy now known, a perfect one, is in the Capell Collection at Trinity College, Cambridge. Both parts of this edition have been reproduced from the Capell copy in photographic facsimile in the Praetorius-Furnivall *Shakspere-Quarto Facsimiles* (1888), Nos. 40 and 41.

The Second Edition (1611), with the two parts in one volume, is that here described. Steevens reprinted it in his *Twenty Plays* (1766), Vol. 2.

The Third Edition (1622), "Printed by Aug. Mathewes for Thomas Dewe," also has the two parts in one volume, with continuous signature-marks, but with a separate title-page for the second part. Both title-pages have the words "Written by W. Shakeſpeare." Of this edition there are copies in the British Museum (2), Capell Collection, Dyce Collection, Edinburgh University, Devonshire, Ellesmere, Boston Public, and White Libraries; also the Howe copy (untraced).

Shakespeare's play, *King John*, though not printed until 1623, was probably written in 1594, being directly adapted from this worthless play, the Third Edition of which fraudulently uses his name on its title-pages. The Second Part, according to the title-page of the First Edition, contains "the death of Arthur Plantaginet, the landing of Lewes, and the poyſning of King Iohn at Swinſtead Abbey."

Pasted to the recto of the second fly-leaf of the copy here described is the following note, in Locker-Lampson's handwriting: "*The troublesome reign of King John. This is the weakest & most wooden of all wearisome chronicles, & its sole vital principle is its power of appeal to the blatant spirit of protestantism which inspired it. There is only one touch of pathos where the dying Arthur w^d fain send a last thoght in search of his mother. This poem c^d not have helped W. S. The crude sketch of the Bastard as he swaggers thro' the long length of its scenes is not the rough husk of the noble creation by W. S.*"

On the verso of the fourth fly-leaf is written, in pencil: "*This may be the quarry from which Shakespeare constructed his drama of the same events. Shakespeare's*

1611   *William Shakespeare*   No. 572

THE
First and second Part of
the troublesome Raigne of
John King of England.

With the discouerie of King Richard Cordelions Base sonne (vulgarly named, The Bastard Fawconbridge:) Also, the death of King *Iohn* at Swinstead Abbey.

As they were (sundry times) lately acted by the Queenes Maiesties Players.

Written by W. Sh.

Imprinted at London by *Valentine Simmes* for *Iohn Helme,* and are to be sold at his shop in Saint Dunstons Churchyard in Fleetestreet.
1611.

No. 572.   Title-page of the Troublesome Raigne of John King of England; the Source Play of Shakespeare's King John; 2d Edition; 1611.

No. 572   *William Shakespeare*   1611

King John was 1st printed in 1st folio. The poet adopted most of the characters, plot, &c. from an earlier play in two parts published in 1591. This book is a reprint of that & again in 1622. It is generally considered that W. S. had no hand in this play."

SHAKESPEARE, WILLIAM.

RICHARD THE SECOND. London, *by Valentine Simmes for Andrew Wife*, 1598.   [573]

Small quarto. Second Edition. Printed with side-notes in italics from the verso of leaf G to the end.

COLLATION BY SIGNATURES: A to I, each 4 leaves; total 36 unnumbered leaves.

COLLATION BY PAGINATION: [title, as reproduced; *See* No. 573], recto of [A]; —[blank], verso of [A]; —[text, with heading] | [conventional head-piece] | Enter King Richard, Iohn of Gant, | with other Nobles and | *Attendants*. |, recto of A 2 to verso of [I 4]; — | *FINIS*. |, verso of [I 4].

CONDITION: Size of leaf, 7 x 5 inches. Bound in red crushed levant morocco, gilt edges; by Bedford. Part of the first word of the title is in facsimile; leaves [H 4], I 3, and [I 4] are extended in the outer margins and have some letters in facsimile; the leaves are stabbed throughout and mended.

OTHER COPIES.

British Museum; Bodleian (Malone copy); Capell Collection; Ellesmere; Boston Public (Bright copy); and White Libraries; also the Howe copy (untraced).

REFERENCES.

Greg, *List of English Plays* (Bibliographical Society; 1900), p. 95; British Museum, *Catalogue*; *Shakespeare* (1897), col. 95; *The Cambridge Shakespeare*, 4 (1894): viii.; Hazlitt, *Manual of Old English Plays* (1892), p. 194; Locker-Lampson, *Catalogue* (1886), p. 105; Boston Public Library, *Catalogue*; *Barton Collection* (1880), p. 36, No. 559; Winsor, *Bibliography* (1876), p. 58; Lowndes, 4 (1869): 2293; Hazlitt, *Hand-Book* (1867), p. 547, No. 8 *b*.

The Steevens-Roxburghe-Daniel-Tite-Locker Lampson copy, with ex-libris of the last. With the arms and crest of the Duke of Roxburghe stamped on the title-page, and also the autograph of George Steevens.

On the last fly-leaf is an autograph note by Tite, as follows: "*This very rare Edition of this Play formerly the Property of Geo: Steevens was bought for me by Mr. Halliwell in Daniells sale July 1864, for the very moderate sum of £138.0.0* [signed] *Willm Tite.*"

Of this play quarto editions were published in 1597, 1598, 1608 (two editions), 1615, and 1634.

Of the First Edition (1597), "Printed by Valentine Simmes for Androw Wife," there are copies in the Capell Collection, Devonshire, and Huth (the Daniel copy) Libraries. This edition was reproduced in the Ashbee-Halliwell *Facsimiles* (1862), No. 6; the Duke of Devonshire's copy was reproduced in the Griggs-Furnivall *Shakspere-Quarto Facsimiles* (1890), No. 17; and the Huth copy, in the Praetorius-Furnivall *Shakspere-Quarto Facsimiles* (1888), No. 18.

1598 William Shakespeare No. 573

THE
Tragedie of King Richard the second.

As it hath beene publikely acted by the Right Honourable the Lord Chamberlaine his seruants.

By William Shake-speare.

Geo. Steevens.

LONDON
Printed by Valentine Simmes for Andrew Wise, and are to be sold at his shop in Paules churchyard at the signe of the Angel.
1598.

No. 573. Title-page of Shakespeare's Richard the Second; 2d Edition; 1598.

The Second Edition (1598), that here described, was reproduced in the Ashbee-Halliwell *Facsimiles* (1869), No. 9.

The Third Edition (1608) is that described in our next number.

Of the Fourth Edition (also 1608), "Printed by W. W. for Mathew Law," in which the title-page reads, | With new additions of the Parlia- | ment Sceane, and the depofing | of King Richard, |, there are copies in the Bodleian (Wright-Malone copy) and the Duke of Devonshire's (the Kemble copy) Libraries. This edition consists of the sheets of the Third Edition reissued with a new title-page. The title-page only of this edition was reproduced in the Ashbee-Halliwell *Facsimiles* (1871), No. 1.

The Fifth Edition (1615) is that described in our No. 575.

The Sixth Edition (1634) is that described in our No. 576.

"An alteration of this play by Nahum Tate, under the original title, was printed in 1681. Ten years later [in 1691 it was again reprinted, when] Tate brought it on the stage at Drury Lane under the title of the *Sicilian Usurper;* but it appears to have been acted only twice, when it was forbidden by authority; on which account the author has added to it a prefatory epistle in vindication of himself, with respect to the prohibition. The scene is laid in England."

Of the 1681 edition, "for Richard Tonfon and Jacob Tonfon," there are copies in the British Museum (2), Bodleian, Birmingham Free, Trinity College (Dublin), Boston Public (2), Hoe, and White Libraries.

Of the 1691 edition, "for James Knapton," there are copies in the British Museum, Bodleian, Devonshire, Harvard University, and Boston Public Libraries. The Boston Public Library Catalogue of the Barton Collection says that this is "the edition of 1681 with a new title-page."

SHAKESPEARE, WILLIAM.

RICHARD THE SECOND. London, *by W. W. for Mathew Law,* 1608.

[574]

Small quarto. Third Edition.

COLLATION BY SIGNATURES: A to K, each 4 leaves (the last blank and lacking); total 40 unnumbered leaves.

COLLATION BY PAGINATION: [title, as reproduced; *See* No. 574], recto of [A]; —[blank], verso of [A];—[text, with heading] | [conventional head-piece] | Enter King Richard, Iohn | of Gaunt, with other Nobles | and Attendants. |, recto of A 2 to verso of K 3; — | FINIS. |, verso of K 3; —[1 blank leaf], [K 4].

CONDITION: Size of leaf, 6¾ x 4¾ inches. Bound in brown straight-grained morocco, gilt edges.

OTHER COPIES.

British Museum; Huth; and White (title-page lacking) Libraries.

REFERENCES.

Greg, *List of English Plays* (Bibliographical Society; 1900), p. 95; British Museum, *Catalogue;* Shakespeare (1897), col. 95; Locker-Lampson, *Catalogue* (1886), p. 106; Huth, *Catalogue,* 4 (1880): 1333; Winsor, *Bibliography of the Original Quartos and Folios of Shakespeare with Particular Reference to Copies in America* (1876), p. 58; Lowndes, 4 (1869): 2293; Hazlitt, *Hand-Book* (1867), p. 548, No. 8 c.

1608   *William Shakespeare*   No. 574

THE
Tragedie of King
Richard the second.

As it hath been publikely acted by the Right
Honourable the Lord Chamberlaine
his seruants.

By *William Shake-speare.*

LONDON,
Printed by W.W. for *Mathew Law*, and are to be
sold at his shop in Paules Church-yard, at
the signe of the Foxe.
1608.

No. 574.   TITLE-PAGE OF SHAKESPEARE'S RICHARD THE SECOND; 3D EDITION; 1608.

The Halliwell Phillipps-Tite-Locker Lampson copy, with ex-libris of the last.
    This edition was reproduced in the Ashbee-Halliwell *Facsimiles* (1870), No. 33, and also (the British Museum copy) in the Praetorius-Furnivall *Shakspere-Quarto Facsimiles* (1888), No. 19.

SHAKESPEARE, WILLIAM.

RICHARD THE SECOND. London, *for Mathew Law*, 1615. [575]

Small quarto. Fifth Edition.

COLLATION BY SIGNATURES: A to K, each 4 leaves (the last blank and lacking); total 40 unnumbered leaves.

COLLATION BY PAGINATION: [title, as reproduced; *See* No. 575], recto of [A]; — [blank], verso of [A]; — [text, with heading] | [type-ornament head-piece] | Enter King Richard, Iohn of | Gaunt, with other Nobles and | Attendants. |, recto of A 2 to verso of K 3; — | *FINIS.* |, verso of K 3; — [1 blank leaf], [K 4].

CONDITION: Size of leaf, 6 11/16 × 4 5/8 inches. Bound in half red calf, red over green edges.

OTHER COPIES.

British Museum; Bodleian (Malone copy); Capell Collection; Edinburgh University; Devonshire; Boston Public; Lenox (Fowle copy); and Hoe Libraries. Winsor locates the Steevens copy in the library of the Marquis of Bute.

REFERENCES.

Hoe, *Catalogue*, 4 (1904): 102; Greg, *List of English Plays* (Bibliographical Society; 1900), p. 95; British Museum, *Catalogue*; *Shakespeare* (1897), col. 95; *The Cambridge Shakespeare*, 4 (1894): viii., ix.; Locker-Lampson, *Catalogue* (1886), p. 106; Boston Public Library, *Catalogue*; *Barton Collection* (1880), p. 37, No. 561; Lenox Library, *Works of Shakespeare* (1880), p. 25, No. 135; Winsor, *Bibliography* (1876), p. 59; Lowndes, 4 (1869): 2293; Hazlitt, *Hand-Book* (1867), p. 548, No. 8 *e*.

The Steevens-Roxburghe-Locker Lampson copy, with the ex-libris of the last, the autograph of George Steevens on the title-page, and the arms and crest of the Duke of Roxburghe stamped on its verso.

This edition was reproduced in the *Ashbee-Halliwell Facsimiles* (1870), No. 45; and was reprinted by Steevens in his *Twenty Plays* (1766), Vol. 2.

Speaking of the first five quarto editions, the Cambridge editor says: "Each of these Quartos was printed from its immediate predecessor. The third [our No. 574, and the Fourth Edition] however contains an important addition, found in all the extant copies of Q_3, amounting to 165 lines, viz. IV. 1. 154—318. This is what is meant by 'the new additions of the Parliament Scene' mentioned in the title-pages of some copies of Q_3 and in that of Q_4 [the present number]. These 'new additions' are found also in the first and following Folios and in Q_5 [our next number]. The play, as given in the first Folio, was no doubt printed from a copy of Q_4 [the present number], corrected with some care and prepared for stage representation. Several passages have been left out with a view of shortening the performance. In the 'new additions of the Parliament Scene' it would appear that the defective text of the Quarto had been corrected from the author's MS. For this part therefore the first Folio is our highest authority: for all the rest of the play the first Quarto affords the best text."

The Deposition Scene, or "new additions" referred to above, is an integral part of the fourth act and is alluded to by the abbot (act iv., sc. 1) when he says "A wofull Pageant haue we heere beheld."

THE
Tragedie of King
Richard the Second:

With new additions of the Parliament Sceane, and the depoſing of King Richard.

As it hath been lately acted by the Kinges Maieſties ſeruants, at the Globe.

By WILLIAM SHAKE-SPEARE.

George Steevens.

At LONDON,
Printed for *Mathew Law*, and are to be ſold at his ſhop in Paules Church-yard, at the ſigne of the Foxe.
1615.

No. 575. TITLE-PAGE OF SHAKESPEARE'S RICHARD THE SECOND; 5TH EDITION; 1615.

THE
LIFE AND
DEATH OF KING
RICHARD THE SECOND.

With new Additions of the *Parliament Scene*, and the Depoſing of King *Richard*.

As it hath beene acted by the Kings Majeſties Servants, at the *Globe*.

By *William Shakeſpeare*.

LONDON,
Printed by IOHN NORTON.
1634.

No. 576. TITLE-PAGE OF SHAKESPEARE'S RICHARD THE SECOND; 6TH EDITION; 1634.

SHAKESPEARE, WILLIAM.

RICHARD THE SECOND. London, *Iohn Norton*, 1634.   [576]

Small quarto. Sixth Edition.

COLLATION BY SIGNATURES: A to K, each 4 leaves; total 40 unnumbered leaves.

COLLATION BY PAGINATION: [title, as reproduced; *See* No. 576], recto of [A]; —[blank], verso of [A]; —[text, with heading] | [type-ornament head-piece] | The Life and Death of | King *Richard* the fecond. | , recto of A 2 to verso of [K 4]; — | FINIS. | , verso of [K 4].

CONDITION: Size of leaf, 6¾ x 5 inches. Bound in brown crushed levant morocco, gilt edges; by Hammond.

OTHER COPIES.

British Museum (2, one imperfect); Bodleian (2); Capell Collection; Dyce Collection; Edinburgh University; Hunterian Museum; Boston Public (Jolley copy); Lenox; and White Libraries.

REFERENCES.

Greg, *List of English Plays* (Bibliographical Society; 1900), p. 95; British Museum, *Catalogue*; *Shakespeare* (1897), col. 95; Boston Public Library, *Catalogue*; *Barton Collection* (1880), p. 37, No. 562; Lenox Library, *Works of Shakespeare* (1880), p. 25, No. 136; Lowndes, 4 (1869): 2294; Hazlitt, *Hand-Book* (1867), p. 548, No. 8*f*.

On the back of the title-page of the copy here described is a long note in faded ink written at "*Shrewsbury*" and signed, "*Jos. Edgerton, C.*"

This edition was printed from the Folio of 1632, "but its readings sometimes agree with one or other of the earlier Quartos, and in a few cases are entirely independent of previous editions." It was reproduced in the Praetorius-Furnivall *Shakspere-Quarto Facsimiles*, No. 20.

SHAKESPEARE, WILLIAM.

HENRY THE FOURTH, PART I. London, *by S.[imon] S.[tafford], for Andrew VVife*, 1599.   [577]

Small quarto. Second Edition.

COLLATION BY SIGNATURES: A to K, each 4 leaves; total 40 unnumbered leaves.

COLLATION BY PAGINATION: [title, as reproduced; *See* No. 577], recto of [A]; —[blank], verso of [A]; —[text, with heading] | [conventional head-piece] | THE HISTORIE OF | Henry the fourth. | , recto of A 2 to verso of [K 4]; — | FINIS. | [conventional tail-piece] | , verso of [K 4].

CONDITION: Size of leaf, 6$\frac{13}{16}$ x 4$\frac{15}{16}$ inches. Bound in red straight-grained morocco, richly panelled sides, gilt edges; by Tuckett. Leaves I 2 to [K 4] are probably in facsimile; and the head-lines are clipped on nearly every page, in some cases being almost entirely cut away. The upper part of the title-page is torn and portions of some of the letters in the first line are lacking.

OTHER COPIES.

British Museum (2); Bodleian (Malone copy); Capell Collection; Huth; Devonshire; Ellesmere; and Hunterian Museum (Glasgow) Libraries. Winsor locates the Steevens copy in the library of the Marquis of Bute.

No. 577 — *William Shakespeare* — 1599

REFERENCES.

Greg, *List of English Plays* (Bibliographical Society; 1900), p. 97; British Museum, *Catalogue*; *Shakespeare* (1897), col. 76; *The Cambridge Shakespeare*, 4 (1894): ix.; Locker-Lampson, *Catalogue* (1886), p. 106; Huth, *Catalogue*, 4 (1880): 1333; Winsor, *Bibliography* (1876), p. 29; Lowndes, 4 (1869): 2278; Hazlitt, *Hand-Book* (1867), p. 548, No. 11 *b*.

The Lettsom-Locker Lampson copy, with the latter's ex-libris.

Quarto editions of this play were issued in 1598, 1599, 1604, 1608, 1613, 1622, 1632, and 1639.

Of the First Edition (1598), "Printed by P. S. for Andrew Wife," there are copies in the British Museum (imperfect, lacking two leaves), Capell Collection, and Duke of Devonshire's Library. This edition was reproduced in the Ashbee-Halliwell *Facsimiles* (1866), No. 10, and also (the Devonshire copy) in the Griggs-Furnivall *Shakspere-Quarto Facsimiles* [1881], No. 8.

The Second Edition (1599), that here described, was reproduced in the Ashbee-Halliwell *Facsimiles* (1866), No. 12.

Of the Third Edition (1604), "Printed by Valentine Simmes, for Mathew Law," there are copies in the Bodleian (Malone copy) Library and Capell Collection, the latter being a fragment. This edition was reproduced in the Ashbee-Halliwell *Facsimiles* (1871), No. 28.

Of the Fourth Edition (1608), "Printed for Mathew Law," there are copies in the British Museum, Bodleian, Devonshire, and White Libraries. This edition was reproduced in the Ashbee-Halliwell *Facsimiles* (1867), No. 34.

The Fifth Edition (1613) is that described in our next number.

The Sixth Edition (1622) is that described in our No. 579.

Of the Seventh Edition (1632), "Printed by John Norton, and are to be fold by William Sheares," there are copies in the British Museum, Capell Collection, Edinburgh University, Boston Public, and White Libraries; also the Howe copy (untraced).

The Eighth Edition (1639) is that described in our No. 580.

In 1700 there appeared an edition entitled "*K. Henry IV. With the Humours of Sir John Falftaff*. . . . As it is Acted at the Theatre in Litttle-Lincolns-Inn-Fields by His Majefty's Servants. Revived, with Alterations. . . . for R. W. and Sold by John Deeve," by the actor and dramatist, Thomas Betterton. Of this edition there are copies in the British Museum (3), Bodleian (2), Ellesmere, Harvard University (title-page lacking), Boston Public, Morgan (Irwin copy), White, and Wrenn Libraries, and the Library of Congress.

The Source Play, entitled *The Famous Victories of Henry the fifth*, an anonymous drama, was written and performed about 1588. From this very popular but valueless play and from Holinshed's *Chronicles* Shakespeare worked up with splendid energy the two parts of *Henry the Fourth*, which form one continuous whole. The *Famous Victories* was first published in 1598, and again in 1617, when two editions appeared.

Of the First Edition (1598), "Printed by Thomas Creede," there is a copy in

HISTORY OF
HENRIE THE FOVRTH;

With the battell at Shrewsburie,
betweene the King and Lord Henry
Percy, surnamed Henry Hotspur of the North.

VVith the humorous conceits of Sir
Iohn Falstalffe.

Newly corrected by *W. Shake-speare.*

AT LONDON,
Printed by S. S. for *Andrew* VVise, dwelling
inPaules Churchyard, at the signe of
the Angell, 1599.

No. 577. Title-page of Shakespeare's Henry the Fourth, Part I.;
2d Edition; 1599.

the Bodleian Library, which has been reproduced by photo-lithography in the Praetorius-Furnivall *Shakspere-Quarto Facsimiles* (1887), No. 39.

Of the Second Edition (1617), "by Barnard Alſop," there are copies in the British Museum and the Capell Collection; also the Howe copy (untraced).

Of the Third Edition (also 1617), "by Barnard Alſop, and are to be ſold by Tymothie Barlow," there are copies in the British Museum, Bodleian, and Devonshire Libraries. This edition differs from the Second only in the title-page.

SHAKESPEARE, WILLIAM.

HENRY THE FOURTH, PART I. London, by *W. W. for Mathew Law*, 1613. [578]

Small quarto. Fifth Edition.

COLLATION BY SIGNATURES: A to K, each 4 leaves; total 40 unnumbered leaves.

COLLATION BY PAGINATION: [title, as reproduced; *See* No. 578], recto of [A]; —[blank], verso of [A];—[text, with heading] | [conventional head-piece] | The Hiſtorie of | Henrie the fourth. |, recto of A 2 to verso of [K 4];—| FINIS. |, verso of [K 4].

CONDITION: Size of leaf, 6⅞ × 5³⁄₁₆ inches. Bound in red crushed levant morocco, gilt edges; by Bedford. The leaves are closely trimmed at the bottom; leaf [I 4] is extended on the upper portion, with head-lines in facsimile.

OTHER COPIES.

British Museum (2, one imperfect, but with variations); Bodleian (Malone copy); Capell Collection; Devonshire; Huth; Lenox (Steevens-Dent-Dyce copy); and Hoe Libraries; also the Howe copy (untraced).

REFERENCES.

Hoe, *Catalogue*, 4 (1904): 101; Greg, *List of English Plays* (Bibliographical Society; 1900), p. 97; British Museum, *Catalogue*; Shakespeare (1897) col. 76; Hazlitt, *Manual of Old English Plays* (1892), p. 103; Locker-Lampson, *Catalogue* (1886), p. 106; Huth, *Catalogue*, 4 (1880): 1333; Lenox Library, *Works of Shakespeare* (1880), p. 14, No. 50; Winsor, *Bibliography* (1876), p. 30; Lowndes, 4 (1869): 2278; Hazlitt, *Hand-Book* (1867), p. 548, No. 11 *e*.

The Locker-Lampson copy, with ex-libris.

In one of the copies of this edition in the British Museum is a note by Halliwell-Phillipps as follows: "In this copy there are variations from the preceding at sig. H 1, line 5 from bottom, and at sig. H 4, verso, line 4; apparently corrections made subsequent to the issuing of earlier copies." These lines read as follows in the copy here described:

"Seemes more then we ſhall find it. Were it good,"

and

"He came but to be Duke of *Lancaſter*,".

In our preceding number these lines read:

"Seemes more, then we ſhall find it : were it good,"

and

"He came but to be Duke of Lancaſter,"

1613   *William Shakespeare*   No. 578

THE
HISTORY OF
Henrie the fourth,

With the Battell at Shrewseburie, betweene the King, and Lord Henrie Percy, sur-named *Henrie Hotspur* of the North.

VVith the humorous conceites of Sir *Iohn Falstaffe*.

Newly corrected by *W. Shake-speare*.

LONDON,
Printed by *W. W.* for *Mathew Law*, and are to be sold at his shop in Paules Church-yard, neere vnto S. *Augustines* Gate, at the signe of the Foxe.
1 6 1 3.

No. 578. Title-page of Shakespeare's Henry the Fourth, Part I.; 5th Edition; 1613.

Hazlitt says: "The impressions of 1598 and 1613 exhibit variations, and the former appears to have been printed twice."

This edition was reproduced in the Ashbee-Halliwell *Facsimiles* (1867), No. 44, and was reprinted by Steevens in his *Twenty Plays* (1766), Vol. 2.

No. 579 — *William Shakespeare* — 1622

THE
HISTORIE
OF
Henry the Fourth.

With the Battell at *Shrewseburie*, betweene the King, and Lord *Henry Percy*, surnamed *Henry Hotspur of the North*.

With the humorous conceits of Sir *Iohn Falstaffe*.

Newly corrected.

By *William Shake-speare*.

LONDON,

¶ Printed by *T. P.* and are to be sold by *Mathew Law*, dwelling in *Pauls* Church-yard, at the Signe of the *Foxe*, neere S. *Austines* gate. 1622.

No. 579. Title-page of Shakespeare's Henry the Fourth, Part I.; 6th Edition; 1622.

SHAKESPEARE, WILLIAM.

HENRY THE FOURTH, PART I. LONDON, *by T. P. and are to be sold by Mathew Law*, 1622. [579]

Small quarto. Sixth Edition.
COLLATION BY SIGNATURES: A to K, each 4 leaves; total 40 unnumbered leaves.
COLLATION BY PAGINATION: [title, as reproduced; *See* No. 579], recto of [A]; —[blank], verso of [A];—[text, with heading] | [conventional head-piece] | The Hiſtorie of | *Henry the Fourth*. | , recto of A 2 to verso of [K 4]; — | FINIS. | , verso of [K 4]. The verso pages of E 2 and K have the head-lines | *The Hiſtory of* | instead of | *The Hiſtorie of* | .
CONDITION: Size of leaf, 7 x 5¹¹⁄₁₆ inches. Bound in red crushed levant morocco, gilt edges.

OTHER COPIES.
British Museum; Bodleian; Capell Collection; Dyce Collection; Edinburgh University; and Boston Public (Halliwell-Phillipps copy) Libraries.

REFERENCES.
Greg, *List of English Plays* (Bibliographical Society; 1900), p. 97; British Museum, *Catalogue*; *Shakespeare* (1897), col. 76; Hazlitt, *Collections and Notes* (1882), p. 555; Boston Public Library, *Catalogue*; *Barton Collection* (1880), p. 21, No. 271; Winsor, *Bibliography* (1876), p. 30; Lowndes, 4 (1869): 2278; Hazlitt, *Hand-Book* (1867), p. 548, No. 11*f*.

In the editions of 1622 (that here described), 1632, and 1639 (our next number) the title-pages are substantially the same, each appearing to have been printed from its immediate predecessor.

SHAKESPEARE, WILLIAM.

HENRY THE FOURTH, PART I. LONDON, *by John Norton, and are to be ſold by Hugh Perry*, 1639. [580]

Small quarto. Eighth Edition.
COLLATION BY SIGNATURES: A to K, each 4 leaves; total 40 unnumbered leaves. Leaves G 2 and G 3 are marked *G* 2 and *G* 3.
COLLATION BY PAGINATION: [title, as reproduced; *See* No. 580], recto of [A]; —[blank], verso of [A];—[text, with heading] | [conventional head-piece] | THE | HISTORY OF HENRY | the Fourth. | , recto of A 2 to verso of [K 4];— | *FINIS.* | , verso of [K 4]. The head-line on the verso of A 2 reads | *The Hiſtory* | instead of | *The Hiſtory of* | .
CONDITION: Size of leaf, 7⁵⁄₁₆ x 5¼ inches. Bound in red crushed levant morocco, gilt edges.

OTHER COPIES.
British Museum; Bodleian; Capell Collection; Edinburgh University; Devonshire; Boston Public; Lenox; Morgan (Libri-Lettsom copy); and White Libraries.

REFERENCES.
Greg, *List of English Plays* (Bibliographical Society; 1900), p. 98; British Museum, *Catalogue*; *Shakespeare* (1897), col. 76; Lenox Library, *Works of Shakespeare* (1880), p. 14, No. 51; Boston Public Library, *Catalogue*; *Barton Collection* (1880), p. 21, No. 273; Lowndes, 4 (1869): 2279; Hazlitt, *Hand-Book* (1867), p. 548, No. 11*h*.

William Shakespeare   1639

THE
HISTORIE
OF
Henry the Fourth:

VVITH THE BATTELL AT
Shrewsbury, betweene the King,
and Lord *Henry Percy*, surnamed
Henry Hotspur of the
North.

With the humorous conceits of Sir
IOHN FALSTAFFE.

Newly corrected,
By
WILLIAM SHAKE-SPEARE.

LONDON,
Printed by JOHN NORTON, and are to be sold by
HVGH PERRY, at his shop next to Ivie-bridge
in the Strand, 1639.

NO. 580. TITLE-PAGE OF SHAKESPEARE'S HENRY THE FOURTH, PART I.;
8TH EDITION; 1639.

SHAKESPEARE, WILLIAM.

HENRY THE FOURTH, PART II. London, *by V. S. for Andrew Wise, and William Aspley*, 1600. [581]

Small quarto. First Edition; sheet E, 4 leaves.

COLLATION BY SIGNATURES: A to K, each 4 leaves; L, 2 leaves (the last blank and lacking); total 42 unnumbered leaves.

COLLATION BY PAGINATION: [title, as reproduced; *See* No. 581], recto of [A]; —[blank], verso of [A];—[text, with heading] | [conventional head-piece] | The ſecond part of Henry the fourth, | *continuing to his death, and coro-* | nation of Henry the | fift. | , recto of A 2 to recto of L; — | *Epilogue.* | , verso of L; — | FINIS. | , verso of L;—[1 blank leaf], [L 2].

CONDITION: Size of leaf, 6 13/16 x 4 7/8 inches. Bound in red crushed levant morocco, gilt edges; by Bedford. The lower outer corner of leaf [E 4] is extended, with the ends of 15 lines in facsimile; and the upper margins of leaves A 2, A 3, and E to [E 4] are extended, with head-lines in facsimile.

OTHER COPIES.

British Museum (sheet E, of 4 leaves, only); Bodleian (Wright-Malone copy, imperfect); Devonshire; and Hunterian Museum Libraries. Winsor locates a copy in the library of the Marquis of Bute.

REFERENCES.

Greg, *List of English Plays* (Bibliographical Society; 1900), p. 98; British Museum, *Catalogue*; *Shakespeare* (1897), col. 78; *The Cambridge Shakespeare*, 4 (1894): xi.; Locker-Lampson, *Catalogue* (1886), p. 106; Winsor, *Bibliography* (1876), p. 31; Lowndes, 4 (1869): 2279.

The Halliwell Phillipps-Locker Lampson copy, with ex-libris of the latter.

On the front fly-leaf appears the following note by Halliwell-Phillipps:

"*There are two editions of the Second Part of Henry the Fourth, 1600, the first with sheet E containing four leaves, as in the present copy, the second with the same sheet consisting of six leaves.*

"*Both editions are of the highest degree of rarity. Since Heber's sale, presuming, as I believe is the case, that the copy noted in Bohn's Lowndes as sold in March, 1856, is the Utterson copy, only two copies have been sold by auction, namely, — 1. Utterson's (sig. E six leaves) sold for £17. 10, but this copy (now Mr. Corser's) has two leaves in facsimile, and 2. one at my sale in May, 1857, also with E six leaves, which sold for £100.*

"*It has been usually stated that the second & six-leaved edition is the rarest, but I believe that this is an error, & that this first edition is one of the very rarest of the old Shakespeare quartos. The Bodley copy of it is imperfect. There are two copies of the six-leaved ed. in the Brit. Mus., but only a fragment of the present one. Both eds. are, however, very rare, & no copy of either was in the Daniel collection.*

"*The present copy is substantially perfect, but a small corner of one leaf & a few head-lines are in facsimile. It has also a special interest of its own in possessing a few short stage-directions in manuscript undoubtedly contemporary with Shakespeare, & in one place, sig. B. 2, a plot as it is probable of the position of the characters on the ancient stage.*

"*June, 1866.*   *J. O. Halliwell.*"

THE
Second part of Henrie
the fourth, continuing to his death,
and coronation of Henrie
the fift.

With the humours of sir Iohn Falstaffe, and swaggering
Pistoll.

As it hath been sundrie times publikely
acted by the right honourable, the Lord
Chamberlaine his seruants.

Written by William Shakespeare.

LONDON
Printed by V.S. for Andrew Wise, and
William Aspley.
1600.

Of this quarto there are two editions.

In the First Edition, that here described, sheet E has but four leaves.

In the Second Edition, described in our next number, sheet E has six leaves. On the printer's discovering that he had omitted the whole of the first scene of act iii., he cancelled leaves E 3 and [E 4], as originally issued, and reprinted them, adding two more leaves in order to include the omitted lines. To allow for this insertion the type already standing was divided, to permit of the interpolation of the omitted matter; so that there are two different impressions for the latter part of act ii. and the beginning of act iii.

The First Edition of this play was reproduced in the Ashbee-Halliwell *Facsimiles* (1866), No. 20. Of the British Museum copy, the distinguishing feature of the First Edition, leaves E 3 and [E 4], were reproduced in the Griggs-Furnivall *Shakspere-Quarto Facsimiles* [1882], No. 9, where they will be found placed at the end of the volume.

SHAKESPEARE, WILLIAM.

HENRY THE FOURTH, PART II. LONDON, *by V. S. for Andrew Wiſe, and William Aſpley*, 1600. [582]

Small quarto. Second Edition; sheet E, 6 leaves.

COLLATION BY SIGNATURES: A to D, each 4 leaves; E, 6 leaves; F to K, each 4 leaves; L, 2 leaves (the last blank and lacking); total 44 unnumbered leaves.

COLLATION BY PAGINATION: Identically the same as in our No. 581.

CONDITION: Size of leaf, 6 11/16 × 4 7/8 inches. Bound in red crushed levant morocco, gilt edges; by Bedford. The leaves are stabbed on the inner margins throughout the book.

OTHER COPIES.

British Museum (2); Bodleian; Capell Collection; Devonshire; Ellesmere; Huth; and White (Heber copy) Libraries.

REFERENCES.

Greg, *List of English Plays* (Bibliographical Society; 1900), p. 98; British Museum, *Catalogue*; *Shakespeare* (1897), col. 78; Hazlitt, *Manual of Old English Plays* (1892), p. 103; Locker-Lampson, *Catalogue* (1886), p. 107; Huth, *Catalogue*, 4 (1880): 1333; Winsor, *Bibliography* (1876), p. 31; Lowndes, 4 (1869): 2279; Hazlitt, *Hand-Book to the Popular, Poetical, and Dramatic Literature of Great Britain* (1867), p. 548, No. 12.

The Locker-Lampson copy.

In this, the Second Edition, sheet E, which was in part reprinted, has six leaves.

The Huth *Catalogue* says: "Slight literal variations have been found in copies of this impression, probably made as the volume was passing through the press."

In this play are many direct references to persons and places familiar to Shakespeare. Three characters are specially noteworthy: Hotspur, the impetuous and ambitious subject of the king; Prince Hal, his son and heir, whose boisterous disposition drives him from court to seek adventures among the haunters of taverns; and Prince Hal's tun-bellied follower, Falstaff, the culmination of Shakespeare's comic power.

"English literature," says Dowden, "knows no humorous creation to set beside Falstaff; and to find his equal — yet his opposite — we must turn to the gaunt figure of [Cervantes'] romantic knight of La Mancha."

The Second Edition was reproduced in the Ashbee-Halliwell *Facsimiles* (1866), No. 21, and also (the Devonshire copy) in the Griggs-Furnivall *Shakspere-Quarto Facsimiles* [1882], No. 9. Steevens reprinted it in his *Twenty Plays* (1766), Vol. 2.

SHAKESPEARE, WILLIAM.

HENRY THE FIFTH. LONDON, *by Thomas Creede, for Tho. Millington, and Iohn Busby*, 1600. [583]

Small quarto. First Edition.

COLLATION BY SIGNATURES: A to G, each 4 leaves (the last blank and lacking); total 28 unnumbered leaves. Leaf G 2 is wrongly marked G 3; and G 3 has no signature-mark.

COLLATION BY PAGINATION: [title, as reproduced; *See* No. 583], recto of [A]; —[blank], verso of [A]; —[text, with heading] | [conventional head-piece] | The Chronicle Hiftorie | of *Henry* the fift: with his battel fought | at *AginCourt* in *France*. Togither with | Auncient *Pistoll.* |, recto of A 2 to recto of [G 3]; — | FINIS. | [conventional tail-piece] |, recto of [G 3]; —[blank], verso of [G 3]; —[1 blank leaf], [G 4].

CONDITION: Size of leaf, 7 × 5¼ inches. Bound in red crushed levant morocco, gilt edges; by Bedford. Leaves A to B 3 are genuine, the remainder being in facsimile; some words in facsimile on leaves B to B 3.

OTHER COPIES.

British Museum; Bodleian (Malone copy); Capell Collection; Devonshire (Steevens copy); and Huth (Heber-Daniel copy) Libraries.

REFERENCES.

Lee, *Life of Shakespeare* (1906), p. 174; Greg, *List of English Plays* (Bibliographical Society; 1900), p. 98; British Museum, *Catalogue*; *Shakespeare* (1897), col. 81; *The Cambridge Shakespeare*, 4 (1894): xii.; Hazlitt, *Manual of Old English Plays* (1893), p. 104; Locker-Lampson, *Catalogue* (1886), p. 107; Huth, *Catalogue*, 4 (1880): 1333; Winsor, *Bibliography* (1876), p. 32; Lowndes, 4 (1869): 2280; Hazlitt, *Hand-Book* (1867), p. 549, No. 13 *a*.

The Locker-Lampson copy, with ex-libris.

Of this play editions were issued in 1600, 1602, and 1608.

The First Edition (1600), that here described, was reproduced in the Ashbee-Halliwell *Facsimiles* (1868), No. 22, and also (the British Museum copy) in the Praetorius-Furnivall *Shakspere-Quarto Facsimiles* (1886), No. 27.

Of the Second Edition (1602), printed by "Thomas Creede, for Thomas Pauier," there are copies in the Capell Collection and the Duke of Devonshire's Library. It was reproduced in the Ashbee-Halliwell *Facsimiles* (1867), No. 24.

The Third Edition (1608) is that described in our next number.

The text of the quarto editions of this play of Shakespeare's was printed from an imperfect draft made up, as Collier and others suppose, from notes hastily taken at

THE CRONICLE

History of Henry the fift,
With his battell fought at *Agin Court* in
France. Togither with *Auntient*
Pistoll.

*As it hath bene sundry times playd by the Right honorable
the Lord Chamberlaine his seruants.*

LONDON

Printed by *Thomas Creede*, for Tho. Millington, and Iohn Busby. And are to be
sold at his house in Carter Lane, next
the Powle head. 1600.

No. 583. Title-page of Shakespeare's Henry the Fifth; 1st Edition; 1600.

the theatre during the performance of the play, and subsequently patched together. The complete text is to be found only in the Folio of 1623. Charles Knight, in commenting on the differences between the text of the quartos and that of the First Folio, says: "Unless we were to reprint the original copy page by page with the text of 1623 it would be impossible to convey a satisfactory notion of the exceeding care with which the play has been recast." The Folio edition has 3500 lines; but the quartos have only 1800.

The text of the edition here described is reprinted in *The Cambridge Shakespeare* (9 : 461–506), with the readings of the Second and Third Editions respectively.

"'Henry V' may be regarded as Shakespeare's final experiment in the dramatisation of English history, and it artistically rounds off the series of his 'histories' which form collectively a kind of national epic."

"It is scarcely necessary," says the Cambridge editor, "to add that 'The famous Victories of Henry the Fift,' [noted by us on p. 814] published in [1598 and] 1617, has nothing to do with Shakespeare's play."

SHAKESPEARE, WILLIAM.

HENRY THE FIFTH. [LONDON], *for* T. P., 1608.   [584]

Small quarto. Third Edition.

COLLATION BY SIGNATURES : A to G, each 4 leaves (the last blank and genuine); total 28 unnumbered leaves. Leaf D 3 has no signature-mark.

COLLATION BY PAGINATION : [title, as reproduced; *See* No. 584], recto of [A]; —[blank], verso of [A]; —[text, with heading] | [conventional head-piece] | The Chronicle Hiftorie | of Henry the fift : with his battell fought | at *AginCourt* in *France*. Togither with | Ancient *Pistoll.* |, recto of A 2 to verso of G 3; — | *FINJS.* | [conventional tail-piece] |, verso of G 3; — [1 blank leaf], [G 4].

CONDITION : Size of leaf, 7⅛ × 5⁵⁄₁₆ inches. Bound in dark green morocco, gilt edges.

OTHER COPIES.

British Museum ; Bodleian (Malone copy); Capell Collection ; Dyce Collection ; Birmingham Free ; Edinburgh University ; Devonshire; Huth; Boston Public; John Carter Brown; Perry (Gwynn copy); Lenox ; Hoe ; Morgan (Irwin copy) ; and Furness (2) Libraries ; also the Howe and the Van Antwerp copies (untraced).

REFERENCES.

Greg, *List of English Plays* (Bibliographical Society; 1900), p. 98; British Museum, *Catalogue*; *Shakespeare* (1897), col. 81; Locker-Lampson, *Catalogue* (1886), p. 107; Boston Public Library, *Catalogue*; *Barton Collection* (1880), p. 23, No. 293; Huth, *Catalogue*, 4 (1880): 1334; Lenox Library, *Works of Shakespeare* (1880), p. 15, No. 60; Winsor, *Bibliography* (1876), p. 33; Lowndes, 4 (1869): 2280; Hazlitt, *Hand-Book* (1867), p. 549, No. 13 *c*.

This edition was reproduced in the Ashbee-Halliwell *Facsimiles* (1870), No. 35, and also (the British Museum copy) in the Praetorius-Furnivall *Shakspere-Quarto Facsimiles* (1886), No. 28. It was reprinted by Steevens in his *Twenty Plays* (1766), Vol. 3.

THE
Chronicle History
of Henry the fift, with his battell fought at *Agin Court* in France. Together with ancient *Pistoll*.

As it hath bene sundry times playd by the Right Honourable the Lord Chamberlaine his Seruants.

Printed for *T. P.* 1608.

SHAKESPEARE, WILLIAM.

[HENRY THE SIXTH, PARTS II. AND III. WITH PERICLES.] THE WHOLE CONTENTION. LONDON, *for* T. P., [1619].   [585]

Small quarto. Third Edition.

COLLATION BY SIGNATURES: A to Z, Aa, each 4 leaves; Bb, 2 leaves (the last blank and genuine); total 98 unnumbered leaves.

COLLATION BY PAGINATION: [title, as reproduced; *See* No. 585*a*], recto of [A]; —[blank], verso of [A]; —[text (*Henry VI.*, Part II.), with heading]|[conventional head-piece] | The firſt part of the Conten- | *tion of the two Famous Houſes of Yorke* | and Lancaſter, with the death of | the good Duke *Humfrey.* |, recto of A 2 to verso of [H 4]; — | *FINIS.* |, verso of [H 4].

[Text of Part II. (*Henry VI.*, Part III.), the first page as reproduced; *See* No. 585*b*], recto of I to verso of [Q 4]; — | *FINIS.* |, verso of [Q 4].

[Text of *Pericles*, the first page as reproduced; *See* No. 585*c*], recto of R to recto of Bb; — | FINIS. |, recto of Bb; — [blank], verso of Bb; —[1 blank leaf], [Bb 2].

CONDITION: Size of leaf, 7¼ × 5½ inches. Bound in red crushed levant morocco, gilt edges; by Bedford. The blank leaf [Bb 2] has been wrongly bound between leaves [Q 4] and R.

OTHER COPIES.

With *Pericles*: British Museum (Garrick copy); Lenox (Loscombe-Halliwell Phillipps-Tite copy); and Hoe Libraries. Without *Pericles*: British Museum; Bodleian; Capell Collection; Dyce Collection; Devonshire (Heber copy); Huth; Birmingham Free (2, one, the First Part, separately); Boston Public; Perry (Gwynne copy); Lenox (2, the Heber and the Utterson-Tite copies, the latter with date changed to 1600); Morgan (McKee copy); and White Libraries; also the Howe and the McKee-Van Antwerp copies (untraced).

REFERENCES.

Greg, *List of English Plays* (Bibliographical Society; 1900), p. 125; *The Cambridge Shakespeare*, 5 (1895): vii.–x.; Hazlitt, *Manual of Old English Plays* (1892), p. 49; Locker-Lampson, *Catalogue* (1886), p. 107; Boston Public Library, *Catalogue*; *Barton Collection* (1880), p. 23, No. 300; Huth, *Catalogue*, 4 (1880): 1339; Lenox Library, *Works of Shakespeare* (1880), pp. 15, 16, Nos. 63–65; Winsor, *Bibliography* (1876), p. 35; Lowndes, 4 (1869): 2281.

The Capell-Locker Lampson copy, with ex-libris of the latter.

The Edition here described contains three plays, viz.:

Henry the Sixth, Part II.   (Part I., leaves A 2 to H 4.)
Henry the Sixth, Part III. (Part II., leaves I to Q 4.)
Pericles.   (Part III., leaves R to Bb.)

The First Edition (1594) of the play, which by subsequent revision came to be known as *Henry the Sixth*, Part II., was "Printed by Thomas Creed, for Thomas Millington," under the title *The Firſt part of the Contention betwixt the two famous Houſes of Yorke and Lancaſter*. Of this edition but a single copy is now known, that in the Bodleian Library (the Tyssen-Malone-Heber copy). It was reproduced in the Praetorius-Furnivall *Shakspere-Quarto Facsimiles* (1889), No. 37.

Of the Second Edition (1600), "Printed by Valentine Simmes for Thomas Millington," which differs from the First only in a very few literal variations and in the title-page, there are copies in the Bodleian (2, one lacking the title-page), Capell Collection (imperfect), Devonshire, and Ellesmere Libraries.

THE
Whole Contention
betweene the two Famous Houses, LANCASTER and YORKE.

With the Tragicall ends of the good Duke Humfrey, Richard Duke of Yorke, and King Henrie the sixt.

Diuided into two Parts: And newly corrected and enlarged. Written by *William Shakespeare,* Gent.

Printed at LONDON, for T. P.

No. 585 *a*. TITLE-PAGE OF SHAKESPEARE'S [HENRY THE SIXTH, PARTS II. AND III.] THE WHOLE CONTENTION; 3D EDITION; [1619].

The Third Edition [1619], "Printed at London, for T. P.," that here described, is entitled *The Whole Contention betweene the two Famous Houses, Lancaster and Yorke.* It is the first edition containing the play as revised by Shakespeare for the

The Second Part.

Containing the Tragedie of Richard Duke of Yorke, and the good *King Henrie the* Sixt.

¶ Enter Richard Duke of Yorke, the Earle of Warwicke, the Duke of Norfolke, Marquesse Mountague, Edward Earle of March, then Crooke backe Richard, and the young Earle of Rutland, with drum and souldiers, with white Roses in their hats.

      Warwicke.
Wonder how the King escap'd our hands.
Yorke. Whilst we pursu'd the horsemen of the
  North,
He slily stole away and left his men:
Whereat the great Lord of *Northumberland,*
Whose warlike eares could neuer brooke re-
  treat,
Charg'd our maine battels front, and there with him
Lord *Stafford* and Lord *Clifford* all abrest
Brake in, and were by th'hands of common souldiers slaine.
 Edward. Lord *Staffords* Father, Duke of Buckingham,
Is either slaine or wounded dangerously,
      I   I

THE HISTORY OF
Pericles, Prince of Tyre.

Enter Gower.

O sing a song that old was sung,
From ashes, ancient *Gower* is come,
Assuming mans infirmities,
To glad your eare, and please your eies;
It hath beene sung at Festiuals,
On Ember eues, and holy-daies
And Lords and Ladies in their liues,
Haue read it for restoratiues :
The purchase is to make men glorious.
Et bonum quo Antiquius eo melius:
If you, borne in these latter times,
When wits more ripe, accept my Rimes;
And that to heare an old man sing,
May to your wishes pleasure bring :
I life would wish, and that I might
Waste it for you like Taper-light.
This *Antioch*, then, *Antiochus* the great,
Built vp this City for his chiefest seate ;
The fairest in all *Syria.*
I tell you what mine Authors say :
This King vnto him tooke a Peere,
Who died, and left a female heire,
So buckesome, blithe, and full of face,

.R   As

No. 585 c. First Page of Shakespeare's Pericles ; [1619].

Second Part of *Henry VI*. This edition contains not only Shakespeare's revision of the *Firſt part of the Contention*, but also, as "The Second Part," his revision of the play previously published in 1595 as *The true Tragedie of Richard Duke of Yorke, and the death of good King Henrie the Sixt*, and *The Hiſtory of Pericles, Prince of Tyre*, as shown by the collation given above. Of this edition the British Museum copy was reproduced in the Praetorius-Furnivall *Shakspere-Quarto Facsimiles* (1886), No. 23. It was reprinted by Steevens in his *Twenty Plays* (1766), Vol. 3.

Another supposed edition, also 1600, with the same title, but said to have been "Printed by W. W. for Thomas Millington," is recorded by Hazlitt (*Collections and Notes;* 1876, p. 98) and Lowndes (4:2281); but neither Greg nor the editor of *The Cambridge Shakespeare* was able to locate a copy. The Cambridge editor says (5:xi.): "The only authority . . . for the existence of an edition of The First Part of the Contention, printed by W. W. in 1600, is the MS. title-page of Malone's copy [Malone, 36: *True Tragedie*, "by W. W."; 1600] in the Bodleian Library." In another place (5:ix.) he says: "The MS. title quoted by Mr. Halliwell from a copy in the Bodleian (Malone, 36) is prefixed to what appears to us unquestionably the same edition as the above" [i.e., *The Firſt part of the Contention*, "by Valentine Simmes; 1600"].

The Locker-Lampson *Catalogue* says the copy here described is "imperfect, wanting titlepage to Pericles." It corresponds in this respect to the Lenox Library copy (No. 64), in which the play ends, and is completed on the verso of leaf Q 4, and *Pericles* begins on the recto of leaf R, with no intervening title-page. In the copy of *The Whole Contention* recently acquired by Mr. Hoe, *Pericles* has the title-page.

The Huth copy, which is bound in two volumes, has, as in the separately bound copy in the present collection (our No. 607), a title-page for *Pericles*. In the Huth *Catalogue* it is described as follows: "After sig. Q, though not mentioned on the first title-page, occurs a second title: 'The Late, And much admired Play, called, Pericles, Prince of Tyre. With the true Relation of the whole History, aduentures, and fortunes of the saide Prince. Written by W. Shakespeare. *Printed for T. P.* 1619.' This is the third [fourth] edition, the second [third] having appeared in 1611. Of 'the whole Contention,' which is not by Shakespeare, but merely one of the plays of which he made use, this is the third or fourth edition. In the impressions of 1594 and 1600 there is no mention of Shakespeare as the author."

Besides the play of *Pericles* which forms an integral part of the copy here described there is in the present collection another copy of the same edition separately bound with a title-page (our No. 607).

Of this play as altered by John Crowne, the First Edition appeared in 1680 under the title *Miſery of Civil-War*. There are copies in the British Museum, Bodleian (2), Huth, Harvard University, and Hoe Libraries, and in the Library of Congress.

The Second Edition by Crowne, entitled *Henry the Sixth. The Second Part; or, The Miſery of Civil War*, was published in 1681. Of this edition there are copies in the British Museum (2), Bodleian (2), Dyce Collection, Devonshire, Hoe, and White Libraries, and the Library of Congress.

SHAKESPEARE, WILLIAM.

[HENRY THE SIXTH, PART III.] THE TRUE TRAGEDIE OF RICHARDE DUKE OF YORKE. Londou, by W. W. for Thomas Millington, 1600. [586]

Small quarto. Second Edition.

COLLATION BY SIGNATURES: A to H, each 4 leaves; total 32 unnumbered leaves. Leaves A 4 and B 4 have signature-marks.

COLLATION BY PAGINATION: [title, as reproduced; See No. 586], recto of [A]; —[blank], verso of [A];—[text, with heading] | [type-ornament head-piece] | THE TRVE TRAGEDIE | OF RICHARD DVKE OF YORKE, | AND THE GOOD KING | HENRIE THE SIXT. |, recto of A 2 to recto of [H 4];—| FINIS. |, recto of [H 4];—[blank], verso of [H 4].

CONDITION: Size of leaf, 6 13/16 × 5 1/8 inches. Bound in red crushed levant morocco, gilt edges; by Bedford. The title-page and leaves E and E 2 have several words in facsimile.

OTHER COPIES.

British Museum (Steevens copy); Bodleian (Malone copy); Devonshire; Ellesmere; and Boston Public (Halliwell-Phillipps copy) Libraries; also the Howe copy (untraced).

REFERENCES.

Greg, *List of English Plays* (Bibliographical Society; 1900), p. 127; British Museum, *Catalogue*; *Shakespeare* (1897), col. 84; *The Cambridge Shakespeare*, 5 (1895): x.; Hazlitt, *Manual of Old English Plays* (1892), p. 239; Locker-Lampson, *Catalogue* (1886), p. 114; Boston Public Library, *Catalogue*; *Barton Collection* (1880), p. 23, No. 301; Winsor, *Bibliography* (1876), p. 36; Hazlitt, *Hand-Book* (1867), p. 506, No. 2 *b*.

The Locker-Lampson copy, with ex-libris.

This is the play which Shakespeare subsequently worked over into *Henry VI., Part III.* It appeared in three different editions: 1595, 1600, and again in 1619, the last time as the Second Part of *The Whole Contention betweene the two Famous Houſes, Lancaſter and Yorke* (our previous number).

The First Edition (1595) appeared under the title *The true Tragedie of Richard Duke of Yorke, and the death of good King Henrie the Sixt, with the whole contention betweene the two Houſes Lancaſter and Yorke*, and was printed "by P. S. for Thomas Millington." The only copy now known of this edition is in the Bodleian Library (Pegge-Chalmers copy). It was reproduced in the Praetorius-Furnivall *Shakspere-Quarto Facsimiles* (1891), No. 38.

The Second Edition (1600) is that here described.

Of the Third Edition [1619], that described as "The Second Part" (leaves I to [Q 4]) in our previous number, the British Museum copy was reproduced in the Praetorius-Furnivall *Shakspere-Quarto Facsimiles* (1886), No. 24. A list of the other copies of this edition will be found under our previous number.

Another edition, also 1600, has been thought to exist, from the fact that, as says the Cambridge editor (5 : x.): "In Malone's Shakespeare (ed. 1790, Vol. I. Pt. I. p. 235), among the 'Dramatick Pieces on which plays were formed by Shakespeare,' an edition of The True Tragedy is mentioned, bearing date '1600, V. S. for Thomas Millington,' but in a note to the 'Third Part of King Henry VI.' (Vol. VI. p. 261) he confesses, 'I have never seen the quarto copy of the *Second* part of The whole

No. 586 *William Shakespeare* 1600

THE
True Tragedie of
Richarde Duke of
Yorke, and the death of good
King Henrie the sixt:

VVith the whole contention betweene the two
Houses, Lancaster and Yorke; as it was
sundry times acted by the Right
Honourable the Earle
of Pembrooke his
seruantes.

Printed at London by *W.W.* for *Thomas Millington*
and are to be sold at his shoppe vnder Saint
Peters Church in Cornewall.
1600.

No. 586. Title-page of The True Tragedie of Richarde Duke of Yorke; Shakespeare's [Henry the Sixth, Part III.]; 2d Edition; 1600.

English Literature [834] Church Catalogue

Contention, &c. printed by *Valentine Simmes* for Thomas Millington, 1600 ; ' and it is extremely doubtful whether such a one exists." As no copy of an edition corresponding to the above description has as yet been located, its existence can safely be deemed fictitious.

SHAKESPEARE, WILLIAM.

[HENRY THE SIXTH, PART III. London, 1619.] [587]

Small quarto. Third Edition.

COLLATION BY SIGNATURES: I to Q, each 4 leaves; total 32 unnumbered leaves.

COLLATION BY PAGINATION: [text, with heading] | [conventional head-piece] | The Second Part. | Containing the Tragedie of | Richard Duke of Yorke, and the | *good King Henrie the* | Sixt. |, recto of I to verso of [Q 4]; — | FINIS. |, verso of [Q 4].

CONDITION: Size of leaf, 7¼ × 5½ inches. Bound with and forming an integral part of our No. 585 (q.v.).

OTHER COPIES.

For a list of other copies of this edition see our No. 585.

REFERENCES.

For a list of references relating to this edition see our No. 585.

SHAKESPEARE, WILLIAM.

RICHARD THE THIRD. London, *by Thomas Creede, for Andrew Wife*, 1598.

[588]

Small quarto. Second Edition.

COLLATION BY SIGNATURES: A to M, each 4 leaves (the last blank and lacking); total 48 unnumbered leaves.

COLLATION BY PAGINATION: [title, as reproduced; *See* No. 588], recto of [A]; — [blank], verso of [A]; — [text, with heading] | [conventional head-piece] | *Enter Richard Duke of Glofter, folus.* |, recto of A 2 to verso of [M 3]; — | FINIS. |, verso of [M 3]; — [1 blank leaf], [M 4].

CONDITION: Size of leaf (extended on lower margin), 7⁷⁄₁₆ × 5⅛ inches. Bound in red morocco, gilt edges; by Bedford. Lower margins extended, with leaves C 2, C 3, M and M 2 possibly supplied from a taller copy; some signature-marks, catch-words, and portions of last lines of text in facsimile; and leaf C 4 probably in facsimile.

OTHER COPIES.

British Museum (2, both imperfect); Bodleian; Capell Collection; Devonshire; and Ellesmere Libraries.

REFERENCES.

Lee, *Life of Shakespeare* (1906), p. 63; Greg, *List of English Plays* (Bibliographical Society; 1900), p. 96; British Museum, *Catalogue; Shakespeare* (1897), col. 99; *The Cambridge Shakespeare*, 5 (1895): xiii., xvii.; Hazlitt, *Manual of Old English Plays* (1892), p. 195; Locker-Lampson, *Catalogue* (1886), p. 107; Winsor, *Bibliography* (1876), p. 61; Lowndes, 4 (1869): 2294; Hazlitt, *Hand-Book to the Popular, Poetical, and Dramatic Literature of Great Britain, From the Invention of Printing to the Restoration* (1867), p. 548, No. 9 b.

The Jolley-Halliwell Phillipps-Tite-Locker Lampson copy, with the ex-libris of the last.

Editions of this play were published in quarto, in 1597, 1598, 1602, 1605, 1612, 1622, 1629, and 1634.

Of the First Edition (1597), " Printed by Valentine Sims, for Andrew Wife," there are copies in the Bodleian (Malone copy, imperfect), Huth (Heber-Daniel copy), and Duke of Devonshire's (Kemble copy) Libraries, and a fragment of two sheets (C and D) in the British Museum; also the Howe copy (untraced). This edition was reproduced in the Ashbee-Halliwell *Facsimiles* (1863), No. 7, and also (the Devonshire copy) in the Griggs-Furnivall *Shakspere-Quarto Facsimiles* [1886], No. 11.

The Cambridge editor attempts to explain the differences between the text of the first quarto edition and that of the First Folio on the theory that the latter was printed from a transcript of the author's original manuscript which had undergone revision at his hands, "with corrections and additions, interlinear, marginal, and on inserted leaves."

The Second Edition (1598), that here described, was reproduced in the Ashbee-Halliwell *Facsimiles* (1867), No. 11. This edition is a reprint of the First.

Of the Third Edition (1602), "Printed by Thomas Creede, for Andrew Wife," there are copies in the British Museum and Capell Collections. "Notwithstanding the words 'newly augmented' [on the title-page], this edition contains nothing that is not found in the second Quarto, from which it is reprinted, except some additional errors of the press." This edition was reproduced in the Ashbee-Halliwell *Facsimiles* (1865), No. 25, and also (the British Museum copy) in the Griggs-Furnivall *Shakspere-Quarto Facsimiles* (1888), No. 42.

The Fourth Edition (1605) is that described in our next number.

The Fifth Edition (1612) is that described in our No. 590.

The Sixth Edition (1622) is that described in our No. 591.

Of the Seventh Edition (1629), "Printed by Iohn Norton, and are to be fold by Mathew Law," there are copies in the British Museum, Bodleian, Capell Collection, Dyce Collection, Edinburgh University, Hunterian Museum, Lenox, and White Libraries; also the Howe copy (untraced). This edition was printed not from the First Folio but from the quarto of 1622.

The Eighth Edition (1634) is that described in our No. 592.

In 1700 an edition of this play, altered by Colley Cibber, as *The Tragical Hiftory of King Richard III., as it is acted at the Theatre Royal*, was published in quarto. Of this edition there are copies in the British Museum, Bodleian, Devonshire, Harvard University, and White Libraries. This version long held the stage to the exclusion of the original play.

In 1594 *The True Tragedie Of Richard the Third*, "by Thomas Creede, fold by William Barley," was published anonymously. Of this play, which bears little resemblance to that which Shakespeare based upon it, there is a copy in the Duke of Devonshire's Library. "The subject," says Sidney Lee, "was already familiar to dramatists. . . . A Latin piece, by Dr. Thomas Legge, had been in favour with academic audiences since 1579." Legge's piece does not seem to have been printed until 1844, when it was appended by the Shakespeare Society to its reprint of *The True Tragedie*.

Throughout Shakespeare's *Richard III.* his effort to emulate Marlowe is undeniable. The play was naturally popular, Burbage's impersonation of Richard being one of the most effective of his performances.

THE TRAGEDIE

of King Richard the third.

Conteining his treacherous Plots againſt his brother *Clarence*: the pitiful murther of his innocent Nephewes: his tyrannicall vſurpation: with the whole courſe of his deteſted life, and moſt *deſerued death.*

As it hath beene lately Acted by the Right honourable the Lord Chamberlaine his ſeruants.

By William Shake-ſpeare.

LONDON

Printed by Thomas Creede, for Andrew Wiſe, dwelling in Paules Church-yard, at the ſigne of the Angell. 1 5 9 8.

No. 588. Title-page of Shakespeare's Richard the Third; 2d Edition; 1598.

No. 589   *William Shakespeare*   1605

THE
TRAGEDIE
of King Richard
the third.

Conteining his treacherous Plots againſt his brother
Clarence : the pittifull murther of his innocent Nephewes : his tyrannicall vſurpation : with the
whole courſe of his deteſted life, and
moſt deſerued death.

*As it hath bin lately Acted by the Right Honourable
the Lord Chamberlaine his ſeruants.*

Newly augmented,

By *William Shake-ſpeare.*

LONDON,
Printed by Thomas Creede, and are to be ſold by *Mathew
Lawe*, dwelling in Paules Church-yard, at the Signe
of the Foxe, neare S. Auſtins gate, 1605.

No. 589.   Title-page of Shakespeare's Richard the Third;
4th Edition; 1605.

SHAKESPEARE, WILLIAM.

RICHARD THE THIRD. LONDON, *by Thomas Creede, and are to be fold by Mathew Lawe*, 1605.   [589]

Small quarto. Fourth Edition.

COLLATION BY SIGNATURES: A to L, each 4 leaves; M, 2 leaves; total 46 unnumbered leaves.

COLLATION BY PAGINATION: [title, as reproduced; *See* No. 589], recto of [A]; — [blank], verso of [A]; — [text, with heading] | [conventional head-piece] | *Enter Richard Duke of Glocefter, folus.* |, recto of A 2 to verso of [M 2]; — | *FINIS.* |, verso of [M 2].

CONDITION: Size of leaf, 7½ × 5⁵⁄₁₆ inches. Bound in red crushed levant morocco, gilt edges; by Bedford. Leaves [A], M, and [M 2] are in facsimile.

OTHER COPIES.

British Museum; and Bodleian (Malone-Halliwell Phillipps copy) Libraries.

REFERENCES.

Greg, *List of English Plays* (Bibliographical Society; 1900), p. 96; British Museum, *Catalogue*; *Shakespeare* (1897), col. 99; Locker-Lampson, *Catalogue* (1886), p. 108; Winsor, *Bibliography* (1876), p. 61; Lowndes, 4 (1869): 2295; Hazlitt, *Hand-Book* (1867), p. 548, No. 9 *d*.

The Tite ?-Locker Lampson copy, with ex-libris of the latter.

This edition was reproduced in the Ashbee-Halliwell *Facsimiles* (1863), No. 30.

SHAKESPEARE, WILLIAM.

RICHARD THE THIRD. LONDON, *by Thomas Creede, and are to be fold by Mathew Lawe*, 1612.   [590]

Small quarto. Fifth Edition.

COLLATION BY SIGNATURES: A to L, each 4 leaves; M, 2 leaves; total 46 unnumbered leaves.

COLLATION BY PAGINATION: [title, as reproduced; *See* No. 590], recto of [A]; — [blank], verso of [A]; — [text, with heading] | [conventional head-piece] | *Enter Richard Duke of Glocefter, folus.* |, recto of A 2 to verso of [M 2]; — | *FINIS.* |, verso of [M 2]. The head-lines on the rectos of leaves C 3, D 3, [F 4], G, H 2, and [I 4] read: | of Richard the thrid. | .

CONDITION: Size of leaf, 7⅛ × 4¹³⁄₁₆ inches. Bound in green crushed levant morocco, gilt edges; by De Coverly. Leaves A–[A 4] and M 2 are supplied from a slightly shorter copy.

OTHER COPIES.

British Museum; Bodleian (Malone copy, with date blurred, looking like 1613); Capell Collection; Forster Collection, South Kensington Museum (imperfect); Edinburgh University; Lenox (2, one the Dyce copy); White; and Furness Libraries. Winsor also locates a copy in the library of the Marquis of Bute.

REFERENCES.

Greg, *List of English Plays* (Bibliographical Society; 1900), p. 96; British Museum, *Catalogue*; *Shakespeare* (1897), col. 99; Locker-Lampson, *Catalogue* (1886), p. 108; Lenox Library, *Works of Shakespeare* (1880), p. 26, No. 143; Winsor, *Bibliography* (1876), p. 62; Hazlitt, *Hand-Book* (1867), p. 548, No. 9 *e*.

No. 590　　　*William Shakespeare*　　　1612

THE
TRAGEDIE
of King Richard
the third.

Containing his treacherous Plots against his brother Clarence : the pittifull murther of his innocent Nephewes: his tyrannicall vsurpation : with the whole courſe of his deteſted life, and moſt deſerued death.

As it hath beene lately Acted by the Kings Maieſties ſeruants.

Newly augmented,
By *William Shake-ſpeare.*

LONDON,
Printed by Thomas Creede, and are to be ſold by Mathew
Lawe, dwelling in Pauls Church-yard, at the Signe
of the Foxe, neare S. Auſtins gate, 1 6 1 2.

No. 590.　Title-page of Shakespeare's Richard the Third;
5th Edition; 1612.

The Locker-Lampson copy, with ex-libris.

This edition was reprinted from the quarto of 1602. It was reproduced in the Ashbee-Halliwell *Facsimiles* (1871), No. 43, and was reprinted by Steevens in his *Twenty Plays* (1766), Vol. 3.

SHAKESPEARE, WILLIAM.

RICHARD THE THIRD. LONDON, *by Thomas Purfoot, and are to be fold by Mathew Law*, 1622. [591]

Small quarto. Sixth Edition.
COLLATION BY SIGNATURES: A to L, each 4 leaves; M, 2 leaves; total 46 unnumbered leaves. Leaf M 2 has a signature-mark.
COLLATION BY PAGINATION: [title, as reproduced; *See* No. 591], recto of [A];— [blank], verso of [A];—[text, with heading] | [conventional head-piece] | *Enter Richard Duke of Gloucester, folus.* |, recto of A 2 to verso of M 2;— | *FINIS.* |, verso of M 2.
CONDITION: Size of leaf, 7⅝₁₆ × 5⅗₁₆ inches. Bound in maroon morocco, with coat of arms in centre of covers, gilt edges.

The leaves are stabbed on the inner margins throughout.

OTHER COPIES.

British Museum (3, one imperfect); Bodleian; and Capell Collections.

REFERENCES.

Greg, *List of English Plays* (Bibliographical Society; 1900), p. 96; British Museum, *Catalogue*; Shakespeare (1897), col. 100; *The Cambridge Shakespeare*, 5 (1895): xiv.; Winsor, *Bibliography* (1876), p. 62; Lowndes, 4 (1869): 2295; Hazlitt, *Hand-Book* (1867), p. 548, No. 9*f*.

The Ives copy, with ex-libris.

This edition was reprinted from that of 1612.

"The edition of 1622," says the Cambridge editor, "is so rare that its very existence has been called in question. ('An impression of 1622 is mentioned in some lists, but the existence of a copy of that date is more than doubtful.' Collier, Ed. 2, Vol. IV. p. 217.) There is however a copy in the Capell collection."

The British Museum copy of this edition was reproduced in the Praetorius-Furnivall *Shakspere-Quarto Facsimiles* (1889), No. 43. Steevens, in his reprint of the quarto of 1612, mentions an edition of 1624, probably a mistake for 1622.

SHAKESPEARE, WILLIAM.

RICHARD THE THIRD. LONDON, *by Iohn Norton*, 1634. [592]

Small quarto. Eighth Edition.
COLLATION BY SIGNATURES: A to L, each 4 leaves; M, 2 leaves; total 46 unnumbered leaves. Leaf K 2 is wrongly marked C 2; and M 2 has a signature-mark.
COLLATION BY PAGINATION: [title, as reproduced; *See* No. 592], recto of [A]; —[blank], verso of [A];—[text, with heading] | [conventional head-piece] | *Enter Richard Duke of Glocester, folus.* |, recto of A 2 to verso of M 2;— | *FJNJS.* |, verso of M 2.

THE TRAGEDIE OF KING RICHARD THE THIRD.

Contayning his treacherous Plots against *his brother* Clarence: *The pittifull murder of his innocent* Nephewes: his tyrannicall Vsurpation: with the whole course of his detested life, and most *deserued death.*

As it hath been lately Acted by the Kings Maiesties *Seruants.*

Newly augmented.

By *William Shake-speare.*

LONDON,
Printed by *Thomas Purfoot,* and are to be sold by *Mathew Law,* dwelling in *Pauls* Church-yard, at the Signe of the *Foxe,* neere S. *Austines* gate. 1622.

1634   *William Shakespeare*   No. 592

THE
TRAGEDIE
OF
KING RICHARD
THE THIRD.

Contayning his treacherous Plots, against his brother *Clarence*: The pitifull murder of his innocent Nephewes: his tyranous vsurpation: with the whole courſe of his deteſted life, and moſt deſerued death.

As it hath beene Acted by the Kings Maieſties Seruants.

VVritten by *William Shake-ſpeare.*

LONDON,
Printed by IOHN NORTON. 1634.

No. 592. TITLE-PAGE OF SHAKESPEARE'S RICHARD THE THIRD;
8TH EDITION; 1634.

CHURCH CATALOGUE   [843]   ENGLISH LITERATURE

No. 592   *William Shakespeare*   1634

CONDITION: Size of leaf, 7 1/16 × 4 7/8 inches. Bound in red crushed levant morocco, gilt edges; by Bedford. Leaf M 2 has a portion of the text in facsimile. The leaves are stabbed and mended on the inner margins throughout.

OTHER COPIES.

British Museum (2, one imperfect); Bodleian (2); Capell Collection; Dyce Collection; Birmingham Free; Edinburgh University; Boston Public; Lenox; and White Libraries; also the Howe copy (untraced).

REFERENCES.

Greg, *List of English Plays Written before 1643 and Printed before 1700* (Bibliographical Society; 1900), p. 96; British Museum, *Catalogue; Shakespeare* (1897), col. 100; Boston Public Library, *Catalogue; Barton Collection* (1880), p. 38, No. 576; Lenox Library, *Works of Shakespeare* (1880), p. 27, No. 145; Lowndes, 4 (1869): 2295; Hazlitt, *Hand-Book* (1867), p. 548, No. 9 *h*.

This edition was printed from the Seventh Edition, that of 1629.

SHAKESPEARE, WILLIAM.

TROILUS AND CRESSIDA.   LONDON, *by G. Eld for R. Bonian and H. Walley*, 1609.

[593]

Small quarto. Second Edition.

COLLATION BY SIGNATURES: A, 4 leaves; ¶2, 1 leaf (inserted between leaves [A] and A 2); B to L, each 4 leaves; M, 1 leaf (imposed with ¶ 2); total 46 unnumbered leaves.

COLLATION BY PAGINATION: [title, as reproduced; *See* No. 593], recto of [A]; —[blank], verso of [A]; —[epistle to the reader, with heading] | A neuer writer, to an euer | reader. Newes. | , recto and verso of ¶ 2; —[text, with heading] | The hiſtory of *Troylus* | and *Creſſeida*. | , recto of A 2 to verso of M ; — | FINIS. | , verso of [M].

CONDITION: Size of leaf, 6 5/8 × 4 5/8 inches. Bound in red crushed levant morocco, gilt edges; by Bedford. The first line on the title-page is cut into.

OTHER COPIES.

British Museum; Bodleian (Malone copy); Capell Collection; Dyce Collection; Huth (Daniel copy); Hoe; and White Libraries.

REFERENCES.

Hoe, *Catalogue*, 4 (1904): 99; Greg, *List of Masques, Pageants, &c.* (Bibliographical Society; 1902), *Essay Introductory*, p. x.; Greg, *List of English Plays* (Bibliographical Society; 1900), p. 101; British Museum, *Catalogue; Shakespeare* (1897), col. 159; *The Cambridge Shakespeare*, 6 (1895) : vii.; Hazlitt, *Manual for the Collector and Amateur of Old English Plays. Edited from the Material formed by Kirkman, Langbain, Downes, Oldys, and Halliwell-Phillipps* (1892), p. 238; Locker-Lampson, *Catalogue* (1886), p. 108; Huth, *Catalogue*, 4 (1880) : 1337; Winsor, *Bibliography* (1876), p. 71; Lowndes, 4 (1869) : 2300; Hazlitt, *Hand-Book to the Popular, Poetical, and Dramatic Literature of Great Britain, to the Restoration* (1867), p. 551, No. 21 *a*.

The Locker-Lampson copy, with ex-libris.

Of this play two editions were published in quarto, both during the same year.

Of the First Edition (1609), "Imprinted by G. Eld for R. Bonian and H. Walley," the title-page reads: *The Hiſtorie of Troylus and Creſſeida*, etc., and is immediately followed by the text. Of this edition there are copies in the British Museum and Devonshire (Pope-Kemble copy) Libraries.

The Second Edition (1609) is that here described. The title, which was changed to *The Famous Hiſtorie of Troylus and Creſſeid*, is followed by a prefatory leaf, "A neuer writer, to an euer reader. Newes.", marked ¶ 2. This edition was reproduced in the Ashbee-Halliwell *Facsimiles* (1863), No. 37, and also in the Griggs-Furnivall *Shakspere-Quarto Facsimiles* [1886], No. 13, which has a facsimile of the title-page of the Capell copy, *The Hiſtorie of Troylus and Creſſeida*, laid in at the end. It was reprinted by Steevens in his *Twenty Plays* (1766), Vol. 3.

This preface, or "Epistle," as it is called in its single head-line, settles the question as to the price at which these quartos were originally issued, viz., a "teſterne," or sixpence. "*Amongst all [his comedies] there is none more witty then this: And had I time I would comment vpon it, though I know it needs not, (for ſo much as will make you thinke your teſterne well beſtowd) but for ſo much worth, as euen poore I know to be ſtuft in it.*"

The estimation in which Shakespeare's plays were held at the time this play was printed is also reflected in this preface, which says: "*this authors Commedies, . . . are ſo fram'd to the life, that they ſerue for the moſt common Commentaries, of all the actions of our liues ſhewing ſuch a dexteritie, and power of witte, that the moſt diſpleaſed with Playes, are pleaſd with his Commedies. . . . So much and ſuch ſauored ſalt of witte is in his Commedies, that they ſeeme (for their height of pleaſure) to be borne in that ſea that brought forth* Venus."

The differences in these two editions are explained by Greg in the "Essay Introductory" of his *List of Masques, Pageants, &c.* (Bibliographical Society; 1902), p. x., as follows, where, speaking of the methods of dramatic publication in vogue in the seventeenth century, he says: "Piracy was of course rife, and though injunctions to stay publication seem at times to have been allowed, a stationer usually did very much as he pleased with any copy that happened to come into his hands. Something of this sort appears to have happened in the case of the 1609 quarto of *Troilus and Cressida*. In 1602–3 the piece was entered to Roberts conditionally upon his obtaining 'authority,' which he seems to have failed to do, since it was re-entered in 1608–9 to Bonian and Walley, who may, as Mr. Fleay suggests, have taken over the copy from Roberts on his leaving business in 1607. They published a quarto in the course of the year with the following seemingly authoritative titlepage: 'The Historie of Troylus and Cresseida. As it was acted by the Kings Maiesties seruants at the Globe. Written by William Shakespeare.' To this, however, the King's company appears to have taken exception, but the only result was the cancelling of the first leaf, which was replaced by a half-sheet containing a new titlepage and an enigmatically defiant preface, the later issue thus at first sight presenting the strange anomaly of a sheet of five leaves. The later titlepage ran: 'The Famous History of Troylus and Cresseid. Excellently expressing the beginning of their loues, with the conceited wooing of Pandarus Prince of Licia. Written by William Shakespeare.'"

This play as altered by John Dryden, with the title *Troilus and Creſſida, or, Truth Found too Late*, was published in quarto in 1679 and again in 1695. Three editions appeared in 1679, but in what order is uncertain.

THE
Famous Historie of
Troylus *and* Cresseid.

Excellently expressing the beginning
of their loues, with the conceited wooing
of *Pandarus* Prince of *Licia.*

Written by William Shakespeare.

LONDON
Imprinted by *G. Eld* for R *Bonian* and *H. Walley,* and
are to be sold at the spred Eagle in Paules
Church-yeard, ouer against the
great North doore.
1609.

No. 593. Title-page of Shakespeare's Troilus and Cressida;
2d Edition; 1609.

Of the First (?) Edition (1679), "for Abel Swall . . . and Jacob Tonſon," there are copies in the Dyce Collection (imperfect), Birmingham Free, Lenox, and Hoe Libraries, and the Library of Congress.

Of the Second (?) Edition (1679), "for Jacob Tonſon . . . and Abel Swall," there are copies in the British Museum, Bodleian, Devonshire, Huth, Harvard University, Boston Public (2), Morgan, White, and Wrenn (2) Libraries.

Of the Third (?) Edition (1679), "for Jacob Tonſon," there is a copy in the Harvard University Library, the full imprint of which reads, | *London,* Printed for *Jacob Tonſon* at the *Judges-Head,* in | *Chancery-Lane* near *Fleet-ſtreet.* 1679.| .

Of the Fourth Edition (1695), "by I. Dawks, for Jacob Tonſon," there are copies in the British Museum (2), Trinity College (Cambridge), Harvard University, Boston Public, and Hoe Libraries.

[SHAKESPEARE, WILLIAM.]

TITUS ANDRONICUS. London, *for Eedward White,* 1611.   **[594]**

Small quarto (really an octavo). Chain-lines perpendicular. Third Edition.

COLLATION BY SIGNATURES: A to K, each 4 leaves; total 40 unnumbered leaves.

COLLATION BY PAGINATION: [title, as reproduced; *See* No. 594], recto of [A]; — [blank], verso of [A]; — [text, with heading] | [conventional head-piece] | ¶ The moſt lamentable Romaine | Tragedie of *Titus Andronicus:* As it was plaid | by the right honorable the Earle of Darbie, Earle | of Pembrooke, and Earle of Suſſex | their Seruants. | , recto of A 2 to verso of [K 4]; — | FINIS. | , verso of [K 4].

CONDITION: Size of leaf, 7⅛ × 5³⁄₁₀ inches. Bound in red crushed levant morocco, with doublure of the same, panelled and elaborately tooled in gilt, gilt edges, red silk and marble-paper end-papers; by the Club Bindery, 1901, finished by Maillard; in flap and slip case.

OTHER COPIES.

British Museum (2, one imperfect); Bodleian (Malone copy); Capell Collection; Devonshire; Huth (Daniel copy); Boston Public (title-page in facsimile); and White Libraries; also the Howe copy (untraced).

REFERENCES.

Greg, *List of English Plays* (Bibliographical Society; 1900), p. 99; British Museum, *Catalogue; Shakespeare* (1897), col. 159; *The Cambridge Shakespeare,* 6 (1895): x.; Hazlitt, *Manual of Old English Plays* (1892), p. 229; Boston Public Library, *Catalogue; Barton Collection* (1880), p. 43, No. 673; Huth, *Catalogue,* 4 (1880): 1338; Winsor, *Bibliography* (1876), p. 70; Lowndes, 4 (1869): 2300; Hazlitt, *Hand-Book* (1867), p. 469, No. 48 *b.*

This play was printed in quarto, in 1594, 1600, and 1611.

Of the First Edition (1594) no copy was known until January, 1905, when a copy was discovered at Lund in Sweden. It was subsequently sold, but its present location has not been reported to us. It is probably in Mr. Folger's collection.

Of the Second Edition (1600), "Printed by I. R. for Edward White," but two copies are known, that belonging to the University of Edinburgh, and that of the Earl of Ellesmere, at Bridgewater House. It was reproduced in the Ashbee-Halliwell

No. 594 *William Shakespeare* 1611

THE
MOST LAMEN-
TABLE TRAGEDIE
of Titus Andronicus.

AS IT HATH SVNDRY
'times beene plaide by the Kings
Maiesties Seruants.

LONDON,
Printed for Eedward White, and are to be solde
at his shoppe, nere the little North dore of
Pauls, at the signe of the
Gun. 1 6 1 1.

No. 594. Title-page of Shakespeare's Titus Andronicus;
3d Edition; 1611.

Facsimiles (1866), No. 15, and also (the Edinburgh University copy) in the Praetorius-Furnivall *Shakspere-Quarto Facsimiles* [1886], No. 29.

The Third Edition (1611), that here described, was reproduced in the Ashbee-Halliwell *Facsimiles* (1867), No. 40, and was reprinted by Steevens in his *Twenty Plays* (1766), Vol. 3.

In 1687 an edition of this play ("Licenſed, Dec. 21. 1686."), entitled *Titus Andronicus, or the Rape of Lavinia. Acted at the Theatre Royall, a Tragedy, Alter'd from Mr. Shakeſpears Works, By Mr. Edw. Ravenſcroft*, was published at London, "by J. B. for J. Hindmarſh." "The plot and much of the language are taken from the original play. The alterations are chiefly in the last act, the horrors of which are intensified." Of this edition of 1687 there are copies in the British Museum (3), Bodleian (3), Birmingham Free, Devonshire, Huth, Harvard University (imperfect), Boston Public, Hoe, and White Libraries; also the Van Antwerp copy (untraced).

The edition here described was reprinted from that of 1600. It is remarkable that the First Folio contains a whole scene (act iii., sc. 2) not to be found in the quartos.

Titus Andronicus and *Henry the Sixth*, Part III., have the distinction of being the only ones attributed to Shakespeare which were performed by other companies than that to which Shakespeare belonged.

[SHAKESPEARE, WILLIAM.]

ROMEO AND JULIET. LONDON, *by Thomas Creede, for Cuthbert Burby*, 1599. [595]

Small quarto. Second Edition.

COLLATION BY SIGNATURES: A to L, each 4 leaves; M, 2 leaves; total 46 unnumbered leaves.

COLLATION BY PAGINATION: [title, as reproduced; *See* No. 595], recto of [A]; — [blank], verso of [A]; — | [conventional head-piece] | The Prologue. | Corus. | [14 lines] | , recto of A2; — [blank], verso of A2; — [text, with heading] | [conventional head-piece] | THE MOST EX-| cellent and lamentable | Tragedie, of *Romeo* and *Iuliet*. | , recto of A3 to recto of [M2]; — | *FINIS*. | [conventional tail-piece] |, recto of [M2]; — [blank], verso of [M2].

CONDITION: Size of leaf, 7 9/16 × 5 5/8 inches. Bound in red crushed levant morocco, gilt edges; by Bedford. The title-page, leaves A2 to B2 inclusive, and a portion of leaf E are in facsimile.

OTHER COPIES.

British Museum; Bodleian (Malone copy); Edinburgh University; Ellesmere; Huth (Steevens-Roxburghe-Daniels copy); and White Libraries; also the Howe copy (untraced).

REFERENCES.

Greg, *List of English Plays* (Bibliographical Society; 1900), p. 96; British Museum, *Catalogue*; *Shakespeare* (1897), col. 141; *The Cambridge Shakespeare*, 6 (1895): xiii.–xv.; Sinker, *Library of Trinity College, Cambridge* (1891), p. 120; Locker-Lampson, *Catalogue* (1886), p. 109; Huth, *Catalogue*, 4 (1880): 1334; Winsor, *Bibliography* (1876), p. 65; Furness, *Variorum Edition* (1871), p. 473; Lowndes, 4 (1869): 2296; Hazlitt, *Hand-Book* (1867), p. 547, No. 7b.

THE MOST EX-
cellent and lamentable
Tragedie, of Romeo
and *Iuliet*.

Newly corrected, augmented, and amended:

As it hath bene sundry times publiquely acted, by the right Honourable the Lord Chamberlaine his Seruants.

LONDON
Printed by Thomas Creede, for Cuthbert Burby, and are to be sold at his shop neare the Exchange.
1 5 9 9.

1599   *William Shakespeare*   No. 595

The Tite-Locker Lampson copy, with the ex-libris of the latter.

Of *Romeo and Juliet* there were six editions printed separately, as follows: 1597, 1599, 1609, n.d. (two editions), and 1637.

Of the First Edition (1597), "Printed by Iohn Danter," there are copies in the British Museum (Garrick copy), Bodleian (Malone copy), Capell Collection, and Devonshire (Stace-Kemble copy) Libraries. This edition was reproduced in the Ashbee-Halliwell *Facsimiles* (1866), No. 5, and also (the British Museum copy) in the Praetorius-Furnivall *Shakspere-Quarto Facsimiles* (1886), No. 25. It was reprinted by Steevens in his *Twenty Plays* (1766), Vol. 4; by Furness in his *Variorum Edition* (pp. 303–364); and in *The Cambridge Shakespeare* (1895), Vol. 9, pp. 639–696.

The editor of *The Cambridge Shakespeare* says (6 : xiii.) that this edition was printed from a manuscript which, in all probability, was obtained from notes taken in shorthand during the representation of the play.

The Second Edition (1599), that here described, was reproduced in the Ashbee-Halliwell *Facsimiles* (1865), No. 13, and also (the British Museum copy) in the Praetorius-Furnivall *Shakspere-Quarto Facsimiles* (1886), No. 26.

"The second Quarto," says the editor of *The Cambridge Shakespeare* (6 : xiv.), "was in all likelihood an edition authorized by Shakespeare and his 'fellows,' and intended to supersede the surreptitious and imperfect edition of 1597. The play so published, we believe . . . to be substantially identical with the play as at first composed; it seems however to have been revised by the author. . . . The words 'newly corrected, augmented, and amended,' found on the title-page of the second Quarto, may be accepted. . . . In fact, the added matter amounts nearly to a quarter of the whole. . . .

"This is unquestionably our best authority; nevertheless in determining the text, (Q_1) must in many places be taken into account. For it is certain that Q_2 [our present number] was not printed from the author's MS., but from a transcript, the writer of which was not only careless, but thought fit to take unwarrantable liberties with the text. In passing through his hands, many passages were thus transmuted from poetry to prose."

The Third Edition (1609) is that described in our next number.

The Fourth Edition (undated), *with* Shakespeare's name on the title-page, is that described in our No. 597.

The Fifth Edition (also undated), but *without* Shakespeare's name on the title-page, is that described in our No. 598.

Of the Sixth Edition (1637), "Printed by R. Young for John Smethwicke," there are copies in the British Museum, Bodleian, Capell Collection, Birmingham Free, Edinburgh University, Huth (Corser copy), Boston Public, Lenox, White, and Wrenn Libraries; also the Howe and the Van Antwerp copies (untraced). This edition was printed from the undated edition.

An edition dated 1607 is mentioned by Knight, probably from the conjectural date given to the undated edition by the catalogue of the British Museum.

"The foundation of this play," says Sinker, "is a poem, copies of which are of extreme rarity: '*The Tragicall Historye of Romeus and Iuliet, written first in Italian by Bandell and now in Englishe by Ar[thur] Br[oke].*' The first edition of this was printed by Richard Tottell in 1562. Our copy of this unfortunately wants the first three leaves; perfect copies are in the Bodleian and in the Huth collection."

Of the First Edition of this poem (1562), "by Richard Tottill," there are copies in the Bodleian, Capell Collection, and Huth Libraries.

Of the Second Edition (1567), "by Richard Tottill," there is a copy in the White Library. This copy, probably unique and lacking all preliminary matter before leaf A, is described in Gray's *General Index to Hazlitt's Handbook and his Bibliographical Collections; 1867–1889* (1893), p. 844.

Of the Third Edition (1587), "by R. Robinſon," there is a copy in the Capell Collection.

This play, as altered by Thomas Otway, was first published in 1680 under the title *The Hiſtory and Fall of Caius Marius*.

Of the First Edition (1680), "for Tho. Fleſher," there are copies in the Bodleian, Devonshire, Huth, Harvard University, Hoe, White, and Wrenn Libraries.

Of the Second Edition (1692), "for R. Bentley," there are copies in the British Museum, Bodleian, Devonshire, and Hoe Libraries.

Of the Third Edition (1696), "for R. Bentley," there are copies in the British Museum, Bodleian, and Boston Public Libraries, and the Library of Congress.

SHAKESPEARE, WILLIAM.

ROMEO AND JULIET. LONDON, *for Iohn Smethvvicke*, 1609. [596]

Small quarto. Third Edition.

COLLATION BY SIGNATURES: A to L, each 4 leaves; M, 2 leaves; total 46 unnumbered leaves. Leaf L 3 has no signature-mark.

COLLATION BY PAGINATION: [title, as reproduced; *See* No. 596], recto of [A]; — [blank], verso of [A]; — | [conventional head-piece] | The Prologue. | Chorus. | [14 lines] |, recto of A 2; — [blank], verso of A 2; — [text, with heading] | [conventional head-piece] | THE MOST EX- | CELLENT AND | Lamentable Tragedie of | ROMEO *and* | IVLIET. |, recto of A 3 to recto of [M 2]; — | *FINIS.* | [conventional tail-piece] |, recto of [M 2]; — [blank], verso of [M 2].

CONDITION: Size of leaf, 6⁵⁄₁₀ × 5 inches. Bound in red morocco, gilt edges; by Bedford.

OTHER COPIES.

British Museum; Bodleian (Heber copy); Capell Collection; and Devonshire Libraries.

REFERENCES.

Greg, *List of English Plays* (Bibliographical Society; 1900), p. 97; British Museum, *Catalogue*; *Shakespeare* (1897), col. 141; Locker-Lampson, *Catalogue* (1886), p. 109; Winsor, *Bibliography* (1876), p. 66; Furness, *New Variorum Edition* (1871), p. 423; Lowndes, 4 (1869): 2296; Hazlitt, *Hand-Book* (1867), p. 547, No. 7 c.

1609 *William Shakespeare* No. 596

THE
MOST EX-
CELLENT AND
Lamentable Tragedie, of
Romeo and Juliet.

As it hath beene sundrie times publiquely Acted,
by the K I N G s Maiesties Seruants
at the Globe.

Newly corrected, augmented, and
amended:

L O N D O N
Printed for I o h n S m e t h v v i c k, and are to be sold
at his Shop in Saint *Dunstanes* Church-yard,
in Fleetestreete vnder the Dyall.
1 6 0 9.

No. 596. Title-page of Shakespeare's Romeo and Juliet;
3d Edition; 1609.

The Halliwell Phillipps-Tite-Locker Lampson copy, with ex-libris of the last.

This edition was printed from that of 1599 (our preceding number).

Halliwell-Phillipps says, "This is a most difficult book to find in perfect condition." It was reproduced in the Ashbee-Halliwell *Facsimiles* (1869), No. 36, and was reprinted by Steevens in his *Twenty Plays* (1766), Vol. 4.

SHAKESPEARE, WILLIAM.

ROMEO AND JULIET. LONDON, *for Iohn Smethwicke*, [n. d.].   [597]

Small quarto. Fourth Edition. With Shakespeare's name on the title-page.

COLLATION BY SIGNATURES : A to L, each 4 leaves ; total 44 unnumbered leaves. Leaves C 3, D 3, E 3, and L 3 have no signature-marks.

COLLATION BY PAGINATION : [title, as reproduced; *See* No. 597], recto of [A]; — | The Prologue.| CHORVS. | [14 lines]| verso of [A];—[text, with heading] | [type-ornament head-piece] | THE MOST EXCEL-| LENT AND LAMENT- ABLE|Tragedie of ROMEO and|IVLIET.|, recto of A 2 to recto of [L 4];—| FINIS. | [conventional tail-piece] | , recto of [L 4]; —[blank], verso of [L 4].

CONDITION : Size of leaf, 7 1/16 × 5 3/16 inches. Bound in half blue straight-grained morocco. The leaves are stabbed on the inner margins throughout.

OTHER COPIES.

Bodleian ; Capell Collection ; Huth ; Boston Public ; and White Libraries ; also the Howe copy (untraced).

REFERENCES.

Boston Public Library, *Catalogue*; Barton Collection (1880), p. 39, No. 592 ; Huth, *Catalogue*, 4 (1880) : 1334 ; Furness, *New Variorum Edition* (1876), pp. 423, 424 ; Winsor, *Bibliography* (1876), p. 66.

Of the edition here described Furness says : "Though this edition has no date, internal evidence conclusively proves that it was printed from Q_3 [the edition of 1609]; and that Q_5 [the edition of 1637] was printed from it." This opinion is shared by Greg and the editor of *The Cambridge Shakespeare*.

Of this edition the title-page only was reprinted in the Ashbee-Halliwell *Facsimiles* (1871), No. 1. The general title to this series of facsimiles as found in this number is as follows : *A Collection of Lithographic Facsimiles of the Early Quarto Editions of the Separate Works of Shakespeare;* including every known edition of all the plays which were issued during the life-time of the Great Dramatist. By Edmund William Ashbee.

SHAKESPEARE, WILLIAM.

ROMEO AND JULIET. LONDON, *for Iohn Smethwicke*, [n. d.].   [598]

Small quarto. Fifth Edition. Without Shakespeare's name on the title-page.

COLLATION BY SIGNATURES : A to L, each 4 leaves ; total 44 unnumbered leaves.

Leaves C 3, D 3, E 3, and L 3 have no signature-marks.

COLLATION BY PAGINATION : [title, as reproduced; *See* No. 598], recto of [A];

1610-19?   *William Shakespeare*   No. 597

THE MOST
EXCELLENT
And Lamentable Tragedie,
of R o m e o and
I v l i e t.

As it hath beene sundrie times publikely Acted,
by the K i n g s Maiesties Seruants
at the G l o b e.

Written by *W. Shake-speare.*

Newly Corrected, augmented, and amended.

LONDON,
Printed for *Iohn Smethwicke*, and are to bee sold at his Shop in
Saint *Dunstanes* Church-yard, in Fleetestreete
vnder the Dyall.

No. 597.   Title-page of Shakespeare's Romeo and Juliet;
4th Edition; [n. d.].
With Shakespeare's name on the title-page.

No. 598   *William Shakespeare*   1610–19?

THE MOST
EXCELLENT
And Lamentable Tragedie, of R o m e o and I v l i e t.

As it hath beene sundrie times publikely Acted,
by the K i n g s Maiesties Seruants
at the G L O B E.

Newly Corrected, augmented, and amended.

L O N D O N,
Printed for *Iohn Smethwicke*, and are to bee sold at his Shop in
Saint *Dunstanes* Church-yard, in Fleetestreete
vnder the Dyall.

No. 598.   Title-page of Shakespeare's Romeo and Juliet;
5th Edition; [n. d.].
Without Shakespeare's name on the title-page.

1610–19? *William Shakespeare* No. 598

—[the rest identically the same as in our preceding number].

CONDITION: Size of leaf, 7¼ × 5⅛ inches. Bound in polished purple morocco, elaborately tooled sides, leather hinges; by Tuckett.

OTHER COPIES.

British Museum Library.

REFERENCES.

Greg, *List of English Plays* (Bibliographical Society; 1900), p. 97; British Museum, *Catalogue; Shakespeare* (1897), col. 141; Locker-Lampson, *Catalogue* (1886), p. 109; Lowndes, 4 (1869): 2297; Hazlitt, *Hand-Book* (1867), p. 547, No. 7 d.

The Halliwell Phillipps-Locker Lampson copy, with ex-libris of the latter.

"This edition was supposed by Mr. Halliwell-Phillipps to be earlier than that of 1609. But from the appearance of the type it cannot be confidently attributed to an earlier date than 1630."

Halliwell-Phillipps says: "It is a curious fact, that, after some copies had been published, having Shakespeare's name on the title, that name was omitted in the copies which were subsequently issued."

This edition was reproduced in the Ashbee-Halliwell *Facsimiles* (1868), No. 46, and also (the British Museum copy) in the Praetorius-Furnivall *Shakspere-Quarto Facsimiles* (1887), No. 36.

SHAKESPEARE, WILLIAM.

JULIUS CÆSAR. London, *by H. H. Jun. for Hen. Herringman, and R. Bentley, and fold by Joseph Knight and Francis Saunders,* [1680]. [599]

Small quarto. First Separate Edition.

COLLATION BY SIGNATURES: A to H, each 4 leaves; total 32 numbered leaves.

COLLATION BY PAGINATION: [title, as reproduced; See No. 599], p. [1];—| Dramatis Perfonæ. |, p. [2];—[text, with heading]| THE | TRAGEDY, | OF | JULIUS CÆSAR. |, pp. 3–64;—| FINIS. |, p. 64.

CONDITION: Size of leaf, 8⁷⁄₁₆ × 6⁹⁄₁₆ inches. Bound in brown crushed levant morocco, gilt edges; by Rivière.

OTHER COPIES.

British Museum; Birmingham Free; Edinburgh University; Huth; Boston Public; Lenox; and White Libraries; and Library of Congress.

REFERENCES.

British Museum, *Catalogue; Shakespeare* (1897), col. 69; *The Cambridge Shakespeare*, 7 (1895): vii.; Boston Public Library, *Catalogue of the Works of William Shakespeare, embraced in the Barton Collection* (1880), p. 24, No. 320; Huth, *Catalogue*, 4 (1880): 1338; Lenox Library, *Works of Shakespeare* (Contributions to a Catalogue of the Lenox Library, No. 5; 1880), p. 16, No. 69; Lowndes, 4 (1869): 2283.

This play appeared for the first time in the First Folio, 1623. "It is more correctly printed," says the Cambridge editor, "than any other play, and may perhaps have been (as the preface falsely implied that all were) printed from the original manuscript of the author." It was not separately printed until it was published in the edition here described. The Second Edition appeared in [1684] and the Third in 1691.

Julius Cæsar.
A
TRAGEDY.

As it is now ACTED
AT THE
Theatre Royal.

WRITTEN BY
WILLIAM SHAKESPEARE.

LONDON.

Printed by *H. H.* Jan. for *Hen. Herringman*, and *R. Bentley* in *Ruſſel-ſtreet* in *Covent-Garden*, and ſold by *Joſeph Knight* and *Francis Saunders* at the *Blew-Anchor* in the Lower Walk of the *New-Exchange* in the *Strand*.

NO. 599.   TITLE-PAGE OF SHAKESPEARE'S JULIUS CÆSAR; 1ST SEPARATE EDITION; [1680].

The First Separate Edition (undated, but 1680) is that here described.

Of the Second Edition (undated, but 1684), "Printed by H. H. jun. for H. Heringman and R. Bentley," there are copies in the British Museum, Edinburgh University, Birmingham Free, Ellesmere, Boston Public, White, and Wrenn Libraries.

Of the Third Edition (1691), "Printed for Henry Herringman, and Richard Bentley," there are copies in the British Museum, Bodleian, Birmingham Free, Boston Public, Valentine, and White Libraries.

Another edition in quarto (undated, but 1696) is given by Lowndes (4:2283). We are unable to find any other record of such an edition or to locate a copy, and it is quite unlikely that there is an edition bearing that date.

Another play with the same title, by William Alexander, Earl of Stirling, was published in his *Monarchicke Tragedies* in 1607 and 1616. Its resemblance to Shakespeare's play is only such as one would expect to find in the treatment of the same subject by different writers.

This play was altered by John Sheffield, Duke of Buckingham, who, says Lounsbury, when he divided it "into two plays [*Julius Cæsar* and *Marcus Brutus*] in order to preserve his darling unities — and even then succeeded but imperfectly — could not resist the temptation to intersperse some love dialogue in the midst of the political action which was going on." Lee in his *Life of Shakespeare* (1906), p. 332, gives the date of Buckingham's alterations as 1692, but his plays do not appear to have been printed until 1723, when they were included in the collected edition of his works.

SHAKESPEARE, WILLIAM.

HAMLET. London, *for Iohn Smethwicke*, 1611. [600]

Small quarto. Fourth Edition.

COLLATION BY SIGNATURES: [A], 2 leaves (the first blank and lacking); B to N, each 4 leaves; O, 2 leaves; total 52 unnumbered leaves.

COLLATION BY PAGINATION: [1 blank leaf], [A];—[title, as reproduced; See No. 600], recto of [A 2];—[blank], verso of [A 2];—[text, with heading] | [conventional head-piece] | The Tragedie of | HAMLET | *Prince of Denmarke.* |, recto of B to recto of O 2; — | FINIS. |, recto of O 2;—[blank], verso of O 2.

CONDITION: Size of leaf, 7 × 5 9/16 inches. Bound in red crushed levant morocco, gilt edges; by Bedford. Leaf [F 4] is in facsimile.

OTHER COPIES.

British Museum; Bodleian; Capell Collection; Dyce Collection; Edinburgh University; Devonshire (Steevens copy, title-page lacking); Huth (Bandinel copy); Boston Public (Heber copy); Hoe; White; and Furness (Daniel-Tite copy) Libraries; also the Howe copy (untraced).

REFERENCES.

Furness, *New Variorum Edition*, 2 (1905): 33; Hoe, *Catalogue*, 4 (1904): 100; Greg, *List of English Plays* (Bibliographical Society; 1900), 100; Lee, *Life of Shakespeare* (1898), pp. 221–225; British Museum, *Catalogue*; *Shakespeare* (1897), col. 54; *The Cambridge Shakespeare*, 7 (1895): xi.–xiii.; Locker-Lampson, *Catalogue* (1886), p. 109; Boston Public Library, *Catalogue*; *Barton Collection* (1880), p. 19, No. 224; Huth, *Catalogue*, 4 (1880): 1337; Winsor, *Bibliography* (1876), p. 27; Lowndes, 4 (1869): 2277; Hazlitt, *Hand-Book* (1867), p. 550, No. 18 d.

No. 600   *William Shakespeare*   1611

The Locker-Lampson copy.

Of this popular play editions were published in quarto in 1603, 1604, 1605, 1611, n. d., and 1637.

Of the First Edition (1603), printed "for N. L. and Iohn Trundell," we can trace but three copies: those in the British Museum (Halliwell-Phillipps copy, lacking the title-page) and the Duke of Devonshire's (Hanmer-Bunbury copy, lacking the last leaf) Libraries, and a copy reported by the Earl of Ellesmere. This edition, which contains 2143 lines, was reproduced in the Ashbee-Halliwell *Facsimiles* (1866), No. 26; and also (the Devonshire copy) in the Griggs-Furnivall *Shakspere-Quarto Facsimiles* [1880], No. 1. It was reprinted by Furness in his *New Variorum Edition* (2: 37–85).

Of the Second Edition (1604), printed "by I. R. for N. L.," which contains 3719 lines, we can locate but three copies, that in the Duke of Devonshire's Library (Malone copy), that in the Huth Library (Plumer copy), and the Jennen-Howe copy (untraced). This edition was reproduced in the Ashbee-Halliwell *Facsimiles* (1867), No. 27; and also (the Devonshire copy) in the Griggs-Furnivall *Shakspere Quarto Facsimiles* [1880], No. 2. The First and Second Editions (1603 and 1604) were reproduced in facsimile from the Devonshire copies by J. Payne Collier in 1858 and 1859, in a privately printed edition limited to forty copies.

Of the Third Edition (1605), printed "by I. R. for N. L.," there are copies in the British Museum (imperfect) and Capell Collection. This edition was merely a reissue of the Second Edition with only the date altered. Furness says: "The title-pages of the two editions [Second and Third] are identical except in date," and the text differs "no more than one copy of the same edition may differ from another." This edition was reproduced in the Ashbee-Halliwell *Facsimiles* (1868), No. 29.

The Fourth Edition (1611), that here described, was reproduced in the Ashbee-Halliwell *Facsimiles* (1870), No. 42. It was also reprinted by Steevens in his *Twenty Plays* (1766), Vol. 4.

Of the Fifth Edition (undated, but c. 1636), "Printed by W. S. for John Smethwicke," there are copies in the British Museum (2), Bodleian, Capell Collection, Huth, Devonshire, Boston Public (title-page in facsimile), Lenox, White, and Furness (Loscombe-Tite copy) Libraries. The editor of *The Cambridge Shakespeare* is convinced that this edition was printed from that of 1611; while Gregg says that it was "printed after the edition of 1611 and before that of 1637."

The Sixth Edition (1637) is that described in our next number.

Besides these, several editions, usually known as Players' Quartos, were printed in 1676, 1683, and 1695. The changes made in these editions have no authority in questions concerning the text, though many emendations usually ascribed to Rowe and Pope are in reality derived from one or another of them.

Of the 1676 edition there are two varieties, one with a four-line, the other with a five-line imprint on the title-page. The British Museum has both varieties. Copies, but with imprint unreported, are also in the Bodleian, Trinity College (Cambridge), Birmingham Free, Hunterian Museum, Boston Public, and White Libraries.

1611 *William Shakespeare* No. 600

THE
TRAGEDY
OF
HAMLET
Prince of Denmarke.

BY

WILLIAM SHAKESPEARE.

Newly imprinted and enlarged to almoſt as much
againe as it was, according to the true
and perfect Coppy.

AT LONDON,
Printed for *Iohn Smethwicke*, and are to be ſold at his ſhoppe
in Saint *Dunſtons* Church yeard in Fleetſtreet.
Vnder the Diall. 1611.

No. 600. TITLE-PAGE OF SHAKESPEARE'S HAMLET; 4TH EDITION; 1611.

Of the 1683 edition there are copies in the British Museum, Trinity College (Cambridge), Birmingham Free, Boston Public, White, and Wrenn Libraries.

Of the 1695 edition there are copies in the British Museum (2, one imperfect), Birmingham Free, Boston Public, and White Libraries.

The story of Hamlet was popular on the English stage as early as 1589 in a play now lost. It was played at Newington Theatre, June 9, 1594, and is several times referred to by contemporaneous writers. Shakespeare's play, which doubtless owed much to this earlier play, was written in 1600 (Furness) or 1602 (Lee).

"The text of Hamlet given in the Folio of 1623," says the editor of *The Cambridge Shakespeare*, "is not derived from any of the previously existing Quartos, but from an independent manuscript. Many passages are found in the Folio which do not appear in any of the Quartos. On the other hand many passages found in the Quartos are not found in the Folio."

"Much more generally interesting than these [unique copies of books in the Capell Collection], however, is *The Hystorie of Hamblet*, printed by Richard Bradocke in 1608; the story on which Shakespeare's tragedy, and perhaps an earlier play, is founded. Seeing, however, that there is an edition of the play as early as 1603, it is clear that at least one earlier edition of the prose romance, perhaps several, must have perished." — SINKER, *Library of Trinity College, Cambridge* (1891), p. 123.

Of this romance Chapters I.–VI. were reprinted by Furness in his *New Variorum Edition* (2:91–113).

SHAKESPEARE, WILLIAM.

HAMLET. LONDON, *by R. Young for John Smethwicke*, 1637. [601]

Small quarto. Sixth Edition.

COLLATION BY SIGNATURES: A to N, each 4 leaves; total 52 unnumbered leaves. Leaf E is wrongly marked D; A 3, H 3, and N 3 have no signature-marks; and those of leaves H, I, I 3, K, L, and L 3 are in italics.

COLLATION BY PAGINATION: [title, as reproduced; *See* No. 601], recto of [A]; —[blank], verso of [A];—[text, with heading] | [conventional head-piece] | THE TRAGEDY | OF HAMLET | PRINCE OF | DENMARK. | , recto of A 2 to recto of [N 4]; — | *FINIS.* |, recto of [N 4]; — [blank], verso of [N 4].

CONDITION: Size of leaf, 7 1/16 × 5 5/8 inches. Bound in red crushed levant morocco, red crushed levant morocco doublure elaborately tooled in gilt, marbled end-papers, gilt edges; by Michel. The leaves are stabbed and neatly mended on the inner margins throughout.

OTHER COPIES.

British Museum; Bodleian; Capell Collection; Devonshire; Dyce Collection (3); Edinburgh University; Boston Public; Lenox; Hoe; Morgan; and White Libraries; also the Howe copy (untraced).

REFERENCES.

Hoe, *Catalogue*, 4 (1904): 101; Greg, *List of English Plays* (Bibliographical Society; 1900), p. 101; British Museum, *Catalogue*; *Shakespeare* (1897), col. 54; Boston Public Library, *Catalogue*; *Barton Collection* (1880), p. 19, No. 226; Lenox Library, *Works of Shakespeare* (1880), p. 13, No. 33; Lowndes, 4 (1869): 2277; Hazlitt, *Hand-Book* (1867), p. 550, No. 18*f*.

1637   *William Shakespeare*   No. 601

THE
TRAGEDY
OF HAMLET
PRINCE OF
DENMARK.

Newly imprinted and inlarged, according to the true
and perfect Copy laſt Printed.

By WILLIAM. SHAKESPEARE.

LONDON,
Printed by *R. Young* for *John Smethwicke*, and are to be ſold at his
Shop in Saint *Dunſtans* Church-yard in Fleet-ſtreet,
under the Diall. 1637.

No. 601.   Title-page of Shakespeare's Hamlet; 6th Edition; 1637.

This edition is printed from the Fifth, though the spelling is considerably modernized and the punctuation amended.

Church Catalogue   [863]   English Literature

[SHAKESPEARE, WILLIAM.] Source Play.

THE TRUE CHRONICLE HISTORY OF KING LEIR. London, *by Simon Stafford for Iohn Wright*, 1605. [602]

Small quarto. Earliest Known Edition.
COLLATION BY SIGNATURES: A to I, each 4 leaves; total 36 unnumbered leaves. Each leaf has a signature-mark.
COLLATION BY PAGINATION: [title, as reproduced; *See* No. 602], recto of [A]; —[blank], verso of [A]; —[text, with heading] | The true Chronicle Hiftorie of King | Leir and his three daughters. |, recto of A 2 to verso of I 4; — | FINIS. |, verso of I 4.
CONDITION: Size of leaf, 6$\frac{13}{16}$ × 5 inches. Bound in red crushed levant morocco, gilt edges; by Bedford.

OTHER COPIES.
British Museum (2, one imperfect); and Huth Libraries.

REFERENCES.
Greg, *List of English Plays* (Bibliographical Society; 1900), p. 132; Hazlitt, *Manual of Old English Plays* (1892), p. 129; Locker-Lampson, *Catalogue* (1886), p. 114; Huth, *Catalogue*, 3 (1880): 827; Hazlitt, *Collections and Notes* (1876), p. 253; Winsor, *Bibliography* (1876), p. 41; Lowndes, 4 (1869): 2284; same, 3: 1328; Hazlitt, *Hand-Book* (1867), p. 470, No. 63.

The Tite(?)-Locker Lampson copy, with ex-libris of the latter.

This is the earliest known edition of this play, which appears to have been licensed to Edward White in 1593.

Pasted on the recto of the second fly-leaf of the copy here described is a clipping from a catalogue: " From this Play Shakespeare is supposed to have drawn the materials for his own Tragedy of Lear. Only two other perfect copies are known, one in the Library of the British Museum and one in that of Mr. Huth." If this statement is true, this must be the copy formerly belonging to Sir William Tite. It was reprinted by Nichols in *Six Old Plays* (1779), and in Steevens' *Twenty Plays* (1766), Vol. 4.

SHAKESPEARE, WILLIAM.

KING LEAR. [LONDON], *for Nathaniel Butter*, 1608. [603]

Small quarto. Second Edition.
COLLATION BY SIGNATURES: A to L, each 4 leaves; total 44 unnumbered leaves. Leaf F 2 is wrongly marked F.
COLLATION BY PAGINATION: [title, as reproduced; *See* No. 603], recto of [A]; —[blank], verso of [A]; —[text, with heading] | [conventional head-piece] | M. VVilliam Shake-fpeare | HIS | Hiftory, of King Lear. |, recto of A 2 to recto of [L 4];
— | FINIS. |, recto of [L 4]; —[blank], verso of [L 4].
CONDITION: Size of leaf, 7$\frac{3}{16}$ × 5$\frac{5}{16}$ inches. Bound in red crushed levant morocco, gilt edges; by Bedford.

OTHER COPIES.
British Museum (3, one with title-page inserted); Bodleian (2, the Malone copies; both imperfect, but with variant readings);

1605 *William Shakespeare* No. 602

THE
True Chronicle Hi.
ftory of King Leir, and his three daughters, Gonorill, Ragan, and Cordella.

As it hath bene diuers and sundry times lately acted.

LONDON,

Printed by Simon Stafford for Iohn Wright, and are to bee sold at his shop at Christes Church dore, next Newgate-Market. 1605.

No. 602.   Title-page of The True Chronicle History of King Leir; Earliest Known Edition; 1605.

M. VVilliam Shake-speare,
HIS
True Chronicle History of the life
and death of King *Lear*, and his
three *Daughters*.

With the vnfortunate life of E D G A R,
sonne and heire to the Earle of *Glocester*, and
his sullen and assumed humour of T O M
of Bedlam.

As it was plaid before the Kings Maiesty at White-Hall, vp-
pon S. Stephens night, in Christmas Hollidaies.

By his Maiesties Seruants, playing vsually at the
Globe on the *Banck-side*.

Printed for *Nathaniel Butter.*
1608.

Capell Collection; Shakespeare Memorial, Stratford; Edinburgh University; Devonshire; Huth; Boston Public (Heber copy); Perry (Gwynn copy); Lenox; Halsey; Hoe; Morgan (Sykes-Ives copy); White; and Furness Libraries; also the Howe and the Van Antwerp copies (untraced).

REFERENCES.

Hoe, *Catalogue*, 4 (1904): 98; Greg, *List of English Plays* (Bibliographical Society; 1900), p. 101; British Museum, *Catalogue*; *Shakespeare* (1897), col. 90; *The Cambridge Shakespeare*, 8 (1895): vii.; Locker-Lampson, *Catalogue* (1886), p. 110; Boston Public Library, *Catalogue*; *Barton Collection* (1880), p. 26, No. 359; Furness, *New Variorum Edition* (1880), p. 355; Huth, *Catalogue*, 4 (1880): 1337; Lenox Library, *Works of Shakespeare* (1880), p. 17, No. 74; Winsor, *Bibliography* (1876), p. 43; Lowndes, 4 (1869): 2284; Hazlitt, *Hand-Book* (1867), p. 550, No. 19 b.

The Locker-Lampson copy, with ex-libris.

This play was published in three quarto editions, two of which appeared in 1608 and the third in 1655.

The First Edition (1608), "Printed for Nathaniel Butter, and are to be fold at his fhop in Pauls Church-yard at the figne of the Pide Bull," hence called the "Pide Bull Edition," is one of the rarest of the early Shakespeare quartos. Of the six copies known to the Cambridge editor (*The Cambridge Shakespeare*, 8 : viii.) no two read exactly alike, though evidently printed from the same forms. There are copies in the British Museum (2, one with facsimile title-page), Bodleian, Capell Collection, Devonshire, Lenox (Heber copy), and White (Lord Mostyn copy) Libraries. This edition was reproduced in the Ashbee-Halliwell *Facsimiles* (1868), No. 31; also (the British Museum copy, and a second sheet K, also in the British Museum) in the Praetorius-Furnivall *Shakspere-Quarto Facsimiles* (1885), No. 33.

The Second Edition (also 1608), that here described, was reproduced in the Ashbee-Halliwell *Facsimiles* (1867), No. 32; also (the British Museum copy) in the Praetorius-Furnivall *Shakspere-Quarto Facsimiles* (1885), No. 34. It was reprinted by Steevens in his *Twenty Plays* (1766), Vol. 2.

The Third Edition (1655) is that described in our next number.

This play, as revised and altered by Nahum Tate, was published in 1681, 1689, and 1699. Of the 1681 edition, "for E. Flefher," there are copies in the British Museum, Bodleian, Birmingham Free, Edinburgh University, Devonshire, Boston Public, Hoe, and White Libraries.

Of the 1689 edition, "for R. Bentley, and M. Magnes," there are copies in the Bodleian, Birmingham Free, and White Libraries.

Of the 1699 edition, "by H. Hills, for R. Wellington," there are copies in the British Museum (2) and Birmingham Free Libraries.

The undated edition in the Boston Public Library entered in the Barton Catalogue (No. 371) under the date "[1692?]" is probably the same as the British Museum copy entered in its catalogue under the date "[1710?]." Mr. White has a copy of this edition, and there is also another in the Bodleian Library.

"In the first Folio," says the Cambridge editor, "*King Lear* was printed from an independent manuscript, and its text is on the whole much superior to that of the Quartos. Each however supplies passages which are wanting in the other."

SHAKESPEARE, WILLIAM.

KING LEAR. London, *Jane Bell*, 1655. [604]

Small quarto. Third Edition.

COLLATION BY SIGNATURES: A to L, each 4 leaves; total 44 unnumbered leaves.

COLLATION BY PAGINATION: [title, as reproduced; *See* No. 604], recto of [A]; —[publisher's advertisement, with heading] | Bookes Printed; | And are to be Sold by *Jane Bell* at the ᵌaſten d | Of Chriſt-Church. |[22 lines]| , verso of [A]; —[text, with heading] | [conventional head-piece] | M. William Shake-ſpeare | *HIS* | Hiſtory of King Lear. | , recto of A 2 to recto of [L 4]; — | *FINIS.* | , recto of [L 4]; — [blank], verso of [L 4].

CONDITION: Size of leaf, 7¼ × 5⁹⁄₁₆ inches. Bound in purple morocco, gilt edges. The upper margins are closely trimmed, and the head-lines are cut into on several folios. The leaves are stabbed on the inner margins throughout. The inner form of sheet E was over-inked.

OTHER COPIES.

British Museum; Bodleian; Capell Collection; Birmingham Free; Edinburgh University; Ellesmere; Boston Public (Jolley-Halliwell Phillipps copy); Lenox; and White Libraries.

REFERENCES.

Greg, *List of English Plays* (Bibliographical Society; 1900), p. 101; British Museum, *Catalogue*; *Shakespeare* (1897), col. 90; Hazlitt, *Manual of Old English Plays* (1892), p. 130; Boston Public Library, *Catalogue*; *Barton Collection* (1880), p. 26, No. 360; Furness, *New Variorum Edition* (1880), p. 358; Lenox Library, *Works of Shakespeare* (1880), p. 17, No. 75; Lowndes, 4 (1869): 2285; Hazlitt, *Hand-Book* (1867), p. 551, No. 19 *c*.

This edition was printed from the Second Edition of 1608.

SHAKESPEARE, WILLIAM.

OTHELLO. London, *by A. M. for Richard Hawkins*, 1630. [605]

Small quarto. Second Edition.

COLLATION BY SIGNATURES: A to M, each 4 leaves; total 48 unnumbered leaves.

COLLATION BY PAGINATION: [title, as reproduced; *See* No. 605], recto of [A]; —[blank], verso of [A]; —[text, with heading] | [conventional head-piece] | *The Tragedy of* Othello *the Moore* | *of* Venice. | , recto of A 2 to recto of [M 4]; — | *FINIS.* | , recto of [M 4]; —[blank], verso of [M 4].

CONDITION: Size of leaf, 6⅞ × 5⁹⁄₁₆ inches. Bound in green morocco, gilt edges; by Bedford. The leaves are stabbed on the inner margins throughout.

OTHER COPIES.

British Museum (2, one imperfect); Bodleian; Capell Collection; Dyce Collection; Edinburgh University; Devonshire; Huth; Boston Public; John Carter Brown; Lenox; Morgan (Asay-Irwin copy); and White Libraries.

REFERENCES.

Greg, *List of English Plays* (Bibliographical Society; 1900), p. 102; British Museum, *Catalogue*; *Shakespeare* (1897), col. 133; Furness, *New Variorum Edition* (1886), p. 341; Locker-Lampson, *Catalogue* (1886), p. 110; Boston Public Library, *Catalogue*; *Barton Collection* (1880), p. 34, No. 517; Huth, *Catalogue*, 4 (1880): 1338; Lenox Library, *Works of Shakespeare* (1880), p. 23, No. 115; Lowndes, 4 (1869): 2291; Hazlitt, *Hand-Book* (1867), p. 551, No. 22 *b*.

M. William Shake-speare,
HIs
True Chronicle History of the life and death of King *Lear*, and his three Daughters.

With the Unfortunat life of E D G A R, sonne and heire to the Earle of *Glocester*, and his sullen assumed humour of TOM of Bedlam.

As it was plaid before the Kings Maiesty at Whit-Hall, vpon S. Stephens night, in Christmas Hollldaies.

By his Maiesties Servants, playing vsually at the Globe on the *Bank-side*.

LONDON.
Printed by *Jane Bell*, and are to be sold at the East-end of *Christ-Church*. 1655.

No. 604. Title-page of Shakespeare's King Lear; 3d Edition; 1655.

THE
Tragœdy of Othello,
The Moore of Venice.

As it hath beene diuerse times acted at the Globe, *and at the* Black-Friers, *by his Maiesties Seruants.*

Written by VVilliam Shakespeare.

LONDON,
Printed by *A. M.* for *Richard Hawkins,* and are to be sold at his shoppe in Chancery-Lane, neere Sergeants-Inne.
1630.

The Locker-Lampson copy, with ex-libris.

The First Edition of this play appeared in 1622, and later editions in 1630 and 1655.

Of the First Edition (1622), "Printed by N. O. [probably Nicolas Okes] for Thomas Walkley," there are copies in the British Museum (2, one imperfect), Bodleian (Wright-Malone copy), Capell Collection, Edinburgh University, Devonshire, Dyce Collection, Huth, Boston Public, Lenox (Bindley-Heber-Daniel copy), and White Libraries; also the Howe copy (untraced). This edition was reproduced in the Ashbee-Halliwell *Facsimiles* (1864), No. 48; also (the British Museum copy) in the Praetorius-Furnivall *Shakspere-Quarto Facsimiles* (1885), No. 31. It was included by Steevens in his *Twenty Plays* (1766), Vol. 4.

The Second Edition (1630), that here described, was reproduced (the British Museum copy) in the Praetorius-Furnivall *Shakspere-Quarto Facsimiles* (1885), No. 32.

The Third Edition (1655) is that described in our next number.

Players' Quartos of this play were published in 1681, 1687, and 1695.

Of the First Edition (1681), "R. Bentley and M. Magnes," there are copies in the Birmingham Free, Ellesmere, Boston Public, and White Libraries.

Of the Second Edition (1687), "R. Bentley and S. Magnes," there are copies in the British Museum, Birmingham Free, Boston Public, and White Libraries.

Of the Third Edition (1695), "for Richard Bentley," there are copies in the British Museum, Bodleian, Birmingham Free, Harvard University, Boston Public, Hoe, and White Libraries.

This was the last of Shakespeare's plays to be issued in separate form before the appearance of the First Folio. It was also one of the two dramas by Shakespeare having an introduction, the other being *Troilus and Cressida*.

In commenting upon the edition here described the editor of *The Cambridge Shakespeare* (8 : xii.) says: "Mr. Collier says: 'It was unquestionably printed from a manuscript different from that used for the Quarto of 1622, or for the Folio of 1623.' But after a minute comparison of the two it appears to us clear that the Quarto of 1630 must have been printed from a copy of the Quarto of 1622, which had received additions and corrections in manuscript. The resemblances between the two are too close to allow of any other supposition. These additions and corrections, though agreeing for the most part with the first Folio, which had appeared in the interval, were derived from an independent source."

SHAKESPEARE, WILLIAM.

OTHELLO. LONDON, *for William Leak*, 1655. [606]

Small quarto. Third Edition.

COLLATION BY SIGNATURES: A to M, each 4 leaves; total 48 leaves.

COLLATION BY PAGINATION: [title, as reproduced; *See* No. 606], recto of [A]; —[blank], verso of [A];—[text, with heading] | [conventional head-piece] | *The Tragedy of* OTHELLO *the Moore* | *of* Venice. |,

No. 606   *William Shakespeare*   1655

THE
Tragœdy of Othello
The MOORE of VENICE

As it hath beene divers times Acted at the Globe, and at the Black-Friers by his Majesties SERVANTS.

Written by William Shakespeare.

The fourth Edition.

LONDON,
Printed for *William Leak* at the *Crown* in *Fleet-street,* between the two Temple Gates, 1 6 5 5.

NO. 606. TITLE-PAGE OF SHAKESPEARE'S OTHELLO; 3D EDITION; 1655.

pp. 1–93; — | FINIS. | , p. 93 ; — [publisher's advertisement, with heading] | Printed or sold by *William Leake*, at the signe of the | Crown in Fleetstreet between the two Temple Gates. | *These Bookes following* | [titles printed in double columns], p. [94]. Page 72 has the head-line | *the Moore of Venice.* | , instead of | *The Tragedy of Othello* | ; and p. 77, | *The Tragedy of* Othello | , instead of | *the Moore of Venice.* | .

CONDITION: Size of leaf, 7 1/10 × 5 inches. Bound in blue crushed levant morocco, gilt edges ; by Rivière. The upper margins are closely clipped and the head-lines cut into on several pages.

OTHER COPIES.

British Museum (2); Bodleian (3); Capell Collection ; Edinburgh University ; Boston Public ; Lenox ; Morgan (Halliwell Phillipps-Asay-Irwin copy); F. K. Trowbridge ; and White Libraries.

REFERENCES.

Greg, *List of English Plays* (Bibliographical Society ; 1900), p. 102; British Museum, *Catalogue*; *Shakespeare* (1897), col. 133; *The Cambridge Shakespeare*, 8 (1895) : xii.; Furness, *New Variorum Edition* (1866), p. 341; Boston Public Library, *Catalogue of the Works of William Shakespeare Original and Translated together with the Shakespeariana Embraced in the Barton Collection* (1880), p. 34, No. 518; Lenox Library, *Works of Shakespeare* (1880), p. 23, No. 116; Lowndes, *Bibliographer's Manual of English Literature*, 4 (1869) : 2291; Hazlitt, *Hand-Book* (1867), p. 551, No. 22 c.

Though called "*The fourth Edition*" on the title-page, this is really the Third of the separately printed editions of *Othello*, which is a reprint of that of 1630. The last leaf contains a list of "*Bookes.*"

SHAKESPEARE, WILLIAM.

PERICLES. LONDON, *for Henry Gosson*, 1609. [607]

Small quarto. Second or "*Eneer Gower*" Edition.

COLLATION BY SIGNATURES : A to I, each 4 leaves (the last blank and lacking); total 36 unnumbered leaves.

COLLATION BY PAGINATION : [title, as reproduced ; *See* No. 607 a], recto of [A]; —[blank], verso of [A]; —[text, first page with conventional head-piece having a face in the centre, as reproduced ; *See* No. 607 b], recto of A 2 to verso of I 3; — | FINIS. | *Gower.* | [18 lines] | FINIS. |, verso of I 3; —[1 blank leaf], [I 4].

CONDITION: Size of leaf, 6¾ × 5 inches. Bound in red morocco, gilt edges; by Bedford.

OTHER COPIES.

British Museum (Garrick copy); and Devonshire (Wright-Kemble copy) Libraries. Lee also locates copies as follows : Public Library of Hamburg ; Marsden J. Perry (Palmer-Fenn-Chaloner Smith copy); also the Halliwell-Phillipps copy (untraced).

REFERENCES.

Lee, *Shakespeare's Pericles, 1609* (Facsimile Edition; 1905), p. 36; Greg, *List of English Plays* (Bibliographical Society ; 1900), p. 103; British Museum, *Catalogue*; *Shakespeare* (1897), col. 138; *The Cambridge Shakespeare*, 9 (1895) : vii.; Hazlitt, *Manual of Old English Plays* (1892), p. 177; Locker-Lampson, *Catalogue* (1886), p. 110; Boston Public Library, *Catalogue*; *Barton Collection* (1880), p. 36, No. 549; Huth, *Catalogue*, 4 (1880) : 1339; Winsor, *Bibliography* (1876), p. 56; Lowndes, 4 (1869) : 2292; Hazlitt, *Hand-Book* (1867), p. 551, No. 20 a.

THE LATE,
And much admired Play,
Called
Pericles, Prince of Tyre.

With the true Relation of the whole Historie, aduentures, and fortunes of the said Prince:

As also,
The no lesse strange, and worthy accidents, in the Birth and Life, of his Daughter
MARIANA.

As it hath been diuers and sundry times acted by his Maiesties Seruants, at the Globe on the Banck-side.

By William ⚜§⚜ Shakespeare.

Imprinted at London for *Henry Gosson*, and are to be sold at the signe of the Sunne in Pater-noster row, &c.
1 6 0 9.

No. 607 a.   Title-page of Shakespeare's Pericles; 2d Edition; 1609.

The Play of Pericles
Prince of Tyre, &c.

Enter Gower.

O sing a Song that old was sung,
From ashes, auncient *Gower* is come,
Assuming mans infirmities,
To glad your eare, and please your eyes:
It hath been sung at Feastiuals,
On Ember-Eues, and Holy dayes:
And Lords and Ladies in their liues,
Haue read it for restoratiues
The purchase is to make men glorious,
Et bonum quo Antiquius eo melius:
If you, borne in these latter times,
When Wits more ripe, accept my Rimes;
And that to heare an olde man sing,
May to your wishes pleasure bring:
I life would wish, and that I might
Waste it for you like Taper-light.
This *Antioch*, then, *Antiochus* the great,
Built vp this Citie, for his chiefest Seat;
The fairest in all *Syria*.
I tell you what my Authors say:
This King vnto him tooke a Peere,
Who dyed, and left a Female-heyre,
So buck-some, blith, and full of face,
As heauen had lent her all his grace:
With whom the Father liking tooke,
And her to Incest did prouoke:
Bad child, worse father to intice his owne.

A 2   To

No. 607   *William Shakespeare*   1609

The Tite-Locker Lampson copy, with ex-libris of the latter.

In the copy here described is a long note in pencil, as follows: "*This copy is that which Cambridge Ed^n calls 4$^{(2)}$, see Line 42 'justifie' in 1st. There are copies of 4$^{(1)}$ in Bod: Capell & B. Mus: & of 4$^{(2)}$ (this) in Duke of Devonshire's & Bri: Mus: & one in Holland. Pericles is not included in the 2 first Editions of the Folio. The text in 3rd Folio is taken from the 6 4to. The Plot of Pericles is founded on Twine's novel called 'the Patterne of Painefull adventures' pub^d in 1576.*"

Tipped in on the recto of the second fly-leaf is a clipping, apparently from the *Athenæum* or the *Spectator*, entitled "Two Editions of 'Pericles' in 1609," by J. O. Halliwell, written from "St. Mary's, West Brompton, July 13." On the verso of the second fly-leaf is a slip tipped in, as follows: "*The three last acts of Pericles, with the possible exception of the socalled chorus, are wholly the work of W. S.*"

The edition here described may be distinguished from the First by the stage direction on leaf A 2, which reads "*Eneer Gower*" instead of "*Enter Gower.*" It was reproduced in the Ashbee-Halliwell *Facsimiles* (1871), No. 39, and also (the British Museum copy) in the Praetorius-Furnivall *Shakspere-Quarto Facsimiles* (1886), No. 22.

This, the Second Edition, may further be distinguished from the First Edition by the following textual differences:

	1ST EDITION	2D EDITION
A 2, recto, line 3,	*Enter Gower.*	*Eneer Gower.*
A 2, verso, line 15,	iuſtifie.	iuſtfiie.
B, verso, line 21,	heate,	heart,
B, verso, last line,	plants	planets
B 2, verso, line 4,	ſpares	feares
E, verso, line 26,	gently	dayly
F 2, verso, line 3,	keep	weepe
G 3, recto, line 20,	Thetis	That is
H 2, verso, line 1,	former	feruor
I 3, verso, last line but 3,	ſo content,	to contend,

Editions of this play were separately published in quarto in 1609 (two editions), 1611, 1619, 1630 (two editions), and 1635.

Of the First or "*Enter Gower*" Edition (1609), "for Henry Goſſon," there are copies in the British Museum, Bodleian (Malone copy), Capell Collection, Huth (Heber-Daniel copy), Boston Public (Steevens-Roxburghe-Jolley copy), W. A. White (Steevens-Perkins copy) Libraries, also the Jennens-Curzon-Howe copy (untraced). Lee locates another copy in the library of John Murray. This edition was reproduced in the Ashbee-Halliwell *Facsimiles* (1862), No. 38; (the British Museum copy) in the Praetorius-Furnivall *Shakspere-Quarto Facsimiles* (1886), No. 21; and (the Bodleian Library copy) in Sidney Lee's *Shakespeare's Pericles, 1609* (1905).

The Second or "*Eneer Gower*" Edition (also 1609) is that here described.

Of the Third Edition (1611), "Printed at London by S. S." (i. e., Simon Stafford), there is an imperfect copy, the Edwards-Halliwell Phillipps copy, which lacks two leaves in sheet D (a part of the second act) in the British Museum. Lee also locates a complete copy in Marsden J. Perry's library. This edition, which was very poorly printed from the Second Edition, was reproduced in the Ashbee-Halliwell *Facsimiles* (1868), No. 41.

The Fourth Edition (1619) is that described in our next number. This edition is found (1) with *The Whole Contention* (*a*) without a title-page, or (*b*) with a title-page; (2) separately, (*a*) without a title-page, or (*b*) with a title-page.

In the Fifth Edition (1630), "by I. N. for R. B. and are to be sould at his shop in Cheapside, at the signe of the Bible," the text is extremely incorrect. There are copies in the British Museum (Garrick copy), Bodleian (Malone copy), Capell Collection, Edinburgh University (Theobald-Halliwell Phillipps copy), Boston Public (Halliwell-Phillipps copy), Lenox (Aldis copy), and Furness Libraries. Lee locates a copy in the Folger Library.

Of the Sixth Edition (1630), "by J. N. for R. B.," there are copies in the British Museum (Halliwell-Phillipps copy), Dyce Collection (Halliwell-Phillipps copy), Edinburgh University (Halliwell-Phillipps copy), Boston Public (Halliwell-Phillipps copy), and Lenox (Heber-Utterson copy) Libraries, and two untraced copies. This edition differs from the Fifth only in its imprint, which has but two lines, while the Fifth has four lines.

The Seventh Edition (1635) is that described in our No. 609.

This play was not included in the First and Second Folios. It was, however, included with other plays wrongly attributed to Shakespeare in the Third and Fourth Folios. "The portions that may confidently be assigned to Shakespeare," says Luce, in his *Handbook* (1906), "are Act III., Act IV., omitting Scenes ii. v. and vi., and Act V. These contain some of the poet's best work, certainly his best sea-sketches."

SHAKESPEARE, WILLIAM.

PERICLES. [LONDON], *Printed for* T. P., 1619. [608]

Small quarto. Fourth Edition.

COLLATION BY SIGNATURES: 1 leaf, without signature-mark; R to Z, Aa, each 4 leaves; Bb, 1 leaf; total 34 unnumbered leaves.

COLLATION BY PAGINATION: [title, as reproduced; *See* No. 608], recto of first leaf; — [blank], verso of first leaf; — [text, with heading] | [conventional head-piece] | THE HISTORY OF | Pericles, Prince of Tyre. |, recto of R to recto of Bb; — | FINIS. |, recto of Bb; — [blank], verso of Bb.

CONDITION: Size of leaf, 7⅜₁₆ x 5¼ inches. Bound in red crushed levant morocco, with doublure of the same, elaborately panelled and tooled in gilt on the outside, with dentelle border inside, gilt edges, red silk and marbled-paper end papers; by the Club Bindery, 1901, finished by Leon Maillard; in flap and slip case. The leaves are stabbed on the inner margins throughout.

OTHER COPIES.

With *The Whole Contention*, and with separate title-page: Hoe Library. With *The Whole Contention*, but without separate title-page: British Museum (Garrick copy); and Lenox (Loscombe-Halliwell Phillipps-Tite copy) Libraries.

No. 608   *William Shakespeare*   1619

THE LATE,
And much admired Play,
CALLED,
Pericles, Prince of Tyre.

With the true Relation of the whole Hi-
ſtory, aduentures, and fortunes of
the ſaide Prince.

Written by W. SHAKESPEARE.

Printed for *T. P.* 1619.

No. 608.   Title-page of Shakespeare's Pericles; 4th Edition; 1619.

Bound separately, with title-page : British Museum (Steevens copy) ; Bodleian (Malone copy) ; Dyce Collection (Farmer copy) ; Devonshire ; Huth ; Boston Public ; Perry (Halliwell-Phillipps copy) ; Lenox ; Trowbridge ; and White Libraries ; also the Jennens-Howe and the Theobald-Warburton-Roxburghe-Halliwell Phillipps-Van Antwerp copies (untraced).

Bound separately, but whether with or without title-page being uncertain : Capell Collection ; and Furness Libraries. Sidney Lee also locates the following copies: Newdegate ; Folger ; Perry (Gwynn copy) ; and 6 other copies untraced, probably reduced to 2 by the location of the Devonshire, Trowbridge, and White copies given above, and one in the possession of the publishers of this catalogue.

REFERENCES.

Lee, *Shakespeare's Pericles, 1609* (Facsimile Edition ; 1905), p. 41 ; Greg, *List of English Plays* (Bibliographical Society ; 1900), p. 104 ; British Museum, *Catalogue*; Shakespeare (1897), col. 139 ; Locker-Lampson, *Catalogue* (1886), p. 107 ; Boston Public Library, *Catalogue* ; Barton Collection (1880), p. 36, No. 551 ; Huth, *Catalogue*, 4 (1880) : 1339 ; Lenox Library, *Works of Shakespeare* (1880), p. 24, No. 127 ; Winsor, *Bibliography* (1876), p. 57 ; Lowndes, 4 (1869) : 2292 ; Hazlitt, *Hand-Book* (1867), p. 551, No. 20 c.

There is also in the present collection another copy, but without the title-page, bound with and forming an integral part of our No. 585 (*The Whole Contention*). It is one of only four known copies so bound.

This, the Fourth Edition of this play, was printed as the third and last part of the volume entitled *The Whole Contention betweene the two Famous Houses, Lancafter and Yorke* (our No. 585), the signature-marks of the three parts being continuous. It is often found bound separately, usually, as in the copy here described, with a title-page (*see* our reproduction), printed on a single leaf without a signature-mark.

SHAKESPEARE, WILLIAM.

PERICLES. LONDON, *Thomas Cotes*, 1635.   [609]

Small quarto. Chain-lines perpendicular. Seventh Edition.

COLLATION BY SIGNATURES : A to H, each 4 leaves ; I, 2 leaves ; total 34 unnumbered leaves. Leaf B 4 has a signature-mark.

COLLATION BY PAGINATION : [title, as reproduced ; *See* No. 609], recto of [A] ; —[blank], verso of [A] ; —[text, with heading] | [conventional head-piece] | THE | HISTORY OF | Pericles, Prince of Tyre. |, recto of A 2 to recto of [I 2] ; — | FINIS. | [conventional tail-piece] |, recto of [I 2] ; —[blank], verso of [I 2].

CONDITION : Size of leaf, 7⅛ x 5¹⁄₁₆ inches. Bound in red crushed levant morocco, gilt edges ; by Rivière. The leaves are stabbed on the inner margins throughout.

OTHER COPIES.

British Museum ; Bodleian ; Capell Collection ; Edinburgh University ; Ellesmere ; Boston Public ; Lenox (Etherege copy) ; Hoe ; Morgan (Halliwell Phillipps-Tite-Asay-Irwin copy) ; W. A. White ; and Furness (Theobald copy, imperfect) Libraries. Sidney Lee also locates other copies as follows : Canterbury Cathedral ; Britwell (Halliwell Phillipps-Crawford copy) ; Perry (Freeling-Kershaw-Halliwell Phillipps copy) ; Folger ; and 7 untraced copies, probably reduced to 3 by the location

THE LATE,
And much admired Play,
CALLED
Pericles, Prince of Tyre.

With the true Relation of the whole History, adventures, and fortunes of the said Prince.

Written by W. SHAKESPEARE,

Printed at *London* by *Thomas Cotes*, 1635.

of the Edinburgh University and Morgan copies, and that here described. For the location of several copies of the various editions of this play we are indebted to Lee's Facsimile Edition of *Shakespeare's Pericles*.

REFERENCES.

Lee, *Shakespeare's Pericles, 1609* (Facsimile Edition; 1905), p. 47; Hoe, *Catalogue*, 4 (1904) : 103; Greg, *List of English Plays* (Bibliographical Society; 1900), p. 104; British Museum, *Catalogue; Shakespeare* (189), col. 139; Boston Public Library, *Catalogue*; *Barton Collection* (1880), p. 36, No. 554; Lenox Library, *Works of Shakespeare* (1880), p. 25, No. 130; Lowndes, 4 (1869) : 2293; Hazlitt, *Hand-Book* (1867), p. 551, No. 20 *e*.

The text of this edition closely follows that of 1630. That of the Third Folio, to which it was appended with six other supposititious plays, is taken from this edition, but with a considerable number of conjectural alterations.

SHAKESPEARE, WILLIAM. (*b*. 1564, *d*. 1616.)

MR. WILLIAM SHAKESPEARES COMEDIES, HISTORIES, & TRAGEDIES. LONDON, *Ifaac Iaggard, and Ed. Blount*, 1623. [610]

Folio. The First Folio Edition.

COLLATION BY SIGNATURES: Comedies: A, 6 leaves; 1 leaf, the title-page, inserted between [A] and A 2; 2 leaves, without signature-marks (verses by Digges and I. M., and names of the actors), inserted between [A 5] and [A 6]; A (repeated), B to Z, Aa, Bb, each 6 leaves; Cc, 2 leaves. Histories: a to g, each 6 leaves; gg, 8 leaves; h to v, each 6 leaves; x, 4 leaves. Tragedies: 2 leaves, without signature-marks; ¶, ¶¶, each 6 leaves; ¶¶¶, 1 leaf; aa to ff, each 6 leaves; gg, 2 leaves; gg (repeated), hh, kk to zz, aaa, bbb, each 6 leaves; total 454 leaves.

The following errors or variations occur in the signature-marks: Comedies: leaf X is marked *X*; and X 2 is *X* 2. Histories: a 3 is wrongly marked Aa 3; and m 3 is l 3. Tragedies: bb 2 is Bb 2; gg (repeated) is Gg; nn is Nn; nn 2 is Nn 2; oo is Oo; oo 2 has no signature-mark; tt 2 is tt 3; xx is x; xx 2 is x 2; xx 3 is x 3; yy 2 is y 2; and yy 3 is y 3.

In some copies there are other errors or variations, viz.: Comedies: V is wrongly marked Vv; and R is R 2 (the cancelled leaf in the Lichfield-Lenox copy). Histories: m 3 is correct. Tragedies: aaa is aa 2 (one of Mr. Morgan's copies). Sidney Lee says (p. xxx.) that in the Comedies leaf B was originally marked A and so appears in a few copies; and that in the Tragedies cc 2 has no signature-mark, and yy 2 and yy 3 are correct in some copies.

COLLATION BY PAGINATION: [blank], recto of [A]; — | To the Reader. | [10 lines of verse] | [signed] | B. I. |, verso of [A]; —[title, with portrait, as reproduced; *See* No. 610], recto of inserted leaf;—[blank], verso of inserted leaf; — | [conventional head-piece] | TO THE MOST NOBLE | AND | INCOMPARABLE PAIRE | OF BRETHREN. | WILLIAM | Earle of Pembroke, &c. Lord Chamberlaine to the | *Kings moſt Excellent Maieſty*. | AND | PHILIP | Earle of Montgomery, &c. Gentleman of his Maieſties | Bed-Chamber. Both Knights of the moſt Noble Order | of the Garter, and our ſingular good | LORDS. | [signed] | Your Lordſhippes moſt bounden, | IOHN HEMINGE. | HENRY CONDELL. |, recto and verso of A 2; — | [conventional head-piece] | *To the great Variety of Readers.* | [signed] | *Iohn Heminge.* | *Henrie Condell.* |, recto of A 3; — [blank], verso of A 3; — | [conventional head-piece] | To the memory of my beloued, | The AVTHOR | MR.

No. 610   William Shakespeare   1623

WILLIAM SHAKESPEARE: | AND | what he hath left vs. | [signed] | BEN: IONSON. | , recto and verso of [A 4]; — | [conventional head-piece] | Vpon the Lines and Life of the Famous | Scenicke Poet, Mafter WILLIAM | SHAKESPEARE. | [signed] | HVGH HOLLAND. | , recto of [A 5]; — [blank], verso of [A 5]; — | [conventional head-piece] | TO THE MEMORIE | of the deceafed Authour Maifter | W. SHAKESPEARE. | [signed] | L. Digges. | [also] | To the memorie of M. W. Shake-fpeare. | [signed] | I. M. | , recto of first unmarked leaf; — [blank], verso of first unmarked leaf; — | The Workes of William Shakefpeare, | containing all his Comedies, Hiftories, and | Tragedies: Truely fet forth, according to their firft | ORJG-JNALL. | The Names of the Principall Actors | in all thefe Playes. | [26 names, in double columns] | , recto of second unmarked leaf; — [blank], verso of second unmarked leaf; — | [conventional head-piece] | A CATALOGVE | of the feuerall Comedies, Hiftories, and Tra- | gedies contained in this Volume. | , recto of [A 6]; — [blank], verso of [A 6].

Comedies: — | [conventional head-piece] | THE | TEMPEST. | , pp. 1 – 19 ; — [epilogue and names of the actors, in double columns, the first with heading] | EPILOGVE, | fpoken by Profpero. | , [the second with heading] | The Scene, an vninhabited Ifland | Names of the Actors. | , p. 19 ; — | [conventional head-piece] | THE | Two Gentlemen of Verona. | , pp. 20 – 38 ; — | The names of all the Actors. | , p. 38 ; — | [conventional head-piece] | THE | Merry Wiues of Windfor. | , pp. 39 – 60 ; — | [conventional head-piece] | MEASVRE, | For Meafure. | , pp. 61 – 84 ; — [names of the actors, in double columns, the first with heading] | The Scene Vienna. | The names of all the Actors. | , p. 84 ; — | [conventional head-piece] | The Comedie of Errors. | , pp. 85 – 100 ; — | [conventional head-piece] | Much adoe about Nothing. | , pp. 101 – 121 ; — | [conventional head-piece] | Loues Labour's loft. | , pp. 122 – 144 ; — | [conventional head-piece] | A | MIDSOMMER | Nights Dreame. | , pp. 145 – 162 ; — | [conventional head-piece] | The Merchant of Venice. | , pp. 163 – 184 ; — | [conventional head-piece] | As you Like it. | , pp. 185 – 207 ; — | [conventional head-piece] | THE | Taming of the Shrew. | , pp. 208 – 229 ; — | [conventional head-piece] | ALL'S | Well, that Ends Well. | , pp. 230 – 254 ; — | [conventional head-piece] | Twelfe Night, Or what you will. | , pp. 255 – 275 ; — [blank], p. [276] ; — | [conventional head-piece] | The Winters Tale. | , pp. 277 – 303 ; — | The Names of the Actors. | , p. 303 ; — [blank], p. [304].

Histories: — | [conventional head-piece] | The life and death of King Iohn. | , pp. 1 – 22 ; — | [conventional head-piece] | The life and death of King Richard | the Second. | , pp. 23 – 45 ; — | [conventional head-piece] | The Firft Part of Henry the Fourth, | with the Life and Death of HENRY | Sirnamed HOT-SPVRRE. | , pp. 46 – 73 ; — | [conventional head-piece] | The Second Part of Henry the Fourth, | Containing his Death: and the Coronation | of King Henry the Fift. | , pp. 74 – 100 ; — | [conventional head-piece] | EPILOGVE. | , p. [101] ; — | [conventional head-piece] | THE | ACTORS | NAMES. | , p. [102] ; — | [conventional head-piece] | The Life of Henry the Fift. | , pp. 69 – 95 ; — | [conventional head-piece] | The firft Part of Henry the Sixt. | , pp. 96 – 119 ; — | [conventional head-piece] | The fecond Part of Henry the Sixt, | with the death of the Good Duke | HVMFREY. | , pp. 120 – 146 ; — | [conventional head-piece] | The third Part of Henry the Sixt, | with the death of the Duke of | YORKE. | , pp. 147 – 172 ; — | [conventional head-piece] | The Tragedy of Richard the Third : | with the Landing of Earle Richmond, and the | Battell at Bofworth Field. | , pp. 173 – 204 ; — | [conventional head-piece] | The Famous Hiftory of the Life of | King HENRY the Eight. | THE PROLOGVE. | , p. 205 ; — [text], pp. 205 – 232 ; — | THE EPILOGVE. | , p. 232.

Tragedies: — | The Prologue. | , recto of first unmarked leaf; — | [conventional head-piece] | THE TRAGEDIE OF | Troylus and Crefsida. | , verso of first unmarked leaf to recto of ¶¶¶ (in all 28 pp.) ; — [blank],

Mr. WILLIAM SHAKESPEARES

COMEDIES, HISTORIES, & TRAGEDIES.

Published according to the True Originall Copies.

Martin Droeshout sculpsit London.

LONDON

Printed by Isaac Iaggard, and Ed. Blount. 1623.

1623   *William Shakespeare*   **No. 610**

verso of ¶¶¶;— | [conventional head-piece] | The Tragedy of Coriolanus. | , pp. 1–30; — | [conventional head-piece] | The Lamentable Tragedy of | Titus Andronicus. | , pp. 31–52 ; — | [conventional head-piece] | THE TRAGEDIE OF | ROMEO and IVLIET. |, pp. 53–79; — | [conventional head-piece] | THE LIFE OF TYMON | OF ATHENS. |, pp. 80–98 ; — | [conventional head-piece] | THE | ACTORS | NAMES. |, p. [99];—[blank], p. [100]; — | [conventional head-piece] | THE TRAGEDIE OF | IVLIVS CÆSAR. |, pp. 109–130; — | [conventional head-piece] | THE TRAGEDIE OF | MACBETH. |, pp. 131–151; — | [conventional head-piece] | THE TRAGEDIE OF | HAMLET, Prince of Denmarke. |, pp. 152–156 and 257–282 [wrongly numbered 280]; — | [conventional head-piece] | THE TRAGEDIE OF | KING LEAR. |, pp. 283–309 ; — | [conventional head-piece] | THE TRAGEDIE OF | Othello, the Moore of Venice. |, pp. 310–339; — | The Names of the Actors. |, p. 339; — | [conventional head-piece] | THE TRAGEDIE OF | Anthonie, and Cleopatra. |, pp. 340–368 ; — | [conventional head-piece] | THE TRAGEDIE OF | CYMBELINE. |, pp. 369–399 [wrongly numbered 993]; — | FINIS. | [conventional tail-piece] | [colophon] | *Printed at the Charges of W. Jaggard, Ed. Blount, I. Smithweeke,* | *and W. Aspley,* 1623. |, p. 399; — [blank], p. [400].

The following errors or variations occur in the pagination : Comedies : p. 50 is wrongly numbered 58 ; 59 is 51 ; 86 is 88; 153 is 151 ; 161 is 163 ; 164 is 162; 165 is 163 ; 189 is 187 ; 249 is 251 ; 250 is 252; and 265 is 273. Histories: 37 is 39 ; 47 and 48 are omitted; 89 is 91 ; 90 is 92; 101 and 102 have no page-numbers; 69–102 are repeated; 165 is 167 ; 166 is 168; and 216 is 218. Tragedies: 77 and 78 are omitted; 81 and 82 are repeated; 99 and 100 have no page-numbers; 101–108 are omitted; 15 leaves (*Troylus and Cressida*) are unnumbered, except the second leaf, which is numbered 79 and 80; 101–108 are omitted ; 157–256 are omitted; 279 is 259; 282 is 280; 308 is 38; 379 is 389; and 399 is 993.

In some copies there are other errors or variations, viz.: Comedies: 193 is 203 and 204 is 194 (the cancelled leaves in the Lichfield-Lenox copy); 214 is 212; and 237 is 233. Histories: 37 is correct. Tragedies: 277 is 273. Sidney Lee says (p. xxix.) that 309 is 307 in some copies.

In the head-lines occur the following errors or variations: Comedies: pp. 37 and 38, | *The Merry Wiues of Windsor.* |, instead of | *The two Gentlemen of Verona.* |; p. 121, | *Much adoe aboat Nothing.* |, instead of | *Much adoe about Nothing.* | ; p. 197, | *As yoa like it.* |, instead of | *As you like it.* |. Tragedies: pp. 79 and 80, the second leaf of *Troilus and Cressida*, has | *The Tragedie of Troylus and Cressida.* |, instead of | *Troylus and Cressida.* |.

CONDITION: Size of leaf, 13⅛ × 8 9/10 inches. Bound in red crushed levant morocco, elaborately tooled in gilt, with heavy centre and corner ornaments and an all-over design of acorns and daisies, vellum end-papers, gilt edges; by Bedford; in brown morocco solander case. The preliminary leaves of the copy here described have been arranged by the binder in the following order : Leaf with verses " To the Reader "; title-page; dedication, A 2 ; "To the memory of my beloued, The author," signed " Ben : Iohnson "; " To the great Variety of Readers," A 3 ; poems, signed " L. Digges " and " I. M."; poem, signed " Hugh Holland "; " The Names of the Principall Actors "; and " A Catalogue of the feuerall Comedies." The binder has also placed the 15 leaves containing *Troylus and Cressida* after *Timon of Athens*, leaf [hh 6].

OTHER COPIES.

British Museum (4); Bodleian (2, one imperfect); Capell Collection ; Trinity College, Cambridge; South Kensington Museum; Dyce Collection ; Forster Collection ; Birmingham Free ; Shakespeare Memorial, Stratford ; Glasgow University ; Trinity College, Dublin ; Crawford ; Devonshire

(Chatsworth copy, reproduced in facsimile, with Introduction and Census of Copies by Sidney Lee; Oxford, 1902); Ellesmere; Huth; Boston Public; John Carter Brown; Lenox (4, one with date changed to 1622); Columbia University; Halsey; Hoe; Morgan (3); W. A. Read; White (Ives copy); Princeton University; Furness; Library of Congress; and other libraries and collections, as given by Sidney Lee in his *Census of Extant Copies*, though several copies recorded by him have since changed ownership.

1905), pp. 8–12; Hoe, *Catalogue*, 4 (1904): 110; Greg (Walter W.), *Bibliographical History of the First Folio*, in *The Library* (Second Series), July, 1903, pp. 258–283; Lee, *Census of Copies of the First Folio* (1902); Greg, *List of English Plays* (Bibliographical Society; 1900), p. 94; British Museum, *Catalogue*; *Shakespeare* (1897), col. 3; Locker-Lampson, *Catalogue* (1886), p. 104; Boston Public Library, *Catalogue*; *Barton Collection* (1880), p. 1, No. 1; Huth, *Catalogue*, 4 (1880): 1330; Lenox Library, *Works of Shakespeare* (1880), pp. 32, 35; Winsor, *Bibliography of the Original Quartos and Folios of Shakespeare with Particular Reference to Copies in America* (1876), pp. 77, 109; Lowndes, 4 (1869): 2253; Hazlitt, *Hand-Book* (1867), p. 546, No. 6 a.

REFERENCES.

Lee, *Notes and Additions to the Census of Copies of the Shakespeare First Folio*, in *The Library* (Second Series), April, 1906, pp. 113–139; *The Original Bodleian Copy of the First Folio of Shakespeare* (Oxford,

In the British Museum is a copy in which the fourth line of the title-page reads | HISTORIES, AND | instead of the more usual | HISTORIES, & | . Sidney Lee says (p. xxx.) the large initial letter in the word | BOte-fwaine. | , on the first leaf of the text, is printed upside down in a few copies.

The Lichfield-Baker-Lenox copy has the date on the title-page changed from 1623 to 1622. This was effected by cutting off the lower margin close up to the date including the lower portion of the last figure. The margin was then extended and the final figure touched up to resemble a 2. This copy contains two impressions of leaf R, pp. 193 and 194 of *As You Like It* (act ii., sc. 7), beginning | *Scena Septima.* | . Both are printed from the same setting of type. The second or cancelled leaf has the page-number 203 instead of 193 and the signature-mark R 2 instead of R. In the same copy are two impressions of leaf [R 6] of the same play, pp. 203 and 204. The second or cancelled leaf has the page-number 194 instead of 204. This leaf was evidently cancelled because of the confusion of the characters in lines 10–12 (act v., sc. 1) in the first column, which read:

> *Orl.* A ripe age : Is thy name *William* ?
> *Clo.* *William*, fir.
> *Clo.* A faire name. Was't borne i'th Forreft heere ?

In the corrected leaf the names of the interlocutors are correctly given as *Clo.*, *Will.*, and *Clo.* respectively. Sidney Lee (p. xxxi.) says that there are other copies of this cancelled leaf in the Boston Public Library and in the copy formerly belonging to Bishop John Vertue of Portsmouth.

In the Tilden-Lenox copy, leaf [q 4], p. 172, in the second column of the last page of *Henry VI.*, Part III. (act v., sc. 6), are several errors, as follows: line 4 reads, | Kong Ned, . . . | , instead of | Yo[u]ng Ned, . . . | ; line 13, | . . . way, add . . . | , instead of | . . . way, and . . . | ; and line 15, | And 'tis . . . | , instead of | And kis . . . | . Sidney Lee (p. xxxi.) says these errors also occur in the Ellesmere and Stratford Memorial Library copies.

In the Brownlowe-Morgan copy are two leaves containing the first page of *Troilus and Cressida*. One of these has "The Prologue" on its recto. The other has on its recto the signature-mark gg 3 and the page-number 77, and on it is printed the last page of *Romeo and Juliet* (act v., sc. 3), followed on its verso by the first page of *Troilus and Cressida*, each printed from a setting of type different from that usually found in copies of this edition. Sidney Lee says (p. xxix.) that the Burdett-Coutts copy also contains an impression of this cancelled leaf.

Leaf [pp 5], pp. 277 (wrongly numbered 273) and 278, *The Tragedie of Hamlet* (act v., sc. 1) in the Tilden-Lenox and Brownlowe-Morgan copies contains several errors corrected in most copies. It may be distinguished by the following readings: p. 277 (wrongly numbered 273), col. 1, line 9 from the bottom reads | . . . iowlos . . . | , instead of | . . . iowles . . . | ; and on p. 278, col. 2, line 30 reads | . . . Brid-bed . . . |, instead of | . . . Bride-bed . . . | . Other errors on these pages are given by Sidney Lee (p. xxxii.), who locates three other copies.

In the Thacher-Chew copy, leaf ff 3, p. 309, the last page of *The Tragedy of King Lear* (act v., sc. 3), col. 2, line 21, the stage direction at the end of the line reads, "He dies." This usually reads, "He dis."; but Mr. Lee says (p. xxxi.) it sometimes reads, "H'e dis."

The Duke of Devonshire's copy (the Chatsworth copy), reproduced by Sidney Lee, contains an erroneous reading at the top of the first column of leaf vv 3, p. 333, *Othello* (act iv., sc. 2), as follows :

"And hell gnaw his bones,
Performances are no kin together."

instead of

"I haue heard too much : and your words and
Performances are no kin together."

This error is due to a compositor's mistake, the first of these lines belonging properly to Emilia's angry speech near the beginning of the preceding column. Mr. Lee (p. xxx.) says that this error occurs in three other copies, only one of which, that of Mr. John Caldwell, of Pittsburg, is in this country.

The Droeshout Portrait. This portrait, which appears in each of the first four Folios, is found in four states, the plate having been altered or touched up from time to time as it became worn. Owing to this, several marked changes are to be observed.

The First or earliest State may be distinguished by the lack of any shadow thrown by the hair on the right-hand side of the collar. Only two copies with the portrait in this state are known, one in the Bodleian Library (Malone Collection), the other in the library of Mr. Marsden J. Perry of Providence, Rhode Island. The former has been reproduced in *The Original Bodleian Copy of the First Folio* (Oxford, 1905), Plate 1.

In the Second State the shadow of the hair is seen on the collar, the moustache and eyebrows have been lengthened, and the lower part of the face has been much roughened by the insertion of numerous dots giving the surface of the chin, especially, an

No. 610   *William Shakespeare*   1623

unshaven appearance. The line of separation between the forehead and hair on the right-hand side of the plate, which in the First State is very faint, has been emphasized by retouching the cross-hatching of the forehead and by giving the inner portion of the hair a lighter tone, probably by partly burnishing down the incised lines of the plate.

In the Third State the changes made were slight. This state may be distinguished (1) by the outer edge of the hair on the right-hand side of the plate, near the centre of which a single hair for a short distance becomes detached, showing the background between it and the main portion of the hair; (2) by lines drawn from the white centres of the eyes toward the right of the plate, that on the right-hand cutting the eyelid. The Third State is uniformly found in the Second and Third Folios, and in some copies of the First Folio.

In the Fourth State, to be found only in the Fourth Folio, the face, hair, shadow on the collar, and clothes have been much darkened by cross-hatching, as a result of which the high lights on the face have been emphasized to an absurd extent. Boaden, speaking of the portrait in this state, says, "I confess it to have become what it has frequently been called — an abominable libel on humanity."

The ten lines of verse written by Ben Jonson in commendation of Droeshout's portrait are differently printed in each of the Four Folios, and may be distinguished by the following variations:

	First Folio 1623	Second Folio 1632	Third Folio 1663	Third Folio 1664	Fourth Folio 1685
Line 2	Shakeſpeare	Shakeſpeare	*Shakeſpeare*	*Shakeſpeare*	*Shakeſpear*
" 3	Grauer	Graver	*Graver*	*Graver*	*Graver*
" 5	wit	VVit	*Wit*	*Wit*	Wit
" 7	face;	Face;	*Face;*	*Face;*	Face;
" 8	braſſe.	Braſſe.	*Braſſe.*	*Braſſe.*	*Braſs.*

Previous to Shakespeare's death numerous editions of his plays, as we have already seen, had been separately issued. No attempt was made to form a collected edition of his works until 1623, when the First Folio was published. "A reprint of the First Folio unwarrantably purporting to be exact," says Sidney Lee, "was published in 1807–8. The best reprint was issued in three parts by Lionel Booth in 1861, 1863, and 1864. The valuable photo-zincographic reproduction undertaken by Sir Henry James, under the direction of Howard Staunton, was issued in sixteen folio parts between February 1864 and October 1865. A reduced photographic facsimile, too small to be legible, appeared in 1876, with a preface by Halliwell-Phillipps." It is hardly necessary to say that the photographic facsimile of "the Chatsworth Copy in the possession of the Duke of Devonshire, K. G., with Introduction and Census of Copies" by Mr. Lee himself supersedes all previous reprints and facsimiles.

Of the collected plays, known as the First Four Folios (1623, 1632, 1663, 1664, and 1685), three of them have variations enough in the imprints to bring the number of editions or issues up to twelve, eleven of which are fully described in this and the numbers which follow (610–620).

The First Folio, says Sidney Lee, "forms the greatest contribution made in a single volume to the secular literature of any age or country." Several attempts have been made since Dibdin's day to locate copies, but none has been so successful as Mr. Lee's exhaustive *Census* made in 1902 in connection with his Facsimile Reprint, which has superseded all other reprints or facsimiles of the First Folio. He then located 158 copies, of which 101 were in England, 52 in the United States, 3 in the British Colonies, and 2 on the Continent. In 1906 he published a supplementary list by which these numbers were increased to 172; 8 of the 14 copies then added being in the United Kingdom, and 6 in the United States. Of the entire number less than a score are perfect copies in good and unrestored condition.

The bibliographical history of the volume has been very fully told by Mr. Lee in his introduction to the Facsimile Reprint, and by Mr. Greg in his "Bibliographical History of the First Folio" (*The Library*, Second Series, Vol. 4, July, 1903, pp. 258–285), to which we are indebted for some of the information here given.

This collected edition of Shakespeare's plays was due to the efforts of two of his intimate friends and fellow actors, John Heming and Henry Condell. As the work was of considerable magnitude, it was undertaken by a syndicate of printers and booksellers; the printers and publishers being William Jaggard and his son Isaac, the booksellers being William Aspley, John Smethwick, and Edward Blount. Previous to this undertaking, sixteen of the plays had been separately published, in quarto form, by different booksellers and publishers. In 1613 Jaggard increased his business by buying out that of James Roberts, who was the owner of the rights to publish several of the plays and also to print the "player's bills" or programmes. The other members of the syndicate were owners of the rights to publish the other plays. Heming and Condell, on their part, undertook to furnish such playhouse transcripts or prompt-books as they had access to. These, together with some transcripts to be found only in private hands, brought the number of plays up to thirty-six, of which twenty were here printed for the first time. One play only of those which had appeared in quarto form (*Pericles*) was not included, probably because the syndicate did not regard it as one of Shakespeare's.

It appears, from the lack of any systematic order in the arrangement of the plays, as well as from peculiarities attaching to the volume itself, that the work of printing began before they had all been brought together. Coming from such various sources, the plays contain numerous corruptions of text and a great variety of style. The texts from which many of the quartos were printed had been obtained from more or less imperfect and unauthorized playhouse transcripts abounding in abridgments or mutilations and copyists' errors; or from crude drafts taken down in shorthand. On the other hand, the plays printed for the first time from prompt-copies of the theatres contain comparatively few faults, and besides are divided into acts and scenes, with stage directions, indications of "the scene," and lists of the dramatis personæ. In transcripts written for private use these features were generally omitted, and the infrequency with which they are given in the First Folio indicate that private transcripts were more frequently used than the prompt-copies of the theatres, doubtless owing to the fire of 1613, which had destroyed the Globe Theatre, where the company and its archives had been housed for fourteen years.

SHAKESPEARE, WILLIAM.

MR. WILLIAM SHAKESPEARES COMEDIES, HISTORIES, AND TRAGEDIES. PUBLISHED ACCORDING TO THE TRVE ORIGINALL COPPIES. THE SECOND IMPRESSION. London, *by Tho. Cotes, for Robert Allot,* 1632. [611]

Folio. The Second Folio, or Allot "Coppies" Edition.

COLLATION BY SIGNATURES: A, 6 leaves; *, 4 leaves; A to Z, Aa, Bb, each 6 leaves; Cc, 2 leaves; a to y, aa, bb, cc (wrongly marked bb), dd to zz, aaa, bbb, ccc, each 6 leaves; ddd, 4 leaves; total 454 leaves.

The following errors or variations occur in the signature-marks: Preliminary leaves: leaf A 3 is wrongly marked A 2. Comedies: S 2 is *S* 2; and Z is *Z*. Histories: i is I; i 3 is I 3; l 3 is h 3; m is M; m 2 is m 3; and u 3 is v 3. Tragedies: cc is bb (repeated); bb 3 (repeated) has no signature-mark; and gg 2 is gg 3.

In some copies there are other errors or variations, viz.: Histories: leaf i 2 is wrongly marked i 3; and u has no signature-mark. Tragedies: bb 3 (repeated) has a signature-mark.

COLLATION BY PAGINATION: [blank], recto of [A]; — | To the Reader. | [10 lines of verse] | [signed] | B. I. |, verso of [A]; — [title, with portrait, as reproduced; *See No.* 611 *a*], recto of [A 2]; — [blank], verso of [A 2]; — | [conventional head-piece] | TO THE MOST NOBLE | AND | INCOMPARABLE PAIRE | OF BRETHREN, | VVilliam | Earle of Pembroke, &c. Lord Chamberlaine to the | *Kings moſt Excellent Majeſtie.* | AND | PHILIP | Earle of Montgomery, &c. Gentleman of his Majeſties | Bed-Chamber. Both Knights of the moſt Noble Order | of the Garter, and our ſingular good | LORDS. | [signed] | Your Lordſhips moſt bounden | *John Heminge.* | *Henry Condell.* |, recto and verso of A 3 [wrongly marked A 2]; — | [conventional head-piece] | *To the great variety of Readers.* | [signed] | *Iohn Heminge.* Henry Condell.* |, recto of A 4; — [blank], verso of A 4; — | [conventional head-piece] | Vpon the Effigies of my worthy | Friend, the Author Maſter William | Shakeſpeare, and his Workes. | [8 lines] | An Epitaph on the admirable Dramaticke | Poet W. SHAKESPEARE. |, recto of [A 5]; — [blank], verso of [A 5]; — | [conventional head-piece] | TO THE MEMORIE | of the deceaſed Author, Maſter | VV. SHAKESPEARE. | [signed] | L. Digges. |, [followed by] | To the Memory of M. *W. Shakeſpeare.* | [signed] | I. M. |, recto of [A 6]; — [blank], verso of [A 6]; — | [conventional head-piece] | The Workes of William Shake- | ſpeare, containing all his Comedies, Hiſto- | ries, and Tragedies: Truly ſet forth, according | to their firſt Originall. | The Names of the Principall Actors | in all theſe Playes. | [26 names, in double columns] |, recto of *; — [blank], verso of *; — | [conventional head-piece] | To the memory of my beloved, | The AVTHOR | MR. VVilliam SHAKESPEARE | AND | what he hath left us. | [signed] | BEN. IONSON. |, recto and verso of * 2; — | [conventional head-piece] | On Worthy Maſter Shake- | ſpeare and his Poems. | [signed] | The friendly admirer of his | Endowments. | *I. M. S.* |, recto and verso of [* 3]; — | [conventional head-piece] | Vpon the Lines and Life of the | Famous Scenicke Poet, Maſter | VV. SHAKESPEARE. | [signed] | Hugh Holland. |, recto of [* 4]; — | [conventional head-piece] | A Catalogue of all the Comedies, | Hiſtories, and Tragedies contained | in this Booke. |, verso of [* 4].

Comedies: — | [conventional head-piece] | THE | TEMPEST. |, pp. 1–19; — [epilogue and names of the actors, in double columns, the first with heading] | EPILOGVE | ſpoken by *Proſpero.* | [the second with heading] | The Scene, an un-inhabited Iſland. | *Names of the Actors.* |, p. 19; — | [conventional head-piece] | THE | Tvvo

Gentlemen of Verona.|, pp. 20–38;—| Names of the Actors.|, p. 38;—|[conventional head-piece]|THE|Merry VVives of VVindfor.|, pp. 39–60;—|[conventional head-piece]|MEASVRE|For Meafure.|, pp. 61–84;—[names of the actors, in double columns, the first with heading]|*The Scæne Vienna.*|*Names of all the Actors.*|, p. 84;—|[conventional head-piece]|The Comedie of Errors.|, pp. 85–100;—|[conventional head-piece]|Much adoe about Nothing.|, pp. 101–121;—|[conventional head-piece]|Loves Labour's loft.|, pp. 122–144;—|[conventional head-piece]|A|MIDSOMMER|Nights Dreame.|, pp. 145–162;—|[conventional head-piece]|The Merchant of Venice.|, pp. 163–184;—|[conventional head-piece]|As you like it.|, pp. 185–207;—|[conventional head-piece]|THE|Taming of the Shrew.|, pp. 208–229;—|[conventional head-piece]|ALL'S|VVell, that Ends VVell.|, pp. 230–254;—|[conventional head-piece]|Tvvelfe Night, Or what you will.|, pp. 255–275;—[blank], p. [276];—|[conventional head-piece]|The VVinters Tale.|, pp. 277–303;—|The Names of the Actors.|, p. 303;—[blank], p. [304].

Histories:—|[conventional head-piece]|The life and death of King Iohn.|, pp. 1–22;—|[conventional head-piece]|The Life and Death of King Richard|the Second.|, pp. 23–45;—|[conventional head-piece]|The Firft Part of Henry the Fourth,|with the Life and Death of HENRY|Sirnamed HOT-SPVRRE.|, pp. 46–73;—|[conventional head-piece]|The Second Part of Henry the Fourth,|Containing his Death: and the Coronation|of King Henry the Fift.|, pp. 74–100;—|[conventional head-piece]|EPILOGVE.|, p. [101];—|[conventional head-piece]|THE|ACTORS|NAMES.|, p. [102];—|[conventional head-piece]|The Life of King Henry the Fift.|, pp. 69–95 [wrongly numbered 59];—|[conventional head-piece]|The firft Part of King Henry the Sixt.|, pp. 96–119;—|[conventional head-piece]|The fecond Part of King Henry the Sixt.|vvith the death of the Good Duke|HVMFREY.|, pp. 120–146;—|[conventional head-piece]|The third Part of King Henry the Sixt.|vvith the death of the Duke of|YORKE.|, pp. 147–172;—|[conventional head-piece]|The Tragedy of Richard the Third:|vvith the Landing of Earle Richmond, and the|Battell at Bofworth Field.|, pp. 173–204;—|[conventional head-piece]|The Famous Hiftory of the Life of|King HENRY the Eight.|*THE PROLOGVE.*|, p. 205;—[text], pp. 205–232;—|THE EPILOGVE.|, p. 232.

Tragedies:—|[conventional head-piece]|The Prologue.|, p. 1;—|[conventional head-piece]|THE TRAGEDIE OF|Troylus and Crefsida.|, pp. 2–29;—|[conventional head-piece]|The Tragedy of Coriolanus.|, pp. 30–59;—|[conventional head-piece]|The Lamentable Tragedy of|Titus Andronicus.|, pp. 60–81;—|[conventional head-piece]|THE TRAGEDIE OF|ROMEO and IVLIET.|, pp. 82–106;—|[conventional head-piece]|THE LIFE OF TYMON|OF ATHENS.|, pp. 107–127;—|[conventional head-piece]|THE|ACTORS|NAMES.|, p. 128;—|[conventional head-piece]|THE TRAGEDIE OF|IVLIVS CÆSAR.|, pp. 129–150;—|[conventional head-piece]|THE TRAGEDIE OF|MACBETH.|, pp. 151–168 and 269–271;—|[conventional head-piece]|THE TRAGEDY OF|HAMLET, Prince of Denmarke.|, pp. 272–302;—|[conventional head-piece]|THE TRAGEDIE OF|KING LEAR.|, pp. 303–329;—|[conventional head-piece]|THE TRAGEDY OF|Othello, the Moore of Venice.|, pp. 330–359;—|THE|ACTORS|*NAMES.*|, p. 359;—|[conventional head-piece]|THE TRAGEDY OF|Anthony, and Cleopatra.|, pp. 360–388;—|[conventional head-piece]|THE TRAGEDY OF|CYMBELINE.|, pp. 398 [wrongly numbered 399] to 419;—|*FINIS.*|[colophon, as reproduced; *See* No. 611*b*]|, p. 419;—[blank], p. [420].

The following errors or variations occur in the pagination: Comedies: p. 46 is wrongly numbered 64; 58 is 80; 153 is 151; 194 is 494; 249 is 251; 250 is 252;

Mr. WILLIAM SHAKESPEARES
COMEDIES, HISTORIES, and TRAGEDIES.

Published according to the true Originall Coppies.

The second Impression.

Printed by Tho. Cotes, for Robert Allot, and are to be sold at his shop at the signe of the blacke Beare in Pauls Church-yard. 1632.

No. 611a. Title-page of the Second Folio of Shakespeare; Allot "Coppies" Edition; 1632.

Reduced; original 10 15/16 × 6 7/16 inches. The Portrait in the Third State.

and 265 is 273. Histories: 47 and 48 are omitted; 89 is 91; 90 is 92; 101 and 102 have no page-numbers; 69–102 are repeated; 94 (repeated) is 49; 95 (repeated) is 59; 164 is 194; and 209 is 120. Tragedies: 85 is 58; 96 is 67; 154 is 134; 169–268 are omitted; 286 is 186; 287 is 187; 341 is 143; 342 is 144; 351 is 151; 352 is 152; 355 is 335; and 389 is 399.

In some copies there are other errors or variations, viz.: Comedies: p. 57 is 79; and 205 is 208. Histories: 20 is 18; 49 is 45; 88 (repeated) is 87 (Lenox copy "A"); 95 is 65 (Lenox copy "A"); and 164 is correct. Tragedies: 85 is correct; 161 is 164; and 164 is 161.

The following errors or variations occur in the head-lines: Comedies: p. 60 reads | *The meery Wives of Windsor.* |, instead of | *The merry Wives of Windsor.* |; pp. 213 and 223 read | *The Taming of a the Shrew.* |, instead of | *The Taming of the Shrew.* |. Histories: p. 115 reads | *The second Part of King Henry the Sixt.* |, instead of | *The first Part of King Henry the Sixth.* |; p. 206, | *The Life and death of Richard the Third.* |, instead of | *The Life of Henry the Eight.* |. Tragedies: p. 294 reads | *The Tragedy of King Lear.* |, instead of | *The Tragedy of Hamlet.* |; pp. 406 and 407 read | *The Tragedy of | Anthony and Cleopatra.* |, instead of | *The Tragedy of Cymbeline.* |.

In some copies there are other errors or variations in the head-lines, as follows: Comedies: p. 50 reads | *The meery Wives of Windsor.* |, instead of | *The merry Wives of Windsor.* |; p. 164, | *The Marchent of Venice.* |, instead of | *The Merchant of Venice.* |. Tragedies: pp. 340 and 341 have | *The Tragedy of Hamlet | the Moore of Venice.* |, instead of | *The Tragedy of Othello | the Moore of Venice.* |; and pp. 406 and 407 read correctly.

CONDITION: Size of leaf, 13¼ × 9 inches. Bound in red crushed levant morocco, gilt edges; by Bedford; in brown morocco solander case.

OTHER COPIES.

"Coppies" edition: Bodleian; Capell Collection (with numerous marginal annotations by Capell); Trinity College, Dublin; and Lenox Libraries; also the Gray copy (noted by Winsor). "Copies" edition: British Museum (3); Bodleian; Trinity College, Cambridge; South Kensington Museum; Dyce Collection; Forster Collection (2); Birmingham Free; Edinburgh University; Hunterian Museum, Glasgow; Crawford; Devonshire; Ellesmere; Huth; Boston Public (2); Yale University; John Carter Brown; Lenox (4); Hagen; Halsey; Hoe (2); Morgan (2); Read; White; Princeton University; Furness; Library of Congress; Wrenn; and other Libraries.

REFERENCES.

Hoe, *Catalogue*, 4 (1904): 113; *The Cambridge Shakespeare*, 1 (1902): xxvii.; Greg, *List of English Plays* (Bibliographical Society; 1900), p. 94; British Museum, *Catalogue*; *Shakespeare* (1897), col. 4; Boston Public Library, *Catalogue*; *Barton Collection* (1880), p. 2, No. 7; Huth, *Catalogue*, 4 (1880): 1330; Lenox Library, *Works of Shakespeare* (1880), pp. 33, 36; Winsor, *Bibliography* (1876), p. 92; Lowndes, 4 (1869): 2256; Hazlitt, *Hand-Book* (1867), p. 547, No. 6 b.

Printed at *London* by *Thomas Cotes*, for *John Smethwick*, *William Aspley*, *Richard Hawkins*, *Richard Meighen*, and *Robert Allot*, 1632.

No. 611 b. COLOPHON OF THE SECOND FOLIO OF SHAKESPEARE; 1632.

No. 611   *William Shakespeare*   1632

The statement made by Lowndes that a copy of the Second Folio exists bearing the date 1631 has never been verified. Lowndes gives no authority for his assertion, and Bohn, in his edition of the *Bibliographer's Manual* (1869), discredits it.

There are two issues of the title-page with Allot's imprint.

In the First Issue, that here described, there is a misprint, "Coppies" for "Copies," in the sixth line. In title-pages with this misprint insufficient space was left between the last line of the title and the first line of the imprint for the impression of the portrait, so that it is usually found to overlap the word "London" of the imprint. This faulty title-page seems to have been discovered before many impressions were struck off, as but very few copies so printed are in existence.

In the Second or "Copies" Issue the title-page was reset, with slight changes, ample space being left for the impression of the portrait.

Copies of the Second Folio vary in the imprints on their title-pages. That of the earliest or the Allot "Coppies" Issue reads as follows:

(*a*) | LONDON, | Printed by *Tho. Cotes,* for *Robert Allot,* and are to be ſold at his ſhop at the ſigne | of the blacke Beare in Pauls Church-yard. 1632. | (our present number; *See* our reproduction No. 611 *a*).

(*b*) In the Allot "Copies" Issue or reprinted title-page the imprint reads: | LONDON, | Printed by *Tho. Cotes,* for *Robert Allot,* and are to be ſold at his ſhop at the ſigne | of the Blacke Beare in Pauls Church-yard. 1632. | .

In some copies the second line of this imprint reads, | Printed by *Tho. Cotes,* for *Robert Allot,* and are to be ſold at the ſigne | , instead of | . . . to be ſold at his ſhop at the ſigne | .

(*c*) The Aspley imprint reads: | LONDON, | Printed by *Tho. Cotes,* for *William Aſpley,* and are to be ſold at the ſigne | of the Parrat in Pauls Church-yard. 1632. | (*See* our reproduction No. 612 *b*).

(*d*) The Hawkins imprint reads: | LONDON, | Printed by *Tho. Cotes,* for *Richard Hawkins,* and are to be ſold at his ſhop | in Chancery Lane, neere Serjeants Inne. 1632. | (*See* our reproduction No. 613).

(*e*) The Meighen imprint reads: | LONDON, | Printed by *Tho. Cotes,* for *Richard Meighen,* and are to be ſold at the middle | Temple Gate in Fleetſtreet. 1632. | (*See* our reproduction No. 614).

(*f*) The Smethwick imprint reads: | LONDON, | Printed by *Tho. Cotes,* for *Iohn Smethwick,* and are to be ſold at his ſhop | in Saint *Dunſtans* Church-yard. 1632. | (*See* our reproduction No. 615).

In the Lenox Library is a copy (the Bliss copy), "C," in which the title-page, "probably cancelled," varies from most copies, as follows: line 6 reads | . . . accodring . . . | , instead of | . . . according . . . | ; line 7, | . . . *Impreſsion*. | , instead of | . . . *Jmpreſsion.* | ; and the imprint, | LONDON, | Printed by *Tho Cotes,* for *Robert Allot,* and are to be ſold at his ſhop at the ſigne | of the blacke Beare in *Pauls* Church yard, 1632. | . This title-page appears to have been due to an attempt to correct the errors and spacing of the letterpress portion of the Allot "Coppies" title-page, the first line being printed from the same setting of type in each.

This attempt proving unsatisfactory it was cancelled and the entire page reset. This reset title-page, with the exception of the imprints, was that used in all subsequent impressions.

The companion-leaf of the title-page, [A 5], "Vpon the Effigies," etc., was also reprinted in the "Copies" Issue and those with the varying imprints.

While it presents a considerable number of literal differences, it may be distinguished by line 13, which reads, | Poet W. SHAKESPEARE. |, as in our No. 611, instead of | Poet, VV. SHAKESPEARE. |, as in our No. 615.

The Utterson-Barton copy in the Boston Public Library and one of the copies, "A," in the Lenox Library also have this reprinted leaf.

The Second Folio appears to have been printed by a syndicate composed of William Aspley and John Smethwick, who had been members of the former syndicate that printed the First Folio; Robert Allot, to whom in 1630 Blount had transferred his rights in the sixteen plays which were first licensed for publication in 1623; and Richard Hawkins and Robert Meighen as new members. The volume was printed by Thomas Cotes. Each member of the syndicate seems to have taken a share of the edition in which his name appears in the imprint, copies of each being found in the present collection. Those with Allot's name are the most common; those with Meighen's the rarest, none of the seven copies in the Lenox collection having the latter's name.

"The second Folio," says the editor of *The Cambridge Shakespeare*, "is a reprint of the first, preserving the same pagination. It differs, however, from the first in many passages, sometimes widely, sometimes slightly, sometimes by accident, sometimes by design. The emendations are evidently conjectural, and though occasionally right, appear more frequently to be wrong. They deserve no more respect than those of other guessers, except such as is due to their author's familiar acquaintance with the language and customs of Shakespeare's day, and possible knowledge of the acted plays."

SHAKESPEARE, WILLIAM.

MR. WILLIAM SHAKESPEARES COMEDIES, HISTORIES, AND TRAGEDIES. PUBLISHED ACCORDING TO THE TRUE ORIGINALL COPIES. THE SECOND IMPRESSION. LONDON, *by Tho. Cotes, for William Afpley,* 1632. [612]

Folio. The Second Folio; Aspley Imprint.

COLLATION BY SIGNATURES: Identically the same as in our preceding number, except that in the Tragedies leaf bb 3 (repeated) has a signature-mark.

COLLATION BY PAGINATION: [blank], recto of [A]; — | To the Reader. | [with manuscript notes, as reproduced; *See* No. 612*a*], verso of [A]; — [title, identically the same as in our next number, except the imprint, as reproduced; *See* No. 612*b*], recto of [A 2]; — [blank], verso of [A 2]; — [dedication], recto and verso of A 3

Shakspeare.

"Age cannot wither him, nor custom stale
His infinite variety: Other Aets cloy.
The appetites they feed, but He makes hungry
Where most he satisfies "   *Ant. & Cleo.*

"Nature never had before so
noble & so true an Interpreter;
never so inward a Secretary
of her Cabinet "
　　Sir Henry Wotton of Lord Bacon

"Natura lo fece, e poi ruppe
la stampa" — *Ariosto.*

When nature such a
mould had introduc'd,
She broke it, & none
like it since produc'd. JP

To the Reader.

This Figure, that thou here seeſt put,
It was for gentle Shakeſpeare cut;
Wherein the Graver had a ſtrife
VVith Nature, to out-doo the life:
O, could he but have dravvne his VVit
As well in Braſſe, as he hath hit
His Face; the Print vvould then ſurpaſſe
All, that was ever vvrit in Braſſe.
But, ſince he cannot, Reader, looke
Not on his Picture, but his Booke.

　　　　　　　　　　　B. I.

His genuine Autograph

By me William Shakspeare

*Imitated by me, at Doctors Commons, 30 May, 1801, by permission.
The detail is more faithful than mere tracing could make it.
In the last syllable the greatest difference will be found, between this
and that done by Mr Steevens, but I have copied every touch exactly.
　　　　　　　　　　　　Boaden.*

No. 612 a.   THE VERSE OF THE SECOND FOLIO OF SHAKESPEARE; 1632.
Reduced; original, including manuscript notes, 12 11/16 × 6 7/8 inches.

[wrongly marked A 2]; — | *To the great variety of Readers.* | , recto of A 4; — [blank], verso of A 4; — | [conventional head-piece] | Vpon the Effigies of my worthy | Friend, the Author Mafter William | Shakefpeare, and his VVorkes. | [9 lines] | Poet, VV. SHAKESPEARE. | , recto of [A 5]; — [the rest identically the same as in our preceding number].

The copy here described has the same errors or variations in the pagination as the preceding number, except that in the Comedies pp. 57 and 205 are correctly numbered, and in the Histories p. 20 is wrongly numbered 18, and 164 is correct.

The errors or variations in the head-lines are the same as in the preceding number, except that in the Comedies p. 50 has | *The meery Wives of Windfor.* | , instead of | *The merry Wives of Windfor.* | ; p. 164 has | *The Marchent of Venice.* | , instead of | *The Merchant of Venice.* | . In the Tragedies the head-lines on pp. 406 and 407 read correctly.

EXTRA-ILLUSTRATED.

Inserted in this folio are 4 portraits — one on the verso of leaf A 4, two on the verso of leaf [A 6], and one on the recto of leaf *; also Baker's engraving "The Birth Place of Shakespeare," at the end of the volume; and pasted to the front fly-leaves, several newspaper clippings, and an impression on red sealing-wax, from a gold seal-ring believed to have belonged to Shakespeare.

CONDITION: Size of leaf, 13 x 8⅞ inches. Bound in old calf, sides panelled in gilt and blind tooling, gilt edges; by C. Kalthoeber; in brown morocco solander case. There are numerous manuscript notes on the fly-leaves, the portrait leaf, and on the margins throughout the book.

OTHER COPIES.

There are copies with the Aspley imprint in the Lenox Library; and that of Harold Murdock, of Philadelphia; also the Lucy-Majoribanks-Van Antwerp copy (untraced).

The copy here described contains two book-plates, that of Johannis Poynder, and that of John Cole Nicholl.

Laid into the copy here described is the following letter, addressed to "*Mefsrs. Dodd, Mead & Co.*":

"*Lenox Library:* | *New York: June 14, 1888.*

Gent^m

The Second Folio with Aspley imprint has long been recognized as 'Of such extraordinary rarity, that few persons, even among those specially interested in Shakesperian bibliography, have ever been able to see it.' This was the language of Halliwell in 1862.

Excepting the Burton-Forrest copy, I know of no other in America except that in this library — to which I am now to add the Dodd, Mead & Co. copy — I suppose.

[signed] | *Yours very truly:* | *Geo: H: Moore* | ."

LONDON,
Printed by Tho. Cotes, for William Aſpley, and are to be ſold at the ſigne of the Parrat in Pauls Church-yard. 1 6 3 2

NO. 612*b*. THE ASPLEY IMPRINT ON THE TITLE-PAGE OF THE SECOND FOLIO OF SHAKESPEARE; 1632.

M^R· WILLIAM SHAKESPEARES COMEDIES, HISTORIES, and TRAGEDIES.

Published according to the true Originall Copies.

The second Impression.

LONDON,
Printed by *Tho. Cotes*, for *Richard Hawkins*, and are to be sold at his shop in Chancery Lane, neere Serjeants Inne. 1 6 3 2.

NO. 613. TITLE-PAGE OF THE SECOND FOLIO OF SHAKESPEARE; HAWKINS IMPRINT; 1632. Reduced; original 11⅝ × 6⅝ inches. The Portrait in its Third State.

SHAKESPEARE, WILLIAM.

MR. WILLIAM SHAKESPEARES COMEDIES, HISTORIES, AND TRAGEDIES. THE SECOND IMPRESSION. LONDON, by Tho. Cotes, for Richard Hawkins, 1632. [613]

Folio. The Second Folio; Hawkins Imprint.

COLLATION BY SIGNATURES: Identically the same as in our No. 611.

COLLATION BY PAGINATION: Identically the same as in our No. 611, except the title-page (as reproduced; See No. 613), and leaf [A 5], which is the same as that in our preceding number.

The copy here described has the same errors or variations in the pagination as in our No. 611, except that in the Tragedies p. 85 is correctly numbered.

The errors or variations in the head-lines are the same as in our No. 611, except that in the Histories p. 206 reads correctly; and in the Tragedies pp. 340 and 341 read | *The Tragedy of Hamlet.* | *the Moore of Venice.* |, instead of | *The Tragedy of Othello* | *the Moore of Venice.* |.

CONDITION: Size of leaf, 12⅝ × 8¾ inches. Bound in red crushed levant morocco, with elaborately tooled gilt panelled sides, gilt over marbled edges; by R. de Coverly; in brown morocco solander case. The verse before the title-page is inlaid.

OTHER COPIES.

Lenox; and J. Pierpont Morgan (Farn copy) Libraries.

On the front fly-leaf of the copy here described is written in an old style of handwriting, "*Thomas Fox Willys, Ejus Liber.*"

SHAKESPEARE, WILLIAM.

MR. WILLIAM SHAKESPEARES COMEDIES, HISTORIES, AND TRAGEDIES. THE SECOND IMPRESSION. LONDON, by Tho. Cotes, for Richard Meighen, 1632. [614]

Folio. The Second Folio; Meighen Imprint.

COLLATION BY SIGNATURES: Identically the same as in our No. 611, except that in the Histories leaf i2 is wrongly marked i3; and in the Tragedies bb3 (repeated) has a signature-mark.

COLLATION BY PAGINATION: Identically the same as in our preceding number, except the imprint on the title-page (as reproduced; See No. 614).

The copy here described has the same errors or variations in the pagination as in our No. 611.

LONDON,
Printed by Tho. Cotes, for Richard Meighen, and are to be sold at the middle Temple Gate in Fleetstreet. 1632.

NO. 614. THE MEIGHEN IMPRINT ON THE TITLE-PAGE OF THE SECOND FOLIO OF SHAKESPEARE; 1632.

No. 614   *William Shakespeare*   1632

The errors or variations in the head-lines are the same as in our No. 611, except that in the Comedies p. 50 has | *The meery Wives of Windsor.* |, instead of | *The merry Wives of Windsor.* |. In the Histories, p. 206, and in the Tragedies, pp. 406 and 407, the head-lines read correctly.

CONDITION: Size of leaf, 13 7/16 × 8 13/16 inches. Bound in red crushed levant morocco, gilt edges; by Rivière; in brown morocco solander case. Leaves [A] and [A 2] and pp. 399–416 have been supplied from a shorter copy; and pp. 417–419 are in facsimile.

OTHER COPIES.

There is another copy with this imprint in the library of Mr. J. Pierpont Morgan.

The copy here described has the ex-libris of F. A. Marshall.

SHAKESPEARE, WILLIAM.

MR. WILLIAM SHAKESPEARES COMEDIES, HISTORIES, AND TRAGEDIES. THE SECOND IMPRESSION. LONDON, *by Tho. Cotes, for Iohn Smethwicke*, 1632.   [615]

Folio. The Second Folio; Smethwick Imprint.

COLLATION BY SIGNATURES: Identically the same as in our No. 611.

COLLATION BY PAGINATION: Identically the same as in our No. 613, except the imprint of the title-page (as reproduced; *See* No. 615).

The copy here described has the same errors or variations in the pagination as in our No. 611, except that in the Comedies p. 57 is wrongly numbered 79, and 205 is 208; in the Tragedies p. 85 is correctly numbered.

The errors or variations in the head-lines are the same as in our No. 611, except that in the Comedies p. 50 has | *The meery Wives of Windsor.* |, instead of | *The merry Wives of Windsor.* |. In the Histories, p. 206, and in the Tragedies, pp. 406 and 407, the head-lines read correctly.

CONDITION: Size of leaf, 13½ × 9 1/16 inches. Bound in old calf, with coat of arms in gilt on the front cover, red edges; in brown morocco solander case. The binder has transposed leaves Bb and [Bb 6].

OTHER COPIES.

Lenox Library (title-page laid in); Beverly Chew; and the Howe copy (untraced).

LONDON,
Printed by *Tho. Cotes*, for *Iohn Smethwick*, and are to be sold at his sho[p] in Saint *Dunstans* Church-yard. 1 6 3 2.

NO. 615. THE SMETHWICK IMPRINT ON THE TITLE-PAGE OF THE SECOND FOLIO OF SHAKESPEARE; 1632.

SHAKESPEARE, WILLIAM.

MR. WILLIAM SHAKESPEARES COMEDIES, HISTORIES, AND TRAGEDIES. THE THIRD IMPRESSION. LONDON, *for Philip Chetwinde*, 1663. [616]

Folio. The Third Folio; Original Title-page of 1663.

COLLATION BY SIGNATURES: A, 4 leaves; b, A to Z, Aa, each 6 leaves; Bb, 8 leaves; Cc to Zz, Aaa to Zzz, Aaaa to Dddd, each 6 leaves; Eeee, 4 leaves; a, 6 leaves; b, *, **, *_**, ****, each 4 leaves; ¶ A, ¶ B, each 6 leaves; ¶ C to ¶ F, each 4 leaves; ¶ G, 6 leaves; total 514 leaves.

Leaf A 3 of the preliminary matter is wrongly marked A 2; Ddd 3 has no signature-mark; and ¶ B 3 is ¶ B 2.

In some copies there are other errors or variations, as follows: leaf Bbb 3 is wrongly marked Bb 3 (one of Mr. Hoe's copies); ¶ A 3 is *_**_** 3 (Morgan and Methuen facsimile copies); ¶ B is ¶ A (correct in most copies); and ¶ G 3 has no signature-mark (Tunno-Hoe copy).

COLLATION BY PAGINATION: [blank], recto of [A]; — | *To the Reader.* | [as reproduced; *See* No. 616 *a*], verso of [A]; — [title, as reproduced; *See* No. 616 *b*], recto of [A 2]; — [blank], verso of [A 2]; — | To the moſt Noble and Incomparable pair of Brethren, | WILLIAM Earl of *Pembroke*, &c. Lord Chamberlain to the | *Kings* moſt Excellent *Majeſtie* ; | And PHILIP Earl of *Montgomery*, &c. Gentleman to His *Ma-* | *jeſties* Bed-Chamber. Both Knights of the moſt Noble Order of | the Garter, and our ſingular good LORDS. | [signed] | Your Lordſhips moſt bounden | *John Heminge,* | *Henry Condell.* |, recto and verso of A 3 [wrongly marked A 2]; — | *To the great variety of Readers.* | [signed] | *J. Heminge. H. Condell.* |, recto and verso of [A 4]; — | [conventional head-piece] | To the Memory of the deceaſed Authour | Mr. VVILLIAM SHAKE-SPEARE. | [signed] | L. Digges. |, recto of b; — | Upon the Effigies of my worthy Friend, the Au- | thour Mr. *W.* Shake-ſpeare, and his *Works.* | [8 lines] | *To the Memory of Mr.* W. Shakeſpeare. | [signed] | *J. M.* |, verso of b; — | To the Memory of my beloved the Authour | Mr. VVILLIAM SHAKESPEARE; | And what he hath left us. | [signed] | BEN. JOHNSON. |, recto of b 2 to recto of b 3; — | *On worthy Mr.* SHAKESPEARE, | *and his* Poems. | [signed] | The friendly admirer of his | Endowments, | *J. M. S.* |, verso of b 3 to verso of [b 4]; — | An EPITAPH | On the admirable Dramatick *Poet,* | *WILLIAM SHAKESPEARE.* |, recto of [b 5]; — | *Upon the Lines and Life of the Famous Scenick* | *Poet Mr.* VV. Shakeſpeare. | [signed] | *Hugh Holland.* |, verso of [b 5]; — | *The* VVorks *of* William Shakeſpeare, *containing* | *all his Comedies, Hiſtories, and Tragedies:* | *Truely ſet forth according to their* | *firſt Original.* | The names of the principal *Actors* in *all* | theſe *Playes.* | [26 names, in double columns] |, recto of [b 6]; — | *A Catalogue of all the Comedies, Hiſtories, and* | *Tragedies contained in this* Book. |, verso of [b 6].

Comedies: — | [conventional head-piece] | THE | TEMPEST. |, pp. 1–19; — [epilogue and names of the actors, in double columns, the first with heading] | EPI-LOCUE | ſpoken by *Proſper.* | [the second with heading] | The Scene an, an [*sic*] uninhabited Iſland. | *Names of the Actors.* |, p. 19; — | [conventional head-piece] | THE | Two Gentlemen of Verona. |, pp. 20–38; — | The Names of the Actours. |, p. 38; — | [conventional head-piece] | THE | Merry VVives of WINDSOR. |, pp. 39 [wrongly numbered 36] to 60; — | [type-ornament head-piece] | MEASURE | For Meaſure. |, pp. 61–84; — | *The Scæne* Vienna. | Names of all the Actors. |, p. 84; — | [type-ornament head-piece] | The Comedie of Errors. |, pp. 85–100; — | [conventional head-piece] | Much adoe about Nothing. |, pp. 101–121; — | [conventional

No. 616   *William Shakespeare*   1663

head-piece] | Love's Labour's loft. |, pp. 122–144; — | [conventional head-piece] | A Midfummers nights DREAM. |, pp. 145–162; — | [conventional head-piece] | The MERCHANT of VENICE. |, pp. 163–184; — | [conventional head-piece] | As you like it. |, pp. 185–207; — | [conventional head-piece] | The Taming of the Shrew. |, pp. 208–229; — | [conventional head-piece] | All's well that ends well. |, pp. 230–254; — | [conventional head-piece] | Twelfe-Night, Or what you will. |, pp. 255–275; — [blank], p. [276]; — | [type-ornament head-piece] | The VVinters Tale. |, pp. 277–303; — | The Name*s* of the Actors. |, p. 303; — [blank], p. [304].

Histories: — | [type-ornament head-piece] | The Life and Death of King John. |, pp. 305–326; — | [type-ornament head-piece] | The Life and Death of King Richard | the Second. |, pp. 327–349; — | [type-ornament head-piece] | The Firft Part of Henry the Fourth, | with the Life and Death of HENRY | Sirnamed HOT-SPURRE. |, pp. 350–375; — | [conventional head-piece] | The Second Part of Henry the Fourth, | Containing his Death: and Coronation of | King Henry the Fift. |, pp. 376–402; — | EPILOGUE. |, p. 403; — | THE | ACTORS | NAMES. |, p. 404; — | [conventional head-piece] | The Life of King HENRY the Fifth. |, pp. 405–431; — | [conventional head-piece] | The firft Part of King HENRY the Sixth, |, pp. 432–455; — | [conventional head-piece] | The fecond Part of King HENRY the Sixth, | With the Death of the good Duke | HUMPHREY. |, pp. 456–482; — | [conventional head-piece] | The third Part of King HENRY the Sixth. | with the death of the Duke of YORK. |, pp. 483–508; — | [conventional head-piece] | The Tragedy of Richard the Third : | With the Landing of the Earl of Richmond, and the Battel' at | Bofworth Field. |, pp. 509–540; — | [conventional head-piece] | The Famous Hiftory of the Life of | King *Henry* the Eighth. |, pp. 541–568; — | The Epilogue. |, p. 568.

Tragedies: — | THE | PROLOGUE. |, p. 560; — | [conventional head-piece] | THE TRAGEDY OF | Troilus and Cref-sida. |, pp. 561–588; — | [conventional head-piece] | The Tragedy of Coriolanus |, pp. 589–619 [wrongly numbered 617]; — | [conventional head-piece] | The Lamentable Tragedy of | Titus Andronicus. |, pp. 620–641; — | [conventional head-piece] | THE TRAGEDIE OF | *ROMEO* and *JULIET*. |, pp. 642–664; — | [type-ornament head-piece] | THE LIFE OF TYMON | OF ATHENS. |, pp. 667–687; — | [type-ornament head-piece] | THE | ACTORS | *NAMES*. |, p. 688; — | [type-ornament head-piece] | THE TRAGEDY OF | JULIUS CÆSAR. |, pp. 689–710; — | [type-ornament head-piece] | THE TRAGEDY OF | MACBETH. |, pp. 711–729; — | [conventional head-piece] | The Tragedy of HAMLET, | Prince of Denmark. |, pp. 730–760; — | [conventional head-piece] | The Tragedy of King LEAR. |, pp. 761–787; — | [conventional head-piece] | The Tragedy of OTHELLO, the | Moore of *Venice*. |, pp. 788–817; — | THE | ACTORS | *NAMES*. |, p. 817; — | [conventional head-piece] | THE TRAGEDY OF | ANTHONY and CLEOPATRA. |, pp. 818–846; — | [conventional head-piece] | The Tragedy of CYMBELINE. |, pp. 847–877; — [blank], p. [878].

Added Plays: — | [conventional head-piece] | The much admired *Play*, CALLED, | PERICLES, PRINCE of TYRE. | *With the true Relation of the whole History, Adventures,* | *and Fortunes of the faid Prince.* | VVritten by VV. SHAKESPEARE, | and publifhed in his life time. |, pp. 1–19; — | THE | ACTORS | *NAMES*. |, p. 20; — | [conventional head-piece] | The *London* PRODIGAL. | Written by *W. Shakefpeare.* |, pp. 1–16; — | [conventional head-piece] | The Hiftory of the Life and Death of THOMAS | Lord CROMWELL. |, pp. 17–31; — | THE | ACTORS | *NAMES*. |, p. 32; — | [conventional head-piece] | The Hiftory of Sir JOHN OLDCASTLE, | *the good* Lord Cobham. |, pp. 33–54; — | [conventional head-piece] | The PURITAN: or, The WIDOW | of *Watling-street*. |, pp. 55–73; — | THE | ACTORS | *NAMES*. | In the *Play* Intituled | The PURITAN WIDOW. | The Scene *London*. |, p. 74; — | [conventional head-piece]

1663   *William Shakespeare*   No. 616

| A YORK-SHIRE TRAGEDY, | *Not ſo New, as Lamentable and True.* |, pp. 75–81 ; — | [conventional head-piece] | The Tragedy of LOCRINE, the eldeſt | Son of King BRUTUS. |, pp. 82–100 ; — | FINIS. | [conventional tail-piece] |, p. 100.

The following errors or variations occur in the pagination: p. 39 is wrongly numbered 36 ; 108 is 56 ; 196 is 194 ; 201 is 103 ; 203 is 103 ; 223 is 123 ; 373 is 374 ; 428 is 433 ; 433 is 428 ; 560–568 are repeated ; 576 is 556 ; 579 is 559 ; 608 is omitted ; 619 is 617 ; 657 and 658 are repeated ; 665 and 666 are omitted ; 714 and 715 are repeated ; 779 is 787 ; 798 is 799 ; 858 is 859 ; 861 is 961 ; 868 is 669 ; 873 is 973 ; 875 is 879 ; and 876 is 990. Added plays: 18 is 16 ; 36 is 41 and 41 is 36, both numbered on the inner margins ; 49 is omitted ; and 53 is repeated.

In some copies there are other errors or variations, as follows: p. 109 is wrongly numbered 111 ; 120 is 119 ; 284 is 282 ; 478 is numbered on the inner margin ; 650 is 649 ; 651 is 650 ; 658 (repeated) is 660 ; 660 is 646 ; 661 is 655 ; and 877 is 881 (in the British Museum copy). Added plays: 12 is wrongly numbered 4 ; 13 is 5 ; 27 is 30 ; 30 is 27 ; and 36 and 41 are correct and numbered on outer margins (in one each of the Hoe and Morgan copies).

The pagination of pp. 649 to 669 (leaves Iii 3 to Lll inclusive) is very erratic. The actual order in most copies is as follows: 649–658, 657–664, 667–669 ; in some copies it is, 649, 649 (repeated), 650, 652–658, 657, 660, 659, 646, 655, 662–664, 667–669 ; while in others the pagination switches bewilderingly from one of these abnormal numberings to the other without any apparent reason.

The following errors or variations occur in the head-lines: pp. 125 and 129 have | *Lov's Labour's loſt.* |, instead of | *Love's Labour's loſt.* | ; p. 186, | *As yon like it.* |, instead of | *As you like it.* | ; pp. 259, 261, 262, and 264, | *Twelfe Night, or What yon will.* |, instead of | *Twelfe Night, or What you will.* | ; pp. 351 and 352, | *The Life and Death of* Henry *the Fourth.* |, instead of | *The firſt Part of King Henry the Fourth.* | ; p. 412, | *The ſecond Part of King Henry the Fourth.* |, instead of | *The Life of Henry the Fifth.* | ; p. 426, | *The firſt Part of King Henry the Sixth.* |, instead of | *The Life of King Henry the Fifth.* | ; p. 434, | *The Life of King Henry the Sixth.* |, and p. 435, | *The Life of King Henry the Fifth.* |, instead of | *The firſt Part of King Henry the Sixth.* | ; pp. 621, 623, 625, 627, 629, 631, and 639, | *The Tragedy of Titus Androuicus.* |, instead of | *The Tragedy of Titus Andronicus.* | ; p. 775, | *The Tragedy of Hamlet.* |, instead of | *The Tragedy of King Lear.* | . In the Added Plays, p. 36 (wrongly numbered 41, with page-number on the inner margin) reads | *the good Lord Cobham.* |, instead of | *The Hiſtory of Sir John Oldcaſtle,* | ; and p. 41 (wrongly numbered 36, with page-number on the inner margin) reads | *The Hiſtory of Sir John Oldcaſtle,* |, instead of | *the good Lord Cobham.* | . There are other slight variations which need not be here noted.

In some copies there are other errors or variations in the head-lines, as follows: p. 623 in two of Mr. Hoe's copies reads | *The Tragedy of Romeo and Juliet.* |, instead of | *The Tragedy of Titus Andronicus.* | ; and in one each of Mr. Hoe's and Mr. Morgan's copies pp. 36 and 41 of the added plays are correctly numbered in the outer margins and the head-lines read correctly.

CONDITION: Size of leaf, 13 9/16 x 8 inches. Bound in red straight-grained morocco, gilt gauffered edges ; by L. Staggemeier & Welcher ; in brown morocco solander case. The binder has wrongly placed leaf [A] between [A 4] and b.

Inserted in the copy here described is an impression of the 1664 title-page, as reproduced in our next number.

OTHER COPIES.

1663 title-page with portrait, but with no additional plays: Birmingham Free ; Huth ; and Boston Public Libraries. 1663 title-page without portrait, but with no additional plays: Ellesmere Library. 1663 title-page without portrait, but with the 1664 title-page and the additional plays: British Museum ; Bodleian ; and J. Pierpont Morgan (Irwin copy) Libraries. 1663

To the Reader.

This *Figure*, that thou here ſeeſt put,
  It was for gentle *Shakeſpeare* cut;
Wherein the *Graver* had a ſtrife
  VVith *Nature*, to out-doe the *Life*:
O, could he but have drawn his *Wit*
  As well in *Braſſe*, as he has hit
His *Face*; the *Print* would then ſurpaſſe
  All, that was ever writ in *Braſſe*.
But ſince he cannot, *Reader*, look
  Not on his *Picture*, but his *Book*.

B. J.

No. 616 a. THE VERSE OF THE THIRD FOLIO OF SHAKESPEARE; 1663.

Mʀ. WILLIAM SHAKESPEARES

Comedies, Histories, and Tragedies.

Published according to the true Original Copies.

The Third Impression.

LONDON,
Printed for *Philip Chetwinde*, 1663.

No. 616   *William Shakespeare*   1663

title-page with the portrait, the 1664 title-page, and the additional plays: Lenox (also 1663 title-page without portrait); Halsey; and the Library of Congress.

REFERENCES.

The Cambridge Shakespeare, 1 (1902): xxviii.; Greg, *List of English Plays* (Bibliographical Society; 1900), p. 94; Sinker, *Library of Trinity College, Cambridge* (1891), p. 117; Boston Public Library, *Catalogue*; Barton Collection (1880), p. 2, No. 8; Lenox Library, *Works of Shakespeare* (1880), p. 34, No. 192; also p. 39; Winsor, *Bibliography* (1876), p. 101; Hazlitt, *Hand-Book* (1867), p. 547, No. 6 c.

The Earl of Aylesford copy, with ex-libris.

In this edition the title-page is found with and without the portrait. In most cases, as in the copy here described, it is lacking. The Lenox Library copy has two title-pages, both dated 1663, one with and one without the portrait. The verses by Jonson, opposite the title-page, are printed in large type (formerly called double English), and the plays end, as in the First and Second Folios, with *Cymbeline*. This is the only Folio Edition in which all the plays are continuously paged.

As is well known, the Third Folio was originally published in 1663, without the seven additional plays, which were added in 1664, when a new title-page was substituted, upon which is given a list of the new plays (*See* our reproduction No. 617 *b*). Some copies with the 1663 title-page, as in that here described, have also the 1664 title-page and the added plays at the end.

In the play of "The Hiſtory of Sir JOHN OLDCASTLE, *the good* Lord Cobham," two whole scenes have been transposed. This transposition occurs after line 48 of the second column of p. 50,

     " True perfect mirrour of Nobilitie.   *Exit*."

This line should have been followed by scenes 2 and 3 of act v. (of later editions, neither the acts nor scenes being indicated in the Third and Fourth Folios). These scenes actually appear on p. 52, scene 2, column 1, lines 4–49, beginning,

     " *Enter Priest and Doll.*"

and ending,

     " *Doll*. O thou art old Sir *John* when all's done ifaith.'

and scene 3, column 1, line 50, to column 2, line 23, beginning,

     " *Enter the hoſt of the houſe with the Irishman.*"

and ending,

     " *Oſt*. Come Gaffer *Club*, unload, unload, and get to ſupper."

In the Fourth Folio the same transposition occurs on pp. 257–259.

"With regard to the plays which it contains in common with the former Folios," says the Cambridge editor, "it is on the whole a tolerably faithful reprint of the second, correcting, however, some obvious errors, making now and then an uncalled-for alteration, and occasionally modernizing the spelling of a word. The printer of course has committed some errors of his own."

SHAKESPEARE, WILLIAM.

MR. WILLIAM SHAKESPEAR'S COMEDIES, HISTORIES, AND TRAGEDIES. THE THIRD IMPRESSION. LONDON, *for P. C.*, 1664.

[617]

Folio. The Third Folio; 1664 Title-page, with Additional Plays.

COLLATION BY SIGNATURES: Identically the same as in our preceding number, except that leaf ¶ B is wrongly marked ¶ A.

COLLATION BY PAGINATION: [blank], recto of [A];—[portrait, by Martin Droeshout, with 10 lines of verse underneath, the verse as reproduced; *See* No. 617 *a*], verso of [A];—[title, as reproduced; *See* No. 617 *b*], recto of [A 2];—[blank], verso of [A 2];—[the rest identically the same as in our preceding number].

The copy here described has the same errors and variations in the pagination as our preceding number, and in addition the following: p. 109 is wrongly numbered 111; 120 is 119; 478 is numbered on the inner margin; 650 is 649; and 651 is 650.

The errors or variations in the head-lines are the same as in our preceding number.

CONDITION: Size of leaf, 13⁹⁄₁₆ × 9

To the Reader.

This *Figure*, that thou here ſeeſt put,
   It was for gentle *Shakeſpeare* cut;
Wherein the *Graver* had a ſtrife
   With *Nature*, to out-doe the *Life* :
O, could he but have drawn his *Wit*
   As well in *Braſſe*, as he has hit
His *Face* ; the *Print* would then ſurpaſſe
   All, that was ever writ in *Braſſe*.
But ſince he cannot, *Reader*, look
   Not on his *Picture*, but his *Book*.

                    B. J.

No. 617 *a*. VERSE BENEATH THE PORTRAIT IN THE THIRD FOLIO OF SHAKESPEARE; 1664.

Mʀ. WILLIAM SHAKESPEAR'S

Comedies, Histories, and Tragedies.

Published according to the true Original Copies.

The third Impression.

And unto this Impression is added seven Playes, never before Printed in Folio.

viz.

Pericles Prince of *Tyre*.
The *London Prodigall*.
The History of *Thomas* Lᵈ· *Cromwell*.
Sir *John Oldcastle* Lord *Cobham*.
The *Puritan Widow*.
A *York-shire* Tragedy.
The Tragedy of *Locrine*.

LONDON, Printed for P. C. 1664.

inches. Bound in old polished calf, red edges; in brown morocco solander case. The binder has placed the leaf of dedication, A 3 (wrongly marked A 2), after the address to the reader [A 4].

OTHER COPIES.

British Museum (3, one without portrait and verses); Bodleian; Capell Collection; Trinity College, Cambridge; South Kensington Museum; Birmingham Free; Trinity College, Dublin; Devonshire; Huth; Boston Public; John Carter Brown; Lenox; Chew; Hagen; Hoe (4; the Tunno, the Daniels, and two others); Morgan (2, one the Griswold copy); Read; Furness (2); Wrenn and other Libraries; also the Howe and the Way-Van Antwerp copies (untraced). The Boston Public, Daniel-Hoe, and Griswold-Morgan copies have each the leaf of portrait and verses of the Fourth Folio.

REFERENCES.

Hoe, *Catalogue*, 4 (1904) : 115; Greg, *List of English Plays* (Bibliographical Society; 1900), p. 94; British Museum, *Catalogue* (1897), col. 4; Boston Public Library, *Catalogue*; *Barton Collection* (1880), p. 2, No. 9; Huth, *Catalogue*, 4 (1880) : 1331; Lenox Library, *Works of Shakespeare* (1880), pp. 34, 40; Winsor, *Bibliography* (1876), p. 101; Lowndes, 4 (1869) : 2257; Hazlitt, *Hand-Book* (1867), p. 547, No. 6 d.

Not long after the publication of the Third Folio it was reissued with a new title-page, with sixty additional leaves appended, containing seven new plays. The names of these plays appear on the new title-page, occupying the space formerly filled by the portrait on the title-page of 1663. Only one of the seven plays (*Pericles*) is to be found in modern editions, all the others now being considered spurious.

In the new title-page the second line is altered from | SHAKESPEARES | to | SHAKESPEAR'S | ; the fifth line, | *The Third Impreſsion.* |, is reset in larger type of slightly different form, | *The third Impreſſion.* |, and below it, in the space formerly occupied by the portrait, appear ten lines giving a list of the newly added plays and a conventional ornament; and the imprint is changed to read | *LONDON*, Printed for *P. C.* 1664. |. The portrait, crowded out by this list, was printed on a separate leaf with Jonson's verses in smaller type (*See* No. 617 a) to face the title-page.

In some copies the binder inserted the 1664 title-page without tearing out the earlier title and verses. Copies in this state, with both title-pages, are of course most highly prized by collectors.

The Daniel-Hoe, Barton (Boston Public Library), and Griswold-Morgan copies of the Third Folio, with the 1664 title-page, have on the opposite leaf the portrait in its Fourth or last State, i.e., heavily cross-hatched, with Jonson's verses below it printed the same as in our reproduction No. 618 a. The leaf with the portrait and lines thus printed really belongs to the Fourth Folio.

This Folio was reproduced in facsimile by Methuen & Co., of London, in 1905.

The plays added to this Folio, excepting *Pericles*, have together with eight other doubtful ones been published by C. F. Tucker Brooke in *The Shakespeare Apocrypha* (1908). "For two hundred years," says he in his introduction, "there has not appeared a reliable version of *Locrine, Mucedorus, Sir John Oldcastle, Thomas Lord Cromwell, The London Prodigal, The Puritan,* or *A Yorkshire Tragedy* — and that, too, notwithstanding the fact that all these plays, except *Mucedorus*, are included in the third and fourth Shakespeare folios, and that all of them in their garbled form have been many times reprinted."

SHAKESPEARE, WILLIAM.

MR WILLIAM SHAKESPEAR'S COMEDIES, HISTORIES, AND TRAGEDIES.... THE FOURTH EDITION. London, *for H. Herringman, and are to be fold by Jofeph Knight and Francis Saunders,* 1685. [618]

Folio. The Fourth Folio; Knight and Saunders Imprint.

COLLATION BY SIGNATURES: 2 leaves, without signature-marks; A, 4 leaves; A (repeated) to Y, each 6 leaves; Z, 4 leaves; Bb and Cc (wrongly marked B and C), Dd to Zz, *Aaa to *Ddd, each 6 leaves; *Eee, 8 leaves; Aaa to Zzz, Aaaa, Bbbb, each 6 leaves; Cccc, 2 leaves; total 458 leaves.

The following errors or variations occur in the signature-marks: Comedies: leaf D 3 is wrongly marked C 3; and U 3 is U 2. Histories: Bb is B; Bb 2 is B 2; Bb 3 is B 3; Cc is C; Cc 2 is C 2; Cc 3 is C 3; Dd 3 is D 3; and Ee 3 has no signature-mark. Tragedies: *Aaa 3 is *Aa 3; *Eee is Eee; and *Eee 2 is Eee 2.

In some copies there are other errors or variations, as follows: Comedies: leaf I has no signature-mark (Methuen facsimile). Histories: Mm 3 is M 3 (Methuen facsimile); and Oo is Pp.

COLLATION BY PAGINATION: [blank], recto of first leaf;—|[portrait of Shakespeare, retouched]|[10 lines of verse, as reproduced; *See* No. 618 *a*]|, verso of first leaf;—[title, as reproduced; *See* No. 618 *b*], recto of second leaf;—[blank], verso of second leaf;—| To the moft Noble and Incomparable pair of Brethren, | William Earl of Pembroke, &c. | Lord Chamberlain to the Kings moft Excellent Majefty; | AND | Philip E. of Montgomery, &c. | Gentleman to his Majefties Bed-Chamber. Both Knights of the moft Noble | Order of the Garter, and our fingular good LORDS, | [signed] | *Your Lordfhips moft bounden,* | JOHN HEMINGE, | HENRY CONDELL. |, recto and verso of A;—| TO THE | Great Variety | OF | READERS, | [signed] | J. Heminge. | H. Condell. |, recto of [A 2];—[poems in memory of Shakespeare, in double columns, the firft with heading] | To the Memory of the deceafed Author | Mr. WILLIAM SHAKESPEAR. |, verso of [A 2] to recto of [A 3];—| AN | EPITAPH | On the admirable Dramatick Poet, | WILLIAM SHAKESPEAR. |, verso of [A 3];—| *Vpon the Lines and Life of the Famous Scenick Poet* | MR. WILLIAM SHAKESPEAR. | [signed] | *Hugh Holland.* |, verso of [A 3]; —| *The* Works *of* WILLIAM SHAKESPEAR; *containing all his Comedies,* | *Hiftories, and Tragedies; Truly fet forth according to their firft Original.* | The Names of the principal *Actors* in all thefe Plays. | [26 lines, in double columns] | *A Catalogue of all the Comedies, Hiftories, and Tragedies contained in this* Book |, recto of [A 4];—[blank], verso of [A 4].

Comedies:—| THE | TEMPEST. |, pp. 1–17;—| EPILOGUE | fpoken by *Profper.* | [20 lines] | The Scene, an uninhabited Ifland. | Names of the *Actors.* | [20 lines] |, p. 17;—| THE | Two Gentlemen of Verona. |, pp. 18–34;—| *The Names of the Actors.* |, p. 34;—| THE | Merry Wives of Windfor. |, pp. 35–54;—| Meafure for Meafure. |, pp. 55–75;—[names of the actors, in double columns, with heading at the top of the first column] | *The Scæne* Vienna. | *The Names of all the Actors.* |, p. 76;—| THE | Comedy of Errors. |, pp. 76–89;—| Much ado about Nothing. |, pp. 90–110;—| Love's Labour,s loft. |, pp. 110–130;—| A Midfummers nights Dream. |, pp. 130–146;—| THE | Merchant of Venice. |, pp. 146–167;—| As you like it. |, pp. 168–188;—| THE | Taming of the Shrew. |, pp. 188–208;—| All's well that ends well. |, pp. 208–230;—| Twelf-Night, Or what you will. |, pp. 230–249;—| THE | WINTERS TALE. |, pp. 250–272;—| THE | Names of the Actors. |, p. [273];—[blank], p. [274].

Histories:— | THE | LIFE and DEATH | OF | KING JOHN. |, pp. 1–20; — | [type-ornament rule] | THE | LIFE and DEATH | OF | KING RICHARD II. |, pp. 20–40; — | The Firſt Part of | HENRY IV, | with the Life and Death of | HENRY | Sirnamed HOT-SPUR. |, pp. 41–63; — | [type-ornament rule] | The Second Part of | HENRY IV, | CONTAINING HIS DEATH: | And Coronation of King | HENRY V. |, pp. 63–86; — | EPILOGUE. | [17 lines] | The Actors Names. |, p. 87; — | THE | LIFE | OF | KING HENRY V. |, pp. 88 [wrongly numbered 87] to 111; — | The Firſt Part of | KING HENRY VI. |, pp. 112–132; — | The Second Part of | KING HENRY VI, | With the Death of the | Good Duke Humphrey. |, pp. 133–156; — | The third Part of | KING HENRY VI, | With the Death of the | DUKE of YORK. |, pp. 157–179; — | THE | TRAGEDY | OF | RICHARD III: | With the Landing of the | EARL of RICHMOND, | And the Battel at | BOSWORTH FIELD. |, pp. 180–207; — | The Famous | HISTORY | Of the LIFE of | KING HENRY VIII. |, pp. 208–232; — | The EPILOGUE. |, p. 232.

Tragedies:— | THE | TRAGEDY | OF | Troilus and Creſſida. |, pp. 233–257; — | THE | TRAGEDY | OF | CORIOLANUS. |, pp. 258–284; — | The Lamentable | TRAGEDY | OF | Titus Andronicus. |, pp. 285–304; — | THE | TRAGEDY | OF | ROMEO and JULIET. |, pp. 305–328; — | THE | LIFE | OF | TIMON of ATHENS. |, pp. 1–19; — | THE | TRAGEDY | OF | JULIUS CÆSAR. |, pp. 20–39; — | THE | TRAGEDY | OF | MACBETH. |, pp. 40–58; — | THE | TRAGEDY | OF | HAMLET | RPINCE of DENMARK. |, pp. 59–86; — | THE | TRAGEDY | OF | KING LEAR. |, pp. 87–111; — | THE | TRAGEDY | OF | OTHELLO, | THE | MOORE of VENICE. |, pp. 111–137; — | THE | TRAGEDY | OF | ANTHONY and CLEOPATRA. |, pp. 138–164; — | THE | TRAGEDY | OF | CYMBELINE. |, pp. 165–192; — | The much Admired | PLAY, | CALLED | PERICLES, | PRINCE of TYRE. | WITH | The true Relation of the whole HISTORY, | Adventures, and Fortunes of the ſaid | PRINCE. | Written by W. SHAKESPEARE, and publiſhed | in his Life time. |, pp. 193–211; — | THE | LONDON PRODIGAL. |, pp. 212–226; — | THE | HISTORY | OF THE | LIFE and DEATH | OF | THOMAS Lord CROMWELL. |, pp. 227–240; — | THE | HISTORY | OF | Sir John Oldcaſtle, | THE GOOD | LORD COBHAM. |, pp. 241–261; — | THE | PURITAN: | OR, THE | VVidow of Watlingſtreet. |, pp. 262–279; — | A Yorkſhire | TRAGEDY, | Not ſo New, as Lamentable and True. |, pp. 280–285; — | THE | TRAGEDY | OF | LOCRINE, | THE | ELDEST SON | OF | KING BRUTUS. |, pp. 286–303; — | FINIS. |, p. 303; — [blank], p. [304]. Leaf L (pp. 123 and 124 of the Comedies) is printed in long primer, with 91 lines to the full column; the work itself being printed in pica, with 74 lines to the full column.

The following errors or variations occur in the pagination: Comedies: p. 33 is wrongly numbered 23; 97 and 98 are omitted; 107 is 109; 109 is 111; 114 is 411; 161 and 162 are omitted; 190 is 186; 191 is 187; 219 is 221; 246 is 234; 255 is 243; 254 and 255 are repeated; and 273 has no page-number. Histories: p. 88 is 87; and 93 is 92. Tragedies: p. 67 is 76.

In some copies there are other errors or variations, as follows: Comedies: p. 96 is 98 (Irwin-Morgan copy); 164 is 160; and 169 is 171. Histories: pp. 88 and 93 are correctly numbered; p. 225 is 224; and 228 is 222.

The following errors or variations occur in the head-lines: Comedies: p. 19 has | *The Tempeſt.* |, instead of | *The Two Gentlemen of* Verona. |; p. 152, | *The Marchant of Venice.* |, instead of | *The Merchant of Venice.* |; and pp. 190 and 191 (wrongly numbered 186 and 187), | *The Taming of a Shrew.* |, instead of | *The Taming of the Shrew.* |. Histories: pp. 114 and 115 have | *The Life of King* Henry *the Sixth.* |, instead of | *The firſt Part of King* Henry the Sixth. | . Tragedies : pp. 134 and 135 have | *The Tragedy of* | *the Moore of* Venice. | , instead of | *The Tragedy of* Othello, | *the Moore of* Venice. | ; and p. 167, | *The Tradgedy of* Cymbeline. | , instead of | *The Tragedy of* Cymbeline. | .

CONDITION : Size of leaf, 14⅛ × 9⅛ inches. Bound in brown calf, diced sides, antique back, marbled edges ; in the style of the end of the eighteenth century.

OTHER COPIES.

Boston Public ; Lenox ; and Hoe Libraries ; and Library of Congress.

REFERENCES.

Hoe, *Catalogue*, 4 (1904) : 121; Lenox Library, *Works of Shakespeare* (1880), p. 35; Winsor, *Bibliography of the Original Quartos and Folios* (1876), p. 106.

The title-page of this edition was printed from two distinct settings of type. The earlier seems to be the one in which the first line begins " M^R " not " M$^{R.}$ ". It has just above the imprint a type-ornament vignette composed of nine pieces instead of a conventional ornament in the centre of which is a fleur-de-lis. Copies of this earlier title-page bear the imprint of " *Joſeph Knight* and *Francis Saunders* " (*See* our reproduction No. 618 *b*). Copies of the later title-page bear two imprints, one containing the name of " *R. Chiſwell* " (*See* our reproduction No. 619), and the other the more usual " *Herringman* " imprint (*See* our reproduction No. 620).

The text is divided into three parts, with separate signature-marks and pagination for each. An examination of the letterpress shows that a copy of the Third Folio was apparently broken into three portions and sent to three different printers. The first printer received the Comedies, pp. 1–304, the latter being blank ; the second, pp. 305–664, the Histories and four of the Tragedies ; and the third, pp. 667 to the end, the eight remaining Tragedies. The fonts of type used by these printers differ somewhat, the large initial letters used at the beginnings of the plays and in the headings of the different acts and scenes being especially noticeable. One leaf, " L, " Comedies, pp. 122, 123, is printed in much smaller type, showing apparently that some lines had been omitted and that these pages were reset in smaller type to include the omitted matter.

Two copies in the Lenox Library have variations which we have seen in no others. In the Astor-Lenox Library copy are several leaves printed without single-rule borders at sides and bottoms, from a different setting of type from those usually found. In the Lenox copy (Knight imprint) is a similar sheet, leaves Oo 3 and [Oo 4]. In every instance these leaves comprise an entire sheet of a gathering. These leaves are also to be distinguished by the following variant readings :

Leaf Ii 3, p. 89, has the catchword | Was | , instead of | VVas | ; p. 90, the catchword | No | , instead of | Not | ; leaf [Ii 4], p. 91, col. 1, line 4, reads | . . . *Dolphin* : . . . | , instead of | . . . *Dolphin* : . . . | ; and p. 92, col. 1, line 1, | . . . may : men . . . | , instead of | . . . may : men . . . | .

Leaf Nn 2, p. 135, col. 2, line 10, reads | . . . Queen . . . | , instead of | . . . Qneen . . . | ; p. 136, col. 1, line 23, | . . . VVho is there ? | , instead of | . . . Who is there ? | ; leaf [Nn 5], p. 141, col. 1, line 30, | *Salis.* Peter ? what mor | , instead of | *Salis.* Peter ? what more ? | ; and p. 142, col. 1, line 1, | *Elian.* VVhat, . . . | , instead of | *Elian.* What, . . . | .

To the Reader:

This *Figure* that thou here feeſt put,
It was for gentle *Shakeſpear* cut ;
Wherein the *Graver* had a ſtrife
With Nature to outdo the Life.
O, could he but have drawn his **W**it
As well in Braſs, as he has hit
His Face ; the Print would then ſurpaſs
All that was ever writ in *Braſs*.
But ſince he cannot, **R**eader, look
Not on his Picture, but his *Book*.

B. J.

No. 618 *a*. Verse beneath the Portrait in the Fourth Folio of Shakespeare ; 1685.

Leaf Oo 3, p. 149, col. 1, lines 41 and 42 read | . . . ſign of a | brave Mind, . . . |, instead of | . . . ſign of | a brave Mind, . . . | ; p. 150, col. 1, lines 52 and 53, | . . . be a good Counſel- | lor, or no ? |, instead of | . . . be a good Councellor, | or no ? | ; leaf [Oo 4], p. 151, col. 1, line 9, | To ſpoyl the City . . . |, instead of | . . . to ſpoyle the City . . . | ; and p. 152, head-line | . . . Second part . . . |, instead of | . . . ſecond Part . . . |.

Leaf Tt 3, p. 209, the catchword is under "Paſſion" in the last line but one, instead of being under "Sir" in the last line ; p. 210, col. 1, lines 53 and 54, read | . . . *and two | or three* . . . |, instead of | . . . *and two or | three* . . . | ; leaf [Tt 4], p. 211, col. 1, line 1, | . . . Taxation ? . . . |, instead of | . . . Taxation ? . . . | ; and p. 212, col. 1, line 1, | . . . the Duke ſhall proſper, . . . |, instead of | . . . the Duke *)* ſhall proſper, . . . |.

Leaf Yy, p. 241, col. 2, line 38, reads | . . . Amen *:* What ho ? |, instead of | . . . Amen : VVhat | ; p. 242, col. 2, line 43, | . . . Air with us. |, instead of | . . . Ayr with us ? | ; leaf [Yy 6], p. 251, col. 2, line 19, | To tender objects ; . . . |,

Mr William Shakespear's
COMEDIES,
HISTORIES,
AND
TRAGEDIES.

Published according to the true Original Copies.

Unto which is added, SEVEN

PLAYS,

Never before Printed in Folio:

VIZ.

Pericles Prince of *Tyre*.
The *London* Prodigal.
The History of *Thomas* Lord Cromwel.

Sir *John* Oldcastle Lord *Cobham*,
The *Puritan* Widow.
A *Yorkshire* Tragedy.
The Tragedy of *Locrine*.

The Fourth Edition.

LONDON,

Printed for *H. Herringman*, and are to be sold by *Joseph Knight* and *Francis Saunders*, at the *Anchor* in the Lower Walk of the *New* Exchange. 1685.

instead of | To tender Objects; . . . | ; and p. 252, col. 1, line 30, | . . . of *Greekiſh* Youth ; . . . | , instead of | . . . of Greekiſh youth ; . . . | .

Leaf *Ccc 2, p. 291, the catchword reads | *Aaron.* Now | , instead of | *Aar.* Now | ; p. 292, col. 1, line 22, | . . . know 'tis he ? | , instead of | . . . know 'tis he ? | ; leaf [*Ccc 5], p. 297, col. 2, line 1, | . . . in thine Arms ? | , instead of | . . . in thine Arms ? | ; and p. 298, col. 1, line 48, | . . . on berries, . . . | , instead of | . . . on Berries, . . . | .

Leaf *Eee 3, p. 317, col. 2, line 12, reads | . . . and *Romeo* Baniſhed, | , instead of | . . . and *Romeo* baniſhed, | ; p. 318, col. 1, line 6, | . . . for *Romeo* is exil'd : | , instead of | . . . for *Romeo* is Exil'd : | ; leaf [*Eee 6], p. 323, col. 1, line 20, | What if it be a Poiſon, . . . | , instead of | What if it be a Poyſon, . . . | ; and p. 324, col. 2, line 42, | . . . with chearful thoughts. | , instead of | . . . with chearful Thoughts. | .

On p. 156 of the Histories the catchword | THE | is followed by a single rule in the Hoe (Knight imprint) copy and in the Lenox copy "A," and by two rules in each of the copies here described and in both of the Morgan copies.

The Fourth Folio was printed from the Third, but with a different pagination. "The spelling," says the Cambridge editor, "is very much modernized, but we have not been able to detect any other evidence of editorial care."

This edition was reproduced in facsimile by Methuen & Co., of London, in 1904.

SHAKESPEARE, WILLIAM.

MR. WILLIAM SHAKESPEAR'S COMEDIES, HISTORIES, AND TRAGEDIES. THE FOURTH EDITION. LONDON, *for H. Herringman, E. Brewſter, R. Chiſwell, and R. Bentley,* 1685. [619]

Folio. The Fourth Folio ; Chiswell Imprint.

COLLATION BY SIGNATURES: Identically the same as in our preceding number, except that in the Comedies leaf D 3 is correctly marked, and in the Histories Oo is Pp.

COLLATION BY PAGINATION: Identically the same as in our preceding number, except the title-page (as reproduced ; *See* No. 619).

The copy here described has the same errors or variations in the pagination as in our preceding number, except that in the Comedies p. 114 is correctly numbered, and in the Histories p. 225 is wrongly numbered 224, and 228 is 222.

The errors or variations in the head-lines are the same as in our preceding number.

CONDITION : Size of leaf, 14 x 9 inches. Bound in red crushed levant morocco, gilt edges ; by Bedford ; in brown morocco solander case. Pages 241–242 and 251–252 (*Troilus and Creſſida*) have been supplied from a narrower copy. The binder has wrongly placed leaf [A 4] between A and [A 2].

OTHER COPIES.

Hoe ; and White Libraries.

In a very exhaustive review upon the orthography of Shakespeare's name in the Lenox Library *Shakeſpeare* it is shown that 42 favor the form "Shakespear," 33 "Shakspere," 111 "Shakspeare," and 282 "Shakespeare," the latter being the form generally used in the Folios and early quartos.

Mr. William Shakespear's
COMEDIES,
HISTORIES,
AND
TRAGEDIES.

Published according to the true Original Copies.

Unto which is added, SEVEN

PLAYS,

Never before Printed in Folio:

VIZ.

Pericles Prince of *Tyre*.
The *London Prodigal*.
The History of *Thomas* Lord *Cromwel*.
} Sir *John Oldcastle* Lord *Cobham*.
The *Puritan Widow*.
A *Yorkshire* Tragedy.
The Tragedy of *Locrine*.

The Fourth Edition.

LONDON,

Printed for *H. Herringman, E. Brewster, R. Chiswell*, and *R. Bentley*, at the *Anchor* in the *New Exchange*; and at the *Crane*, and *Rose* and *Crown* in St. *Pauls* Church-Yard, and in *Russel*-Street *Covent-Garden*. 1 6 8 5.

SHAKESPEARE, WILLIAM.

MR. WILLIAM SHAKESPEAR'S COMEDIES, HISTORIES, AND TRAGEDIES. THE FOURTH EDITION. London, *for H. Herringman, E. Brewſter, and R. Bentley*, 1685.   [620]

Folio. The Fourth Folio; the usual or Herringman Imprint.

COLLATION BY SIGNATURES: Identically the same as in our No. 618, except that in the Histories leaf Oo is wrongly marked Pp.

COLLATION BY PAGINATION: Identically the same as in our No. 618, except the imprint of the title-page (as reproduced; *See* No. 620).

The copy here described has the same errors or variations in the pagination as in our No. 618, except that in the Comedies p. 114 is correctly numbered, and in the Histories 225 is 224.

The errors or variations in the headlines of the copy here described are the same as in our No. 618.

CONDITION: Size of leaf, 14 9/16 × 9 inches. Bound in maroon crushed levant morocco, gilt edges; by Bradstreet; in brown morocco solander case. The binder has wrongly placed leaf [A 4] between A and [A 2].

OTHER COPIES.

British Museum (4, one without title-page); Bodleian; Capell; Trinity College, Cambridge (3, one without portrait); Birmingham Free; Trinity College, Dublin; Devonshire; Ellesmere; Huth; John Carter Brown; Lenox (2, one the Astor copy); Chew; Hagen; Halsey; Morgan (2); Read; Princeton University; Furness (2); Wrenn; and other Libraries; also the Howe and the Van Antwerp copies (untraced).

REFERENCES.

Hoe, *Catalogue*, 4 (1904): 119; Greg, *List of English Plays* (Bibliographical Society; 1900), p. 95; British Museum, *Catalogue*; *Shakespeare* (1897), col. 6; Boston Public Library, *Catalogue*; *Barton Collection* (1880), p. 2, No. 10 (Knight and Saunders imprint); Lenox Library, *Works of Shakespeare* (1880), pp. 35, 40; Winsor, *Bibliography* (1876), p. 106; Lowndes, 4 (1869): 2258; Hazlitt, *Hand-Book* (1867), p. 547, No. 6 *e*.

The information regarding differences in signature-marks, pagination, and head-lines in the foregoing numbers (610–620) is based upon our examination *de visu* of twelve First Folios, twenty-one Second Folios, twelve Third Folios, and twelve Fourth Folios; including, in addition to those here described, the copies in the Lenox Library, those in the Hoe and the Morgan collections, and the facsimile reprints.

LONDON,

Printed for *H. Herringman, E. Brewſter*, and *R. Bentley*, at the *Anchor* in the *New Exchange*, the *Crane* in St. *Pauls* Church-Yard, and in *Ruſſel*-Street *Covent-Garden.* 1 6 8 5.

No. 620.   USUAL IMPRINT OF THE FOURTH FOLIO OF SHAKESPEARE; 1685.
Reduced; original 1 9/16 × 6 3/8 inches.

SUPPOSITITIOUS OR SPURIOUS WORKS.

The earliest and only prose work which has been ascribed to Shakespeare is *A Compendious or briefe examination of certayne ordinary complaints, of diuers of our country men in thefe our dayes: . . . By W. S. [i.e., W. Stafford], Gentleman",* published "at London, . . . by Thomas Marfhe," in 1581. Of this Edition there are copies in the Bodleian (6, one imperfect), Boston Public (2), and Hoe Libraries.

This work was reprinted in 1751, with a preface in which an attempt was made to show that it was written by "Wm. Shakespeare, Gent." "The reference by Stafford [the real author of this treatise on political economy] in his dedication to queen Elizabeth to her 'clemency, in pardoninge certayne my vndutifull misdemeanour,' he having been engaged in a conspiracy against her, has led the editors of this [the 1751] edition to ascribe the work to Shakespeare, on the ground that his deer-stealing was the misdemeanor referred to." Of this later edition there are copies in the British Museum (2) and Boston Public Libraries.

Certain plays in which it was thought Shakespeare's hand could be traced, as well as others to which the publishers had attached his name evidently with a view to increasing their sales, were, from time to time, ascribed to that dramatist. In 1664 seven of these plays were appended to the Folio edition of that year (our No. 617). Of these but one, *Pericles,* is now included in the collected editions of his plays. The following list of these Supposititious Plays is arranged in the order in which they were originally published.

(1) Of *The Araygnement of Paris,* first published in 1584, "by Henrie Marfh," there are copies in the British Museum, Capell Collection, and Duke of Devonshire's Library. This play is now generally ascribed to George Peele. "The ascription," says Greg (*List of English Plays; Appendix II.,* p. li.), "rests on the authority of Nash's preface to Greene's *Menaphon.*"

(2) Of *The Lamentable and True Tragedie of M. Arden of Feuerfham in Kent,* editions were published in 1592, 1599, and 1633. There is a copy of the last edition in the present collection, described below.

(3) Of *The Lamentable Tragedie of Locrine* but a single edition in quarto was published, that of 1595 (our No. 622).

(4) Of *The Raigne of King Edvvard the third,* editions were published in 1596 and 1599, a copy of the First Edition (1596) being in the present collection (our No. 623).

(5) *A Moft pleafant Comedie of Mucedorus* first appeared in 1598, and seems to have been the most popular play of its day, having passed through no fewer than seventeen editions, the Fourth of which (1611) is in the present collection (our No. 624).

(6) *The firft part Of the true and honorable hiftorie of the life of Sir John Oldcaftle, the good Lord Cobham,* one of the seven plays added to the Folio of 1664, first appeared in two quarto editions in 1600, the Second of which is in the present collection (our No. 625).

(7) *The True Chronicle Hiſtorie of the whole life and death of Thomas Lord Cromwell* was one of the seven plays added to the Third Folio in 1664. The First Quarto Edition of this play appeared in 1602. Of the Second and last edition, which appeared in 1613, there is a copy in the present collection (our No. 626).

(8) *The London Prodigall* was also one of the seven plays added to the Folio of 1664. But one edition of this play was published in quarto, that of 1605, a copy of which is in the present collection (our No. 627).

(9) *The Puritaine Or The VViddow of Watling-ſtreete*, also one of the plays added to the Third Folio in 1664, was published only once in quarto, in 1607. There is a copy in the present collection (our No. 628).

(10) *The Merry Devill of Edmonton* appeared in several editions, the First in 1608. There are copies of the Third (1617) and Fifth (1631) editions in the present collection (our Nos. 629 and 630).

(11) *A Yorkſhire Tragedy* was one of the seven plays added to the Folio edition of 1664. But two editions of this play were published in quarto, the First in 1608, the Second in 1619, both of which are in the present collection (our Nos. 631 and 632).

(12) *A Pleaſant Commodie, of faire Em the Millers daughter of Mancheſter* appeared in two editions in quarto, the earlier without date. Of the Second Edition (1631) there is a copy in the present collection (our No. 633).

(13) *The Two Noble Kinſmen*, now generally ascribed to Beaumont and Fletcher, first appeared in the quarto edition of 1634. There is a copy in the present collection (our No. 634).

(14) *The Birth of Merlin: or, The Childe hath found his Father*, was printed for the first time in the quarto edition of 1662. The title-page says, "Written by William Shakeſpear, and William Rowley," but there is no reason to suppose that Shakespeare had any hand in it. There are copies of this edition in the British Museum (2), Bodleian, Capell Collection, Dyce Collection (2), Devonshire, Ellesmere, Boston Public, Lenox, and Hoe Libraries.

Even during the eighteenth and nineteenth centuries several plays appeared also falsely attributed to Shakespeare: *Double Falſehood* (1728); *George a Greene* (1744); *Vortigern*, Ireland's forgery (1799); and *Fifth of November* (1830). Copies of each of these plays are in the Boston Public Library. C. F. Tucker Brooke, in his recently published *Shakespeare Apocrypha* (1908), which may well be consulted, gives a list of forty-two different plays (pp. ix.–xi.), roughly arranged according to date of attribution. He has also appended to the text of the plays a very full bibliography (pp. 438–456) of this interesting branch of Shakespeariana.

The Shakespeare Apocrypha designedly omits *Pericles* and *Titus Andronicus* "because they have established their position in practice, if not in universal opinion, among the genuine works;" but it includes Nos. 2–14 of the above list and the recently discovered *Sir Thomas More*.

"The exact likelihood of Shakespeare's connexion with any member of this various group must be determined by careful individual examination. . . .

"There can, indeed, be no stronger vindication of the honesty and intelligence of the editors of the first Shakespeare Folio, Hemings and Condell, than careful study of the works which they excluded. As all attempts to deprive the poet of a large interest in any of the thirty-six plays published by them have so far failed, so it seems in the highest degree improbable that their list will ever be augmented by more than the genuine act or two of *Pericles* and a few broken fragments which Shakespeare would doubtless have been the last of all men to include among his works."

[SHAKESPEARE, WILLIAM.] Suppositious Play.

ARDEN OF FEVERSHAM. LONDON, *by Eliz. Allde*, 1633. [621]

Small quarto. Third Edition.

COLLATION BY SIGNATURES: A to I, each 4 leaves; total 36 unnumbered leaves. Leaf I is marked *I*.

COLLATION BY PAGINATION: [title, as reproduced; *See* No. 621], recto of [A];— [woodcut], verso of [A];—[text, with heading] | [type-ornament head-piece] | The Tragedie of Mafter *eArden* | of Feverfham. |, recto of A 2 to verso of [I 4];— | FINIS. |, verso of [I 4].

CONDITION: Size of leaf, 6¾ × 4⅞ inches. Bound in red crushed levant morocco, gilt edges; by Leighton.

OTHER COPIES.

British Museum (2); Bodleian; Edinburgh University; Dyce Collection (2); Devonshire; Ellesmere; Huth; Hoe; and White Libraries.

REFERENCES.

Brooke, *Shakespeare Apocrypha* (1908), p. 440; Hoe, *Catalogue*, 1 (1903) : 9; Greg, *List of English Plays* (Bibliographical Society; 1900), p. 124; British Museum, *Catalogue* (under *Arden,* Thomas); Hazlitt, *Manual of Old English Plays* (1892), p. 17; same, *Collections and Notes on Early English Literature; 1474–1700* (1887), p. 132; Locker-Lampson, *Catalogue* (1886), p. 112; Lowndes, 4 (1869) : 2302; Hazlitt, *Hand-Book to the Popular, Poetical, and Dramatic Literature of Great Britain* (1867), p. 466, No. 31 *c*.

The Roxburghe-Jolley-Locker Lampson copy, with the ex-libris of the two latter, and with the arms of the Duke of Roxburghe stamped on the title-page.

Editions of this play, published anonymously, and at one time often attributed to Shakespeare, were issued in quarto in 1592, 1599, and 1633.

Of the First Edition (1592), "for Edward White," there are copies in the Bodleian Library and Dyce Collection, the latter imperfect at the end.

Of the Second Edition (1599), by "I. Roberts for Edward White," there are copies in the Duke of Devonshire's and the Earl of Ellesmere's libraries.

The Third Edition (1633) is that here described.

"The plan of this play is formed on a true history, then pretty recent, of one Arden, a gentleman of Faversham, in the reign of Edward VI., who was murdered as he was playing a game at tables with the said Mosbie. The fact is related by Holinshed and Baker, in Beard's *Theatre,* and in Jacob's *History of Faversham.* 'They have the play in manuscript at Canterbury, but I never cou'd see it in print.' — *Oldys.* In 1866, at any rate, the room in which this murder was committed was shown at Faversham, as well as the spot, or at least the lane, where Black Will at first tried to waylay Arden."

THE
LAMENTABLE
AND TRVE TRAGEDY
OF MASTER ARDEN OF FEVERSHAM IN KENT:

VVho was moſt wickedly murdered by the meanes of his diſloyall and wanton wife, who, for the love ſhe bare to one *Mosby*, hired two deſperate Ruffins, *Blacke-Will*, and *Shakebag*, to kill him.

Wherein is ſhewed the great malice and diſſimulation of a wicked woman, the unſatiable deſire of filthy luſt, and the ſhamefull end of all murderers.

LONDON,
Printed by Eliz. Allde dwelling neere Chriſts-Church. 1633.

No. 621. Title-page of Arden of Feversham; 3d Edition; 1633.

No. 622   *William Shakespeare*   1595

[SHAKESPEARE, WILLIAM.] Suppositious Play.

LOCRINE. London, *Printed by Thomas Creede,* 1595.   [622]

Small quarto. Sole Edition.

COLLATION BY SIGNATURES: A, 4 leaves (the first blank and lacking); B to K, each 4 leaves; total 40 unnumbered leaves.

COLLATION BY PAGINATION: [1 blank leaf], [A]; —[title, as reproduced; *See* No. 622], recto of [A 2]; —[blank], verso of [A 2]; —[text, with heading] | [conventional head-piece] | The lamentable Tragedie | of *Locrine,* the eldeſt ſonne of King *Brutus,* diſcour- | ſing the warres of the *Britaines* and *Hunnes,* | *with their diſcomfiture, the* Britaines *victory* | with their accidents, and the death | of *Albanact.* |, recto of A 3 to verso of [K 4]; — | FINIS. |, verso of [K 4].

CONDITION: Size of leaf, 6⅞ × 5 inches. Bound in green morocco, gilt, some leaves red, edges, with George Daniel's monogram on the front cover.

OTHER COPIES.

British Museum (3); Bodleian; Capell Collection; Birmingham Free; Devonshire; Ellesmere; and Morgan Libraries; also the Howe copy (untraced).

REFERENCES.

Brooke, *Shakespeare Apocrypha* (1908), p. 442; Greg, *List of English Plays* (Bibliographical Society; 1900), p. 102; British Museum, *Catalogue;* *Shakespeare* (1897), col. 179; Hazlitt, *Manual of Old English Plays* (1892), p. 131; Locker-Lampson, *Catalogue* (1886), p. 112; Hazlitt, *Hand-Book* (1867), p. 621.

The Daniel-Tite-Locker Lampson copy, with ex-libris of the last.

On the recto of the second fly-leaf is a memorandum: "*Some suppose this was written by Marlowe.* [signed] *F. L.*"

This is one of the seven pseudo-Shakespeare plays added to the Folio of 1664.

This play, but one edition of which was published in quarto, in 1595, has been incorrectly attributed to Shakespeare. The initials "*VV. S.*" on the title-page probably stand for Wentworth Smith; but the author is supposed to be Charles Tylney.

"There is no further pretence," says Hazlitt, "for assigning this drama to Shakespeare. On the title-page of an existing copy, it is expressly given to Charles Tylney by Sir George Buck, Master of the Revels, whose information was on more than one account peculiarly likely to be correct."

[SHAKESPEARE, WILLIAM.] Suppositious Play.

EDWARD THE THIRD. London, *for Cuthbert Burby,* 1596.   [623]

Small quarto. First Edition.

COLLATION BY SIGNATURES: [A], 4 leaves (the first blank and lacking); B to I, each 4 leaves; K, 2 leaves; total 38 unnumbered leaves. As a rule the letter of the signature-mark is omitted on the second and third leaves of each sheet, C 3 being the only exception.

COLLATION BY PAGINATION: [1 blank leaf], [A]; —[title, as reproduced; *See* No. 623], recto of [A 2]; —[blank], verso of [A 2]; —[text, with heading] | THE

1595   *William Shakespeare*   No. 622

THE

Lamentable Tragedie of

Locrine, the eldeſt ſonne of King *Brutus*, diſcour-
ſing the warres of the *Britaines*, and *Hunnes*,
with their diſcomfiture:

The Britaines *victorie with their Accidents, and the
death of* Albanact. *No leſſe pleaſant then
profitable.*

Newly ſet foorth, ouerſeene and corrected,
By *VV. S.*

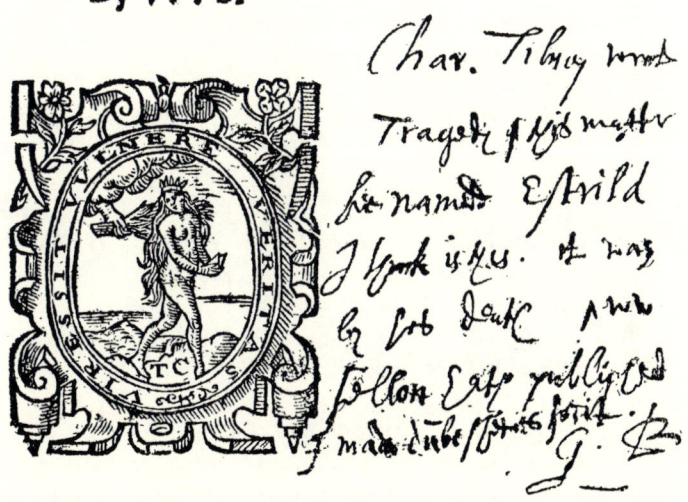

LONDON
Printed by Thomas Creede.
1 5 9 5.

No. 622. Title-page of Locrine; Sole Edition; 1595.

RAIGNE OF | K: Edward the third. |, recto of [A]3 to verso of [K 2]; — | FINIS. |, verso of [K 2].

Condition: Size of leaf, 6%₁₀ × 4%₁₀ inches. Bound in red crushed levant morocco, gilt top and fore edges; by Bedford. A short copy; the upper margins extended, and parts of letters supplied in facsimile, on

Church Catalogue   [921]   English Literature

No. 623   *William Shakespeare*   1596

leaves [B]3, [E]3, [F]3, G, [G]3, and [I 4]; K and [K 2] are in facsimile; and the signature-marks are cut off from sheets H and I, except [H]3.

OTHER COPIES.

British Museum; Bodleian (imperfect); Capell Collection; and Devonshire Libraries.

REFERENCES.

Brooke, *Shakespeare Apocrypha* (1908), p. 441; Greg, *List of English Plays* (Bibliographical Society; 1900), p. 127; British Museum, *Catalogue*; *Shakespeare* (1897), col. 179; Hazlitt, *Manual of Old English Plays* (1892), p. 71; Locker-Lampson, *Catalogue* (1886), p. 113; Hazlitt, *Hand-Book* (1867), p. 176.

The Locker-Lampson copy, with ex-libris.

Laid into this copy is an autograph letter of Tennyson's, written from "Farringford, Freshwater, Isle of Wight," and dated "*6 December 1875.*"

"*My dear Furnivall. I have not reconsidered the subject since you wrote last, but my first impreſsion remains. In spite of Delius calling it a clever imitation I cannot but think that no small dramatist c.^d have done Shakespeare so well, & no great Dramatist w^d have done it, but w.^d have followd his own line. If not Shakespeare in the best parts of the Play — who? Let Delius or another tell.* [signed] *Yours always, Alfred Tennyson.*"

Another letter laid in, "*From* F. J. FURNIVALL, 3, *St. George's Square, Primrose Hill, London, N. W.,*" dated December 7, 1875, reads as follows:

"*Dear Mr Locker. I wish you'd have a good turn at* Edw. III. *& give me your opinion on it. If you've the 1st ed.^{n}, I shall ask you to lend it me some day, to reprint. These Shakspere plays & questions interest me tremendously now. Having only taken up Sh. lately, after years & years of our dull E. E. men, he does 'stain' 'em all with a vengeance. Dear old Chaucer seems to fade, evergreen as he is.* [signed] *Since^y yrs, F. J. F.*"

Another slip: "*The raigne of King Edward the 3rd. Edward Capell thought W. S. had a hand in this. It seems to me to be more in the manner of Marlow, but a feeble composition, compared with either Marvell* [sic] *or Shakespeare.*"

Pasted to the recto of the second fly-leaf is the following note: "*Swinburne says that the Yorkshire Tragedy is a coarse crude & vigorous impromptu in wch. we possibly might think W. S. had a hand, or rather finger, if we had a reason to suppose that during the last 10 or 12 years of his life he was likely to have taken part in any such dramatic improvisation. Schlegel classed it among W. S.'s best & maturest works.*"

On the recto of the third fly-leaf, in pencil: "*This play settles the date of 94 Sonnet.*"

Editions of this play were published in 1596 and 1599.

The First Edition (1596) is that here described.

Of the Second Edition (1599), "by Simon Stafford for Cuthbert Burby," there

1596   *William Shakespeare*   No. 623

THE
RAIGNE OF
KING EDVVARD
the third:

As it hath bin sundrie times plaied about the Citie of London.

LONDON,
Printed for Cuthbert Burby.
1 5 9 6.

No. 623. Title-page of Edward the Third; 1st Edition; 1596.

are copies in the British Museum, Bodleian, Capell Collection, Dyce Collection, Ellesmere, and White Libraries.

   This is a good play, and was once thought to have been written by Shakespeare. The Second Edition is said to differ considerably from the First. It was reprinted by Capell in his *Prolusions*, 1760.

No. 624 *William Shakespeare* 1611

[SHAKESPEARE, WILLIAM.] Suppositious Play.

MUCEDORUS. LONDON, *for William Iones*, 1611. [624]

Small quarto. Fourth Edition.

COLLATION BY SIGNATURES: A to F, each 4 leaves (the last, probably blank, lacking); total 24 unnumbered leaves. Leaf A 2 is marked A ii.

COLLATION BY PAGINATION: [title, as reproduced; *See* No. 624], recto of [A]; — [blank], verso of [A]; — | [conventional head-piece] | The Prologue. |, recto of A ii.; — | [conventional head-piece] | Ten perfons may | eafily play it. |, verso of A ii.; — [text, with heading] | [conventional head-piece] | A moft pleafant Comedie of | *Mucedorus* the Kinges Sonne of *Valencia*, and | *Amadine* the Kings Daughter of *Aragon*. |, recto of A 3 to verso of F 3; — | FINIS. | [conventional tail-piece] |, verso of F 3; — [1 leaf, probably blank], [F 4].

CONDITION: Size of leaf, 6 13/16 × 4 13/16 inches. Bound in red crushed levant morocco, gilt edges; by Rivière. The lower outer corner of leaf C is extended, with a few words in facsimile.

OTHER COPIES.

The Bodleian Library.

REFERENCES.

Brooke, *Shakespeare Apocrypha* (1908), p. 444; British Museum, *Catalogue* (under *Mucedorus*); Greg, *List of English Plays* (Bibliographical Society; 1900), p. 128; Hazlitt, *Manual of Old English Plays* (1892), p. 161; same, *Collections and Notes* (1876), p. 297.

The Locker-Lampson copy, with ex-libris.

This seems to have been one of the most popular of the plays attributed to Shakespeare. Editions appeared in 1598, 1606, 1610, 1611, 1613, 1615, 1618, 1619, 1621, 1626, [1629?], 1631, 1634, 1639, 1663, 1668, and one edition without date [1640–50?].

Of the First Edition (1598), "for William Iones," there are copies in the British Museum (the Garrick copy) and Devonshire Libraries.

Of the Second Edition (1606), "for William Iones," there is a copy in the Dyce Collection.

Of the Third Edition (1610), amplified with new additions, imprinted at London "for William Iones," there are copies in the British Museum and Capell Collection.

The Fourth Edition (1611) is that here described.

Of the Fifth Edition (1613), "for William Iones," there are copies in the British Museum and Boston Public Libraries.

Of the Sixth Edition (1615), by "N. O. for William Jones," there is a copy in the British Museum.

Of the Seventh Edition (1618), "for Iohn Wright," there is a copy in the Huth Library.

Of the Eighth Edition (1619), "for Iohn Wright," there are copies in the British Museum, Bodleian, Devonshire, and Boston Public Libraries.

Of the Ninth Edition (1621), "for Iohn Wright," Greg (*List of English Plays; Addenda & Corrigenda*, p. cxxx.) locates a copy in the Municipal Library at Danzig.

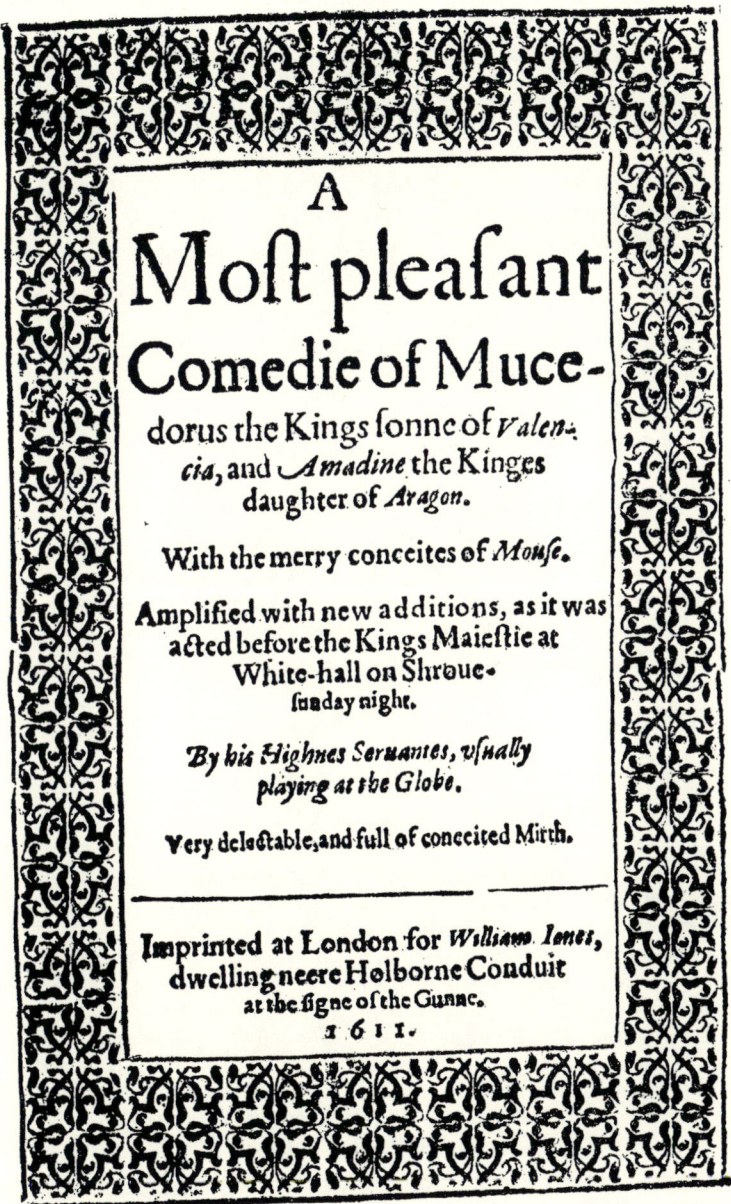

No. 624. Title-page of Mucedorus; 4th Edition; 1611.

No. 624 *William Shakespeare* 1611

Of the Tenth Edition (1626), "for Iohn Wright," there is a copy in the Dyce Collection.

Of an edition, probably the Eleventh [1629?], lacking the title-page, the only copy known is in the Capell Collection. Mr. Greg gives the probable date of this edition as 1629. It is doubtless the same as that recorded, without location, by Hazlitt (*Hand-Book*, p. 468, No. 40).

Of the Twelfth Edition (1631), "for Iohn Wright," there is a copy in the British Museum.

Of the Thirteenth Edition (1634), "for Iohn Wright," the Roxburghe copy is in the British Museum.

Of the Fourteenth Edition (1639), "for John Wright," there are copies in the Capell Collection, Boston Public, and Morgan (Griswold copy) Libraries.

Of an undated edition, probably the Fifteenth [1640–50?], "for Francis Coles," there are copies in the British Museum and Capell Collection.

Of the Sixteenth Edition (1663), "for Francis Coles," there are copies in the Bodleian and Boston Public Libraries.

Of the Seventeenth Edition (1668), "printed by E. O. for Francis Coles," there are copies in the British Museum (2, one imperfect), Bodleian, Capell Collection, Boston Public, and Lenox Libraries.

"Collier thought that one passage in this piece, 44 lines, was from the pen of Shakespear. *The Wandering Prince and Princess; or, Mucedorus and Amadine*, is a ballad founded on it. See Rowe's *Tragi-Comœdia*, 1653, for an account of a catastrophe, which occurred at Witney in Oxfordshire, while some rustics were performing *Mucedorus*, or rather probably a scene from it."

[SHAKESPEARE, WILLIAM.] Supposititious Play.

SIR JOHN OLDCASTLE. LONDON, *for T. P.*, 1600. [625]

Small quarto. Second Edition.

COLLATION BY SIGNATURES: A to K, each 4 leaves; total 40 unnumbered leaves.

COLLATION BY PAGINATION: [title, as reproduced; *See* No. 625], recto of [A]; —[blank], verso of [A]; —|[conventional head-piece]| The Prologue.|, recto of A 2; —[blank], verso of A 2; —[text, with heading] | [type-ornament head-piece] | The true and honorable Hiſtorie, of | *the life of Sir Iohn Old-Caſtle, the* | good Lord Cobham.|, recto of A 3 to recto of [K 4]; —| FINIS.|, recto of [K 4]; —[blank], verso of [K 4].

CONDITION: Size of leaf, 7 x 5⁵⁄₁₆ inches. Bound in red morocco, with Almon W. Griswold's coat of arms on the front cover, gilt edges; by Bedford.

OTHER COPIES.

British Museum (2); Bodleian (Malone copy, 222); Capell Collection; Dyce Collection (2); Shakespeare Memorial, Stratford; Devonshire; Huth; Boston Public; Perry (Gwynn copy); Lenox; Hoe; Morgan (Inglis-Asay-Irwin copy); White; and Wrenn Libraries; also the Howe and the Locker Lampson-Van Antwerp copies (untraced).

REFERENCES.

Brooke, *Shakespeare Apocrypha* (1908), p. 445; Greg, *List of English Plays* (Bibliographical Society; 1900), p. 102; British Museum, *Catalogue*; *Shakespeare* (1897), col. 180; Hazlitt, *Manual of Old English Plays* (1892), p. 212; Locker-Lampson, *Catalogue* (1886), p. 112; Boston Public Library, *Catalogue*; *Barton Collection* (1880), p. 48, No. 716; Huth, *Catalogue*, 4 (1880) : 1339; Lenox Library, *Works of Shakespeare* (1880), p. 30, No. 176; Hazlitt, *Hand-Book* (1867), p. 468, No. 46.

The Griswold copy.

This is one of the seven pseudo-Shakespeare plays added to the Folio of 1664.

Of this play two editions were published, both during the same year.

Of the First Edition (1600), by "V. S. for Thomas Pauier," without the name of Shakespeare as the author on the title-page, there are copies in the Bodleian (Malone, 768) and Ellesmere Libraries.

The Second Edition (also 1600) is that here described.

There were two editions in 1600; on the title-page of most copies of the latter and less correct the name of Shakespeare occurs as the author. It appears from Henslowe's *Diary* that this play was written in 1599 by Munday, Drayton, Wilson, and Chettle. Of the second part, licensed August 11, 1600, no copy is known to exist; it appears to have completed the story, including Oldcastle's martyrdom.

[SHAKESPEARE, WILLIAM.] Supposititious Play.

THOMAS LORD CROMWELL. LONDON, *Thomas Snodham*, 1613. [**626**]

Small quarto. Second Edition.

COLLATION BY SIGNATURES: A to G, each 4 leaves (the last blank and genuine); total 28 unnumbered leaves.

COLLATION BY PAGINATION: [title, as reproduced; *See* No. 626], recto of [A]; —[blank], verso of [A]; — [text, with heading] | [type-ornament head-piece] | The life and death of the Lord | *Cromwell.* |, recto of A 2 to recto of [G 3]; — | FINIS. |, recto of [G 3]; — [blank], verso of [G 3]; —[1 blank leaf], [G 4].

CONDITION: Size of leaf, 7 x 5⅜₆ inches. Bound in olive green morocco, gilt edges; by Bedford.

OTHER COPIES.

British Museum (3); Bodleian; Capell Collection; Dyce Collection; Devonshire; Huth; and White Libraries; also the Howe copy (untraced).

REFERENCES.

Brooke, *Shakespeare Apocrypha* (1908), p. 441; Greg, *List of English Plays* (Bibliographical Society; 1900), p. 103; British Museum, *Catalogue*; *Shakespeare* (1897), col. 179; Hazlitt, *Manual of Old English Plays* (1892), p. 137; Locker-Lampson, *Catalogue* (1886), p. 113; Huth, *Catalogue*, 4 (1880) : 1340; Hazlitt, *Hand-Book* (1867), p. 469, No. 55 *b*.

The Locker-Lampson copy, with ex-libris.

In this copy is a manuscript slip pasted to the recto of the second fly-leaf, as follows: "*Thomas Ld Cromwell is a piece of such utterly shapeless, spiritless, bodiless, soulless, senseless, helpless, worthless rubbish, that there is no known writer of W. S's age to whom it c^d be inscribed* [sic] *without the infliction of an unwarrantable insult on that writer's memory.* [signed] *A. C. Swinburne.*

"∴ *This is said apropos of Schlegel's statement that it sh^d be classed among his best and maturest works.*"

The first part

Of the true & honorable history, of the Life of
Sir Iohn Old-castle, the good Lord Cobham.

As it hath bene lately acted by the Right honorable the Earle of Notingham Lord High Admirall of England, his Seruants.

Written by William Shakefpeare.

London printed for T.P.
1600.

No. 625. Title-page of Sir John Oldcastle; 2d Edition; 1600.

1613   *William Shakespeare*   No. 626

This is one of the seven pseudo-Shakespeare plays added to the Folio of 1664.

Editions of this play appeared in quarto in 1602 and 1613.

Of the First Edition (1602), "for William Iones," there are copies in the Bodleian and Lenox Libraries, the latter being the Roxburghe-Heber copy. There is also the Howe copy (untraced).

The Second Edition (1613) is that here described.

[SHAKESPEARE, WILLIAM.] Supposititious Play.

THE LONDON PRODIGAL. LONDON, *by T. C. for Nathaniel Butter*, 1605.

[627]

Small quarto. Sole Edition.

COLLATION BY SIGNATURES: A to G, each 4 leaves; total 28 unnumbered leaves. Leaf B 2 is marked *B 2*; and F 3 is *F* 3.

COLLATION BY PAGINATION: [title, as reproduced; *See* No. 627], recto of [A]; — [blank], verso of [A]; — [text, with heading] | [conventional head-piece] | THE LONDON | Prodigall. |, recto of A 2 to verso of [G 4]; — | *FINIS.* |, verso of [G 4]. Sheets E and F contain 35 lines to the full page; the rest of the work, 38 lines.

CONDITION: Size of leaf, 6⅞ × 4¾ inches. Bound in red crushed levant morocco, with Almon W. Griswold's coat of arms on the front cover, gilt edges; by Bedford.

OTHER COPIES.

British Museum; Bodleian; Capell Collection; Devonshire; Ellesmere; Huth (Heber-Daniel copy); Lenox; and White Libraries.

REFERENCES.

Brooke, *Shakespeare Apocrypha* (1908), p. 443; Greg, *List of English Plays* (Bibliographical Society; 1900), p. 103; British Museum, *Catalogue*; *Shakespeare* (1897), col. 179; Hazlitt, *Manual of Old English Plays* (1892), p. 131; Locker-Lampson, *Catalogue* (1886), p. 112; Huth, *Catalogue*, 4 (1880): 1339; Lenox Library, *Works of Shakespeare* (1880), p. 30, No. 173; Hazlitt, *Hand-Book* (1867), p. 470, No. 60.

The Griswold copy.

This is one of the seven pseudo-plays added to the Folio of 1664.

Of this play but a single edition, that here described, was printed in quarto. It has been falsely attributed to Shakespeare.

[SHAKESPEARE, WILLIAM.] Supposititious Play.

THE PURITAN. LONDON, *G. Eld*, 1607.

[628]

Small quarto. Sole Edition.

COLLATION BY SIGNATURES: A to H, each 4 leaves (the first blank and lacking); total 32 unnumbered leaves.

COLLATION BY PAGINATION: [1 blank leaf], [A]; — [title, as reproduced; *See* No. 628], recto of [A 2]; — [blank], verso of [A 2]; — [text, with heading] | The Puritaine Widdow. |, recto of A 3 to recto of [H 4]; — | *FINIS.* |, recto of [H 4]; — [blank], verso of [H 4].

CONDITION: Size of leaf, 7⅛ × 5⁵⁄₁₆

No. 626   *William Shakespeare*   1613

THE
True Chronicle Hi-
ſtorie of the whole life and death
of *Thomas* Lord *Cromwell*.

As it hath beene ſundry times publikely Acted by the Kings Maieſties
Seruants.

Written by W.S.

LONDON;
Printed by THOMAS SNODHAM.
1613.

No. 626.   TITLE-PAGE OF THOMAS LORD CROMWELL; 2D EDITION; 1613.

THE LONDON Prodigall.

As it was plaide by the Kings Maiesties seruants.

By VVilliam Shakespeare.

LONDON.

Printed by T. C. for *Nathaniel Butter*, and
are to be sold neere S. *Austins gate*,
at the signe of the pyde Bull.
1605.

No. 628 *William Shakespeare* 1607

THE PVRITAINE

Or

THE VVIDDOVV
of Watling-ſtreete.

Acted by the Children of Paules.

Written by W. S.

Imprinted at London by G. E ld.
1607.

No. 628.   Title-page of The Puritan; Sole Edition; 1607.

inches. Bound in brown polished morocco, gilt edges.

OTHER COPIES.

British Museum (2); Bodleian; Capell Collection; Shakespeare Memorial, Stratford (imperfect); Ellesmere; Huth (thick-paper Heber-Daniel copy); Boston Public (title and last page in facsimile); Lenox; Hoe; and White Libraries; also the Howe copy (untraced).

REFERENCES.

Brooke, *Shakespeare Apocrypha* (1908), p. 446; Hoe, *Catalogue*, 4 (1904) : 104; Greg, *List of English Plays* (Bibliographical Society; 1900), p. 103; British Museum, *Catalogue; Shakespeare* (1897), col. 180; Hazlitt, *Manual of Old English Plays* (1892), p. 187; Locker-Lampson, *Catalogue* (1886), p. 113; Boston Public Library, *Catalogue; Barton Collection* (1880), p. 48, No. 717; Huth, *Catalogue*, 4 (1880) : 1339; Lenox Library, *Works of Shakespeare* (1880), p. 31, No. 177; Lowndes, 4 (1869) : 2304; Hazlitt, *Hand-Book* (1867), p. 471, No. 70.

The Heber-Tite-Halliwell Phillipps-Locker Lampson copy, with ex-libris of the last. This is one of the seven pseudo-Shakespeare plays added to the Folio of 1664. But one edition of this play was published in quarto, that here described.

"This play is one of the seven erroneously attributed to Shakespear. The character of George Pyeboard is supposed with good reason to have been borrowed from George Peele the dramatist and the exploits narrated in his so-called *Jests*, 1607."

[SHAKESPEARE, WILLIAM.] Suppositious Play.

THE MERRY DEVIL OF EDMONTON. LONDON, *by G. Eld, for Arthur Iohnſon*, 1617. [629]

Small quarto. Third Edition.

COLLATION BY SIGNATURES: A, 4 leaves (the first blank and lacking); B to F, each 4 leaves; total 24 unnumbered leaves. Leaf E 3 has no signature-mark.

COLLATION BY PAGINATION : [1 blank leaf], [A]; —[title, as reproduced; *See* No. 629], recto of [A 2]; —[blank], verso of [A 2]; —[text, with heading] | [conventional head-piece] | The merry Deuill | of Edmonton. |, recto of A 3 to recto of [F 4]; — | FINIS. |, recto of [F 4]; — [blank], verso of [F 4].

CONDITION : Size of leaf, 6⅞ x 5 1/16 inches. Bound in green crushed levant morocco, gilt edges.

OTHER COPIES.

British Museum; Bodleian (2); Capell Collection; and Devonshire Libraries.

REFERENCES.

Greg, *List of English Plays* (Bibliographical Society; 1900), p. 135; Hazlitt, *Manual of Old English Plays* (1892), p. 155; same, *Collections and Notes* (1876), p. 139; Lowndes, 4 (1869) : 2303; Hazlitt, *Hand-Book* (1867), p. 471, No. 72 *b*.

On the fly-leaf facing the title-page is written the following:
"*Anon.*
"*Said by Kirkman, 1671, to be by Shakspere. Entered Stat. Hall by H. Moseley 1653, as by W. Shakspere. Coxeter saw a MS. with M. Drayton's name as author. Original entry at Stat. Hall in 1608 as written by T. B. supposed to be Tony Brewer — as same initials were placed to his Country Girl.*"

No. 629　　　　　　*William Shakespeare*　　　　　　1617

THE
MERRY DIVEL
OF
EDMONToN.

As it hath beene fundry times Acted,
by his *Maiefties Seruants*, at the
Globe on the Banke-fide.

AT LONDON.
Printed by *G. Eld*, for *Arthur Iohnfon*, dwelling at the figne of the white-Horfe in Paules Church-yard, ouer againft the great North Doore of Paules.
1617.

No. 629. Title-page of The Merry Devil of Edmonton; 3d Edition; 1617.

"Of this charming comedy the plot is founded on the history of one Peter Fabel, of whom a prose account appears to have been printed as early as 1533, and of whom more particular mention is made in Fuller's *Church History* and in the Chronicles of Henry VI.'s reign. This comedy, in the original entry on the Stationers' books in 1608, is said to have been written by T. B., which letters have been rashly taken to stand for Tony or Anthony Brewer. The same letters are prefixed to that author's *Country Girl.* H. Moseley again entered it September 9, 1653, as the production of Shakespear; but that statement is of no authority. The *Merry Devil of Edmonton* is mentioned in the *Black Book* by T. M., 1604, as if it were then a popular comedy; the *Merry Pranks of Fabyl*, noticed by Weever (*Anc. Fun. Mon.*, 1631, p. 334), above referred to, was seen by Warton in the study of Collins the Poet. In Hazlitt's Dodsley."

This popular play appeared in several editions, as follows: 1608, 1612, 1617, 1626, 1631, and 1655.

Of the First Edition (1608), "by Henry Ballard for Arthur Iohnſon," there are copies in the Capell Collection, Devonshire, and White Libraries.

Of the Second Edition (1612), "by Thomas Creede, for Arthur Iohnſon," there is a copy in the Huth Library (Corser copy).

The Third Edition (1617) is that here described.

Of the Fourth Edition (1626), "by A. M. for Francis Falkner," there are copies in the British Museum, Capell Collection, Dyce Collection, and Boston Public Library.

The Fifth Edition (1631) is that described in our next number.

Of the Sixth Edition (1655), "for William Gilbertſon," there are copies in the British Museum, Capell Collection, Dyce Collection, and Morgan Library.

[SHAKESPEARE, WILLIAM.] Suppositious Play.
THE MERRY DEVIL OF EDMONTON. London, *by T. P. for Francis Falkner*, 1631.
[630]

Small quarto. Fifth Edition.

COLLATION BY SIGNATURES: A, 4 leaves (the first blank and lacking); B to F, each 4 leaves; total 24 unnumbered leaves.

COLLATION BY PAGINATION: [1 blank leaf], [A];—[title, as reproduced; *See* No. 630], recto of [A 2];—[blank], verso of [A 2];—[text, with heading] | [conventional head-piece]| *The Merry Deuill of* | Edmonton. |, recto of A 3 to recto of [F 4];— | FINIS. |, recto of [F 4];— [blank], verso of [F 4].

CONDITION: Size of leaf, 7³⁄₁₆ × 5¼ inches. Bound in red crushed levant morocco, gilt edges; by Bedford.

OTHER COPIES.

British Museum (2); Bodleian (2); Capell Collection; Ellesmere; and Boston Public Libraries.

REFERENCES.

Brooke, *Shakespeare Apocrypha* (1908), p. 443; Greg, *List of English Plays* (Bibliographical Society; 1900), p. 135; Hazlitt, *Manual for the Collector and Amateur of Old English Plays* (1892), p. 155; Boston Public Library, *Catalogue*; *Barton Collection* (1880), p. 47, No. 710; Hazlitt, *Collections and Notes* (1876), p. 139; Lowndes, 4 (1869): 2303.

The Merry Deuill
OF
EDMONTON.

As it hath been sundry times
Acted, by his *Maiesties*
Seruants, at the Globe on
the Bancke-side.

LONDON.
¶ Printed by *T. P.* for *Francis Falkner*, and are to be
sold at his Shoppe neere vnto *S. Margarites*-hill
in Southwarke. 1631.

No. 630.   TITLE-PAGE OF THE MERRY DEVIL OF EDMONTON;
5TH EDITION; 1631.

The copy here described formerly belonged to Frederick Locker-Lampson and contains his ex-libris. *See* the Catalogue of "The Rowfant Library" (1886), p. 113.

[SHAKESPEARE, WILLIAM.] Supposititious Play.

A YORKSHIRE TRAGEDY. London, *by R. B. for Thomas Pauier*, 1608. [631]

Small quarto. First Edition.

COLLATION BY SIGNATURES : A to D, each 4 leaves (the last blank and genuine) ; total 16 unnumbered leaves. Leaf D 3 has no signature-mark.

COLLATION BY PAGINATION : [title, as reproduced ; *See* No. 631], recto of [A] ; — [blank], verso of [A] ; — [text, with heading] | [conventional head-piece] | ALL'S ONE, | *OR*, | One of the foure Plaies in one, called | a *York-ſhire* Tragedy : as it was plaid | by the Kings Maieſties Plaiers. |, recto of A 2 to verso of [D 3] ; — | *FINIS.* | [conventional tail-piece] |, verso of [D 3] ; — [1 blank leaf], [D 4].

CONDITION : Size of leaf, 6¾ × 5 inches.

Bound in brown crushed levant morocco, gilt edges ; by Hammond.

OTHER COPIES.

British Museum ; Bodleian ; and Devonshire Libraries.

REFERENCES.

Brooke, *Shakespeare Apocrypha* (1908), p. 447 ; Greg, *List of English Plays* (Bibliographical Society ; 1900), p. 103 ; British Museum, *Catalogue* ; *Shakespeare* (1897), col. 182 ; Hazlitt, *Manual of Old English Plays* (1892), p. 260 ; Locker-Lampson, *Catalogue* (1886), p. 113 ; Lowndes, 4 (1869) : 2304 ; Hazlitt, *Hand-Book* (1867), p. 471, No. 72 *a* [73 *a*].

The Locker-Lampson copy, with ex-libris.

This is one of the seven pseudo-Shakespeare plays added to the Folio of 1664. Two editions were printed in quarto, the first in 1608, the second in 1619.

The First Edition (1608) is that here described.

The Second Edition (1619) is that described in our next number.

"This play is sometimes erroneously ascribed to Shakespear, whose name was surreptitiously placed on the title-pages of the early editions. . . . The play is founded on the murder of Mistress Caverly at York, in August, 1605, by her husband, of which an account was printed the same year. This is what is meant by the statement on the title that the incident was not quite fresh."

[SHAKESPEARE, WILLIAM.] Supposititious Play.

A YORKSHIRE TRAGEDY. [London], *for T. P.*, 1619. [632]

Small quarto. Second Edition.

COLLATION BY SIGNATURES : 2 leaves, without signature-marks (the first blank and lacking) ; A, B, C, each 4 leaves ; D, 2 leaves ; total 16 unnumbered leaves. Leaf D 2 has a signature-mark.

COLLATION BY PAGINATION : [1 blank leaf] ; — [title, as reproduced ; *See* No. 632], recto of second leaf ; — [blank], verso of second leaf ; — [text, with heading] | [type-ornament head-piece] | ALL'S ONE, | OR, | *One of the foure Plaies in one,*

A YORKSHIRE Tragedy.

Not so New as Lamentable and true.

Acted by his Maiesties Players at the *Globe*.

VVritten by VV. Shakspeare.

At LONDON
Printed by *R. B.* for *Thomas Pauier* and are to bee sold at his shop on Cornhill, neere to the exchange.
1608.

A YORKSHIRE TRAGEDIE.

Not so New, as Lamentable and True.

Written by W. SHAKESPEARE.

Printed for T. P. 1619.

No. 632. TITLE-PAGE OF A YORKSHIRE TRAGEDIE; 2D EDITION; 1619.

No. 632   *William Shakespeare*   1619

called a | Yorkſhire Tragedy. As it was plaid by | the Kings Maieſties Players. |, recto of A to verso of D 2 ; — | *FINIS.* |, verso of D 2.

CONDITION : Size of leaf, 6¾ × 5⁵⁄₁₆ inches. Bound in salmon crushed levant morocco, gilt edges ; by Bedford.

OTHER COPIES.

British Museum (3) ; Bodleian ; Capell Collection ; Dyce Collection ; Edinburgh University ; Devonshire ; Ellesmere ; Huth ; Boston Public ; Perry (Gwynne copy) ; Lenox ; Hoe ; Morgan (Irwin copy) ; and White Libraries ; also the Howe copy (untraced).

REFERENCES.

Hoe, *Catalogue*, 4 (1904) : 104 ; Greg, *List of English Plays* (Bibliographical Society ; 1900), p. 103 ; British Museum, *Catalogue* ; *Shakespeare* (1897), col. 182 ; Locker-Lampson, *Catalogue* (1886), p. 114 ; Boston Public Library, *Catalogue* ; *Barton Collection* (1880), p. 49, No. 722 ; Huth, *Catalogue*, 4 (1880) : 1340 ; Lenox Library, *Works of Shakespeare* (1880), p. 31, No. 181 ; Hazlitt, *Hand-Book* (1867), p. 471, No. 72 *b* [73 *b*].

The copy here described was formerly in the library of Frederick Locker-Lampson, and contains his ex-libris.

[SHAKESPEARE, WILLIAM.]   Suppositious Play.

FAIR EM. LONDON, *for Iohn Wright*, 1631.   [633]

Small quarto. Second Edition.

COLLATION BY SIGNATURES : A to F, each 4 leaves (the last, probably blank, lacking) ; total 24 unnumbered leaves.

COLLATION BY PAGINATION : [title, as reproduced ; *See* No. 633], recto of [A] ; — [blank], verso of [A] ; — [text, with heading] | A Pleaſant Comedie of faire *Em*, | The Millers daughter of Mancheſter. | With the loue of *William* | the Conquerour. |, recto of A 2 to verso of F 3 ; — | FINIS. |, verso of F 3 ; — [1 leaf, probably blank], [F 4].

CONDITION : Size of leaf, 7³⁄₁₆ × 5⁵⁄₁₆ inches. Bound in red crushed levant morocco, gilt edges ; by Bedford. The leaves are stabbed on the inner margins throughout.

OTHER COPIES.

British Museum (3) ; Bodleian ; Capell Collection ; Dyce Collection ; Ellesmere ; Huth ; Boston Public ; Hoe ; Morgan (Irwin copy) ; White ; and Wrenn Libraries.

REFERENCES.

Brooke, *Shakespeare Apocrypha* (1908), p. 442 ; Hoe, *Catalogue*, 2 (1903) : 186 ; Greg, *List of English Plays* (Bibliographical Society ; 1900), p. 137 ; Hazlitt, *Manual of Old English Plays* (1892), p. 79 ; Locker-Lampson, *Catalogue* (1886), p. 92 ; Boston Public Library, *Catalogue* ; *Barton Collection* (1880), p. 46, No. 707 ; Huth, *Catalogue*, 2 (1880) : 503 ; Hazlitt, *Hand-Book* (1867), p. 325, No. 4 *b*.

The Locker-Lampson copy, with ex-libris.

On the recto of the second fly-leaf is a note in pencil by Locker-Lampson, as follows :

"*Some give this Play to Greene. Some to Shakespeare in derisive immitation of Greene. Mountenay is intended for Marlowe.*"

Of this play two editions were issued in quarto, one without date, the other dated 1631.

Of the First Edition (undated), "for T. N. and I. W.," the only copy known

A Pleaſant COMEDIE Of FAIRE EM,

The Millers Daughter of Mancheſter:

With the loue of *William* the Conquerōr.

As it was ſundry times publiquely acted in the Honourable Citie of London, by the right Honourable the Lord *Strange* his Seruants.

LONDON,
Printed for *Iohn Wright*, and are to be ſold at his ſhop at the ſigne of the Bible in Guilt-ſpur ſtreet without New-gate. 1 6 3 1.

is that in the Bodleian Library. Malone supposed this edition to be the earlier, and Greg says, "This edition is considerably the earlier."

The Second Edition (1631) is that here described.

[SHAKESPEARE, WILLIAM.] Supposititious Play.

THE TWO NOBLE KINSMEN. LONDON, by Tho. Cotes, for Iohn Waterſon, 1634. [634]

Small quarto. Sole Edition.

COLLATION BY SIGNATURES: [A], 1 leaf; B to M, each 4 leaves; N, 1 leaf; total 46 leaves. The title-page and last leaf were imposed together. Leaves F 3 and L 3 have no signature-marks.

COLLATION BY PAGINATION: [title, as reproduced; *See* No. 634], recto of [A]; — | PROLOGVE. |, verso of [A]; — [text, with heading] | [type-ornament head-piece] | The Two Noble | Kinſmen. |, pp. [1]–88; — | EPILOGVE. |, p. [89]; — | FINIS. |, p. [89]; — [blank], p. [90].

CONDITION: Size of leaf, 7½ × 5⅝ inches. Bound in red crushed levant morocco, gilt edges; by Bedford. Many leaves uncut on the lower margins; a fine, crisp, perfect copy.

OTHER COPIES.

British Museum (2); Bodleian; Capell Collection; Dyce Collection; Birmingham Free; Devonshire; Ellesmere; Huth; Boston Public; Lenox (imperfect); Hoe; Trowbridge; White; and Wrenn Libraries; also the Howe and the McKee-Van Antwerp copies (untraced).

REFERENCES.

Brooke, *Shakespeare Apocrypha* (1908), p. 446; Greg, *List of English Plays* (Bibliographical Society; 1900), p. 9; British Museum, *Catalogue* (1897), col. 181; Hazlitt, *Manual of Old English Plays* (1892), p. 241; Locker-Lampson, *Catalogue* (1886), p. 43; Boston Public Library, *Catalogue*; Barton Collection (1880), p. 48, No. 718; Huth, *Catalogue*, 2 (1880): 528; Lenox Library, *Works of Shakespeare* (1880), p. 31, No. 178; Lowndes, 4 (1869): 2304; Hazlitt, *Hand-Book to the Popular, Poetical, and Dramatic Literature of Great Britain* (1867), p. 204, No. 7.

The Locker-Lampson copy, with ex-libris.

Of this play but a single edition was printed in quarto, the one here described. It was reprinted in Beaumont and Fletcher's *Fifty Comedies* (1679), of which there are copies in the British Museum (3), Bodleian, University Library (Cambridge), Dyce Collection, and Boston Public Libraries.

On the recto of the second fly-leaf of the copy here described is a note by Locker-Lampson: "*This play is supposed to be by Fletcher, especially the 4th act.*"

Immediately below this is the following note in a different handwriting:

"*The story of this play is taken from Palamon and Arcite, but the latter part which in Chaucer is full of dramatic power & interest here becomes mere narrative.*"

"*The first & the last acts of the Two Noble Kinsmen which in point of composition is perhaps the most superb work in the language, and beyond all doubt Shakespeare's, would have been the most gorgeous rhetoric, had they not happened to be something far better. The supplications of the widow'd Queens to Theseus, the invocations of their tutelar divinities by Palamon & Arcite, the death of Arcite,*

1634 *William Shakespeare* No. 634

THE TWO NOBLE KINSMEN:

Preſented at the Blackfriers
by the Kings Maieſties ſervants,
with great applauſe:

Written by the memorable Worthies
of their time;
{ M^r. *John Fletcher*, and } Gent.
{ M^r. *William Shakſpeare*. }

Printed at *London* by *Tho. Cotes*, for *Iohn Waterſon*:
and are to be ſold at the ſigne of the *Crowne*
in *Pauls* Church-yard. 1 6 3 4.

No. 634. Title-page of The Two Noble Kinsmen;
Sole Edition; 1634.

&c. are finished in a more elaborate style of excellence, than any other almost of W. S's most felicitous scenes."

In criticism of the above Locker-Lampson has written:

"I do not know who says this, but certainly the invocation to Mars is very fine (see P. 71). Richard Edwards wrote a play called Palamon & Arcyte (1566)."

"Opinions differ as to the share which Shakespear had in this drama. See Mr. Dyce's remarks in his edition of the poet, 1868, and in his Beaumont and Fletcher. The story is taken from Chaucer's *Knight's Tale*. Compare *Palamon and Arcite*.

"This drama was revived after the Restoration, it is stated by Langbaine on the authority of Cadman the publisher, by Davenant, under the title of *The Rivals*, and printed in this altered form, 4to, 1668. The scene, Arcadia. It was acted nine days successively to full houses, at the Duke of York's Theatre. Miss Davis acted in it 'a shepherdess, being mad for love, especially in singing several wild and mad songs, " My lodging it is on the cold ground," etc. She performed that so charmingly, that, not long after, it rais'd her from her bed on the cold ground to a bed royal.' See *Roscius Anglicanus*, 1708."

There are copies of *The Rivals* (1668), "for William Cademan," in the British Museum, Bodleian, Dyce Collection, Harvard University, Boston Public, and doubtless other libraries.

SHAKESPEARIANA. Preston, Thomas. (*b.* 1537, *d.* 1598.)

A LAMENTABLE TRAGEDY... OF CAMBISES KING OF PERCIA.
LONDON, by Iohn Allde, [1570].   [635]

Small quarto. First Edition. Printed in black-letter.

COLLATION BY SIGNATURES: A to E, each 4 leaves; F, 4 leaves (the last, probably blank, lacking); total 24 unnumbered leaves.

COLLATION BY PAGINATION: [title, as reproduced; *See* No. 635], recto of [A]; —[blank], verso of [A]; —[prologue, with heading] | *The Prologue entreth.* |, recto of A. ij.; — | FINIS. |, recto of A. ij.; —[text, with running head-lines] | A Commedy of | king Cambises. |, verso of A. ij. to recto of [F. iij.]; — | Amen. ꝗ Thomas Preston. | [colophon] | *Imprinted at London by Iohn Allde.* |, recto of [F.iij.]; —[blank], verso of [F. iij.]; — [1 leaf, probably blank], [F. iiij.].

CONDITION: Size of leaf, 6⅝ x 4⅝ inches. Bound in red crushed levant morocco, gilt edges; by Pratt. The titlepage is mounted; the margins of some leaves are extended, with a few letters supplied in facsimile.

OTHER COPIES.

British Museum (Garrick copy).

REFERENCES.

Greg, *List of English Plays* (Bibliographical Society; 1900), p. 85; Hazlitt, *Manual of Old English Plays* (1892), p. 34; Locker-Lampson, *Catalogue* (1886), p. 95; Huth, *Catalogue*, 4 (1880): 1183; Lowndes, 4 (1869): 1960; Hazlitt, *Hand-Book* (1867), p. 479.

The Locker-Lampson copy, with ex-libris.

A lamentable tragedy

mixed ful of pleaſant mirth, conteyning the life of CAMBISES king of PERCIA, from the beginning of his kingdome vnto his death, his one good deed of execution, after that many wicked deeds and tirannous murders, committed by and through him, and laſt of all, his odious death by Gods Iuſtice appointed. Don in ſuch order as foloweth. By *Thomas Preſton.*

The diuiſion of the partes.

Councel, Huf, Praxaſpes, Murder, Lob, the 3. Lord.	For one man.	Prologue, Siſamnes, Diligence, Crueltie, Hob, Preparatiō the 1. Lord.	For one man.
Lord, Ruf, Commons cry, Cōmōs cōplaint, Lord ſmirdis, Venus.	For one man.	Ambidexter, Triall.	For one man.
Knight, Snuf, Small habilitie, Proof, Execution, Attendance, ſecond Lord,	For one man.	Meretrix, Shame, Otian, Mother, Lady, Queene.	For one man.
Cambiſes, Epilogus.	For one man.	Yung childe, Cupid.	For one man

No. 635. Title-page of Preston's Cambises King of Percia; 1st Edition; [1570].

No. 635   *William Shakespeare*   1570

There were two editions of this play published, both without date, the first in 1570, the second about 1608. The First Edition (1570) is that here described.

Of the Second Edition (no date, but about 1608), "by Edward Allde," there are copies in the British Museum (2), Bodleian (Malone copy, also leaves F ij. and F iij. of another copy, containing the colophon), Dyce Collection, Devonshire, Ellesmere, Huth, and White Libraries.

"It is to this play that Shakespeare is supposed to allude in the 'Midsummer Night's Dream,' when Peter Quince says: 'Marry our play is — The most lamentable comedy and most cruel death of Pyramus and Thisby,' thus parodying the title of 'A lamentable Tragedie, mixed full of plesant mirth.'"

"This is the piece," says Hazlitt, "which gave rise to the phrase 'King Cambyses' vein,' employed by Shakespear."

SHAKESPEARIANA. Harvey, Gabriel. (*b.* c. 1545, *d.* 1630.)

FOVRE LETTERS, AND CERTAINE SONNETS. London, *by Iohn Wolfe, 1592.*

[636]

Small quarto.

COLLATION BY SIGNATURES: A to I, each 4 leaves; K, 2 leaves; total 38 leaves.

COLLATION BY PAGINATION: [title, as reproduced; *See* No. 636], recto of [A]; — | The particular Contents. | [10 lines]|, verso of [A];— | To all courteous mindes, that will voutchsafe|the readinge.|, pp. [1]-[2];—[the four letters], pp. 3-61; —[22 numbered sonnets, the first with heading]| GREENES MEMORIALL, OR | certaine Funerall Sonnets.|, pp. 61-74;— [2 poems in Latin], p. 74;—[sonnet]| To the right worſhipfull, my ſingular good frend, | M. Gabriell Haruey, Doctor | of the Lawes.| [signed]| *Your deuoted frend, during life,* | Edmund Spencer. | [dated]|| *Dublin: this xviij. of Iuly: 1586.*|, p. 75;—| *FINIS.*|, p. 75;—[blank], p.[76]. Page 26 is wrongly numbered 29; and the numbers 39 and 40 are omitted in the pagination. The page-numbers are in mixed roman and italic figures.

CONDITION: Size of leaf, $6\frac{7}{8} \times 4\frac{7}{8}$ inches. Bound in dark green morocco, gilt edges; by Pratt.

OTHER COPIES.

British Museum (2); Bodleian (3); Ellesmere; and White Libraries.

REFERENCES.

Grolier Club, *Langland to Wither* (1893), p. 112, No. 135; Corser, *Collectanea Anglo-Poetica*, Part 7 (Chetham Society, Vol. CI.; 1877), p. 180; New Shakspere Society, Publications for 1874, Series IV., *Shakspere Allusion-Books*, Part I., pp. xxii., 123-149; Lowndes, 2 (1869): 1007; Hazlitt, *Hand-Book* (1867), p. 257, No. 4; Collier, *Rarest Books*, 2 (1866): 124; *Bibliotheca Anglo-Poetica* (1815), p. 147, No. 343.

The Locker-Lampson copy, with ex-libris.

On the first fly-leaf is written in Frederick Locker-Lampson's handwriting:

"*See p. 48. If this is intended for Shakespeare it w^d prove that G. Harvey was the 1st writer to recognize his excellence, in fact that he was the only one to do so.*

"*He refers to Greene going on the stage* [p. 9], '*The King of the Paper stage had played his last part & was gone to join Tarleton.*'

FOVRE LETTERS,
and certaine Sonnets:

Especially touching Robert Greene, *and other parties, by him abused*:

But incidently of diuers excellent persons, and some matters of note.

To all courteous mindes, that will vouchsafe the reading.

LONDON
Imprinted by Iohn Wolfe,
1 5 9 2.

No. 636. Title-page of Harvey's Fovre Letters, and certaine Sonnets; 1592.

No. 636   *William Shakespeare*   1592

"*Nash satirized Harvey & the Puritans* [*in his*]—'*Strange News of the intercepting certaine letters, & a Convoy of Verses as they were going privilie to victuall the low countries,*' *dated 1592. The book is sometimes called Pierce Pennelefse* (*1593*)."

Two supposed allusions to Shakespeare are found in Harvey's Third Letter. The first occurs on p. 23 in the words " the worſt of the foure " in the sentence, " Green, vile *Greene*, would thou weareſt halfe ſo honeſt, as the worſt of the foure, whom thou vpbraideſt : or halfe ſo learned, as the vnlearnedſt of the three."

This bitter attack on Greene was occasioned by a passage in his "famous new worke, intituled, *A Quippe for an vpſtart Courtier*" (1592). It was considered by Harvey to be a contemptuous allusion to his father, who was a rope-maker at Saffron-Walden in Essex, a circumstance of which he had the weakness to be ashamed. This controversy between Harvey on the one hand and Greene and Nash on the other, of which D'Israeli gives an interesting and amusing account in the second volume of his *Calamities of Authors*, assumed such bitterness that it was at last put an end to by the authorities, who seized and destroyed their numerous pamphlets. This step doubtless greatly assisted in giving the work here described its present rarity.

The second allusion is near the end of the letter (p. 48) :

" Good ſweete Oratour, be a deuine Poet indeede : and vſe heauenly Eloquence indeede : and employ thy golden talent with amounting vſance indeede : and with heroicall Cantoes honour right Vertue, & braue valour indeede : as noble Sir Philip Sidney, and gentle Maiſter Spencer haue done, with immortall Fame : and I will beſtow more complements of rare amplifications vpon thee, then euer any beſtowed vppon them : or this Tounge euer affoorded : or any Aretiniſh mountaine of huge exaggerations can bring-foorth. . . . I cordially recommend to the deere Louers of the Muſes : and namely to the profeſſed Sonnes of the-fame ; *Edmond Spencer, Richard Staniburſt, Abraham France, Thomas Watſon, Samuell Daniell, Thomas Naſh*, and the reſt : whome I affectionately thancke for their ſtudious endeuours, commendably employed in enriching, & poliſhing their natiue Tongue, neuer ſo furniſhed, or embelliſhed, as of-late. . . . The right Noouice of pregnante, and aſpiring conceit, wil not ouer-skippe any precious gemme of Inuention, or any beautifull floure of Elocution, that may richly adorne, or gallantly bedecke the trimme garland of his budding ſtile. I ſpeake generally to euery ſpringing wit : but more ſpecially to a few : and at this inſtante ſingularly to one [Shakespeare] : whom I ſalute with a hundred bleſſings : and entreate with as many prayers, to loue them, that loue all good wittes : and hate none, but the Diuell, and his incarnate Impes, notoriouſly profeſſed."

One of the "certaine Sonnets," the last in the volume, is Spenser's fine sonnet of compliment addressed " To the right worſhipfull, my ſingular good frend, M. Gabriell Haruey, Doctor of the Lawes," and dated, " *Dublin: this xviij. of Iuly: 1586.*", or six years before its appearance here.

"There is no tract in the English language," says Lowndes, " which contains so many cotemporary literary notices of the Elizabethan reign ; and as such, it is of the highest value to the antiquarian, critic, and philologer."

The Third Letter (pp. 15–50) was reprinted in the New Shakspere Society's Publications for 1874, Series IV., *Shakspere Allusion-Books*, Part I., pp. 123-149.

1598   *Shakespeariana*   No. 637

SHAKESPEARIANA. Meres, Francis. (*b.* 1565, *d.* 1647.)

PALLADIS TAMIA. WITS TREASVRY BEING THE SECOND PART OF WITS COMMON WEALTH. LONDON, *by P. Short, for Cuthbert Burbie*, 1598.   [637]

Small octavo. First Edition.
COLLATION BY SIGNATURES: [A], 4 leaves; B to Z, Aa to Vv, each 8 leaves; total 340 leaves. Leaves B 4, E 4, G 4, M 4, O 4, P 4, S 4, and Ee 4 have no signature-marks; Z 2 is marked z 2; Z 3 is z 3; Z 4 is z 4; and Sf 2 is fS 2.

COLLATION BY PAGINATION: [title, as reproduced; *See* No. 637], recto of [A]; — [blank], verso of [A]; — [table of authors, with heading] | [type-ornament head-piece] | The Authours both fa- | cred and profane, out of | *which thefe fimilitudes are* | for the moſt part | *gathered.* |, recto of [A 2] to verso of [A 4]; — [text, with heading] | [type-ornament head-piece] | THE SECOND | part of Wits Com- | mon-wealth. |, recto of folio [1] to recto of folio 333; — | FINIS. |, recto of folio 333; — | A Table of the Common places | *into which thefe Similitudes* | are digeſted. |, verso of folio 333 to verso of folio [336]; — | FINIS. |, verso of folio [336]. Folio 5 is wrongly numbered 9; 77 is 76; 79 is 78; 141 is 131; 143 is 133; 297 is 397; 329 is 339; and 331 is 301.

CONDITION: Size of leaf, 5¼ × 3⅛ inches. Bound in polished calf, sprinkled edges. The title-page and table of contents (sheet A) are lacking, the former supplied in a rough pen-and-ink facsimile.

OTHER COPIES.

British Museum (2, one the Grenville copy); Bodleian (2); Capell Collection; and White Libraries; also the Chew copy (with engraved title-page only, dated 1636, and no preliminary matter).

REFERENCES.

Lee, *Life of Shakespeare* (1906), p. 178; Grolier Club, *Langland to Wither* (1893), p. 148, No. 172; Locker-Lampson, *Catalogue* (1886), p. 78; Boston Public Library, *Catalogue*; *Barton Collection* (1880), p. 76, in No. 1052; New Shakspere Society, Publications for 1874, Series IV., *Shakspere Allusion-Books*, Part I., pp. xxiii., 152–167; Lowndes, 3 (1869): 1537; Hazlitt, *Hand-Book to the Popular, Poetical, and Dramatic Literature of Great Britain* (1867), p. 389.

The Collier-Locker Lampson copy, with ex-libris of the latter and the former's autograph on the crude pen-and-ink facsimile title-page.

Hazlitt records a copy (*Collections and Notes*, 1876, p. 289) in which "there is a duplicate of leaf B, exhibiting a different setting-up." This was most likely the first leaf of the text of the Second or 1834 Edition.

Meres' *Palladis Tamia* was written as a second part of John Bodenham's *Politeuphuia* (1597), "for Nicholas Ling." Meres says of the *Politeuphuia* in his address "To the Reader" in the 1634 edition of his own work "that thrice within one yeare it hath runne thorow the Preſſe." And another writer says, "Such was its popularity, that it was from time to time 'newly corrected and amended', and passed through eighteen editions before the Restoration." The *Politeuphuia* and *Palladis Tamia* both have the secondary title, *Wits Common wealth*.

There appear to have been two other works belonging to this series: the Third Part, *Wits Theatre of the Little World* (1598), "by I. R. for N. L."; and the

Fourth Part, *Palladis Palatium*, published anonymously, but written by William Wrednot (1604), "by G. Eld for Francis Burton."

The First Edition of *Palladis Tamia* (1598), that here described, has head-lines on the verso and recto pages respectively, as follows: | *The ſecond part of* | *Wits Common-wealth.* | .

The Second Edition (1634), a small duodecimo (A, 8 leaves, B to Ii, each 12 leaves, Kk, 4 leaves, the last probably blank), "by William Stanſby, and are to be ſold by Richard Royſton," appeared as *Wits Common Wealth. The Second Part.* This edition contains on leaves A 2 to [A 4] an address "To the Reader" not to be found in the First Edition. The head-lines on verso and recto pages respectively read | *Wits Common* .| *Wealth* | . Of this edition there are copies in the British Museum, Bodleian, Huth, and White Libraries. To some copies of this edition is prefixed an engraved title-page by Droeshout, entitled | WITTS | ACADEMY | A | *Treaſurie of* | *Goulden* | *Sentences* | *Similes and* | *Examples.* | . . . | *Printed at London* | *for Richard Royſton* | 1636. | . Each of the copies in the Bodleian and Huth Libraries has the letterpress title-page dated 1634 and this engraved title-page. There are copies with this engraved title-page only in the British Museum and Boston Public Libraries. Mr. Chew's copy of the First Edition has this title-page only.

Hazlitt (*Collections and Notes*, 1876, p. 289) records a copy examined by him in which this engraved title-page is dated 1635.

"Of the many testimonies paid to Shakespeare's literary reputation at this period of his career, the most striking was that of Francis Meres. Meres was a learned graduate of Cambridge University, a divine and schoolmaster, who brought out in 1598 a collection of apophthegms on morals, religion, and literature which he entitled 'Palladis Tamia.' . . . Shakespeare figured in Meres's pages as the greatest man of letters of the day. . . . Shakespeare's name was thenceforth of value to unprincipled publishers, and they sought to palm off on their customers as his work the productions of inferior pens."

Palladis Tamia contains, on folio 282 (edition of 1634, p. 623), the earliest printed list of Shakespeare's plays, as quoted below.

Mention by contemporaneous writers is of great importance in ascertaining the chronology of Shakespeare's writings. No single work has contributed more information upon this point than the work here described. Meres enumerates twelve plays. The "*Loue labours wonne*" in his list is generally believed to have been the earlier form of *All's Well that Ends Well*, but some have attempted to identify it with *The Taming of the Shrew*, others with *Much Ado about Nothing*.

Folios 279–287 (Second Edition, pp. 616–635) contain | A comparatiue diſcourſe of | our Engliſh Poets, with the | *Greeke, Latine, and Ita-* | *lian Poets.* | , in the course of which all the principal English poets of the day are mentioned. The principal passages referring to Shakespeare are as follows:

"The Engliſh tongue is mightily enriched, and gorgeouſlie inueſted in rare ornaments and reſplendent abiliments by ſir *Philip Sidney, Spencer, Daniel, Drayton, Warner, Shakeſpeare, Marlow* and *Chapman*. .

1598   *Shakespeariana*   No. 637

Palladis Tamia.

WITS
TREASVRY

Being the Second part
of *Wits Common*
wealth.

BY
Francis Meres Maister
of Artes of both Vni-
uerſities.

Viuitur ingenio, catera mortis erunt.

AT LONDON
Printed by P. Short, for Cuthbert Burbie, and
are to be ſolde at his ſhop at the Royall
Exchange, 1 5 9 8.

No. 637.   Title-page of Meres' Palladis Tamia; 1st Edition; 1598.
Reproduced from the British Museum copy.

"'As the foule of *Euphorbus* was thought to liue in *Pythagoras*: fo the fweete wittie foule of *Ouid* liues in mellifluous & hony-tongued *Shakeſpeare*, witnes his *Venus* and *Adonis*, his *Lucrece*, his fugred Sonnets among his priuate friends, &c. [When this was written Shakespeare's Sonnets were still unpublished, and only circulated among his friends in manuscript.]

"As *Plautus* and *Seneca* are accounted the beſt for Comedy and Tragedy among the Latines: fo *Shakeſpeare* among ẙ Engliſh is the moſt excellent in both kinds for the ſtage; for Comedy, witnes his *G̃tlemẽ of Verona*, his *Errors*, his *Loue labors loft*, his *Loue labours wonne*, his *Midfummers night dreame*, & his *Merchant of Venice* : for Tragedy his *Richard the 2. Richard the 3. Henry the 4. King Iohn, Titus Andronicus* and his *Romeo* and *Iuliet*.

"As *Epius Stolo* faid, that the Mufes would fpeake with *Plautus* tongue, if they would fpeak Latin : fo I fay that the Mufes would fpeak with *Shakefpeares* fine filed phrafe, if they would fpeake Englifh."

The above extract, taken in connection with the date at which it was published, would seem to refute sufficiently the opinion of some modern critics that Shakespeare was not appreciated by his contemporaries.

Five sections, including the "comparatiue difcourfe" (folios 275-288), are reprinted in the New Shakspere Society's Publications for 1874, Series IV., *Shakspere Allusion-Books*, Part I., pp. 152-167.

SHAKESPEARIANA.

THE RETVRNE FROM PERNASSVS: OR THE SCOURGE OF SIMONY. LONDON, *by G. Eld, for Iohn Wright*, 1606.   [638]

Small quarto.

COLLATION BY SIGNATURES : A to H, each 4 leaves; I, 2 leaves (the last, probably blank, lacking); total 34 unnumbered leaves.

COLLATION BY PAGINATION : [title, as reproduced; *See* No. 638], recto of [A]; — [blank], verso of [A]; — | The Pro1 logue. | , recto of A 2 to recto of [A 3]; — [type-ornament tail-piece], recto of [A 3]; — | The names of the Actors. | , verso of [A 3]; — [text, with running head-lines] | *The returne from Pernaffus*. | , recto of [A 4] to verso of I ; — | FINIS. | , verso of I ; — [1 leaf, probably blank], [I 2].

CONDITION: Size of leaf, 6¾ × 4⅞ inches. Bound in green crushed levant morocco, gilt edges; by Bedford.

OTHER COPIES.

Bodleian (2); Capell Collection; Ellesmere; Huth; Boston Public; Hoe; and White Libraries.

REFERENCES.

Nicoll and Seccombe, 1 (1907) : 221 ; Hoe, *Catalogue*, 4 (1904) : 35 ; Greg, *List of Masques, Pageants, &c.* (Bibliographical Society ; 1902), *Essay Introductory*, p. xi. ; Greg, *List of English Plays* (Bibliographical Society ; 1900), p. 133 ; Hazlitt, *Manual of Old English Plays* (1892), p. 193 ; Locker-Lampson, *Catalogue* (1886), p. 93 ; Huth, *Catalogue*, 4 (1880) : 1238 ; Lowndes, 4 (1869) : 1786 ; Hazlitt, *Hand-Book* (1867), p. 470, No. 66 ; also p. 656, No. 23.

The Sykes-Locker Lampson copy, with ex-libris of the latter.

The First (?) Edition (1606) is that here described.

Of the Second (?) Edition (1606), "by G. Eld, for Iohn Wright" (A-H, each 4 leaves), there are copies in the British Museum (3), Bodleian, Capell Collection, Dyce Collection (2), Devonshire, Hoe, and White Libraries.

Hazlitt says there were "two editions the same year, with the same title (except as regards the arrangement of the lines in the imprint), but with rather important differences as regards the text: in the second many errors are corrected. It is a curious piece, with numerous allusions to contemporary writers, but it was written and acted a few years before it was published."

He also says that this work, as altered and adapted by Robert Wild, was published in 1689 as *The Benefice, a Comedy.*

This very witty dramatic satire contains some curious notices of Shakespeare, Marlowe, Spenser, Drayton, Churchyard, Ben Jonson, and other dramatists and poets of the time, some of whom are treated with much severity.

In act i., sc. 2 (verso of leaf B), we read:

> "*Ing.* . . . Good men and true, ſtand togither: heare your cenſure, what's thy iudgement of *Spencer*?
>   *Iud.* A ſweeter ſwan then euer ſong in Poe[try],
>   A ſhriller Nightingale then euer bleſt
>   The prouder groues of ſelfe admiring Rome.
>   Blith was each vally, and each ſheapeard proud,
>   While he did chaunt his rurall minſtralſye.
>   Attentiue was full many a dainty eare.
>   Nay hearers hong vpon his melting tong,
>   While ſweetly of his Faiery Queene he ſong."

In the same scene (verso of leaf B 2) Judicio is made to say of Shakespeare:

> "*Iud.* Who loues *Adonis* loue, or *Lucre's* rape,
> His ſweeter verſe contaynes hart robbing life,
> Could but a grauer ſubiect him content,
> Without loues fooliſh lazy languiſhment."

In act iv., sc. 3 (recto of G 3), Kemp, the celebrated actor, says:

> "Why heres our fellow *Shakeſpeare* puts them all downe, I and *Ben Ionſon* too. O that *Ben Ionſon* is a peſtilent fellow, he brought vp *Horace* giuing the Poets a pill, but our fellow *Shakeſpeare* hath giuen him a purge that made him beray his credit:"

Speaking of the methods employed in dramatic publications of the seventeenth century, Greg says: "The habit of reprinting titlepages in order to make a book appear up to date was also, of course, common. One of the most interesting cases is that of the *Tragical Reign of Selimus* which originally appeared anonymously from the press of Thomas Creede in 1594, the unsold copies being re-issued more than forty years later, namely in 1638, as printed 'by Iohn Crooke for Richard Serger,' the new titlepage also bearing T. G. as the author's initials, no doubt with the object of leading the public to suppose that it was from the pen of Thomas Goffe, whose tragedies on oriental and classical themes had then lately appeared. The reverse case, that of two distinct editions in which the titlepages alone are printed from the same setting up of the type, though naturally far less frequent, nevertheless occurs, and is rather difficult to explain, since it is not easy to see why the titlepage should have been kept in type after the rest had been distributed. One instance, I think, occurs in the two editions of the anonymous comedy *Albumazar*, printed in 1615. The

THE
RETVRNE FROM PERNASSVS:
Or
The Scourge of Simony.

Publiquely acted by the Students in Saint Iohns Colledge in *Cambridge.*

AT LONDON
Printed by *G. Eld,* for *Iohn Wright,* and are to bee sold at his shop at Christ church Gate.
1606.

No. 638.   Title-page of The Retvrne from Pernassvs; 1st Edition; 1606.

editions are certainly distinct, having collations respectively A² B–L⁴ and A–I⁴, but so far as I am aware the titlepages are identical. Since, however, I only know of one library which contains copies of both editions (U.L.C.), I should be inclined to suspect that one copy had the title properly belonging to the other edition, were it not for the fact that the identical case repeats itself in connection with the *Return from Parnassus*, copies of the two editions of which, published in 1606, may be compared both at the Bodleian and at Trinity College, Cambridge. Here we find that while the two editions have respectively the collations A–H⁴ I² and A–H⁴, the titlepages are again printed from the same setting up of the type. There is even a third case in the 1609 *Pericles* [our No. 607] . . . though here one of the editions is unfortunately represented by a single copy, the proper titlepage to which may have perished and been replaced from a copy of the other edition."

SHAKESPEARIANA. Boaden, James. (*b.* 1762, *d.* 1839.)

AN INQUIRY INTO THE AUTHENTICITY OF VARIOUS PICTURES AND PRINTS . . . OF SHAKSPEARE. LONDON, *for Robert Triphook,* 1824. [639]

Octavo.

COLLATION BY SIGNATURES: 2 leaves, without signature-marks; a, 4 leaves; B to O, each 8 leaves (the last blank and genuine); total 110 leaves.

COLLATION BY PAGINATION: [halftitle], recto of first leaf; —[blank], verso of first leaf; —[title] | AN | INQUIRY | INTO THE | AUTHENTICITY | OF VARIOUS | PICTURES AND PRINTS, | WHICH, FROM THE DECEASE OF THE POET TO OUR OWN TIMES, | HAVE BEEN OFFERED TO THE PUBLIC | AS | PORTRAITS | OF | SHAKSPEARE: | CONTAINING | A CAREFUL EXAMINATION OF THE EVIDENCE ON WHICH | THEY CLAIM TO BE RECEIVED; | BY WHICH THE PRETENDED PORTRAITS HAVE BEEN REJECTED, | THE GENUINE CONFIRMED AND ESTABLISHED. | ILLUSTRATED BY | ACCURATE AND FINISHED ENGRAVINGS, | BY THE ABLEST ARTISTS, | FROM SUCH ORIGINALS AS WERE OF INDISPUTABLE | AUTHORITY. | BY JAMES BOADEN, ESQ. | "We will draw the curtain, and shew you the PICTURE." | TWELFTH NIGHT. | *LONDON:* | PRINTED FOR ROBERT TRIPHOOK, 23, OLD BOND-STREET. | 1824. |, recto of second leaf; — [imprint], verso of second leaf; —[preface and contents], pp. [i.]–[vii.]; —[blank], p. [viii.]; —[introduction], pp. [1]–7; —[blank], p. [8]; —[text in several portions, the first with heading] | MARTIN DROESHOUT'S | PRINT OF SHAKSPEARE. |, pp. [9]–206; —[1 blank leaf], [O 8].

PLATES: 5 portraits of Shakespeare (the last lacking), as follows:

[1] Mezzotint; bust, directed, facing, and looking to the front; with inscription: | *Engraved by Cha*ˢ *Turner Mezzotinto Engraver in ordinary to His Majesty.* | WILLIAM SHAKESPEAR | *From the original Picture by Cornelius Iansen* | in the Collection of His Grace the Duke of Somerset. | *London, Pub*ᵈ *Jan*ʸ *1, 1824, by Rob*ᵗ *Triphook Bookseller Old Bond Street.* | ; facing the title-page.

[2] Line engraving; bust, directed and facing slightly to the left, looking to the front; with inscription : | *I. Swaine fc.* | SHAKSPEARE | *from the First Folio Edition.* |; facing p. [9].

[3] Stipple engraving; bust, directed, facing, and looking to the front; with inscription : | *E Scriven sc.* | *Drawn by M*ʳ

Iohn Boaden from the Stratford Bust. | ; facing p. [25].

[4] Stipple engraving; bust, directed, facing, and looking to the front; with inscription: | *Scriven Sculp! | From M*̣ *Ozias Humphry's Drawing of the | Chandos Picture made for the late M*̣ *Malone | in the Year 1783.*| ; facing p. [39].

[5] Line engraving; half-length, directed, facing, and looking to the front; with inscription, in verse: | *This Shadowe is renowned Shakefpear's? Soule of th'age* | [7 lines]| *W. M. fculpfit.* | From the Edition of his Poems, 1640. | ; facing p. [113]. This portrait is lacking in the copy here described.

EXTRA-ILLUSTRATED.

Inserted in this work are 12 portraits, as follows:

[1] Line engraving; India proof; similar to [2] above; with inscription: | *Engraved by H. Cook.* | WILLIAM SHAKESPEARE. | *Engraved from the Portrait by M. Droeshout, | in the Folio Edition 1623.* | ; facing p. 23.

[2] Line engraving; inlaid to size; view of Shakespeare's monument at Stratford; with inscription, at top: | DRAMATIC BIOGRAPHY.| ; at bottom: | *Shakspeare's Monument at Stratford on Avon — R. Cooper Sculp.* | ; facing p. 27.

[3] Line engraving; bust, directed slightly to the left, facing and looking to the front; with inscription, at top: | Engraved for the Univerfal Magazine. | ; at bottom: | WILLIAM SHAKESPEAR.| *Printed for I. Hinton at the King's Arms in Newgate Street.* | ; facing p. 33.

[4] Stipple engraving; proof; bust, directed, facing, and looking slightly to the left; with inscription: | *Holl sculp.*| ; facing p. 53.

[5] Stipple engraving; bust; directed, facing, and looking to the front; with inscription at the bottom, to the right: | *Engraved on Steel by Hopwood.*| ; in the centre: | *Shakspeare.*| ; facing p. [66].

[6] Line engraving; similar to the lacking plate [5]; with inscription, at top: | To Face the Firft Page N° 3 of Shakespeares Will. | ; at bottom: | *This Shadowe is renowned Shakefpear's? Soule of th'age* | [7 lines]] | ; facing p. [113].

[7] Line engraving; India proof; similar to the lacking plate [5]; with inscription: | *This Shadowe . . .* | [7 lines] | *W. M. fculpfit.*| ; facing p. 119.

[8] Stipple engraving; bust, directed, facing, and looking to the front; with inscription: | *William Shakspear* [facsimile signature] | *Engraved by T. W. Harland from the portrait by N. Hilliard.*| ; facing p. [123].

[9] Stipple engraving; half-length, directed and facing slightly to the right, looking to the front; with inscription: | *William Shakspear* [facsimile signature] | WILLIAM SHAKESPEARE. | A. Fullarton & C̣° London & Edinburgh| ; facing p. 137.

[10] Lithograph; half-length, directed, facing, and looking to the front; with no inscription; facing p. 145.

[11] Lithograph; inlaid to size; with inscription: | Shakspeare's Monument, Stratford Church. | ; facing p. 176.

[12] Line engraving; medal of Shakespeare; profile of bust, looking to the left; with inscription around bust: | GULIELMUS SHAKSPEARE | ; at bottom, to the right: | *J. Bate, exc!* | ; facing p. 199.

CONDITION: Size of leaf, 9 × 5½ inches. Bound in half blue crushed levant morocco, gilt top, other edges uncut; by Bradstreet.

REFERENCES.

Hoe, *Catalogue*, 1 (1905): 62; Lenox Library, *Shakespeare* (1880), p. 64, No. 375; Boston Public Library, *Catalogue*; Barton Collection (1880), p. 79, No. 1088 (2 copies); Lowndes, 1 (1869): 223.

This work was also published in a large-paper edition, in quarto, of 143 pages.

Of all the portraits of Shakespeare, the greater number of which are more or less ideal, indisputably the most satisfactory if not authentic of them all is the Droeshout engraving, first published on the title-page of the First Folio edition in 1623 (our No. 610).

SHAKESPEARIANA. Wivell, Abraham. (*b.* 1786, *d.* 1849.)

AN INQUIRY INTO THE HISTORY, AUTHENTICITY, & CHARACTERISTICS OF THE SHAKSPEARE PORTRAITS. LONDON, *Published by the Author*, 1827. [640]

Octavo.

COLLATION BY SIGNATURES: 2 leaves, without signature-marks; A to Z, AA to II, each 4 leaves; total 130 leaves.

COLLATION BY PAGINATION: [title] | AN INQUIRY | INTO THE | History, Authenticity, & Characteristics | OF THE | SHAKSPEARE PORTRAITS, | IN WHICH THE CRITICISMS OF | MALONE, STEEVENS, BOADEN, & OTHERS, | Are Examined, Confirmed, or Refuted. | [6 lines] | Together with an Exposé of the spurious Pictures and Prints. | BY ABRAHAM WIVELL, | *PORTRAIT PAINTER.* | London: | PUBLISHED BY THE AUTHOR, 40, CASTLE STREET EAST, | OXFORD STREET, | AND SOLD BY ALL BOOKSELLERS. | 1827. |, recto of first leaf; — [imprint], verso of first leaf; — [contents], recto and verso of second leaf; — [dedication and introduction], pp. [i.]–vi.; — [text in several sections, the first with heading] | ADVERTISEMENT | TO | The Preface | OF | *Mr. RICHARDSON's PROPOSALS, &c.* | 1794. |, pp. [7]–254; — | *Directions for placing the Engravings to this Work.* | [8 lines] | ERRATA. | [21 lines] |, p. [255]; — [blank], p. [256].

PLATES: 8 plates, portraits of Shakespeare, as called for in the binder's directions; and 1 plate of facsimiles (facing p. 39).

EXTRA-ILLUSTRATED.

Inserted in this work are 12 plates, portraits of Shakespeare, facing pp. [29], 35, 52, 62, 147, [197], 229, 239 (same as at p. 62), [240], [243], 251, and 253.

CONDITION: Size of leaf, 8 13/16 × 5 5/8 inches. Bound in half blue crushed levant morocco, gilt top, other edges uncut; by Bradstreet.

SHAKESPEARIANA (BIBLIOGRAPHY). Halliwell-Phillipps, James Orchard. (*b.* 1820, *d.* 1889.)

SHAKESPERIANA. A CATALOGUE OF THE EARLY EDITIONS OF SHAKESPEARE'S PLAYS. LONDON, *John Russell Smith*, 1841. [641]

Octavo.

COLLATION BY SIGNATURES: [A], 2 leaves; B to F, each 4 leaves; G, 2 leaves; total 24 numbered leaves.

COLLATION BY PAGINATION: [title] | Shakesperiana. | A CATALOGUE | OF THE EARLY EDITIONS OF | Shakespeare's Plays, | AND OF THE | COMMENTARIES AND OTHER PUBLICATIONS | ILLUSTRATIVE OF HIS WORKS. | BY | JAMES ORCHARD HALLIWELL, . . . | . . . | LONDON: | JOHN RUSSELL SMITH, | 4, OLD COMPTON STREET, SOHO SQUARE. | M DCCC XLI. |, p. [1]; — [imprint], p. [2]; — [preface], pp. [3]–4; — [text], pp. [5]–46; — [imprint] | GREENWICH: PRINTED BY HENRY S. RICHARDSON. |, p. 46; — [publisher's advertisement], pp. [1]–2.

CONDITION: Size of leaf, 8¾ × 5⅝ inches. Bound in publisher's cloth, uncut edges.

REFERENCE.

Lenox Library, *Shakespeare* (1880), p. 68, No. 412.

No. 641   *William Shakespeare*   1841

Of this work a few copies were printed on India paper.

It has been superseded by Lowndes' *Bibliographer's Manual* (1869) and Greg's *List of English Plays* (1900).

"Something of the same kind was undertaken by Mr. Wilson, and published in 1827; but, besides being very concise in the list of early editions of the plays, it offers us no correct accounts of the different impressions."

SHAKESPEARIANA. Smirke, *Sir* **Robert** (*b*. 1752, *d*. 1845), *and others*.

ILLUSTRATIONS OF SHAKESPEAR'S PLAYS. LONDON, *Frederick Warne and Co.;* NEW YORK, *Scribner, Welford and Co.,* [n. d.].   [642]

Folio.

COLLATION BY SIGNATURES: 53 unnumbered leaves, without signature-marks.

COLLATION BY PAGINATION: [half-title] | ILLUSTRATIONS | OF | SHAKSPEARE'S PLAYS. |, p. [1]; — [blank], p. [2]; — [title] | ILLUSTRATIONS | OF | SHAKSPEARE'S PLAYS. | FIFTY ORIGINAL DESIGNS BY | R. SMIRKE, R.A.; T. STOTHARD, R.A.; E. H. CORBOULD, | ETC. ETC. | ENGRAVED ON STEEL | BY | CHARLES HEATH, W. GREATBACH, | ETC. | WITH PORTRAIT, AND LETTERPRESS DESCRIPTIONS OF THE PLATES. | [publishers' device] | LONDON: | FREDERICK WARNE AND CO. | BEDFORD STREET, COVENT GARDEN. | NEW YORK: SCRIBNER, WELFORD AND CO. |, p. [3]; — [imprint] | LONDON: | SAVILL, EDWARDS AND CO., PRINTERS, CHANDOS STREET, | COVENT GARDEN. |, p. [4]; — | CONTENTS. |, p. [5]; — [blank], p. [6]; — [50 pages of letterpress, taken from the plays, versos blank, alternating with the plates].

PLATES: 51 plates, India-paper proofs, including a portrait of Shakespeare as frontispiece, as called for in the table of contents.

CONDITION: Size of leaf, 16¾ × 11¼ inches. Bound in cloth, bevelled boards, gilt edges.

SHAKESPEARE, WILLIAM. Dyce, Alexander, *editor*.

THE WORKS OF WILLIAM SHAKESPEARE. THIRD EDITION. LONDON, *Chapman and Hall*, 1875–1876.   9 vols., octavo, viz.:   [643]

VOL. I. 1875.

COLLATION BY SIGNATURES: 5 leaves, without signature-marks; A to Z, AA to MM, each 8 leaves; NN, 3 leaves; total 288 numbered leaves.

COLLATION BY PAGINATION: [half-title], p. [i.]; — [imprint], p. [ii.]; — [title] | THE WORKS OF | WILLIAM SHAKESPEARE. | THE TEXT REVISED | BY | THE REV. ALEXANDER DYCE. | IN NINE VOLUMES. | VOL. I. | *THIRD EDITION*. | LONDON: | CHAPMAN AND HALL, 193 PICCADILLY. 1875. |, p. [iii.]; — [blank], p. [iv.]; — [dedication, contents, preface to the Third Edition, and preface to the Second Edition], pp. [v.]–xxv.; — [blank], p. [xxvi.]; — [preface to the edition of 1857], pp. [1]–11; — [blank], p. [12]; — | SOME AC-

1875-76 — William Shakespeare — No. 643

COUNT | OF THE | LIFE OF SHAKE- SPEARE. |, pp. [13]–137; — | APPEN- DIX. |, pp. 138–148; — [titles, notes, and extracts from early editions], pp. 149–170; — [*The Tempest, The Two Gentlemen of Verona, The Merry Wives of Windsor*, and *Measure for Measure*, with half-title, text, and notes to each], pp. [171]–546. The pagination is as follows: 1–16, 16ª–16ᵈ, 17–546.

Vol. 2. 1875.

COLLATION BY SIGNATURES: [A], 4 leaves (the first blank and genuine); B to Z, AA to EE, each 8 leaves (the last blank and genuine); total 220 leaves.

COLLATION BY PAGINATION: [1 blank leaf], [A]; — [half-title], recto of [A 2]; — [imprint], verso of [A 2]; — [title, same as in Vol. 1, except volume-number], recto of [A 3]; — [blank], verso of [A 3]; — [contents], recto of [A 4]; — [blank], verso of [A 4]; — [*The Comedy of Errors, Much Ado about Nothing, Love's Labour's Lost, A Midsummer-Night's Dream,* and *The Merchant of Venice*, with half-title, text, and notes to each], pp. [1]–429; — [imprint], p. [430]; — [1 blank leaf], [EE 8].

Vol. 3. 1875.

COLLATION BY SIGNATURES: [A], 4 leaves (the first blank and genuine); B to Z, AA to LL, each 8 leaves; MM, 2 leaves; total 270 leaves.

COLLATION BY PAGINATION: [1 blank leaf], [A]; — [half-title], recto of [A 2]; — [imprint], verso of [A 2]; — [title, same as in Vol. 1, except volume-number], recto of [A 3]; — [blank], verso of [A 3]; — [contents], recto of [A 4]; — [blank], verso of [A 4]; — [*As You Like It, The Taming of the Shrew, All's Well That Ends Well, Twelfth-Night,* and *The Winter's Tale*, with half-title, text, and notes to each], pp. [1]–531; — [blank], p. [532].

Vol. 4. 1875.

COLLATION BY SIGNATURES: [A], 4 leaves (the first blank and genuine); B to Z, AA to LL, each 8 leaves; MM, 4 leaves (the last blank and genuine); total 272 leaves.

COLLATION BY PAGINATION: [1 blank leaf], [A]; — [half-title], recto of [A 2]; — [imprint], verso of [A 2]; — [title, same as in Vol. 1, except volume-number], recto of [A 3]; — [blank], verso of [A 3]; — [contents], recto of [A 4]; — [blank], verso of [A 4]; — [*King John, King Richard the Second, The First Part of King Henry the Fourth, The Second Part of King Henry the Fourth,* and *King Henry the Fifth*, with half-title, text, and notes to each], pp. [1]–534; — [1 blank leaf], [MM 4].

Vol. 5. 1875.

COLLATION BY SIGNATURES: [A], 4 leaves (the first blank and genuine); B to Z, AA to PP, each 8 leaves; QQ, 2 leaves; total 302 leaves.

COLLATION BY PAGINATION: [1 blank leaf], [A]; — [half-title], recto of [A 2]; — [imprint], verso of [A 2]; — [title, same as in Vol. 1, except volume-number], recto of [A 3]; — [blank], verso of [A 3]; — [contents], recto of [A 4]; — [blank], verso of [A 4]; — [*The First Part of King Henry the Sixth, The Second Part of King Henry the Sixth, The Third Part of King Henry the Sixth, King Richard the Third,* and *King Henry the Eighth*, with half-title, text, and notes to each], pp. [1]–595; — [blank], p. [596].

No. 643   *William Shakespeare*   1875-76

VOL. 6. 1875.

COLLATION BY SIGNATURES: [A], 4 leaves (the first blank and genuine); B to Z, AA to YY, each 8 leaves; ZZ, 4 leaves (the last blank and genuine); total 360 leaves.

COLLATION BY PAGINATION: [1 blank leaf], [A];—[half-title], recto of [A 2];—[imprint], verso of [A 2];—[title, same as in Vol. 1, except volume-number], recto of [A 3];—[blank], verso of [A 3];—[contents], recto of [A 4];—[blank], verso of [A 4];—[*Troilus and Cressida, Coriolanus, Titus Andronicus, Romeo and Juliet, Timon of Athens,* and *Julius Cæsar,* with half-title, text, and notes to each], pp. [1]-710;—[1 blank leaf], [ZZ 4].

VOL. 7. 1875.

COLLATION BY SIGNATURES: [A], 4 leaves (the first blank and genuine); B to Z, AA to ZZ, 3 A, 3 B, 3 C, each 8 leaves; total 388 leaves.

COLLATION BY PAGINATION: [1 blank leaf], [A];—[half-title], recto of [A 2];—[imprint], verso of [A 2];—[title, same as in Vol. 1, except volume-number], recto of [A 3];—[blank], verso of [A 3];—[contents], recto of [A 4];—[blank], verso of [A 4];—[*Macbeth, Hamlet, King Lear, Othello, Antony and Cleopatra,* and *Cymbeline,* with half-title, text, and notes to each], pp. [1]-767;—[blank], p. [768].

VOL. 8. 1876.

COLLATION BY SIGNATURES: [A], 4 leaves (the first blank and genuine); B to Z, AA to GG, each 8 leaves; HH, 4 leaves; total 240 leaves.

COLLATION BY PAGINATION: [1 blank leaf], [A];—[half-title], recto of [A 2];—[imprint], verso of [A 2];—[title, same as in Vol. 1, except volume-number and date of imprint], recto of [A 3];—[blank], verso of [A 3];—[contents], recto of [A 4];—[blank], verso of [A 4];—[*Pericles, The Two Noble Kinsmen, Venus and Adonis, Lucrece, Sonnets, A Lover's Complaint,* and *The Passionate Pilgrim,* with half-title, text, and notes to each], pp. [1]-468;—[*The Phœnix and Turtle*], pp. [469]-471;—[blank], p. [472].

VOL. 9. 1876.

COLLATION BY SIGNATURES: [A], 4 leaves; B to Z, AA to KK, each 8 leaves; LL, 2 leaves (the last blank and genuine); total 262 numbered leaves.

COLLATION BY PAGINATION: [half-title], p. [i.];—[imprint], p. [ii.];—[title, same as in Vol. 8, except volume-number], p. [iii.];—[blank], p. [iv.];—[preface], p. [v.];—[blank], p. [vi.];—| NOTE. |, pp. [vii.]-viii.;—[text, with heading] | A | GLOSSARY TO SHAKESPEARE. |, pp. [1]-514;—[1 blank leaf], [LL 2].

EXTRA-ILLUSTRATED.

Inserted in Vols. 1-8 are 190 engravings, nearly all by Starling, after various artists.

CONDITION: Size of leaf, 8½ x 5½ inches. Bound in half red crushed levant morocco, gilt tops; by R. W. Smith.

The First Edition of Dyce's Shakespeare was published in 1857 in six volumes; the Second, in nine volumes in 1866 and 1867, the ninth volume bearing the latter date.

During a long life of study Dyce united the patient learning of an antiquary with a real appreciation of the beauties of the early English poets and dramatists. In dealing with Shakespeare his mind, as a general rule, was fixed on restoring rather than amending the original text, so that few commentators have excelled him in satisfying both the poetic student and the archaic scholar.

SHAKESPEARE, WILLIAM (BIBLIOGRAPHY). Winsor, Justin. (*b.* 1831, *d.* 1897.)

A BIBLIOGRAPHY OF THE ORIGINAL QUARTOS AND FOLIOS OF SHAKESPEARE. BOSTON, *James R. Osgood and Company*, 1876.
[644]

Folio. No. 14 of 250 copies printed.

COLLATION BY SIGNATURES: 55 numbered leaves, without signature-marks.

COLLATION BY PAGINATION: [title] | A | BIBLIOGRAPHY | OF THE | ORIGINAL QUARTOS AND FOLIOS | OF | SHAKESPEARE | WITH | PARTICULAR REFERENCE TO COPIES IN AMERICA | BY | JUSTIN WINSOR | SUPERINTENDENT OF THE BOSTON PUBLIC LIBRARY | WITH | Sixty-Eight Heliotype Facsimiles | BOSTON | JAMES R. OSGOOD AND COMPANY | (LATE TICKNOR & FIELDS, AND FIELDS, OSGOOD, & CO.) | 1876 |, p. [1]; — [copyright and edition notices], p. [2]; — [list of illustrations], pp. 3–4; — [introduction], pp. 5–20; — [half-title] | THE QUARTOS BEFORE THE FOLIO | OF 1623 | WITH | COMPARISONS OF THE TEXT OF THE PLAYS IN THAT FOLIO |, p. [21]; — [key to copies in America], p. [22]; — [text], pp. [23]–74; — [half-title] | THE FOLIOS OF SHAKESPEARE | 1623, 1632, 1663–64, 1685 |, p. [75]; — [blank], p. [76]; — [text in several sections, the first with heading] | THE FIRST FOLIO, 1623. |, pp. 77–109; — [blank], p. [110].

PLATES: 68 facsimile title-pages, etc., at the end, as called for in the list of illustrations.

CONDITION: Size of leaf, 14⅜ x 10¼ inches. Bound in red cloth, uncut edges, with paper title-label.

This work is largely a history and description of the Barton Collection now in the Boston Public Library. Much attention is paid to the records of prices obtained at sales, public and private, and copies are located as far as possible, especially in the United States. In the interval since its publication many copies have changed hands, so that this portion of the work, valuable in its day, is now chiefly of value from a historical standpoint. Of the 68 facsimile title-pages, etc., appended to the text, 30 are reproductions of originals in the Barton Collection. Of the remaining 38, 33 are taken from the Ashbee pen-and-ink facsimiles and Halliwell's folio edition, and the remaining 5 from other sources.

SHELLEY, PERCY BYSSHE. (*b.* 1792, *d.* 1822.)

THE CENCI. [LEGHORN] ITALY, *for C. and J. Ollier*, LONDON, 1819.
[645]

Octavo. First Edition.

COLLATION BY SIGNATURES: 4 leaves, without signature-marks (the first blank and genuine); **, [1] to 13, each 4 leaves; total 60 numbered leaves.

COLLATION BY PAGINATION: [1 blank leaf]; — [title] | THE CENCI. | A TRAGEDY, | IN FIVE ACTS. | *By* PERCY B. SHELLEY. | ITALY. | PRINTED FOR C. AND J. OLLIER | VERE STREET, BOND STREET. | LONDON. | 1819. |, p. [i.]; — [blank], p. [ii.]; —|

No. 645   *Percy Bysshe Shelley*   **1819**

DEDICATION | TO | LEIGH HUNT ESQ. | [signed] | Your affectionate friend, | PERCY B. SHELLEY. | [dated] | *Rome, May 29. 1819.* |, pp. [iii.]–v.; —[blank], p. [vi.]; —[preface], pp. vii.–xiv.; —[half-title] | THE CENCI. |, p. [1]; — | DRAMATIS PERSONÆ. |, p. [2]; — [text, with heading] | THE CENCI |, pp. [3]–104; — | THE END. |, p. 104. CONDITION: Size of leaf, 9¹/₁₀ × 5⅞ inches. Bound in the original boards, uncut edges; with title-label lettered: | THE | CENCI. | 4*s.* 6*d.* bds. | .

REFERENCES.

Slater, *Early Editions* (1894), p. 256, No. 14; Forman, *The Shelley Library, an Essay in Bibliography*, 1 (1886) : 90; Locker-Lampson, *Catalogue* (1886), p. 174; Huth, *Catalogue*, 4 (1880) : 1344; Lowndes, 4 (1869) : 2375.

This is the one book of Shelley's of which a second edition appeared during his lifetime. He began writing it at Rome, May 14, 1819, and finished it at Villa Valsovano, about the middle of August. It was printed at Leghorn, under his personal supervision, to ensure its correctness, as Shelley had been much annoyed by the many mistakes that crept into his text when he was prevented by distance from correcting the proofs. Only 250 copies were printed. It contains a few errors of the press due undoubtedly to the Italian compositors' ignorance of English. *The Cenci* was not published in England until the spring of 1820, and then without the intended frontispiece.

"The list of *errata*," says Forman, "which is in my possession, is in the handwriting of Mrs. Shelley. As it has never as far as I am aware been printed, I give it here:

"'Preface. p. viii, line 2, the words *The Papal government* until the words *a matter of some difficulty* — inclusive — to be printed as a note.

P. xii, line 2 from the bottom, dele the word *most*.

P. 3, l. 5 from the bottom, for *so* read *as*.

P. 4, l. 9, for *respited from hell*, read, *respited me from hell*.

P. 6, last line, for *But that there*, read, *And but that there*.

P. 8, l. 6, for *have* read *had*.

P. 8, l. 15, for *shall* read *shalt*.

P. 10, l. 1, for *yet* read *thus*.

P. 11, l. 2 from the bottom, for *slave* read *vassal*.

P. 18, l. 9, for *dare not one* read *dare no one*.

P. 55, l. 2 from the bottom, read thus

      Ors. Why, that were well. I must be gone; good night!
      When next we meet may all be done ——
        Giac. And all
      Forgotten — Oh, that I had never been!

"Except as regards the punctuation of the last item, the whole of these corrections were duly made in the second edition."

"Universal approbation,'" says Dowden (Globe Edition, p. 347), "soon stamped *The Cenci* as the best tragedy of modern times. . . . The Fifth Act is a masterpiece. It is the finest thing he ever wrote, and may claim proud comparison not only with any contemporary, but preceding, poet."

SHELLEY, PERCY BYSSHE.

QUEEN MAB. LONDON, *Printed and published by W. Clark*, 1821.   [646]

Octavo.   First Published Edition.

COLLATION BY SIGNATURES : [1] to 11, each 8 leaves; 12, 4 leaves; total 92 leaves.

COLLATION BY PAGINATION : [title] | Queen Mab.| BY | PERCY BYSSHE SHELLEY.| London: | PRINTED AND PUBLISHED BY W. CLARK, | 201, STRAND.| 1821.|, p. [1];—[blank], p. [2];—[text, with heading] | Queen Mab.|, pp. [3]-89;—[blank], p. [90]; —[half-title]| NOTES.|, p. [91];— [publisher's note, 7 lines, signed] | W. CLARK.|, p. [92];— | NOTES.|, pp. [93]-182;—[publisher's advertisements, with heading]| BOOKS, | PUBLISHED BY | W. CLARK, 201, STRAND.| QUEEN MAB, . . . |,[etc.], p.[183];—[blank], p. [184].

CONDITION : Size of leaf, $8\frac{15}{16}$ × $5\frac{9}{16}$ inches. Bound in the original boards, uncut edges; with title-label lettered : | QUEEN | Mab.| WITH | NOTES | AND | *Translations*. | 12s. 6d. bds.| .

REFERENCES.

Slater, *Early Editions* (1894), p. 253, No. 6; Forman, *The Shelley Library, an Essay in Bibliography*, 1 (1886) : 36, 46, No. 22; also Nos. 23-26; Lowndes, *Bibliographer's Manual*, 4 (1869) : 2374.

"The poem," says Forman, "was finished in February 1813; and the notes were put together after that date." An edition of 250 copies was then privately printed on fine crown octavo paper. It contained title-page, leaf of dedication, pp. 1-122 of text, half-title to the notes, and text of notes, pp. 125-240. After Shelley's death, Carlile, one of the numerous publishers of the piratical editions of *Queen Mab*, advertised in *The Republican*, in 1822, that he had 180 copies of Shelley's edition.

The First Published Edition is that here described. Some copies of this edition were printed on thick, fine paper. Some copies have the dedication (lacking in the copy here described, and upon the omission of which Shelley congratulated himself), inserted either after the title-page or at the end of the notes. Translations of the notes in French, Latin, and Greek are supplied in the foot-notes. There are two issues of the text. The First Issue contains the whole text and notes intact. In the Second Issue a few of the most aggressive passages have been mutilated by omission of words and even verses. These occur at p. 39, lines 15, 16; p. 54, line 17; p. 55, lines 26-28; p. 65, line 1; p. 77, line 26; p. 82, line 26; p. 98, line 25; p. 146, line 17; p. 147, line 25; p. 171, lines 23 and 24. "The omissions at pages 146 and 147-8 are such as to involve the overrunning of the pages up to 160 inclusive." Forman says he has "not the slightest doubt about the two kinds of copy having been printed from the same types at the same period."

From a note in the British Museum copy it appears that Clark, the publisher, sold only fifty copies of this edition; that he was prosecuted for publishing the work, and tried and convicted in the Old Bailey, but was pardoned on giving up the remainder of the copies to the Society for the Suppression of Vice.

Some of Clark's sheets passed into the hands of Carlile, who, the year after, reissued them with the imprint | London : | Printed and Published by R. Carlile, | 55, Fleet Street. | 1822. | . Some of the copies with this imprint are of the unmutilated issue and have the dedication after the title-page, while others have it after the notes. Carlile did not even cancel the half-title to the notes, on the verso of which was Clark's name. He also issued some copies without the notes.

In 1823 Carlile again reissued Clark's unmutilated sheets, with a new title-page dated 1823, and with the dedication at the end.

The work therefore may contain a title-page, 1 leaf; dedication, 1 leaf; poem, pp. 3–89; half-title to notes, 1 leaf; notes, pp. 93–182; and advertisements of books, 1 leaf.

Clark's edition of 1821 may be found : (*a*) on thick paper or ordinary paper ; (*b*) with or without the dedication ; (*c*) with or without the notes ; (*d*) with the unmutilated text and notes or with the mutilated text and notes.

Carlile's edition of the same sheets of the unmutilated text, with a new title-page dated 1822, may be found : (*a*) with the dedication after the title-page or at the end ; and (*b*) with or without the notes.

Carlile's edition of 1823 is usually found with the unmutilated text and the dedication at the end.

The rhythm of *Queen Mab* was founded on Southey's *Thalaba*, and the first few lines bear a striking resemblance in spirit, though not in idea, to that poem.

SIDNEY, Sir PHILIP. (*b.* 1554, *d.* 1586.)

THE COVNTESSE OF PEMBROKES ARCADIA. LONDON, *for William Ponsonbie*, 1590. [647]

Small quarto. First Edition.

COLLATION BY SIGNATURES: A, 4 leaves (the first blank and genuine); B to Z, Aa to Zz, each 8 leaves ; total 364 leaves.

COLLATION BY PAGINATION : [1 blank leaf], [A]; — [title, as reproduced ; *See* No. 647], recto of [A2]; — [blank], verso of [A2]; — | [type-ornament head-piece] | TO MY DEARE LADIE | AND SISTER, THE COVN- | TESSE OF PEMBROKE. | [signed] | Your louing Brother | *Philip Sidnei.* | , recto of A3 to recto of [A4]; — [note, with heading] | [conventional head-piece] | *THe diuision and summing of the* | *Chapters was not of Sir Philip* | Sidneis *dooing, but aduentured* | *by the ouer-seer of the print, for* | *the more ease of the Readers.* . . . | , verso of [A4]; — [text in 3 books, the first with heading] | [conventional head-piece] | THE COVN- TESSE OF | PEMBROKES ARCADIA WRIT- | TEN BY SIR PHILIP | SIDNEI. | THE FIRST BOOKE. | , recto of folio 1 to verso of folio 97 ; — | *The end of the first Booke.* | , verso of folio 97 ; — | [type-ornament head-piece] | THE SECOND BOOKE | OF THE COVNTESSE OF | PEMBROKES ARCADIA. | , recto of folio 98 to verso of folio 243 ; — | *The end of the second Booke.* | , verso of folio 243 ; — | [type-ornament head-piece] | THE THIRDE BOOKE | OF THE COVN- TESSE OF | PEMBROKES ARCADIA. | , recto of folio 244 to verso of folio 360 ; — | * * * | [conventional tail-piece] | , verso of folio 360. Folio 232 is wrongly numbered 240 ; 329 is 389 ; and 330 is 390.

CONDITION : Size of leaf, 7¾ × 5⅝ inches. Bound in green crushed levant morocco, elaborately tooled sides, tan morocco doublure with elaborate gilt borders, marbled fly-leaves, gilt edges; by Bedford; in red straight-grained morocco solander case.

OTHER COPIES.

British Museum; Capell Collection; Huth; Halsey; and Hoe Libraries.

REFERENCES.

Hoe, *Catalogue*, 4 (1904) : 175; *The Bibliographer*, 1 (1902) : 379; Lee (Sidney), *Great Englishmen of the Sixteenth Century* (1904), pp. 101, 102, *note*; Grolier Club, *Langland to Wither* (1893), p. 187, No. 214; Sommer (H. Oskar), *Countess of Pembroke's Arcadia, 1590* (Facsimile Edition; 1891), Introduction, p. 2; Huth, *Catalogue*, 4 (1880) : 1355; Locker-Lampson, *Catalogue* (1886), p. 116; Lowndes, 4 (1869) : 2395; Hazlitt, *Hand-Book* (1867), p. 557, No. 1*a*; Collier, *Rarest Books*, 4 (1866) : 50–56.

On the recto of the fifth fly-leaf of the copy here described is written in an old handwriting: "*May. 29. 1590. . . . publiſhed by D. Guin, Doctor in Phyſick, fellow of S. Johns in Oxon.*

"*Sir Philip Sidnie, or as it is now spelt, Sidney was born the 29th of November 1554, and died of a wound received before the Town of Zutphen, on the 22ᵈ Sept 1586. — The Arcadia was published after his death 1590 by his sister, the Counteſ of Pembroke. — I found this copy of the first edition in Paris 1837.*"

On the verso of folio 311 is a blank space enclosed by a type-ornament border. In this copy there has been neatly written in, in imitation of print, the following:

"'The Epitaph.

His being was in her alone :
    And he not being, she was none.
They ioi'd one ioy, one griefe they griu'd,
One loue they lou'd, one life they liu'd.
The hand was one, one was the ſword,
That did his death, her death afford.
    As all ẏ rest, ſo now the ſtone
That tombes the two is iuſtly one.

ARGALVS, & PARTHENIA."

In subsequent editions the text was much altered and improved, the manuscript used for this being imperfect and otherwise faulty. In the short prefatory notice we are told: "*The diuiſion and ſumming of the Chapters was not of Sir Philip Sidneis dooing, but aduentured by the ouer-ſeer of the print, for the more eaſe of the Readers.*" This "diuiſion and ſumming of the Chapters" was omitted in the Second Edition. It appears that Lady Pembroke herself revised the text for the new edition, which was printed in folio in 1593 (our next number).

The work was in circulation in manuscript for some time before it was put into type from one of the copies which had been procured by Ponsonby, the publisher. There seems to have been an intention to put it to press late in 1586. Sidney, before his departure for Flanders, placed in Greville's hands a corrected copy of what was known as the "old Arcadia," which copy he forwarded to Lady Sidney.

"In the 4to before us, the whole work is divided into three Books, and those

Books into chapters. The first Book has nineteen chapters, the second twenty-nine chapters, and the third nineteen chapters. There is no *Finis*, or words equivalent to it, at the end of the volume, but three asterisks to indicate that the work was incomplete.

"What Lady Pembroke did towards finishing her brother's work may be seen only by a comparison of the 4to, 1590, with the second edition in folio, 1593, where, after Sidney's dedication, comes an address 'To the Reader,' subscribed H. S., avowing the manner in which her Ladyship had perfected what had been left incomplete. Among the additions, we may presume on the authority of manuscripts left in her hands and in those of Sidney's friends, is the Epitaph upon Argalus and Parthenia. In the 4to, 1590, a blank space was left for it on folio 311 b, and in some copies it has been partly supplied [but fully so in the copy here described] in writing of the time; but the whole of it, consisting of only eight lines, may be seen in Book 3 of the later impressions: it occurs on p. 294 of the folio of 1598. Lady Pembroke, instead of including the whole 'Arcadia' in three Books, as in 1590, divided it, rather unequally, into five Books in 1593."

Of the edition here described 300 impressions were reproduced in photographic facsimile, from the copy in the British Museum, with a bibliographical introduction, in which all the early and some modern editions are described, by H. Oskar Sommer, in 1891.

Sir Philip Sidney, at an early age a soldier and a statesman of high promise, was of aristocratic kindred on both sides. He was educated at Shrewsbury, where he met Fulke Greville, his lifelong friend and subsequent biographer. From Shrewsbury he went to Christ College, Oxford, but left there when seventeen. He spent three years completing his education by continental travel, visiting Paris, Vienna, and Venice. At these places he associated with statesmen and scholars, and made an earnest study of European politics. On his return he was introduced at court, where he won the favor of Queen Elizabeth, who considered him "one of the jewels of her crown." In 1557, at the age of twenty-two, he was sent to carry messages of congratulation to the newly seated Elector Palatine, at Heidelberg, and to Rudolph II., at Prague. On his return he visited Antwerp, to congratulate William the Silent on the birth of a son. William was captivated with him, and pronounced him one of the greatest and ripest statesmen in Europe. He returned to England the following year, was knighted in 1583, and lived partly at court and partly at his country-seat at Penshurst, in Kent, until 1585, when he accompanied Leicester on his expedition to the Netherlands, where he was appointed Governor of Flushing. He was wounded at the battle of Zutphen, September 22, 1586, and died at Arnheim fifteen days later, at the early age of thirty-two.

In 1578 Sidney met Spenser at Leicester's house, a meeting which resulted in a deep and tender friendship, which has been immortalized in Spenser's *Astrophel, a Pastoral Elegy*, published as an appendix to his *Colin Clouts Come Home Againe* (our No. 661).

THE COVNTESSE OF PEMBROKES ARCADIA,

WRITTEN BY SIR PHILIPPE SIDNEI.

LONDON
Printed for William Ponſonbie.
Anno Domini, 1590.

No. 647. TITLE-PAGE OF SIDNEY'S COVNTESSE OF PEMBROKES ARCADIA; 1ST EDITION; 1590.

No. 647   Sir Philip Sidney   1590

In literature Sidney is distinguished as the author of *Astrophel and Stella* (1591), the first important body of English sonnets — 110 in number — in which the poet chronicles his love for Penelope Devereux, sister of the Earl of Essex. Some of these sonnets were the special favorites of Charles Lamb. His most famous work is his prose romance, *The Counteſſe of Pembrokes Arcadia* (our present number). It was written in 1580, or thereabouts, for the especial delectation of his sister, Mary Herbert, Countess of Pembroke, and her coterie at "delicious Penshurst." It abounds with marvellous adventures, rainbow descriptions, pastoral scenes filled with nobles and countrymen, and stately kings and queens, all products of a brain inflamed with youthful theories and love-fancies, rather than with the high moral purpose which his friend Fulke Greville ascribed to it. His *Apology for Poetrie* (1595), which displays the finest quality of his intellect, has become a classic. None of his writings were published until after his death, being circulated in manuscript until 1590, when *The Counteſſe of Pembrokes Arcadia* was first published.

"Sidney's sister, Pembroke's mother," collaborated with him and suggested the composition of the *Arcadia*. She is the Urania of Spenser's *Colin Clout*. Among the works of her pen is *The Tragedie of Antonie* (our No. 507), a translation of Robert Garnier's *Marc Antoine*.

"The text of the *Arcadia* suffers from the author's casual methods of composition. Much of it survives in an unrevised shape. He seems to have himself prepared for press the first two books, and the opening section of the third — about a half of the whole. This portion of the romance was printed in 1590, and ended abruptly in the middle of a sentence. Subsequently there was discovered a very rough draft of portions of a long continuation, forming the conclusion of the third book, with the succeeding fourth and fifth books. This supplement survived in 'several loose sheets (being never after reviewed or so much as seen altogether by himself) without any certain disposition or perfect order.' With a second edition of the authentic text these unrevised sheets were printed in 1593. Sidney's sister, the Countess of Pembroke, supplied the recovered books with 'the best coherences that could be gathered out of those scattered papers,' but no attempt was made to fill an obvious hiatus in the middle of the third book at the point where the original edition ended and the rough draft opened. Nor did the editor or publisher venture to bring the unfinished romance to any conclusion. What close was designed for the story by the author was 'only known to his own spirit.' The editors of later editions, bolder than their predecessors, sought to remedy such defects. The gap in the third book was in 1621 filled by a 'little essay' from the pen of a well-known Scottish poet, Sir William Alexander, Earl of Stirling. Finally, in 1628 a more adventurous spirit, Richard Beling, or Bellings, a young barrister of Lincoln's Inn, endeavoured to terminate the story in a wholly original sixth book. It is with these additions that subsequent re-issues of the *Arcadia* were invariably embellished. Other efforts were made to supplement Sidney's unfinished romance. One by Gervase Markham, an industrious literary hack, came out as early as 1607. Another, by 'a young gentlewoman,' Mrs. A. Weames, was published in 1651. The neglect of these fragmentary contributions by publishers of the full work, calls for no regret."

SIDNEY, Sir PHILIP.

THE COVNTESSE OF PEMBROKES ARCADIA. London, *for William Ponſonbie*, 1593. [648]

Small folio. Second Edition.

COLLATION BY SIGNATURES: ¶, 4 leaves (the first blank and lacking); A to Z, Aa to Rr, each 6 leaves; Ss, 4 leaves (the last blank and lacking); total 248 leaves. The first four leaves of each sheet have signature-marks. Leaf H 2 is wrongly marked I 2.

COLLATION BY PAGINATION: [1 blank leaf], [¶]; — [title, as reproduced; *See* No. 648 *a*], recto of [¶ 2]; — [blank], verso of [¶ 2]; — | [conventional head-piece] | TO MY DEARE LADY AND | SISTER, THE COVNTESSE | OF PEMBROKE. | [signed] | *Your louing brother.* | Philip Sidney. |, recto and verso of ¶ 3; — | [conventional head-piece] | To the Reader. | [signed] | H. S. |, recto and verso of ¶ 4; — [text in 5 books, the first with heading] | [conventional head-piece] | THE COVNTESSE OF PEMBROKES | ARCADIA VVRITTEN BY | SIR PHILIP SIDNEI. | THE FIRST BOOKE. |, recto of folio 1 to verso of folio 49; — | *The end of the firſt Booke.* | [type-ornament tail-piece] |, verso of folio 49; — | [conventional head-piece] | ☙ THE SECOND BOOKE OF THE | COVNTESSE OF PEMBROKES | ARCADIA. |, recto of folio 50 to verso of folio 120; — | *The end of the ſecond Eclogues.* |, verso of folio 120; — | [type-ornament head-piece] | ☙ THE THIRDE BOOKE OF THE | COVNTESSE OF PEMBROKES | ARCADIA. |, recto of folio 121 to recto of folio 201; — | The ende of the third Booke. | [two conventional tail-pieces] |, recto of folio 201; — | [conventional head-piece] | ☙ THE FOVRTH BOOKE OF THE | COVNTESSE OF PEMBROKES | ARCADIA. |, verso of folio 201 to verso of folio 222; — | The ende of the fourth Booke. | [two conventional tail-pieces] |, verso of folio 222; — | [conventional head-piece] | ☙ THE FIFTH BOOKE OF THE | COVNTESSE OF PEMBROKES | ARCADIA. |, recto of folio 223 to verso of folio 243; — | FINIS. | [conventional tail-piece] |, verso of folio 243; — [colophon, as reproduced; *See* No. 648 *b*], verso of folio 243; — [1 blank leaf], [Sſ 4]. Folio 44 is wrongly numbered 50. In some copies folio 49 is wrongly numbered 46.

CONDITION: Size of leaf, $10\frac{7}{8} \times 7\frac{5}{16}$ inches. Bound in red crushed levant morocco, elaborately tooled in gilt, gilt edges; by Rivière; in pasteboard slip case.

OTHER COPIES.

Britwell; and Hoe Libraries.

REFERENCES.

Hoe, *Catalogue*, 4 (1904): 176; *The Bibliographer*, 1 (1902): 381; Sommer, *Countess of Pembroke's Arcadia*, 1590 (Facsimile Edition; 1891), *Introduction*, pp. 4, 6–7; Lowndes, 4 (1869): 2395; Hazlitt, *Hand-Book* (1867), p. 557, No. 1 *b*.

"The second edition of the 'Arcadia,' in folio, was published by William Ponsonbie in 1593. This edition is as rare as the editio princeps, if not more so; there is no copy of it at the British Museum. . . . As concerns the text of the 'Arcadia,' this edition is the one on which all later editions are based, the text of the original edition having been slightly altered in the 'Eclogues' adjoined to each book, and augmented by two books. . . .

"The statements concerning the relationship of the quarto to the first and all other folio editions generally given by bibliographers and literary scholars are erroneous. There do not exist numberless variations between the two texts, and it is equally wrong to assert 'that not a few original poems are found in the 4to which are not

THE
COVNTESSE
OF PEMBROKES
ARCADIA.

WRITTEN BY SIR
Philip Sidney Knight.

NOW SINCE THE FIRST EDI-
tion augmented and ended.

LONDON.
Printed for William Ponsonbie.
Anno Domini. 1 5 9 3.

reprinted when the Countess of Pembroke revised the whole.' Nobody seems to have ever compared the two texts, and the erroneous statements seem to be caused by the words in the preface in the folio edition ' To the Reader : ' ' The disfigured face, gentle Reader, wherewith this worke not long since appeared to the common view, . . . to take in hand the wiping away those spottes wherewith the beauties therof were vnworthely blemished.' The main differences of the two texts are these :

" 1. The folio contains a part of the third book, and a fourth and fifth book, not to be found in the quarto.

" 2. The additions of ' the ouerseer of the print ' added in the quarto, such as the division of the books into chapters and the summaries of the contents preceding them, are omitted in the folio.

" 3. Some poems, but only such as are subjoined to the end of the books under the heading of ' Eclogues,' are differently placed or replaced by others. Thus it occurred that Sir John Harrington states in his ' Ariosto,' 1591, that the quarto does not contain the following poem :

> " ' Who doth desire that chaste his wife should be,
> First be he true, for truth doth truth deserue :
> Then such be he, as she his worth may see,
> And one man still credit with her preserue.

> " ' Not toying kinde, nor causlesly vnkinde,
> Not sturring thoughts, nor yet denying right
> Not spying faults, nor in plaine errors blinde,
> Neuer hard hand, nor euer raines too light.

> " ' As farre from want, as farre from vaine expence,
> (The one doth force, the later doth entise)
> Allow good company, but kepe from thence
> Al filthy mouth's that glory in their vice.
> This done, thou hast no more, but leaue the rest
> To vertue, fortune, time & womans brest.'

"On the other hand, the prose text of the quarto is with very insignificant orthographical differences reprinted in the folio, and all poems occurring in the text are to be found unaltered in the same places in the folio where they stand in the quarto."

In the above quotation from Sommer's Introduction the spelling in the extracts from the *Arcadia* has been made to conform to the original text.

LONDON.
Printed for William Ponsonbie, dwelling in Paules Church yard, neere vnto the great north doore of Paules.
Anno Domini. 1593.

No. 648 b. Colophon of Sidney's Covntesse of Pembrokes Arcadia; 2d Edition; 1593.

No. 649   *Tobias George Smollett*   1769

[SMOLLETT, TOBIAS GEORGE.]   (*b*. 1721, *d*. 1771.)

THE HISTORY AND ADVENTURES OF AN ATOM. LONDON, *for Robinſon and Roberts,* 1749 [1769].   2 vols., duodecimo, viz.:   [649]

VOL. 1.

COLLATION BY SIGNATURES : [A], 4 leaves; B to K, each 12 leaves; L, 6 leaves; total 118 numbered leaves.

COLLATION BY PAGINATION : [half-title], p. [i.];—[blank], p. [ii.];—[title, as reproduced ; *See* No. 649], p. [iii.] ;—[blank], p. [iv.] ;—| ADVERTISE-MENT | FROM THE | PUBLISHER to the READER. |[signed]| S. ETHERINGTON. |, pp. [v.]–viii.;—[text, with heading]| THE | Hiſtory and Adventures|OF AN|ATOM. | The EDITOR'S Declaration. |, pp. [1]–227;—| END of the FIRST VOLUME. |, p. 227 ;—[blank], p. [228].

VOL. 2.

COLLATION BY SIGNATURES : [A], 2 leaves; B to I, each 12 leaves (the last blank and lacking); total 98 leaves.

COLLATION BY PAGINATION : [half-title], p. [i.];—[blank], p. [ii.];—[title, same as in Vol. 1, except volume-number], p. [iii.];—[blank], p. [iv.];—[text], pp. [1]–190;—| FINIS. |, p. 190;—[1 blank leaf], [I 12].

CONDITION : Size of leaf, 6⅜ x 3¹¹⁄₁₆ inches. Bound in light polished calf, gilt edges ; by Bedford.

    This is the First Edition of this work.

    The History and Adventures of an Atom is a ferocious satire on the English political system. Its temper is borrowed mainly from *Gulliver's Travels* (our No. 678) and its local color and nomenclature from the accounts of Japan given by the Jesuits and other travellers whose works Smollett had consulted while preparing his *Compendium of Voyages and Travels* (1757).

    Lowndes says: "A key to this work, which exhibits, under fictitious characters, the conduct and dissensions of the several political parties, from 1754 to 1768, will be found in 'A Second Journey round the Library of a Bibliomaniac, by William Davis, 1825.'"

    Smollett was one of the trio of proto-novelists, the other members of which were Fielding and Richardson. As a novelist pure and simple he was their inferior, but as a professional man of letters he was by far their superior. A poet, playwright, historian, publicist, topographer, translator, satirist, periodical critic, lampooner, and novelist, he wrote skillfully on almost every conceivable subject, and for a short period between Pope and Johnson was a kind of literary Protector. Born in 1721, he received a fairly good education at Dumbarton and Glasgow, and went to London at eighteen years of age with the manuscript of his tragedy, *The Regicide,* in his pocket. Failing to get it accepted he joined the navy, which he soon quitted in disgust.

    The success of *Pamela* and *Joseph Andrews* (our No. 380) led him to try his hand at prose fiction, and in 1748 he brought out *Roderick Random,* modelled after Le Sage's immortal *Gil Blas,* in the earlier chapters of which, the best he ever wrote, he is known to have included some material of an autobiographical nature. In 1851 appeared *Peregrine Pickle,* and two years later his third novel, *Ferdinand Count Fathom,* than which few novels have been more imitated. From 1756 he conducted

1769   *Tobias George Smollett*   No. 649

THE
HISTORY
AND
ADVENTURES
OF AN
ATOM.

IN TWO VOLUMES.

VOL. I.

LONDON:
Printed for ROBINSON and ROBERTS, N°. 25,
in Pater-noster Row.
MDCCXLIX.

No. 649.   TITLE-PAGE OF SMOLLETT'S HISTORY AND ADVENTURES OF AN ATOM; 1ST EDITION; [1769].

The Critical Review. His *History of England,* translation of *Don Quixote,* and other works of compilation, translation, and abridgment followed one another in rapid succession. In 1762 his health broke down, and he spent the greater part of the next two years in France and Italy, chiefly at Nice. In 1766 he published his *Travels through France and Italy.* Two years later, upon his return to London, appeared the work here described. In 1769 he left England for the last time and settled at Monte Novo near Leghorn, where in the autumn of 1770 he wrote *Humphry Clinker,* the "most pleasant gossiping novel that was ever written." He died September 17, 1771.

No. 650   *Edmund Spenser*   1569

[SPENSER, EDMUND.] (*b.* 1552, *d.* 1599.) Noodt, Jan van der.
A THEATRE FOR WORLDLINGS. LONDON, *Henry Bynneman*, 1569.
[650]

Small octavo. Text in black-letter, with side-notes in roman.
COLLATION BY SIGNATURES: A to R, each 8 leaves; S, 2 leaves; total 138 leaves.
COLLATION BY PAGINATION: [title, as reproduced; *See* No. 650], recto of [A j.]; —[royal coat of arms], verso of [A j.]; —[commendatory verses, the first with heading] | [type-ornament head-piece] | *In commendationem operis ab* | Nobiliff. & virtutis Studiofifsimo Do- | *mino, Ioanne vander Noodt* | *Patricio Antuerpienfi* | *æditi, Carmen.* | M. RABILAE. Poete Brabant. | , recto and verso of A ij.; — | TO THE MOSTE | high, puiffant, noble, ver- | tuous, and righte Chriftian Princeffe | *Elizabeth, by the grace of God* | Quene of Englande, Fraunce, | and Ireland. &c. | [signed] | *Your Maiesties most humble feruant* | *Iean vander Noodt.* | [dated] | At London your Maiefties Citie and feate | royal. The. 25. of May. 1569. | , recto of A iij. to recto of B j.; — | Epigrams. | [on verso pages, illustrated with woodcuts on recto pages], verso of B j. to verso of [B vij.]; — | Sonets. | [on verso pages, illustrated with woodcuts on recto pages], recto of [B viij.] to recto of [D vj.]; — [blank], verso of [D vj.]; — [text, in black-letter, with heading] | [type-ornament head-piece] | A BRIEFE DE- | claration of the Authour | vpon his vifions, takẽ out of the holy fcrip- | tures, and dyuers Oratois, Poetes, | *Philofophers, and true histories.* Tran- |

flated out of French into En- | glifhe by Theodore Roeft. | [with running head-lines] | A Theatre | for worldlings. | , recto of [D vij.] to verso of S j.; — [colophon] | [type-ornament head-piece] | Imprinted at Lon- | *don by Henrie Bynneman,* | dwelling in Knight riders ftreat, at | *the figne of the Marmaid.* | ANNO. 1569. | CVM PRIVILEGIO AD IMPRI- | MENDVM SOLVM. | [conventional tail-piece] | , recto of [S ij.]; — [printer's device], verso of [S ij.].
CONDITION: Size of leaf, 5 × 3½ inches. Bound in red crushed levant morocco, gilt over red edges; by Bedford. The leaves are closely trimmed on the upper and outer margins, many head-lines and side-notes being cut into.
OTHER COPIES.
British Museum; Huth; and White Libraries.
REFERENCES.
Dictionary of National Biography, 53 (1898): 385, 386; Grolier Club, *Langland to Wither* (1893), p. 169, No. 192; Locker-Lampson, *Catalogue* (1886), p. 86; Corser, *Collectanea Anglo-Poetica*, Part 10 (Chetham Society, Vol. CVIII.; 1880), pp. 312–319; Lowndes, 5 (1869): 2752; Hazlitt, *Hand-Book* (1867), p. 625, No. 2; Collier, *Rarest Books in the English Language*, 4 (1866): 84; *Bibliotheca Grenvilliana*, 2 (1842): 756; *Bibliotheca Anglo-Poetica* (1815), p. 369, No. 779.

The Locker-Lampson copy, with ex-libris.
The "Sonets," leaves [B. viij.] to [D. vj.], are the first specimens in print of Spenser's poetry. He afterward inserted them in his *Complaints*, 1591 (our No. 658).
"On 22 July 1569 the well-known printer and publisher, Henry Bynneman, obtained a license to issue an English version by one Theodore Roest of an edifying moral tract, originally written in Flemish prose by an Antwerp physician named John Van der Noodt, who had taken refuge in England from religious persecution. A French translation was issued in London in 1568. The work appeared in its English form next year with the running title 'A Theatre for Worldlings' (London, b. l. 8vo), a dedication addressed to the queen and signed by Van der Noodt

was dated 25 May. There followed, as a further introduction to the book, twenty-one woodcuts in illustration of some poems by Petrarch and Du Bellay which Van der Noodt had studied when compiling his tract, and opposite each woodcut was placed a translation into English verse of the appropriate Italian or French poem. The six poems assigned to Petrarch, which were in Van der Noodt's volume entitled 'Epigrams,' were renderings of the six stanzas of Petrarch's canzone, beginning 'Standomi un giorno solo a la finestra,' and each consisted of either fourteen or twelve lines alternately rhymed. The fourteen sonnets or 'Visions' of Du Bellay — four of which were described as taken 'out of the Revelations of St. John' — were unrhymed in the English version. Van der Noodt in his preface writes of these poems as his own work, but there can be little doubt that they were the products of Spenser's youthful pen, and were inserted by the publisher as letterpress for the illustrations. In a collection of verse avowedly by Spenser, and published in 1591 under the title of 'Complaints' [our No. 658], these twenty stanzas were reprinted with some revision; Du Bellay's sonnets were supplied with rhymes, and others were substituted for the four 'out of the Revelations of St. John,' while Petrarch's poems were renamed 'Visions,' and were each made of the uniform length of fourteen lines. The poems were promising performances for an undergraduate." Spenser at the time this volume was published was only about sixteen years of age.

Edmund Spenser, the author of *The Faerie Queene*, was a Londoner by birth. He was educated at the newly founded Merchant Taylors' School, from which he went, in May, 1569, to Pembroke Hall (now College) as sizar. His first appearance in print took place at about the same time, some poems of his being inserted in Van der Noodt's *Theatre for Worldlings* (our present number). At the university Spenser read widely and became not only a considerable Latin and Greek scholar but an expert in the French and Italian literatures. His two most intimate associates were Gabriel Harvey, the author of *Foure Letters, and certaine Sonnets* (our No. 635), and Edward Kirk, both of whom, recognizing his budding genius, shared and encouraged his literary tastes.

In 1576 he took his degree of M.A. and left the university. For a time he is said to have sojourned with his kinsfolk at or near Hurstwood, where he fell in love with a damsel to whom he gives the feigned name Rosalind. This ill-requited passion did much to stimulate his poetic impulse. By Harvey's advice he went to London, where he soon became a member of the Earl of Leicester's household. His chief duties while in Leicester's service seem to have been to deliver dispatches to the Earl's correspondents in foreign countries. Among the places which he visited while carrying out these duties were Ireland, Spain, and Rome. In April, 1580, he was again at Leicester's house in London.

Spenser's association with Leicester led to his forming the acquaintance of Sir Philip Sidney, Leicester's nephew, an acquaintance which ripened into a deep and tender friendship. In his correspondence with Harvey in 1579 and 1580 he mentions several poems which have not been preserved, at least in any form that can be positively identified. Of his two poems, *The Shepheardes Calender* (our next number) and *The Faerie Queene* (our No. 655), the former was completed and the latter begun while he was still under Leicester's roof.

The Shepheardes Calender was sent to press without delay, and appeared under the modest pseudonym "Immerito." Ten years passed before any part of *The Faerie Queene* was ready for the press. Meres recognized the merit of *The Shepheardes Calender*, and Drayton said of it that "Master Edmund Spenser had done enough for the immortality of his name had he only given us his Shepherd's Calendar."

In July, 1580, Spenser was appointed secretary to Lord Grey (personified as "Sir Artegall" in Book 5 of *The Faerie Queene*), then going to Ireland as Lord Deputy. With the exception of two short visits to England, Ireland henceforth remained his home until within a month of his death in 1598. Here, though he found the country far from congenial, he held several official positions and secured much landed property. His main solace, however, was in literary work, to which he devoted all his leisure time. He continued *The Faerie Queene*, of which he had written only Book 1 and part of Book 2. By the end of 1586 he had probably written his elegy on "Astrophel," i.e. Sir Philip Sidney, which first appeared in *Colin Clouts Come home againe* in 1595, and his fine sonnet to his friend Harvey which was appended to his *Fowre Hymnes* (our No. 662). In June, 1588, Spenser resigned his position as Clerk of the Court of Chancery in Dublin, and purchased the post of Clerk of the Council of Munster. Having acquired a landed property, he took up his residence in the old castle of Kilcolman on his estate. He there continued his work on *The Faerie Queene*, and in 1589 showed the draft of the first three books to his friend and neighbor Sir Walter Raleigh, who was enchanted with it.

About November, 1589, Spenser visited London and lost no time in placing his manuscript in the hands of William Ponsonby the publisher, who procured a license for its publication December 3, 1589. *The Faerie Queene*, the only great poem written in England since Chaucer died, was in design a moral treatise. Three of the twelve books, the only ones then completed, treating of Holiness, Temperance, and Chastity, were published in quarto the next year. The success achieved by the publication of *The Shepheardes Calender* was more than sustained by *The Faerie Queene*, and Spenser's right to supremacy among the English poets of that time was rendered indisputable. A Second Edition appeared in 1596 (our No. 656).

Spenser remained in England several months, during which he wrote *Proſopopoia, or Mother Hubberds Tale* (in our No. 658) and *Daphnaïda* (our No. 659), a pastoral elegy on the death of the niece of the mistress of the robes.

In February a pension was bestowed on him by the Queen. Soon afterward he returned to Kilcolman, where he penned a charming account of his travels and court experiences, which he entitled *Colin Clouts Come home againe* (our No. 661). Here under disguised names is given a vivid description of the literary men and women whose sympathies he had won. Shakespeare is doubtless here alluded to under the name of "Aetion." This work, though its dedication is dated December 27, 1591, was not published until 1595.

Edmund Spenser

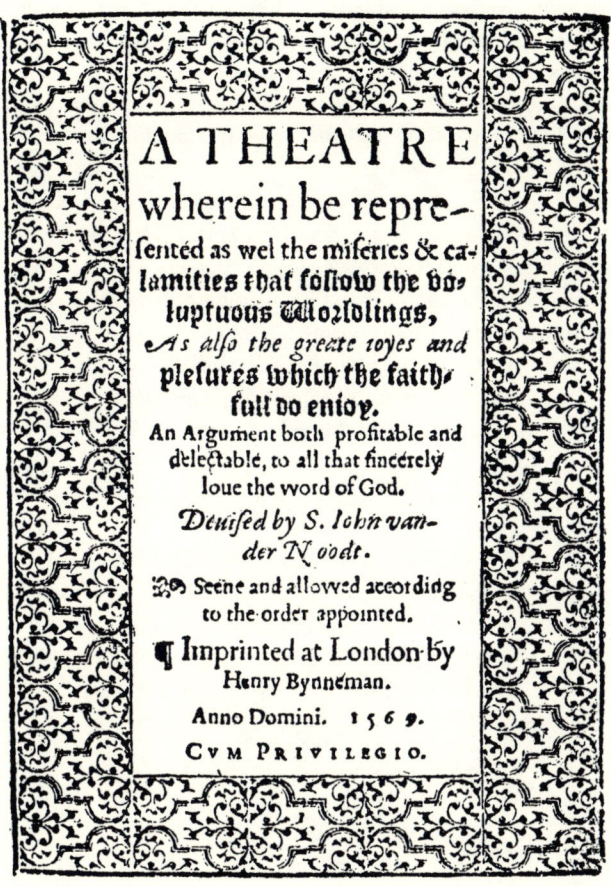

No. 650. Title-page of Van der Noodt's Theatre for Worldlings; 1569.

The success of *The Faerie Queene* led Ponsonby to make a collection of Spenser's small poems, which appeared in 1591 under the title *Complaints, Containing sundrie Small Poemes of the Worlds Vanitie* (our No. 658). The best of the poems in this volume, mostly made up of rewritten juvenile efforts, was "Muiopotmos, or The Fate of the Butterflie," the most airily fanciful of any of Spenser's writings. In 1594 Spenser sent to Ponsonby his *Amoretti and Epithalamion* (our No. 660), which appeared in 1595. The same year Ponsonby issued *Colin Clouts Come home againe* (our No. 661), with an appendix containing elegies on Spenser's late friend Sir Philip Sidney.

In 1594 Spenser had completed three more books of *The Faerie Queene*, which he himself carried to London, together with some small pieces. *The Second Part of* the *Faerie Queene* (our No. 657) was licensed to be printed January 20, 1595/6, and appeared soon afterward in quarto. This contained the Fourth, Fifth, and Sixth Books, upon Friendship, Justice, and Courtesy respectively. The popularity of this second volume was as pronounced as that of its predecessor. His reflections on the fate of Mary Queen of Scots in the Fourth Book, under the name of "Duessa," were exceedingly offensive to King James, who was anxious to have Spenser prosecuted for the aspersions upon his mother.

The dedication to his *Fowre Hymnes* (our No. 662) is dated from Greenwich, September 1, 1596, where he was with the Court. Here he wrote two new poems celebrating "heavenly love" and "heavenly beauty," the other two having been long in circulation in manuscript. The following November he wrote one of his latest and most fascinating minor poems, *Prothalamion* (our No. 663), in honor of the double wedding of two daughters of the Earl of Worcester.

Early in 1597 Spenser returned to Kilcolman, depressed and in failing health. On September 30th he was appointed Sheriff of Cork. In Tyrone's Rebellion, which broke out in October, Kilcolman Castle was burned over the poet's head, and he fled to Cork with his wife and four children. In December he was sent to London with a dispatch by Sir Thomas Norris, the President of Munster, and died at Westminster only a month after his arrival, January 16, 1598/9. He was buried in Westminster Abbey, only a few yards from the grave of Chaucer, whom he ever delighted to acknowledge as his poetic master.

The secret of Spenser's enduring popularity with poets and lovers of poetry lies especially in this, that he excels in the poet's peculiar gift, the instinct for verbal music.

[SPENSER, EDMUND.]

THE SHEPHEARDES CALENDER.   LONDON, *Hugh Singleton*, 1579.   [651]

Small quarto. First Edition. The poems printed in black-letter, the arguments in italic, and the commentaries in roman.

COLLATION BY SIGNATURES: ¶, A to N, each 4 leaves; total 56 leaves. Leaves C iij., I 3, K 3, M 3, and N 3 have no signature-marks; leaves ¶iiij., A 4, B 4, E 4, F 4, G 4, I 4, K 4, and L 4 have signature-marks.

COLLATION BY PAGINATION: [title, as reproduced; *See* No. 651 *a*], recto of [¶]; —[verse, with heading] | [type-ornament head-piece] | TO HIS BOOKE. | [signed] | *Jmmeritô.*|, verso of [¶]; — | ¶ *To the moſt excellent and learned both* | Oꝛatoꝛ and Poete, Mayſter Gabꝛiell Haruey, his | verie ſpecial and ſingular good frend E. K. commen-|deth the good lyking of this his labour, | and the patronage of the | new Poete. | [signed] | *Your owne aſſuredly to* | *be commaunded* E. K. | [dated] | . . . *from my lodging at London* | *thys* 10. *of Aprill.* 1579. |, recto of ¶ ij. to verso of ¶ iij.; — | *The generall argument of* | the whole booke. |, recto and verso of ¶ iiij.; — [type-ornament tail-piece], verso of ¶ iiij.; — [text in 12 sections, the first with running head-line] | *Januarye.* |, recto of folio 1 to recto of folio 52; — [colophon, as reproduced; *See* No. 651 *b*], verso of folio 52.

THE
Shepheardes Calender
Conteyning twelue Æglogues proportionable to the twelue monethes.

Entitled
TO THE NOBLE AND VERTV-
ous Gentleman most worthy of all titles
both of learning and cheualrie M.
Philip Sidney.

AT LONDON.
Printed by Hugh Singleton, dwelling in
Creede Lane neere vnto Ludgate at the
signe of the gylden Tunne, and
are there to be solde.
1579.

No. 651 a. Title-page of Spenser's Shepheardes Calender;
1st Edition; 1579.

Folio 38 is wrongly numbered 37; and 40 is 39.

ILLUSTRATIONS: 12 woodcuts, one to each month, on the recto pages of folios 1, 3, 8, 16, 26, 31, 35, 39, and 44, and the verso pages of folios 11, 22, and 48.

CONDITION: Size of leaf, 6⅞ × 4¹¹⁄₁₆ inches. Bound in old red morocco, gilt edges. The title-page has been split, its verso and a few letters of the imprint being in facsimile, as are also portions of leaves ¶ ij., ¶ iij., and ¶ iiij. The colophon is in

No. 651 Edmund Spenser 1579

*Imprinted at London by Hugh
Singleton, dwelling in Creede lane
at the signe of the gylden
Tuon neere vnto
Ludgate.*

No. 651 *b*.   FACSIMILE COLOPHON OF SPENSER'S SHEPHEARDES CALENDER;
1ST EDITION; 1579.

facsimile, printed on an old piece of paper upon which had previously been printed a signature-mark "A" (*See* our reproduction).
OTHER COPIES.
British Museum (Heber-Grenville copy); Bodleian; Capell Collection; and Huth Libraries.
REFERENCES.
Sinker, *Library of Trinity College,*

Cambridge (1891), p. 122; Sommer, *Shepheardes Calender, 1579* (Facsimile Edition; 1890), *Introduction*, p. 11; Huth, *Catalogue,* 4 (1880) : 1385; Lowndes, 5 (1869) : 2478; Hazlitt, *Hand-Book* (1867), p. 572, No. 1 *a*; *Bibliotheca Grenvilliana*, 2 (1842) : 681; *Bibliotheca Heberiana*, Part 4 (1834), p. 311, No. 2627; Watt, *Bibliotheca Britannica,* 2 (1824) : 872 *c*.

The Gott copy, with ex-libris.
Of *The Shepheardes Calender,* which gave a new impulse to English literature, editions were published in 1579, 1581, 1586, 1591, and 1597, all but that of 1591

being in the present collection. Each of these editions was published anonymously, and it was not until that of 1611 that Spenser's name appeared on the title-page. In 1653 an edition appeared with a Latin translation in verse.

To each of the twelve months is prefixed a woodcut appropriate to its season, with the suitable sign of the zodiac in the heavens. These blocks were used in the first five quarto editions (1579, the edition here described; 1581, our next number; 1586, our No. 653; 1591; and 1597, our No. 654), and appeared for the last time in the sixth or folio edition of 1611.

This work is interesting (1) because it is the earliest work of importance by the writer of the *Faerie Queene;* (2) because it marks a turning-point in English literature; and (3) because of the mysterious circumstances attending its publication, the so-called friend of Spenser, "E. K.," whose commentary appeared with the *Calender*, giving rise to many suppositions and disputes, though now it has been proved, as far as possible, that Spenser wrote it himself.

Grenville, in a manuscript note in his copy, now in the British Museum, says: "This first edition is so rare that I have not as yet been able to ascertain any other copy except that in Trinity College, Cambridge, though probably others are to be found. For even the third edition of 1586, Sir M. Sykes gave £21 at the Roxburghe Sale. The Shepheard's Calendar was reprinted a fourth and fifth time in 1591 and 1597. All these Quarto old editions are valuable, but the first very peculiarly so."

"*The Shepherd's Calendar* was hailed with enthusiasm as the advent of a 'new poet.' Not only was it a complete work in a form then new to English literature, but the execution showed the hand of a master. There had been nothing so finished, so sustained, so masterful in grasp, so brilliant in metre and phrase, since Chaucer. It was felt at once that the poet for whom the age had been waiting had come."

The edition here described was reproduced in photographic facsimile from the copy in the British Museum, in 1890, with bibliographical and critical introductions by H. Oskar Sommer.

[SPENSER, EDMUND.]

THE SHEPHEARDES CALENDER. LONDON, *by Thomas Eaſt, for Iohn Harriſon the younger*, 1581. [652]

Small quarto. Second Edition. The poems printed in black-letter, the arguments in italic, and the commentaries in roman.

COLLATION BY SIGNATURES: *₀*, A to N, each 4 leaves; total 56 leaves. Leaf E iiij. has a signature-mark.

COLLATION BY PAGINATION: [title, as reproduced; *See* No. 652 a], recto of [*₀*]; — [verse, with heading] | TO HIS BOOKE. | [18 lines] | [signed] | *Immeritô.* |, verso of [*₀*]; — | ¶ *To the moſt excellent and learned both* | Orator and Poet, Maiſter Gabriell Haruey, his very | ſpeciall and ſingular good friend E. K commendeth the | *good liking of this his labour, and the patro-*

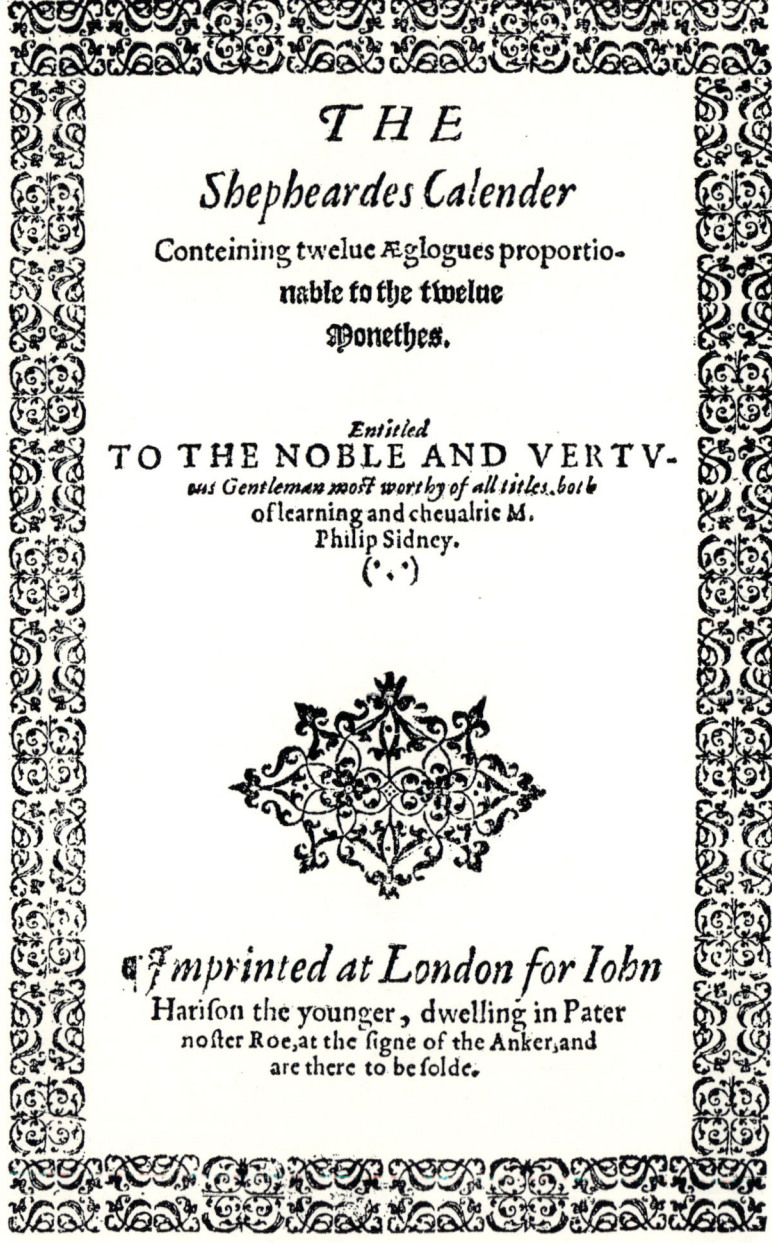

No. 652 a. Title-page of Spenser's Shepheardes Calender; 2d Edition; 1581.

| nage of the newe Poet. | [signed] | *Your owne assuredly to* | *be commaunded E. K.* | [dated] | . . . *From* | *my lodging at London this 10. of Aprill. 1579.* |, recto of *⁎*⁎* ii. to verso of *⁎*⁎* iii. ; — | [type-ornament head-piece] | *The generall Argument of* | *the whole Booke.* |, recto and verso of [*⁎*⁎* iiij.]; — [text in 12 sections, the first with running head-line] | *Januarie.* |, recto of folio 1 to recto of folio 52 ; — [colophon, as reproduced ; *See* No. 652 *b*], recto of folio 52 ; — [blank], verso of folio 52.

ILLUSTRATIONS : 12 woodcuts, one to each month, on the recto pages of folios 1, 3, 8, 16, 26, 31, 35, 40, and 44, and on the verso pages of folios 11, 22, and 48.

CONDITION : Size of leaf, 7¼₆ × 5 inches. Bound in maroon crushed levant morocco, gilt over red edges ; by Rivière.

OTHER COPIES.

British Museum (Grenville copy); Capell Collection ; Britwell ; and Huth Libraries.

REFERENCES.

Sinker, *Library of Trinity College, Cambridge* (1891), p. 122 ; Sommer, *Shepheardes Calender, 1579* (Facsimile Edition ; 1890), Introduction, p. 12 ; Huth, *Catalogue*, 4 (1880) : 1386 ; Lowndes, 5 (1869) : 2478 ; Hazlitt, *Hand-Book* (1867), p. 572, Nos. 1 *b* and *c* ; *Bibliotheca Heberiana*, Part 4 (1834), p. 311, Nos. 2628, 2629 ; *Bibliotheca Grenvilliana*, 2 (1842) : 681.

¶Imprinted at London by Thomas East, for Iohn Harrison the younger, dwelling in Pater noster Roe, at the signe of the Anker, and are there to bee solde.
1581.

No. 652 *b*. COLOPHON OF SPENSER'S SHEPHEARDES CALENDER ; 2D EDITION ; 1581.

The variation between the imprint and the colophon in this the Second Edition has given rise to the statement by Hazlitt that there were two impressions in the same year, but such was not the case (see Huth *Catalogue*).

[SPENSER, EDMUND.]

THE SHEPHEARDES CALENDER. *Harrison the yonger*, 1586. LONDON, *by Iohn Wolfe, for Iohn* [653]

Small quarto. Third Edition. The poems printed in black-letter, the arguments in italic, and the commentaries in roman.

COLLATION BY SIGNATURES : 4 leaves, without signature-marks ; A to N, each 4 leaves ; total 56 leaves. Leaf E 3 is wrongly marked 3 ; I 2 is 2 ; E iiii. has a signature-mark ; and I 3 has none.

COLLATION BY PAGINATION : [title, as reproduced ; *See* No. 653], recto of first leaf ; — [verse, with heading] | [type-ornament head-piece] | TO HIS BOOKE. | [18

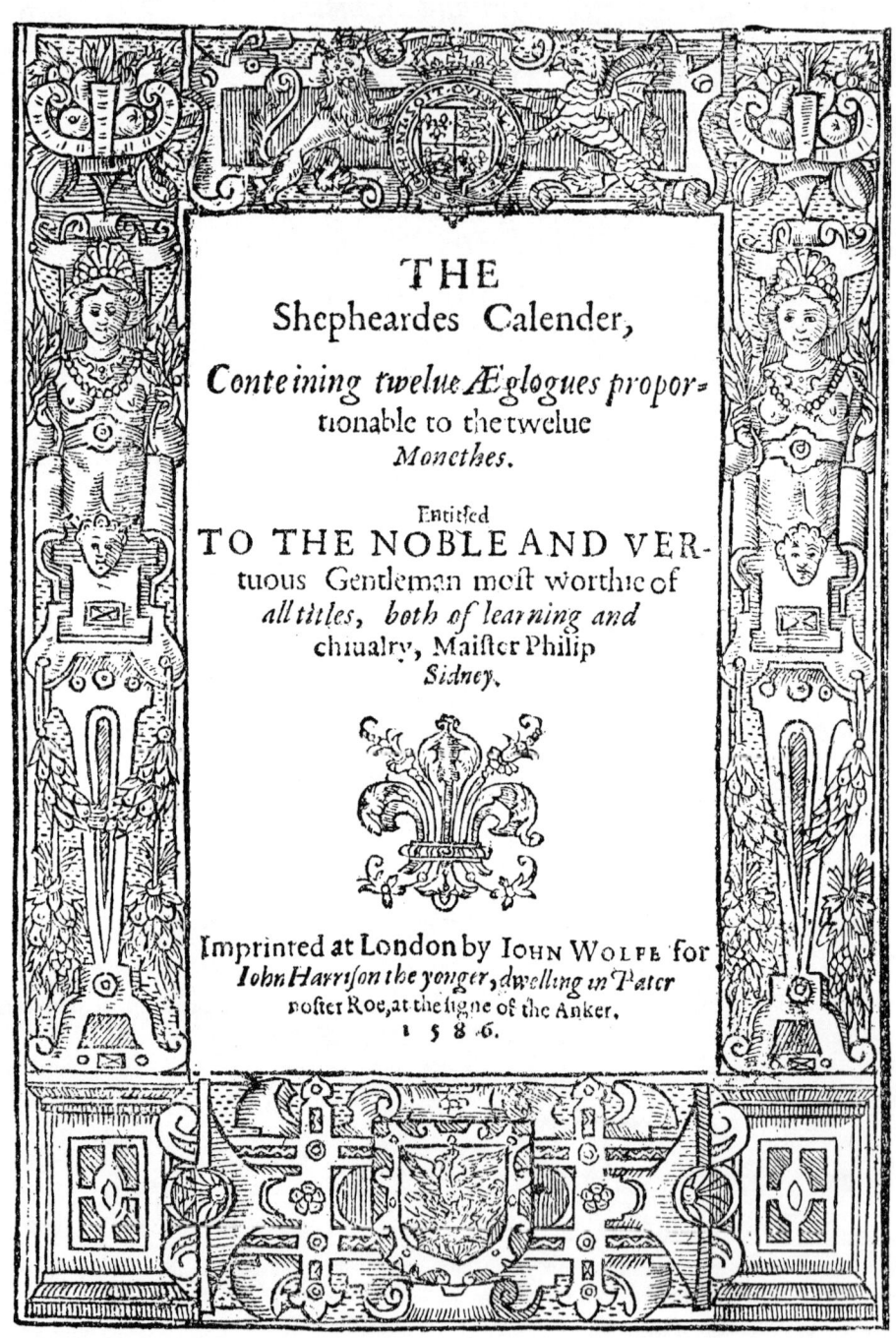

No. 653. Title-page of Spenser's Shepheardes Calender; 3d Edition; 1586.

lines] | [signed] | *Immeritò*. | [type-ornament tail-piece] | , verso of first leaf ; — | ¶ *To the moſt excellent and learned both* | Orator and Poet, Maiſter Gabriel Haruey, his | very ſpeciall and ſingular good friend E. K. commendeth | the good liking of this his good labour, and the | *patronage of the newe Poet.* | [signed] | *Your owne aſſuredly to* | *be commaunded E. K.* | [dated] | . . . From my lodging at London this 10. of Aprill. 1579. | , recto of second leaf to recto of third leaf ; — | The generall Argument | of the whole booke. | , verso of third leaf to recto of folio 1 ; — [text in 12 sections, the first with running head-lines] | Ianuarie. | , recto of folio 1 to recto of folio 52 ; — [colophon] | ¶ Imprinted at London by Thomas Eaſt, for | *Iohn Harriſon the younger, dwelling in Pa-* | ter noſter Roe, at the ſigne of the Anker, | and are there to be ſold. | 1586. | , recto of folio 52 ; — [blank], verso of folio 52. The verso of folio 7 is numbered 8 on the inner margin ; folio 8 has no number ; and 11 is wrongly numbered 12.

ILLUSTRATIONS : 12 woodcuts, one to each month, on the recto pages of folios 1, 3, [8], 16, 26, 31, 35, 40, and 44, and the verso pages of folios 11 [wrongly numbered 12], 22, and 48.

CONDITION : Size of leaf, 7 x 5⅛ inches. Bound in olive green crushed levant morocco, with elaborate floriated gilt tooling, gilt over red edges ; by C. S. [Cobden-Sanderson], 1889. The title-page is extended on the fore and lower edges, part in facsimile.

OTHER COPIES.

British Museum (Grenville copy); Britwell Library ; Capell Collection ; and White Libraries.

Of the Fourth Edition (1591) there are copies in the British Museum ; Britwell ; Devonshire ; Ellesmere ; Capell Collection ; and Hoe Libraries.

REFERENCES.

Grolier Club, *Langland to Wither* (1893), p. 199, No. 228 ; Sinker, *Library of Trinity College, Cambridge* (1891), p. 122 ; Sommer, *Shepheardes Calender, 1579* (Facsimile Edition ; 1890), *Introduction*, p. 12 ; Locker-Lampson, *Catalogue* (1886), p. 120 ; Lowndes, 5 (1869) : 2478 ; Hazlitt, *Hand-Book* (1867), p. 572, No. 1 *d*.

The copy here described was formerly in the library of Frederick Locker-Lampson, and contains his ex-libris, colored by hand.

[SPENSER, EDMUND.]

THE SHEPHEARDS CALENDER. *Harriſon the yonger*, 1597. LONDON, *by Thomas Creede, for Iohn*

Small quarto. Fifth Edition. The poems printed in black-letter, the arguments in italic, and the commentaries in roman.

COLLATION BY SIGNATURES: A to O, each 4 leaves ; total 56 leaves. Leaves G 3 and O 3 have no signature-marks.

COLLATION BY PAGINATION : [title, as reproduced ; *See* No. 654], recto of [A]; — [verse, with heading] | [type-ornament head-piece] | TO HIS BOOKE. | [18 lines] | [signed] | *Immeritò* | [type-ornament tail-piece] | , verso of [A] ; — | To the moſt excellent and learned, both Orator and Poet, maſter | *Gabriel Haruey,* his verie ſpeciall and ſingular good friend *E. K.* com- | *mendeth the good lyking of this his good labour, and the* | *patronage of the new Poet.* | [signed] | *Your owne aſſuredly to be* | *commaunded.* *E. K.* | [dated] | . . . From my lodging at London the tenth of Aprill. 1579. | , recto of A 2 to recto of [A 4] ; — | [type-ornament head-piece] | The generall Argument of the | whole Booke. | , verso of [A 4]

THE
SHEPHEARDS
Calender:

CONTEYNING TWELVE
Aeglogues, proportionable to the
twelue Moneths.

ENTITVLED,
To the Noble and vertuous Gentleman, most worthy of all tytles, both of learning and chiualrie,
Maister *Philip Sidney.*

LONDON
Printed by Thomas Creede, for Iohn Harrison the yonger, dwelling in Pater noster Row, at the signe of the Anchor.
1597.

1597   *Edmund Spenser*   **No. 654**

to verso of B;—[text in 12 sections, the first with running head-lines] | Ianuarie. |, pp. 1–101;—[blank], p. [102].

ILLUSTRATIONS: 12 woodcuts, one to each month, on pp. 1, 5, 15, 21, 30, 43, 49, 59, 67, 77, 85, and 94.

CONDITION: Size of leaf, 7⅝₁₆ × 5⅞₁₆ inches. Bound in red crushed levant morocco, gilt edges; by Bedford.

OTHER COPIES.

British Museum; Britwell; Duke of Devonshire; Hoe (2); Morgan; and White Libraries.

REFERENCES.

Hoe, *Catalogue*, 4 (1904) : 213; Grolier Club, *Langland to Wither* (1893), p. 200, No. 230; Sommer, *Shepheardes Calender, 1579* (Facsimile Edition; 1890), Introduction, p. 13; also p. 14, *note*; Lowndes, 5 (1869) : 2478; Hazlitt, *Hand-Book* (1867), p. 572, No. 1*f*; *Bibliotheca Anglo-Poetica* (1815), p. 305, No. 640.

The Yorke-Locker Lampson copy, with ex-libris of each.

"According to the General Catalogue of the British Museum Library," says Sommer, writing in 1890, "there exist about ten different editions of the complete works, and about fifteen of the poetical works of Spenser; so that altogether the 'Shepheardes Calendar' has been printed thirty-five times in three hundred years." The best known editions of Spenser's complete works are Todd's (1805), Collier's (1862), Hales' (1869), and Grosart's (1882).

SPENSER, EDMUND.

THE FAERIE QVEENE. LONDON, *for William Ponsonbie*, 1590.   **[655]**

Small quarto. First Edition, First Issue.

COLLATION BY SIGNATURES: A to Z, Aa to Pp, each 8 leaves; *Qq*, 4 leaves; total 308 leaves. Leaf A 5 has a signature-mark.

COLLATION BY PAGINATION: [title, as reproduced; *See* No. 655], recto of [A]; — | TO THE MOST MIGH- | TIE AND MAGNIFI- | CENT EMPRESSE ELI- | ZABETH, BY THE | GRACE OF GOD QVEENE | OF ENGLAND, FRANCE | AND IRELAND DE- | FENDER OF THE FAITH | &c. | Her most humble | Seruant : | *Ed. Spenser.* |, verso of [A];—[text in 3 books, the first with heading] | [conventional head-piece] | The first Booke of | the Faerie Queene. | *Contayning* | The Legend of the Knight | *of the Red Crosse,* | OR | *Of Holinesse.* |, pp. [1]–183;—| *Finis Lib. I.* |, p. 183;—[woodcut of a mounted knight killing a dragon], p. [184];—| [conventional head-piece] | The second Booke | of the Faerie Queene. | *Contayning* | The Legend of Sir Guyon. | OR | *Of Temperaunce.* |, pp. 185–387;—[conventional tail-piece], p. 387; —[blank], p. [388];—| [conventional head-piece] | The thirde Booke | of the Faerie Queene. | *Contayning* | The Legend of Britomartis. | OR | *Of Chastity.* |, pp. 389–589;—| FINIS. |, p. 589;—[blank], p. [590];—| A | Letter of the Authors expounding his | *whole intention in the courfe of this worke : which* | for that it giueth great light to the Reader, for | the better vnderstanding is hereunto | annexed. | *To the Right noble, and Valorous, Sir Walter* | Raleigh knight, Lo. Wardein of the Stanneryes, and | her Maiesties lieutenant of the County of Corne- | wayll. | [signed] | Yours most humbly affectionate. | Ed. Spenser. | [dated] | *23. Ianuary. 1589.* |, pp. 591–595;—| ¶ A Vision vpon this conceipt of the | Faery Queene. | [14 lines] | Another of the same. | [14 lines] | [signed] | W. R. |, p. 596;—[poem, with heading] | To the learned Shepeheard. | [signed] | Hobynoll. |, pp. 597–598;—[poem, 10

No. 655　　　　　　*Edmund Spenser*　　　　　　1590

lines, signed] | R. S. | [10 lines] | H. B. | , p. 598; — [poem of 4 stanzas, signed] | W. L. |, p. 599; — [poem of 4 stanzas, signed] | Ignoto. |, p. 600; — [10 sonnets by Spenser, addressed to various people, the first with heading] | *To the right honourable Sir* Chriſtopher Hatton, | Lord high Chauncelor of England. &c. |, pp. 601–605; — | FINIS. |, p. 605; — [errata, with heading] | Faults eſcaped in the Print. |, p. 606; — [15 sonnets by Spenser, addressed to various people, 8 of those on pp. 601–605 being repeated], recto of *Q q* to verso of [*Q q* 4].

Page 79 is wrongly numbered 81; 82 is 84; 83 is 85; 86 is 88; 87 is 89; 90 is 92; 91 is 93; 94 is 96; 309 is 319; 317 is 217; 403 is 408; 439 is 493; 486 is 488; 487 is 489; 510 is 600; 562 is 592; and 586 is 589.

CONDITION: Size of leaf, 7⅚₁₆ × 5⅛ inches. Bound in red crushed levant morocco, gilt edges; by Bedford.

OTHER COPIES.

There are other copies, but of which issue is uncertain, in the British Museum (Grenville copy); Bodleian; Britwell; Capell Collection; Rylands; Crawford; Devonshire; Huth; Lenox; Halsey; Hoe (2, one having but 600 pages, the other 606); Morgan; and White Libraries.

REFERENCES.

Nicoll and Seccombe, 1 (1907): 181; Hoe, *Catalogue*, 4 (1904): 208; Lee, *Great Englishmen of the Sixteenth Century* (1904), pp. 192, 195, 202; Grolier Club, *Langland to Wither* (1893), p. 200, No. 231; Sinker, *Library of Trinity College, Cambridge* (1891), p. 122; Quaritch, *General Catalogue*, 1 (1887): 773, No. 8304; 4 (1887): 2181, Nos. 22286, 22287; Locker-Lampson, *Catalogue* (1886), p. 119; Huth, *Catalogue*, 4 (1880): 1386; Lowndes, 5 (1869): 2476; Hazlitt, *Hand-Book* (1867), p. 573, No. 2 *a*; *Bibliotheca Anglo-Poetica* (1815), p. 302, No. 634.

The Locker-Lampson copy, with ex-libris.

On the recto of the second fly-leaf is written in pencil: "*The 1ˢᵗ Book is an allegory. The Red Croſs Knight is the militant Xtian whom Una, the True Church, loves, whom Duessa, the type of Popery, seduces, who is reduced almost to despair but rescued by the intervention of Una & the assistance of Faith, Hope & Charity, & though in none of the other books is the allegory so clearly conceived, or so steadily preserved the book may be read without its being perceived or remembered.*

"*5 Book. Arthegal is Sir Arthur Gray. Gloriana is the type of Q. Elizabeth, as also is Belphœbe. The three last books show signs of wearineſs, & are inferior.*

"*Una 'herself much whiter' (than the aſs) is absurd. See P. No poet had a more exquisite sense of the beautiful. See 604 to Rawleigh.*"

In this, the First Issue of the First Edition, lines 4 and 5 of p. 332 (Book 2, Canto 10, stanza 24, of modern editions) have blank spaces left for the insertion of Welsh and English words, as follows:

"How oft that day did ſad *Brunchildis* ſee
　The greene ſhield dyde in dolorous vermell?
　　That not　　　　　　he mote ſeeme to bee.
But　　　　　　　　　　　　　"

In the Second Issue of this edition (our next number) the last two lines read:

"That not *Seuith guiridh* he mote ſeeme to bee.
But rather *y Seuith gogh*, ſigne of ſad crueltee."

In the Second Edition (our No. 656) these lines read:

> "That not *Scuith guiridh* it mote feeme to bee.
> But rather *y Scuith gogh*, figne of fad crueltee."

These blank spaces are usually cited as tests of the First or Original Issue. They were filled up in the Second Issue soon after the publication of the First, and long before the Second Edition with its suppressions and changes was published in 1596.

In both editions of the First Part (Books I.–III.) the text of the poem ends on p. 589, the first stanza on p. 588 being identical in each. In the First Edition that stanza is followed by *five* others, in which the amorous embracements of Amoret and Sir Scudamore are warmly described. In the Second Edition these stanzas were suppressed, and *three* others of a milder character substituted.

The 10 sonnets on pp. 601–605 are inscribed to the following persons: p. 601, to Sir Christopher Hatton and to the Earle of Essex; p. 602, to the Earle of Oxenford and to the Earle of Northumberland; p. 603, to the Earle of Ormond and Offory and to the Lo. Ch. Howard; p. 604, to the Lord Grey of Wilton and to Sir Walter Raleigh; p. 605, to the Lady Carew and to "all the gratious and beautifull Ladies in the Court." Page 606 contains "Faults efcaped in the Print."

The four unnumbered leaves at the end contain 15 sonnets, as follows: recto of Qq, to Sir Christopher Hatton and to Lo. Burleigh; verso of Qq, to the Earle of Oxenford and to the Earle of Northumberland; recto of Qq 2, to the Earle of Cumberland and to the Earle of Essex; verso of Qq 2, to the Earle of Ormond and Offory and to the Lo. Ch. Howard; recto of Qq 3, to the Lord of Hunsdon and to the Lord Grey of Wilton; verso of Qq 3, to the Lord of Buckhurst and to Sir Fr. Walsingham, Knight; recto of [Qq 4], to Sir Iohn Norris and to Sir Walter Raleigh; verso of [Qq 4], to the Countesse of Pembroke.

Of the sonnets on pp. 601–605, those to the Lady Carew and "To all the gratious and beautifull Ladies in the Court" are not included in those given in the unnumbered leaves. Of the 15 sonnets on leaves Qq–[Qq 4], seven are new: those to Lo. Burleigh, Earle of Cumberland, Lord of Hunsdon, Lord of Buckhurst, Sir Fr. Walsingham, Sir Iohn Norris, and the Countesse of Penbroke. One of these is addressed to Sir Francis Walsingham, who died in 1590, so it is possible that the leaves containing this sonnet may have been printed before those containing but 10 sonnets (pp. 601–605).

We have seen another copy (the Majoribanks copy), in which pp. 601–606, [Pp 6]–[Pp 8], are also followed by the four unnumbered leaves, Qq–[Qq 4].

A Second Edition of this volume (our No. 656) was issued in 1596, to accompany the First Edition of the Second Part, Books IV.–VI., which was published that year.

The volume here described contains the first three books of *The Faerie Queene*. The next three books were published in 1596 (our No. 657). The first complete edition in folio (1609) contains two additional cantos belonging to some later book, presumably never completed.

The whole poem, as originally planned, was to have contained twelve books of twelve cantos each. In his letter to Sir Walter Raleigh (pp. 591–595) Spenser describes the poem, the greater part of which was yet to be written, as "*a continued Allegory, or darke conceit.*" As we now have them, the stories in the several books have no definite relation to one another, it being Spenser's purpose to reserve the central event, which was the occasion of the different adventures of the poem, until they had all been related.

Notwithstanding its monotony and tediousness, "the patient reader is rewarded at every turn by episodes which are informed by a wealth of fancy and of musical diction that gives the 'Faerie Queene' a place among English narrative poems not far below the greatest of them — Milton's 'Paradise Lost.' 'The nobility of the Spencers,' wrote Gibbon in his Memoirs, 'has been illustrated and enriched by the trophies of Marlborough, but I exhort them to consider the 'Fairy Queen' as the most precious jewel of their coronet.'"

"Except Milton, and possibly Gray, Spenser was the most learned of English poets, and signs of his multifarious reading in the classics and modern French and Italian literature abound in his writings. Marot inspired his 'Shepheards Calender.' The 'Faerie Queene' was avowedly written in emulation of Ariosto's 'Orlando,' and Sackville's 'Induction' to the 'Mirror for Magistrates' gave many hints for the general outline. Throughout the great work Homer and Theocritus, Virgil and Cicero, Petrarch and Tasso, Du Bellay, Chaucer, and many a modern romance writer of Western Europe, are laid under repeated contribution. . . . But Spenser's subtle æsthetic sense permitted him to assimilate nothing that did not enhance the pictorial beauty of his spacious achievement."

"Only one Englishman contrived a wholly successful allegory. Spenser was not he. John Bunyan, in the *Pilgrim's Progress*, alone among Englishmen possessed just that definite measure of imagination which enabled him to convert with absolute sureness personifications of virtues and vices into speaking likenesses of men and women and places. Bunyan's great exercise in the allegorical art is rarely disfigured by inconsistencies or incoherences. His scenes and persons — Christian and Faithful, The House Beautiful and Vanity Fair — while they are perfectly true to analogy, — are endowed with intelligible and life-like features. The moral significance is never doubtful, while the whole picture leaves the impression of a masterpiece of literary fiction."

"In all senses the work is great. The scale on which Spenser planned his epic allegory has indeed no parallel in ancient or modern literature. All that has reached us is but a quarter of the contemplated whole. Yet the *Faerie Queene* is, in its extant shape, as long as Homer's *Iliad* and *Odyssey* combined with Virgil's *Aeneid*. Even epics of more recent date, whose example Spenser confesses to have emulated, fell far behind his work in its liberality of scale. In the unfinished form that it has come down to us, Spenser's epic is more than twice as long as Dante's *La Divina Commedia* or Tasso's *Gierusalemme Liberata;* Ariosto's *Orlando Furioso*, with which Spenser was thoroughly familiar, was brought to completion in somewhat fewer lines. Nor did Spenser's great successors compete with him in length. Milton's

1590   *Edmund Spenser*   No. 655

THE FAERIE
QVEENE.

Difposed into twelue books,
Fashioning
XII. Morall vertues.

LONDON
Printed for William Ponfonbie.
1 5 9 0.

No. 655.   Title-page of Spenser's Faerie Qveene; 1st Edition,
1st Issue; 1590.

Church Catalogue   [991]   English Literature

No. 655   *Edmund Spenser*   1590

Paradise Lost, the greatest of all English epics, fills, when joined to its sequel *Paradise Regained,* less than a third of Spenser's space. Had the *Faerie Queene* reached a twenty-fourth book, as the poet at the outset thought possible, not all the great epics penned in ancient or modern Europe would, when piled one upon the other, have reached the gigantic dimensions of the Elizabethan poem."

" Of the many beauties and excellences of the poem every generation from the date of its appearance has testified through the mouths of its choicest spirits. For Spenser has not been the poet of a school of singers, but the poet of all true poets from Dryden and Pope and Byron to Milton, Keats, and Wordsworth."

SPENSER, EDMUND.

THE FAERIE QVEENE.   London, *for William Ponsonbie,* 1590.   [655 A]

Small quarto. First Edition, Second Issue.

COLLATION BY SIGNATURES: Identically the same as in our preceding number.

COLLATION BY PAGINATION: Identically the same as in our preceding number, except the imprint on the title-page (as reproduced; *See* No. 655 A).

CONDITION: Size of leaf, $7\frac{9}{16}$ × $5\frac{3}{8}$ inches. Bound in maroon crushed levant morocco, gilt over marbled edges; by Lortic.

The Second Issue differs from the First only in having the Welsh and English words supplied in lines 4 and 5 of p. 332, as described in our note to the preceding number. The imprint on the title-page was also reset, as appears below.

LONDON
Printed for William Ponsonbie.
1590.

No. 655 A.   IMPRINT ON THE TITLE-PAGE OF SPENSER'S FAERIE QVEENE; 1ST EDITION, 2D ISSUE; 1590.

[SPENSER, EDMUND.]

THE FAERIE QVEENE.   [BOOKS I.-III.]   London, *for William Ponsonbie,* 1596.   [656]

Small quarto. Second Edition.

COLLATION BY SIGNATURES: A to Z, Aa to Oo, each 8 leaves; total 296 leaves.

COLLATION BY PAGINATION: [title, as reproduced; *See* No. 656], recto of [A];

— | [conventional head-piece] | TO | THE MOST HIGH, | MIGHTIE | And | MAGNIFICENT | EMPRESSE RENOVV- | MED FOR PIETIE, VER- | TVE, AND ALL GRATIOVS | GOVERNMENT ELIZABETH . . . | [16 lines] |, verso

1596   *Edmund Spenser*   No. 656

THE FAERIE
QVEENE.

Difposed into twelue bookes,

Fashioning

XII. Morall vertues.

LONDON
Printed for VVilliam Ponfonbie.
1596.

No. 656.   Title-page of Spenser's Faerie Qveene; 2d Edition; 1596.

No. 656   *Edmund Spenser*   **1596**

of [A];—[text in 3 books, the first with heading] | [conventional head-piece] | THE FIRST | BOOKE OF THE | FAERIE QVEENE. | *Contayning* | THE LEGENDE OF THE | KNIGHT OF THE RED CROSSE, | OR | OF HOLINESSE. | , pp. [1]–183; — | *FINIS LIB. I.* | [conventional tail-piece] | , p. 183; —[woodcut of a mounted knight killing a dragon], p. [184];— | [conventional head-piece] | THE SECOND | BOOKE OF THE | FAERIE QVEENE. | Contayning, | THE LEGEND OF SIR GVYON. | OR | *Of Temperaunce.* | , pp. 185–387;—[conventional tail-piece], p. 387; —[blank], p. [388]; — | [conventional head-piece] | THE THIRD | BOOKE OF THE | FAERIE QVEENE. | Contayning, | THE LEGEND OF BRITOMARTIS. | OR | *Of Chaſtitie.* | , pp. 389–589; — | A Viſion vpon this conceipt of the | *Faery Queene.* | [14 lines] | Another of the fame. | [14 lines] | [signed] | W. R. | , p. 589; —[poem, with heading] | To the learned Shepheard. | [signed] | Hobynoll. | , p. 590. Page 10 is wrongly numbered 18; the numbers 79 and 80 are omitted in the pagination, and 95 and 96 are repeated; 102 is 120; 311 is 331; 468 is 478; 497 is 597; 510 is 600; and 586 is 589.

Inserted in this work as an extra-illustration is a copperplate portrait of Spenser, engraved by G. Van de Gucht, inlaid to size; facing the title-page.

CONDITION: Size of leaf, 7 3/16 × 5 9/16 inches. Bound in maroon crushed levant morocco, gilt over marbled edges; by Lortic.

OTHER COPIES.

British Museum (2, one the Grenville copy); Britwell; Capell Collection; Forster Collection; Rylands; Edinburgh University; Hoe (Evelyn copy); and Morgan Libraries; and the Library of Congress.

REFERENCES.

Hoe, *Catalogue*, 4 (1904): 209; Grolier Club, *Langland to Wither* (1893), p. 202, No. 232; Sinker, *Library of Trinity College, Cambridge* (1891), p. 122; Lowndes, 5 (1869): 2476; Hazlitt, *Hand-Book* (1867), p. 573, No. 2 b; *Bibliotheca Grenvilliana*, 2 (1842): 681; *Bibliotheca Anglo-Poetica* (1815), p. 303, No. 636.

This, the Second Edition of Books I.–III. of the *Faerie Queene*, was printed to accompany the First Edition of the second portion, containing Books IV.–VI. (our next number), published the same year. Although a paginary reprint, it differs from the First Edition, especially at the end of the volume, all the complimentary matter, consisting of sonnets, verses, etc., in that edition commencing with sheet Pp being omitted, with the exception of the three commendatory verses given in the above collation. The last five stanzas of Book III., because of their too freely amorous character, were rewritten and reduced to three. Lines 4 and 5 on p. 332 are here completed by the insertion and correction of the necessary Welsh and English words.

SPENSER, EDMUND.

THE SECOND PART OF THE FAERIE QVEENE. LONDON, *for VVilliam Ponſonby*, 1596.   **[657]**

Small quarto. First Edition.

COLLATION BY SIGNATURES: A to Z, Aa to Ii, each 8 leaves; Kk, 4 leaves; total 260 leaves.

COLLATION BY PAGINATION: [title, as reproduced; *See* No. 657], recto of [A]; —[blank], verso of [A]; —[text, books 4–6, the first with heading] | [conventional head-piece] | THE FOVRTH | BOOKE OF THE | FAERIE QVEENE. | *Containing* |

1596   Edmund Spenser   No. 657

THE SECOND
PART OF THE
FAERIE QVEENE.

Containing

THE FOVRTH,
FIFTH, AND
SIXTH BOOKES.

By Ed. Spenser.

Imprinted at London for VVilliam
Ponsonby. 1596.

No. 657.   TITLE-PAGE OF THE SECOND PART OF THE FAERIE QVEENE;
1ST EDITION; 1596.

No. 657   *Edmund Spenser*   1596

The Legend of CAMBEL and TELAMOND, | OR | OF FRIENDSHIP. |, pp. [1]–181; — [blank], p. [182]; — | [conventional head-piece] | THE FIFTH | BOOKE OF THE | FAERIE QVEENE. | *Contayning*, | THE LEGEND OF ARTEGALL | OR | OF IVSTICE. |, pp. 183–353; — [blank], p. [354]; — | [conventional head-piece] | THE SIXTE | BOOKE OF THE | FAERIE QVEENE. | *Contayning* | THE LEGEND OF S. CALIDORE | OR | OF COVRTESIE. |, pp. 355–518; — | FINIS. |, p. 518. The numbers 3 and 4 are omitted in the pagination; p. 30 is wrongly numbered 28; 31 is 29; 153 is 15; and the numbers 366 and 367 are repeated.

CONDITION: Size of leaf, 7⅜ x 5⅚ inches. Bound in red crushed levant morocco, gilt edges; by Bedford.

OTHER COPIES.

British Museum (2, Grenville copies); Bodleian; Britwell; Capell Collection; Forster Collection; Rylands; Crawford; Devonshire; Huth; Lenox; Halsey; Hoe (2, one the Evelyn copy); Morgan; and White Libraries; and the Library of Congress.

REFERENCES.

Hoe, *Catalogue*, 4 (1904) : 209; Grolier Club, *Langland to Wither* (1893), p. 202, No. 233; Sinker, *Library of Trinity College, Cambridge* (1891), p. 122; Locker-Lampson, *Catalogue* (1886), p. 119; Huth, *Catalogue*, 4 (1880) : 1386; Lowndes, 5 (1869) : 2476; Hazlitt, *Hand-Book* (1867), p. 573, No. 2, ii.; *Bibliotheca Grenvilliana*, 2 (1842) : 680; *Bibliotheca Anglo-Poetica* (1815), p. 302, No. 634.

The copy here described was formerly in the library of Frederick Locker-Lampson and contains his ex-libris.

SPENSER, EDMUND.

COMPLAINTS. CONTAINING SUNDRIE SMALL POEMES OF THE WORLDS VANITIE. LONDON, *for VVilliam Ponſonbie*, 1591.

[658]

Small quarto. First Edition.

COLLATION BY SIGNATURES: A to Z, each 4 leaves (the last blank and genuine); total 92 unnumbered leaves. Leaf G 2 is wrongly marked G 4; A 3, E 2, and T 3 have no signature-marks. In some copies leaf G 4 is correctly marked, and Y 2 is wrongly marked Y 3.

COLLATION BY PAGINATION: [title, as reproduced; *See* No. 658 *a*], recto of [A]; — | A note of the ſundrie Poemes contained | in this Volume. |, verso of [A]; — | [conventional head-piece] | The Printer to the | *Gentle Reader.* |, recto and verso of A 2; — | [conventional head-piece, with title in a mortiſe] | THE RVINE OF TIME. | Dedicated | To the right Noble and beauti- | *full Ladie, the La. Marie* | Counteſſe of Pembrooke. | [ſigned] | Your Ladiſhips euer | humblie at commaund. | *E. S.* | [conven- tional tail-piece] |, recto of [A 3] to recto of [A 4]; — [blank], verso of [A 4]; — [poem, with running head-lines] | *The Ruines of Time.* |, recto of B to verso of [D 4]; — | FINIS. |, verso of [D 4].

| THE | Teares of the Mu- | ſes. | By ED. SP. | [device, same as in our reproduced title-page] | LONDON. | Imprinted for *VVilliam* | *Ponſonbie*, dwelling in Paules | Churchyard at the ſigne of | *the Biſhops head.* | 1591. | [in same border as in our reproduced title-page], recto of [E]; — [blank], verso of [E]; — | TO THE RIGHT HONOR- ABLE | the Ladie *Strange.* | [ſigned] | Your La: humbly euer. | Ed. Sp |, recto of [E 2]; — [text, with running head-lines] | *The Teares of the Muſes.* |, verso of [E 2] to verso of [G 4]; — | FINIS. |, verso of [G 4]; — | Long ſince dedicated | *To the most noble and excellent Lord*, | the

No. 658 a.   Title-page of Spenser's Complaints; 1st Edition; 1591.

No. 658   *Edmund Spenser*   1591

Earle of Leicefter, late | deceafed. |, recto of H ; — [poem, with running head-lines] | *Virgils Gnat.* |, verso of H to verso of [K 4] ; — | FINIS. |, verso of [K 4].

[Title-page, as reproduced ; *See* No. 658 *b*], recto of [L] ; — [blank], verso of [L] ; — | [conventional head-piece] | To the right Honourable, the | Ladie *Compton* and | *Mountegle.* | [signed] | Your La: euer | humbly ; | *Ed. Sp.* |, recto and verso of L 2 ; — [text, with heading] | *Profopopoia :* or | *Mother Hubberds Tale.* |, recto of L 3 to verso of [Q 4] ; — | FINIS. |, verso of [Q 4] ; — [poem, with heading] | *Ruines of Rome : by Bellay.* |, recto of R to verso of [S 4] ; — | FINIS. |, verso of [S 4].

| MVIOPOTMOS, | Or | The Fate of the Butterflie. | By ED. SP. | Dedicated to the moft faire and | vertuous Ladie : the Ladie | *Carey.* | [device, same as in our reproduced title-page] | LONDON. | Imprinted for VVilliam | Ponfonbie, dwelling in Paules | Churchyard at the figne of | *the Bifhops head.* | 1590. | [in same border as in our reproduced title-page], recto of [T] ; — [blank], verso of [T] ; — | [conventional head-piece] | To the right worthy and vertuous | Ladie ; the La *: Carey.* | [signed] | Your La : euer | humbly ; | *E : S.* |, recto and verso of T 2 ; — [poem, with heading] | *Muiopotmos :* or | *The Fate of the Butterflie.* |, recto of [T 3] to recto of X 2 ; — | FINIS. |, recto of X 2 ; — [blank], verso of X 2 ; — [poem, with running head-lines] | *Vifions of the worlds vanitie.* |, recto of X 3 to verso of Y ; — | FINIS. |, verso of Y ; — [poem, with heading] | *The Vifions of Bellay.* |, recto of Y 2 to verso of Z ; — | FINIS. |, verso of Z ; — [poem, with heading] | *The Vifions of Petrarch* | *formerly tranflated.* |, recto of Z 2 to verso of Z 3 ; — | FINIS. |, verso of Z 3 ; — [1 blank leaf], [Z 4].

CONDITION : Size of leaf, 7⁹⁄₁₆ × 5¼ inches. Bound in old calf.

OTHER COPIES.

British Museum (Grenville copy) ; Bodleian ; Capell Collection ; Dyce Collection ; Rylands ; Devonshire ; Ellesmere ; Huth ; Boston Public (Barton) ; Lenox ; Halsey ; Hoe ; Morgan ; and White Libraries.

REFERENCES.

Nicoll and Seccombe, 1 (1907) : 185 ; Hoe, *Catalogue*, 4 (1904) : 215 ; Grolier Club, *Langland to Wither* (1893), p. 204, No. 235 ; Sinker, *Library of Trinity College, Cambridge* (1891), p. 122 ; Locker-Lampson, *Catalogue* (1886), p. 118 ; Huth, *Catalogue*, 4 (1880) : 1387 ; Lowndes, 5 (1869) : 2478 ; Hazlitt, *Hand-Book* (1867), p. 573, No. 5 ; Collier, *Rarest Books*, 4 (1866) : 83 ; Hazlitt, *Collections and Notes* (1876), p. 398 ; *Bibliotheca Grenvilliana*, 2 (1842) : 681.

The Locker-Lampson copy, with ex-libris.

"The great success of the first three books of *The Faerie Queene* induced the publisher to apply to Spenser for material for a further volume. This appeared early in 1591, entitled *Complaints*, forming a collection of nine miscellaneous poems. Of these *Muiopotmos, or The Fate of the Butterfly*, swept by a gust of wind into a spider's web, is a delightful exercise of lyrical fancy (admirably criticised by Lowell) ; *The Ruines of Time* is an elegiac tribute to the Countess of Pembroke, lamenting the deaths of Sidney, Leicester, and Warwick ; *The Tears of the Muses*, a lament upon the low state of learning in England ; while the vigorous though desponding *Mother Hubberd's Tale*, perhaps the most direct of Spenser's writings, contains a poignant satire in decasyllabic couplets upon certain aspects of the English court."

These poems were printed while their author was in Ireland, but seem from the dedication to have been prepared by him for publication. "'The Teares of the Mufes' contains in the second stanza on F 2 recto what is thought to be the earliest notice of Shakespeare, 'Our pleafant *Willy*,' as Spenser here calls him, in his twenty-eighth year when the poem was published."

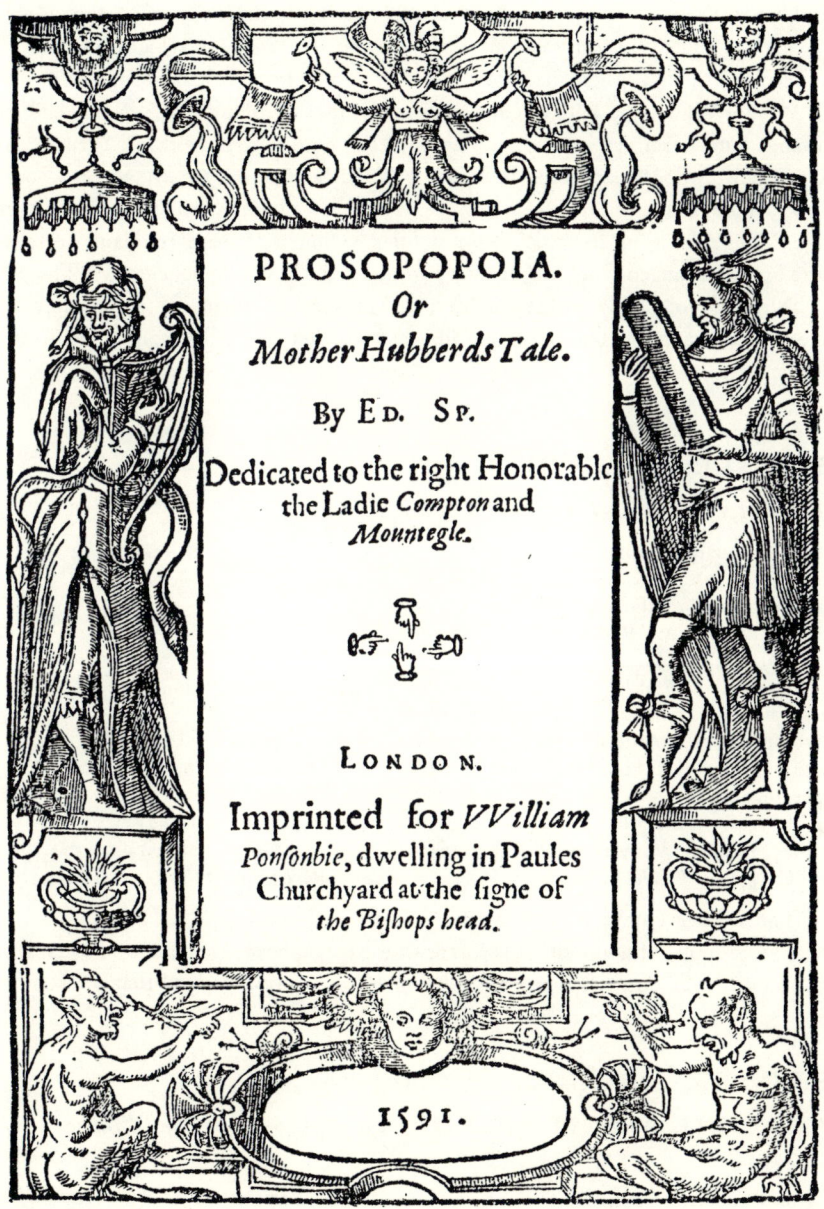

No. 658 b.   Title-page of Spenser's Prosopopoia.   Or Mother Hubberds Tale; 1st Edition; 1591.

"T. M. in his *Father Hubbard's Tales*, 1604, says, 'Why I call these Father Hubbards Tales is not to haue them called in againe as the Tales of Mother Hubbard' — whence it may appear that Spenser's *Mother Hubbard*, to which this must surely be received as an allusion, has not come down to us in its original shape."

"The Vifions of Bellay" and "The Vifions of Petrarch" at the end of the volume here described are unquestionably the very earliest work of Spenser extant. They had previously appeared in Van der Noodt's *Theatre for Worldlings* (our No. 650), though not in the form given here, and without proper acknowledgment.

"The Vifions of Bellay," there entitled "Sonets," were in blank verse; they here appear changed into the ordinary form of the rhyming sonnet. "The Vifions of Petrarch" originally printed in rhyme, but some of them containing only twelve lines, here reappear, but with an additional couplet added to such of them as were deficient.

SPENSER, EDMUND.

DAPHNAÏDA. LONDON, *for William Ponfonby*, 1591.   [659]

Small quarto. First Edition.

COLLATION BY SIGNATURES: A, B, C, each 4 leaves; total 12 unnumbered leaves.

COLLATION BY PAGINATION: [title, as reproduced; *See* No. 659], recto of [A]; —[blank], verso of [A];—|[conventional head-piece]|| To the right Hono-|rable and vertuous Lady *Helena*| *Marquefse of* North-hampton.|[signed]|| *Your Honors humbly euer.*| E. Sp.|, recto and verso of *A* 2;— [text, with heading]|[conventional head-piece]|*Daphnaïda.*|, recto of A 3 to verso of [C 4];—| *FINIS.*|, verso of [C 4].

CONDITION: Size of leaf, 7 9/16 × 5 1/4 inches. Bound with No. 658.

OTHER COPIES.

British Museum (2, Grenville copies); Bodleian; and Boston Public Libraries.

REFERENCES.

Locker-Lampson, *Catalogue* (1886), p. 119; Hazlitt, *Collections and Notes* (1876), p. 398; Lowndes, 5 (1869): 2479; Hazlitt, *Hand-Book* (1867), p. 573, No. 4; *Bibliotheca Grenvilliana*, 2 (1842): 681.

The Locker-Lampson copy, with ex-libris.

The Second Edition, with a separate title-page, appears in Spenser's *Fowre Hymnes*, 1596 (our No. 662), though not mentioned on the title-page of that work.

SPENSER, EDMUND.

AMORETTI AND EPITHALAMION. [LONDON], *for William Ponfonby*, 1595.   [660]

Small octavo. First Edition.

COLLATION BY SIGNATURES: ¶, 4 leaves; A to H, each 8 leaves; total 68 unnumbered leaves. Leaf ¶ 2 is wrongly marked ¶; A 4 has a signature-mark; and A has none.

COLLATION BY PAGINATION: [title, as reproduced; *See* No. 660], recto of [¶]; —[blank], verso of [¶];—|[conventional head-piece]|| *To the Right Worfhip-*| full Sir Robart Need-| *ham Knight·*|[signed] | W. P |, recto of ¶ 2 [wrongly marked ¶]

Daphnaïda.

An Elegie vpon the

death of the noble and vertuous
Douglas Howard, *Daughter and*
heire of *Henry* Lord *Howard*, Viscount *Byndon, and* wife of Ar-
thure Gorges *Esquier*.

Dedicated to the Right honorable the Lady
Helena, Marquesse of *Northampton*.

By Ed. Sp.

At London
Printed for William Ponsonby, *dwelling in*
Paules Churchyard at the signe of the
Bishops head **1591**.

AMORETTI
AND
Epithalamion.

Written not long since by Edmunde Spenser.

Printed for William Ponsonby. *1595.*

No. 660. Title-page of Spenser's Amoretti and Epithalamion; 1st Edition; 1595.

to recto of [¶3];—[blank], verso of [¶3]; —[verses to the author, with heading] | *G: W. senior, to the Author* |, recto of [¶4]; —[blank], verso of [¶4];—[verses to the author, signed] | *G. W. I.* |, recto of [A]; —[blank], verso of [A];—[89 numbered sonnets, the first with heading] | *SONNET. I.* |, recto of A 2 to recto of [F 6];—[poem on Cupid], verso of [F 6] to recto of G 2;— | *FINIS.* |, recto of G 2;—[blank], verso of G 2.

| [Type-ornament head-piece] | Epithalamion. | [device, same as on our reproduced title-page] | [type-ornament tail-piece] |, recto of [G 3];—[blank], verso of [G 3];

—[text], recto of [G 4] to verso of [H 7]; —| *FINIS* |, verso of [H 7];—[colophon] | [type-ornament head-piece] | *Imprinted by P. S. for Wil-* | liam Ponsonby. | [type-ornament tail-piece] |, recto of [H 8];— [blank], verso of [H 8].

Condition: Size of leaf, 4⅝ × 3¹⁄₁₆ inches. Bound in polished green morocco, gilt edges; by Bedford.

Other Copies.

British Museum (Grenville copy); Bodleian; Capell Collection; Rylands; Edinburgh University; Huth (mislaid); and White Libraries.

1595   *Edmund Spenser*   No. 660

REFERENCES.

Nicoll and Seccombe, 1 (1907) : 185, 202; Sinker, *Library of Trinity College, Cambridge* (1891), p. 122; Locker-Lampson, *Catalogue* (1886), p. 118; Lowndes, 5 (1869): 2479; Hazlitt, *Hand-Book* (1867), p. 573, No. 7; *Bibliotheca Grenvilliana*, 2 (1842) : 681.

The Tite-Locker Lampson copy, with ex-libris of the latter.

Written in ink on the recto of the third fly-leaf is what appears to be an autograph signature of Thomas Moore, the Irish poet.

This volume was written during Spenser's residence in Ireland. Not more than seven perfect copies are known.

"In 1594 his *Amoretti and Epithalamion* went to Ponsonby for publication. The sonnets are rather disappointing in their lack of individuality, but the *Epithalamion* (written in alternately rhyming decasyllabics), which crowns the series of *Amoretti*, is perhaps the most splendid hymn of triumphant love in the language."

"Certain Amoretti were addressed, though not by name, to the Elizabeth Boyle, who, in 1594, became Spenser's wife; but many of them are either purely ideal or not poems of love at all."

SPENSER, EDMUND.

COLIN CLOVTS COME HOME AGAINE. London, *for VVilliam Ponfonbie*, 1595.   [661]

Small quarto. First Edition.

COLLATION BY SIGNATURES : A to K, each 4 leaves; total 40 unnumbered leaves.

COLLATION BY PAGINATION : [title, as reproduced; *See* No. 661], recto of [A]; —[blank], verso of [A];—|[conventional head-piece]| TO THE RIGHT | worthy and noble Knight | Sir *VValter Raleigh*, Captaine of her Maiefties | Guard, Lord Wardein of the Stanneries, | *and Lieutenant of the Countie of* | *Cornwall.* | [signed] | Yours euer humbly. | *Ed. Sp.* | [dated] | ... From my houfe | of Kilcolman, the 27. of December. | 1591. |, recto and verso of A 2; —[poem, with heading] | [type-ornament head-piece]| COLIN CLOVTS | come home againe. |, recto of A 3 to verso of E 2;—| FINIS. |, verso of E 2;— [half-title] | [type-ornament head-piece] | ASTROPHEL.| A Paftorall Elegie vpon |the death of the moft Noble and valorous| Knight, Sir *Philip Sidney.* | Dedicated | *To the most beautifull and vertuous Ladie, the Counteffe* | *of* Effex. | [type-ornament tail-piece]|, recto of [E 3];—[blank], verso of [E 3]; —[poem, with heading] | [conventional head-piece] | Aftrophel. |, recto of [E 4] to recto of G 3;—| *The mourning Mufe of* Theftylis. |, recto of G 3 to recto of H 2;—| *A pastorall Aeglogue vpon the death of Sir* Phillip | Sidney Knight, *&c.* |, recto of H 2 to verso of [H 4];—[elegy and 2 epitaphs upon Sir Philip Sidney, the first with heading] | [type-ornament head-piece]| An Elegie, or friends paf-|fion, for his *Astrophill.* |, recto of I to recto of [K 4];—| FINIS.| [colophon] | LONDON |Printed by T. C. for William Ponfonbie. | 1595. |, recto of [K 4]; —[blank], verso of [K 4].

CONDITION : Size of leaf, 7½ x 5⅝ inches. Bound in maroon crushed levant morocco, gilt edges ; by Lortic.

OTHER COPIES.

British Museum (Grenville copy); Bodleian ; Capell Collection ; Dyce Collection ; Rylands ; Huth ; Boston Public

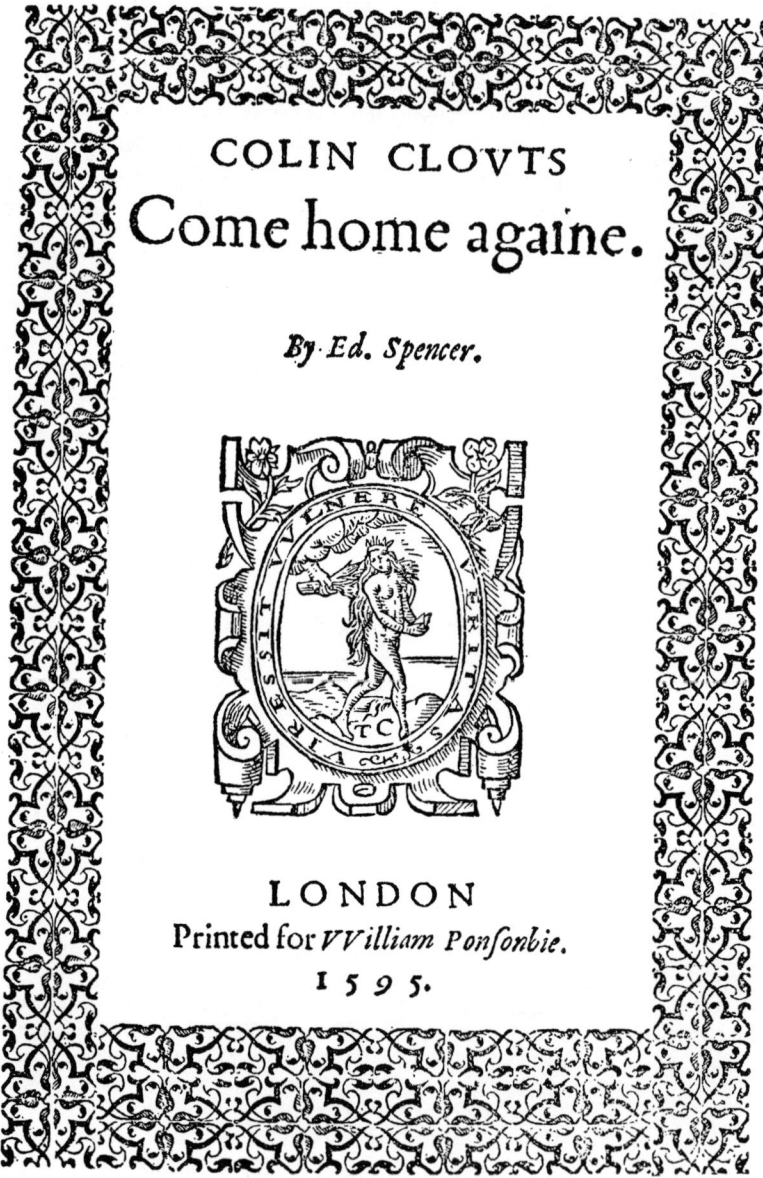

No 661. Title-page of Spenser's Colin Clovts Come home againe; 1st Edition; 1595.

(Barton); Halsey; Hoe (2, one the Evelyn copy); Morgan; and White Libraries; and the Library of Congress.

REFERENCES.

Hoe, *Catalogue*, 4 (1904) : 209; Grolier Club, *Langland to Wither* (1893), p. 206, No. 236; Sinker, *Library of Trinity College* (1891), p. 122; Locker-Lampson, *Catalogue* (1886), p. 119; Huth, *Catalogue*, 4 (1880) : 1387; Lowndes, 5 (1869) : 2479; Hazlitt, *Hand-Book* (1867), p. 573, No. 6; *Bibliotheca Grenvilliana*, 2 (1842) : 681; *Bibliotheca Anglo-Poetica* (1815), p. 452, No. 947.

This fascinating narrative of Spenser's journey to Court and of what he saw there was written immediately after his return to Kilcolman, in 1591. It contains an interesting allusion to Shakespeare under the name of " Aetion " on leaf C 2, as follows:

" And there though laſt not leaſt is *Aetion*,
A gentler ſhepheard may no where be found:
Whoſe *Muſe* full of high thoughts inuention,
Doth like himſelfe Heroically ſound."

Contemporary references to Shakespeare are few in number.

" With this is printed ' The Mourning Muse of Thestylis,' by Lodowick Bryskett, of which no separate edition is known. It includes also ' An Elegie, or friends passion for his Astrophell ' [by Matthew Roydon?] Brysket's Poem was licensed to John Wolfe in 1587 separately, and very probably printed by him; but no such impression has yet come to light."

SPENSER, EDMUND.

FOWRE HYMNES. LONDON, *for VVilliam Ponſonby*, 1596. [662]

Small quarto. First Edition.

COLLATION BY SIGNATURES : A to I, each 4 leaves; K, 2 leaves; total 38 leaves. Leaf I iij. has no signature-mark.

COLLATION BY PAGINATION : [title, as reproduced; *See* No. 662 *a*], recto of [A]; — [blank], verso of [A]; — | [conventional head-piece] | TO THE RIGHT HO- | NORABLE AND MOST VER- | tuous Ladies, the Ladie Margaret Counteſſe | of Cumberland, and the Ladie Marie | Counteſſe of Warwicke. | [signed] | *Your Honors moſt bounden euer* | *in all humble ſeruice.* | Ed. Sp. | , recto and verso of *A ij*.; — [4 poems, the first with heading] | [type-ornament head-piece] | AN HYMNE IN | HONOVR OF | LOVE. | , pp. 1 – 45; — [blank], p. [46].

[Title of *Daphnaïda*, as reproduced; *See* No. 662 *b*], p. [47]; — [blank], p. [48]; — | [conventional head-piece] | TO THE RIGHT | HONORABLE AND VER- | tuous Lady *Helena Marqueſſe* of | Northhampton. | [signed] | *Your Honours humbly euer.* | Ed. Sp. | [dated] | . . . London *this firſt of* | *Ianuarie*. 1591. | , pp. 49 – [50]; — [text, with heading] | [type-ornament head-piece] | DAPHNAIDA. | , pp. 51 – 71; — | *FINIS*. | , p. 71; — [blank], p. [72]. Page 50 has no page-number.

CONDITION : Size of leaf, 7⅛ × 5⅚ inches. Bound in maroon crushed levant morocco, gilt edges; by Lortic.

OTHER COPIES.

British Museum (Grenville copy); Bodleian; Dyce Collection; Rylands; Ellesmere; Huth; Boston Public; Halsey; Hoe (2); and White Libraries.

Fowre Hymnes,
MADE BY
EDM. SPENSER.

LONDON,
Printed for VVilliam Ponsonby.
1596.

No. 662 a.   TITLE-PAGE OF SPENSER'S FOWRE HYMNES; 1ST EDITION; 1596.

Daphnaïda.

AN ELEGIE VPON THE DEATH OF THE NOBLE AND VERTVOVS DOVGLAS

Howard, daughter and heire of *Henry* Lord *Howard*, Viscount *Byn-don*, and wife of *Arthur Gorges* Esquier.

Dedicated to the Right honorable the Ladie *Helena*, Marquesse of *Northampton*.

By *Ed. Sp.*

AT LONDON
Printed for William Ponsonby,
1596.

No. 662*b*. Title-page of Spenser's Daphnaïda; 2d Edition; 1596.

No. 662   *Edmund Spenser*   1596

REFERENCES.

Hoe, *Catalogue*, 4 (1904) : 216; Grolier Club, *Langland to Wither* (1893), p. 208, No. 238; Locker-Lampson, *Catalogue* (1886), p. 120; Huth, *Catalogue*, 4 (1880) : 1387; Hazlitt, *Collections and Notes* (1876), p. 399; Lowndes, 5 (1869) : 2479; Hazlitt, *Hand-Book* (1867), p. 574, No. 8; *Bibliotheca Grenvilliana*, 2 (1842) : 682; *Bibliotheca Anglo-Poetica* (1815), p. 453, No. 948.

With this work appears the Second Edition of *Daphnaïda*, the First having been printed in 1591 (our No. 659).

SPENSER, EDMUND.

PROTHALAMION. LONDON, *for VVilliam Ponſonby*, 1596.   [663]

Small quarto. First Edition.

COLLATION BY SIGNATURES: A, 4 leaves; B, 2 leaves; total 6 leaves.

COLLATION BY PAGINATION : [title, as reproduced; *See* No. 663], recto of [A]; —[blank], verso of [A]; —[text, with heading] | [type-ornament head-piece] | 1 | *Prothalamion.* |, pp. 1–10; — | FINIS. | [type-ornament tail-piece] |, p. 10. Each page has a type-ornament head- and tail-piece.

CONDITION : Size of leaf, 7⅛ × 5¾₁₆ inches. Bound in maroon crushed levant morocco, gilt edges; by Lortic. The first leaf of sheet B is duplicated.

OTHER COPIES.

British Museum (Grenville copy); Bodleian; Devonshire; Huth; Boston Public; Hoe; and White Libraries.

REFERENCES.

Hoe, *Catalogue*, 4 (1904) : 217; Grolier Club, *Langland to Wither* (1893), p. 208, No. 237; Locker-Lampson, *Catalogue* (1886), p. 120; Huth, *Catalogue*, 4 (1880) : 1387; Hazlitt, *Collections and Notes* (1876), p. 399; Lowndes, 5 (1869) : 2479; Hazlitt, *Hand-Book* (1867), p. 574, No. 9; *Bibliotheca Grenvilliana*, 2 (1842) : 682; *Bibliotheca Anglo-Poetica* (1815), p. 453, No. 949.

In some copies the catchword on the recto of leaf B 2 is wrongly printed "To" instead of "From."

SPENSER, EDMUND.

BRITTAIN'S IDA. LONDON, *for Thomas Walkley*, 1628.   [664]

Small octavo. First Edition.

COLLATION BY SIGNATURES: A, 4 leaves (the first, probably blank, lacking); B, C, each 8 leaves; total 20 unnumbered leaves.

COLLATION BY PAGINATION : [1 leaf, probably blank], [A]; — [title, as reproduced; *See* No. 664], recto of [A 2]; — [blank], verso of [A 2]; — | [type-ornament head-piece] | TO THE RIGHT | Noble Lady *MARY*, | Daughter to the moſt Illuſtri- | ous Prince GEORGE, Duke | of *Buckingham.* | [signed] | The humbleſt of your | deuoted Seruants. | *Thomas Walkley.* |, recto and verso of *A* 3 ; — [verses, with heading] | Martial. |, recto and verso of [A 4] ; — [text, with heading] | [type-ornament head-piece] | Brittain's Ida. |, recto of B to verso of [C 8] ; — | FINIS. |, verso of [C 8]. Each page has a type-ornament head- and tail-piece.

Prothalamion
Or
A Spousall Verse made by
Edm. Spenser.
IN HONOVR OF THE DOV-
ble mariage of the two Honorable & vertuous
Ladies, *the Ladie* Elizabeth *and the Ladie* Katherine
Somerset, Daughters to the Right Honourable the
Earle of *Worcester* and espoused to the two worthie
Gentlemen M. *Henry Gilford*, and
M. *William Peter* Esquyers.

AT LONDON.
Printed for *VVilliam Ponsonby.*
1596.

No. 663. Title-page of Spenser's Prothalamion; 1st Edition; 1596.

No. 664 Edmund Spenser 1628

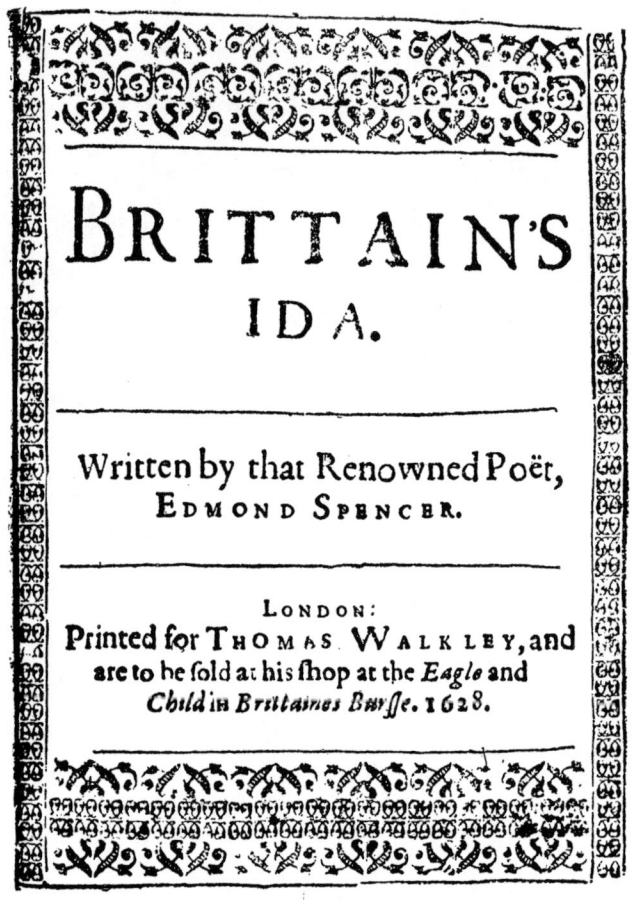

No. 664. Title-page of Spenser's Brittain's Ida; 1st Edition; 1628.

CONDITION: Size of leaf, 5 × 3 7/16 inches. Bound in green crushed levant morocco, gilt edges; by Bedford.

OTHER COPIES.
Rylands; and Huth Libraries.

REFERENCES.
Locker-Lampson, *Catalogue* (1886), p. 121; Huth, *Catalogue*, 4 (1880) : 1387; Lowndes, 5 (1869) : 2479; Hazlitt, *Hand-Book* (1867), p. 574, No. 10.

The Farmer-Locker Lampson copy, with ex-libris of the latter.

On the recto of the first fly-leaf of the copy here described is a clipping from a sale catalogue, as follows:

"The only authority for Brittain's Ida being the production of Spenser is the title of this excessively rare edition, a copy of which sold for £11 in Mr. Halliwell's sale. It is certainly extraordinary that Gabriel Harvey the Editor of the 1611 edition, should not have known of its existence. Mr. Bright thought it written by Shakespeare and Mr. Halliwell-Phillipps mentions it as 'a poem of considerable merit, written in the style of Shakespeare's Venus and Adonis . . . but the attribution to Spenser is extremely doubtful.'"

On the verso of the fourth fly-leaf is written in an old handwriting: "*R. Farmer. This is the original Edition.* See Warton *on* Spenser, *V. 1. p. 123.*"

"Dedicated by the Publisher to the Lady Mary, daughter of the Duke of Buckingham, whom he informs that he has been 'certainly assured by the ablest, and most knowing men, that it must be a work of Spencers.'"

"Mr. Grosart, in his letter to Lord Coleridge, 1869, assigns this poem to Phineas Fletcher."

STANBRIDGE, JOHN. (*b.* 1463, *d.* 1510.)

VOCABULA MAGISTRI STĀBRIGI PRIMŪ IAM EDITA SUA SALTEM EDITŌE. London, *Wynkyn de Worde*, [1520]. [665]

Small quarto. Printed in black-letter.

Collation by Signatures: A, 6 leaves; B, 4 leaves; C, 6 leaves; D, 4 leaves; total 20 unnumbered leaves.

Collation by Pagination: [title, as reproduced; *See* No. 665 *a*], recto of [A]; —[preface, with heading] | ⁋ Ad lectorem epiſtola. |, verso of [A]; —[vocabulary], recto of A ii. to recto of [D iiii.]; — | ⁋ Finis. | [colophon, as reproduced; *See* No. 665 *b*]|, recto of [D iiii.]; —[device of Wynkyn de Worde, as reproduced; *See* No. 665 *c*], verso of [D iiii.].

Condition: Size of leaf, 7 3/10 × 5 inches. Bound in brown crushed levant morocco, gilt edges.

Other Copies.

Huth Library.

References.

Quaritch, *General Catalogue*, 6 : 3921, No. 37934; Hazlitt, *Collections and Notes* (1887), p. 238; same (1882), p. 715; Huth, *Catalogue*, 4 (1880) : 1394; Dibdin, *Typographical Antiquities*, 2 (1812) : 91.

The James Comerford copy, with ex-libris.

The text is printed in the form of Latin hexameters for committal to memory, with the English equivalent in small type above.

John Stanbridge, a noted schoolmaster, who took an active part in establishing early grammar-schools, was the author of several grammatical treatises which passed through numerous editions.

Wynkyn de Worde, a native of Lorraine, accompanied Caxton from Bruges to England. He had doubtless been associated with Caxton during the greater part of that printer's career, and on his death in 1491 succeeded to the business. The use of Caxton's types led Blades to ascribe to him several books which were probably not printed until after Caxton's death. De Worde attained great distinction not only from the number of books which he printed but also because of their typographical excellence. Of Stanbridge's treatises Dibdin records no fewer than nineteen editions published by this printer alone.

No. 665 *a*. Title-page of Stanbridge's Vocabula magistri stãbrigi; [1520].

No. 665 *b*. Colophon of Stanbridge's Vocabula magistri stãbrigi; [1520].

No. 665 c. Device of Wynkyn de Worde, in Stanbridge's Vocabula Magistri Stābrigi; [1520].

[STERNE, LAURENCE.] (*b.* 1713, *d.* 1768.)

A SENTIMENTAL JOURNEY THROUGH FRANCE AND ITALY.
London, *for* T. Becket *and* P. A. De Hondt, 1768. 2 vols., small octavo, viz.: [666]

Vol. I.

Collation by Signatures: 2 leaves, without signature-marks; a, B to N, each 8 leaves; O, 6 leaves; total 112 numbered leaves.

Collation by Pagination: [half-title] | A | SENTIMENTAL JOURNEY, | &c. &c. |, p. [i.]; — [blank], p. [ii.]; —[title, as reproduced; *See* No. 666], p. [iii.]; — [blank], p. [iv.]; — [list of subscribers, with heading] | SUBSCRIBERS. | * *Imperial Paper.* |, pp. [v.]-xx.; —[text, with heading] | A | SENTIMENTAL JOURNEY, | &c. &c. |, pp. [1]-203; — | END OF VOL. I. |, p. 203;—[blank] p. [204].

A

SENTIMENTAL JOURNEY

THROUGH

FRANCE AND ITALY.

BY

Mr. YORICK.

VOL. I.

LONDON:

Printed for T. Becket and P. A. De Hondt, in the Strand. MDCCLXVIII.

No. 666. Title-page of Sterne's Sentimental Journey; 1st Edition; 1768.

Vol. 2.

Collation by Signatures: 2 leaves, without signature-marks; B to O, each 8 leaves; total 106 leaves. Leaf F 3 has no signature-mark.

Collation by Pagination: [half-title], p. [i.]; — [blank], p. [ii.]; — [title, same as in Vol. 1, except volume-number], p. [iii.]; — [blank], p. [iv.]; — [text, the first chapter with heading] | THE | FILLE DE CHAMBRE | PARIS. |, pp. [1]-208; — | END OF VOL. II. |, p. 208. Page 34 is wrongly numbered 33; and 35 is 34.

PLATE: 1 copperplate engraving in the text, on p. 38.

CONDITION: Size of leaf, 6 1/16 × 3 13/16 inches. Bound in old sprinkled calf, red edges.

REFERENCES.

Locker-Lampson, *Catalogue* (1886), p. 176; Huth, *Catalogue*, 4 (1880): 1399; Lowndes, 5 (1869): 2509.

The Locker-Lampson copy, with ex-libris.
The copy here described is a large-paper impression which has been cut down.

[SURTEES, ROBERT SMITH.] (*b.* 1803, *d.* 1864.)

JORROCKS'S JAUNTS AND JOLLITIES. LONDON, *Walter Spiers*, 1838.

[667]

Octavo. First Edition.

COLLATION BY SIGNATURES: [A], 4 leaves; B to Z, each 8 leaves; 2A, 4 leaves (the last blank and lacking); total 184 leaves.

COLLATION BY PAGINATION: [half-title], recto of [A]; — [blank], verso of [A]; — [title] | JORROCKS'S | JAUNTS AND JOLLITIES; | OR, THE | HUNTING, SHOOTING, RACING, DRIVING, SAILING, EATING, | ECCENTRIC, AND EXTRAVAGANT EXPLOITS | OF THAT | RENOWNED SPORTING CITIZEN, | MR. JOHN JORROCKS, | OF ST. BOTOLPH LANE AND GREAT CORAM STREET. | WITH TWELVE ILLUSTRATIONS BY PHIZ. | LONDON : | WALTER SPIERS, | NEW SPORTING MAGAZINE OFFICE, | 399, OXFORD STREET. | 1838. |, recto of [A 2]; — [blank], verso of [A 2]; — [preface], recto of [A 3]; — [blank], verso of [A 3]; — [contents], recto of [A 4]; — [blank], verso of [A 4]; — [text in 10 papers, with half-title to each], pp. [1]-358; — [1 blank leaf], [2A 4].

PLATES: Frontispiece and 11 plates, without inscriptions other than "*Page 21*," etc.; facing pp. 21, 23, 37, 56, 72, 79, 115, 145, 263, 309, and 317.

CONDITION: Size of leaf, 8 11/16 × 5 1/2 inches. Bound in red crushed levant morocco, leather hinges, gilt top, other edges uncut.

REFERENCES.

Slater, *Early Editions* (1894), p. 281, No. 1; Thomson, *Life of Hablôt K. Browne*, "*Phiz*" (1884), p. 204.

This work originally appeared in ten papers, or articles, in the pages of the *New Sporting Magazine*, between the months of July, 1831, and September, 1834, after which it was published in volume form, bound in pictorial cloth.

Two of the designs are very fine specimens of Browne's art as an illustrator. "'The Meet,' though rather inclined to caricature, has many well-drawn horses and dogs, the tiny figures in the distance being cleverly inserted. The other, representing Jorrocks riding through the fog with a mailcoach lamp strapped to his back, in order to pierce the thick atmosphere, is a delightfully fine piece of etching work."

Robert Smith Surtees, the sporting novelist, having qualified as a solicitor, bought a partnership in a London firm. The business having been misrepresented he found difficulty in recovering the purchase-money. He next took rooms in Lincoln's Inn Fields, and began to contribute to the old *Sporting Magazine*. In 1831, with

No. 667 *Robert Smith Surtees* 1838

Rudolph Ackermann, he started the *New Sporting Magazine,* which he edited until 1836. Between 1831 and 1834 he developed in its pages the humorous character of Mr. John Jorrocks, a sporting grocer. The success of these sketches led Chapman & Hall to undertake a similar scheme, which resulted in Dickens' *Pickwick Papers* (our No. 321). Surtees' papers were collected and published in 1838, as *Jorrocks's Jaunts* (our present number). At Lockhart's suggestion he tried his hand as a novelist, and wrote *Handley Cross* (our No. 670), in which Jorrocks reappears. The humorous illustrations by Leech in this and some of his later novels, "*Ask Mamma*" (our No. 671) and *Mr. Facey Romford's Hounds* (our No. 673), are among the most successful of that artist's productions. At the time of his death Surtees had just prepared for serial publication his last novel, *Mr. Facey Romford's Hounds* (our No. 673). Leech himself died before it was fully issued, and the illustrations were finished by "Phiz," Hablôt K. Browne. Surtees had a positive objection to seeing his name in print, and his *Horseman's Manual* (1831), his first production, is the only one of his books in which his name appears on the title-page.

[SURTEES, ROBERT SMITH.]

HAWBUCK GRANGE. LONDON, *for Longman, Brown, Green, and Longmans,* 1847.   [668]

Octavo. First Edition.

COLLATION BY SIGNATURES: [A], 4 leaves; B to X, each 8 leaves; Y, 6 leaves (the last blank and lacking); total 170 leaves.

COLLATION BY PAGINATION: [half-title], recto of [A];—[imprint], verso of [A];—[title]| HAWBUCK GRANGE; | OR, THE | SPORTING ADVENTURES OF THOMAS SCOTT, ESQ. | BY THE AUTHOR OF | "HANDLEY CROSS; OR, THE SPA HUNT," | &c.| WITH EIGHT ILLUSTRATIONS BY PHIZ. | LONDON : | PRINTED FOR | LONGMAN, BROWN, GREEN, AND LONGMANS,| PATERNOSTER-ROW. |1847.|, recto of [A 2];—[blank], verso of [A 2];—[preface], recto of [A 3];—[blank], verso of [A 3];—[contents], recto of [A 4];—[blank], verso of [A 4];—[text], pp. [1]–329;—[imprint], p. [330]; —[1 blank leaf], [Y 6].

PLATES : 8 plates, as follows :

[1] | *Hawbuck Grange as seen from the South.* |; facing the title-page.

[2] | *Hold hard!* |; facing p. 39.

[3] | *Lord Lionel discourses on hare hunting.*|; facing p. 96.

[4] | *Cake and the Cutlets.*| ; facing p. 132.

[5] | *Who-hoop!* |; facing p. 166.

[6] | *Muff refuses the Brush.*|; facing p. 236.

[7] | *Captain Rasher demonstrating.* | ; facing p. 243.

[8] | *Ware Sheep! Ware Sheep!* | ; facing p. 327.

CONDITION : Size of leaf, 8⅝ x 5½ inches. Bound in red crushed levant morocco, leather hinges, gilt top, other edges uncut. The plates facing pp. 236, 243, and 327 should face pp. 226, 253, and 323 respectively.

REFERENCES.

Slater, *Early Editions* (1894), p. 283, No. 5; Thomson, *Life of Hablôt K. Browne,* "*Phiz*" (1884), p. 211.

This work originally appeared in a series of sketches in *Bell's Life in London and Sporting Chronicle* during the winter of 1846–1847, after which it was printed in volume form, in scarlet cloth.

"From his earliest years of designing, 'Phiz' exhibited an aptitude for illustrating hunting scenes, and achieved a fame which clung to him through life. Possessing a personal knowledge of the field, he was enabled to make illustrations of scenes he had often witnessed, and thus the eight etchings of hunting incidents in 'Hawbuck Grange' (1847) are the great attraction of the volume."

[SURTEES, ROBERT SMITH.]

MR. SPONGE'S SPORTING TOUR. London, *Bradbury and Evans*, 1853.

[669]

Octavo. First Edition.

COLLATION BY SIGNATURES: [*a*], 4 leaves; *b*, 2 leaves; B to Z, AA, BB, CC, each 8 leaves; DD, 4 leaves; total 210 numbered leaves.

COLLATION BY PAGINATION: [half-title], p. [i.];—[blank], p. [ii.];—[title] | MR. SPONGE'S | SPORTING TOUR. | BY THE | AUTHOR OF "HANDLEY CROSS," JORROCKS'S JAUNTS," | ETC. ETC. | [vignette] | WITH ILLUSTRATIONS BY JOHN LEECH. | LONDON: | BRADBURY AND EVANS, 11, BOUVERIE STREET. | 1853. |, p. [iii.];—[imprint], p. [iv.];—[dedication, preface, contents, list of engravings on steel, and list of engravings on wood], pp. [v.]–[xii.];—[text], pp. [1]–408.

PLATES: 13 engravings on steel, colored, and 84 woodcuts in the text, as called for in the lists of illustrations, except that the woodcut on p. 229 should be on p. 230, and that there is an extra woodcut on p. 182; also 4 engraved initials not included in the list of woodcuts; all by Leech.

CONDITION: Size of leaf, $8\frac{11}{16} \times 5\frac{1}{2}$ inches. Bound from the original parts, in red crushed levant morocco, leather hinges, gilt top, other edges uncut; by Bradstreet. With the original wrappers and advertising pages, on white paper, in all 33 leaves, bound in at the end, as follows: Parts I.–XIII., 2, 2, 2, 2, 2, 2, 4, 2, 2, 2, 6, 5 (and 2 slips) leaves respectively. Published in 13 monthly parts (the last a double number), in red wrappers, at one shilling each, with pictorial title designed by Leech: | Mr SPONGE'S | SPORTING TOUR | BY THE | *Author of* | *"Handley-Cross"* | *"Jorrocks's Jaunts"* | *&c. &c. &c.* | *with* | *illustrations by* | *John Leech.* | BRADBURY AND EVANS, 11, BOUVERIE STREET, LONDON. |.

REFERENCE.

Slater, *Early Editions* (1894), p. 284, No. 6.

This work, originally issued in parts, was afterward issued in volume form with a pictorial cover, also designed by Leech.

In 1862 Leech exhibited at Egyptian Hall a series of sketches in oil.

"A story is told of a visit of a sporting lord who took his huntsman — whose judgment of hounds and horses was celebrated for its acumen — to give his verdict on the Leech Exhibition in general, and on dogs and horses in particular.

"'Ah, my lord, nothin' but a party as knows 'osses could have drawed them there 'unters.'"

[SURTEES, ROBERT SMITH.]

HANDLEY CROSS; OR, MR. JORROCKS'S HUNT. London, *Bradbury and Evans*, 1854. [670]

Octavo. First Edition.

COLLATION BY SIGNATURES: [A], 6 leaves (the first, probably a half-title, lacking); B to Z, AA to MM, each 8 leaves; NN, 4 leaves (the last blank and lacking); total 282 leaves.

COLLATION BY PAGINATION: [1 leaf, probably a half-title], [A]; — [title] HANDLEY CROSS; | OR, | MR. JORROCKS'S HUNT. | BY | THE AUTHOR OF "MR. SPONGE'S SPORTING TOUR," | "ASK MAMMA," ETC. ETC. | [vignette] | WITH ILLUSTRATIONS BY JOHN LEECH. | LONDON: | BRADBURY AND EVANS, 11, BOUVERIE STREET. | 1854. |, p. [i.]; — [imprint], p. [ii.]; — [dedication, preface, contents, list of engravings on steel, and list of engravings on wood], pp. [iii.]–[x.]; — [text], pp. [1]–550; — [1 blank leaf], [NN 4]. Page 37 is wrongly numbered 73.

PLATES: Frontispiece and 16 engravings on steel, colored, and 84 woodcuts in the text, as called for in the lists of illustrations, except that the plate which should face p. 532 faces the title-page, and that the woodcuts on pp. 51 and 132 should be on 50 and 133. There are also 15 engraved initials and 1 tail-piece not included in the list of woodcuts.

CONDITION: Size of leaf, 8⅝ × 5½ inches. Bound in red crushed levant morocco, leather hinges, gilt top, other edges uncut; by Bradstreet. With the original cloth back and side, with sporting devices, mounted on a guard and bound in at the end.

REFERENCE.

Slater, *Early Editions* (1894), p. 284, No. 7.

This work was originally published in seventeen monthly parts (March, 1853, to October, 1854), in red wrappers designed by Leech. On the completion of the work in parts it was published in volume form, in fancy red cloth, with sporting devices on the side and back.

[SURTEES, ROBERT SMITH.]

"ASK MAMMA." London, *Bradbury and Evans*, 1858. [671]

Octavo. First Edition.

COLLATION BY SIGNATURES: [A], 6 leaves; B to Z, AA, BB, CC, each 8 leaves; DD, 6 leaves; total 212 numbered leaves.

COLLATION BY PAGINATION: [title] | "ASK MAMMA;" | OR, | THE RICHEST COMMONER IN ENGLAND. | BY THE | AUTHOR OF "HANDLEY CROSS," "SPONGE'S SPORTING TOUR," | ETC. ETC. | [vignette] | WITH ILLUSTRATIONS BY JOHN LEECH. | LONDON: | BRADBURY AND EVANS, 11, BOUVERIE STREET. | 1858. |, p. [i.]; — [imprint], p. [ii.]; — [dedication, preface, contents, list of engravings on steel, and list of engravings on wood], pp. [iii.]–[xii.]; — [text], pp. [1]–412.

PLATES: Frontispiece and 12 engravings on steel, colored, and 69 woodcuts in the text, as called for in the lists of illustrations. There are also 2 engraved initials not included in the list of woodcuts.

CONDITION: Size of leaf, 8⅝ × 5⅝ inches. Bound from the original parts, in red crushed levant morocco, leather hinges,

1858   *Robert Smith Surtees*   No. 671

gilt top, other edges uncut. With the original front wrappers bound in at the end, with the exception of Part II., which is placed in front. Published in 13 monthly parts, in red wrappers, at one shilling each, with pictorial title designed by Leech: | "ASK MAMMA" | or | THE RICHEST COMMONER | IN | ENGLAND | By The Author of | "Handley Crofs" "Sponge's | Sporting Tour" &c, &c, | with illustrations | by John Leech | BRADBURY AND EVANS, 11, BOUVERIE STREET, LONDON. | .

REFERENCE.

Slater, *Early Editions* (1894), p. 285, No. 8.

This work, originally issued in parts, was afterward published in volume form with the above title.

[SURTEES, ROBERT SMITH.]

"PLAIN OR RINGLETS?" LONDON, *Bradbury and Evans*, 1860. [672]

Octavo. First Edition.

COLLATION BY SIGNATURES: [A], 6 leaves (the first, probably a half-title, lacking); B to Z, AA, BB, CC, each 8 leaves; DD, 4 leaves (the last blank and lacking); total 210 leaves.

COLLATION BY PAGINATION: [1 leaf, probably a half-title], [A]; — [title] | "PLAIN OR RINGLETS?" | BY THE | AUTHOR OF "HANDLEY CROSS," "SPONGE'S SPORTING TOUR," | "ASK MAMMA," ETC. ETC. | [vignette] | WITH ILLUSTRATIONS BY JOHN LEECH. | LONDON: BRADBURY AND EVANS, 11, BOUVERIE STREET. | 1860. | , p. [i.]; — [imprint], p. [ii.]; — [dedication, contents, list of steel engravings, and list of wood engravings], pp. [iii.]-[x.]; — [text], pp. [1]-406; — [1 blank leaf], [DD 4].

PLATES: Engraved pictorial title-page and 12 engravings on steel, colored; and 44 woodcuts in the text, as called for in the lists of illustrations. There are also 10 engraved initials not included in the list of woodcuts.

CONDITION: Size of leaf, 8¾ x 5⅝ inches. Bound from the original parts, in red crushed levant morocco, leather hinges, gilt top, other edges uncut; by Bradstreet. With the original wrappers bound in at the end. Published in 13 monthly parts (the last a double number), in red wrappers, at one shilling each, with pictorial title designed by Leech: | PLAIN | or | RINGLETS | By the Author of | "Handley Crofs" "Sponge's Tour" | "Ask Mamma" &c. &c. | with illustrations by | John Leech | BRADBURY AND EVANS, 11, BOUVERIE STREET, LONDON. | BRADBURY AND EVANS, PRINTERS, WHITEFRIARS. | .

REFERENCE.

Slater, *Early Editions* (1894), p. 286, No. 9.

This work was originally issued in parts, and afterward in book form, in red cloth with sporting designs on the sides and back. The leaf giving the list of illustrations is sometimes found at the end of the volume instead of after the table of contents.

"Leech seems to have left no phase of human life and character untouched: whether he deals with the aristocrat or the plebeian, the Duchess or the beggar, the very poor or the very rich, the beautiful or the ugly, he is ever true to Nature; turning away from our vices, dealing lovingly with us in all ways, touching our follies lightly, humorously, and always good-naturedly — in short, invariably reflecting in his work his own disposition to what is pure, manly, and true."

[SURTEES, ROBERT SMITH.]

MR. FACEY ROMFORD'S HOUNDS. London, *Bradbury and Evans*, 1865.

[673]

Octavo. First Edition.

COLLATION BY SIGNATURES: [A], 4 leaves; B to Z, AA, BB, each 8 leaves; CC, 4 leaves; total 200 leaves.

COLLATION BY PAGINATION: [half-title], p. [i.];—[blank], p. [ii.];—[title] | MR. FACEY ROMFORD'S | HOUNDS. | BY THE | AUTHOR OF "HANDLEY CROSS," "MR. SPONGE'S SPORTING TOUR," | "ASK MAMMA," ETC. ETC. | [vignette] WITH ILLUSTRATIONS BY JOHN LEECH AND HABLOT K. BROWNE. | LONDON: | BRADBURY AND EVANS, 11, BOUVERIE STREET. | 1865. | [*The Right of Translation is reserved.*] |, p. [iii.];—[imprint], p. [iv.];—[contents and list of engravings], pp. [v.]-[vii.];—[blank], p. [viii.];—[text], pp. [1]-391;—[blank], p. [392].

PLATES: 24 engravings on steel, colored, 14 of which are by Leech and 10 by "Phiz," as called for in the list of illustrations.

CONDITION: Size of leaf, 8⅝ × 5⅝ inches. Bound from the original parts, in red crushed levant morocco, leather hinges, gilt top, other edges uncut; by Bradstreet. With front wrappers bound in at the end, except that of Part II., which is placed in the front. Parts IX., X., and XII. are numbered in ink on the wrappers of | PART V. | [SEPTEMBER.] |, etc. Published in 12 monthly parts, from May to April, in red wrappers, at one shilling each, with pictorial title designed by Leech: | Mr. | ROMFORD'S | HOUNDS | *By the author of* | "*Handley Cross,*" | "*Mr Sponge's Sporting Tour,*" | *&c. &c.* | *with illustrations* | *by John Leech* | BRADBURY AND EVANS, 11, BOUVERIE STREET, LONDON. |.

REFERENCES

Slater, *Early Editions* (1894), p. 286, No. 10; Frith, *John Leech, His Life and Work*, 2 (1891): 130.

"This novel appeared in parts, in red pictorial wrappers designed by Leech. The work, though written throughout by Surtees, was practically posthumous, as the author died immediately after the publication of the first number. Curiously enough, Leech also died before the work had made much progress, and the task of designing the further illustrations was entrusted to 'Phiz.' These illustrations consist of twenty-four engravings on steel (coloured), of which the first fourteen (inclusive of front) were designed by Leech, and the remainder by Browne."

When issued in book form it appeared in fancy cloth, with sporting designs on side and back.

"The period of Leech's pictorial activity (1840 – 64) covers the middle of the century. He comes, for practical purposes, between Cruikshank and Du Maurier, and in that order plays an indispensable part in the progressive transformation of humorous art from the broad brutalities of the earlier men to the gentler and more subdued satire now in vogue. As Cruikshank refines upon Gillray and Rowlandson, so Leech refines upon Cruikshank, but to a much greater extent. His humour is to the full as keen, his sense of fun as marked; but it is less grotesque, less boisterous, less exaggerated, nearer to truth and to ordinary experience."

[SWIFT, JONATHAN.] (b. 1667, d. 1745.)

A TALE OF A TUB. LONDON, *for John Nutt*, 1704. [674]

Octavo. First Edition.

COLLATION BY SIGNATURES: A, 6 leaves; B to X, each 8 leaves; Y, 2 leaves (the last blank and genuine); total 168 leaves.

COLLATION BY PAGINATION: [blank], recto of [A];—[list of Swift's books, "which will be speedily published"], verso of [A];—[title, as reproduced; *See* No. 674], recto of [A 2];—[blank], verso of [A 2];—| TO | The Right Honourable, | JOHN | *Lord* SOMMERS.| [signed] | *My* LORD, | *Your Lordship's most Obedient,* | *and most Faithful Servant,* | The Bookseller. |, recto of A 3 to verso of [A 5];—| THE | BOOKSELLER | TO THE | READER. |, recto and verso of [A 6];—| THE | Epistle Dedicatory, | TO | His Royal Highness | PRINCE POSTERITY.| [signed] | *SIR,* | *Your Highness's* | *Most devoted,* &c. | [dated] | Decemb.| 1697.|, pp. 1–11;—[blank], p. [12];—| THE | PREFACE. |, pp. 13–31;—[blank], p. [32];—[text, with heading] | A | TALE | OF A | TUB, &c. |, pp. 33–221;—| FINIS. |, p. 221;—[blank], p. [222].

| A | Full and True Account | OF THE | BATTEL | Fought last *FRIDAY,* | Between the | *Antient* and the *Modern* | BOOKS | IN | St. *JAMES*'s | LIBRARY.| LONDON: | Printed in the Year, MDCCIV.|, p. [223]; —[blank], p.[224];—| THE | BOOKSELLER | TO THE | READER.|, pp. [225]–[226];—| THE | PREFACE | OF THE | AUTHOR.|, pp. [227]–[228];—[text, with heading] | A Full and True | ACCOUNT | OF THE | BATTEL | *Fought last FRIDAY,* &c.|, pp. 229–278;—| FINIS.|, p. 278.

| A | DISCOURSE | Concerning the | Mechanical Operation | OF THE | SPIRIT. | IN A | LETTER | *To a FRIEND.* | A | FRAGMEMT.| *LONDON:* | Printed in the Year, MDCCIV.|, p. [279];—[blank], p. [280];—| THE | BOOKSELLER's | Advertisement.|, p. [281];—[blank], p. [282];—[text, with heading] | A | DISCOURSE | Concerning the | Mechanical Operation | OF THE | SPIRIT, &c.|, pp. 283–322;—| FINIS.|, p. 322;—[1 blank leaf], [Y 2].

CONDITION: Size of leaf, 7 7/16 × 4 7/16 inches. Bound in sprinkled calf, inlaid panelled sides, gilt edges; by Bedford.

OTHER COPIES.

British Museum; Bodleian; and Trinity College, Dublin.

REFERENCES.

Bartholomew, *Richard Bentley; a Bibliography* (1908), p. 39, No. 132; Jackson, *Bibliography,* in *Prose Works of Jonathan Swift,* 12 (Bohn's Libraries, 1908): 114; Nicoll and Seccombe, 2 (1907): 597; Hoe, *Catalogue,* 3 (1905): 124; Locker-Lampson, *Catalogue* (1886), p. 176; Lowndes, 5 (1869): 2558.

The Locker-Lampson copy, with ex-libris.

On the verso of the first fly-leaf is written in pencil: "*Charles I. Fox said that no one could be an ill-tempered man who wrote so much nonsense as Swift did. A predominant quality of Swift's satire is shewn in the precise & business-like air with which he carries on an Argument that is absolutely baseless. The gravity and minuteness not only add to the humour, but give a wonderful air of plausibility to the statements themselves, & then there is a remarkable* intensity *about him.*"

"*This volume was completed by Swift as early as 1697, but not published till 7 years after. F. L.*"

Three editions appeared in 1704, the Fourth in 1705, and the Fifth in 1710.

No. 674   Jonathan Swift   1704

This is Swift's first great satire. It was drafted in 1695, and nearly finished about a year later. Though published anonymously, its authorship was soon guessed by the wits, among whom Swift's position was henceforth assured.

"In the tale, to the alarm of most of those of his contemporaries who could understand him, Swift discussed the growing pretensions of science, the impotence of human reason, the immeasurable follies of mankind with an almost apathetic disregard for the decencies or conventionalities of his age and country. Irreverent as it was, the satire was an unmistakable defence of the Church of England, against the opponents of which, whether Papists, Nonconformists, or Free-thinkers, the author poured forth an inextinguishable torrent of hatred and abuse."

The *Battle of the Books*, which forms a part of this volume, was written in 1697. In it Swift supports the side taken by his patron, Sir William Temple, in the *Letters of Phalaris* controversy, in which he first shows to the world his amusing gift of allegorical irony.

Jonathan Swift, the greatest satirist of his own or perhaps of any age, was born in Dublin, November 30, 1667. His early dependence upon an unfeeling uncle did much to encourage in him that bitterness which he afterward displayed toward all mankind. He was educated at Trinity College, Dublin, where he failed to distinguish himself as a student. On leaving the university he entered the family of Sir William Temple, at Moor Park in Surrey, as his private secretary. Swift's abilities were soon recognized and he was intrusted with important missions. He took his M.A. degree at Oxford in 1692, and two years later, not meeting with the advancement he desired, left Temple's employment and returned to Ireland, where he was ordained. He was soon induced to return to Moor Park, where he remained until Temple's death, in 1699, after which he prepared Temple's memoirs and correspondence for publication. To his service with Temple, who was frequently visited by William III. and consulted on public affairs, Swift owed his subsequent distinction as a politician and the foundation of his literary renown, which was laid at that time.

His first prose composition was *The Battle of the Books* (here described), a satirical contribution to the Phalaris controversy which had been raised by Perrault respecting the comparative merits of the ancients and moderns. In 1700 he was appointed to the rectory of Agher, in Meath, with the united vicarages of Laracor and Rathbeggan. In 1704 appeared his *Tale of a Tub* (here described), a "crusade against bad writing and bad writers, which Swift carried on more or less for the whole of his middle and later years." In 1701–1704 he again visited England, where he counted Pope, Addison, and Steele among his friends. In 1709 *Baucis and Philemon* (our next number) was published. This, his best poem, he frankly tells us owes much to the corrections of Addison. In 1710 he was living in London, actively engaged as a writer of ministerial pamphlets, all of which were published anonymously. At the same time he was also writing his *Journal to Stella*, "that unique exemplar of a giant's playfulness," which, though written for the private pleasure of one person, has ever since had an irresistible attraction for the many.

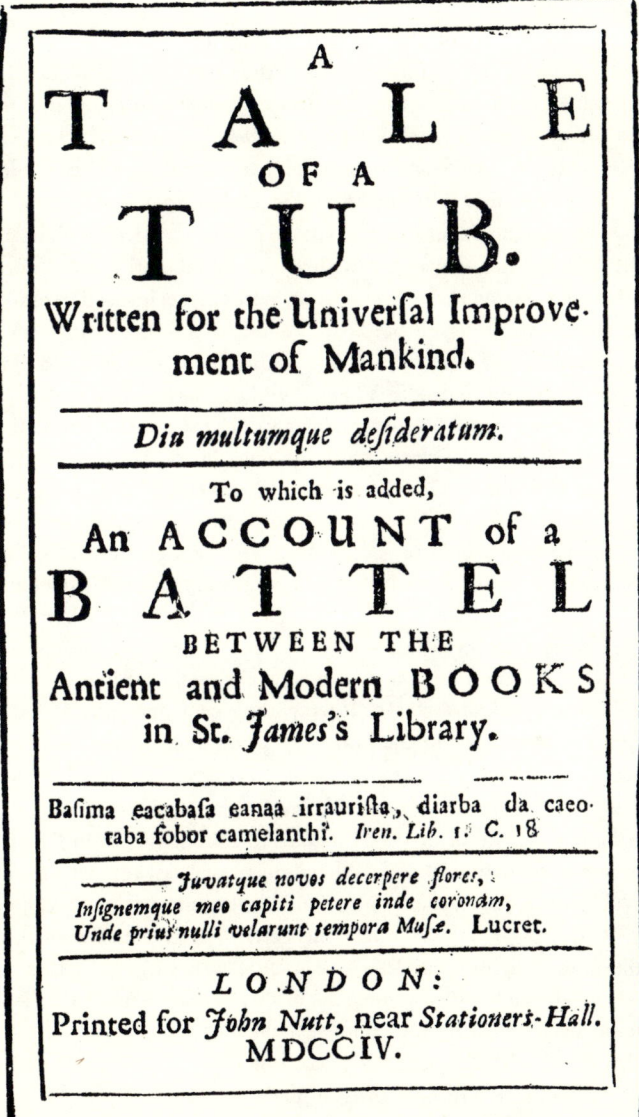

No. 674.   Title-page of Swift's Tale of a Tub; 1st Edition; 1704.

No. 674　　　　　　　　*Jonathan Swift*　　　　　　　　1704

In 1713 Swift was appointed Dean of St. Patrick's, Dublin, where he went in June of that year, but was soon recalled to England to reconcile the difficulties between Oxford and Bolingbroke. Notwithstanding his political activities he found time to enter into the literary life of the day and to form numerous lasting friendships. Many of his best poems belong to this period. After the dismissal of Oxford and the death of Queen Anne (1714) he returned to Ireland, where he spent the next twelve years.

Before the appearance of *The Tale of a Tub* (1704) Swift had invited two ladies to Laracor — Esther Johnson, whom he has immortalized as "Stella," and Mrs. Dingley, her chaperone. When he was in Dublin they resided near him, and during his absence in London superintended his household. At the height of his political influence he had become acquainted with Esther Vanhomrigh ("Vanessa"), who insensibly became enamoured of him, but without reciprocation on his part. As a friend he must have preferred Stella to Vanessa. On the death of Vanessa's mother, in 1714, she followed him to Dublin. Unable to marry Stella without destroying Vanessa, or to openly welcome Vanessa without destroying Stella, he found himself involved in a most miserable embarrassment. For a time he temporized, but at length, in 1716, consented to a private marriage with Stella, insisting, out of tenderness for Vanessa, that their union should be kept a strict secret. This secrecy compelled the unfortunate Stella to bear the unmerited opprobrium of passing as his mistress. Swift in the meantime endeavored to soothe Miss Vanhomrigh by addressing to her *Cadenus* [*Decanus*] *and Vanessa* (our No. 677), a history of their attachment and the best example of his serious poetry. In 1717 she retired from Dublin to Marley Abbey, where after three years of separation Swift began to pay her regular visits. In 1723, worn out with his evasions, she wrote to Stella, who replied avowing her marriage. Vanessa died within a few weeks, leaving the poem and correspondence for publication. Stella followed her to the grave five years after without any public recognition of her marriage.

In 1724 Swift attained great popularity by the publication of the *Drapier Letters*, in which he attacked William Wood's grant to coin halfpence in Ireland. Scarcely had the excitement following their publication passed away, when in 1726 appeared *Gulliver's Travels* (our No. 678), infinitely the most famous and popular of all his works. "*Gulliver's Travels* (omitting certain passages)," says Leslie Stephen, "is almost the most delightful children's book ever written. . . . The charm of Gulliver for the young depends upon an obvious quality, which is indicated in Swift's report of the criticism by an Irish bishop, who said that 'the book was full of improbable lies, and for his part he hardly believed a word of it.'"

Swift's subsequent writings scarcely merit mention. In 1738 he began to show a failure of his faculties, and in 1742 it became necessary to have guardians appointed to care for his person and estate. He gradually grew worse, and after three years spent in a state of speechless torpor died October 19, 1745, and was buried by Stella's side in his own cathedral. So passed away Swift, preëminently the British satirist of his age; a master of humor, irony, and invective without a superior.

Baucis and *Philemon*;

A

POEM.

On the ever lamented Loss

Of the two *YEW-TREES*,

In the Parish of *CHILTHORNE*,

NEAR THE

County Town of *SOMERSET*.

Together with

Mrs. *Harris's* Earnest Petition.

By the Author of the Tale of a Tub. *viz*
Jonathan Swift. D.D.

AS ALSO

An ODE upon *Solitude*.

By the Earl of Roscommon.

LONDON:
Printed and Sold by *H. Hills*, in *Black-fryars*, near the Water-side, 1709.

No. 675. TITLE-PAGE OF SWIFT'S BAUCIS AND PHILEMON;
1ST EDITION; 1709.

No. 675   *Jonathan Swift*   1709

[SWIFT, JONATHAN.]

BAUCIS AND PHILEMON; A POEM. LONDON, H. *Hills*, 1709.
[675]

Octavo. First Edition.
COLLATION BY SIGNATURES: A, 8 numbered leaves.
COLLATION BY PAGINATION : [title, as reproduced; *See* No. 675], p. [1];— [blank], p. [2];—[text, with heading] | *The Metamorphoſis of* Baucis *and* Philemon, | *Burleſqu'd; from the* 8th *Book of* Ovid. |, pp. 3 – 9; — | *To their Excellencies,* &c. | The Humble Petition of *Frances Harris,* | Who muſt ſtarve, and die a Maid, if it | (miſcarries.|, pp. 9 – 14;—| AN | ODE | UPON | SOLITUDE.|, pp. 15 – 16;—| FINIS.|, p. 16.

CONDITION : Size of leaf, 7 1/16 × 4 3/8 inches. Bound in half red morocco.

OTHER COPIES.

There is a copy of this edition in the Bodleian Library.

REFERENCES.

Jackson, *Bibliography,* in *Prose Works of Jonathan Swift,* 12 (Bohn's Libraries, 1908): 121; Locker-Lampson, *Catalogue* (1886), p. 177.

The Locker-Lampson copy, with ex-libris.

Jackson records an edition in quarto, with title, "Baucis and Philemon, Imitated from Ovid. Printed An. Dom. M DCC IX.", without printer's name or place, beginning, "In ancient Times, as Story tells." It was reprinted in *Miscellanies,* 1711 (our next number), pp. 377 – 387. The edition here described seems to have been unknown to Lowndes, as he mentions only that of the year following (1710).

Falkiner says (*Prose Works of Swift;* 1908; Bohn's Libraries, Vol. 12, p. 11) that at the family seat, Narford, in Norfolk, of Sir Andrew Fountaine, one of the punning coterie at Dublin, calling themselves Castilians, of which Swift was also a member, "Forster found with his lineal descendant, Mr. Fountaine, some most valuable MSS. of Swift, including the Castilian records, and the original Baucis and Philemon, as written before Addison 'corrected it by expurgating some of its wittiest couplets.'"

[SWIFT, JONATHAN.]

MISCELLANIES IN PROSE AND VERSE. LONDON, *for John Morphew,* 1711.
[676]

Octavo. First Edition.
COLLATION BY SIGNATURES: A, 8 leaves (the fifth, probably blank, lacking); B to Z, Aa to Dd, each 8 leaves; total 216 leaves. Leaf B 4 is wrongly marked C 4; L 4, N 3, R 3, and S 2 have no signature-marks; and U 2, U 3, and U 4 have large lower-case letters.
COLLATION BY PAGINATION : [title, as reproduced; *See* No. 676], recto of [A]; — [blank], verso of [A];— | THE | PUBLISHER | TO THE | READER.|, recto of A 2 to verso of A 4;—[1 leaf, probably blank], [A 5];— | THE | CONTENTS.|, recto of [A 6] to recto of [A 8];—[blank], verso of [A 8];—[text in several sections, the first with heading] | A | DISCOURSE | OF THE | *Conteſts and Diſſentions* | Between

Jonathan Swift

MISCELLANIES
IN
PROSE
AND
VERSE.

LONDON:
Printed for JOHN MORPHEW, near *Stationers Hall.* MDCCXI.

No. 676. TITLE-PAGE OF SWIFT'S MISCELLANIES IN PROSE AND VERSE; 1ST EDITION; 1711.

No. 676   *Jonathan Swift*   **1711**

the | NOBLES and the COMMONS | IN | ATHENS and ROME, | WITH THE | Confequences they had upon both thofe | STATES. |, pp. 1–91;—[blank], p. [92];—[1 blank leaf], pp. [93]–[94];— | THE | SENTIMENTS | OF A | *Church of England-Man* | With Refpect to | RELIGION and GOVERNMENT. |, pp. 95–151;— | AN | ARGUMENT | To prove that the | *Abolifhing of* CHRISTIANITY | IN | ENGLAND, | [4 lines] |, pp. 152–181;— | A | PROJECT | FOR THE | *Advancement of Religion*, | AND THE | Reformation of Manners. | By a Perfon of QUALITY. |, pp. 182–230;— | A | MEDITATION | UPON A | Broom-Stick. | [3 lines] |, pp. 231–234;— | *Various Thoughts*, | Moral and Diverting. |, pp. 235–245;—[blank], p. [246];— | A | *Tritical Effay* | UPON THE | Faculties of the Mind. |, pp. 247–259;—[blank], p. [260];— | PREDICTIONS | FOR THE | YEAR 1708. |, pp. 261–282;— | THE | ACCOMPLISHMENT | Of the Firft of | Mr. *Bickerftaff*'s Predictions. | Being an | ACCOUNT | Of the Death of | Mr. *PARTRIGE*, the Almanack-maker. | Upon the 29th Inftant. |, pp. 283–289;—[blank], p. [290];— | A | VINDICATION | OF | *Ifaac Bickerftaff* Efq; |, pp. 291–304;— | A | Famous Prediction | OF | MERLIN, | THE | *BRITISH* Wizard. |, pp. 305–312;—[blank], p. [313];— | ADVERTISEMENT. |, p. 314;— | A | LETTER | [4 lines] | *concerning the* SACRA- | MENTAL TEST. |, pp. 315–350;— | VERSES | Wrote in a | LADY's *Jvory Table-Book*. |, pp. 351–352;— | TO THEIR | EXCELLENCIES | THE | *Lords Juftices of* IRELAND. | *The Humble Petition of* Frances Harris, | . . . |, pp. 353–360;—[ballad to Lady B—— B——], pp. 361–363;— | *V——*'s HOUSE | *Built from the Ruins of* White- | Hall *that was Burnt.* |, pp. 364–371; — | THE | DESCRIPTION | OF A | Salamander. |, pp. 372–376;— | *BAVCIS* | AND | *PHILEMON*. | *Imitated, From the Eighth Book of* OVID. |, pp. 377–387;— | TO | Mrs. BIDDY FLOYD. |, p. 388; — | THE | HISTORY | OF | V————'s House. |, pp. 389–391;— | A | *Grubftreet* ELEGY On the fuppofed Death of | *PATRIGE* | THE | ALMANACK-MAKER. |, pp. 392–398;— | *Apollo* Outwitted. | [2 lines] |, pp. 399–403;— | A | DESCRIPTION | OF THE | MORNING. |, pp. 404–405;— | A | DESCRIPTION | OF A | *CITY SHOWER*. |, pp. 406–410;— | [3 lines] | THE | VIRTUES | OF | *Sid Hamet* the MAGICIAN'S | ROD. |, pp. 411–416. Page 168 is wrongly numbered 861.

CONDITION : Size of leaf, 7⅞ × 4¹⁵⁄₁₆ inches. Bound in sprinkled calf, inlaid panelled sides, marbled edges ; by Bedford.

REFERENCE.

Jackson, *Bibliography*, in *Prose Works of Jonathan Swift*, 12 (Bohn's Libraries, 1908) : 123.

A cheap edition, containing only 66 pages, was also published in 1711 by E. Curll, at one shilling.

The Second Edition appeared in 1713.

[SWIFT, JONATHAN.]

CADENUS AND VANESSA. A POEM. LONDON, *J. Roberts*, 1726.

[677]

Octavo. First Edition.

COLLATION BY SIGNATURES : A to E, each 4 leaves (the last blank and genuine); total 20 numbered leaves.

COLLATION BY PAGINATION : [half-title] | [type-ornament rule] | *CADENVS* | AND | *VANESSA*. | A | POEM. | [type-ornament rule] | A [signature-mark] |, p. [1];— [blank], p. [2];—[title, as reproduced; See No. 677], p. [3];—[blank], p. [4]; —[text, with heading] | [conventional head-piece] | *CADENVS* | AND | *VANESSA*. |, pp.

1726   *Jonathan Swift*   No. 677

CADENUS

AND

VANESSA.

A

POEM.

LONDON,

Printed: And Sold by *J. Roberts* at the *Oxford-Arms* in *Warwick-Lane,* 1726.   Price 6 *d.*

No. 677. Title-page of Swift's Cadenus and Vanessa; 1st Edition; 1726.

[5]-37; — | *FINIS.* | [conventional tailpiece] |, p. 37; — [blank], p. [38]; — [1 blank leaf], [E 4].

CONDITION: Size of leaf, 7⁹⁄₁₆ x 4¹¹⁄₁₆ inches. Bound in half olive green crushed levant morocco, gilt top, other edges sprinkled; by De Coverly. Lower fore-edges of pp. 7 and 21 uncut.

OTHER COPIES.

There is another copy of this edition in the Bodleian Library.

REFERENCES.

Jackson, *Bibliography*, in *Prose Works of Jonathan Swift*, 12 (Bohn's Libraries; 1908) : 143 ; Nicoll and Seccombe, *A History of English Literature*, 2 (1907) : 599 ; Hoe, *Catalogue*, 3 (1905) : 126; Locker-Lampson, *Catalogue* (1886), p. 177.

The Locker-Lampson copy, with ex-libris.

Although "Vanessa" (Hester Vanhomrigh) died in 1723, the present poem did not appear until 1726, when it was published by four or more different booksellers. Jackson assigns the edition here described the first place. It contains some variations from the others, notably the addition on p. 35 of the ten lines beginning "But what Succeſs *Vaneſſa* met." Another edition claiming to be printed "From the Original Copy" was printed at Dublin "in the Year 2726" [*sic*]. Still another edition, "Printed for T. Warner, in Paternoster Row, MDCCXXVI.", is described in *The Antiquarian Magazine* for January, 1885.

"The Fourth Edition" (also 1726), "for N. Blandford, and ſold by J. Peele," has added, "A True and Faithful Inventory." The Fifth and Sixth Editions also appeared the same year, and Jackson records a Seventh published at "Edinburgh, 1726 (Allan Ramsay), paged 83 –114."

"On October 20th, 1710, Swift first mentions in his journal-letter to Stella the name of Mrs. Vanhomrigh as that of his hostess. Esther Vanhomrigh ("Vanessa"), the daughter, became Swift's devoted slave. Swift flattered this clever and impressionable girl by playing at being her tutor. She startled him after a time by confessing that love had taken the place of admiration in her heart. Swift tried to convince her of the impropriety of a romantic passion and to indicate a more rational kind of intimacy in his remarkable poem of *Cadenus* [i.e., Decanus] *and Vanessa*, begun in 1712 and finished in 1713. Poor Hessy's infatuation was not amenable to such treatment. She followed Swift to Ireland, and he was reduced to expedients for temporising with her and mollifying Stella. In 1723 Vanessa is said to have written to Stella or to Swift (there are discrepancies between the versions of Sheridan and Lord Orrery, neither of whom is distinguished by minute accuracy), asking whether the report that they were married was true. Swift rode down to Vanessa's retreat at Colbridge, threw down her letter in a great rage, and left without speaking a word. Vanessa died shortly afterwards, having revoked a will in Swift's favour. Swift hid himself for two months in the South of Ireland. Stella also was shocked, but when some one remarked that the deceased must have been a remarkable woman to inspire such a poem as *Cadenus and Vanessa*, observed that there was nothing surprising about it, for the Dean, as all the world knew, could write finely upon a broomstick."

1726   Jonathan Swift   No. 678

[SWIFT, JONATHAN.]

[GULLIVER'S TRAVELS.] TRAVELS INTO SEVERAL REMOTE NATIONS OF THE WORLD. IN FOUR PARTS. LONDON, *for Benj. Motte*, 1726. The 4 parts in 2 vols., octavo, viz.:   [678]

VOL. I.

PART I.

COLLATION BY SIGNATURES: A to K, each 8 leaves; L, 2 leaves; total 82 numbered leaves.

COLLATION BY PAGINATION: [title, as reproduced; *See* No. 678], p. [i.]; — [blank], p. [ii.]; — [contents], p. [iii.]; — [blank], p. [iv.]; — | [conventional head-piece] | THE | PUBLISHER | TO THE | READER. | [signed] | RICHARD SYMPSON. |, pp. [v.]–ix.; — [blank], p. [x.]; — [title] | TRAVELS | INTO SEVERAL | REMOTE NATIONS | OF THE | WORLD. | PART I. | A VOYAGE to LILLIPUT. | [vignette] | *LONDON:* | Printed in the Year MDCCXXVI. |, p. [xi.]; — [blank], p. [xii.]; — | [conventional head-piece] | THE | CONTENTS. |, pp. [xiii.]–xvi.; — [text, with heading] | [conventional head-piece] | TRAVELS. | PART I. | *A* VOYAGE *to* LILLIPUT. |, pp. [1]–148. Page 124 is wrongly numbered 24.

PLATES: Portrait and map, as follows:

Portrait of Gulliver in an oval, with inscription below: | *Sturter. Sheppard. Sc.* | *Captain Lemuel Gulliver, of* | Redriff Ætat. fuæ 58. |; facing the title-page of Vol. I.

Map of Lilliput, etc., with inscription in the upper left-hand corner: | Plate. I Part. I *Page*. I. |; facing p. [1].

PART 2.

COLLATION BY SIGNATURES: [A], 3 leaves; B to L, each 8 leaves; M, 2 leaves; total 85 leaves.

COLLATION BY PAGINATION: [title] | TRAVELS | INTO SEVERAL | Remote Nations | OF THE | WORLD. | *By Captain* LEMUEL GULLIVER. | PART II. | A VOYAGE to BROBDINGNAG. | *LONDON:* | Printed in the Year, MDCCXXVI. |, recto of [A]; — [blank], verso of [A]; — | [conventional head-piece] | THE | CONTENTS. |, recto of [A 2] to verso of [A 3]; — [text, with heading] | [conventional head-piece] | TRAVELS. | PART II. | A Voyage to BROBDINGNAG. |, pp. [1]–164.

MAP: Map of Brobdingnag, etc., with inscription in the upper right-hand corner: | Plate, II Part, II *Page*. 1. |.

VOL. 2.

PART 3.

COLLATION BY SIGNATURES: A, 3 leaves; B to K, each 8 leaves; L, 4 leaves; M, 2 leaves; total 81 leaves.

COLLATION BY PAGINATION: [title] | TRAVELS | INTO SEVERAL | Remote Nations | OF THE | WORLD. | *By Captain* LEMUEL GULLIVER. | PART III. | A VOYAGE to LAPUTA, BALNIBARBI, | GLUBBDUBDRIB, LUGGNAGG and | JAPAN. | PART IV. | A VOYAGE to the HOUYHNHNMS. | *LONDON:* | Printed for BENJAMIN MOTTE, at the | *Middle-Temple-Gate.* MDCCXXVI. |, recto of [A]; — [blank], verso of [A]; — | [type-ornament head-piece] | THE | CONTENTS. |, recto of A 2 to verso of [A 3]; — [text, with heading] | [conventional head-piece] | TRAVELS. | PART III. | *A* VOYAGE *to* LAPUTA, BAL- | NIBARBI, LUGGNAGG, | GLUBBDUBDRIB and JA- | PAN. |, pp. [1]–155; — [blank], p. [156]. Page 74 is wrongly numbered 44.

PLATES: 2 maps and 1 plate, as follows:

Map of Iesso, Japon, Lugnagg, Laputa, and Balnibarbi, with inscription in upper left-hand corner: | Plate III. Part. III. *Page*. I. |; facing p. [1].

No. 678   *Jonathan Swift*   1726

Map of Balnibarbi, with inscription at the top : | Plate IIII. Part. III. *Page.* 39. | ; facing p. 39.

Plate of hieroglyphics, with inscription at the top : | Plate. V. Part. III. *Page.* 74. | ; facing p. 74 [wrongly numbered 44].

PART 4.

COLLATION BY SIGNATURES: A, 4 leaves ; B to N, each 8 leaves ; O, 4 leaves ; total 104 leaves.

COLLATION BY PAGINATION: [title] | TRAVELS | INTO SEVERAL | Remote Nations | OF THE | WORLD. | *By Captain* LEMUEL GULLIVER. | PART IV. | A VOYAGE to the HOUYHNHNMS. | *LONDON:* | Printed in the Year, M DCC XXVI. | , recto of [A]; —[blank], verso of [A]; — | [type-ornament head-piece] | THE | CONTENTS. | , recto of A 2 to verso of [A 4]; —[text, with heading] | [conventional head-piece] | TRAVELS. | PART IV. | *A* VOYAGE *to the Country of* | *the* HOUYHNHNMS. | , pp. [1]-199 ; — | *FINIS.* | , p. 199 ; — [blank], p. [200].

MAP: Map of Houyhnhnms Land, with inscription in the upper left-hand corner : | Plate. VI. Part. IIII. *Page.* I. | ; facing p. [1].

CONDITION : Size of leaf, 9¼ × 5⅜ inches. Bound in mottled calf, Vol. 1 with yellow edges, Vol. 2 with sprinkled edges.

OTHER COPIES.

British Museum (large-paper copy) ; Bodleian ; Forster Collection (large-paper ; Ford-Malone copy ; interleaved and with Ford's manuscript alterations and additions, taken from Swift's own list of corrections) ; Sion College ; University Library, Cambridge ; and Hoe (2, one a large-paper copy) Libraries.

REFERENCES.

Jackson, *Bibliography*, in *Prose Works of Jonathan Swift*, 12 (Bohn's Libraries, 1908) : 143 ; same, 8 (1899) : xxx. ; Hoe, *Catalogue*, 3 (1905) : 127 ; Locker-Lampson, *Appendix to Catalogue* (1900), p. 97 ; South Kensington Museum, *Forster Collection* ; *A Catalogue of Printed Books* (1888), p. 479, No. 8551 ; *Notes and Queries*, Sixth Series, Vol. 12 (1885), pp. 198, 350, 398, 473 ; Locker-Lampson, *Catalogue* (1886), p. 178 ; Huth, *Catalogue*, 4 (1880) : 1420 ; Lowndes, 5 (1869) : 2560 ; *Bibliotheca Grenvilliana*, 2 (1842) : 704.

First Edition. Large-paper copy.

Four editions of *Gulliver's Travels* were published in 1726, of which this is the First.

In the First Edition (1726 ; Jackson "Edition A"), that here described, the second volume has not the words "Vol. II." on the title-page. The portrait is in its First State, with inscription in a compartment below the portrait : | *Captain Lemuel Gulliver, of* | Redriff Ætat. suæ 58. | ; but none around the oval. Each part has its own series of signature-marks, and is separately paged, Part III. ending on p. 155.

In another edition of the same date (Jackson "Edition AA") the words "Vol. II. Part III." and the word "Glubbdubdribb" (not "Glubdubdrib") appear on the title-page of the second volume. Each part has also a distinct series of signature-marks and is separately paged, but Part III. ends on p. 154. The portrait is in its Second State, with inscription around the oval : | CAPTAIN LEMUEL GULLIVER OF REDRIFF. ÆTAT. SUÆ LVIII. | ; and in the compartment below the portrait are two lines of Latin, a quotation from Persius. Of this edition there are copies in the British Museum, Forster Collection (Vol. 1 only), and Hoe Libraries.

In still another edition, also 1726 (Jackson "Edition B"), the title-page of

TRAVELS

INTO SEVERAL

Remote Nations

OF THE

WORLD.

In Four PARTS.

By *LEMUEL GULLIVER,*
Firſt a Surgeon, and then a Captain of ſeveral SHIPS.

Vol. I.

LONDON
Printed for Benj. Motte, *at the Middle* Temple-Gate *in* Fleet-ſtreet.
MDCCXXVI.

No. 678. Title-page of Swift's [Gulliver's Travels] Travels into several Remote Nations of the World; 1st Edition; 1726.

Vol. 2 is the same as in the preceding edition ("AA"), but each volume has only one set of signature-marks and one pagination. In most copies of this edition Vol. 2 is called the "Second Edition." True copies of this volume are extremely scarce. Of this edition there are copies in the British Museum (Vol. 1 only), Forster Collection, University Library (Cambridge), Trinity College (Dublin), and Hoe Libraries.

Further differences in these editions ("A," "AA," and "B") will be found in the Hoe *Catalogue,* where full collations are given; though what is here described as the First Edition is there considered to be "Presumably the second edition." Inserted at the end of Vol. 2 of Mr. Hoe's copy of "AA" is a leaf, verso blank, containing a Key, dated "Jan. Feb. March. 1743."

In 1727 there appeared a spurious volume purporting to be a continuation of the *Travels,* divided into two parts, "A Second Voyage to Brobdingnag," and "A Voyage to Sevarambia, &c." With a view to deceiving the readers of the genuine edition, it was cleverly printed to imitate it, and is entitled | TRAVELS | INTO SEVERAL | Remote Nations | OF THE | WORLD. | *By Capt.* LEMUEL GULLIVER. | VOL. III. | [2 lines in Latin] | *LONDON*: Printed in the Year M.DCC.XXVII. |. "This is an impudent forgery. It consists chiefly of a translation of the 'Histoire des Sevarambes,' by Denys Vairasse d'Alais, published, 1677–1679." Of this volume there are copies in the British Museum, Dyce Collection, Forster Collection (the Mitford copy, with his manuscript notes), and Hoe Libraries.

Gulliver's Travels, as appears by Motte's advertisement in *The Daily Journal* of October 28, 1726, was published on that day, a "few" copies being "printed on a Royal Paper." The whole impression was sold within a week and was universally read from the cabinet-council to the nursery. It was reprinted serially in *Parker's Penny Post* from November 28, 1726, to November 3, 1727. In order to avoid responsibility for passages which might give offence, Motte before publishing Swift's manuscript made such alterations in it that Swift says, "The style is debased, the humour quite lost, and the matter insipid." Slight corrections were made in the second edition published in 1727, more important ones in the Dublin edition of 1735; but the alterations, substitutions, and additions made by Ford from Swift's own list appear in full and in their proper order for the first time in Temple Scott's edition of *The Prose Works of Swift,* Vol. 8 (Bohn's Libraries, 1889).

An anonymous translation in French appeared at The Hague early in 1727, and soon after at Paris, another by the Abbé des Fontaines. A Dutch translation in three volumes was published at The Hague the same year.

"'Gulliver' is among the most original of works of fiction, as well as one of the most witty of satires. No other writer has succeeded in giving such verisimilitude to an altogether impossible narrative. In the 'Voyage to Lilliput' and the 'Voyage to Brobdingnag' especially, if we once accept the scale on which the countries and their inhabitants are drawn [viz. 1 to 12, and 12 to 1], there is nothing in what follows to throw any strain upon our credulity. . . . The first two voyages at least may be read with delight, even by those who know nothing of the persons and events which are held up to ridicule."

[n. d.]   *Richard Tarlton*   No. 679

[TARLTON, RICHARD.]   (*b.* ——, *d.* 1588.)

A PRETTIE NEW BALLAD. London, *for Henry Kyrkham*, [n. d.].
[679]

Folio.

COLLATION BY SIGNATURES: 2 numbered leaves, without signature-marks.

COLLATION BY PAGINATION: | [type-ornament head-piece] | [text, with heading] | A prettie new Ballad, intytuled: | The Crowe sits upon the wall, | Please one and please all. | To the tune of, Please one and please all. | [16 stanzas of poetry, printed in black-letter, signed] | R T |, recto pages of folios [1]-2; — | FINIS. | [conventional tail-piece] | [colophon] | *Imprinted at London for Henry Kyrkham, dwelling at the little North doore of Paules,* | *at the syne of the blacke Boy.* |, recto of folio 2; — [imprint] | *J. Davy & Sons, Printers, 137, Long Acre, London.* | [*Ten Copies only.*] |, verso of folio 2. The verso of folio [1] is blank.

This reprint has upon the recto of folio [1], under the heading, a mounted India-proof wood portrait of Queen Elizabeth.

CONDITION: Size of leaf, 14¾ × 10¹¹⁄₁₆ inches. Bound with No. 309.

Of the original edition of this ballad, printed about 1570, only one copy is known, that in the Huth library (*Catalogue*, Vol. 4, p. 1428). " Reprinted in ' Anc. Ballads,' &c., 1867."

[THACKERAY, WILLIAM MAKEPEACE.]   (*b.* 1811, *d.* 1863.)

THE SNOB. Cambridge, *W. H. Smith*, 1829.   [680]

Duodecimo.

COLLATION BY SIGNATURES: 5 leaves, without signature-marks; A, 2 leaves; B, 1 leaf; C, 2 leaves; D, D (repeated), E to L, each 3 leaves; total 37 numbered leaves. Leaves I and K have no signature-marks.

COLLATION BY PAGINATION: [title, as reproduced; *See* No. 680], p. [i.]; — [imprint], p. [ii.]; — | TO | ALDERMAN ABBOTT, | [9 lines] |, p. [iii.]; — [blank], p. [iv.]; — [preface], pp. [v.]-vi.; — [index], pp. [vii.]-ix.; — [quotation, 5 lines], p. [x.]; — [text of the first number, with heading] | VOL I. | Fifth Edition. | THE SNOB. | [quotation, same as on the title-page] |

No. 1. THURSDAY, APRIL 9, 1829. PRICE 2½ d. |, pp. [1]-4;

No. 2. Third Edition. Thursday, April 16; pp. [5]-10;

No. 3. Thursday, April 23; pp. [11]-16;

No. 4. Fourth Edition. Thursday, April 30, 1829; pp. [17]-22;

No. 5. Fourth Edition. Thursday, May 7, 1829; pp. [23]-28;

No. 6. Thursday, May 14, 1829; pp. [29]-34;

No. 7. Thursday, May 21, 1829; pp. [35]-40;

No. 8. Thursday, May 28, 1829; pp. [41]-46;

No. 9. Thursday, June 4, 1829; pp. [47]-52;

No. 10. Third Edition; Thursday, June 11, 1829; pp. [53]-58;

No. 11. Second Edition; Thursday, June 18, 1829; pp. [59]-64;

| FINIS. | [imprint] | *Printed for the Editors, by Weston Hatfield;* | And pub-

No. 680   *William Makepeace Thackeray*   1829

lished by W. H. Smith, Rose Crescent, Cambridge.|, p. 64.

CONDITION: Size of leaf, 7 7/10 × 4 5/8 inches. Bound in the original light green boards, with title on the front cover similar to that reproduced, but enclosed by a type-ornament border; in wine-colored crushed levant morocco solander case. The numbers are printed on various colored papers, viz.: preliminary leaves, yellow; Nos. 1–3, pink; No. 4, blue; Nos. 5–6, pink; No. 7, blue; No. 8, yellow; Nos. 9–11, pink.

REFERENCES.

Thackeray's Works (Biographical Edition, 13 vols.; 1903), 13 : 531, *note*, 691; Melville, *Life of Thackeray*, 1 (1899): 55; also 2 : 336; Slater, *Early Editions* (1894), p. 316, No. 1; Johnson, *Early Writings of Thackeray* (1888), pp. 2–9; Johnson, *Hints to Collectors* (1885), p. 11, No. 1.; Shepherd, *Bibliography of Thackeray* (1880), p. 1, No. 1.

This copy is complete, and consists of eleven numbers, printed on variously tinted papers. Several numbers (Slater says all copies) are headed with the words "Second Edition," "Third Edition," etc., at the top of the first page, but Nos. 3, 6, 7, 8, and 9 are not so marked in the copy here described.

Mr. Robert Bowes in *The Athenæum* for June 11, 1887 (p. 766), states that there is a set of the eleven numbers without any designation of edition, and therefore the First, in the Cambridge Free Library. He further says that a comparison of the different editions of the same number show that they are printed from the same settings of type, with the exception of the Fourth Edition of No. 6, which "must have been entirely reset." Slater having never seen any of the First editions is therefore in error in concluding that there were none.

The Snob was a little weekly undergraduate paper, which made its first appearance April 9, 1829, and ran through eleven numbers, the last appearing June 18th. Among Thackeray's known contributions to this periodical is a parody of Tennyson's prize poem entitled "Timbuctoo," which probably represents Thackeray's first appearance in print, when he was only eighteen years of age. He is believed to have been responsible for a considerable portion of the contents of the publication, though it is not possible to say with certainty which contributions were from his pen. Several epigrammatic verses and some letters full of misspellings and malapropisms, from "Dorothea Julia Ramsbottom," are almost unmistakably his.

William Makepeace Thackeray was born at Calcutta, July 18, 1811, and was sent to England in 1817 in a ship which touched at St. Helena. Five years later he entered Charterhouse School, London, remaining there until 1828. In February of the next year he was entered at Trinity College, Cambridge, where he remained until the end of the Easter term in 1830, leaving without a degree. After a year spent in travel, during which he met Goethe at Weimar, he entered the Middle Temple in November, 1831, with the intention of studying law, but soon gave up law for journalism, in which he was actively engaged for the next few years, contributing to several London journals.

An unfortunate connection with two newspapers, *The National Standard* and *The Constitutional*, in which he was successively a partner from 1833 to 1837, together with unlucky investments and the failure of an India bank, caused his financial ruin.

THE SNOB:

A LITERARY AND SCIENTIFIC JOURNAL.

NOT

―――――――

" CONDUCTED BY MEMBERS OF THE UNIVERSITY."

―――――――

Tityre, tu patulæ recubans sub tegmine fagi
Sylvestrem ?   Virgil.

―――――――

Cambridge:
PUBLISHED BY W. H. SMITH, ROSE CRESCENT.

1829.

No. 680.   Title-page of The Snob; 1829.

Thrown upon his own resources, he studied art and contributed articles to several magazines. From 1832 to 1837 he wrote principally for *Fraser's Magazine*. In 1836 appeared his first publication, *Flore et Zephyr* (our No. 682), a collection of nine satirical drawings. In 1842 he was associated with *Punch*, for which he was prose writer, poet, and draughtsman as occasion required until 1854. During his connection with this periodical he was regarded as the most important rival of the witty and brilliant Douglas Jerrold. In 1860 he became editor of the *Cornhill Magazine,* and though he resigned that position with the April number in 1862, he continued to contribute to its columns up to the time of his death, on Christmas Eve, 1863, his uncompleted story, *Denis Duval,* appearing posthumously in it.

The public was slow to appreciate the merits of Thackeray's literary productions. He had been writing for many years before his work received the stamp of decided approval given to it in 1848, when, at thirty-seven years of age, he wrote *Vanity Fair.* From that time to the close of his life his popularity continued to increase, and it may with safety be said that his writings are more highly esteemed to-day than they were at the time of his death.

A master of style, a cultured gentleman, artistic by temperament and training, beloved by his friends, endowed with profound insight into human nature, he possessed many of the elements capable of striking responsive chords in his fellow men. It was these traits of his character which caused his writings to abound in those touches of nature which make the whole world kin.

COLLECTIONS. It is not surprising that it has been one of the favorite pursuits of Thackeray's admirers to collect early editions of his writings. Among such collections worthy of note, in New York are those of F. R. Halsey, J. Pierpont Morgan, Harry B. Smith, and P. A. Valentine; in Philadelphia, those of the Drexel Institute and Major William H. Lambert, the latter of which is believed to be the most complete in the world; while in Cleveland, Frederick S. Dickson has a fine collection.

AUTHORITIES. Thackeray's works in book form were largely made up of papers gathered from his numerous contributions to periodicals. The first of these appeared in this country as early as 1838, where a few of his other early productions were also published for the first time in book form. Several bibliographies of Thackeray have already appeared, but the definitive bibliography has yet to appear. Richard H. Shepherd in 1880 brought out his *Bibliography,* which records 139 items from Thackeray's pen and 34 relating to him. In it is included a record not only of such works as had appeared in book form, but also of many of the articles in *Fraser's Magazine, Punch,* and the *Cornhill Magazine* that had not at that time appeared in any of the editions of Thackeray's collected works. Five years later, in 1885, Charles Plumptre Johnson published his *Hints to Collectors of Original Editions of Thackeray.* He records 31 titles with collations and notes, giving variations to be found in different editions and issues. In 1888 the same author, in his *Early Writings of Thackeray,* gives an interesting account, with extracts, of Thackeray's contributions to *The Snob* and *The Gownsman,* of his unfortunate connection with *The National Standard* and *The Constitutional,* of his contributions to *Fraser's Magazine,* and of the early American editions of his works. J. H. Slater in his *Early Editions of Some Popular Modern Authors* (1894) gives 40 titles (pp. 314-334) arranged in chronological order, closing his list with *Etchings* published in 1878.

At the end of Vol. 2 of Lewis Melville's *Life of Thackeray* (1899) will be found a bibliography of Thackeray's writings. This is divided into four parts: books separately published; contributions to periodicals; miscellanea; and volumes of biographical information. The second of these parts is the one most carefully worked out. In the *Bibliography* by W. J. Williams appended to the Biographical Edition of Thackeray's *Works* the titles are arranged in the order in which they first made their appearance in book form. Full tables of contents of volumes containing miscellaneous papers are given, with references to the periodicals in which each of the several parts first appeared. The latest and most carefully prepared of Thackeray bibliographies is that of Frederick S. Dickson, appended to General James Grant Wilson's *Thackeray in the United States*. Unfortunately it deals only with such works as have appeared in this country, either in periodicals or in book form. It contains a long list of Thackerayana, and does for the periodicals of the United States what Melville and Williams have done for those of England. We are informed that the compiler of this valuable bibliography has in manuscript a complete bibliography of Thackeray.

Of the various editions of Thackeray's *Works*, that published by the Macmillan Company, 1904, etc., with notes by Melville, is the most nearly complete of any which has yet appeared, the notes containing much valuable bibliographical information.

[THACKERAY, WILLIAM MAKEPEACE.]

THE GOWNSMAN. CAMBRIDGE, *W. H. Smith, and sold by Simpkin and Marshall*, 1830. [681]

Crown octavo.

COLLATION BY SIGNATURES: [A], 4 leaves; 1 leaf, without signature-mark; B to F, F (repeated), G to L, L (repeated), M to P, P (repeated), each 4 leaves; 1 leaf, without signature-mark; total 74 numbered leaves.

COLLATION BY PAGINATION: [title, as reproduced; *See* No. 681], p. [i.];—[imprint], p. [ii.];—| DEDICATION.| TO ALL PROCTORS.|[17 lines]|, p. [iii.];—[blank], p. [iv.];—[preface, dated] |ST. JOHN'S, *June 9th*, 1830.|, pp. [v.]-vi.;—[index], pp. [vii.]-ix.;—[quotation, 2 lines], p. [x.];—[text in 17 numbers, the first with heading]| THE GOWNSMAN.|[quotation, 3 lines]| No. 1. THURSDAY, NOVEMBER 5. PRICE 3*d*.|, pp. [1]-138. The numbers 35-40 are repeated and 43-48 are omitted in the pagination.

Each number contains one sheet of 4 leaves, except the last, which has 5 leaves.

CONDITION: Size of leaf, 7$\frac{3}{16}$ × 4½ inches. Bound in the original pink boards, the front cover with title lined as reproduced but reset in smaller type and enclosed by a type-ornament border; in the same case with the preceding number.

REFERENCES.

Melville, *Life of Thackeray*, 1 (1899): 57; *Three Hundred Notable Books* (1899), p. 60; Slater, *Early Editions* (1894), p. 316, No. 2; Johnson, *Early Writings of Thackeray* (1888), pp. 9-13.

The Gownsman, the successor of *The Snob*, made its first appearance Thursday, November 5, 1829, and was continued weekly until February 25, 1830, making in all seventeen numbers, after which it ceased to appear.

It is difficult to determine precisely Thackeray's connection with this periodical.

No. 681 *William Makepeace Thackeray* 1830

THE GOWNSMAN,

(FORMERLY CALLED)

"THE SNOB,"

A Literary and Scientific Journal,

NOW

CONDUCTED BY MEMBERS OF THE UNIVERSITY

Sir, here is newly come to court Laertes; believe me an absolute Gentleman,—full of most excellent differences.
HAMLET.

VOL. 2.

CAMBRIDGE:

PUBLISHED BY W. H. SMITH, ROSE CRESCENT,
AND SOLD BY SIMPKIN AND MARSHALL, LONDON,
AND MAY BE HAD OF ALL BOOKSELLERS.

1830.

No. 681. Title-page of The Gownsman; 1830.

It seems more than probable that he was its actual editor and did a large part of the writing for it. Trollope has suggested that he wrote the dedication:

"To all Proctors,
Both past, present, and future, . .
Whose taste it is our privilege to follow,
Whose virtues it is our duty to imitate,
And whose presence it is our interest to avoid."

William Makepeace Thackeray

"It is stated," says Johnson, "on the authority of Mr. Edward Fitzgerald, who was a great friend of Thackeray's, that his contributions to *The Gownsman* were signed '☉,' a signature which he afterwards used for his famous article on his friend George Cruikshank [our No. 691], which appeared in the *Westminster Review* in 1840. This, if conceded, at once identifies Thackeray's writings for *The Gownsman*."

Thackeray has been credited with the following items:

(1) Dedication, p. [iii.].
(2) Letter from Dorothea Julia Ramsbottom, pp. [10]–12.
(3) Last paragraph on p. 13 signed θ.
(4) "I'd be a tadpole," pp. 14–15.
(5) "From Anacreon," p. 39.
(6) "An Extract from the Diary of the Late Thomas Timmins," p. 41.

[THACKERAY, WILLIAM MAKEPEACE.]

FLORE ET ZEPHYR. London, *J. Mitchell*, 1836. [682]

Folio. A collection of 9 unnumbered plates, including the wrapper title, without signature-marks; drawn by Thackeray, and signed with the pseudonym | THÉOPHILE WAGSTAFF |, and lithographed by Edward Morton, impressions on India paper, with titles as follows:

[1] Wrapper title, as reproduced; *See* No. 682.
[2] | LES DELASSEMENTS DE ZEPHYR. |.
[3] | FLORE DEPLORE L'ABSENCE DE ZEPHYR |.
[4] | TRISTE ET ABATTU, LES SÉDUCTIONS DES NYMPHES LE TENTENT EN VAIN. |.
[5] | JEUX INNOCENS DE ZEPHYR ET FLORE. |.
[6] | LA DANSE FAIT SES OFFRANDES SUR L'AUTEL DE L'HARMONIE |.
[7] | LA RETRAITE DE FLORE. |.
[8] | DANS UN PAS-SEUL IL EXPRIME SON EXTRÊME DESESPOIR. |.
[9] | RECONCILIATION DE FLORE & ZEPHYR. |.

CONDITION: Size of plates, 13⅝ × 9¹³⁄₁₆ inches; size of wrappers, 14¾ × 10½ inches. Bound in blue crushed levant morocco, gilt top; by the Club Bindery, 1899. With the original brown paper wrappers bound in, the front wrapper with title as reproduced. The plates, which in this copy are slightly tinted, are mounted on guards and stilted to match the wrappers. The vignette on the wrapper title is also by Thackeray, and is here counted as a plate.

REFERENCES.

Williams, *Bibliography*, in Thackeray, *Works* (Biographical Edition, 13 vols.; 1903), 13 : 721; Melville, *Life of Thackeray*, 2 (1899) : 297; same, 2 : 204–206, 212; Slater, *Early Editions* (1894), p. 317, No. 3; Johnson, *Hints to Collectors* (1885), p. 12, No. 11.; Shepherd, *Bibliography of Thackeray* (1880), p. 3, No. 3.

This work consists of nine lithographed plates drawn by Thackeray, in folio, representative of scenes in the life of a ballet girl. There is no letterpress. Each plate bears Thackeray's monogram, "W. T." The British Museum copy is uncolored, but most copies are slightly tinted.

Shepherd and Williams, in their bibliographies, give the plates in a different order from that in which they are arranged in the copy here described, viz.:

FLORE ET ZEPHYR
Ballet Mythologique
DÉDIÉ À

par *Théophile Wagstaff*

LONDON, PUBLISHED MARCH 1ST 1836 BY J. MITCHELL. LIBRARY, 33, OLD BOND ST
à Paris chez Rittner & Goupil Boulevard Montmartre

Printed by Graf & Soret

NO. 682. WRAPPER TITLE OF THACKERAY'S FLORE ET ZEPHYR; 1836.
Reduced; original 9⅛ × 5⅜ inches.

"Vignette Title.
1. La Danse fait ses offrandes sur l'autel de l'Harmonie.
2. Jeux Innocens de Zéphyr et Flore.
3. Flore deplore l'absence de Zéphyr.
4. Dans un pas-seul il exprime son extrême desespoir.
5. Triste et abattu, les séductions des Nymphes le tentent en vain.
6. Reconciliation de Flore & Zéphyr.
7. La Retraite de Flore.
8. Les Delassements de Zéphyr."

The plates, being unnumbered, seem to have been differently placed when bound. Of three copies which we have examined side by side no two agree in their arrangement and none follow the order given by Shepherd or Williams. These also varied in size, the wrappers measuring 14¾ × 10½, 12⅞ × 9⅛, and 11¾ × 8¹³⁄₁₆ inches respectively. The first of these, the copy here described, seems to have the wrappers of the size in which they were originally printed. The lithographic impressions of the plates vary in size, being from 6½ to 8 inches long and from 5½ to 6⅜⁄₁₆ inches wide. Seven of these are mounted within printed panels, below which appear the inscriptions.

We have also seen two impressions of the title-page which differ from the one here described: (*a*) a copy which appears to be a proof before any letters, printed on plate paper 15⅛ × 11¹⁄₁₆ inches; (*b*) a copy identically the same as our reproduction but printed on what is said to be India paper and mounted on a blank wrapper.

This work was reprinted in the Biographical Edition. It deservedly takes a high rank among Thackeray's artistic works.

[THACKERAY, WILLIAM MAKEPEACE.]

KING GLUMPUS. London, 1837. [683]

Foolscap octavo.

COLLATION BY SIGNATURES: 8 numbered leaves, without signature-marks.

COLLATION BY PAGINATION: [title, as reproduced; *See* No. 683], p. [1];—[blank], p. [2];—|DRAMATIS PERSONÆ.|, p. [3];—[blank], p. [4];—[text, with heading]|KING GLUMPUS.|, pp. [5]-16.

PLATES: 3 plates from drawings by Thackeray, as follows:

[1]| KING GLUMPUS.|; facing the title-page.

[2]| LADY POPKINS.|; facing p. 9.
[3]| LORD LOLLYPOP |; facing p. 13.

CONDITION: Size of leaf, 7⅛ × 4⅜ inches. Bound in the original blank yellow wrappers; in red crushed levant morocco solander case.

REFERENCES.

Wilson, *Thackeray in the United States*, 2 (1904): 112, 121; Melville, *Life of Thackeray*, 2 (Chicago and New York, 1899): 297.

This little one-act piece, a burlesque interlude somewhat after the style of *Bombastes Furioso*, was probably intended for an amateur performance, and is one of the few pieces written by Thackeray for the stage. "The illustrations were reproduced

No. 683   *William Makepeace Thackeray*   1837

KING GLUMPUS:

AN INTERLUDE

IN ONE ACT.

———◆◆◆———

[For private circulation only.]

LONDON:
———
1837.

No. 683.   Title-page of Thackeray's King Glumpus; 1837.

in *The Autographic Mirror*, vol. ii. (1865)"; and "a fac-simile reprint was issued in 1898 by Mr. W. T. Spencer, 27, New Oxford Street, London." It was also reprinted, with the illustrations, in the *Bookman*, New York, Vol. 8 (December, 1898), pp. 342–346, with an introductory note by Luther S. Livingston.

   King Glumpus and *The Exquisites* are among the most recently discovered of Thackeray's works. Copies of both these works are in the library of Major William

H. Lambert of Philadelphia. There is an article on the authorship of these two pieces by Luther S. Livingston, containing a letter by Frederick S. Dickson, in the *Bookman*, Vol. 8 (February, 1899), pp. 567–569.

In the *Athenæum* for February 23, 1907 (p. 225), is a long communication by W. Roberts on the two booklets *King Glumpus* and *The Exquisites*. It is there stated that "there is no secret about the identity of the illustrator, W. M. Thackeray," but the claim is made that the text of both was written by John Barrow, who died at Chipping Norton, December 9, 1898. This claim is based upon a statement made by Mrs. Ellicott, widow of the Bishop of Gloucester and a relative of Thackeray, her father, Admiral Becher, being an intimate friend of Barrow. She "recalls his gift to her family of copies of the two booklets" (which are inherited). "Mrs. Ellicott tells me," says Roberts, "that Barrow's authorship of the two booklets was a perfectly well-known 'secret' to her father and herself, and that the question of authorship was never at any time in doubt among the members of her family. Mrs. Ellicott also remembers Thackeray well, and possesses a number of most interesting letters from him. . . .

"There is more literary merit in 'King Glumpus' than in 'The Exquisites'; but one does not usually look for much literary merit in either an 'interlude' or a 'farce' written for the private gratification and amusement of a small circle of intimates. Both were printed expressly for private circulation. . .

"Only one copy of 'King Glumpus' has so far appeared in the saleroom, and this realized 101 *l.* at Messrs. Hodgson's on August 1st, 1906. This was an exceedingly interesting presentation copy, and an inscription on the first fly-leaf bears out the theory that Thackeray was *not* the author, inasmuch as nothing is said in the sale catalogue which claims Thackeray to have written the inscription, which runs thus: 'Miss Emily Parker from her never-to-be-sufficiently-admired friend The Author.' If this handwriting were in the well-known autograph of Thackeray, that fact would have been stated. The auctioneers, however, reached one conclusion of interest, namely, that 'a comparison of the title-page of the above with the title-page of "The Exquisites" reveals a marked similarity, which certainly points to the fact that they were issued from the same press.' "

[THACKERAY, WILLIAM MAKEPEACE.]

THE YELLOWPLUSH CORRESPONDENCE. PHILADELPHIA, *E. L. Carey & A. Hart*, 1838. [684]

Duodecimo. First Edition.

COLLATION BY SIGNATURES: [1], 1 leaf; 2 to 19, each 6 leaves; 20, 5 leaves; total 114 leaves.

COLLATION BY PAGINATION: [title, as reproduced; *See* No. 684], recto of [1]; —[imprint], verso of [1]; —[text, with heading]|THE|YELLOWPLUSH CORRESPONDENCE.|, pp. [13]–238.

CONDITION: Size of leaf, 7½ × 4½ inches. Bound in the original boards, cloth back, with paper title-label lettered: | THE

THE

YELLOWPLUSH

CORRESPONDENCE.

Wm Makepeace Thackeray

PHILADELPHIA:
E. L. CAREY & A. HART.
1838.

No. 684.   Title-page of Thackeray's Yellowplush Correspondence;
1st Edition; 1838.

| YELLOWPLUSH | CORRESPON- | DENCE. | .

REFERENCES.

Dickson, *Bibliography*, in Wilson, *Thackeray in the United States*, 2 (1904): 229; Williams, *Bibliography*, in Thackeray, *Works* (Biographical Edition, 13 vols.; 1903), 13 : 721; Melville, *Life of Thackeray*, 1 (1899) : 113; 2 : 315; Johnson, *Early Writings of Thackeray* (1888), p. 62; Shepherd, *Bibliography of Thackeray* (1880), p. 4, No. 4.

The copy here described is complete; no preliminary leaves, except a title-page, seem to have been printed.

This is the first collected edition of Thackeray's writings that appeared on either side of the Atlantic. It contains "Fashnable Fax and Polite Annygoats," "Miss Shum's Husband," "Diamond Cut Diamond," "Skimmings from 'The Dairy of George IV.,'" "Foring Parts," "Mr. Deuceace at Paris," and "The End of Mr. Deuceace's History."

These papers first appeared in *Fraser's Magazine* (Vols. 16–18), in November, 1837, and from January to July, 1838. They were first published in book form, with other papers, in England, in *Comic Tales and Sketches*, Vol. 1, 1841 (our No. 693). It is almost needless to say that the papers were carefully revised before their republication in this later volume.

[THACKERAY, WILLIAM MAKEPEACE, *illustrator*.] Addison, Charles Greenstreet. (*b.* ——, *d.* 1866.)

DAMASCUS AND PALMYRA. LONDON, *Richard Bentley*, 1838. 2 vols., octavo, viz.: [685]

VOL. 1.

COLLATION BY SIGNATURES; [A], 8 leaves; b, 6 leaves; B to Z, AA to EE, each 8 leaves; FF, 4 leaves; total 234 numbered leaves.

COLLATION BY PAGINATION: [half-title] | A JOURNEY TO THE EAST. |, p. [i.]; — [imprint], p. [ii.]; — [title] | DAMASCUS AND PALMYRA: | A JOURNEY TO THE EAST. | WITH A SKETCH OF | THE STATE AND PROSPECTS OF SYRIA, | UNDER IBRAHIM PASHA. | BY CHARLES G. ADDISON, | OF THE INNER TEMPLE. | IN TWO VOLUMES. | VOL. I. | LONDON: | RICHARD BENTLEY, NEW BURLINGTON STREET; | Publisher in Ordinary to Her Majesty. | 1838. |, p. [iii.]; — [blank], p. [iv.]; — [dedication, introduction, contents, and errata], pp. [v.]–[xxviii.]; — [text, with heading] | A JOURNEY, | ETC., ETC. |, pp. [1]–440.

PLATES: 9 colored lithographs, after designs by Thackeray, as follows:

[1] | DANCING DERVISH. | ; facing the title-page.
[2] | GREEK PEASANT. | ; facing p. 36.
[3] | TURKISH RECRUIT. | ; facing p. 178.
[4] | ARABAT, OR TURKISH LADIES CARRIAGE. | ; facing p. 198.
[5] | TURKISH LADY. | ; facing p. 216.
[6] | DANCER AT THE CAFÉS. | ; facing p. 235.
[7] | MUSICIAN OF THE HAREM. | ; facing p. 246.
[8] | MUEZZIN CALLING TO PRAYERS. | ; facing p. 255.
[9] | TURKISH GENTLEMAN. | ; facing p. 344.

VOL. 2.

COLLATION BY SIGNATURES: [A], 2 leaves; b, 4 leaves; B to Z, AA to HH, each 8 leaves; II, 2 leaves; total 248 numbered leaves.

COLLATION BY PAGINATION: [half-title], p. [i.]; — [imprint], p. [ii.]; — [title, same as in Vol. 1, except volume-number], p. [iii.]; — [blank], p. [iv.]; — [contents], pp. [v.]–x.; — [half-title] | A JOURNEY TO THE EAST. |, p. [xi.]; — | ERRATA. | [6 lines] |, p. [xii.]; — [text], pp. [1]–484.

No. 685   *William Makepeace Thackeray*   1838

PLATES: 9 colored lithographs, after designs by Thackeray, as follows:
- [1] | SCENE IN THE BAZAAR. | [in which Thackeray has represented himself seated in the doorway smoking]; facing the title-page.
- [2] | EGYPTIAN SOLDIER. | ; facing p. 26.
- [3] | SYRIAN MERCHANT. | ; facing p. 96.
- [4] | BON BON SELLER. | ; facing p. 114.
- [5] | AN EASTERN LADY WAITING ON HER GUESTS. | ; facing p. 128.
- [6] | DAMASCENE LADY. | ; facing p. 172.
- [7] | SHERBET SELLER. | ; facing p. 190.
- [8] | THE BEDOUIN SHEIKH. | ; facing p. 330.
- [9] | LADY OF DAMASCUS. | ; facing p. 384.

Besides the title each plate bears the imprint: "*Madeley lith. 3 Wellington S.t Strand.*"

CONDITION: Size of leaf, 9 × 5⅝ inches. Bound in the original green cloth, uncut edges.

REFERENCE.

Slater, *Early Editions; a Bibliographical Survey of the Works of Some Popular Modern Authors* (1894), p. 315.

This is one of the rare copies containing eighteen illustrations by Thackeray; there are usually but ten.

Damascus and Palmyra was reviewed by *The Athenæum* for February 17 and 24, 1838 (pp. 119–121, 142, 143), but no reference is made to the illustrations.

During 1838 Thackeray was engaged both as a writer and as an illustrator. It was during this year that he illustrated Douglas Jerrold's *Men of Character.* Two years later, in 1840, he was employed as a writer and artist by the Anti-Corn Law agitators; his drawings while in their service being reproduced in Sir Henry Cole's *Fifty Years of Public Work.*

The earliest notice of Thackeray's work yet discovered is in a review of Douglas Jerrold's *Men of Character* in the *Athenæum* for February 24, 1838 (pp. 138, 139). The critic concludes as follows:

"According to the prevailing fashion the work is illustrated by etchings *after* Cruikshank, which are only remarkable for the badness of the drawing, and the total absence of humour. They will not serve, we fear, to place the artist among the 'men of character.'"

[THACKERAY, WILLIAM MAKEPEACE.] Cruikshank, George.

THE COMIC ALMANACK, FOR 1839. LONDON, *for Charles Tilt,* [1838].

[686]

Duodecimo. First Edition.

COLLATION BY SIGNATURES: [A] to H, each 4 leaves; total 32 numbered leaves.

COLLATION BY PAGINATION: [title] | THE | COMIC | ALMANACK, | FOR 1839 : | AN EPHEMERIS IN JEST AND EARNEST, | CONTAINING | "ALL THINGS FITTING FOR SUCH A WORK." | BY RIGDUM FUNNIDOS, GENT. | [vignette] | ADORNED WITH A DOZEN OF "RIGHTE MERRIE" CUTS, | PERTAINING TO THE MONTHS, AND | AN HIEROGLYPHIC, | BY GEORGE CRUIKSHANK. | LONDON : | IMPRINTED FOR CHARLES TILT, BIBLIOPOLIST, | IN FLEET STREET. | WHITEHEAD AND CO. PRINTERS, 76, FLEET

STREET.|, p. [1];—[calendar for 12 months], pp. 2–47;—[miscellany], pp. [48]–64.

PLATES: 12 plates (one for each month), designed, etched, and signed by George Cruikshank; facing pp. 3, 7, 11, 15, 19, 23, 27, 31, 35, 39, 43, and 49; 1 woodcut hieroglyphic on p. 50; and numerous woodcuts.

CONDITION: Size of leaf, 6⅝ × 4¾₁₆ inches. Bound in blue crushed levant morocco, gilt top, other edges uncut; by Rivière. With the original paper wrappers and 16 unnumbered leaves of publishers' advertisements, with signatures B and C,

with heading | COMIC ALMANACK ADVERTISEMENT SHEET.|, bound in as originally published.

REFERENCES.

Douglas, *Works of George Cruikshank* (1903), p. 268; Williams, *Bibliography*, in Thackeray, *Works* (Biographical Edition, 13 vols.; 1903), 13 : 722, 733; Melville, *Life of Thackeray*, 2 (1899) : 297; Johnson, *Hints to Collectors* (1885), p. 13, No. III.; Shepherd, *Bibliography of Thackeray* (1880), p. 7, No. 10; Reid, *Descriptive Catalogue of the Works of George Cruikshank*, 1 (1871) : 154, Nos. 1930–1941.

In this almanac appeared for the first time Thackeray's story *Stubbs's Calendar; or, The Fatal Boots*, on pp. [4]–5, [8]–9, [12]–13, etc., to and including p. 49; in all, 24 pages. It is illustrated with twelve plates by Cruikshank.

It was first reprinted in *Comic Tales and Sketches*, 1841, Vol. 2 (our No. 693), appeared in volume form in 1850 (our next number), and later as *The Fatal Boots*, in Thackeray's *Miscellaneous Writings* (1855), Vol. 2.

THACKERAY, WILLIAM MAKEPEACE.

STUBBS'S CALENDAR. NEW-YORK, *Stringer & Townsend*, 1850. [687]

Sixteenmo.

COLLATION BY SIGNATURES: [1], 2 leaves; [2] to 7, each 8 leaves; 8, 6 leaves; total 56 numbered leaves.

COLLATION BY PAGINATION: [title]| STUBBS'S CALENDAR: | OR, | THE FATAL BOOTS. | BY | W. M. THACKERAY, | AUTHOR OF "VANITY FAIR," "MRS. PERKINS'S BALL," | ETC., ETC., ETC. | ILLUSTRATED BY GEORGE CRUIKSHANK. | NEW-YORK: | STRINGER & TOWNSEND.|1850.|, p. [1];— [blank], p. [2];—[contents], pp. [3]–4; —[text, with heading]|STUBBS'S CALENDAR; | OR, | THE FATAL BOOTS.|, pp. [5]–112.

PLATES: 6 plates, designed, etched, and signed by George Cruikshank; facing the title-page and pp. 40, 54, 76, 88, and 102.

CONDITION: Size of leaf, 5¹⁵⁄₁₆ × 4¹⁄₁₆ inches. Bound in the original yellow boards, with title on the front cover same as the title-page, but with vignette between lines 7 and 8; in yellow crushed levant morocco solander case.

REFERENCES.

Dickson, *Bibliography*, in Wilson, *Thackeray in the United States*, 2 (1904) : 238; Douglas, *Works of George Cruikshank* (1903), p. 268; Reid, *Descriptive Catalogue of the Works of George Cruikshank*, 1 (1871) : 154, Nos. 1930–1941.

This tale first appeared in Cruikshank's *Comic Almanack* for 1839 (our preceding number), where it was illustrated with twelve designs by that famous artist. In this edition the publishers seem to have had an insufficient number of sets of plates to properly illustrate their edition, and to have contented themselves with using only six in each copy, making it necessary for the collector to get two or perhaps more copies if he wishes to obtain all the illustrations.

The plates in this edition have no titles, those given in the list below being taken from the *Comic Almanack* in which they first appeared. The full complement is as follows, those contained in the copy here described being indicated by asterisks:

(1) JANUARY. — The birth of the Year.
(2) FEBRUARY. — Cutting Weather — Squally.*
(3) MARCH. — Showery.
(4) APRIL. — Fooling.*
(5) MAY. — Restoration Day.
(6) JUNE. — Marrow Bones and Cleavers.*
(7) JULY. — Summery Proceedings.
(8) AUGUST. — DOGS have their DAYS.*
(9) SEPTEMBER. — Plucking a Goose.
(10) OCTOBER. — Mars and Venus in opposition.*
(11) NOVEMBER. — A General Post Delivery.*
(12) DECEMBER. — "The winter of our discontent."

[THACKERAY, WILLIAM MAKEPEACE.]

THE EXQUISITES. LONDON, 1839. [688]

Foolscap octavo.

COLLATION BY SIGNATURES: 2 leaves, without signature-marks; A to E, each 4 leaves (the last blank and genuine); total 22 leaves.

COLLATION BY PAGINATION: [title, as reproduced; *See* No. 688], recto of first leaf; — [blank], verso of first leaf; — | DRAMATIS PERSONÆ.|, recto of second leaf; — [blank], verso of second leaf; — [text, with heading] | THE EXQUISITES, &c.|, pp. [1]–37; — [blank], p. [38]; — [1 blank leaf], [E4].

PLATES: 4 plates, from drawings by Thackeray; facing the title-page and pp. 7, 21, and 25.

CONDITION: Size of leaf, 7¼ × 4⁹⁄₁₆ inches. Bound in the original blank yellow stiff paper wrappers; in red crushed levant morocco solander case.

REFERENCES.

Wilson, *Thackeray in the United States*, 2 (1904): 125; Melville, *Life of William Makepeace Thackeray*, 2 (1899): 297.

"'The Exquisites,' a farce in two acts, with etchings, . . . was printed for private circulation in 1839. The play, it is believed, has never been acted. . . . The small book had been offered in Mr. Taylor's catalogue, but a few months before being sent to London, for two shillings sixpence, it was sold by the Messrs. Sotheby [December 17, 1898] for fifty-eight pounds sterling, — about two hundred and eighty-five dollars!" A second copy, with colored plates, was sold in London by Hodgson, March 9, 1904, for eighty-five pounds. There is a copy of *The Exquisites* in the collection of Major William H. Lambert, of Philadelphia.

For a discussion as to the authorship of this piece see *The Bookman*, Vol. 8 (February, 1899), pp. 567–569; also *The Athenæum* (February 23, 1907), pp. 225–226.

THE EXQUISITES:

A Farce

IN TWO ACTS.

"Whate'er they did was done with so much ease,
"In them alone 'twas natural to please:
"Their motions all accompanied with grace,
"And paradise was open'd in their face."—*Dryden.*

[For private circulation only.]

LONDON:

1839.

No. 688. Title-page of Thackeray's Exquisites; 1839.

[THACKERAY, WILLIAM MAKEPEACE.] Cruikshank, George.

THE COMIC ALMANACK, FOR 1840. London, *for Charles Tilt*, [1839].
[689]

Duodecimo. First Edition.
COLLATION BY SIGNATURES: [B] to I, each 4 leaves; total 32 numbered leaves.
COLLATION BY PAGINATION : · [title] | THE | COMIC | ALMANACK, | FOR 1840 : | AN EPHEMERIS IN JEST AND EARNEST, | CONTAINING | "ALL THINGS FITTING FOR SUCH A WORK." | BY RIGDUM FUNNIDOS, GENT. | [vignette] | ADORNED WITH A DOZEN OF "RIGHTE MERRIE" CUTS, | PERTAINING TO THE MONTHS, AND | AN HIEROGLYPHIC, | BY GEORGE CRUIKSHANK. | LONDON : | IMPRINTED FOR CHARLES TILT, BIBLIOPOLIST, | IN FLEET STREET. | WHITEHEAD AND CO. PRINTERS, 76, FLEET STREET. |, p. [1]; — [calendar for 12 months], pp. 2–47; — [miscellany], pp. [48]–64.
PLATES : 12 plates (one for each month), designed, etched, and signed by George Cruikshank; facing pp. 3, 7, 11, 15, 19, 23, 27, 31, 35, 39, 43, and 47; 1 woodcut hieroglyphic on p. [60]; and numerous woodcuts.
CONDITION : Size of leaf, 6$\frac{9}{16}$ x 4$\frac{9}{16}$ inches. Bound in blue crushed levant morocco, gilt top, other edges uncut; by Rivière. With the original paper wrappers and 16 unnumbered and 4 numbered leaves of publishers' advertisements bound in as originally published.

REFERENCES.

Douglas, *Works of George Cruikshank* (1903), p. 268; Williams, *Bibliography*, in Thackeray, *Works* (Biographical Edition, 13 vols.; 1903), 13 : 733; Melville, *Life of Thackeray*, 2 (1899) : 297; Johnson, *Hints to Collectors* (1885), p. 14, No. IV.; Shepherd, *Bibliography of Thackeray* (1880), p. 8, No. 15; Reid, *Descriptive Catalogue of the Works of George Cruikshank*, 1 (1871) : 158, Nos. 2038–2049.

This almanac contains the first appearance of Thackeray's story *Barber Cox, and the Cutting of His Comb*, better known by its later title *Cox's Diary*, on pp. [4]–5, [8]–9, [12]–13, etc., to and including p. [48]; in all, 23 pages.

It was reprinted as *Cox's Diary* in Thackeray's *Miscellaneous Writings* (1855), Vol. I. It was first separately reprinted with Cruikshank's plates and twelve initials by J. P. Atkinson in Thackeray's *Works*, London, 1879, Vol. 17.

THACKERAY, WILLIAM MAKEPEACE. Manuscript.

THE CHRONICLE OF THE DRUM. Paris, 1840. [690]

The original autograph manuscript (the first page as reproduced; *See* No. 690), written on 5 quarto and 8 octavo leaves, some written on both sides of the leaf, in all 20 pages.
CONDITION : Mounted (8 leaves to size) in a quarto volume bound in red crushed levant morocco, gilt edges; lettered along the back : | CHRONICLE OF THE DRUM — THACKERAY'S AUTOGRAPH MS. |

REFERENCE.

Dickson, *Bibliography*, in Wilson, *Thackeray in the United States*, 2 (1904) : 262.

Chronicle of the Drum. Part II

At Paris hard by the Maine barriers
  Whoever will choose to repair
Midst a dozen of wooden-legged warriors
  May hap'ly fall in with old Pierre.
On the sunshiny bench of a tavern
  He sits and he prates of old wars
And moistens his pipe of tobacco
  With a drink that is named after Mars.

The beer makes his tongue run the quicker
  And as long as his tap never fails
Thus over his favorite liquor
  Old Peter will tell his old tales.
Says he, in my life's ninety summers
  Strange changes & chances I've seen
So here's to all gentlemen-drummers
  That ever have thumped on a skin.

Brought up in the art military
  For four generations we are.
My ancestor drummed for king Harry
  The Huguenot lad of Navarre.
And as each man in life has his station
  According as fortune may fix
While Condé was waving the baton
  My grandsire was trolling the sticks.

Ah! those were the days for commanders
  What glories my grandfather won
Ere bigots & lackies and panders
  The fortunes of France had undone.

No. 690. First Page of Thackeray's Autograph Manuscript of
The Chronicle of the Drum; 1840.
Slightly reduced; original 9 × 4½ inches.

This was the printer's copy. On the back of the eighth page we read: "*Dear Sir: Part II. will come in the first days of January. Call the poem The Chronicle of the Drum. Part I. Truly yrs W. M. T.*" "Part II." begins on p. 10 and ends on p. 20, at the bottom of which is the date "*Paris 1 January.*" On the back of p. 16 we read: "*All*" and the address | *Mr Cunningham | 1 St Martin's Place | Trafalgar Sq^r | London.* | The Paris postmark is dated "31 Dec 40," and the London one "1 Ja 1841."

Laid in is an autograph MS. page from the *Virginians*, beginning " *Chap. 49.*"

This fine martial poem was first printed in *The Second Funeral of Napoleon* (our No. 694), in 1841.

It was separately published, with a portrait and thirty-four illustrations, by Charles Scribner's Sons, at New York, in 1882. There is also an edition with a London imprint, 1886.

[THACKERAY, WILLIAM MAKEPEACE.]

AN ESSAY ON THE GENIUS OF GEORGE CRUIKSHANK. LONDON, Henry Hooper, 1840. [691]

Octavo.

COLLATION BY SIGNATURES: 2 leaves, without signature-marks; A, B, C, each 8 leaves; D, 6 leaves; total 32 leaves.

COLLATION BY PAGINATION: [title] | AN | ESSAY ON THE GENIUS | OF | GEORGE CRUIKSHANK. | WITH NU-MEROUS ILLUSTRATIONS OF HIS WORKS. | *(FROM THE WESTMINSTER REVIEW, No. LXVI.)* | WITH ADDITIONAL ETCHINGS. | HENRY HOOPER, 13 PALL MALL EAST. | MDCCCXL. |, recto of first leaf; — [imprint], verso of first leaf; — | ILLUSTRATIONS. |, pp. [i.]–ii.; — [text, with heading] | GEORGE CRUIK-SHANK'S WORKS. |, pp. [1]–59; — [blank], p. [60].

PLATES: 17 etchings and 39 woodcuts in the text, all by George Cruikshank; as called for in the list of illustrations except that there are two on p. 32.

CONDITION: Size of leaf, 8⅝ × 5⁷⁄₁₆ inches. Bound in the original publisher's green cloth, lettered along the back: | GEORGE CRUIKSHANK |.

REFERENCES.

Williams, *Bibliography*, in Thackeray, *Works* (Biographical Edition, 13 vols.; 1903), 13 : 722; Melville, *Life of Thackeray*, 2 (1899) : 298; Slater, *Early Editions* (1894), p. 319, No. 7; Johnson, *Hints to Collectors* (1885), p. 16, No. VI.; Shepherd, *Bibliography of Thackeray* (1880), p. 11, No. 20.

This is a reprint of an article which appeared in the *Westminster Review* (Vol. 34) for June, 1840, pp. 1–60. It was published in book form immediately after its appearance in the *Review*, and was originally issued in cloth, with uncut edges. It contains one additional plate, while to the list of George Cruikshank's works two books have been added, thus raising the number to 47, if allowance is made for the omission of No. 34 in the numbered list and the inclusion of Bowring's *Minor Morals*, mentioned in the note at the foot of p. ii. Some copies do not contain all the plates, that entitled "Philoprogenitiveneſs" in particular, which in the copies we have seen is printed on white instead of tinted paper, is often lacking.

It was reprinted, with 24 woodcuts and 10 etchings, in Thackeray's *Works* (1879), Vol. 18.

In 1884 the work was again reprinted, with 40 illustrations and with a prefatory note on Thackeray as an artist and art-critic, by W. E. Church.

[THACKERAY, WILLIAM MAKEPEACE.] Meadows, Joseph Kenny.

HEADS OF THE PEOPLE. LONDON, *Robert Tyas*, 1840–1841. 2 vols., octavo, viz.:

[692]

VOL. 1. 1840.

COLLATION BY SIGNATURES: 4 leaves, without signature-marks; A to Z, AA to ZZ, a to d, each 4 leaves; total 204 numbered leaves. Leaf L has no signature-mark.

COLLATION BY PAGINATION: [title] | HEADS OF THE PEOPLE: | OR, | Portraits of the English. | DRAWN BY KENNY MEADOWS. | WITH ORIGINAL ESSAYS BY DISTINGUISHED WRITERS. | LONDON: | ROBERT TYAS, 50 CHEAPSIDE. | MDCCCXL. |, p. [i.]; — [imprint], p. [ii.]; — [preface], pp. [iii.]–vi.; — [contents], pp. [vii.]–viii.; — [text, with heading] | HEADS OF THE PEOPLE. |, pp. [1]–400. The numbers 145 and 146 are omitted in the pagination; and 153 and 154 are repeated.

PLATES: Frontispiece, engraved title-page, and 50 plates, all except the engraved title-page colored by hand; engraved by Orrin Smith, from drawings by Kenny Meadows.

VOL. 2. 1841.

COLLATION BY SIGNATURES: 3 leaves, without signature-marks; A to U, V, W, X, Y, Z, AA to UU, VV, WW, XX, each 4 leaves; [Y], 1 leaf; total 196 numbered leaves. Leaf K is wrongly marked H; and II is H H.

COLLATION BY PAGINATION: [title] | HEADS OF THE PEOPLE: | [5 lines] | ROBERT TYAS, 8 PATERNOSTER ROW. | MDCCCXLI. |, p. [i.]; — [imprint], p. [ii.]; — [preface], pp. [iii.]–iv.; — [contents], pp. [v.]–vi.; — [text, with heading] | HEADS OF THE PEOPLE: | BEING | Portraits of the English. |, pp. [1]–385; — [imprint], p. [386].

PLATES: Frontispiece, engraved title-page, and 56 plates, all except the engraved title-page colored by hand; engraved by Orrin Smith, from drawings by Kenny Meadows.

CONDITION: Size of leaf, 8 7/16 × 5 5/16 inches. Bound from the original parts, in red crushed levant morocco, gilt edges; by Rivière. Vol. 1 has the original wrappers of No. II. and one leaf of publisher's advertisements bound in at the front; and Vol. 2 has the original front wrapper of No. VII., New Series, bound in at the front, and one leaf of publisher's advertisements bound in at the end.

REFERENCES.

Williams, *Bibliography*, in Thackeray, *Works* (Biographical Edition, 13 vols.; 1903), 13 : 733; Melville, *Life of Thackeray*, 2 (1899): 339; Slater, *Early Editions* (1894), p. 319, No. 8; Shepherd, *Bibliography of Thackeray* (1880), pp. 12, 13, Nos. 24–26.

In the copy here described the illustrations have been specially colored by hand.

Among the contributors to the text of this work (a series of sketches by Joseph

Kenny Meadows, the artist) were Douglas Jerrold and Thackeray, the latter of whom wrote three pieces for it:

"Captain Rook and Mr. Pigeon. By William Thackery," Vol. 1, pp. [305]-320;

"The Fashionable Authoress. By William Thackeray," Vol. 2, pp. [73]-84; and

"The Artists. By Michael Angelo Titmarsh," Vol. 2, pp. [161]-176.

These papers were separately printed under the title *Character Sketches* in Thackeray's *Miscellaneous Writings* (1856), Vol. 2; they also appeared in *Novels by Eminent Hands* (our No. 716). "Captain Rook and Mr. Pigeon" had previously appeared in the *Corsair*, September, 1839.

[THACKERAY, WILLIAM MAKEPEACE.]

COMIC TALES AND SKETCHES. London, *Hugh Cunningham*, 1841. 2 vols., large duodecimo, viz.: [693]

VOL. 1.

COLLATION BY SIGNATURES: [A], 4 leaves; B to N, each 12 leaves; O, 6 leaves; total 154 numbered leaves.

COLLATION BY PAGINATION: [title] | COMIC | TALES AND SKETCHES. | EDITED AND ILLUSTRATED | BY | MR. MICHAEL ANGELO TITMARSH, | ... | IN TWO VOLUMES. | VOL. I. | LONDON: | HUGH CUNNINGHAM, ST. MARTIN'S PLACE, | TRAFALGAR SQUARE. | 1841. |, p. [i.]; — [blank], p. [ii.]; — [preface], pp. [iii.]-vii.; — [blank], p. [viii.]; — [text, with heading] | PAPERS BY MR. YELLOWPLUSH, | SOMETIME | FOOTMAN IN MANY GENTEEL FAMILIES. |, pp. [1]-299; — [blank], p. [300].

PLATES: 6 plates, tinted, as follows: engraved title, as frontispiece, and facing pp. 32, 131, 157, 189, and 245.

VOL. 2.

COLLATION BY SIGNATURES: [A], 2 leaves; B to Q, each 12 leaves; R, 5 leaves; total 187 leaves.

COLLATION BY PAGINATION: [title, same as in Vol. 1, except volume-number], recto of [A];—[blank], verso of [A];— [contents], recto of [A 2];—[blank], verso of [A 2];—[text, with heading] | SOME PASSAGES | IN THE | LIFE OF MAJOR GAHAGAN. |, pp. [1]-150; — | THE PROFESSOR. | A TALE OF SENTIMENT. |, pp. 151-183; — [blank], p. [184]; — | THE | BEDFORD-ROW CONSPIRACY. |, pp. [185]-277; — [blank], p. [278]; — | STUBBS'S CALENDAR; | OR, | THE FATAL BOOTS. |, pp. [279]-370.

PLATES: 6 plates, tinted, as follows: facing the title-page and pp. 26, 43, 99, 181, and 220.

CONDITION: Size of leaf, 7⅝ × 4¹¹⁄₁₆ inches. Bound in maroon crushed levant morocco, gilt tops, other edges uncut; by Bradstreet. In the first and fourth leaves of Vol. 1 and the first two leaves of Vol. 2 the quality of the paper differs from that of the rest of the work.

REFERENCES.

Williams, *Bibliography*, in Thackeray, *Works* (Biographical Edition, 13 vols.;

1903), 13 : 722; Melville, *Life of Thackeray*, 2 (1899) : 298; Slater, *Early Editions* (1894), p. 320, No. 10; Johnson, *Hints to Collectors* (1885), p. 17, No. VII.; Shepherd, *Bibliography of Thackeray* (1880), p. 13, No. 27; Reid, *Descriptive Catalogue of the Works of George Cruikshank*, 1 (1871) : 154, Nos. 1930–1941.

The preface is dated "*Paris, 1 April,* 1841."

This work is a collection of papers which had originally appeared in *Fraser's Magazine,* the *New Monthly Magazine, Bentley's Miscellany,* and the *Comic Almanack* for 1839. *The Fatal Boots* as originally published in the *Comic Almanack* for 1839 (our No. 686) was illustrated by Cruikshank.

Nos. 1 to 5 inclusive of the *Yellowplush Papers* were first reprinted from *Fraser's Magazine* in *The Yellowplush Correspondence,* Philadelphia, 1838 (our No. 684); but "Fashnable Fax and Polite Annygoats," which was the first number in that volume, was here omitted, and two new articles added, viz., "Mr. Yellowplush's Ajew" and "Epistles to the Literati."

"This book, like most of Thackeray's early works, did not sell well at first, but after he had made his name as the author of 'Vanity Fair,' the stock was looked up, and a new title-page printed, which refers to the writer as the author of 'Vanity Fair,' &c., and bears no date. Care must therefore be taken to see that the title corresponds *exactly* with that set out above."

[THACKERAY, WILLIAM MAKEPEACE.]

THE SECOND FUNERAL OF NAPOLEON AND THE CHRONICLE OF THE DRUM. LONDON, *Hugh Cunningham,* 1841. [694]

Sixteenmo.

COLLATION BY SIGNATURES : [A], 2 leaves; B to H, each 8 leaves; I, 6 leaves; total 64 leaves.

COLLATION BY PAGINATION : [title, as reproduced; *See* No. 694], recto of [A]; —[blank], verso of [A];—[contents], recto of [A 2];—[blank], verso of [A 2]; —[text, with heading]|MR. TITMARSH TO MISS SMITH|ON|THE SECOND FUNERAL OF NAPOLEON.|, pp. [1]–84;—[half-title]|THE|CHRONICLE OF THE DRUM.|, p. [85];—[blank], p. [86];—[text, with heading]|THE|CHRONICLE OF THE DRUM.|, pp. [87]–122;—[publisher's advertisement]| PREPARING FOR IMMEDIATE PUBLICATION. | DINNER REMINISCENCES : |[6 lines]|, p. [123];—[blank], p. [124].

PLATES : 4 full-page woodcuts; facing the title-page and pp. 40, 58, and 60.

CONDITION : Size of leaf, 5 7/16 × 4 11/16 inches. Bound in the original gray paper wrappers, the front cover with title : | THE SECOND FUNERAL | OF | [vignette of Napoleon lying in state] | AND | THE CHRONICLE OF THE DRUM. | BY MR. M. A. TITMARSH.| LONDON : | HUGH CUNNINGHAM, ST. MARTIN'S PLACE, | TRAFALGAR SQUARE. | ; in green straight-grained morocco solander case. The date in the imprint of the cover title has apparently been cut off.

REFERENCES.

Williams, *Bibliography,* in Thackeray, *Works* (Biographical Edition, 13 vols.; 1903), 13 : 723; Melville, *Life of Thackeray*, 2 (1899) : 298; Slater, *Early Editions* (1894), p. 320, No. 9; Johnson, *Hints to Collectors* (1885), p. 18, No. VIII.; Shepherd, *Bibliography of Thackeray* (1880), p. 13, No. 28.

No. 694   *William Makepeace Thackeray*   1841

THE

SECOND FUNERAL OF NAPOLEON:

In Three Letters

TO MISS SMITH, OF LONDON

AND

THE CHRONICLE OF THE DRUM.

BY

MR. M. A. TITMARSH.

LONDON:
HUGH CUNNINGHAM, ST. MARTIN'S PLACE,
TRAFALGAR SQUARE.
1841.

No. 694.   Title-page of Thackeray's Second Funeral of Napoleon and The Chronicle of the Drum; 1841.

"'Have you read Thackeray's little book — "The Second Funeral of Napoleon?" If not, pray do; and buy it, and ask others to buy it: as each copy sold puts 7½d. in T.'s pocket: which is very empty just now, I take it. I think this book is the best thing he has done.' — Edward Fitzgerald to W. H. Thompson, 18th February 1841."

"The plates are not referred to in the work, and were evidently added after it was written. This little work seems, from the newspaper notices of the period, to have been well received by the press, but we learn, from the prefatory note in No. 73 of 'The Cornhill' (where the pamphlet was reprinted 'from the original MS.,' but with numerous errors), that it was not a success. The British Museum copy is much cut down, but has the cover.

"This is a case where it is of importance to have the cover, as the illustration on it was certainly by Thackeray, and has not been reprinted. It is interesting to compare this sketch of Napoleon with that, also by Thackeray, at p. 43 of Vol. II. of the 'Comic Tales and Sketches,' published the same year, and very soon after this."

The Chronicle of the Drum, the original MS. of which is in the present collection (our No. 690), was reprinted for the first time, with a prefatory note, from the original manuscript in the *Cornhill Magazine* (Vol. 13) for January, 1866.

THACKERAY, WILLIAM MAKEPEACE.

THE IRISH SKETCH-BOOK. LONDON, *Chapman and Hall*, 1843. 2 vols., duodecimo, viz.: [695]

VOL. 1.

COLLATION BY SIGNATURES: [A], 4 leaves; B to O, each 12 leaves; total 160 leaves.

COLLATION BY PAGINATION: [half-title], recto of [A]; — [blank], verso of [A]; — [title] | THE | IRISH SKETCH-BOOK. | BY | MR. M. A. TITMARSH. | WITH NUMEROUS ENGRAVINGS ON WOOD, | DRAWN BY THE AUTHOR. | IN TWO VOLUMES. | VOL. I. | LONDON: | CHAPMAN AND HALL, 186, STRAND. | MDCCCXLIII. |, p. [i.]; — [imprint], p. [ii.]; — | TO DR. CHARLES LEVER, | OF TEMPLEOGUE HOUSE, NEAR DUBLIN. | [signed] | Most sincerely and gratefully yours, | W. M. THACKERAY. | [dated] | LONDON, *April* 27, 1843. |, p. [iii.]; — [blank], p. [iv.]; — [contents], pp. [v.]-vi.; — [text in 15 chapters, the first with heading] | A | SUMMER DAY IN DUBLIN, | OR | THERE AND THEREABOUTS. |, pp. [1]-311; — [imprint], p. [312].

PLATE: 1 plate, from a drawing by Thackeray, with inscription: | A CAR TO KILLARNEY. |; facing the title-page.

There are also 18 woodcuts by Thackeray printed in the text.

VOL. 2.

COLLATION BY SIGNATURES: [A], 4 leaves (the first blank and genuine); B to O, each 12 leaves; P, 8 leaves; total 168 leaves. Leaf 13 (really 15) has no signature-mark.

COLLATION BY PAGINATION: [1 blank leaf], [A]; — [half-title], p. [i.]; — [blank], p. [ii.]; — [title, same as in Vol. 1, except volume-number], p. [iii.]; — [imprint], p. [iv.]; — [contents], pp. [v.]-vi.; — [text, with heading] | THE IRISH SKETCH-BOOK. |, pp. [1]-327; — [note, 4 lines], p. [328].

PLATE: 1 plate, from a drawing by Thackeray, with inscription: | A PLEASURE-BOAT AT THE GIANT'S CAUSEWAY. |; facing the title-page.

There are also 20 woodcuts by Thackeray printed in the text.

CONDITION: Size of leaf, 7$\frac{15}{16}$ × 4$\frac{3}{4}$ inches. Bound in the original publishers' green cloth, lettered on the back: | THE | IRISH | SKETCH BOOK | M. A. TITMARSH | I. [–II.] |.

REFERENCES.

Williams, *Bibliography*, in Thackeray, *Works* (Biographical Edition, 13 vols.; 1903), 13 : 723; Locker-Lampson, *Appendix to Catalogue* (1900), p. 104; Melville, *Life of Thackeray*, 2 (1899) : 299; Slater, *Early Editions* (1894), p. 321, No. 11; Johnson, *Hints to Collectors* (1885), p. 19, No. IX.; Shepherd, *Bibliography of Thackeray* (1880), p. 16, No. 37.

No. 695   *William Makepeace Thackeray*   1843

This, the First Edition of *The Irish Sketch-book*, is illustrated by the author.

In June, 1842, Thackeray visited Ireland, where he made a sort of grand tour, in the course of which he met Charles Lever. *The Irish Sketch-book*, the first of Thackeray's works brought out by Chapman & Hall, was the result of that visit. Like most of his writings, at that time it was signed with his familiar pseudonym, "Michael Angelo Titmarsh"; but the dedication to Charles Lever, dated "London, April 27, 1843," was signed with his real name: "Laying aside for a moment the travelling-title of Mr. Titmarsh, let me . . . subscribe myself, my dear Lever, most sincerely and gratefully yours, W. M. Thackeray."

The first American edition, New York, J. Winchester, with 41 woodcuts, though undated, really appeared the next year (1844).

[THACKERAY, WILLIAM MAKEPEACE.]

MRS. PERKINS'S BALL.   LONDON, *Chapman & Hall*, [1847].   [696]

Pott quarto. First Edition.

COLLATION BY SIGNATURES: A to F, each 4 leaves; total 24 leaves.

COLLATION BY PAGINATION: [engraved title, inserted as a plate] | M^{RS} PERKINS'S BALL | BY M. A. TITMARSH | CHAPMAN & HALL, 186 STRAND. |; —[text in several portions, the first with heading] | THE MULLIGAN (OF BALLYMULLIGAN), | AND HOW WE WENT TO | MRS. PERKINS'S BALL. |, pp. [1]–46; —[blank], p. [47]; —[imprint], p. [48].

Inserted before the title is a half-title, verso blank, as follows: | MRS. PERKINS'S BALL. |.

PLATES: 22 plates, each in two states, colored and uncolored, by the author; as frontispiece, title-page, and facing pp. 3, 7, [11], [13], [15], [17], [19], [21], [23], [25], [27], [29], [31], [33], [35], [37], a two-page plate, between pp. [38] and [39], facing pp. [41], [43], and [45]; all without inscriptions except the uncolored frontispiece.

CONDITION: Size of leaf, 8$\frac{9}{16}$ × 6 inches.

Bound in lavender crushed levant morocco, leather hinges, gilt edges, with lavender moiré doublure and fly-leaves; by Champs. With the original pink glazed paper covers bound in, with title: | M^{RS} PERKINS'S BALL | BY | Mr M. A. *Titmarsh*. | Mrs *Perkins* | At Home | *Friday Evening 19 Dec^{r}* | *Pocklington Square.* | LONDON : | CHAPMAN AND HALL, 186 STRAND. | MDCCCXLVII. | PRICE 7s. 6d. PLAIN; OR, 10s. 6d. COLOURED. |; the whole enclosed by a type-ornament border, with printers' imprint below.

REFERENCES.

Williams, *Bibliography*, in Thackeray, *Works* (Biographical Edition, 13 vols.; 1903), 13:724; Melville, *Life of Thackeray*, 1 (1899):244; same, 2:299; Slater, *Early Editions* (1894), p. 322, No. 14; Locker-Lampson, *Catalogue* (1886), p. 182; Johnson, *Hints to Collectors* (1885), p. 20, No. x.; Shepherd, *Bibliography of Thackeray* (1880), p. 28, No. 75.

"Three editions of this book were published in pink boards, crown 4to, 1847, but the first can be told by reason of the fact that it is the only one which contains no letterpress under the plate facing the title. . . . There are or should be 22 full-page illustrations by the author (including title-page and front). This is one of the well-known 'Christmas Books.'"

1847 — William Makepeace Thackeray — No. 696

This Christmas Book of Thackeray's was first sketched at Malta, in 1844, when he was there in quarantine. It was published the same year as his novel *Vanity Fair*, and was favorably received.

Melville in speaking of it says: "Like its annual successors, *Our Street, Dr. Birch and his Young Friends, The Kickleburys on the Rhine*, it ... was such a success that Thackeray determined to take advantage of its popularity by issuing in book-form, through Messrs. Bradbury & Evans, the *Snob Papers* and *The Great Hoggarty Diamond*. In both these volumes his own name was printed on the title-page; but he had still a sneaking fondness for his favorite pseudonym, and all his Christmas Books, including *The Rose and the Ring*, bore the superscription of M. A. Titmarsh."

The following is a complete list of Thackeray's Christmas Books:

    Mrs. Perkins's Ball, 1847 (our present number).
    Our Street, 1848 (our No. 698).
    Doctor Birch and His Young Friends, 1849 (our No. 700).
    The Kickleburys on the Rhine, 1850 (our No. 704).
    The Rose and the Ring, 1855 (our No. 711).

THACKERAY, WILLIAM MAKEPEACE.

THE BOOK OF SNOBS. London, *Punch Office*, 1848. [697]

Crown octavo.

COLLATION BY SIGNATURES: [A], 4 leaves; B to M, each 8 leaves; N, 2 leaves; total 94 numbered leaves.

COLLATION BY PAGINATION: [publishers' advertisements], pp. [i.]–[ii.]; — [half-title], p. [iii.]; — [blank], p. [iv.]; — [title] | THE | BOOK OF SNOBS. | BY | W. M. THACKERAY, | [2 lines] | [vignette] | LONDON : | PUNCH OFFICE, 85, FLEET STREET. | MDCCCXLVIII. |, p. [v.]; — [imprint], p. [vi.]; — [contents], pp. [vii.]–viii.; — [text, with heading] | THE SNOBS OF ENGLAND. | BY ONE OF THEMSELVES. |, pp. [1]–180.

ILLUSTRATIONS: 65 small woodcuts and initials printed in the text.

CONDITION: Size of leaf, 7¼ x 4¹³⁄₁₆ inches. Bound in the original stiff green paper wrappers, with title: | THE | BOOK OF SNOBS. | [woodcut] | By | W. M. Thackeray. | LONDON : PUNCH OFFICE, 85, FLEET STREET. | [PRICE 2s. 6d.] | ; in a green straight-grained morocco solander case.

REFERENCES.

Dickson, *Bibliography*, in Wilson, *Thackeray in the United States*, 2 (1904) : 239; Williams, *Bibliography*, in Thackeray, *Works* (Biographical Edition, 13 vols.; 1903), 13 : 724; Locker-Lampson, *Appendix to Catalogue* (1900), p. 104; Melville, *Life of Thackeray*, 2 (1899) : 299; Slater, *Early Editions* (1894), p. 323, No. 16; Johnson, *Hints to Collectors* (1885), p. 24, No. XIV.; Shepherd, *Bibliography of Thackeray* (1880), p. 28, No. 76.

This book was issued in green pictorial wrappers, with designs by the author.

It was first printed in *Punch* (Vols. 10–12), from 1846 to 1847, as a serial, with illustrations by the author, under the title "*The Snobs of England. By one of* themselves. With illustrations." When reprinted in book form, seven chapters (xvii. to xxiii., inclusive), chiefly political, were omitted. Thackeray, in a note, gave his reason for their omission, as follows: "On re-perusing these papers, I have found them so stupid, so personal, so snobbish, in a word, that I have withdrawn them from this collection." These suppressed chapters were reprinted in a supplementary volume of his collected works (Vol. 26, 1886).

The *Snob Papers* are written in admirable style, and with a freshness and vigor of portraiture that may be said to have made Thackeray famous. The work was re-issued in Thackeray's *Miscellaneous Writings* (Vol. 1) and also separately in yellow wrappers in 1855.

[THACKERAY, WILLIAM MAKEPEACE.]

"OUR STREET." LONDON, *Chapman and Hall*, 1848. [698]

Superroyal sixteenmo. First Edition.

COLLATION BY SIGNATURES: A to G, each 4 leaves; total 28 leaves.

COLLATION BY PAGINATION: [title, inserted as a plate] | "OUR STREET." | BY | MR. M. A. TITMARSH. | [vignette] | LONDON.| CHAPMAN AND HALL, 186 STRAND. | MDCCCXLVIII. | ; — [text, with heading] | OUR STREET. | , pp. [1]-54; — [publishers' advertisement], p. [55]; — [imprint], p. [56]. Page 21 has no page-number.

PLATES: 16 plates, each in two states, colored and uncolored, by the author, as follows: frontispiece, title-page, and facing pp. 8, 10, [13], [17], [21], [23], 28, 33, 37, [39], 42, 49, 51, and 52. There is also a woodcut on p. 45.

CONDITION: Size of leaf, 7⅛ × 5 9/16 inches. Bound in blue crushed levant morocco, elaborately tooled in gilt, gilt edges, with cadet blue moiré doublure and fly-leaves; by Champs. With the original pink glazed paper covers bound in, with title: | OUR STREET | [vignette, different from inside title] | BY MR. M. A. TITMARSH. | LONDON : | CHAPMAN AND HALL, 186 STRAND. | MDCCCXLVIII. | PRICE 5*s.* PLAIN ; OR, 7*s.* 6*d.* COLOURED. | ; the whole enclosed by a type-ornament border.

REFERENCES.

Wilson, *Thackeray in the United States*, 2 (1904): 107; Williams, *Bibliography*, in Thackeray, *Works* (Biographical Edition, 13 vols.; 1903), 13 : 724; Melville, *Life of Thackeray*, 2 (1899) : 299; Slater, *Early Editions* (1894), p. 323, No. 15; Johnson, *Hints to Collectors* (1885), p. 23, No. XIII.; Shepherd, *Bibliography of Thackeray* (1880), p 33, No. 87.

This was the second of Thackeray's Christmas Books.

It was originally published in pink glazed boards. There were two editions, both published in 1848, the First with colored plates, the Second with the plates plain. No list of plates was issued with the book, and they should be counted to see if they are all present. The illustration on the cover was not repeated.

The original manuscript of about one half of the work is in the collection of Major W. H. Lambert of Philadelphia.

THACKERAY, WILLIAM MAKEPEACE.

VANITY FAIR. LONDON, *Bradbury and Evans*, 1848. [699]

Octavo. First Edition, First Issue.

COLLATION BY SIGNATURES: [A] to Z, AA to RR, each 8 leaves; total 320 numbered leaves. Leaf N has no signature-mark.

COLLATION BY PAGINATION: [blank], p. [i.]; — [publishers' advertisement of *The Great Hoggarty Diamond*], p. [ii.]; — [title, as reproduced; *See* No. 699], p. [iii.]; — [imprint], p. [iv.]; — [dedication], p. [v.]; — [blank], p. [vi.]; — [preface, with heading] | BEFORE THE CURTAIN. |, pp. [vii.] - ix.; — [blank], p. [x.]; — [contents and list of plates], pp. [xi.] - xvi.; — [text, with heading] | VANITY FAIR. | A NOVEL WITHOUT A HERO. |, pp. [1] - 624.

PLATES: 40 plates, as called for in the list of plates; also numerous initials and small woodcuts in the text.

CONDITION: Size of leaf, 8 11/16 x 5½ inches. Bound from the original parts, in blue crushed levant morocco, gilt top, other edges uncut; by Tout. With wrappers and advertising pages on yellow and white paper, in all 74 leaves and 3 slips, bound in at the end, as follows: Nos. I-XX., 12, 4, 4, 2, 4, 2, 2, 2, 2, 2, 2, 2, 4 (1 slip), 2, 4, 6, 4, 10, and 4 (2 slips) leaves respectively. Published in 20 numbered monthly parts (the last a double number), from January, 1847, to July, 1848, in yellow wrappers, at one shilling each, with pictorial title: | [vignette] | VANITY FAIR: | PEN AND PENCIL SKETCHES OF ENGLISH SOCIETY. | BY W. M. THACKERAY, | [2 lines] | LONDON: | PUBLISHED AT THE PUNCH OFFICE, 85, FLEET STREET. | J. MENZIES, EDINBURGH; J. M'LEOD, GLASGOW; J. M'GLASHAN, DUBLIN. | 1847. | [Bradbury & Evans, Printers, Whitefriars.] |.

REFERENCES.

Dickson, *Bibliography*, in Wilson, *Thackeray in the United States*, 2 (1904): 236; Williams, *Bibliography*, in Thackeray, *Works* (Biographical Edition, 13 vols.; 1903), 13: 724; Melville, *Life of Thackeray*, 2 (1899): 299; Slater, *Early Editions* (1894), p. 323, No. 17; Johnson, *Hints to Collectors* (1885), p. 22, No. XII.; Shepherd, *Bibliography of Thackeray* (1880), p. 29, No. 78.

The title on the wrappers differs from that on the title-page. The pictorial title-page was not repeated in the work as afterward published in cloth. This copy is of the earliest issue, and contains two title-pages, one engraved, both with the date 1848, and the illustrated advertisement of *The Great Hoggarty Diamond*, which, however, did not appear until 1849. It has the short title *Vanity Fair* on p. [1] in small rustic open-letter type, and on p. 336 is a woodcut of the Marquis of Steyne. These features appear in no other early issue or edition, the woodcut being suppressed and the type moved up from there to the end of the chapter (pp. 336 - 340) to fill the vacancy so caused.

The wrappers in this copy all have the numbers printed at the upper left-hand corner, "I.]", "II.]", etc., except XIV., XV., XVII., XVIII., and XIX. & XX., which do not have the bracket at their right. Nos. I. - XV. have "[PRICE 1*s*.]" at the upper right-hand corner; Nos. XVI. - XVIII., "PRICE 1*s*."; and Nos. XIX. & XX. (a double number), "PRICE 2*s*." All except XVI., XVIII., and XIX. & XX. have the dates printed at the bottom, viz.: Nos. I. - XII., "1847"; Nos. XIII. - XV., and XVII., "1848." We have seen an unbound copy, in

No. 699   *William Makepeace Thackeray*   1848

VANITY FAIR.

𝔄 Novel without a 𝔥ero.

BY

WILLIAM MAKEPEACE THACKERAY.

WITH ILLUSTRATIONS ON STEEL AND WOOD BY THE AUTHOR.

LONDON:
BRADBURY AND EVANS, 11, BOUVERIE STREET.
1848.

No. 699. Title-page of Thackeray's Vanity Fair; 1st Edition, 1st Issue; 1848.

English Literature   [1064]   Church Catalogue

parts, all with printed numbers and dates, except XVI., which had no printed date. We have also seen a loose wrapper, No. XVII., without a printed date. In later issues wrappers appear to have been printed without numbers or dates, and with pages 2, 3, and 4 blank, the numbers and dates to be filled in with a pen to correspond with the part inserted. The cover reproduced in Melville's *Life of Thackeray* is one of these and is not a first issue. The advertisements on pp. 2, 3, and 4 of the wrappers and on the inserted sheets and slips in the copy here described, with a very few exceptions agree with the list of those given in *The Boston Evening Transcript* (September 2, 1908, p. 19) as belonging to the first issues.

This novel was published the same year (1848), by Harper & Brothers, in New York, in two parts, in green wrappers, with vignette and facsimile of signature on the wrapper, and with engraved title-page and 32 plates.

The history of *Vanity Fair* was almost identical with that of Dickens' *Pickwick Papers:* the earlier numbers failed to attract attention, and the advisability of stopping its publication was seriously considered; but fortunately, later in the year, the sales increased with great rapidity, and the success of the venture was assured. There has been much speculation as to what caused this change. In January, 1848, when more than half the book had already been issued, a favorable notice appeared in the *Edinburgh Review*. "*Vanity Fair*," predicted the reviewer, "is as sure of immortality as ninety-nine hundredths of modern novels are sure of annihilation." Its increased popularity has been thought by some to have been due to this notice in the *Edinburgh Review*, by others to Charlotte Brontë's eulogistic dedication of *Jane Eyre* to Thackeray, and by still others to the success of the first Christmas Book; but it is more likely that it was due to a combination of these favorable events.

"It is curious," observes Mr. Dickson in a private communication, "how much notice has been taken of the omission of the woodcut of the Marquis of Steyne from the second edition of Vanity Fair. Mr. Layard reprinted it in his article on 'Suppressed Plates' in the *Pall Mall Magazine* for July, 1899, and later in the book he made on the subject. Mr. Melville gives it in his *Life of Thackeray* in 1899, while the *Bookman*, London, February, 1903, prints it again, and yet almost any illustrated edition of *Vanity Fair* contains this cut save only the second edition of 1848 and that of 1849. It is in the first Library edition of the Works, 1867, 1869, the de luxe edition of 1878, and the Standard edition of 1883. On the other hand, three of Thackeray's drawings and two full pages of text which appeared on pages 44, 45 of the first and second editions of 1848 and also in the issue of 1849, have been dropped entirely since then and have been printed in no other editions to date. Even the Kensington edition, which claims to be printed from the first edition of all the works, omits this matter, and, as far as I know, no one has called attention to this suppression. As this matter was retained during Thackeray's lifetime, I for one would like to know who had the hardihood to suppress these drawings and these passages after he was dead."

Portions of the original manuscript, about three fourths in all, are in the library of Mr. J. Pierpont Morgan.

[THACKERAY, WILLIAM MAKEPEACE.]

DOCTOR BIRCH AND HIS YOUNG FRIENDS. London, *Chapman and Hall*, 1849. [700]

Superroyal sixteenmo. First Edition.

COLLATION BY SIGNATURES: [A], 2 leaves; B to G, each 4 leaves; [H], 2 leaves; total 28 leaves.

COLLATION BY PAGINATION: [title] | DOCTOR BIRCH | AND | HIS YOUNG FRIENDS. | [vignette] | BY | MR. M. A. TITMARSH. | LONDON: | CHAPMAN AND HALL, 186, STRAND. | 1849. |, recto of [A]; — [imprint], verso of [A]; — [list of illustrations], recto of [A 2]; — [blank], verso of [A 2]; — [text, with heading] | DOCTOR BIRCH. |, pp. [1]-44; — | EPILOGUE. | [in verse], pp. [45]-49; — [imprint], p. [50]; — [publishers' advertisement], p. [51]; — [blank], p. [52].

PLATES: 16 plates, including engraved title-page, by the author; each in two states, colored and uncolored; as called for in the list of illustrations.

Inserted as an extra-illustration is a plate with inscription: | W. M. THACKERAY. | BY HIMSELF. |, a sepia drawing; facing the letterpress title-page.

CONDITION: Size of leaf, 7 7/16 × 5 1/8 inches. Bound in mauve crushed levant morocco, leather hinges, elaborately tooled gilt panelled sides, gilt edges, with mauve moiré doublure and fly-leaves; by Champs. With the original pink glazed paper covers bound in, with title: | DOCTOR BIRCH | AND | HIS YOUNG FRIENDS. | [vignette] | BY MR. M. A. TITMARSH. | WITH SIXTEEN ILLUSTRATIONS BY THE AUTHOR. | LONDON: CHAPMAN & HALL, 186, STRAND. | 1849. |; the whole enclosed by a type-ornament border; also 2 leaves of book advertising matter, published by James Gilbert, mounted on guards, bound in at the end.

REFERENCES.

Williams, *Bibliography*, in Thackeray, *Works* (Biographical Edition, 13 vols.; 1903), 13 : 725; Locker-Lampson, *Appendix to Catalogue* (1900), p. 104; Melville, *Life of Thackeray*, 2 (1899) : 300; Slater, *Early Editions* (1894), p. 325, No. 21; Johnson, *Hints to Collectors* (1885), p. 26, No. XVI.; Shepherd, *Bibliography of Thackeray* (1880), p. 37, No. 102.

This was the third of Thackeray's Christmas Books, the first being *Mrs. Perkins's Ball* (our No. 696). The Epilogue is in verse. Of the original manuscript of this work, about two thirds, including the Epilogue, is in the collection of Major William H. Lambert of Philadelphia.

THACKERAY, WILLIAM MAKEPEACE.

THE HISTORY OF SAMUEL TITMARSH AND THE GREAT HOGGARTY DIAMOND. London, *Bradbury & Evans*, 1849. [701]

Superroyal sixteenmo.

COLLATION BY SIGNATURES: [A], 6 leaves; B to N, each 8 leaves; total 102 leaves.

COLLATION BY PAGINATION: [half-title], p. [i.]; — [blank], p. [ii.]; — [title] | THE HISTORY | OF | SAMUEL TITMARSH | AND | THE GREAT HOGGARTY DIAMOND. | BY | W. M. THACKERAY, | . . . | LONDON: |

1849   *William Makepeace Thackeray*   No. 701

BRADBURY & EVANS, 11, BOUVERIE STREET. | MDCCCXLIX. | , p. [iii.]; —[imprint], p. [iv.]; —[preface, contents, and list of illustrations], pp. [v.]-[xii.]; —[text, with heading] | THE | HISTORY OF SAMUEL TITMARSH | AND | THE GREAT HOGGARTY DIAMOND. | , pp. [1]-189; —[imprint], p. [190]; —[publishers' advertisements], pp. [191]-[192].

PLATES : 10 plates, including engraved title-page and 9 uncolored plates, by the author, as called for in the list of illustrations.

EXTRA-ILLUSTRATED.

Inserted in this work are 2 portraits, as follows :

[1] Sepia drawing by F. Reason, 1886, with inscription : | W. M. THACKERAY. | AGED 53 YEARS | 1864 | ; facing the title-page.

[2] Sepia drawing of Thackeray, seated with mask and jester's bauble ; facing p. [v.].

CONDITION : Size of leaf, 6 13/16 x 4 3/4 inches. Bound in orange crushed levant morocco, leather hinges, gilt edges, with orange moiré doublure and fly-leaves ; by Champs. With the original glazed paper covers bound in, with title : | THE HISTORY | OF | SAMUEL TITMARSH, | AND | THE GREAT HOGGARTY DIAMOND. | [vignette] | BY W. M. THACKERAY. | LONDON : | Bradbury & Evans, 11, bouverie Street. | , the whole enclosed by a green floriated border.

REFERENCES.

Dickson, *Bibliography*, in Wilson, *Thackeray in the United States*, 2 (1904) : 237 ; Williams, *Bibliography*, in Thackeray, *Works* (Biographical Edition, 13 vols.; 1903), 13 : 726 ; Melville, *Life of Thackeray*, 2 (1899) : 300 ; Slater, *Early Editions* (1894), p. 325, No. 20 ; Locker-Lampson, *Catalogue* (1886), p. 182 ; Johnson, *Hints to Collectors* (1885), p. 27, No. XVII. ; Shepherd, *Bibliography of Thackeray* (1880), p. 37, No. 104.

This work originally appeared in *Fraser's Magazine* (Vol. 24), from September to December, 1841, under the title *The History of Samuel Titmarsh and the Great Hoggarty Diamond. Edited and Illustrated by Sam's Cousin, Michael Angelo.*

"The complete work contains two title-pages, the first illustrated and the second plain; a half-title precedes both, with full-page plate, 'The Rosolio,' to face. Unless a copy exactly answers this description it is not complete."

The work was first published in book form in New York by Harper & Brothers, no date, but really 1848, it being No. 122 of *Harper's Library of Select Novels.* This volume follows the original as it appeared in *Fraser's.* Dickson was able to locate but one copy of the New York edition, that in the Boston Athenæum Library. The first London edition, here described, was published February, 1849, in pictorial boards, with numerous illustrations by the author.

"Care should be taken," says Johnson, "to see that both title-pages are present. The cover should be preserved, as it has an illustration on it, not repeated in the book. There are also, at the end, some interesting press notices of 'Vanity Fair' and of the early numbers of 'Pendennis,' which should be preserved."

"The excellencies of this story were quite overlooked by the general reading public. . . . There were, however, a few critics who were less blind than the public, and amongst these was John Stirling, who wrote to his mother : . . . 'I got hold of the two first numbers of *The Hoggarty Diamond*, and read them with extreme delight. What is there better in Fielding or Goldsmith ? The man is a true genius, and . . . might produce masterpieces which would last as long as any we have, and delight millions of unborn readers.'"

No. 702   *William Makepeace Thackeray*   1849

THACKERAY, WILLIAM MAKEPEACE. Bevan, Samuel.

SAND AND CANVAS. LONDON, *Charles Gilpin*, 1849.   [702]

Octavo.
COLLATION BY SIGNATURES : [A], 6 leaves; B to Z, 2A, each 8 leaves; 2B, 2 leaves; total 192 leaves.
COLLATION BY PAGINATION : [title] | SAND AND CANVAS; | A | NARRATIVE OF ADVENTURES IN EGYPT, | WITH A SOJOURN | AMONG THE ARTISTS IN ROME. | BY SAMUEL BEVAN. | LONDON : | CHARLES GILPIN, 5, BISHOPSGATE STREET, WITHOUT. | MDCCCXLIX. |, p. [i.]; — [imprint], p. [ii.]; — [dedication], p. [iii.]; — [blank], p. [iv.]; — [preface and contents], pp. [v.]-xii. ; — [text], pp. [1]-370 ; — [publisher's advertisement], pp. [371]-[372]. Page 185 is wrongly numbered 186.
PLATES : Engraved pictorial title-page, by Herbert White, and 7 full-page woodcuts, by W. C. Harrison, as follows :
[1] | THE AUTHOR'S ENTRY INTO ALEXANDRIA. | ; facing p. 26.

[2] | THE PASHA'S NATIVE BAND. | ; facing p. 36.
[3] | A HALT IN THE DESERT. | ; facing p. 60.
[4] | THE DEAD DROMEDARY. | ; facing p. 120.
[5] | THE "ROUND OF BEEF." | ; facing p. 126.
[6] | ARTISTS ON THE PINCIAN. | ; facing p. 222.
[7] | FRIENDS' MEETING AT ROME. | ; facing p. 348.
There are also 5 woodcuts in the text, on pp. 55, 227, 229, 234, and 246.
CONDITION : Size of leaf, 8⅝ x 5½ inches. Bound in publisher's blue cloth, uncut edges.

REFERENCE.

Williams, *Bibliography*, in Thackeray, *Works* (Biographical Edition, 13 vols.; 1903), 13 : 738.

The Montgomerie Miller copy, with ex-libris.
In this work appeared for the first time Thackeray's ballad "The Three Sailors" (pp. 340-342). An interesting account of the occasion upon which it was written and recited by its author accompanies it as an appropriate setting. The occasion was a holiday dining-party, in which Thackeray, who at the time happened to be in Rome on his return from his journey from Cornhill to Grand Cairo, was voted into the chair. After a considerable portion of the evening had been consumed in long-winded speeches, came "a call for a song from the chair, amid a vociferous shout of 'Viva Titmarsh!' and a deafening clatter of dessert furniture. Our great friend assured us he was unable to sing, but would endeavour to make amends by getting up a recitation, if some one in the mean time would make a beginning. Whilst a few, therefore, on the right of the chair, were tantalizing the company by a tortured version of one of Calcott's glees, the F. C., busy with his tablets under the table, produced the following affecting narrative, of which he soon after delivered himself in a fittingly lugubrious tone of voice. . . . It is needless to say that the recital of M. A. Titmarsh was received with all the applause it merited."
In some copies the plate "The Author's Entry into Alexandria" has a single-

rule border but no title. There being no directions to the binder for the plates, they appear to have been placed without much regard to order in different copies.

The ballad was reprinted in the *North British Review*, Vol. 40 (February, 1864), p. 254, as "Little Billee," by which title it is now best known.

THACKERAY, WILLIAM MAKEPEACE.

THE HISTORY OF PENDENNIS. LONDON, *Bradbury and Evans*, 1849–1850. 2 vols., octavo, viz.: [703]

VOL. 1. 1849.

COLLATION BY SIGNATURES: [A], 4 leaves; B to Z, AA, BB, each 8 leaves; total 196 numbered leaves.

COLLATION BY PAGINATION: [half-title], p. [i.]; — [blank], p. [ii.]; — [title] | THE HISTORY | OF | PENDENNIS. | HIS FORTUNES AND MISFORTUNES, HIS FRIENDS AND HIS | GREATEST ENEMY. | BY | WILLIAM MAKEPEACE THACKERAY. | WITH ILLUSTRATIONS ON STEEL AND WOOD BY THE AUTHOR. | VOL. I. | LONDON: | BRADBURY AND EVANS, 11, BOUVERIE STREET. | 1849. |, p. [iii.]; — ['imprint], p. [iv.]; — [contents and list of plates], pp. [v.]–viii.; — [text, with heading] | PENDENNIS. |, pp. [1]–384.

PLATES: Engraved title-page and 23 engravings, as called for in the list of plates; also numerous initials and woodcuts in the text, all by the author. The plate which should face p. 12 has been bound in this copy as a frontispiece.

VOL. 2. 1850.

COLLATION BY SIGNATURES: [A], 6 leaves; B to Z, AA, each 8 leaves; BB, 2 leaves; total 192 numbered leaves.

COLLATION BY PAGINATION: [title, same as in Vol. 1, except volume-number and date of imprint], p. [i.]; — [imprint], p. [ii.]; — [dedication, preface, contents, and list of plates], pp. [iii.]–xii.; — [text, with heading] | PENDENNIS. |, pp. [1]–372.

Inserted before the title-page is a half-title, | THE | HISTORY OF PENDENNIS. | .

PLATES: Engraved title-page and 23 engravings, as called for in the list of plates; also numerous initials and woodcuts in the text, all by the author. The plate which should face p. 370 is bound in this copy as a frontispiece.

Inserted as an extra-illustration is a pen-and-ink portrait of Dr. John Elliotson from a rare woodcut; laid in to face p. [iii.].

CONDITION: Size of leaf, 8⅝ × 5½ inches. Bound from the original parts, in blue crushed levant morocco, gilt tops, other edges uncut; by Rivière. With wrappers and advertising pages, in all 61 leaves and 1 slip, bound in at the end, as follows: Vol. 1, Nos. I.–XII., 3, 6, 2, 3, 2, 3, 4, 2, 4, 3, 2, and 2 leaves respectively; Vol. 2, Nos. XIII.–XXIV., 2, 2, 2, 2, 2, 2, 2, 2, 2, 3, and 4 (1 slip) leaves respectively. Originally published in 24 numbered monthly parts (the last a double number), from November, 1848, to December, 1850, in yellow wrappers, at one shilling each, with title: | THE HISTORY | OF | PENDENNIS. | [vignette by Thackeray] | HIS FORTUNES AND MISFORTUNES, | HIS FRIENDS AND HIS GREATEST ENEMY. | BY | W. M. THACKERAY, | . . . | LONDON: BRADBURY & EVANS, 11, BOUVERIE STREET. | J. MENZIES, EDINBURGH; T. MURRAY, GLASGOW; AND J. M'GLASHAN, DUBLIN. | Bradbury & Evans,] 1848 [–1850] [Printers, Whitefriars. | .

No. 703   *William Makepeace Thackeray*   1849-50

REFERENCES.

Dickson, *Bibliography*, in Wilson, *Thackeray in the United States*, 2 (1904): 237; Williams, *Bibliography*, in Thackeray, *Works* (Biographical Edition, 13 vols.; 1903), 13:726; Melville, *Life of Thackeray*, 2 (1899):300; Slater, *Early Editions* (1894), p. 324, No. 19; Johnson, *Hints to Collectors* (1885), p. 25, No. xv.; Shepherd, *Bibliography of Thackeray* (1880), p. 36, No. 99.

This work was originally issued in parts. After the appearance of the eleventh number (dated September, 1849) the publication was suspended during three months on account of the illness of the writer. The twelfth number, therefore, bears the date of January, 1850. On its completion it was issued in two volumes in cloth. The illustration of the pictorial title-page when repeated on the inside varies considerably from that on the wrappers. The preface is dated "Kensington, Nov. 26th, 1850."

Pendennis was published in New York by Harper & Brothers, in eight parts, from 1849 to 1850, with 113 woodcuts and the vignettes on the wrappers. "The title-pages furnished with parts iv. and viii.," says Dickson, "are dated 1850. None of the parts are dated and all of the records of Harper & Brothers were destroyed by fire in 1853. 'Littell's Living Age,' under date of October 27, 1849, acknowledges the receipt of parts i. and ii. This edition contains all the woodcuts of the first London edition, but none of the plates. Vol. i., as made up from the parts, contained thirty-nine chapters, but when Mr. Thackeray revised his work for publication in book form, he cut out a portion of chapter xvi., and a still larger portion of chapter xvii., and consolidated the two into one, leaving but thirty-eight chapters in all, and sacrificing at the same time two illustrations. The New York edition of 1850 contains all these suppressed paragraphs and the two illustrations, which are, however, omitted from all later editions published in either England or America. The missing sketches are on pages 157 and 158 of the New York edition, and on pages 149 and 150 of the London edition."

[THACKERAY, WILLIAM MAKEPEACE.]

THE KICKLEBURYS ON THE RHINE. LONDON, *Smith, Elder, & Co.*, 1850.   [704]

Superroyal sixteenmo.   First Edition.

COLLATION BY SIGNATURES: [A], 2 leaves; B to F, each 8 leaves; G, 5 leaves; total 47 leaves.

COLLATION BY PAGINATION: [half-title], recto of [A]; — [blank], verso of [A]; — [title, inserted as a plate] | THE KICKLEBURYS | ON THE RHINE. | [vignette] | BY MR. M. A. TITMARSH. | LONDON : SMITH, ELDER, & CO., | 65, CORNHILL. | MDCCCL. | ; — [list of illustrations], recto of [A 2]; — [blank], verso of [A 2]; — [text, with heading] | THE | KICKLEBURYS ON THE RHINE. |, pp. [1] – 87; — [blank], p. [88]; — [publishers' advertisements], pp. [89] – [90].

PLATES: 15 plates, including vignette title-page, each in two states, colored and uncolored, by Thackeray; as called for in the list of illustrations.

1850   *William Makepeace Thackeray*   No. 704

Inserted is the preface of the Second Edition, 8 leaves, pages [i.]–xv., p. xvi. being blank, with heading : | PREFACE TO THE SECOND EDITION | BEING | AN ESSAY ON THUNDER AND SMALL BEER. | [signed] | M. A. TITMARSH. | [dated] | *January* 5. | ; preceding the text. Inserted as an extra-illustration is also a stipple portrait of Thackeray, by B. Lander; facing p. [i.] of the inserted preface.

CONDITION : Size of leaf, 7 x 5⅛ inches. Bound in pink crushed levant morocco, leather hinges, elaborately tooled gilt panelled sides, gilt edges, with pink moiré doublure and fly-leaves; by Champs. With the original pink glazed paper covers bound in, with title : | THE KICKLEBURYS | ON | THE RHINE. | [vignette] | BY MR. M. A. TITMARSH. | LONDON : SMITH, ELDER, & CO., 65 CORNHILL. | MDCCCL. | PRICE 5*s*. PLAIN ; OR 7*s*. 6*d*. COLOURED. | ; the whole enclosed by a type-ornament border.

REFERENCES.

Williams, *Bibliography*, in Thackeray, *Works* (Biographical Edition, 13 vols.; 1903), 13 : 726; Locker-Lampson, *Appendix to Catalogue* (1900), p. 105 ; Melville, *Life of Thackeray*, 2 (1899) : 301 ; Slater, *Early Editions* (1894), p. 326, No. 23 ; Johnson, *Hints to Collectors of Original Editions of the Works of William Makepeace Thackeray* (1885), p. 30, No. xx.

This was Thackeray's fourth Christmas Book. Inserted in this copy are the pages containing the preface to the Second Edition, published in 1851. This preface, "being an Essay on Thunder and Small Beer," was written in answer to the famous criticism which appeared in the *Times*, probably from the pen of Samuel Phillips, the author of the now almost forgotten novel *Caleb Stukely*. The *Times*' review was absurd in the highest degree, and Thackeray's reply to it was written in so scathing and severe a tone, though in so intensely amusing a manner, that it is difficult to believe it came from his pen.

[THACKERAY, WILLIAM MAKEPEACE.]

REBECCA AND ROWENA. LONDON, *Chapman and Hall*, 1850.   [705]

Superroyal sixteenmo. First Edition.

COLLATION BY SIGNATURES : [A] to O, each 4 leaves ; total 56 leaves.

COLLATION BY PAGINATION : [half-title], p. [i.] ; — [blank], p. [ii.] ; — [title] | REBECCA | AND | ROWENA. | A | ROMANCE UPON ROMANCE | BY MR. M. A. TITMARSH. | [vignette] | WITH ILLUSTRATIONS BY RICHARD DOYLE. | LONDON : | CHAPMAN AND HALL, 186, STRAND. | 1850. | [the first 5 lines engraved], p. [iii.] ; — [imprint], p. [iv.] ; — [preface and contents], pp. [v.]–viii. ; — [text, with heading] | REBECCA AND ROWENA. |, pp. [1]–102 ; — [publishers' advertisement], p. [103] ; — [blank], p. [104].

PLATES : 8 plates, each in two states, colored and uncolored, by Richard Doyle ; facing the title-page and pp. 30, 39, 42, 54, 76, 80, and 84. Also 2 woodcuts in the text by the same artist.

EXTRA-ILLUSTRATED.

Inserted in this work are 3 portraits, as follows :

[1] | W. M. *Thackeray* | ENGRAVED BY SARTAIN. — THE ORIGINAL BY S. LAWRENCE. | ; facing the title-page.

[2] Pen-and-ink portrait of Dr. Elliotson, by H. Lindsay ; facing p. [v.].

[3] Pen-and-ink portrait of Richard Doyle, by H. Lindsay ; facing p. vi.

CONDITION : Size of leaf, 7 1/16 x 5 9/16

No. 705   *William Makepeace Thackeray*   1850

inches. Bound in blue crushed levant morocco, leather hinges, gilt edges, with blue moiré doublure and fly-leaves; by Champs. With the original pink glazed paper pictorial covers bound in, with title: | REBECCA | AND | ROWENA | A | ROMANCE UPON ROMANCE. | [vignette] | Mʳ MICHAEL ANGELO TITMARSH | ILLUSTRATED BY RICHARD DOYLE. | LONDON: | CHAPMAN AND HALL, 186, STRAND. | 1850. | *Price 5s. plain, or 7s. 6d. coloured.* | [all but the last 4 lines engraved].

REFERENCES.

Dickson, *Bibliography*, in Wilson, *Thackeray in the United States*, 2 (1904): 235; Williams, *Bibliography*, in Thackeray, *Works* (Biographical Edition, 13 vols.; 1903), 13:726; Locker-Lampson, *Appendix to Catalogue* (1900), p. 105; Melville, *Life of Thackeray*, 2 (1899): 300; Slater, *Early Editions* (1894), p. 326, No. 22; Johnson, *Hints to Collectors* (1885), p. 28, No. XVIII.; Shepherd, *Bibliography of Thackeray* (1880), p. 40, No. 111.

This work was originally published in pink pictorial boards, the illustration on the cover not being repeated in the work itself. The illustration on the title-page is generally left uncolored, even when the plates are colored.

"In some of the parts of 'David Copperfield,'" says Johnson, "an interesting advertisement of this book is to be found, giving, as a kind of second title, 'A Story for Christmas (and indeed any other season), containing Perilous Adventures, Tremendous Battles, Tender Love-making, Profound Historical Knowledge, and a (tolerably) happy ending.' This is dated 1st December, 1849."

Rebecca and Rowena was written as a continuation of Scott's *Ivanhoe*. The preface is dated "Kensington, December 20th, 1849." Owing to an illness of the author, the illustrations were made by Richard Doyle, then twenty-six years of age. Proposals for a continuation of *Ivanhoe* in "A letter to Monsieur Alexander Dumas by Monsieur Angelo Titmarsh" appeared in *Fraser's Magazine* (Vol. 34), August and September, 1846. It was reprinted in *Littell's Living Age* (Vols. 10 and 11) for September 12 and October 10, 1846. This is the foundation of *Rebecca and Rowena*, which contains material alterations. The original has never been reprinted in English, but it was translated into Spanish and published at Madrid in 1882.

THACKERAY, WILLIAM MAKEPEACE.   Marvy, Louis.

SKETCHES AFTER ENGLISH LANDSCAPE PAINTERS.   LONDON, David Bogue, [1850?].   [706]

Quarto

COLLATION BY SIGNATURES: 23 unnumbered leaves, without signature-marks.

COLLATION BY PAGINATION: [title] | SKETCHES | AFTER | ENGLISH LANDSCAPE PAINTERS. | BY | L. MARVY. | WITH SHORT NOTICES BY W. M. THACKERAY. | LONDON: | DAVID BOGUE, 86, FLEET STREET. |, p. [1]; —[imprint], p. [2]; —[preface], p. [3]; —[blank], p. [4]; —[contents], p. [5]; —[blank], p. [6]; —

[text in numerous parts, the first with heading] | SIR AUGUSTUS WALL CALLCOTT. |, pp. [7]-[46].

PLATES: 20 plates, as called for in the contents.

CONDITION: Size of leaf, 12⅜ × 9⅛ inches. Bound in green crushed levant morocco, gilt edges; by Rivière.

REFERENCES.

Melville, *Life of Thackeray*, 2 (1899): 219, *note*; Johnson, *Hints to Collectors* (1885), p. 29, No. XIX.; Shepherd, *Bibliography of Thackeray; a Bibliographical List arranged in Chronological Order* (1880), p. 41, No. 113.

A later edition of this work, also undated, bears the imprint of Richard Griffin.

The letterpress consists of a preface and twenty short biographical notices of eminent painters. The volume is unpaged.

"During 1848, Louis Marvy, a young French artist, in whose *atelier* in Paris, and with whose family Thackeray had spent many happy hours, fled to England to take refuge from the revolutionary storm. Here he had engraved some *Sketches after English Landscape Painters*, hoping, by this means, to obtain enough money to enable him to pursue his more ambitious designs. The publisher to whom the engraving had been submitted would not entertain the proposal of the skilful but unknown painter, unless the letterpress was written by Thackeray, who agreed readily enough, and furnished a number of short notices of Turner, Calcott, Redgrave, Cattermole, Constable, Gainsborough, and other famous painters."

"Thackeray," says Dr. John Brown, "was one of the best of art-critics. . . . It would not be easy to imagine better criticisms of art than those from Mr. Thackeray's hand. . . . He is more objective, cool, and critical than Mr. Ruskin."

THACKERAY, WILLIAM MAKEPEACE.

THE HISTORY OF HENRY ESMOND. LONDON, *for Smith, Elder, & Company*, 1852. 3 vols., crown octavo, viz.: [707]

VOL. I.

COLLATION BY SIGNATURES: [A], 4 leaves; *b*, B to X, each 8 leaves; total 172 numbered leaves.

COLLATION BY PAGINATION: [half-title] | ESMOND. | A STORY OF QUEEN ANNE'S REIGN. | BY | W. M. THACKERAY, | *Author of " Vanity Fair," " Pendennis," &c.* | VOLUME I. | ☞ The Author of this work gives notice that he reserves to | himself the right of tranflating it. |, p. [1]; —[blank], p. [2]; —[title] |THE HISTORY | OF | HENRY ESMOND, ESQ. | A COLONEL IN THE SERVICE OF HER MAJESTY | Q. ANNE. | WRITTEN BY HIMSELF. | [Latin quotation]

| IN THREE VOLUMES. | VOLUME THE FIRST. | *LONDON:* | PRINTED FOR SMITH, ELDER, & COMPANY, | OVER AGAINST ST. PETER'S CHURCH IN CORNHILL, | 1852. |, p. [3]; —[imprint], p. [4]; —[dedication], p. [5]; —[blank], p. [6]; —[contents], pp. [7]-8; —[preface], pp. [9]-21; —[blank], p. [22]; —[half-title] | BOOK I. | THE EARLY YOUTH OF HENRY ESMOND, UP TO | THE TIME OF HIS LEAVING TRINITY | COLLEGE, IN CAMBRIDGE. |, p. [23]; —[blank], p. [24]; —[text, with heading] | THE HISTORY | OF | HENRY ESMOND. | BOOK THE FIRST. |, pp. [25]-344.

VOL. 2.

COLLATION BY SIGNATURES: [A], 4 leaves (the first blank and genuine); B to X, each 8 leaves; total 164 leaves.

COLLATION BY PAGINATION: [1 blank leaf], [A];—[half-title], p. [i.];—[blank], p. [ii.];—[title, same as in Vol. 1, except volume-number], p. [iii.];—[imprint], p. [iv.];—[contents], pp. [v.]–vi.;—[half-title] | BOOK II. | CONTAINS MR. ESMOND'S MILITARY LIFE AND | OTHER MATTERS APPERTAINING TO THE | ESMOND FAMILY. |, p. [1];—[blank], p. [2];—[text], pp. [3]–319;—[blank], p. [320].

VOL. 3.

COLLATION BY SIGNATURES: [A], 4 leaves (the first blank and genuine); B to X, each 8 leaves; Y, 2 leaves; total 166 leaves.

COLLATION BY PAGINATION: [1 blank leaf], [A];—[half-title], p. [i.];—[blank], p. [ii.];—[title, same as in Vol. 1, except volume-number], p. [iii.];—[imprint], p. [iv.];—[contents], pp. [v.]–vi.;—[half-title] | BOOK III. | CONTAINING THE END OF MR. ESMOND'S | ADVENTURES IN ENGLAND. |, p. [1];—[blank], p. [2];—[text], pp. [3]–324.

CONDITION: Size of leaf, 7 9/16 x 5 inches. Bound in the original brown cloth, uncut edges, with white paper title-labels, lettered: | ESMOND. | A Story of Queen Anne's | Reign. | BY | W. M. THACKERAY. | IN THREE VOLS. | VOL. I. [–III.] | SMITH, ELDER, & Co., | 65, Cornhill. |.

With publishers' catalogue, 16 numbered pages, with heading, | A | CATALOGUE OF BOOKS | [2 lines] | PUBLISHED BY | SMITH, ELDER AND CO., |, bound in at the end of Vol. 3.

REFERENCES.

Williams, *Bibliography*, in Thackeray, *Works* (Biographical Edition, 13 vols.; 1903), 13 : 727 (the note "*Fraser's Magazine*" belongs to *The Luck of Barry Lyndon*, on the next page); Melville, *Life of Thackeray*, 2 (1899) : 301; Slater, *Early Editions* (1894), p. 326, No. 24; Sinker, *Library of Trinity College, Cambridge* (1891), p. 36; Locker-Lampson, *Catalogue* (1886), p. 183; Johnson, *Hints to Collectors* (1885), p. 31, No. XXI.; Shepherd, *Bibliography of Thackeray* (1880), p. 42, No. 117.

The Locker-Lampson copy, with ex-libris.

This is the First Edition of *Henry Esmond*, Thackeray's masterpiece, which ranks among the greatest works of historical fiction of any age or country. It was originally issued in cloth with white labels, and was published in America the same year.

Inserted in Vol. 1 of this copy is an autograph letter by Thackeray, dated "*Kensington Sep.r 16. 1848*," as follows: "*Dear M.rs Alexander, I get so many applications of the nature of the enclosed that I have made a vow not to answer them. It looks very conceited to be sending about autographs and I don't like being made a Lion of. But if you choose to send any note of mine (this one for example) to gratify a young lady who is no doubt very pretty & accomplished & has, I am sure, a remarkable good taste there is nothing I know to prevent you so that the matter rests entirely with you, and not with* [signed] *Yours very sincerely* | *W M Thackeray*."

The complete manuscript of *Esmond*, partly, and that very largely, in his own writing, partly in that of his daughter, and partly in that of another amanuensis, is in the library of Trinity College, Cambridge. Sinker, in his *Library of Trinity College, Cambridge*, gives a facsimile page (facing p. 115) of this precious manuscript.

THACKERAY, WILLIAM MAKEPEACE.

THE HISTORY OF HENRY ESMOND. LONDON, *for Smith, Elder, & Company*, 1852. 3 vols., crown octavo, viz. : [707 A]

VOL. 1.

COLLATION BY SIGNATURES: Identically the same as in our preceding number.

COLLATION BY PAGINATION: Identically the same as in our preceding number.

EXTRA-ILLUSTRATED.

Inserted in this volume are 2 portraits, 3 plates, and 8 vignettes, as follows:

PORTRAITS: [1] | *W. M. Thackeray.* | ; etched by Hollyer, with facsimile signature; facing the title-page.

[2] | QUEEN ANNE. | ; engraved by Cochran, after Kneller, published Dec. 1, 1836; facing p. [5].

PLATES: 3 full-page illustrations, after drawings by Du Maurier, engraved by Swain; facing pp. 36, 221, and 337.

VIGNETTES: 8 vignettes, after drawings by Du Maurier, engraved by Swain; mounted to size and facing pp. 63, 70, 115, 177, 206, 241, 263, and 292.

VOL. 2.

COLLATION BY SIGNATURES: Identically the same as in our preceding number.

COLLATION BY PAGINATION: Identically the same as in our preceding number.

EXTRA-ILLUSTRATED.

Inserted in this volume are 3 portraits, 1 plate, and 9 vignettes, as follows:

PORTRAITS: [1] | *W. M. Thackeray* | ; engraved by Alais, with facsimile signature; on India paper; facing the title-page.

[2] | *Sir Richard Steele.* | ; engraved by Bragg, after Richardson, published September, 1821; facing p. 30.

[3] | ADDISON. | ; engraved by Holl; inlaid to size and facing p. 192.

PLATE: | BEATRIX | ; engraved by Swain, after a drawing by Du Maurier; facing p. 115.

VIGNETTES: 9 vignettes engraved by Swain, after drawings by Du Maurier; mounted to size and facing pp. 5, 24, 45, 70, 106, 171, 196, 285, and 313.

VOL. 3.

COLLATION BY SIGNATURES: Identically the same as in our preceding number.

COLLATION BY PAGINATION: Identically the same as in our preceding number.

EXTRA-ILLUSTRATED.

Inserted in this volume are 2 portraits, 4 plates, and 7 vignettes, as follows:

PORTRAITS: [1] | *W. M. Thackeray* | ; etching with facsimile signature; facing the title-page.

[2] | *James Stuart* | ; engraved by Freeman, published at Glasgow; facing p. 292.

PLATES: 4 plates, engraved by Swain, after drawings by Du Maurier; facing pp. 28, 121, 220, and 316.

VIGNETTES: 7 vignettes, engraved by Swain, after drawings by Du Maurier; mounted to size and facing pp. 53, 84, 157, 178, 190, 260, and 301.

CONDITION: Size of leaf, $7\frac{3}{8} \times 4\frac{15}{16}$ inches. Bound in wine-colored crushed levant morocco, gilt tops, other edges uncut; by Bradstreet. With 1 unnumbered leaf of publishers' advertisement and 8 numbered leaves of book catalogue, bound in at the end of the third volume, the first with heading: | JUST PUBLISHED, | In One Volume, crown 8vo, price 10*s*. 6*d*. | THE SCHOOL FOR FATHERS. | An Old English Story. | BY T. GWYNNE. |, and the publishers' book catalogue dated "*October* 1852."

THACKERAY, WILLIAM MAKEPEACE.

THE ENGLISH HUMOURISTS OF THE EIGHTEENTH CENTURY.
LONDON, *Smith, Elder, & Co.*, 1853. [708]

Crown octavo. First English Edition. COLLATION BY SIGNATURES: [A], 4 leaves; B to X, each 8 leaves; Y, 4 leaves; total 168 leaves.

COLLATION BY PAGINATION: [half-title], recto of [A]; — [blank], verso of [A]; — [title] | THE | ENGLISH HU-MOURISTS | OF THE | EIGHTEENTH CENTURY. | A Series of Lectures, | DE-LIVERED IN ENGLAND, SCOTLAND, AND THE UNITED STATES OF | AMERICA. | BY | W. M. THACKERAY, | . . . | LONDON : | SMITH, ELDER, & CO. 65, CORNHILL. | BOMBAY: SMITH, TAYLOR, & CO. | 1853. | [*The author of this work reserves to himself the right of authorising* | *a translation of it.*] | , recto of [A 2]; — [imprint], verso of [A 2]; — [contents], recto of [A 3]; — [blank], verso of [A 3]; — | ERRATA. | [17 lines] | , recto of [A 4]; — [blank], verso of [A 4]; — [text, with heading] | THE ENGLISH HUMOURISTS | OF THE | EIGHTEENTH CENTURY. | , pp. [1]-322 ; — [press notices of *Esmond*], pp. [323]-[328].

EXTRA-ILLUSTRATED.

Inserted in this work are 68 portraits, 35 of them India proofs.

CONDITION: Size of leaf, $7\frac{5}{16}$ × $4\frac{7}{8}$ inches. Bound in blue crushed levant morocco, gilt top, other edges uncut; by Rivière. With publishers' catalogue, 8 numbered leaves, dated "*June* 1853," bound in at the end.

REFERENCES.

Dickson, *Bibliography*, in Wilson, *Thackeray in the United States*, 2 (1904): 243; Williams, *Bibliography*, in Thackeray, *Works* (Biographical Edition, 13 vols.; 1903), 13: 731; Melville, *Life of Thackeray*, 1 (1899): 274; 2: 301; Slater, *Early Editions* (1894), p. 327, No. 25; Johnson, *Hints to Collectors* (1885), p. 32, No. XXII.; Shepherd, *Bibliography of Thackeray* (1880), p. 42, No. 118.

The copy here described is the First English Edition. At the end are a number of interesting press notices of *Esmond*, which should be preserved. The Second Edition has the same date, but contains the words "Second Edition" on the title-page.

In addition to the lectures contained in this, the First English Edition, an American edition, published the same year, by Harper & Brothers, New York, includes an additional lecture on "Charity and Humour," which was first delivered in New York on behalf of a charity.

The English Humourists and *The Four Georges* (notwithstanding some objections were raised to the latter at the time they were delivered) have both taken their place in the classical literature of the nineteenth century.

"The *raison d'être* of the lectures was the desire [of Thackeray] to make a good provision for his wife and daughters; and the subject selected seems only natural since his great fondness for the Queen Anne writers dates back to the early years of his life. Allusions to Steele and Addison and Pope and Swift, and Stella, Venessa [*sic*], Dr. Johnson, Richard Savage, and others, real or unreal, may be found in some of his earliest writings, especially in *Catherine* and *Barry Lyndon*."

The original manuscript of the lecture on Swift is in the collection of Major W. H. Lambert of Philadelphia.

THACKERAY, WILLIAM MAKEPEACE.

THE NEWCOMES. LONDON, *Bradbury and Evans*, 1854–1855. 2 vols., octavo, viz.: [709]

VOL. 1. 1854.

COLLATION BY SIGNATURES: [A], *b*, each 2 leaves; B to Z, AA, each 8 leaves; BB, 6 leaves; total 194 leaves.

COLLATION BY PAGINATION: [half-title], p. [i.]; —[blank], p. [ii.]; —[title] | THE NEWCOMES. | MEMOIRS OF A MOST RESPECTABLE FAMILY. | EDITED BY | ARTHUR PENDENNIS, ESQ. | WITH ILLUSTRATIONS ON STEEL AND WOOD BY RICHARD DOYLE. | VOL. I. | LONDON: | BRADBURY AND EVANS, 11, BOUVERIE STREET. | 1854. |, p. [iii.]; — [imprint], p. [iv.]; —[contents and list of plates], pp. [v.]–viii.; —[text, with heading] | THE NEWCOMES. |, pp. [1]–380.

PLATES: Engraved pictorial title-page and 23 engravings, as called for in the list of plates; also numerous initials and woodcuts in the text; all by Richard Doyle.

VOL. 2. 1855.

COLLATION BY SIGNATURES: [A], 4 leaves; B to Z, AA, each 8 leaves; BB, 4 leaves; total 192 numbered leaves. Leaf R2 is wrongly marked R.

COLLATION BY PAGINATION: [half-title], p. [i.]; —[blank], p. [ii.]; —[title, same as in Vol. 1, except volume-number and date of imprint], p. [iii.]; —[imprint], p. [iv.]; —[contents and list of plates], pp. [v.]–viii.; —[text], pp. [1]–375; —[blank], p. [376].

PLATES: Engraved pictorial title-page and 23 engravings, as called for in the list of plates; also numerous initials and woodcuts in the text; all by Richard Doyle.

CONDITION: Size of leaf, $8\frac{11}{16}$ × $5\frac{1}{2}$ inches. Bound from the original parts, in blue crushed levant morocco, gilt tops, other edges uncut; by Rivière. With wrappers and advertising pages, in all 55 leaves, bound in at the end, as follows: Vol. 1, Nos. 1–12, 2, 2, 4, 2, 3, 3, 2, 2, 2, 2, 2, and 3 leaves respectively; Vol. 2, Nos. 13–23, 2, 4, 3, 3, 2, 2, 2, 2, 2, 2, and 2 leaves respectively. Originally published in 24 numbered monthly parts (the last a double number), from October, 1853, to August, 1855, in yellow wrappers, at one shilling each, with pictorial title designed by Richard Doyle: | MR. THACKERAY'S NEW MONTHLY WORK. | THE | NEWCOMES | MEMOIRS | OF | A MOST | Respectable | FAMILY | EDITED BY | ARTHUR PENDENNIS ESQ^{re} | ILLUSTRATED BY RICHARD DOYLE. | LONDON: BRADBURY AND EVANS, 11, BOUVERIE STREET. | 1853 [–1855]. | .

REFERENCES.

Dickson, *Bibliography*, in Wilson, *Thackeray in the United States*, 2 (1904): 243, 244; Anne Thackeray Ritchie, *Introduction* to *The Newcomes* (Biographical Edition, 13 vols.; 1903), p. xxxix.; Locker-Lampson, *Appendix to Catalogue* (1900), p. 105; Williams, *Bibliography*, in Thackeray, *Works* (Biographical Edition, 13 vols.; 1903), 13:731; Melville, *Life of Thackeray*, 2 (1899): 4, 301; Slater, *Early Editions* (1894), p. 327, No. 26; Johnson, *Hints to Collectors* (1885), p. 33, No. XXIII.; Shepherd, *Bibliography of Thackeray* (1880), p. 43, No. 121.

This novel originally appeared in parts, and was afterward published in two volumes in slate-colored cloth, but the design on the wrappers was not repeated. It also appeared in *Harper's Magazine* (Vols. 7–11), from November, 1853, to October,

No. 709   *William Makepeace Thackeray*   1854-55

1855, with the exception of March, 1854, with 113 woodcuts; after which it was published in book form in two volumes, in 1855, with 133 woodcuts.

"There is another cry of 'suppressed plate' in *The Newcomes*. Mr. Eyre Crowe in *With Thackeray in America*, p. 174, states that Thackeray was much displeased at one of Doyle's cuts which represented the Charterhouse boys playing marbles, and the irate author is stated to have exclaimed, 'Why, they would as soon have thought of cutting off their heads as play marbles at the Charterhouse.' 'This wood-cut was, I noticed,' says Mr. Crowe, 'suppressed altogether in subsequent editions.' Mr. Walter Jerrold quotes this anecdote in his introduction to *The Newcomes*, London, Dent, 1902, pp. viii., ix., and adds, without quotation marks, 'The offending illustration — along with many other delightful drawings in the text and illustrative chapter initials — is not to be found in subsequent issues of the story.' As a matter of fact, I know of no edition pretending to contain the original illustrations that omits this drawing. It is in Vol. I., p. 35 of the first edition of 1854, and on the same page of the second edition of 1855, and it is on page 43 of both the Library edition of 1869 and the edition de luxe of 1878. What Mr. Jerrold means by his reference to other delightful drawings being missing in subsequent issues I do not know, for the Library edition of Vol. III., 1869, has all the 51 drawings of the first edition and contains in addition two drawings by Doyle not to be found in either the first edition or the second. One is of Clive walking with children on page 41, and the other is the cut on the last page of the volume." — DICKSON (in a private communication).

Wilson says in his *Thackeray in the United States* (2:92) that during Thackeray's second visit to America Dr. Henry W. Bellows in conversation with him regarding *The Newcomes* said, "'You have constructed your Colonel Newcome out of two characters already familiar to all students of good literature, — Don Quixote and Sir Roger de Coverley.' Thackeray started. 'You have touched on the very truth,' said he. 'I had been reading the Don's memoirs and the Sir Roger papers in the "Spectator" just before attacking that last task. I tried to make the Colonel a creation of my own, but I was conscious all the while that my beloved old heroes were blending in my mind. No one else has guessed it, so far as I know.'"

"Northern reviewers," says Mrs. Ritchie, "were generally favourable to him. 'Thackeray's peculiar style,' says this one [Burne Jones], 'reaches perfection in the "Newcomes," and to appreciate it properly, the degrees through which this writer has passed should be examined.' He then proceeds to compare my father to Fielding, 'whose breadth of treatment, impossible for the modern novelist, is represented in Mr. Thackeray's works by a subtlety of handling which is almost equally admirable.'"

The manuscript of *The Newcomes*, which is preserved at Charterhouse (Godalming) in the Museum, is partly in Thackeray's handwriting, partly in that of his eldest daughter, and partly in that of Mr. Eyre Crowe. This novel was written in the interval between Thackeray's two visits to America, the preface having been begun July 7, 1853, and the very last page, according to Mrs. Ritchie, having been written at Paris, June 20, 1855.

THACKERAY, WILLIAM MAKEPEACE.

BALLADS. London, *Bradbury & Evans*, 1855. [710]

Crown octavo. First Edition.

COLLATION BY SIGNATURES: [A], 2 leaves; B to L, each 8 leaves; total 82 leaves.

COLLATION BY PAGINATION: [half-title], recto of [A];—[blank], verso of [A];—[title] | BALLADS. | BY | W. M. THACKERAY, | ... | [vignette] | LONDON: | BRADBURY & EVANS, | 11, BOUVERIE STREET. | 1855. |, recto of [A 2];—[imprint], verso of [A 2]; —[text, with heading] | BALLADS. |, pp. [1]–159;—[blank], p. [160].

CONDITION: Size of leaf, 7⅛ × 4¾ inches. Bound in blue crushed levant morocco, gilt top; by Rivière. With the original yellow paper wrappers bound in, with title: | BALLADS | BY | W. M. THACKERAY | [vignette] | LONDON: | BRADBURY & EVANS | BOUVERIE ST. | 1856. |; the whole enclosed by an engraved border, above which is | PRICE EIGHTEENPENCE. |.

REFERENCES.

Wilson, *Thackeray in the United States*, 1 (1904): 181; Dickson, *Bibliography*, in Wilson, *Thackeray in the United States*, 2 (1904): 245; Williams, *Bibliography*, in Thackeray, *Works* (Biographical Edition, 13 vols.; 1903), 13 : 731; Slater, *Early Editions* (1894), p. 329, III.; Johnson, *Hints to Collectors* (1885), p. 35, No. xxv. *a*.

The wrapper appears to be from a later edition.

This is one of the selections made from the *Miscellaneous Writings* of Thackeray. It is the first separate appearance of the *Ballads* in book form. They had originally appeared in various periodicals and in other works of Thackeray. An American edition was published by Ticknor & Fields, Boston, the same year, with an introduction by the author, dated "Boston, 27th October, 1855," which Dickson says was "the first edition of the *Ballads* published separately." Thackeray, on the other hand, in his preface to the Boston edition says: "They are published simultaneously in England and America, where a public which has been interested in the writer's prose stories, he hopes, may be kindly disposed to his little volume of verses."

"The *Ballads*' ... first appearance was in the *Miscellanies*, 1855, and later in the year they were published separately in yellow wrappers. They appeared separately in the Boston volume at the time the *Miscellanies* were published in London." — DICKSON (in a private communication).

[THACKERAY, WILLIAM MAKEPEACE.]

THE ROSE AND THE RING. London, *Smith, Elder, and Co.*, 1855. [711]

Superroyal sixteenmo. First Edition.

COLLATION BY SIGNATURES: [A], 2 leaves; B to I, each 8 leaves; 8 leaves, without signature-marks; total 74 numbered leaves.

COLLATION BY PAGINATION: [title] | THE | ROSE AND THE RING; | OR, THE | HISTORY OF PRINCE GIGLIO AND PRINCE BULBO. | A Fire-Side

No. 711   *William Makepeace Thackeray*   1855

Pantomime for Great and Small Children. | [vignette] | BY MR. M. A. TITMARSH, | ... | LONDON : | SMITH, ELDER, AND CO., 65, CORNHILL. | 1855. |, p. [i.]; —[imprint], p. [ii.]; — | PRELUDE. |, pp. [iii.]–iv.; —[text, with heading] | THE ROSE AND THE RING. |, pp. [1]–128 ; —[publishers' advertisements], pp. [1]–16.

PLATES: 8 plates, by the author; facing the title-page and pp. 43, 53, 68, 93, 95, 115, and 127; also 48 woodcuts in the text, also by Thackeray.

Inserted as an extra-illustration is a sepia portrait by F. Reason, 1886, with inscription : | W. M. THACKERAY | AGED 13 YEARS | 1824 | ; facing p. [iii.].

CONDITION: Size of leaf, 6⅞ × 5³⁄₁₆ inches. Bound in green crushed levant morocco, leather hinges, gilt edges, with green moiré doublure and fly-leaf; by Champs.

With the original pink glazed paper covers bound in, with title, enclosed by a type-ornament border, which though reset in different type is lined the same as the title-page, except lines 8–10, which are as follows : | LONDON : SMITH, ELDER, AND CO., 65, CORNHILL. | MDCCCLV. | PRICE FIVE SHILLINGS. |.

REFERENCES.

Dickson, *Bibliography*, in Wilson, *Thackeray in the United States*, 2 (1904): 245 ; Williams, *Bibliography*, in Thackeray, *Works* (Biographical Edition, 13 vols.; 1903), 13: 731 ; Locker-Lampson, *Appendix to Catalogue* (1900), p. 105 ; Melville, *Life of Thackeray*, 2 (1899): 301 ; Slater, *Early Editions* (1894), p. 328, No. 28 ; Johnson, *Hints to Collectors* (1885), p. 34, No. XXIV. ; Shepherd, *Bibliography of Thackeray* (1880), p. 45, No. 126.

This, the last of Thackeray's Christmas Books, was originally published in pink boards. As there is no list of the plates, they should be counted. They are never found colored. A Third Edition appeared the same year.

There was a long interval between the appearance of this work and its predecessor, *The Kickleburys on the Rhine* (our No. 704), which was published in 1850. *The Rose and the Ring* was begun in Rome in 1854, the preface being dated in December of that year. It was also published by Harper & Brothers, of New York, in 1855, with 59 illustrations.

The original manuscript, with drawings in color, among which are many that have never been printed, is in the collection of Major W. H. Lambert of Philadelphia. "This," says Dickson, "is undoubtedly the choicest Thackeray manuscript in existence."

Locker-Lampson, in his poem *The Rose and the Ring*, explains the circumstances under which this book was written.

THACKERAY, WILLIAM MAKEPEACE.

BARRY LYNDON. LONDON, *Bradbury & Evans*, 1856.   [712]

Crown octavo.

COLLATION BY SIGNATURES: [A], 2 leaves ; B to U, each 8 leaves ; X, 4 leaves ; total 158 leaves.

COLLATION BY PAGINATION : [title] | THE MEMOIRS OF | BARRY LYN-

DON, ESQ., | OF THE KINGDOM OF IRELAND. | CONTAINING | AN ACCOUNT OF HIS EXTRAORDINARY ADVENTURES ; MISFORTUNES ; HIS SUFFERINGS | IN THE SERVICE OF HIS LATE PRUSSIAN MAJESTY ; HIS VISITS TO MANY OF THE | COURTS OF EUROPE ;

HIS MARRIAGE, AND SPLENDID ESTABLISH-MENTS IN | ENGLAND AND IRELAND; AND THE MANY CRUEL PERSECUTIONS, | CONSPIRACIES, AND SLANDERS OF WHICH HE HAS BEEN | A VICTIM. | BY | W. M. THACKERAY, | ... | [vignette] | LONDON: | BRADBURY & EVANS, 11, BOUVERIE STREET. | 1856. |, recto of [A]; — [imprint], verso of [A]; — [contents], recto of [A2]; — [blank], verso of [A2]; — [text, with heading] | THE | MEMOIRS OF BARRY LYNDON, ESQ. |, pp. [1]–305; — [blank], p. [306]; — [publishers' advertisement], pp. [307]–[312].

Inserted before the title-page is a half-title, presumably printed for this copy, with verso blank, as follows: | THE MEMOIRS OF | BARRY LYNDON, ESQ. |.

CONDITION: Size of leaf, 7⅜ × 5¹⁵⁄₁₆ inches. Bound in blue crushed levant morocco, gilt top, other edges uncut; by Rivière. With original yellow paper wrappers bound in, with title: | MEMOIRS | OF | BARRY LYNDON, ESQ., | BY | W. M. THACKERAY. | [vignette] | LONDON: | BRADBURY & EVANS | BOUVERIE ST. | 1856. |; the whole enclosed by an engraved border, above which is | PRICE THREE SHILLINGS. |.

REFERENCES.

Williams, *Bibliography*, in Thackeray, *Works* (Biographical Edition, 13 vols.; 1903), 13:728 (727, by mistake under *Esmond*); Slater, *Early Editions* (1894), p. 330, No. 29, X.; Johnson, *Hints to Collectors* (1885), p. 36, No. XXV.*h*; Shepherd, *Bibliography of Thackeray* (1880), p. 18, No. 43.

This work originally appeared as *The Luck of Barry Lyndon*, in *Fraser's Magazine* (Vols. 29–30), from January to September, November, and December, 1844. It is one of the selections from the *Miscellaneous Writings* of Thackeray, published in yellow wrappers.

An American edition, printed directly from *Fraser's*, was published by D. Appleton & Co., New York, in two volumes, in 1853. In the London edition, here described, many passages that appeared in *Fraser's Magazine* were omitted.

THACKERAY, WILLIAM MAKEPEACE.

BURLESQUES. A LEGEND OF THE RHINE: REBECCA AND ROWENA. LONDON, *Bradbury & Evans*, 1856. [713]

Crown octavo.

COLLATION BY SIGNATURES: B to I, each 8 leaves; K, 1 leaf; total 65 numbered leaves.

COLLATION BY PAGINATION: [title] | BURLESQUES. | A LEGEND OF THE RHINE: | REBECCA AND ROWENA. | BY | W. M. THACKERAY, | ... | [vignette] | LONDON: | BRADBURY & EVANS, 11, BOUVERIE STREET, | 1856. |, p. [1]; — [imprint], p. [2]; — [contents], p. [3]; — [blank], p. [4]; — [text, with heading] | A LEGEND OF THE RHINE. |, pp. [5]–65; — [blank], p. [66]; — [half-title] | REBECCA AND ROWENA; | OR, ROMANCE UPON ROMANCE. |, p. [67]; — [blank], p. [68]; — [text, with heading] | REBECCA AND ROWENA. |, pp. [69]–129; — [blank], p. [130].

Inserted before the title-page is a half-title, presumably printed for this copy, with verso blank, as follows: | BURLESQUES. |.

CONDITION: Size of leaf, 7⅜ × 4⅞ inches. Bound in blue crushed levant morocco, gilt top, other edges uncut; by Rivière. With the original yellow paper wrappers bound in, with title: | BUR-

No. 713   *William Makepeace Thackeray*   1856

LESQUES. | A LEGEND | OF THE RHINE. | REBECCA & ROWENA. | BY | W. M. THACKERAY. | [vignette] | LONDON : | BRADBURY & EVANS | BOUVERIE ST. | 1856. | ; the whole enclosed by an engraved border, above which is | PRICE EIGHTEENPENCE | .

REFERENCES.

Dickson, *Bibliography*, in Wilson, *Thackeray in the United States*, 2 (1904) : 242; Williams, *Bibliography*, in Thackeray, *Complete Works* (Biographical Edition, 13 vols.; 1903), 13 : 728; Slater, *Early Editions* (1894), pp. 328, 329, No. 29, v.

This is one of the selections from the *Miscellaneous Writings* of Thackeray, published in yellow wrappers.

The Legend of the Rhine first appeared in George Cruikshank's *Table Book* (Parts 6–12), in 1845 (our No. 287), with three illustrations by that artist. *Rebecca and Rowena* had already appeared in separate form in 1850 (our No. 705). Both of these pieces were published with *Jeames's Diary, A Legend of the Rhine, and Rebecca and Rowena*, in New York, by D. Appleton & Co., in 1853.

"The first reprint of *The Legend of the Rhine* was with *The Kickleburys Abroad; Rebecca and Rowena; The Second Funeral of Napoleon*, Leipzig, Bernard Tauchnitz, 1851, afterwards appearing as Vol. II. of the Tauchnitz edition of the *Miscellanies*." — DICKSON (in a private communication).

THACKERAY, WILLIAM MAKEPEACE.

A LITTLE DINNER AT TIMMINS'S: AND THE BEDFORD-ROW CONSPIRACY. LONDON, *Bradbury & Evans*, 1856.   [714]

Crown octavo.

COLLATION BY SIGNATURES : B to F, each 8 leaves; G, 4 leaves; total 44 leaves.

COLLATION BY PAGINATION : [title] | A | LITTLE DINNER AT TIMMINS'S : | AND | THE BEDFORD-ROW CONSPIRACY. | BY | W. M. THACKERAY, | . . . | [vignette] | LONDON : | BRADBURY & EVANS, 11, BOUVERIE STREET. | 1856. | , p. [1]; —[imprint], p. [2]; —[contents], p. [3]; —[blank], p. [4]; —[text, with heading] | A LITTLE DINNER AT TIMMINS'S. | , pp. [5]–34; —[text, with heading] | THE BEDFORD-ROW CONSPIRACY. | , pp. [35]–82; —[publishers' advertisements], pp. [83]–[88].

Inserted before the title-page is a half-title, presumably printed for this copy, with verso blank, as follows : | A LITTLE DINNER AT TIMMINS'S : | AND | THE BEDFORD-ROW CONSPIRACY. | .

CONDITION : Size of leaf, 7 7/16 × 4 7/8 inches. Bound in blue crushed levant morocco, gilt top, other edges uncut; by Rivière. With the original yellow paper wrappers bound in, with title : | A LITTLE DINNER | AT | TIMMINS'S : | AND | THE BEDFORD-ROW CONSPIRACY. | BY | W. M. THACKERAY. | [vignette] | LONDON : | BRADBURY & EVANS | BOUVERIE ST. | 1856. | ; the whole enclosed by an engraved border, above which is | PRICE ONE SHILLING. | .

REFERENCES.

Dickson, *Bibliography*, in Wilson, *Thackeray in the United States*, 2 (1904) : 240; Williams, *Bibliography*, in Thackeray, *Works* (Biographical Edition, 13 vols.; 1903), 13 : 723, 728; Melville, *Life of Thackeray*, 2 (1899) : 322, 332; Slater, *Early Editions* (1894), p. 329, No. 29, VI.; Johnson, *Hints to Collectors* (1885), p. 36, No. XXV. j.

This is one of the *Miscellaneous Writings* of Thackeray, issued in yellow wrappers.

The *Little Dinner at Timmins's* first appeared with eight illustrations in seven numbers of *Punch* (Vols. 14 and 15), from May 27 to July 29, 1848.

The *Bedford-Row Conspiracy*, which before its appearance here had been reprinted in *Comic Tales and Sketches* in 1841 (our No. 693), first appeared in the *New Monthly Magazine* (Vol. 58) for January, March, and April, 1840.

Both these works had previously been printed with the *Shabby Genteel Story* by D. Appleton & Co., New York, in 1852; but in the first edition the *Little Dinner at Timmins's* was incomplete, as it lacked the first three numbers. Thackeray called the attention of the publishers to this omission, and a new edition was prepared supplying the omitted numbers, thus giving the volume 283 instead of 267 pages, as originally issued.

THACKERAY, WILLIAM MAKEPEACE.

THE MEMOIRS OF MR. CHARLES J. YELLOWPLUSH, AND THE DIARY OF C. JEAMES DE LA PLUCHE. London, *Bradbury & Evans*, 1856.   [715]

Crown octavo.

COLLATION BY SIGNATURES: [A], 2 leaves; B to N, each 8 leaves; O, 6 leaves; total 104 leaves.

COLLATION BY PAGINATION: [title] | THE MEMOIRS | OF | MR. CHARLES J. YELLOWPLUSH, | AND | THE DIARY OF | C. JEAMES DE LA PLUCHE, ESQ. | BY | W. M. THACKERAY, | . . . | [vignette] | LONDON: | BRADBURY & EVANS, 11, BOUVERIE STREET. | 1856. |, p. [i.]; —[imprint], p. [ii.]; —[contents], pp. [iii.]–iv.; —[text, with heading] | THE MEMOIRS | OF | MR. CHARLES J. YELLOWPLUSH, | SOMETIME | FOOTMAN IN MANY GENTEEL FAMILIES. |, pp. [1]–151; —[blank], p. [152]; —[half-title] | THE DIARY | OF | C. JEAMES DE LA PLUCHE, ESQ. |, p. [153]; —[blank], p. [154]; —[text, with heading] | THE DIARY | OF | C. JEAMES DE LA PLUCHE, ESQ. |, pp. [155]–202; —[publishers' advertisement], p. [203]; —[blank], p. [204].

Inserted before the title-page is a half-title, presumably printed for this copy, with verso blank, as follows: | THE MEMOIRS OF | MR. CHARLES JAMES YELLOWPLUSH. |.

CONDITION: Size of leaf, 7⅛ × 4¾ inches. Bound in blue crushed levant morocco, gilt top, other edges uncut; by Rivière. With the original yellow paper wrappers bound in, with title: | THE MEMOIRS OF | MR CHARLES JAMES YELLOWPLUSH | THE DIARY OF | C. JEAMES DE LA PLUCHE E$^{SQ}_·$ | BY | W. M. THACKERAY. | [vignette] | LONDON: | BRADBURY & EVANS | BOUVERIE ST. | 1856. |; the whole enclosed by an engraved border, above which is | PRICE TWO SHILLINGS |.

REFERENCES.

Dickson, *Bibliography*, in Wilson, *Thackeray in the United States*, 2 (1904): 229, 236; Williams, *Bibliography*, in Thackeray, *Works* (Biographical Edition, 13 vols.; 1903), 13: 722, 728; Slater, *Early Editions* (1894), p. 329, No. 29, VIII.; Johnson, *Hints to Collectors* (1885), p. 35, No. XXV. *e*; Shepherd, *Bibliography of Thackeray* (1880), p. 4, No. 4; p. 13, No. 27; p. 26, No. 67.

This is one of the selections from the *Miscellaneous Writings* of Thackeray published in yellow wrappers from 1855 to 1857.

The *Diary* was here first published in full in a separate form. It originally appeared in *Punch* (Vols. 9 and 10), from August 2, 1845, to February 7, 1846. It was reprinted, with the exception of the second paper, in New York, by William Taylor & Co., in 1846, with nineteen woodcuts, all the illustrations that had appeared in *Punch*.

Of the *Memoirs*, which first appeared in *Fraser's Magazine* (Vols. 16–18, and 21) for November, 1837, January to August, 1838, and January, 1840, numbers one to eight were first separately printed in *The Yellowplush Correspondence*, Philadelphia, 1838 (our No. 684). The entire work was printed as *The Yellowplush Papers* in *Comic Tales and Sketches*, in London, 1841 (our No. 693), from which it was here reprinted. The volume here described contains: "Miss Shum's Husband," "The Amours of Mr. Deuceace," "Skimmings from 'The Dairy of George IV.,'" "Foring Parts," "Mr. Deuceace at Paris," "Mr. Yellowplush's Ajew," and "Epistles to the Literati."

The Philadelphia edition of *The Yellowplush Correspondence* was the first collection of Thackeray's writings that appeared in book form on either side of the Atlantic.

"The *Diary* was reprinted without the illustrations, excepting in the case of the incomplete New York edition of 1846, until it appeared in the Library edition of the *Works* in 1869. The editor of this edition for reasons only known to himself rejected some of the illustrations and in their place printed cuts from the suppressed numbers of *The Book of Snobs*. In the Macmillan edition of 1903, under the capable editorship of Mr. Melville, the *Diary* appeared for the first time complete and with all the illustrations originally printed in *Punch*." — DICKSON (in a private communication).

THACKERAY, WILLIAM MAKEPEACE.

NOVELS BY EMINENT HANDS, AND CHARACTER SKETCHES.
LONDON, *Bradbury & Evans*, 1856. [716]

Crown octavo.

COLLATION BY SIGNATURES: [A], 2 leaves; B to H, each 8 leaves; total 58 leaves.

COLLATION BY PAGINATION: [title] | NOVELS BY EMINENT HANDS, | AND | CHARACTER SKETCHES. | BY | W. M. THACKERAY, | . . . | [vignette] | LONDON: | BRADBURY & EVANS, 11, BOUVERIE STREET, | 1856. |, recto of [A]; —[imprint], verso of [A]; —[contents], recto of [A 2]; —[blank], verso of [A 2]; —[text, with heading] | NOVELS BY EMINENT HANDS. |, pp. [1]–59; —[blank], p. [60]; —[half-title] | CHARACTER SKETCHES. |, p. [61]; —[blank], p. [62]; —[text, with heading] | CHARACTER SKETCHES. |, pp. [63]–112.

Inserted before the title-page is a half-title, presumably printed for this copy, with verso blank, as follows: | NOVELS | BY | EMINENT HANDS. |.

CONDITION: Size of leaf, 7$\frac{3}{16}$ × 4¾ inches. Bound in blue crushed levant morocco, gilt top, other edges uncut; by Rivière. With the original yellow paper wrappers bound in, with title: | NOVELS

1856   *William Makepeace Thackeray*   No. 716

| BY | EMINENT HANDS. | CHARACTER SKETCHES. | BY | W. M. THACKERAY. | [vignette] | LONDON : | BRADBURY & EVANS | BOUVERIE ST. | 1856. | ; the whole enclosed by an engraved border, above which is | PRICE EIGHTEENPENCE. | .

REFERENCES.

Dickson, *Bibliography*, in Wilson, *Thackeray in the United States*, 2 (1904): 242; Williams, *Bibliography*, in Thackeray, *Works* (Biographical Edition, 13 vols.; 1903), 13 : 731, 733, 737 ; Slater, *Early Editions* (1894), p. 329, No. 29, IV.; Johnson, *Hints to Collectors* (1885), p. 35, No. XXV. g.; Shepherd, *Bibliography of Thackeray* (1880), p. 31, No. 84; 43, No. 120.

This is one of the selections from the *Miscellaneous Writings* of Thackeray.

The *Character Sketches* had previously appeared in Kenny Meadows' *Heads of the People* (our No. 692), but are here collectively published for the first time.

Novels by Eminent Hands originally appeared in *Punch* (Vol. 13) for August 28, September 4, 11, 25, and October 9, 1847; Vol. 20, p. 75, and Vols. 12–13, on various dates from April 3 to July 24, 1847. These were first reprinted in volume form, as *Punch's Prize Novelists*, in New York, by D. Appleton & Co., in 1853. Those here printed are: "George de Barnwell," "Phil. Fogarty," "Barbazure," "Lords and Liveries," and "Codlingsby."

These "novels" were parodies of the styles of popular authors. Lever, on reading *Phil. Fogarty*, declared that he might as well shut up shop, and actually altered the character of his novels. Thackeray wished to close the series with similar articles on Dickens and himself, but as the proprietors of *Punch* refused to publish a parody of Dickens the series came to an end without them.

From 1853 to 1857 several of the pieces which were included in Thackeray's *Miscellaneous Writings* (4 vols., 1855–57) were published in yellow wrappers, as follows :

(1) *The Snob Papers*, 1855.
(2) *The Fatal Boots and Cox's Diary*, 1855.
(3) *Ballads*, 1855 (our No. 710).
(4) *Novels by Eminent Hands, and Character Sketches*, 1856 (our present number).
(5) *A Legend of the Rhine: Rebecca and Rowena*, 1856 (our No. 713).
(6) *A Little Dinner at Timmins's: and The Bedford-Row Conspiracy*, 1856 (our No. 714).
(7) *Major Gahagan's Tremendous Adventures*, 1856.
(8) *Memoirs of Mr. Charles J. Yellowplush; The Diary of C. Jeames De La Pluche, Esq.*, 1856 (our preceding number).
(9) *Sketches and Travels in London*, 1856 (our next number).
(10) *Memoirs of Barry Lyndon*, 1856 (our No. 712).
(11) *A Shabby Genteel Story*, 1857 (our No. 719).
(12) *The History of Samuel Titmarsh and the Great Hoggarty Diamond*, 1857.
(13) *The Fitz-Boodle Papers: and Men's Wives*, 1857 (our No. 718).

THACKERAY, WILLIAM MAKEPEACE.

SKETCHES AND TRAVELS IN LONDON. London, *Bradbury & Evans*, 1856. [717]

Crown octavo.

COLLATION BY SIGNATURES: [A], 2 leaves; B to M, each 8 leaves; total 90 numbered leaves.

COLLATION BY PAGINATION: [title] | SKETCHES | AND | TRAVELS IN LONDON. | BY | W. M. THACKERAY, | ... | [vignette] | LONDON: | BRADBURY & EVANS, 11, BOUVERIE STREET. | 1856. |, p. [i.]; — [imprint], p. [ii.]; — [contents], pp. [iii.]-iv.; — [text, with heading] | SKETCHES AND TRAVELS IN LONDON. |, pp. [1]-176.

Inserted before the title-page is a half-title, presumably printed for this copy, with verso blank, as follows: | SKETCHES | AND | TRAVELS IN LONDON. |.

CONDITION: Size of leaf, 7 9/16 × 4 3/4 inches. Bound in blue crushed levant morocco, gilt top, other edges uncut; by Rivière. With the original yellow paper wrappers bound in, with title: | SKETCHES | & | TRAVELS | IN LONDON. | BY | W. M. THACKERAY. | [vignette] | LONDON: | BRADBURY & EVANS | BOUVERIE ST. | 1856. |; the whole enclosed by an engraved border, above which is | PRICE TWO SHILLINGS |.

REFERENCES.

Dickson, *Bibliography*, in Wilson, *Thackeray in the United States*, 2 (1904): 241; Williams, *Bibliography*, in Thackeray, *Works* (Biographical Edition, 13 vols.; 1903), 13: 729, 730; Slater, *Early Editions* (1894), pp. 328, 329, No. 29, IX.; Johnson, *Hints to Collectors* (1885), p. 35, No. xxv.*f.*; Shepherd, *Bibliography of Thackeray* (1880), p. 32, No. 86; p. 38, No. 109.

This is one of the selections from the *Miscellaneous Writings* (Vol. 2, 1856) of Thackeray, published with yellow wrappers. The volume is made up of several series of articles from *Punch*. "Mr. Brown's Letters to His Nephew" (pp. 1–84) first appeared in various numbers of *Punch* (Vol. 16, p. 115, to Vol. 17, p. 69) from March 24 to August 18, 1849, under the title "Mr. Brown's Letters to a Young Man about Town." The three articles (pp. 85–99) "On a Lady in an Opera Box," "On the Pleasures of being a Fogy," and "On the Benefits of being a Fogy," first appeared in *Punch* (Vol. 18, pp. 151–198), in 1850, as "The Proser." "Child's Parties: and a Remonstrance Concerning Them" (pp. 100–109) also first saw the light in *Punch* (Vol. 16, pp. 13–36), January 13 and 27, 1849. All of these (pp. 1–109) were first separately printed at New York in 1853, by D. Appleton & Co., in *Mr. Brown's Letters to a Young Man about Town; with The Proser and Other Papers*, with a preface by the author, dated "New York, December, 1852."

In several numbers of *Punch*, from November 27 to December 31, 1847, January 8 to March 11, 1848, and that for March 9, 1850, Thackeray contributed a series of articles entitled "Travels in London." They comprised "The Curate's Walk" (in two parts), "A Dinner in the City" (in three parts), "A Club in an Uproar," "Waiting at the Station," and "A Night's Pleasure" (in six parts). All of these, with the exception of "A Club in an Uproar," are reprinted in the volume here described (pp. 110–160). The volume concludes with "Going to See a Man

Hanged" (pp. 160–176), which originally appeared in *Fraser's Magazine* for August, 1840. "Travels in London" and this last article were first separately printed at New York in 1853, by D. Appleton & Co., in a volume entitled *Punch's Prize Novelists, The Fat Contributor, and Travels in London*.

"Mr. Thackeray omitted from the *Miscellanies* the initial paper of the *Sketches and Travels in London*, and the editor of the Library edition of the *Works* in 1869 omitted the illustration to 'The Curate's Walk' and replaced it with that designed for the introductory paper. This blunder was perpetuated through all editions until the appearance of that edited by Mr. Melville and published by Macmillan in 1904. Here for the first time the *Sketches and Travels in London* are presented complete and with all the illustrations as they appeared in *Punch*." — DICKSON (in a private communication).

THACKERAY, WILLIAM MAKEPEACE.

THE FITZ-BOODLE PAPERS: AND MEN'S WIVES. LONDON, *Bradbury & Evans*, 1857. [718]

Crown octavo.

COLLATION BY SIGNATURES: [A], 2 leaves; B to O, each 8 leaves; P, 6 leaves; total 112 numbered leaves.

COLLATION BY PAGINATION: [title] | THE FITZ-BOODLE PAPERS: | AND | MEN'S WIVES. | BY | W. M. THACKERAY, | ... | [vignette] | LONDON: | BRADBURY & EVANS, 11, BOUVERIE STREET. | 1857. |, p. [i.]; — [imprint], p. [ii.]; — [contents], pp. [iii.]–iv.; — [text, with heading] | THE FITZ-BOODLE PAPERS. |, pp. [1]–50; — [half-title] | MEN'S WIVES. |, p. [51]; — [blank], p. [52]; — [text, with heading] | MEN'S WIVES. |, pp. [53]–219; — [blank], p. [220].

Inserted before the title-page is a half-title, presumably printed for this copy, with verso blank, as follows: | THE FITZ-BOODLE PAPERS: | AND | MEN'S WIVES. |; also as an extra-illustration a portrait of Thackeray, engraved by Fowle after Lawrence, with facsimile signature; facing the title-page.

CONDITION: Size of leaf, 7⅜ x 4⅞ inches. Bound in half maroon crushed levant morocco, gilt top, other edges uncut; by Bradstreet. With the original yellow paper wrappers bound in, with title: | THE | FITZ-BOODLE | PAPERS: | AND | MEN'S WIVES. | BY | W. M. THACKERAY. | LONDON: | BRADBURY & EVANS | BOUVERIE ST. | ; the whole enclosed by an engraved border, above which is | PRICE TWO SHILLINGS AND SIXPENCE. | .

REFERENCES.

Dickson, *Bibliography*, in Wilson, *Thackeray in the United States*, 2 (1904): 239, 240; Williams, *Bibliography*, in Thackeray, *Works* (Biographical Edition, 13 vols.; 1903), 13 : 727; Melville, *Life of Thackeray*, 1 (1899) : 209; 2 : 302; Slater, *Early Editions* (1894), p. 330, No. 29, XIII.; Johnson, *Hints to Collectors* (1885), p. 36, No. xxx k.

The Fitz-Boodle Papers were contributed to *Fraser's Magazine* (Vols. 25–27), in 1842 and 1843. They were first published in separate form, under the title *The Confessions of Fitz-Boodle; and Some Passages in the Life of Major Gahagan*, by D. Appleton & Co., New York, in 1852.

Men's Wives first appeared in *Fraser's Magazine* (Vols. 27 and 28), from March to June, and August to October, 1843. It was first published, as issued, in separate form by D. Appleton & Co., New York, in 1852.

"But Fitz cannot be forgiven for writing those scandalous chronicles of his friends' private lives — *Men's Wives*. Curiously enough, it is the last one of these, the ———'s [*Executioner's*] *Wife*, which has never been reprinted in his collected works, the story of a heartless coquette and of a brother's revenge, that seems to me the most admirable. The others are stories of mean lives without any redeeming sun-rays to enliven the surrounding gloom. The scoundrel Walker, the blackguard Boroski, the humbug Sir George, the foolish Ravenswing, . . . the dragon-like Mrs. Berry, and . . . Mrs. Dennis Haggarty . . . are so many people whom we would rather not know, and of whom we would certainly rather not read."

The edition here described does not include "The ———'s Wife," which appeared in *Fraser's*. This paper was reprinted in Thackeray's *Works*, Vol. 12, Boston, 1899, and in *Stray Papers*, Philadelphia, 1901, but is not to be found in the Biographical Edition, New York, 1903.

THACKERAY, WILLIAM MAKEPEACE.

A SHABBY GENTEEL STORY. LONDON, *Bradbury & Evans*, 1857.

[719]

Crown octavo.

COLLATION BY SIGNATURES: [A], 4 leaves; B to G, each 8 leaves; H, 2 leaves; total 54 numbered leaves.

COLLATION BY PAGINATION: [half-title], p. [1];—[blank], p. [2];—[title] | A SHABBY GENTEEL STORY. | BY | W. M. THACKERAY, | ... | [vignette] | LONDON: | BRADBURY & EVANS, 11, BOUVERIE STREET. | 1857. |, p. [3];—[imprint], p. [4];—[contents], p. [5];—[blank], p. [6];—[text, with heading] | A SHABBY GENTEEL STORY. |, pp. [7]–108.

EXTRA-ILLUSTRATED.

Inserted in this work are the following: Portrait of Thackeray, proof before letters, facing the title-page; 9 woodcut initials by Wallace, mounted to size, and facing pp. [7], 19, 31, 46, 53, 69, 77, 83, and 97; and 5 vignettes by Wallace, mounted to size, and facing pp. 10, 50, 57, 75, and 91.

CONDITION: Size of leaf, 7$\frac{3}{16}$ x 4$\frac{13}{16}$ inches. Bound in half maroon crushed levant morocco, gilt top, other edges uncut; by Bradstreet. With the original yellow paper wrappers bound in, with title: | A | SHABBY- | GENTEEL | STORY. | BY | W. M. THACKERAY. | [vignette] | LONDON: | BRADBURY & EVANS | BOUVERIE ST. | ; the whole enclosed by an engraved border, above which is | PRICE ONE SHILLING AND SIXPENCE. |.

REFERENCES.

Dickson, *Bibliography*, in Wilson, *Thackeray in the United States*, 2 (1904): 240; Williams, *Bibliography*, in Thackeray, *Works* (Biographical Edition, 13 vols.; 1903), 13: 728; Melville, *Life of Thackeray*, 2 (1899): 302; Slater, *Early Editions* (1894), p. 328, No. 29, XI.; Johnson, *Hints to Collectors* (1885), p. 35, No. xxv.*l.*; Shepherd, *Bibliography of Thackeray* (1880), p. 12, No. 23.

This is one of the selections from the *Miscellaneous Writings* of Thackeray, published in yellow wrappers. In the edition here described it was reprinted, with a brief note of fourteen lines at the end by the author, signed "W. M. T.," and dated "London, April 10th, 1857," as follows:

"When the republication of these Miscellanies was announced, it was my intention to complete the little story, of which only the first part is here written. Perhaps novel-readers will understand, even from the above chapters, what was to ensue. Caroline was to be disowned and deserted by her wicked husband : that abandoned man was to marry somebody else : hence, bitter trials and grief, patience and virtue, for poor little Caroline, and a melancholy ending — as how should it have been gay ? The tale was interrupted at a sad period of the writer's own life. The colours are long since dry; the artist's hand is changed. It is best to leave the sketch, as it was when first designed seventeen years ago. The memory of the past is renewed as he looks at it —

die Bilder froher Tage,
Und manche liebe Schatten steigen auf."

This story originally appeared in *Fraser's Magazine* (Vols. 21 and 22), from June to August and October, 1840. It was first separately printed with other tales by D. Appleton & Co., New York, in 1852.

THACKERAY, WILLIAM MAKEPEACE.

THE VIRGINIANS. LONDON, *Bradbury & Evans*, 1858–1859. 2 vols., octavo, viz.:

VOL. 1. 1858.

COLLATION BY SIGNATURES: [A], 4 leaves; B to Z, AA, BB, each 8 leaves; total 196 leaves.

COLLATION BY PAGINATION: [half-title], p. [i.]; — [blank], p. [ii.]; — [title] | THE VIRGINIANS. | A TALE OF THE LAST CENTURY. | BY | W. M. THACKERAY, | . . . | WITH ILLUSTRATIONS ON STEEL AND WOOD BY THE AUTHOR. | VOL. I. | LONDON : | BRADBURY & EVANS, 11, BOUVERIE STREET. | 1858. |, p. [iii.]; — [imprint], p. [iv.]; — [contents and list of plates], pp. [v.]–viii.; — [text, with heading] | THE VIRGINIANS. |, pp. [1]–382; — [publishers' advertisement], p. [383]; — [blank], p. [384].

PLATES: Engraved title-page and 23 engravings, as called for in the list of plates; also numerous initials and small woodcuts in the text. The last two plates have been transposed by the binder.

VOL. 2. 1859.

COLLATION BY SIGNATURES: [A], 4 leaves; B to Z, AA, each 8 leaves; BB, 4 leaves; total 192 numbered leaves.

COLLATION BY PAGINATION: [title, same as in Vol. 1, except volume-number and date of imprint], p. [i.]; — [imprint], p. [ii.]; — [dedication], p. iii.; — [blank], p. [iv.]; — [contents and list of plates], pp. [v.]–viii.; — [text, with heading] | THE VIRGINIANS. |, pp. [1]–376.

PLATES: Engraved title-page and 23 engravings, as called for in the list of plates; also numerous initials and small woodcuts in the text.

No. 720   *William Makepeace Thackeray*   1858-59

Inserted before the title-page is a half-title, presumably printed for this copy, with verso blank, as follows : | THE VIRGINIANS. | .

CONDITION : Size of leaf, 8⅝ x 5⁹⁄₁₆ inches. Bound from the original parts, in blue crushed levant morocco, gilt tops, other edges uncut; by Rivière. With wrappers and advertising pages on yellow and white paper, in all 54 leaves, and 1 slip, bound in at the end, as follows: Vol. 1, Nos. 1–12, 2 (1 slip), 3, 2, 2, 2, 2, 2, 2, 2, 2, 2, and 2 leaves; Vol. 2, Nos. 13–24, 2, 3, 3, 2, 4, 2, 2, 4, 2, 2, 2, and 1 leaf respectively. Published in 24 numbered monthly parts, from November, 1857, to October, 1859, in yellow wrappers, at one shilling each, with pictorial title: | THE VIRGINIANS | A TALE OF THE LAST CENTURY. | BY W. M. THACKERAY. | [vignette] | Author of "Esmond," | "Vanity Fair," | "The Newcomes," | &c. &c. | LONDON : | BRADBURY AND EVANS, 11, BOUVERIE STREET. | 1857 [–9]. | ☞ The Author reserves the right of Translation. | .

The line reserving the right of translation does not appear on the first ten numbers.

REFERENCES.

Wilson, *Thackeray in the United States*, 2 (1904) : 108 ; Dickson, *Bibliography*, in Wilson, *Thackeray in the United States*, 2 (1904) : 246–247 ; Williams, *Bibliography*, in Thackeray, *Works* (Biographical Edition, 13 vols.; 1903), 13 : 733 ; Melville, *Life of Thackeray*, 2 (1899) : 302 ; Slater, *Early Editions* (1894), p. 330, No. 30 ; Johnson, *Hints to Collectors* (1885), p. 37, No. XXVI.; Shepherd, *Bibliography of Thackeray* (1880), p. 46, No. 130.

On p. 207 of Vol. 1, line 15 from the bottom, occurs the word "actresses," changed in later editions to "ancestresses"; on p. [371] Chapter XLVII. is wrongly numbered XLVIII.; and on p. [378] Chapter XLVIII. is numbered XLIX. Both these errors were corrected in the Second Edition.

This novel, originally issued in parts, was afterward published in two volumes, cloth, dated 1858 and 1859 respectively. Each volume has two title-pages, one engraved and the other in letterpress, and in each case the engraved title-page is faced by a full-page plate.

The work appeared serially in the *New York Semi-Weekly Tribune* from November 20, 1857, to October, 1859; in the *New York Weekly Tribune* from November 21, 1857, to October 27, 1859; and in *Harper's Magazine* from December, 1857, to November, 1859. Dickson, in his *Bibliography*, gives an interesting account of the dispute which arose between the rival publishers of this work. It was then published in book form by Harper & Brothers in 1859, with 136 woodcuts.

"'I hear,' observed Thackeray to Douglas Jerrold, 'that you have said "The Virginians" is the worst novel I ever wrote.' 'You are wrong,' replied Jerrold ; 'I said it is the worst novel anybody ever wrote.' 'And yet,' remarked Mr. Curtis, 'the work has taken its rightful place among the masterpieces of the English language, although surpassed by his three more important publications.'"

Mr. Thackeray's original note-book of *The Virginians*, with memoranda and sketches, is in the collection of Major William H. Lambert of Philadelphia. There is also a single page of the original manuscript of this story, beginning "*Chap. 49.*," in No. 690 of the present collection.

Mrs. Ritchie says : "It was the last of my father's books that he illustrated for himself, and we still have the designs and sketches he made, as well as the manuscript of the book itself."

1859   William Makepeace Thackeray   No. 721

THACKERAY, WILLIAM MAKEPEACE.   Yates, Edmund.
(*b.* 1831, *d.* 1894.)

MR. THACKERAY, MR. YATES, AND THE GARRICK CLUB.
[LONDON], 1859.   [721]

Octavo.

COLLATION BY SIGNATURES: 8 numbered leaves, without signature-marks.

COLLATION BY PAGINATION: [title] | MR. THACKERAY, MR. YATES, | AND | THE GARRICK CLUB. | THE | CORRESPONDENCE AND FACTS. | STATED BY | EDMUND YATES. | PRINTED FOR PRIVATE CIRCULATION. | 1859. |, p. [1]; —[imprint], p. [2]; —[text, with heading] | MR. THACKERAY, MR. YATES, | AND | THE GARRICK CLUB. |, pp. [3]–15; —[blank], p. [16].

CONDITION: Size of leaf, 8⅝ × 5⅝ inches. Bound in red crushed levant morocco, gilt top, other edges uncut; by Rivière. Laid in are pp. [385]–392 from | TIME | JANUARY 1880. |, and frontispiece, containing a reprint of the text, with title: | AN OLD CLUB SCANDAL. | BY THE EDITOR [Edmund Yates]. | .

REFERENCES.

Melville, *Life of Thackeray*, 2 (1899): 37–53; Slater, *Early Editions* (1894), p. 79, No. XVII.; 331, No. 31; Merivale and Marzials, *Life of W. M. Thackeray* (1891), pp. 195–198; Shepherd, *Bibliography of Thackeray* (1880), p. 46, No. 129.

The work here described relates to a controversy which arose from an article on Thackeray, written by Yates, which appeared in a periodical called *Town Talk* in June, 1858. It followed a pen-and-ink sketch of Dickens which Yates had previously written that met with great success. Thackeray, feeling injured, on the 14th of June wrote a fierce letter demanding a retraction. Yates applied for advice to Dickens, who was also a member of the Garrick Club, whereupon Thackeray appealed to the committee, on the plea that as he had met Yates only at the club it was the club's duty to protect him from Yates's insults. At the general meeting in July action was taken involving the expulsion of Yates unless he made an "ample apology." On his refusal to do this he was turned out. The affair created a coolness between Thackeray and Dickens that was terminated only a week before Thackeray's death. Melville gives a full account of the controversy, and reprints Yates's article and Thackeray's letters.

THACKERAY, WILLIAM MAKEPEACE.

WILLIAM MAKEPEACE THACKERAY AT CLEVEDON COURT.
BRISTOL, *Lavars*, [c. 1860].   [722]

Quarto.

COLLATION BY SIGNATURES: 17 unnumbered leaves, without signature-marks.

COLLATION BY PAGINATION: [title] | WILLIAM MAKEPEACE THACKERAY | AT CLEVEDON COURT. | Lavars Lith. Bristol. [this line on the wrapper only] |, p. [1]; —[facsimile autograph letter], p [2]; —[1 blank leaf], pp. [3]–[4]; —[15 plates, verso pages blank], pp. [5]–[34].

PLATES: 15 plates, reproductions of the

sketches made by Thackeray at Clevedon Court, with descriptions in his facsimile autograph below.

Inserted is an autograph letter signed, in regard to a reading upon Sterne and Goldsmith, 7 lines in all.

CONDITION: Size of leaf, 11 9/16 x 9 1/8 inches. Bound in green crushed levant morocco, gilt edges; by Rivière. With the original blue glazed paper wrappers bound in, the front cover with title as above.

The Daly copy.

This work is a reproduction of the famous sketches made by Thackeray at Clevedon Court, with descriptions in Thackeray's facsimile autograph below each sketch.

A few copies were privately printed for presentation only. An autograph letter of Thackeray's, in reference to Sterne and Goldsmith, dated "*Kensington. Wednesday,*" is inserted, which reads as follows: "*Dear Madam: Sterne & Goldsmith are perhaps the pleasantest gentlemen to bring into your drawing room and if you please I will read the paper at 5 o'clock.* [signed] *always faithfully yours | W M Thackeray.*"

THACKERAY, WILLIAM MAKEPEACE.

THE FOUR GEORGES. LONDON, *Smith, Elder and Co.*, 1861. [723]

Crown octavo. First Edition, First Issue.

COLLATION BY SIGNATURES: 2 leaves, without signature-marks; 1 to 14, each 8 leaves; 15, 2 leaves; total 116 leaves.

COLLATION BY PAGINATION: [half-title], recto of first leaf; — [blank], verso of first leaf; — [title, as reproduced; *See* No. 723], recto of second leaf; — [blank], verso of second leaf; — [half-title] | I. — GEORGE THE FIRST. |, p. [1]; — [blank], p. [2]; — [text in 4 parts, with half-title to each], pp. [3]–226; — [imprint], p. [227]; — [blank], p. [228].

PLATES: 2 plates, engraved by Swain; facing the title-page and p. 59; also 13 small woodcuts in the text.

CONDITION: Size of leaf, 7 7/16 x 4 15/16 inches. Bound in the original green cloth, uncut edges.

REFERENCES.

Dickson, *Bibliography*, in Wilson, *Thackeray in the United States*, 2 (1904): 249; Williams, *Bibliography*, in Thackeray, *Works* (Biographical Edition, 13 vols.; 1903), 13: 734; Melville, *Life of Thackeray*, 2 (1899): 302; Slater, *Early Editions* (1904), p. 331, No. 33; Johnson, *Hints to Collectors* (1885), p. 39, No. XXVIII.; Shepherd, *Bibliography of Thackeray* (1880), p. 48, No. 36.

This, the First English Edition, was published November, 1861, in green cloth.

There are two issues of the edition here described, of which the First is by far the rarer. Only the genuine First Issue has the words "Sketches of Manners, Morals, Court, and Town Life" on the title-page. All the other issues have a half-title, but not the above words. According to Johnson, the copy in the British Museum is of the Second Issue. He says he had looked at some ten or twelve copies, and found only one with the title-page as here given.

The work consists of the series of lectures that Thackeray first delivered on his second visit to the United States, from October, 1855, to April, 1856. On his

1861   *William Makepeace Thackeray*   No. 723

THE FOUR GEORGES:

SKETCHES OF MANNERS, MORALS, COURT,

AND TOWN LIFE.

BY

W. M. THACKERAY,

AUTHOR OF "LECTURES ON THE ENGLISH HUMOURISTS,"
ETC. ETC.

WITH ILLUSTRATIONS.

LONDON:
SMITH, ELDER AND CO., 65, CORNHILL.

M.DCCC.LXI.

[*The right of Translation is reserved.*]

No. 723.   Title-page of Thackeray's Four Georges; 1st Edition,
1st Issue; 1861.

return to England he delivered them in London and other cities. They first appeared in print in the *Cornhill Magazine* (Vol. 2), from July to October, 1860, and were reprinted in *Harper's Magazine* (Vol. 2), from August to November, and in Littell's *Living Age* (Vols. 66 and 67), August 11th, September 1st, October 13th, and November 10th of the same year.

They were first published in book form by Harper & Brothers, New York, in November, 1860, with sixteen illustrations.

A portion of the original manuscript, "George the Third," partly written in this country, is in the library of the Drexel Institute, Philadelphia, having been presented to that institution by the late George W. Childs.

THACKERAY, WILLIAM MAKEPEACE.

A LEAF OUT OF A SKETCH-BOOK. LONDON, *Emily Faithfull & Co.*, 1861. [724]

Small duodecimo. Author's Edition.

COLLATION BY SIGNATURES: 12 numbered leaves, without signature-marks (the last blank and genuine).

COLLATION BY PAGINATION: [half-title], p. [1]; — [blank], p. [2]; — [title, as reproduced; *See* No. 724], p. [3]; — [blank], p. [4]; — [text, with heading] | A | LEAF OUT OF A | SKETCH-BOOK. |, pp. [5]–21; — [blank], p. [22]; — [1 blank leaf]. Pages 15 and 19 are blank, and pp. 16 and 20 are full-page woodcuts, from drawings by the author.

CONDITION: Size of leaf, 6⅝ × 4⅛ inches. In the original green paper wrappers, the front cover with title similar to that reproduced, but surrounded by a type-ornament and rule border, with | 25 Copies for the Author's Use. | below the border; in blue crushed levant morocco solander case.

REFERENCE.

Melville, *Life of Thackeray*, 2 (1899): 338; (reprinted in) Thackeray, *Works* (Biographical Edition, 13 vols.; 1903), 13 : 643.

This is the first separate issue of this work, which originally appeared in the *Victoria Regia*, with two illustrations, in 1861, pp. 118–125. The edition was limited to "25 Copies for the Author's Use."

THACKERAY, WILLIAM MAKEPEACE.

LOVEL THE WIDOWER. LONDON, *Smith, Elder and Co.*, 1861. [725]

Post octavo.

COLLATION BY SIGNATURES: 2 leaves, without signature-marks; 1 to 16, each 8 leaves; 17, 2 leaves; total 132 leaves.

COLLATION BY PAGINATION: [title] | LOVEL THE WIDOWER. | BY | W. M. THACKERAY, | WITH ILLUSTRATIONS. |

LONDON: | SMITH, ELDER AND CO., 65, CORNHILL. | M.DCCC.LXI. | [*The right of Translation is reserved.*] |, recto of first leaf; — [blank], verso of first leaf; — [contents], recto of second leaf; — [blank], verso of second leaf; — [text, with heading] | LOVEL THE WIDOWER. |, pp.

A

LEAF OUT OF A SKETCH-BOOK.

BY

WILLIAM MAKEPEACE THACKERAY.

LONDON:
EMILY FAITHFULL & CO., VICTORIA PRESS.
1861.

NO. 724.   TITLE-PAGE OF THACKERAY'S LEAF OUT OF A SKETCH-BOOK; 1861.

[1]-258;—[imprint], p. [259];—[blank], p. [260].

PLATES: 6 full-page woodcuts; facing the title-page and pp. 82, 101, 175, 184, and 241; also 6 small woodcuts in the text, of which 2 are initials.

CONDITION: Size of leaf, 7⅝ × 4⅞ inches. Bound in red crushed levant morocco, gilt top, other edges uncut; by Bradstreet. With 8 numbered leaves of publishers' advertisements, with heading |

NEW AND STANDARD WORKS | PUBLISHED BY | SMITH, ELDER AND CO. | [dated] | 65, *Cornhill, London*, | *November*, 1861. | bound in at the end.

REFERENCES.

Wilson, *Thackeray in the United States*, 2 (1904): 199; Dickson, *Bibliography*, in Wilson, *Thackeray in the United States*, 2 (1904): 248, 249; Williams, *Bibliography*, in Thackeray, *Works* (Biographical Edition,

No. 725   *William Makepeace Thackeray*   1861

13 vols.; 1903), 13: 734; Melville, *Life of Thackeray*, 2 (1899) : 166, 303; Slater, *Early Editions* (1894), p. 331, No. 32; Johnson, *Hints to Collectors* (1885), p. 38, No. XXVII.; Shepherd, *Bibliography of Thackeray* (1880), p. 47, No. 135.

    This story was adapted from *The Wolves and the Lamb*, a play which Thackeray submitted to the managers of the Haymarket and Olympic theatres in 1854, but which neither of them would produce. The play was well written, the dialogue delightful, and the characters grandly drawn; only there was too much dialogue, too little action, and no dramatic incident. It was first printed in the Library Edition of Thackeray's works (Vol. 22), 1869.

    Lovel the Widower first appeared in the *Cornhill Magazine* (Vol. 1), from January to June, 1860, and was reprinted in *Harper's Magazine* (Vols. 20 and 21), from February to July, 1860. It was first separately printed in New York, June 30, 1860, by Harper & Brothers, with thirteen woodcuts. The edition here described, with six full-page illustrations by the author, issued in embossed violet cloth, did not appear until November, 1861.

    When Thackeray opened his new house at No. 2, Palace Green, Kensington, with a house-warming, in February, 1862, the rejected play, *The Wolves and the Lamb*, was admirably acted by amateurs, among whom was the author himself. The play was performed a second time in the same house.

THACKERAY, WILLIAM MAKEPEACE.

THE ADVENTURES OF PHILIP. LONDON, *Smith, Elder and Co.*, 1862. 3 vols., post octavo, viz. :

[726]

VOL. I.

COLLATION BY SIGNATURES : 4 leaves, without signature-marks; 1 to 20, each 8 leaves; 21, 5 leaves; total 169 leaves.

COLLATION BY PAGINATION : [half-title], recto of first leaf; —[blank], verso of first leaf; —[title] | THE | ADVENTURES OF PHILIP | ON HIS WAY THROUGH THE WORLD ; | SHEWING | WHO ROBBED HIM, WHO HELPED HIM, AND WHO PASSED HIM BY. | BY | W. M. THACKERAY, | . . . | IN THREE VOLUMES. | VOL. I. | LONDON : | SMITH, ELDER AND CO., 65, CORNHILL. | M.DCCC.-LXII. | , recto of second leaf; — | [*The right of Translation is reserved.*] | , verso of second leaf; —[dedication], recto of third leaf ; —[blank], verso of third leaf ; — [contents], recto of fourth leaf ; —[blank], verso of fourth leaf; —[text, with heading] | PHILIP. |, pp. [1]-329; —[imprint], p. [330].

EXTRA-ILLUSTRATED.

    Inserted in this volume are the following : Portrait of Thackeray, an etching, facing the title-page ; 3 engravings by Frederick Walker, facing pp. 192, 255, and 293; 4 engravings by Thackeray, facing pp. 44, 47, 99, and 145; and 16 woodcut initials, mounted to size, by Thackeray, facing pp. [1], 17, 32, 45, 66, 92, 113, 138, 148, 166, 183, 206, 237, 257, 286, and 299.

Vol. 2.

COLLATION BY SIGNATURES: 2 leaves, without signature-marks; 22 to 40, each 8 leaves; total 154 leaves.

COLLATION BY PAGINATION: [title, same as in Vol. 1, except volume-number], recto of first leaf; — | [*The right of Translation is reserved.*] |, verso of first leaf; — [contents], recto of second leaf; — [blank], verso of second leaf; — [text], pp. [1]-304.

Vol. 3.

COLLATION BY SIGNATURES: 2 leaves, without signature-marks; 41 to 58, each 8 leaves; 59, 7 leaves; total 153 leaves.

COLLATION BY PAGINATION: [title, same as in Vol. 1, except volume-number], recto of first leaf; — | [*The right of Translation is reserved.*] |, verso of first leaf; — [contents], recto of second leaf; — [blank], verso of second leaf; — [text], pp. [1]-301; — [imprint], p. [302].

EXTRA-ILLUSTRATED.

Inserted in this volume are the following: Portrait of Thackeray, etched by S. Hollyer, facing the title-page; 6 engravings by Frederick Walker, facing pp. 52, 79, 120, 200, 234, and 263; and 13 woodcut initials by Thackeray, mounted to size, facing pp. [1], 25, 53, 71, 86, 118, 140, 164, 185, 209, 220, 255, and 264.

EXTRA-ILLUSTRATED.

Inserted in this volume are the following: Engraved portrait of Thackeray, facing the title-page; 7 engravings by Frederick Walker, facing pp. 29, 60, 114, 179, 220, 280, and 302; and 13 woodcut initials by Thackeray, mounted to size, facing pp. [1], 18, 48, 69, 95, 126, 141, 170, 188, 215, 234, 257, and 281.

CONDITION: Size of leaf, 7¾ x 5 inches. Bound in brown crushed levant morocco, gilt tops, other edges uncut; by Bradstreet. With one sheet of publishers' advertisements, including this work, with woodcut, bound in at the end.

REFERENCES.

Wilson, *Thackeray in the United States*, 2 (1904): 107; Dickson, *Bibliography*, in Wilson, *Thackeray in the United States*, 2 (1904): 251; Williams, *Bibliography*, in Thackeray, *Works* (Biographical Edition, 13 vols.; 1903), 13:734; Melville, *Life of Thackeray*, 2 (1899): 303; Slater, *Early Editions* (1894), p. 332, No. 34; Johnson, *Hints to Collectors* (1885), p. 40, No. XXIX.; Shepherd, *Bibliography of Thackeray* (1880), p. 48, No. 137.

This work, of which this is the First Edition, originally appeared as a serial in the *Cornhill Magazine* (Vols. 3–6), from January, 1861, to August, 1862. It was first published in book form in London, July 21, 1862, in dark red cloth, with a dedication to "M. I. Higgins," dated "Kensington, July, 1862." The illustrations by the author and by Frederick Walker, which appeared in its serial form, were not reprinted in this edition.

Thackeray has here left an admirable picture of his beloved Bohemia. "'Philip,'" says Mrs. Ritchie, in her introduction to the Biographical Edition, "did not have the success it deserved. To me it seems to contain some of the wisest and most beautiful things my father ever wrote.

"I can remember hearing him say how much of his own early life was written down in its pages."

The original manuscript of *The Adventures of Philip* is in the collection of Major W. H. Lambert of Philadelphia.

THACKERAY, WILLIAM MAKEPEACE.

THE STUDENTS' QUARTER. LONDON, *John Camden Hotten*, [1864].
[727]

Crown octavo. First Edition.
COLLATION BY SIGNATURES: [A], 2 leaves; a, 1 leaf; B to M, each 8 leaves; N, 5 leaves; total 96 numbered leaves.
COLLATION BY PAGINATION: [title] | THE | STUDENTS' QUARTER | OR | PARIS FIVE-AND-THIRTY YEARS SINCE. | BY THE LATE | WILLIAM MAKEPEACE THACKERAY. | Not included in his Collected Writings. | WITH ORIGINAL COLOURED ILLUSTRATIONS. | LONDON: | JOHN CAMDEN HOTTEN, PICCADILLY. |, p. [i.]; — [imprint], p. [ii.]; — [preface], pp. [iii.]–iv.; — [contents], p. [v.]; — [blank], p. [vi.]; — [text, with heading] | THE STUDENTS' QUARTER. |, pp. [17]–202.

PLATES: 5 colored plates, each with Thackeray's well-known mark (a pair of spectacles) in the lower right-hand corner; facing the title-page and pp. 24, 56, 124, and [160].

CONDITION: Size of leaf, 7⅜ × 4⅞ inches. Bound in the original publisher's blue cloth, uncut edges.

REFERENCES.

Wilson, *Thackeray in the United States*, 1 (1904): 203; Dickson, *Bibliography*, in Wilson, *Thackeray in the United States*, 2 (1904): 344; Melville, *Life of Thackeray*, 2 (1899): 314; Slater, *Early Editions* (1894), p. 332, No. 36; Shepherd, *Bibliography of Thackeray* (1880), p. 10.

This work was originally published in cloth, with colored illustrations.

"Of the eight Letters," Shepherd says, "seven were reprinted in substance in the *Paris Sketch-Book* in 1840, with here and there a slight omission or alteration, hardly of sufficient interest to note. The only letter, therefore, 'not included in Thackeray's "Collected Writings" is that which stands as the fifth, and is entitled "More Aspects of Paris Life"' (pp. 113–132), and dated August 31. . . .

"It should be added that the coloured illustrations which figure in this volume were not executed to accompany the letterpress, even if, as seems probable, they are rightly attributed to Thackeray's pencil."

The volume here described, published after Thackeray's death, is made up of articles from his pen mainly if not wholly contributed to *The Corsair*, which are here separately printed for the first time:

(1) "Off to France," pp. 17–42. This paper first appeared in *The Corsair*, August 24, 1839, pp. 380–382; and afterward in *The Paris Sketch Book*, 1840, Vol. 1, pp. 1–22, as "An Invasion of France."

(2) "A Week of Fêtes," pp. 43–62; in *The Corsair*, October 5, 1839, pp. 473–475; and in *The Paris Sketch Book*, Vol. 1, pp. 59–75, as "The Fêtes of July."

(3) "French Fiction," pp. 63–84; in *The Corsair*, September 14, 1839, pp. 429, 430; and in *The Paris Sketch Book*, Vol. 2, pp. 102–124, as "Madam Sand and the New Apocalypse" (first half).

(4) "The Story of 'Spiridion,'" pp. 85–112; in *The Corsair*, September 21, 1839, pp. 445–447; and in *The Paris Sketch Book*, Vol. 2, pp. 124–151, as "Madam Sand and the New Apocalypse" (second half).

(5) "More Aspects of Paris Life," pp. 113–132; in *The Corsair*, October 26, 1839, pp. 521–523; but not in *The Paris Sketch Book*.

(6) "A French Jack Sheppard," pp. 133–159; in *The Corsair*, October 19, 1839, pp. 504–506; and in *The Paris Sketch Book*, Vol. I, pp. 142–164, as "Cartouche." It also appeared in *Fraser's Magazine*, October, 1839, Vol. 20, pp. 447–453, as "The French Plutarch. I. Cartouche."

(7) "A Ramble in the Picture Galleries," pp. 160–182; in *The Corsair*, December 28, 1839, pp. 665–667; and in *The Paris Sketch Book*, Vol. I, pp. 76–97, as "On the French School of Painting."

(8) "Another Ramble in the Picture Galleries," pp. 183–202; in *The Corsair*, January 18, 1840, pp. 716, 717; and in *The Paris Sketch Book*, Vol. I, pp. 97–114, as "On the French School of Painting." This and the preceding article previously appeared in *Fraser's Magazine*, December, 1839, Vol. 20, pp. 679–688, as "On the French School of Painting."

"In a private letter to his partner, dated London, July 26, Willis writes: 'I have engaged a contributor to the "Corsair." Who do you think? The author of "Yellowplush" and "Major Gahagan." I have mentioned it in my jottings, that our readers may know all about it. He has gone to Paris, and will write letters from there, and afterwards from London, for a guinea a *close column* of the "Corsair" —cheaper than I ever did anything in my life. I will see that he is paid for a while to see how you like him. For myself, I think him the very best periodical writer alive. He is a royal, daring, fine creature too.'"

THACKERAY, WILLIAM MAKEPEACE. [Hotten, John Camden.]
(*b.* 1832, *d.* 1873.)

THACKERAY THE HUMOURIST AND THE MAN OF LETTERS.
LONDON, *John Camden Hotten*, 1864. [728]

Post octavo.

COLLATION BY SIGNATURES: [A], 4 leaves; B to P, each 8 leaves; total 116 numbered leaves.

COLLATION BY PAGINATION: [title] | THACKERAY | THE | HUMOURIST AND THE MAN OF LETTERS. | The Story of His Life, | INCLUDING | A SELECTION FROM HIS CHARACTERISTIC SPEECHES, NOW | FOR THE FIRST TIME GATHERED TOGETHER. | BY THEODORE TAYLOR, ESQ., | Membre de la Société des Gens de Lettres. | WITH PHOTOGRAPH FROM LIFE BY ERNEST EDWARDS, B.A., AND | ORIGINAL ILLUSTRATIONS. | [vignette] | LONDON: | JOHN CAMDEN HOTTEN, PICCADILLY. | 1864. |, p. [i.]; — [imprint], p. [ii.]; —[preface], pp. [iii.]–iv.; —[contents], pp. [v.]–vii.; —[blank], p. [viii.]; —[text, with heading] | THACKERAY; | THE | HUMOURIST AND THE MAN OF LETTERS. | THE STORY | OF HIS LIFE AND LABOURS. |, pp. [1]–223; —[blank], p. [224].

PLATES: Frontispiece; 2 engravings, facing pp. 48 and 83; and a facsimile page of Thackeray's handwriting, facing p. 188.

CONDITION: Size of leaf, 7⅝ × 4¹⁵⁄₁₆

No. 728   *William Makepeace Thackeray*   1864

inches. Bound in the original publisher's green cloth, uncut and unopened edges. With 14 unnumbered leaves of publisher's advertisements bound in at the end.

REFERENCE.

Shepherd, *Bibliography of Thackeray* (1880), p. 57, No. 18.

THACKERAY, WILLIAM MAKEPEACE.

DENIS DUVAL. LONDON, *Smith, Elder and Co.*, 1867.   [729]

Crown octavo.

COLLATION BY SIGNATURES: 2 leaves, without signature-marks; 1 to 17, each 8 leaves; 18, 2 leaves; total 140 leaves.

COLLATION BY PAGINATION: [title] | DENIS DUVAL. | BY | W. M. THACKERAY, | [2 lines] | LONDON: | SMITH, ELDER AND CO., 65, CORNHILL. | 1867. |, recto of first leaf; — | [*The right of Translation is reserved.*] |, verso of first leaf; —[contents], recto of second leaf; —[blank], verso of second leaf; —[text, with heading] | DENIS DUVAL. |, pp. [1]–253; —[blank], p. [254]; — | NOTES ON DENIS DUVAL. |, pp. [255]–275; —[imprint], p. [276].

Inserted before the title-page is a half-title, verso blank, as follows: | DENIS DUVAL. |. Inserted at the end are 39 leaves, from Vol. 24 of "The Standard Edition" of Thackeray's Works, as follows: [half-title, verso blank] | THE | WRITINGS OF W. M. THACKERAY. | ;—[text, with heading] | THE WRITINGS | OF | W. M. THACKERAY. | BY LESLIE STEPHEN. |, pp. [359]–433; —[blank], p. [434]. After p. 426 are 3 pages of facsimile manuscript of Thackeray.

EXTRA-ILLUSTRATED.

Inserted in this work are the following:

Portrait of Thackeray, engraved by Joseph Brown, after Lawrence, with facsimile signature; facing the title-page.

Portrait of Thackeray in his library, engraved by Armytage from a photograph; facing inserted p. [359].

Four engravings by Swain, after drawings by Walker; facing pp. 12, 92, 186, and 243.

Also 8 initial letters, mounted to size: 2 by Thackeray, facing pp. [1] and 94; 4 by Ralston, facing pp. 14, 61, 125, and 188; and 2 by Walker, facing pp. 158 and 218.

CONDITION: Size of leaf, 7⅜ × 4⅞ inches. Bound in blue crushed levant morocco, gilt top, other edges uncut; by Bradstreet.

REFERENCES.

Dickson, *Bibliography*, in Wilson, *Thackeray in the United States*, 2 (1904): 252; Williams, *Bibliography*, in Thackeray, *Works* (Biographical Edition, 13 vols.; 1903), 13 : 735; Melville, *Life of Thackeray*, 2 (1899): 303; Slater, *Early Editions* (1894), p. 333, No. 37; Johnson, *Hints to Collectors of Original Editions of the Works of William Makepeace Thackeray* (1885), p. 42, No. XXXI.; Shepherd, *Bibliography of Thackeray* (1880), p. 50, No. 139.

This work originally appeared as a serial in *The Cornhill Magazine* (Vol. 9), from March to June, 1864, and was reprinted in *Harper's Magazine* (Vols. 28–29) for April, May, July, and August, 1864. The same year it first appeared at New York in book form, preceded by a short biographical sketch, "In Memoriam," by Charles Dickens, and illustrated with a portrait and eight woodcuts.

This is the First English Edition of Thackeray's last work, left unfinished at his death. It was issued without illustrations, though there had been illustrations in the magazine. The notes at the end are by Fred. Greenwood, at that time editor of *The Cornhill Magazine.*

THACKERAY, WILLIAM MAKEPEACE.

ETCHINGS. LONDON, *H. Sotheran & Co.*, 1878. [730]

Octavo. First Edition.

COLLATION BY SIGNATURES: 10 unnumbered leaves, without signature-marks.

COLLATION BY PAGINATION: [title] | *Etchings | by the late | William Makepeace Thackeray, | while at Cambridge, | Illustrative of | University Life, etc., etc. | Now First Published from the | Original Plates. | 1878. | London. H. Sotheran & C°., Piccadilly.* | [engraved entirely in script], p. [1]; —[blank], p. [2]; —| LIST OF SUBJECTS. |, p. [3]; —[blank], p. [4]; —[11 colored plates, on 8 leaves, verso pages blank], pp. [5]–[20].

PLATES: 11 plates, in two states, plain and colored, as follows:

[1] | *A Family Picture — the departue for Cambridge.* | .
[2] | *Another Family Picture — being the arrival from Cambridge.* | .
[3] | *Worldly Study* | .
[4] | *Imposition* | .
[5] | *The First Term* | .
[6] | *Second Term* | .
[7] [*Work Within*], without inscription.
[8] [*Pleasure Without*], without inscription.
[9] | *The Collera Morbus* | .
[10] | *Scene from the Deluge* | .
[11] | *Ah! Mr. Goldfinch . . .* | .

CONDITION: Size of leaf, 8 9/16 × 5 7/16 inches. Bound in half maroon crushed levant morocco, gilt top, other edges uncut. With the original front gray paper wrapper bound in, with title : | Etchings | [5 lines in script, same as the title-page] | Now First Published from the | Original Plates. | .

REFERENCES.

Melville, *Life of Thackeray,* 2 (1899): 304; Slater, *Early Editions* (1894), p. 334, No. 40; Johnson, *Hints to Collectors* (1885), p. 46, No. XXXV.; Shepherd, *Bibliography of Thackeray* (1880), p. 51, No. 143.

The plates in a few copies of this work were colored. Of the etchings here given, those most worthy of mention are "The Departure for Cambridge," "The Arrival from Cambridge," "The First Term," a student hard at work, and "The Second Term," the same student on a sofa with its back turned toward the spectator, who is able to see only the cigar and boots of the lounger.

THACKERAY, WILLIAM MAKEPEACE. Trollope, Anthony. (*b.* 1815, *d.* 1882.)

THACKERAY. LONDON, *Macmillan and Co.*, 1879. [731]

Crown octavo. First Edition.

COLLATION BY SIGNATURES: [A], 4 leaves; B to O, each 8 leaves; P, 2 leaves; total 110 leaves.

COLLATION BY PAGINATION: [half-title] | English Men of Letters | EDITED BY JOHN MORLEY | THACKERAY | [publishers' device] |, p. [i.]; —[blank], p. [ii.]; —[title] | THACKERAY | BY | ANTHONY TROLLOPE | London : | MAC-

No. 731   *William Makepeace Thackeray*   1879

MILLAN AND CO.| 1879.| *The Right of Translation and Reproduction is Reserved.*|, p. [iii.];—[imprint], p. [iv.];—[contents], pp. [v.]-vi.;—[half-title]| THACKERAY|, p. [vii.];—[blank], p. [viii.];—[text, with heading]| THACK-ERAY.|, pp. [1]-210;—[publishers' advertisement], pp. [1]-2.

CONDITION: Size of leaf, 7⅝ x 5⅛ inches. Bound in publishers' drab cloth, with paper title-label lettered:| Thackeray | Anthony | Trollope.|.

THACKERAY, WILLIAM MAKEPEACE.

EXTRACTS FROM THE WRITINGS OF W. M. THACKERAY. LONDON, *Smith, Elder, & Co.*, 1881.   [732]

Crown octavo.

COLLATION BY SIGNATURES: [A], 8 leaves (the first blank and genuine); B to Z, AA, BB, CC, each 8 leaves; total 208 leaves. Leaf 1 is marked *1.

COLLATION BY PAGINATION: [1 blank leaf], [A];—[half-title], p. [i.];—[blank], p. [ii.];—[title]| EXTRACTS | FROM | THE WRITINGS|OF|W. M. THACK-ERAY | *CHIEFLY PHILOSOPHICAL AND RE-FLECTIVE* |[quotations]| LONDON | SMITH, ELDER, & CO., 15 WATER-LOO PLACE|1881|, p. [iii.];—[blank], p. [iv.];—[contents], pp. [v.]-xiv.;—[text in numerous portions, the first with heading]| PARENTS AND CHIL-DREN.|, pp. [1]-395;—[blank], p. [396];—[publishers' advertisements], pp. [397]-[400].

PLATE: Portrait of Thackeray in his study, engraved by Armytage from a photograph; facing the title-page.

CONDITION: Size of leaf, 7⅞ x 5 inches. Bound in publisher's green cloth, uncut edges.

REFERENCES.

Dickson, *Bibliography*, in Wilson, *Thackeray in the United States*, 2 (1904): 262; Johnson, *Hints to Collectors* (1885), p. 48, No. XXXVII.

The portrait of Thackeray in his library, contained in this compilation, is a good one, and the choice of passages is excellent. This edition was reissued, with a new title-page, by J. B. Lippincott & Co., of Philadelphia, in 1882.

THACKERAY, WILLIAM MAKEPEACE.

A COLLECTION OF LETTERS OF THACKERAY. NEW YORK, *Charles Scribner's Sons*, 1887.   [733]

Superroyal octavo. No. 131 of 500 copies printed.

COLLATION BY SIGNATURES: 6 leaves, without signature-marks (the first blank and genuine); [1] to 11, each 8 leaves; [12], 8 leaves (the last blank and genuine); total 102 numbered leaves.

COLLATION BY PAGINATION: [1 blank leaf];—[half-title], p. [i.];—[edition notice], p. [ii.];—[rubricated title]| A COLLECTION OF | LETTERS OF THACKERAY | 1847-1855 | NEW YORK|CHARLES SCRIBNER'S SONS | MDCCCLXXXVII |, p. [iii.];—[copyright notice], p. [iv.];—| PUBLISHERS' NOTE.|, pp. [v.]-vi.;—[list of illustrations], pp. vii.-ix.;—[blank], p. [x.];—[introduction], pp. [1]-2;—[half-title] |

LETTERS. |, p. [3];—[blank], p. [4]; —[text], pp. [5]–183;—[blank], p. [184];—[index], pp. [185]–189;—[blank], p. [190];—[1 blank leaf], [12₈].

PLATES: 4 portraits and 14 plates, as follows:

4 portraits of Thackeray; facing the title-page (India proof) and pp. 118, 158 (India proof), and 178.

14 photogravures; facing pp. 18, 28, 40, 54, 62, 68, 72, 82, 94, 114, 130, 138, 148, and 154.

There are also numerous small illustrations in the text.

CONDITION: Size of leaf, 9$\frac{15}{16}$ × 7$\frac{1}{16}$ inches. Bound in boards, cloth back, gilt top, other edges uncut. With 3 facsimile letters, bound in at pp. 80, 110, and 142.

These letters originally appeared in *Scribner's Magazine*, Vol. 1 (1887), pp. 387, 551, and 672, and Vol. 2 (1887), pp. 18, 131, 321, and 412. They extend from 1847 to 1855.

In the introduction, written by Mrs. Brookfield, the recipient of most of the letters contained in this volume, she says:

"The letters which form this collection were most of them written by Mr. Thackeray to my husband, the late Rev'd W. H. Brookfield, and myself, from about 1847, and continuing during many years of intimate friendship, beginning from the time when he first lived in London, and when he especially needed our sympathy. His happy married life had been broken up by the malady which fell upon his young wife after the birth of her youngest child; his two remaining little girls were under his mother's care, at Paris. Mr. Thackeray was living alone in London. 'Vanity Fair' was not yet written when these letters begin. His fame was not yet established in the world at large; but amongst his close personal friends, an undoubting belief in his genius had already become strongly rooted. No one earlier than my dear gifted husband adopted and proclaimed this new faith. The letters now so informally collected together are not a consecutive series; but they have always been carefully preserved with sincere affection by those to whom they were written. Some of them are here given without the omission of a word; others are extracts from communications of a more private character; but if every one of these letters from Thackeray could be rightly made public, without the slightest restriction, they would all the more redound to his honour."

THACKERAY, WILLIAM MAKEPEACE. Johnson, Charles Plumptre.

THE EARLY WRITINGS OF WILLIAM MAKEPEACE THACKERAY.
LONDON, *Elliot Stock*, 1888. [734]

Square royal octavo. One of 50 large-paper copies printed on Van Gelder hand-made paper.

COLLATION BY SIGNATURES: 7 leaves, without signature-marks; 1 to 4, each 8 leaves; 1 leaf, without signature-mark; total 40 leaves. Leaves 3—2 and 4 have no signature-marks.

COLLATION BY PAGINATION: [half-title], p. [i.];—[blank], p. [ii.];—

No. 734 *William Makepeace Thackeray* **1888**

[title] | | The Early Writings | OF | William Makepeace Thackeray | BY | CHARLES PLUMPTRE JOHNSON | *WITH ILLUSTRATIONS AFTER W. M. THACKERAY* | *CHINNERY, F. WALKER AND R. DOYLE* | LONDON | ELLIOT STOCK, 62, PATERNOSTER ROW, E.C | 1888 | , p. [iii.]; — [edition notice], p. [iv.]; — [dedication, contents, list of illustrations, and introduction], pp. [v.]–xiv.; — [text, with heading] | THE EARLY WRITINGS | OF | WM. MAKEPEACE THACKERAY. | , pp. [1]–64; — [publisher's advertisement], p. [65]; — [blank], p. [66]. Pages 17, 35, 50, and 59 are blank.

PLATES: 4 photogravures, each in two states, plain and on India paper; and numerous illustrations in the text; all as called for in the list of illustrations.

CONDITION: Size of leaf, 9⅞ × 7⅜ inches. Roxburghe binding, gilt top, other edges uncut.

This work originally appeared in *The Athenæum* as *Notes and Queries for a Bibliography of the Writings of W. M. Thackeray*. In it are reprinted several pieces from *The Snob* and *The Gownsman* which have been attributed to Thackeray; an account of his unfortunate connections with *The National Standard* and *The Constitutional* and his later connection with *Fraser's Magazine;* and at the end a chapter is devoted to the first American editions of his works in *Appleton's Popular Library of the Best Authors*, and other publications.

THACKERAY, WILLIAM MAKEPEACE.

READING A POEM.   LONDON, *The Chiswick Press*, 1891.   **[735]**

Sixteenmo. First Edition No. 269 of 321 copies printed for private circulation only.

COLLATION BY SIGNATURES: [A], 6 leaves; B to E, each 8 leaves; [F], 2 leaves; total 40 leaves.

COLLATION BY PAGINATION: [half-title] | | [conventional head-piece] | PRIVATELY PRINTED OPUSCULA | Issued to Members of the Sette | of Odd Volumes | No. XXVII | READING A POEM | [type-ornament] | , p. [i.]; — [publisher's note], p. [ii.]; — [title] | READING A POEM | BY | WM. MAKEPEACE THACKERAY | COMMUNICATED BY | *BROTHER CHARLES PLUMPTRE JOHNSON* | TO THE SETTE AT A MEETING HOLDEN AT | LIMMER'S HOTEL, ON FRIDAY THE | 1ST OF MAY, 1891 | IMPRINTED AT | THE CHISWICK PRESS, TOOKS COURT | CHANCERY LANE, LONDON | MDCCCXCI | , p. [iii.]; — [blank], p. [iv.]; — [dedication], p. [v.]; — [blank], p. [vi.]; — [edition notice], p. [vii.]; — [blank], p. [viii.]; — [introduction], pp. [ix.]–xi.; — [blank], p. [xii.]; — [text, with heading] | READING A POEM. | BY MR. MICHAEL ANGELO TITMARSH. | , pp. [1]–50; — | O. V. | A | BIBLIOGRAPHY | OF THE | PRIVATELY PRINTED OPUSCULA | *Issued to the Members of the Sette of Odd Volumes.* | , pp. [51]–56; — | MISCELLANIES. | , pp. [57]–60; — | Ye Sette of Odd Volumes. | [a list of members], pp. [61]–66; — [imprint], p. [67]; — [blank], p. [68].

PLATE: 1 plate, proof on India paper, by W. D. Almond; facing the title-page.

Inserted as an extra-illustration is a pen-and-ink portrait of Thackeray; facing the title-page.

CONDITION: Size of leaf, 5⁷⁄₁₀ × 4⅜ inches. Bound in mauve crushed levant morocco, leather hinges, gilt top, other edges uncut; by Bradstreet. With the original vellum wrappers, sides and back, bound in, with rubricated title: | *THE SETTE OF ODD VOLUMES* | [conventional ornament] | Reading a Poem | A Sketch by | WM. MAKEPEACE THACKERAY | COMMUNICATED TO THE SETTE AT A MEETING | HOLDEN AT LIMMER'S HOTEL, ON FRIDAY | THE 1ST OF MAY, 1891, BY | BROTHER CHARLES PLUMPTRE JOHNSON | [printer's device] | IMPRINTED AT THE CHISWICK PRESS, TOOKS | COURT, CHANCERY LANE, LONDON. MDCCCXCI | ; and the seal of the Odd Volumes on the back wrapper; with title along the back: | O.V. | XXVII | Reading a Poem | 1891 | .

REFERENCES.

Dickson, *Bibliography*, in Wilson, *Thackeray in the United States*, 2 (1904) : 279; Williams, *Bibliography*, in Thackeray, *Works* (Biographical Edition, 13 vols.; 1903), 13 : 743; Melville, *Life of Thackeray*, 2 (1899) : 307, 311.

This sketch originally appeared in *The Britannia* for May 1, 1841, and is here separately printed by C. P. Johnson for the first time, as No. XXVII. of "The Sette of Odd Volumes," and distributed to members of that book club. It was also privately printed in an edition of one hundred copies for Mr. Edward G. Kennedy, a member of the Grolier Club, in 1897.

"There was also an edition published by A. Wessels Co., New York, 1903." — DICKSON (in a private communication).

This little play in two scenes, says Melville (2 : 165), "deals with the days when 'Bungay' and 'Bacon' issued *Keepsakes* and *Spring Annuals*, and would pay large sums to obtain the poems — or the *names* — of titled ladies and gentlemen . . .

"That Thackeray ever attempted to have this performed I think unlikely, but it is certainly amusing; and in the quaint satire on the remarkably ephemeral *Annuals* there are discernible many touches of the hand that afterward wrote *Pendennis*."

THACKERAY, WILLIAM MAKEPEACE. Crowe, Eyre.

WITH THACKERAY IN AMERICA. NEW YORK, *Charles Scribner's Sons,* 1893. [736]

Octavo.

COLLATION BY SIGNATURES: 10 leaves, without signature-marks; 1 to 11, each 8 leaves; 12, 6 leaves; total 104 leaves. Leaf 3_2 is wrongly marked D 2.

COLLATION BY PAGINATION: [blank], recto of first leaf; —[publishers' advertisement], verso of first leaf; —[blank], p. [i.]; —[frontispiece], p. [ii.]; —[title] | WITH THACKERAY | IN AMERICA | BY | EYRE CROWE, A.R.A. | *ILLUSTRATED* | NEW YORK | CHARLES SCRIBNER'S SONS | 1893 | , p. [iii.]; — [copyright notice and imprint], p. [iv.]; —[dedication, preface, contents, and list of illustrations], pp. [v.]–xvi.; —[half-title], p. [xvii.]; —[blank], p. [xviii.]; —[text, with heading] | WITH THACKERAY IN AMERICA |, pp. [1]–176; —[index], pp. [177]–179; —[blank], p. [180]; — [publishers' advertisements], pp. [1]–8.

Besides the frontispiece there are numerous woodcuts in the text, all as called for in the list of illustrations.

CONDITION: Size of leaf, 8¼ x 6¹/₁₀ inches. Bound in publishers' cloth.

This volume contains 118 illustrations and a facsimile of Thackeray's handwriting.

THACKERAY, WILLIAM MAKEPEACE.

MR. THACKERAY'S WRITINGS IN "THE NATIONAL STANDARD," AND "CONSTITUTIONAL." LONDON, *W. T. Spencer*, 1899. [737]

Octavo. One of 500 copies printed.

COLLATION BY SIGNATURES: [A], 2 leaves; B, 4 leaves; [1] to 7, each 8 leaves; 8, 4 leaves; 9 to 20, each 8 leaves; total 162 leaves.

COLLATION BY PAGINATION: [half-title], recto of [A]; — [edition notice], verso of [A]; — [title] | MR. THACKERAY'S | WRITINGS IN | "THE NATIONAL STANDARD," | AND | "CONSTITUTIONAL." | *With Facsimiles of all the Illustrations by the author: — and a special Portrait | from the Monumental Bust in Westminster Abbey.* | TO WHICH IS ADDED AN | ELEGIAC POEM (1864), | BY | SEBASTIAN EVANS, M.A. | [vignette] | LONDON: | W. T. SPENCER, 27, New Oxford Street, W.C. | 1899 |, recto of [A 2]; — [blank], verso of [A 2]; — [dedication], recto of B; — [blank], verso of B; — [preface], recto of [B 2]; — [blank], verso of [B 2]; — [contents], recto of [B 3]; — [blank], verso of [B 3]; — | COPY OF THE ORIGINAL TITLE PAGE | [of the *National Standard*], recto of [B 4]; — [note], verso of [B 4]; — [text], pp. [1]-105; — [blank], p. [106]; — [half-title] | "THE CONSTITUTIONAL, | (AND PUBLIC LEDGER):" | LONDON: 1836-1837. |, p. [107]; — [blank], p. [108]; — [note], p. 109; — [blank], p. [110]; — [text, with heading] | "THE CONSTITUTIONAL, &c." |, pp. [111]-297; — [blank], p. [298]; — [half-title] | TO THE MEMORY | OF | WILLIAM MAKEPEACE THACKERAY | A POEM BY | SEBASTIAN EVANS, M.A. |, p. [299]; — [blank], p. [300]; — [note], p. [301]; — [blank], p. [302]; — | COPY OF ORIGINAL TITLE-PAGE | [of the elegiac poem], p. [303]; — [blank], p. [304]; — [text of poem, with heading] | William Makepeace Thackeray. | *December 24th*, 1863. |, pp. [305]-312.

PLATE: Portrait of Thackeray, with facsimile signature; facing the title-page.

There are also numerous woodcuts in the text.

CONDITION: Size of leaf, 8⁹⁄₁₆ × 5¹¹⁄₁₆ inches. Bound in half red straight-grained morocco, gilt top, other edges uncut.

REFERENCES.

Wilson, *Thackeray in the United States*, 2 (1904): 107; Melville, *Life of Thackeray*, 2 (1899): 311, 321; Johnson, *Early Writings of Thackeray* (1888), pp. 19-34; Shepherd, *Bibliography of Thackeray* (1880), p. 1, No. 2.

In this work are collected for the first time in separate form Thackeray's contributions, during the years 1833-1837, to the two unsuccessful weekly journals in which he was interested, not only as contributor but also as editor and part owner. The first of these, *The National Standard*, appeared from January 5, 1833, to February 1, 1834. Thackeray's editorship began about the nineteenth number, and he appears to have done a variety of work upon it. Shepherd traces thirteen articles to his pen, which appeared from May 4th to August 24th, when his contributions appear to have ceased.

The second of these journals, *The Constitutional*, in which Thackeray met with financial ruin, was begun September 15, 1836, and continued to July 1, 1837, the date of the last number. Of this Laman Blanchard was editor, and Thackeray the

Paris correspondent. Between September 27th and February 18th he contributed forty-four pieces.

There is a complete file of the *Constitutional* in the collection of Major William H. Lambert of Philadelphia.

"Mr. Spencer, the editor of the 1899 volume, missed one number by Thackeray, the letter dated 'Paris Feb'y 8th' and printed in *The Constitutional* for February 11, 1837, fol. 3, cols. 5 and 6. This letter has never been reprinted." — DICKSON (in a private communication).

THOMSON, JAMES. (*b.* 1700, *d.* 1748.)

THE SEASONS. LONDON, *for James Wallis*, 1805. [738]

Octavo.

COLLATION BY SIGNATURES: 1 leaf, without signature-mark; a, 8 leaves; 2 leaves, without signature-marks; B, C, D, each 8 leaves; E, 4 leaves; 2 leaves, without signature-marks; F to K, each 8 leaves; L, 4 leaves; 3 leaves, without signature-marks; M to P, each 8 leaves; Q, 4 leaves (the last lacking); R, S, T, each 8 leaves; U, 2 leaves; 1 leaf, without signature-mark; X, 4 leaves; Y, 2 leaves; total 157 leaves.

COLLATION BY PAGINATION: [title] | THE | SEASONS, | BY | JAMES THOMSON: | WITH | HIS LIFE | BY | SAMUEL JOHNSON, L.L.D. | AND | *A COMPLETE GLOSSARY AND INDEX.* | EMBELLISHED WITH ENGRAVINGS ON WOOD, | BY BEWICK, | FROM THURSTON'S DESIGNS. | LONDON : | PRINTED FOR JAMES WALLIS, PATERNOSTER-ROW. | 1805. |, recto of first leaf; — [blank], verso of first leaf; — [text, with heading] | LIFE OF THOMSON. |, pp. [i.]-xvi.; — [half-title] | SPRING. | [woodcut] | [6 lines of verse] |, p. [xvii.]; — [blank], p. [xviii.]; — | THE ARGUMENT. |, p. [xix.]; — [blank], p. [xx.]; — [text, with heading] | SPRING. |, pp. [1]-57; — [blank], p. [58]; — [half-title] | SUMMER. | [woodcut] | [4 lines of verse] |, p. [59]; — [blank], p. [60]; — | THE ARGUMENT. |, p. [61]; — [blank], p. [62]; — [text, with heading] | SUMMER. |, pp. [63]-149; — [blank], p. [150]; — [half-title] | AUTUMN. | [woodcut] | [4 lines of verse] |, p. [151]; — [blank], p. [152]; — | THE ARGUMENT. |, p. [153]; — [blank], p. [154]; — [text, with heading] | AUTUMN. |, pp. [155]-221; — [blank], p. [222]; — [half-title] | WINTER. | [woodcut] | [4 lines of verse] |, p. [223]; — [blank], p. [224]; — | THE ARGUMENT. |, p. [225]; — [blank], p. [226]; — [text, with heading] | WINTER. |, pp. [227]-278; — [half-title] | HYMN. | [woodcut] | [4 lines of verse] |, p. [279]; — [blank], p. [280]; — [text, with heading] | A HYMN. |, pp. [281]-286; — | THE | INDEX AND GLOSSARY. |, pp. [287]-[292].

ILLUSTRATIONS: 9 woodcuts by Bewick.

CONDITION: Size of leaf, 8 15/40 x 5 5/8 inches. Bound in light polished calf, sprinkled edges. Pages 225-226, containing the Argument for "Winter," are lacking.

REFERENCES.

Newcastle-upon-Tyne, Public Library, *Catalogue Bewick Collection* (1904), p. 35, No. 115; Thomson, *Life and Works of Thomas Bewick* (1882), p. 217; same, *Catalogue* (Stephens, *Notes*; 1881), p. 26; Hugo, *Bewick Collector*, 1 (1866): 84, Nos. 203, 204.

No. 738   *James Thomson*   1805

There were two editions of *The Seasons* published in 1805: one in royal octavo on very thick paper with remarkably fine impressions of the plates and with twenty pages of preliminary matter; the other in octavo with sixteen preliminary pages. The title-pages also differ, that of the thick-paper edition reading, according to Hugo: "The Seasons, By J. Thomson. Embellished with Engravings on Wood By Bewick, From Thurston's Designs. London: Printed for James Wallis, Paternoster-Row, By T. Bensley, Bolt Court, Fleet Street, 1805."

The copy here described, according to Hugo, *Bewick Collector* (Nos. 203–204), has the title-page of the octavo edition and the text of the royal octavo edition.

"The blocks in this volume," says Thomson, "are quite different in workmanship from those in the Birds; they are so much like several of Bewick's pupils' work as to make it exceedingly doubtful if the master did more than superintend the execution."

Dr. Johnson says: "The reader of 'The Seasons' wonders that he never saw before what Thomson shows him, and that he never yet has felt what Thomson impresses. . . . His descriptions of extended scenes and general effects bring before us the whole magnificence of Nature, whether pleasing or dreadful. The gaiety of Spring, the splendour of Summer, the tranquillity of Autumn, and the horror of Winter, take in their turns possession of the mind."

TUCKERMAN, HENRY THEODORE. (*b.* 1813, *d.* 1871.)

BOOK OF THE ARTISTS.   NEW YORK, G. P. *Putnam & Sons;* LONDON, Sampson Low & Co., 1867.   [739]

Superroyal quarto. Largest-paper copy. One of 25 copies printed.

COLLATION BY SIGNATURES: 4 leaves, without signature-marks (the first blank and genuine); [1] to 40, each 8 leaves; total 324 leaves. Leaves 30 and 32 have no signature-marks. Notwithstanding the signature-marks, this work is imposed in quarto.

COLLATION BY PAGINATION: [1 blank leaf];—[title] | Book of the Artists. | AMERICAN ARTIST LIFE, | COMPRISING BIOGRAPHICAL AND CRITICAL SKETCHES | OF AMERICAN ARTISTS: PRECEDED BY AN HIS- | TORICAL ACCOUNT OF THE RISE AND | PROGRESS OF ART IN AMERICA. | BY | HENRY T. TUCKERMAN. | WITH AN APPENDIX CONTAINING AN ACCOUNT OF NOTABLE PICTURES | AND PRIVATE COLLECTIONS. | [publishers' device] | NEW YORK: | G. P. PUTNAM & SON, 661 BROADWAY | LONDON: SAMPSON LOW & CO. | 1867. |, p. [i.];—[copyright notice and imprint], p. [ii.];—[quotations], p. [iii.]; —[blank], p. [iv.];—[contents], pp. [v.]–vi.;— | PUBLISHERS' ADVERTISEMENT. |, p. [vii.];—[blank], p. [viii.];— | PLAN AND PURPOSE OF THIS WORK. |, pp. [ix.]–xi.;— [blank], p. [xii.];— | INTRODUCTION. | ART IN AMERICA. |, pp. [7]–39;— [blank], p. [40];—[text, with heading] | AMERICAN ARTIST LIFE. |, pp. [41]–619;—[blank], p. [620];—[appendix], pp. [621]–633;—[blank], p. [634]; —[index], pp. [635]–639;—[blank], p. [640].

PORTRAITS: 58 portraits (57 photographs and 1 stipple engraving) of American artists, all but two mounted to size.

CONDITION: Size of leaf, 14¼ × 11¼ inches. Folded sheets, in portfolio.

REFERENCE.

Allibone, 3 (1881): 2467, No. 22.

WALTON, IZAAK. (*b.* 1593, *d.* 1683.)

THE LIVES OF DONNE, WOTTON, HOOKER, AND HERBERT.
LONDON, *by Tho. Newcomb for Richard Marriott*, 1670.   4 parts in 1 vol., octavo, viz.:

[740]

[PART 1.]

COLLATION BY SIGNATURES: A, 8 leaves (the first and eighth blank and genuine); B to F, each 8 leaves; G, 4 leaves; total 52 leaves. Leaf D4 has no signature-mark.

COLLATION BY PAGINATION: [1 blank leaf], [A]; — [title, as reproduced; *See* No. 740 *a*], recto of [A 2]; — [blank], verso of [A 2]; — | To the Right Honorable | And | Reverend Father in GOD | GEORGE | *Lord Bifhop of Winchefter*, . . . | [2 lines] | [signed] | *Izaak Walton.* |, recto of *A* 3 to verso of *A* 4; — | To the Reader. | [signed] | *J. W.* |, recto of [A 5] to recto of [A 7]; — | ERRATA. |, verso of [A 7]; — [1 blank leaf], [A 8]; — | *The Copy of a Letter writ to* | *Mr. Ifaac Walton, by Doctor* | *King Lord Bifhop of* Chi- | chefter. | [dated] | Chichefter, | *Novem.* 17. | 1664. |, pp. 1 – 8; — [text, with heading] | THE | LIFE | OF | Dr. JOHN DONNE, | [2 lines] |, pp. 9 – 81; — | An EPITAPH written by Dr. | *Corbet*, late Bifhop of *Oxford*, | on his Friend Dr. *Donne.* |, p. 82; — [2 elegies], pp. 83 – 88; — | FINIS. |, p. 88.

PLATE: Portrait of Donne, engraved by Lombart; facing p. 9.

[PART 2.]

COLLATION BY SIGNATURES: A, 4 leaves; B to E, each 8 leaves; F, 4 leaves; total 40 numbered leaves. Leaf A 2 is wrongly marked B 2.

COLLATION BY PAGINATION: [title] | THE | LIFE | OF | Sr HENRY WOTTON, | [4 lines] | *LONDON*, | Printed by *Thomas Newcomb*, for *Richard Marriot*, | and fold by moft Bookfellers. 1670. |, p. [1]; — [blank], p. [2]; — [text, with heading] | THE | LIFE | OF | Sir HENRY WOTTON. |, pp. 3 – 77; — | AN | ELEGIE | ON | Sir HENRY WOTTON, | WRIT | By Mr *ABRAM COWLEY.* |, pp. 78 – 79; — | FINIS. |, p. 79; — [blank], p. [80].

PLATE: Portrait of Wotton, engraved by Dolle; facing the title-page.

[PART 3.]

COLLATION BY SIGNATURES: A, 4 leaves; B to H, each 8 leaves; total 60 numbered leaves. Leaf H 2 is wrongly marked F 2; and H 4 is F 4.

COLLATION BY PAGINATION: [title] | The LIFE | OF | Mr. RICH. HOOKER, | [8 lines] | *LONDON*, | Printed by *Tho: Newcomb*, for *Rich: Marriot*, | fold by moft *Bookfellers.* M.DC.LXX. |, p. [1]; — [blank], p. [2]; — [complimentary verses, with heading] | To . . . Mr. | *Ifaac Walton*, upon his . . . | . . . Life of . . . | . . . Mr. | *Richard Hooker.* | [signed] | *Sam: Woodford.* | [dated] | Benfted Hants. | Mar. 10. 16$\frac{69}{70}$. |, pp. 3 – 6; — | THE LIFE | OF | Mr. RICHARD HOOKER. | [with introduction], pp. 7 – 110; — [epitaph] | . . . in memory of Mr. *Hooker*, | by Sir *William Cooper*, . . . | [2 lines] |, p. 111 [wrongly numbered 11]; — | APPENDIX |, pp. 112 – 122; — | GEORGE CRANMER'S | LETTER unto | Mr. *Richard Hooker.* | February 1598. |, pp. 123 – 140. Page 111 is wrongly numbered 11; and the numbers 57 – 76 are omitted in the pagination.

PLATE: Portrait of Hooker, by Dolle; facing the title-page.

[PART 4.]

COLLATION BY SIGNATURES: A to F, each 8 leaves; G, 4 leaves; total 52 numbered leaves.

COLLATION BY PAGINATION: [title] | The LIFE | OF | Mr. GEORGE HERBERT. | [4 lines] | *LONDON*, | Printed by *Tho: Newcomb*, for *Richard Marriott*, | fold by moft Bookfellers. M.DC.LXX. |, p. [1]; — | IMPRIMATUR, | Sam: Parker *Reveren-*

THE LIVES

Of
- Dr *John Donne*,
- Sir *Henry Wotton*,
- Mr *Richard Hooker*,
- Mr *George Herbert*.

Written by I Z A A K W ALTON.

To which are added some Letters written by Mr. *George Herbert*, at his being in *Cambridge*: with others to his Mother, the Lady *Magdalen Herbert*, written by *John Donne*, afterwards Dean of St. *Pauls*.

Eccles. 44. 7.
These were honourable men in their Generations.

LONDON,
Printed by *Tho. Newcomb* for *Richard Marriott*.
Sold by most Booksellers. 1670.

No. 740 a.   Title-page of Walton's Lives of Donne, Wotton, Hooker, and Herbert; 1st Collected Edition; 1670.

1670 — Izaak Walton — No. 740

diſſimo in | Chriſto Patri ac Domino, Domi- | no Gilberto Archi-ep: Cantuar : | à Sac: Domeſt. | April 21. | 1670. |, p. [2]; — [complimentary verses, with heading] | To . . . | . . . Mr. | Izaack Walton, upon his Ex- | cellent Life of Mr. George | Herbert. | [signed] | Sam: Woodforde. |, pp. 3 – 5 ; — | The LIFE | OF | Mr. GEORGE HER- BERT. |[with introduction], pp. 6 – 80 ; — [note], pp. 81 – 82.

| LETTERS | WRITTEN BY | Mr. GEORGE HERBERT, | [2 lines] | With others to his Mother, the Lady | MAGDA- LEN HERBERT : | WRITTEN BY | John Donne, | [2 lines] | LONDON, | Printed by Tho: Newcomb, for Richard Marriott, | Sold by moſt Bookſellers. M.DC.LXX. |, p. [83] ; — [blank], p. [84] ; — [text in numerous portions, the first with heading] | Mr. GEORGE HER- | BERT to N. F. the | TRANSLATOUR of Val- | [deſſo's] Book. |, [etc.], pp. 85 – 103 ; — | FINIS. |, p. 103 ; — [verse, with heading] | On Mr. George Her- bert's Book, | Intituled, The Temple of Sa- | cred Poems, ſent to a Gen- | tlewoman. |, p. 104.

PLATE : Portrait of Herbert, engraved by R. White ; facing the title-page.

CONDITION : Size of leaf, 7 1/16 × 4 11/16 inches. Bound in green crushed levant mo- rocco, gilt edges ; by Stikeman.

OTHER COPIES.

British Museum ; Trinity College, Cam- bridge ; Devonshire ; Ellesmere ; Huth ; Lenox ; and Halsey Libraries.

REFERENCES.

Locker-Lampson, Catalogue (1886), p. 127 ; Hazlitt, Collections and Notes (1882), p. 632 ; Allibone, 3 (1881) : 2566 ; Huth, Catalogue, 5 (1880) : 1561 ; Lowndes, Bib- liographer's Manual of English Literature, 5 (1869) : 2829.

First Collected Edition.

The Foote copy, with ex-libris.

This was a presentation copy from the author, and contains an autograph inscrip- tion on the verso of the first blank leaf, as reproduced (See No. 740 b). Walton seems to have given away a number of copies of this work, in each of which he had corrected some of the errors of the press with his own hand.

NO. 740 b. AUTOGRAPH OF IZAAK WALTON.

WALTON, IZAAK.

THE LIVES OF DONNE, WOTTON, HOOKER, HERBERT, AND SANDERSON. YORK, Wilson, Spence, and Mawman, 1796. [741]

Quarto. First Zouch Edition.

COLLATION BY SIGNATURES : 2 leaves, without signature-marks (the first blank and genuine) ; [A] to F, f, each 4 leaves ; 4 leaves, without signature-marks ; G to Z, Aa to Xx, each 4 leaves ; xx, 2 leaves ; Yy, Zz, 3A to 3Z, 4A, each 4 leaves (the last blank and lacking) ; total 292 leaves. Leaves N 2, Q 2, and R 2 have no signature-marks ; Pp is marked PP ; and Pp 2 is PP 2.

COLLATION BY PAGINATION : [1 blank

THE
LIVES

OF

DR. JOHN DONNE; SIR HENRY WOTTON;

MR. RICHARD HOOKER; MR. GEORGE HERBERT;

AND

DR. ROBERT SANDERSON.

BY ISAAC WALTON.

WITH

NOTES, AND THE LIFE OF THE AUTHOR.

BY THOMAS ZOUCH, M.A.

THESE WERE HONOURABLE MEN IN THEIR GENERATIONS.   ECCLES. xliv. 7.

YORK:
PRINTED BY WILSON, SPENCE, AND MAWMAN.
SOLD BY J. ROBSON, NEW BOND-STREET, B. WHITE, FLEET-STREET, T. PAYNE, AT THE MEWS-GATE, AND T. EGERTON, WHITEHALL, LONDON; J. COOKE, OXFORD; J. DEIGHTON, CAMBRIDGE; AND WILSON, SPENCE, AND MAWMAN, J. TODD, AND H. SOTHERAN, YORK.
Anno 1796.

No. 741.   TITLE-PAGE OF WALTON'S LIVES OF DONNE, WOTTON, HOOKER, HERBERT, AND SANDERSON; 1ST ZOUCH EDITION; 1796.
Reduced; original 7 15/16 × 5 11/16 inches.

leaf]; —[title, as reproduced; *See* No. 741], recto of second leaf; —[blank], verso of second leaf; — | TO THE RIGHT HONOURABLE | SIR RICHARD PEPPER ARDEN, | [signed] | THOMAS ZOUCH. | [dated] | WYCLIFFE, JAN. 16, 1796. |, p. [i.]; —[blank], p. [ii.]; —[preface, contents, and directions for placing the plates], pp. [iii.]–[vii.]; —[blank], p. [viii.]; —[life of Walton], pp. [ix.]–liv.; —[errata], p. [lv.]; —[blank], p. [lvi.]; —[half-title] | WALTON'S LIVES. |, p. [1]; —[blank], p. [2]; —[dedication, preface, verses by Cotton, and copy of a letter written to Walton by the Bishop of Chichester], pp. [3]–22; —[life of Donne, with half-title, introduction, verses, appendix, and errata], pp. [23]–116; —[life of Wotton, with half-title, elegy, and appendix], pp. [117]–[191]; —[blank], p. [192]; —[life of Hooker, with half-title, complimentary verses, preface, introduction, epitaph, errata, and appendix], pp. [193]–314; —[life of Herbert, with half-title, complimentary verses, introduction, appendix, and errata], leaf [xx 2] and pp. [313]–406; —[life of Sanderson, with half-title, dedication, preface, and appendix], pp. [407]–508; — | ADDENDA. |, pp. [509]–512; —[in-dex], pp. [513]–518; —[1 blank leaf], [4A 4]. The numbers 313 and 314 are repeated in the pagination; leaf xx 2 has no page-number; and p. 395 is wrongly numbered 397.

PLATES: 7 portraits and one view, bound in as called for in the directions for placing the plates, except that the portrait of Hooker faces p. [1] instead of p. 193.

EXTRA-ILLUSTRATED.

Inserted in this work are:

[1] Portrait of Sir Julius Cæsar, Knt., published Oct. 11, 1810, by Robt. Wilkinson; facing p. 158.

[2] View of Old St. Paul's (?), after Hollar, engraved by W. Byrne; facing p. 78.

CONDITION: Size of leaf, 11⅛ x 8¾ inches. Bound in green crushed levant morocco, gilt top, other edges uncut; by Stikeman. The binder has improperly folded sheet [A] so that the dedication and preface follow instead of precede the contents and directions for placing the plates. He has also placed the leaf of errata [f 4] after p. [2].

REFERENCES.

Allibone, 3 (1881): 2566; Lowndes, 5 (1869): 2829.

On the recto of leaf [A] is the following inscription, written in ink: | *James Tate.* | *Richmond, Yorkshire.* | *From the Editor.* | [Thomas Zouch].

WALTON, IZAAK.

THE LIVES OF DONNE, WOTTON, HOOKER, HERBERT, AND SANDERSON. LONDON, *John Major*, 1825. [742]

Post octavo.

COLLATION BY SIGNATURES: [a], b, each 4 leaves; c, 2 leaves; B to [Z], Aa to Zz, 3 A to 3 T, each 4 leaves; total 262 numbered leaves. The letter n is omitted in the first series of signature-marks.

COLLATION BY PAGINATION: [title] | THE | LIVES | OF | DR. JOHN DONNE, SIR HENRY WOTTON, | MR. RICHARD HOOKER, | MR. GEORGE HERBERT, | AND | DR. ROBERT SANDERSON: | BY IZAAK WALTON. | TO WHICH ARE ADDED, | THE AUTOGRAPHS OF THOSE EMINENT MEN, | NOW FIRST COLLECTED; | AN INDEX, AND ILLUSTRATIVE NOTES. | [printer's device] | [quotation] | LONDON: | JOHN MAJOR, FLEET-STREET, | ADJOINING SERJEANTS'-INN. | MDCCCXXV. |, p. [i.]; —[quotation and imprint], p. [ii.];

—[preface, list of embellishments, and dedication], pp. [iii.]–xviii.

| THE LIFE | OF | DR. JOHN DONNE, | LATE DEAN OF ST. PAUL'S CHURCH, | LONDON. | [vignette] | LONDON : | JOHN MAJOR, | MDCCCXXV. |, p. [xix.] ; —[blank], p.[xx.]; —[introduction, text, epitaph, and elegy], pp. [1]–86.

| THE LIFE | OF | SIR HENRY WOTTON, KNIGHT, | LATE | PROVOST | OF | ETON COLLEGE. | [vignette] | LONDON : | JOHN MAJOR, | MDCCCXXV. |, p. [87]; —[blank], p. [88]; —[text and elegy], pp. [89]–160.

| THE LIFE | OF | MR. RICHARD HOOKER : | THE AUTHOR OF THOSE LEARNED BOOKS | OF THE | LAWS OF ECCLESIASTICAL POLITY. | [vignette] | LONDON : | JOHN MAJOR, | MDCCCXXV. |, p. [161]; —[blank], p. [162] ; —[introduction, text, and appendix], pp. [163]–268.

| THE LIFE | OF | MR. | GEORGE HERBERT, | PREBENDARY OF SALISBURY CATHEDRAL. | [vignette] | LONDON : | JOHN MAJOR, | MDCCCXXV. |, p. [269]; —[blank], p. [270]; —[introduction and text], pp. [271]–348.

| THE LIFE | OF | DR. ROBERT SANDERSON, | LATE BISHOP OF LINCOLN. | [vignette] | LONDON : | JOHN MAJOR, | MDCCCXXV. |, p. [349]; —[blank], p. [350]; —[dedication, preface, and text], pp. [351]–438 ; —[notes and index], pp. [439]–503 ; —[printer's device and imprint], p. [504]. Page 328 is wrongly numbered 283.

PLATES : 5 portraits and 6 plates ; also 52 woodcuts in the text ; all as called for in the list of illustrations.

CONDITION : Size of leaf, 7^{15}⁄$_{16}$ × 5 inches. Bound in brown crushed levant morocco, gilt top, other edges uncut ; by Matthews.

WALTON, IZAAK.

THE LIVES OF DONNE, WOTTON, HOOKER, HERBERT AND SANDERSON. LONDON, *William Pickering*, 1827.   [743]

Thirtytwomo. Large-paper copy.

COLLATION BY SIGNATURES : 4 leaves, without signature-marks (the first blank and lacking) ; 1 to 27, each 8 leaves ; 28, 6 leaves (the last blank and lacking) ; total 226 leaves. Leaves 4 and 8 have no signature-marks.

COLLATION BY PAGINATION : [1 blank leaf] ; —[title] | THE | LIVES | OF | DONNE, WOTTON, HOOKER, | HERBERT AND | SANDERSON. | WRITTEN BY | IZAAK WALTON. | [quotation, 2 lines] | LONDON | WILLIAM PICKERING | M.DCCC.XXVII. |, p. [i.] ; —[imprint], p. [ii.] ; —[preface and contents], pp. [iii.]–[v.] ; —[blank], p. [vi.] ; —[dedication, address to the reader, and copy of a letter to Walton from the Bishop of Chichester], pp. [i.]–xiii. ; —[blank], p. [xiv.]; —[life of Donne, with half-title and introduction], pp. [xv.]–xix. and [1]–74 ; —[life of Wotton], pp. [75]–139; —[elegy on Wotton], pp. [140]–141 ; —[blank], p. [142] ; —[life of Hooker, with address to the reader, introduction, appendix, and Cranmer's letter], pp. [143]–245 ; —[blank], p. [246] ; —[life of Herbert, with introduction], pp. [247]–315; —[letters], pp. [316]–329 ; —[blank], p. [330]; —[life of Sanderson, with dedication and preface], pp. [331]–411 ; —[letters], pp. [412]–422.

PLATE : Portraits of Donne, Wotton, Hooker, Herbert, and Sanderson, engraved by Aug. Fox, after Stothard, a group ; facing the title-page.

CONDITION : Size of leaf, 4⅝ × 2¾ inches. Bound in red crushed levant morocco, gilt top, other edges uncut; by Rivière.

In some copies there occur the following variations from the copy here described: Leaves 4 and 8 have signature-marks, but 1 and 18 have none; pp. 1–4 (title, etc.) are numbered in arabic instead of roman characters; the D is supplied at the end of the word LEARNED in the heading on p. 143; p. xiii. is wrongly numbered xii.; and pp. 413–422 are wrongly numbered 433–442.

REFERENCES.

Allibone, 3 (1881) : 2566; Lowndes, *Bibliographer's Manual of English Literature*, 5 (1869) : 2830.

This edition was intended as a companion volume to Pickering's editions of *The Complete Angler*, 1825 and 1826. A few copies were printed on India paper.

WALTON, IZAAK.

THE LIFE OF DR. SANDERSON, LATE BISHOP OF LINCOLN.
LONDON, *for Richard Marriott*, 1678. [744]

Small octavo.   First Edition.

COLLATION BY SIGNATURES: A, a to o, A to S, each 8 leaves; T, 4 leaves; total 268 leaves.

COLLATION BY PAGINATION: [blank], recto of [A]; —[portrait of Dr. Sanderson], verso of [A]; —[title, as reproduced; See No. 744], recto of [A 2]; —[blank], verso of [A 2]; — | TO THE | RIGHT REVEREND, | AND | HONOURABLE, | GEORGE | Lord Bifhop of Winchefter, |[3 lines]|[signed] | *Izaak Walton* |, recto of *A* 3 to verso of *A* 4; — | THE | PREFACE. |, recto of [A 5] to recto of [A 8]; —[license to print] | *May the 7th.* 1678. | [signed] | *WILL. JANE*, Chaplain | to the Right Reverend | Father in God, *Henry* Lord | Bifhop of *London*. |, verso of [A 8]; —[text, with heading] | THE | LIFE | OF | Dr. *Robert Sanderfon*, |[2 lines]|, recto of a to verso of n 3; — | Poftfcript. |, recto of n 4; —[blank], verso of n 4; — | Dr. *PIERCE*'s | LETTER. | [dated] | *North-Tidworth*, | *March* 5. 167$\frac{7}{8}$. |, recto of [n 5] to recto of o 2; —[blank], verso of o 2; — | THE | BISHOP | OF | LINCOLN'S | LETTER· | [dated] | *London*, *May* 10. | 1678. |, recto of o 3 to verso of [o 7]; — | ERRATA. | [9 lines]|, recto of [o 8]; —[blank], verso of [o 8].

| Bifhop *Sanderfon*'s | JUDGMENT | Concerning | SUBMISSION | TO | Ufurpers.

| *LONDON*, | Printed by for *Richard Marriott*. | M DC LXXVIII. |, recto of [A]; —[blank], verso of [A]; —[text, with heading] | Bifhop *Sanderfon*'s | JUDGMENT | Concerning | SUBMISSION | TO | USURPERS. |, pp. 1–45; —[blank], p. [46].

| PAX | Ecclefiæ. | BY THE | RIGHT REVEREND | FATHER in GOD | *ROBERT SANDERSON*, | LATE | Lord *Bifhop of* Lincoln. | *LONDON*, | Printed for *Richard Marriott*. 1678. |, recto of [D]; —[blank], verso of [D]; —[text, with heading] | PAX | ECCLESIÆ. |, pp. 47–84.

| Bifhop *Sanderfon*'s | JUDGMENT | IN ONE | VIEW | FOR THE | SETTLEMENT | OF THE | CHURCH. | LONDON, | Printed for *Richard Marriott*. | 1678. |, p. [85]; —[blank], p. [86]; —[text, with heading] | Bifhop *Sanderfon*'s | JUDGMENT | IN ONE | VIEW. |, pp. 87–167; —[blank], p. [168].

| REASONS | Of the prefent | JUDGMENT | OF THE | Univerfity of *OXFORD*, | Concerning | The | *Solemn League and Covenant*. | *Negative Oath*. | *Ordinances concerning Difci-* | *pline and Worfhip*. | [4 lines] | *LONDON*, | Printed for *Richard Marriott*. | 1678. |, recto of [L 7]; —[blank], verso of [L 7]; —[text in several portions, the first with heading] | A Solemn League and | Covenant for Refor- | mation

THE LIFE OF Dr. SANDERSON, LATE Bishop of Lincoln.

Written by IZAAK WALTON.

To which is added, Some short Tracts or Cases of Conscience, written by the said Bishop.

ECCLES. 3.
Mysteries are revealed to the meek.

LONDON,
Printed for *Richard Marriott.* 1678.

No. 744. Title-page of Walton's Life of Dr. Sanderson; 1st Edition; 1678.

1678   *Izaak Walton*   No. 744

and Defence of | Religion, . . . | [5 lines] |, recto of [L8] to p. 253;—[blank], p. [254].

  | A | SERMON | OF | RICHARD HOOKER | Author of thofe | LEARNED BOOKS | OF | *Ecclefiaftical Politie*, | Found in the Study of the late | Learned Bifhop *Andrews*. | LONDON, | Printed for *Richard Marriott*. | 1678. |, recto of [S];—[blank], verso of [S];—[text, with heading] | A | SERMON | OF | *Richard Hooker, &c.* |, pp. 255–276;— | FINIS. |, p. 276.

  PORTRAIT: Portrait, with inscription: | *R. White fculpfit.* | *Vera Effigies Reverendi* | *Patris* ROBERTI SANDERSON | *Lincolnien-sis Episcopi, Æt. 76.* |; facing the title-page.

  CONDITION: Size of leaf, 6⅞ x 4¼ inches. Bound in old mottled calf, sprinkled edges.

OTHER COPIES.

British Museum (3); Trinity College, Cambridge; Devonshire; Ellesmere; Huth; Lenox; and Hoe Libraries.

REFERENCES.

Hoe, *Catalogue*, 5 (1905): 76; Marston, *Walton and Some Earlier Writers on Fish and Fishing* (1894), p. 234; Hazlitt, *Collections and Notes* (1882), p. 632; Huth, *Catalogue*, 5 (1880): 1561.

This was the last of the unrivalled collection of devotional biographies written by Walton, which are unapproached alike in graceful simplicity and in humble admiration and piety. Walton must have been well over eighty years of age when he wrote it. Five years later he died, and was buried in Winchester Cathedral.

"In his 'Epistle Dedicatory' of his Life of Dr. Sanderson, Bishop of Lincoln, Walton, addressing Dr. George Morley, Bishop of Winchester, thanks him for having introduced him to 'Dr. Sanderson, Mr. Chillingworth and Dr. Hammond,' men whose merits ought never to be forgotten; and he mentions that his friendship for Dr. Sanderson 'was begun almost forty years past.'"

WOLLSTONECRAFT (*afterward* GODWIN), MARY. (*b.* 1759, *d.* 1797.)

ORIGINAL STORIES FROM REAL LIFE. LONDON, *for J. Johnfon*, 1791.   [745]

  Duodecimo.

  COLLATION BY SIGNATURES: A, 6 leaves; B to H, each 12 leaves; I, 6 leaves; total 96 leaves.

  COLLATION BY PAGINATION: [title] | ORIGINAL STORIES | FROM | *REAL LIFE*; | WITH | CONVERSATIONS, | CALCULATED TO | REGULATE THE AFFECTIONS, | AND | FORM THE MIND | TO | TRUTH AND GOODNESS. | BY MARY WOLLSTONECRAFT. | LONDON: | PRINTED FOR J. JOHNSON, NO. 72, ST. | PAUL'S CHURCH-YARD. | 1791. |, p. [i.];—[blank], p. [ii.];—[preface], pp. [iii.]–vi.;—[introduction], pp. [vii.]–viii.;—[contents], pp. [ix.]–[xii.];—[text, with heading] | MORAL CONVERSATIONS | AND | STORIES. |, pp. [1]–177;—[publisher's catalogue of books], pp. [178]–[180].

  PLATES: 6 engravings by Blake; facing the title-page and pp. 24, 75, 93, 114, and 172.

  CONDITION: Size of leaf, 6½ x 3⅞ inches. Bound in light polished calf, gilt edges; by Rivière.

This author is best known by her *Vindication of the Rights of Woman* (1792), a plea for equality of education, noted for its unreserved plainness of speech.

YARRELL, WILLIAM. (b. 1784, d. 1856.)

A HISTORY OF BRITISH BIRDS. LONDON, John Van Voorst, 1843. 3 vols., royal octavo, viz.:

VOL. 1.

COLLATION BY SIGNATURES: [A], b, B to R, each 8 leaves; s, 9 leaves; T, U, each 8 leaves; x, 9 leaves; Y, Z, 2 A to 2 D, each 8 leaves; 2 E, 9 leaves; 2 F to 2 L, each 8 leaves (the last blank and lacking); total 283 numbered leaves. Leaves s 7, x 7, and 2 E 3 have signature-marks; 2 B, 2 I 2, and 2 L have none.
COLLATION BY PAGINATION: [half-title], p. [i.]; — [blank], p. [ii.]; — [title] | A | HISTORY | OF | BRITISH BIRDS. | BY | WILLIAM YARRELL, F.L.S. V.P.Z.S. | [coat of arms] | ILLUS-TRATED BY 520 WOOD-ENGRAVINGS. | IN THREE VOLUMES. — VOL. I. | LONDON: | JOHN VAN VOORST, PATERNOSTER ROW. | M.DCCC.-XLIII. |, p. [iii.]; — [imprint], p. [iv.]; — [preface], pp. [v.]-xii.; — [index], pp. [xiii.]-xxxii.; — [text, with heading] | BRITISH BIRDS. |, pp. [1]-525; — [imprint], p. [526]; — [1 blank leaf], [2L 8]. Pages 268* and 269* follow p. 268; 316* and 317* follow 316; and 420* and 421* follow 420.

VOL. 2.

COLLATION BY SIGNATURES: [A], 2 leaves; B to P, each 8 leaves; Q, 9 leaves; R to Z, 2 A to 2 U, each 8 leaves; total 339 leaves. Leaves E 2, K 2, M, Q 2, and 2 A 2 have no signature-marks; and Q 5 has a signature-mark.
COLLATION BY PAGINATION: [half-title], recto of [A]; — [blank], verso of [A]; — [title, same as in Vol. 1, except vignette and volume-number], recto of [A 2]; — [imprint], verso of [A 2]; — [text, with heading] | BRITISH BIRDS. |, pp. [1]-669; — [imprint], p. [670]; — | TEMPORARY | INDEX TO ENGLISH NAMES | OF VOLUME II. |, pp. [671]-672. Pages 232* and 233* follow p. 232.

VOL. 3.

COLLATION BY SIGNATURES: [A], 2 leaves; B to Z, 2 A to 2 L, each 8 leaves; total 266 leaves. Leaves C 2, T 2, U 2, and x 2 have no signature-marks.
COLLATION BY PAGINATION: [half-title], recto of [A]; — [blank], verso of [A]; — [title, same as in Vol. 1, except vignette and volume-number], recto of [A 2]; — [imprint], verso of [A 2]; — [text, with heading] | BRITISH BIRDS. |, pp. [1]-528.
There are 520 woodcuts in the text of the three volumes.
CONDITION: Size of leaf, 8¹⁵⁄₁₆ x 6¼ inches. Bound in half blue crushed levant morocco, gilt tops, other edges uncut; by Bradstreet. Large-paper copy. Published in 37 monthly numbered parts, at five shillings each, from July, 1837, to June, 1843, in brown wrappers, with title: | A | HISTORY | OF | BRITISH BIRDS. | BY | WILLIAM YARRELL, F.L.S. | SECRETARY TO THE ZOOLOGICAL SOCIETY. | ILLUSTRATED BY A WOODCUT OF EACH SPECIES, | AND NUMEROUS VIGNETTES. | LONDON: | JOHN VAN VOORST, 1, PATERNOSTER ROW; | CHEAPSIDE END. |. With wrappers and one advertising page bound in at the end, in all 75 leaves, as follows: Vol. 1, Parts I.-XI., July 1, 1837, to March 1, 1839; Vol. 2, Parts XII.-XXV., May 1, 1839, to June 1, 1841; Vol. 3, Parts XXVI.-XXXVII., August 2, 1841, to June 1, 1843; each 2 leaves except Part XXXVII., which has 3 leaves.

REFERENCE.

Lowndes, 5 (1869): 3015.

1843   *William Yarrell*   No. 746

Large-paper copy. This is the Second Edition with the First Supplement incorporated. This work was published in three sizes, octavo, royal octavo, and imperial octavo.

The titles of the wrappers vary greatly. Two different vignettes are used, and some are entirely without them.

YARRELL, WILLIAM.

SUPPLEMENT TO THE HISTORY OF BRITISH BIRDS. LONDON, *John Van Voorst,* 1845.   [747]

Royal octavo.

COLLATION BY SIGNATURES: [A], 4 leaves (the first blank and lacking); [B], 4 leaves; C, D, each 8 leaves; E, 4 leaves (the last blank and lacking); total 28 numbered leaves.

COLLATION BY PAGINATION: [1 blank leaf], pp. [1]-[2];—[title] | SUPPLEMENT | TO THE | HISTORY | OF | BRITISH BIRDS. | BY | WILLIAM YARRELL, F.L.S. V.P.Z.S. | [vignette] | ILLUSTRATED WITH WOOD-ENGRAVINGS. | LONDON: | JOHN VAN VOORST, PATERNOSTER ROW. | M.DCCC.XLV. |, p. [3];—[blank], p. [4];—[preface], p. [5];—[blank], p. [6];—[text, with heading] | SUPPLEMENT | TO THE | HISTORY OF BRITISH BIRDS. |, pp. 7-53;—[imprint], p. [54].

There are 13 woodcuts in the text.

CONDITION: Size of leaf, 8 15/16 × 6¼ inches. Bound with Vol. 3 of the preceding number.

YARRELL, WILLIAM.

SECOND SUPPLEMENT TO THE HISTORY OF BRITISH BIRDS. LONDON, *John Van Voorst,* 1856.   [748]

Royal octavo.

COLLATION BY SIGNATURES: [A], 2 leaves (the first blank and lacking); b, 4 leaves; B to E, each 8 leaves; F, 6 leaves; total 44 numbered leaves.

COLLATION BY PAGINATION: [1 blank leaf], [A];—[title] | SECOND SUPPLEMENT | TO THE | HISTORY | OF | BRITISH BIRDS: | BEING ALSO A | FIRST SUPPLEMENT TO THE SECOND EDITION. | BY WILLIAM YARRELL, V.P.L.S. F.Z.S. | [printer's device] | ILLUSTRATED WITH 18 WOOD-ENGRAVINGS. | LONDON: | JOHN VAN VOORST, PATERNOSTER ROW. | M.DCCC.LVI. |, p. [i.];—[imprint], p. [ii.];—[preface], pp. [iii.]-x.;—[text, with heading] | SECOND SUPPLEMENT | TO THE | HISTORY OF BRITISH BIRDS. |, pp. [1]-71;—[imprint], p. [72];—[publisher's advertisements], pp. [1]-4.

There are 18 woodcuts in the text.

CONDITION: Size of leaf, 8 15/16 × 6¼ inches. Bound with Vol. 3 of No. 746.

ZOUCH, THOMAS.

THE LIFE OF ISAAC WALTON. LONDON, *Septimus Prowett,* 1823.
See No. 110.

INDEX

(References are to numbers only)

ABBOT, The; Scott; 1st edition, 1820. 537
À Beckett, Gilbert A. Comic Blackstone; 1st edition; London, 1844. 1
Comic History of England; 1st edition; London, 1847-48. 2
Comic History of Rome; 1st edition; London, 1852. 3
À Beckett, Gilbert A., *editor*. CRUIKSHANK. Table-book; 1st edition, 1845. 287
Accedence commenc't grammar; Milton; 1st edition, 1669. 497
Addison, Charles G. Damascus and Palmyra; London, 1838. 685
Adventures of Hunch-back; London, 1814. 119
Adventures of Philip; Thackeray; 1st edition, 1862. 726
Adventures of Ulysses; Lamb; 1st edition, 1808. 427

Æsop. Fables; London, 1793. 4
Æsop *and others*. Beauties of Æsop and other fabulists; London, 1786. 142
Bewick's select fables; 1871. 130
— *same*; 1879. 131
Fables of Æsop, and others; 1st edition; Newcastle, 1818. 179
— *same*; 2d edition; Newcastle, 1823. 180
Select fables; 2d edition, 2d impression; Newcastle, 1784. 128
— *same*; Charnley edition; Newcastle, 1820. 129
Agamemnon, translated by John Studley; Seneca; 1581. *in* 504
Age of intellect; Moore; London, 1819. 242
Ainsworth, William H. Guy Fawkes; 1st edition; London, 1841. 8
Jack Sheppard; 1st edition; London, 1839. 6
Rookwood; 4th edition; London, 1836. 5
Saint James's; London, 1846. 9
Tower of London; 1st edition; London, 1840. 7

À Kempis, Thomas. *See* Kempis, Thomas à.
Akenside, Mark. Poetical works; Aldine edition; London, 1835. *in* 195
Akerman, John Y. Tales of other days; 1st edition; London, 1830. 262
Album verses; Lamb; 1st edition, 1830. 441

Aldine edition of the British poets; 53 vols.; London, 1830-53. 195
Aldine presses. ANDREWS. Choice collection of books from the Aldine presses; 1885. 11
All the Year Round, Extra Christmas numbers of; 1859-67. 357
Allot, Robert. Englands Parnassus; 1st edition; London, 1600. 10
Amelia; Fielding; 1st edition, 1752. 382
— *same*; 1832. *in* 267
American angler's guide; Brown; 4th edition, 1857. 100
American engravers. *See* Engravers, American.
American notes; Dickens; 1st edition, 1st issue, 1842. 336
American Revolution. ANDREWS. Essay on the portraiture of the American Revolutionary war; 1896. 18
Among my books; Andrews; 1894. 15
Amoretti and Epithalamion; Spenser; 1st edition, 1595. 660
Anatomie of the English nunnery at Lisbon; Robinson; 3d edition, 1630. 511
Anatomy of melancholy; Burton; 1st edition, 1621. 210
Anderdon, John L. River Dove; London, 1845. 92
— *same*; London, 1847. 93
Andrews, William L. Among my books; N. Y., 1894. 15
Bibliopegy in the United States; N. Y., 1902. 28
Bradford map of the city of New York; N. Y., 1893. 14
Choice collection of books from the Aldine presses; N. Y., 1885. 11
English XIX century sportsman and bibliopole; N. Y., 1906. 28 B
Essay on the portraiture of the American Revolutionary war; N. Y., 1896. 18
Fragments of American history; N. Y., 1898. 21
Gossip about book collecting; N. Y., 1900. 24
Iconography of the Battery and Castle Garden; N. Y., 1901. 26
Jacob Steendam; a memoir of the first poet in New Netherland; N. Y., 1908. 29

Vol. I., Nos. 1-416; II., 417-748.

Andrews, William L. (*continued*). James Lyne's survey; or, The Bradford map of the city of New York; N. Y., 1900. 25
Jean Grolier; N. Y., 1892. 12
Journey of the Iconophiles around New York; N. Y., 1897. 19
New Amsterdam, New Orange, New York; N. Y., 1897. 20
Paul Revere and his engraving; N. Y., 1901. 27
Roger Payne and his art; N. Y., 1892. 13
Sextodecimos et infra; N. Y., 1899. 22
Short historical sketch of the art of bookbinding; N. Y., 1895. 17
Stray leaf from the correspondence of Washington Irving and Dickens; N. Y., 1894. 16
Trio of eighteenth century French engravers of portraits in miniature; N. Y., 1899. 23
Andrews, William L., *editor*. BERNERS. Treatyse of fysshynge wyth an angle; N. Y., 1903. 28 A
Angler's guide; Salter; 2d edition, 1815. 75
— *same*; 3d edition, 1815. 76
— *same*; 9th edition, 1841. 77
Angler's rambles; Jesse; 1836. 84
Angling:
  ANDERDON. River Dove; 1845. 92
  — *same*; 1847. 93
  ANDREWS. An English XIX century sportsman and bibliopole; 1906. 28 B
  BADDELEY. London angler's book; 1834. 82
  BERNERS. Book containing the treatises of hawking; hunting; coat-armour; fishing; and blasing of arms (reprint); 1810. 74
  — Treatyse of fysshynge wyth an angle; 1827. 78
  — *same*; 1903. 28 A
  BEST. Concise treatise on the art of angling; 1st edition, 1787. 72
  BLACKER. Art of fly making; 1855. 97
  BOOSEY. Piscatorial reminiscences and gleanings; 1835. 83
  BOUSSUET. De natura aquatilium carmen; 1558. 32
  BOWDICH. Fresh-water fishes of Great Britain; 1828. 79
  BOWLKER. Art of angling, greatly enlarged and improved; 1829. 80
  BROOKES. Art of angling; 3d edition, 1770. 70
  BROWN. American angler's guide; 4th edition, 1857. 100
  BROWNE. Angling sports; 3d edition, 1773. 71
  BURNAND. Incompleat angler; 1887. 107
  Concise but comprehensive treatise on the art of angling; London, c. 1809. 73
  COTTON. Compleat angler, Part 2; 1st edition, 1676. *in* 38
  — *same*. *in* 39
    See also WALTON and COTTON.

Angling (*continued*):
  Fly-fisher's entomology; 5th edition, 1856. 98
  HALFORD. Floating flies and how to dress them; 1886. 106
  HAMILTON. Recollections of fly fishing for salmon, trout, and grayling; 1884. 104
  HERBERT. Frank Forester's fish and fishing; 1850. 94
  — *same*; new edition, 1859. 96
  — *same*; Supplement; 1850. 95
  HOFLAND. British angler's manual; 1st edition, 1839. 88
  JESSE. Angler's rambles; 1836. 84
  — Scenes and tales of country life; 1844. 91
  MARBURY. Favorite flies and their histories; 1892. 109
  MAYER. Sport with gun and rod in American woods and waters; 1883. 103
  NOBBES. Compleat troller; 1st edition, 1682. 68
  OPPIANUS. Halieuticks; 1722. 31
  — Oppiani poetæ alieuticon seu de piscibus; 1508. 30
  PENN. Maxims and hints for an angler; 1st edition, 1833. 81
  PHILLIPS. True enjoyment of angling; 1843. 89
  SABIN. Bibliographical catalogue of the Waltonian library of Robert W. Coleman; 1866. 115
  SAGE. Ristigouche and its salmon fishing; 1888. 108
  SALTER. Angler's guide; 2d edition, 1815. 75
  — *same*; 3d edition, 1815. 76
  — *same*; 9th edition, 1841. 77
  SAUNDERS. Compleat fisherman; 1724. 69
  SCOTT. Fishing in American waters; 1869. 101
  SCROPE. Days and nights of salmon fishing in the Tweed; 1st edition, 1843. 90
  SOLTAU. Trout flies of Devon and Cornwall; 2d edition, 1856. 99
  STEWART. Caution to anglers; 1871. 102
  VENABLES. Experienc'd angler; 1st edition, 1662. 67
  — *same*; 4th edition, 1676. *in* 39
  WALTON. Compleat angler; 1st edition, 1653. 33
  — *same* (Bagster's reprint); 1810. 34
  — *same*; 2d edition, 1655. 35
  — *same*; 3d edition, 1661. 36
  — *same*; 4th edition, 1668. 37
  WALTON and COTTON. Compleat angler; Walton's 5th and Cotton's 1st edition, 1676. 38
  — *same*. *in* 39
  — *same*; Bagster's 1st edition (4to), 1808. 48
  — *same* (medium 8vo). 49
  — *same*; Bagster's 2d edition, 1815. 50
  — *same*; Bethune's 1st edition, 1847. 62
  — *same*; Bethune's 2d edition, 1880. 65

Vol. I., Nos. 1-416; II., 417-748.

Angling (continued):
  WALTON *and* COTTON. Compleat angler; Browne's 1st edition, 1750.   40
  — *same*; Browne's 2d edition, 1759.   41
  — *same*; Browne's 3d edition, 1772.   43
  — *same*; Causton's edition, 1851.   63
  — *same*; Gosden's edition, 1822.   51
  — *same*; Hawkins' 1st edition, 1760.   42
  — *same* (reprint); 1824.   54
  — *same*; Hawkins' 3d edition, 1775.   44
  — *same*; Hawkins' 4th edition, 1784.   45
  — *same*; Hawkins' 5th edition, 2d issue, 1792.   46
  — *same*; Hawkins' 6th edition, 1797.   47
  — *same* (reprint); 1826.   56
  — *same*; Hawkins' 7th and Bagster's 1st edition (4to), 1808.   48
  — *same* (medium 8vo).   49
  — *same*; Hawkins' 8th and Bagster's 2d edition, 1815.   50
  — *same*; Hawkins' 9th or Gosden's edition, 1822.   51
  — *same*; Hawkins' 11th edition (reprint), 1825.   55
  — *same*; Hawkins-Rennie edition, 1836.   59
  — *same*; Lea and Dove edition; edited by R. B. Marston, 1888.   66
  — *same*; Major's 1st edition, 1823.   52
  — *same*; Major's 2d edition, 1824.   53
  — *same*; Major's 3d edition (reprint), 1839.   60
  — *same*; Major's 4th edition, 1844.   61
  — *same* (reprint); 1866.   64
  — *same*; Marston's Lea and Dove edition, 1888.   66
  — *same*; Pickering's 2d edition, 1826.   57
  — *same*; Pickering's 3d edition, 1836.   58
  — *same*; Rennie's edition, 1836.   59
  WALTON, COTTON, *and* VENABLES. Universal angler; Walton's 5th, Cotton's 1st, and Venable's 4th edition; 1676.   39
  WELLS. Fly-rods and fly-tackle; 1885.   105
  WESTWOOD. Chronicle of the "Compleat Angler"; 1864.   114
  WESTWOOD *and* SATCHELL. Chronicle of the "Compleat Angler" (reprint); 1888.   *in* 66
  WOOD. Bibliography of "The Complete Angler"; 1900.   116
  YARRELL. History of British fishes; 1836.   85
  — *same*; Supplement; 1839.   86
  — *same*; Second Supplement; 1860.   87
  See also Sports.
Angling sports; Browne; 3d edition, 1773.   71
Anne of Geierstein; Scott; 1st edition, 1829.   551
Anstey, Christopher. New Bath guide; London, 1832.   269
Antiquary, The; Scott; 1st edition, 1816.   532

Antonie, Tragedie of, doone into English by the Countesse of Pembroke; Garnier; 2d edition, 1595.   507
Apel, T. A. Der Freischütz travestie; 1st edition; London, 1824.   247
Apocalipsis cum figuris; Dürer; 4th edition; Nurnberge, 1511.   376
Arabian Nights:
  PAYNE, *translator*. Book of the thousand nights and one night; 1882–84.   117
  — Tales from the Arabic; 1884.   118
  SMIRKE, *illustrator*. Adventure of Hunch-back, and the stories connected with it; 1814.   119
Arden of Feversham, The lamentable and true tragedy of Master; 3d edition, 1633.   621
Areopagitica; a speech for the liberty of unlicenc'd printing; Milton; 1st edition, 1644.   490
Aretino, Leonardo. *See* Bruni, Leonardo.
Art of angling; Brookes; 3d edition, 1770.   70
Art of angling, greatly enlarged; Bowlker; 1829.   80
Art of fly making; Blacker; 1855.   97
Arthur, Morte d'. *See* Malory, *Sir* Thomas.
Arthur O'Leary; Lever; 1st edition, 1844.   452
Ascham, Roger. The scholemaster; 3d edition; London, 1573.   120
Ask mamma; Surtees; 1st edition, 1858.   671

BACON, Francis. Essayes; 1st edition; London, 1597.   121
— *same*; 2d edition; London, 1598.   122
Baddeley, John. London angler's book; London, 1834.   82
Bagster, Samuel, *publisher*:
  WALTON. Compleat angler; 1st edition (reprint), 1810.   34
  WALTON *and* COTTON. Compleat angler; 1st edition (4to), 1808.   48
  — *same* (medium 8vo).   49
  — *same*; 2d edition, 1815.   50
Baisers, Les; Dorat; 2d issue, 1770.   369
— *same*; 1880.   370
Baldwin, William, *editor*. Myrrour for magistrates; 2d edition; London, 1563.   499
Ballads:
  Collection of old ballads; London, 1723–25.   123
  DICKENS. Loving ballad of Lord Bateman; 1839.   330
  TARLTON. Prettie new ballad, intytuled: The Crowe sits upon the wall; n. d.   679
  THACKERAY. Ballads; 1st edition, 1855.   710
Barber Cox, and the cutting of his comb; Thackeray; 1st edition, 1839.   *in* 689
Barham, Richard H. Ingoldsby legends; 1st edition; London, 1840–47.   282

Vol. I., Nos. 1–416; II., 417–748.

Barker, Matthew H. Greenwich Hospital; London *and* Dublin, 1826. 254
    Land and sea tales; London, 1836. 277
    Tough yarns; London, 1835. 276
Barnaby Rudge; Dickens; 1st edition, 1841. *in* 334
Barnes, *Dame* Juliana. *See* Berners, *Dame* Juliana.
Barrington; Lever; 1st edition, 1863. 469
Barry Lyndon; Thackeray; 1856. 712
Basile, Giovanni B. The Pentamerone; 1st edition; London, 1848. 289
Bateman, Loving ballad of Lord; Dickens; 1st issue, 1839. 330
Battle of life; Dickens; 1st edition, 1st issue, 1846. 342
Battle of the books; Swift; 1st edition, 1704. *in* 674
Baucis and Philemon; Swift; 1st edition, 1709. 675
Beattie, James. Poetical works; Aldine edition; London, 1853. *in* 195
Beauties of Æsop and other fabulists; London, 1786. 142
Beauties of natural history; Buffon; 1804. 166
Beauty and the beast; Lamb; "Surprise" edition, 1813. 431
  — *same;* "Surprize" edition, 1813. 432
Beckett, Gilbert A. à. *See* À Beckett, Gilbert A.
Beckford, Peter. Thoughts on hunting; London, 1820. 181
Bedford-Row conspiracy; Thackeray; 1841. *in* 693
  — *same;* 1856. *in* 714
Bee and the wasp; Frankum; 1st edition, 1832. 271
Bembo, Pietro. Gli Asolani; Vinegia, 1515. 124
Berners, *Dame* Juliana. Book containing the treatises of hawking; hunting; coat-armour; fishing; and blasing of arms (reprint); London, 1810. 74
    Treatyse of fysshynge wyth an angle; London, 1827. 78
  — *same;* N. Y., 1903. 28 A
Berquin, Arnaud. Blossoms of morality; London, 1796. 127
Best, Thomas. Concise treatise on the art of angling; 1st edition; London, 1787. 72
Bethune, George W., *editor:*
    Walton *and* Cotton. Compleat angler; 1st edition, 1847. 62
  — *same;* 2d edition, 1880. 65
    See also Sabin, Bibliographical catalogue (115).
Betrothed, The; Scott; 1st edition, 1825. *in* 547
Betting-book, The; Cruikshank; 1852. 295
Bevan, Samuel. Sand and canvas; London, 1849. 702
Bewick, John, *illustrator:*
    Berquin. Blossoms of morality; 1796. 127

Bewick, John, *illustrator (continued)*:
    Trusler. Proverbs exemplified, and illustrated by pictures from real life; 1790. 125
    Wynne. Tales for youth, in thirty poems; 1794. 126
Bewick, John *and* Thomas, *illustrators:*
    Æsop and others. Bewick's select fables; 1871. 130
  — *same;* 1879. 131
  — Select fables; 2d edition, 2d impression, 1784. 128
  — *same;* Charnley edition, 1820. 129
    Campe. New Robinson Crusoe; 2d edition, 1789. 132
    Emblems of mortality; 1789. 133
    Goldsmith *and* Parnell. Poems; 1804. 138
    Le Grand d'Aussy. Fabliaux or tales, abridged from French manuscripts; 1st edition, 1796-1800. 134
  — *same;* 2d edition, 1815. 135
    Somerville. The Chase; 1st edition, 1796. 136
  — *same;* 2d edition, 1802. 137
Bewick, Thomas. Description of more than three hundred animals; London, 1812. 177
    General history of quadrupeds; 1st edition; Newcastle, 1790. 144
  — *same;* 2d edition; Newcastle, 1791. 145
  — *same;* 3d edition; Newcastle, 1792. 146
  — *same;* 4th edition; Newcastle, 1800. 147
  — *same;* 5th edition; Newcastle, 1807. 148
  — *same;* 6th edition; Newcastle *and* London, 1811. 149
  — *same;* 7th edition; Newcastle, London, *and* York, 1820. 150
  — *same;* 8th edition; Newcastle, London, *and* York, 1824. 151
    History of British birds; 1st edition, 1st impression; Newcastle, 1797-1804. 154
  — *same;* 1st edition, 2d impression; Newcastle, 1797-1804. 154 A
  — *same;* Newcastle, 1804. 155
  — *same;* 2d edition; Newcastle, 1805. 156
  — *same;* 3d edition; Newcastle, 1809. 157
  — *same;* 5th edition; Newcastle, 1821. 158
  — *same;* Supplement (imperial 8vo); Newcastle, 1821. 159
  — *same;* Supplement (8vo); Newcastle, 1821. 160
  — *same;* 6th edition; Newcastle, 1826. 161
  — *same;* Addenda; Newcastle, 1826. 162
  — *same;* 7th edition; Newcastle, 1832. 163
  — *same;* 8th edition; Newcastle, 1847. 164
    Holograph letter, ordering paper, dated Newcastle, July 26, 1821. 183
    Natural history of British birds; Alnwick, 1809. 168

Vol. I., Nos. 1-416; II., 417-748.

Bewick, Thomas (*continued*). Natural history of British quadrupeds; Alnwick, 1809.   171
Natural history of fishes; Alnwick, 1809.   173
Natural history of foreign birds; Alnwick, 1809.   169
Natural history of foreign quadrupeds; Alnwick, 1809.   172
Natural history of reptiles, serpents, and insects; Alnwick, 1809.   174
Natural history of water birds; Alnwick, 1809.   170
Wood engravings from a pretty book of pictures; Newcastle, 1779.   140

Bewick, Thomas, *illustrator*:
ÆSOP *and others*. Beauties of Æsop and other fabulists; 1786.   142
— Fables of Æsop, and others; 1st edition, 1818.   179
— *same*; 2d edition, 1823.   180
BECKFORD. Thoughts on hunting; 1820.   181
BUFFON. Beauties of natural history; 1804.   166
CONSETT. Tour through Sweden, Swedish-Lapland, Finland and Denmark; 1st edition, 1789.   143
GAY. Fables; 4th edition, 1811.   176
HODGSON. Hive of ancient and modern literature; 4th edition, 1812.   153
— Hive of modern literature; 1st edition, 1795.   152
Lilliputian magazine; London, 1783.   141
MINSHULL. Essayes and characters of a prison and prisoners; 1821.   184
New lottery book of birds and beasts, for children; Newcastle, 1771.   139
Oxford sausage; or, Select poetical pieces; London, 1814.   178
PERCY. Hermit of Warkworth; 2d edition, 1807.   167
REAY. Short treatise on that useful invention called the sportsman's friend; 1801.   165
SCOTT. British field sports; 1820.   182
THOMSON. The Seasons; 1805.   738
THORNTON. New family herbal; 1st edition, 1810.   175

Bewick, Thomas:
MEMOIR of Thomas Bewick, written by himself; Newcastle *and* London, 1862.   185
THOMSON. Life and works of Thomas Bewick; 1882.   186

Bewick, Thomas *and* John, *illustrators*:
ÆSOP *and others*. Bewick's select fables; 1871.   130
— *same*; 1879.   131
— Select fables; 2d edition, 2d impression, 1784.   128
— *same*; Charnley edition, 1820.   129

Bible. BIBLE in Greek; 1st edition; Venetiis, 1518.   187
Bibliographical Decameron; Dibdin; 1817.   314
Bibliography:
DIBDIN. Bibliographical Decameron; 1817.   314
— Bibliographical tour in England and Scotland; 1838.   318
— Bibliographical tour in France and Germany; 1821.   315
— Library companion; 2d edition, 1825.   316
— Typographical antiquities; 1st edition, 1810-19.   313
HALLIWELL-PHILLIPPS. Shakesperiana; a catalogue of the early editions of Shakespeare's plays; 1841.   641
JOHNSON. Early writings of Thackeray; 1888.   734
SABIN. Bibliographical catalogue of the Waltonian library of Robert W. Coleman; 1866.   115
WESTWOOD. Chronicle of the "Compleat Angler"; 1864.   114
WESTWOOD *and* SATCHELL. Chronicle of the "Compleat Angler" (reprint); 1888.   *in* 66
WINSOR. Bibliography of the original quartos and folios of Shakespeare; 1876.   644
WOOD. Bibliography of "The Complete Angler"; 1900.   116
Bibliomania; or, Book-madness; Dibdin; 3d edition, 1842.   319
Bibliopegy in the United States; Andrews; 1902.   28
Biglow papers, The; Lowell; 2d English edition, 1861.   301
Birds:
EYTON. Catalogue of British birds; 1836.   378
— History of the rarer British birds; 1836.   377
YARRELL. History of British birds; 1843.   746
— *same*; Supplement; 1845.   747
— *same*; Second Supplement; 1856.   748
See *also* Bewick, Thomas, History of British birds; *also* his Natural history of British birds.
Black dwarf, The; Scott; 1st edition, 1816.   *in* 533
Blacker, William. Art of fly making; London, 1855.   97
Blackmantle, Bernard, *pseudonym*. See Westmacott, Charles M.
Bleak House; Dickens; 1st edition, 1853.   350
Blossoms of morality; Berquin; 1796.   127
Boaden, James. Inquiry into the authenticity of various pictures of Shakspeare; London, 1824.   639

Vol. I., Nos. 1-416; II., 417-748.

Bobbin, Tim, *pseudonym*. *See* Collier, John.
Boccaccio, Giovanni. The Decameron; London, 1886. 189
— *same*; London, 1887. 190
— Le Decameron; Londres, 1757-61. 188
Book Collecting. ANDREWS. Gossip about book collecting; 1900. 24
Book of snobs; Thackeray; 1st edition, 1848. 697
Book of the artists; Tuckerman; 1867. 739
Bookbinding:
 ANDREWS. Bibliopegy in the United States; 1902. 28
 — Roger Payne and his art; 1892. 13
 — Short historical sketch of the art of bookbinding; 1895. 17
Bookbindings. BEMBO. Gli Asolani (in an original Grolier binding); 1515. 124
Book-making:
 ANDREWS. Bibliopegy in the United States; 1902. 28
 — Sextodecimos et infra; 1899. 22
Books of Hours. *See* Hours, Books of.
Boosey, Thomas. Piscatorial reminiscences and gleanings; London, 1835. 83
Boots at the Holly-tree Inn; Dickens; 1st reading edition, 1858. *in* 354
Boussuet, François. De natura aquatilium carmen; Lugduni, 1558. 32
Bow Street, Illustrations to Mornings at, with short extracts; Wight; 1827. 252
Bow Street, More mornings at; Wight; 1827. 257
Bow Street, Mornings at; Wight; 2d edition, 1824. 251
Bowdich, *Mrs.* Sarah W. Fresh-water fishes of Great Britain; London, 1828. 79
Bowles, William L. *and others*. Selected sonnets; Bristol, 1796. 417
Bowlker, Charles. Art of angling, greatly enlarged and improved; Ludlow, 1829. 80
Bowring, *Sir* John. Minor morals for young people; London, 1834-39. 274
Boz, *pseudonym*. *See* Dickens, Charles.
Bracciolini, Poggio. Historia Fiorentina; 1st edition; Vinegia, 1476. 191
Bramleighs of Bishop's Folly; Lever; 1st edition, 1868. 477
Brathwait, Richard. The English gentleman; 1st edition; London, 1630. 192
 The English gentlewoman; 1st edition; London, 1631. 193
Bray, *Mrs.* Anna E. K. S. Life of Thomas Stothard; London, 1851. 194
Bride of Lammermoor; Scott; 1st edition, 1819. *in* 536
British angler's manual; Hofland; 1st edition, 1839. 88

British poets; Aldine edition; 53 vols.; London, 1830-53. 195
Brittain's Ida; Spenser; 1st edition, 1628. 664
Brookes, Richard. Art of angling; 3d edition; London, 1770. 70
Brough, Robert B. Life of Sir John Falstaff; 1st edition; London, 1858. 298
Brown, John J. American angler's guide; 4th edition; N. Y., 1857. 100
Browne, Hablôt K. ("Phiz"), *illustrator*:
 DICKENS. Bleak House; 1st edition, 1853. 350
 — Dombey and son; 1st edition, 1848. 345
 — Little Dorrit; 1st edition, 1857. 353
 — Martin Chuzzlewit; 1st edition, 1st issue, 1844. 339
 — Master Humphrey's clock; 1st edition, 1840-41. 334
 — Nicholas Nickleby; 1st edition, 1839. 331
 — Pic nic papers; 1841. 335
 — Pickwick papers; 1st edition, 1837. 321
 — *same*; Victorian edition, 1887. 322
 — Sketches of young couples; 1st edition, 1840. 333
 — Sketches of young gentlemen; 1st edition, 1838. 329
 — Sketches of young ladies (Caswell); 1st edition, 1837. 323
 — Strange gentleman; 1st edition, 1837. 324
 — Tale of two cities; 1st edition, 1859. 356
 LEVER. Barrington; 1st edition, 1863. 469
 — Charles O'Malley; 1st edition, 1841. 450
 — Confessions of Con. Cregan; 1st edition, 1850. 459
 — Daltons, The; 1st edition, 1852. 461
 — Davenport Dunn; 1st edition, 1859. 467
 — Dodd family abroad; 1st edition, 1854. 462
 — Harry Lorrequer; 1st edition, 1839. 449
 — Knight of Gwynne; 1st edition, 1847. 457
 — Luttrell of Arran; 1st edition, 1865. 472
 — Martins of Cro' Martin; 1st edition, 1856. 465
 — Nuts and nutcrackers; 1st edition, 1845. 453
 — O'Donoghue, The; 1st edition, 1845. 454
 — One of them; 1st edition, 1861. 468
 — Our mess; 1st edition, 1843-44. 451
 — Roland Cashel; 1st edition, 1850. 460
 — Saint Patrick's eve; 1st edition, 1845. 455
 — Tales of the trains; 1st edition, 1845. 456
 SURTEES. Hawbuck Grange; 1st edition, 1847. 668
 — Jorrocks's jaunts and jollities; 1st edition, 1838. 667
 — Mr. Facey Romford's hounds; 1st edition, 1865. 673
Browne, Moses. Angling sports; 3d edition; London, 1773. 71

Vol. I., Nos. 1-416; II., 417-748.

Browne, Moses, *editor:*
  WALTON and COTTON. Compleat angler; 1st edition, 1750. 40
  — *same;* 2d edition, 1759. 41
  — *same;* 3d edition, 1772. 43
Browne, *Sir* Thomas. Religio medici; 1st unauthorized edition; London, 1642. 196
Bruni, Leonardo. Historia Fiorentina; Vinegia, 1476. 197
Bryskett, Lodowick. Mourning muse of Thestylis (only known impression); 1595. *in* 661
Buffon, Georges L. L. Beauties of natural history; London, 1804. 166
Bunyan, John. Pilgrim's progress; 1st edition; London, 1678. 198
  — *same;* 3d edition; London, 1679. 199
  — *same;* 4th edition, 2d issue; London, 1680. 200
  — *same;* 5th edition; London, 1680. 201
  — *same;* 6th edition; London, 1681. 202
  — *same;* 9th edition; London, 1683. 203
  — *same;* Second Part; 1st edition; London, 1684. 204
  — *same;* 3d edition; London, 1690. 207
  — *same;* Spurious Second Part; 1st edition; London, 1683. 205
  — *same;* 2d edition; Edinburgh, 1684. 206
  Voyage d'un chrestien vers l'eternité; 1st edition in French; Amsterdam, 1685. 208
Burlesques; Thackeray; 1856. 713
Burnand, *Sir* Francis C. Incompleat angler; London, 1887. 107
Burns, Robert. Poems, chiefly in the Scottish dialect; 1st edition; Kilmarnock, 1786. 209
  Poetical works; Aldine edition; London, 1830–39. *in* 195
Burton, Robert. Anatomy of melancholy; 1st edition; Oxford, 1621. 210
Butler, Samuel. Hudibras, First Part; 1st edition; London, 1663. 211
  — *same;* 2d edition; London, 1663. 212
  — *same;* 3d edition; London, 1663. 213
  — *same;* 1st unauthorized edition, 1st issue; London, 1663. 214
  — *same;* 2d unauthorized edition, London, 1663. 215
  — *same;* Second Part; 1st edition; London, 1664. 216
  — *same;* 2d edition; London, 1664. 217
  — *same;* 3d spurious edition; London, 1663. 218
  — *same;* Third Part; 1st edition; London, 1678. 219
  — *same;* 2d edition; London, 1678. 220
  — *same,* in Three Parts; London, 1800. 221
  Poetical works; Aldine edition; London, 1835. *in* 195

Byron, George Gordon, 6*th Baron.* HUNT. Lord Byron and some of his contemporaries; 1828. 413

CADENUS and Vanessa; Swift; 1st edition, 1726. 677
Cæsar, Caius Julius. C. Julii Cæsaris quæ extant ex emendatione Jos. Scaligeri; 2d edition; Lugduni Batavorum, 1635. 222
Cambises King of Percia, Lamentable tragedy of; Preston; 1st edition, 1570. 635
Campe, Joachim H. New Robinson Crusoe; 2d edition; London, 1789. 132
Care-killer, The; Jonathan Jolly, *pseudonym;* 1st edition, 1807. 425
Carew, Richard, *translator.* TASSO. Godfrey of Bulloigne; 1594. 223
Castle Dangerous; Scott; 1st edition, 1832. *in* 553
Caswell, Edward. Sketches of young ladies; 1st edition; London, 1837. 323
Cat's tail, The; Southey; 1831. 266
Causton, Henry K., *editor.* WALTON and COTTON. Compleat angler; 1851. 63
Caution to anglers; Stewart; 1871. 102
Caxton, William, *editor.* Cronycle of Englonde; London, 1515. 225
Caxton, William, *printer.* CICERO. Treatises on Old age, Friendship, and the Declamation of noblesse; 1481. 224
Caxton, William, *translator.* LE FEVRE. Recuile of the histories of Troie; 1553. 226
Cenci, The; Shelley; 1st edition, 1819. 645
Centlivre, *Mrs.* Susannah. Works; London, 1760–61. 227
Cervantes Saavedra, Miguel. Don Quixote de la Mancha, El Ingenioso hidalgo; 1st edition, 1st issue; Madrid, 1605. 228
  — *same;* 2d edition; Madrid, 1605. 229
  — *same;* 3d edition; Madrid, 1608. 230
  — *same,* Segunda parte del Ingenioso Cavallero; 1st edition; Madrid, 1615. 231
  Don Quichote, History of; London, 1620. 232
  Don Quixote; Roscoe's Novelist's Library; London, 1833. *in* 267
Chamisso, Ludwig C. A. von. Peter Schlemihl; London, 1824. 248
Character of the Long Parliament; Milton; 1681. 498
Character sketches; Thackeray; 1856. *in* 716
Charles O'Malley; Lever; 1st edition, 1841. 450
Chase, The; Somerville; 1st edition, 1796. 136
  — *same;* 2d edition, 1802. 137
Chaucer, Geoffrey. Poetical works; Aldine edition; London, 1845. *in* 195
Chester, Robert. Love's martyr; or, Rosalins complaint; 1st edition; London, 1601. 558

Vol. I., Nos. 1–416; II., 417–748.

Child's dream of a star; Dickens; 1st edition, 1871. 363
Child's history of England; Dickens; 1852-54. 349
Child's story; Dickens; 1852. *in* 347
Chimes, The; Dickens; 1st edition, 1st issue, 1845. 341
Christmas carol; Dickens; 1st edition, 1st issue, 1843. 337
— *same*; 1st edition, 2d issue, 1843. 338
Christmas stories; 1st edition; Oxford, 1823. 243
Christmas Stories:
  DICKENS. Battle of life; 1846. 342
  — Chimes, The; 1845. 341
  — Christmas carol; 1843. 337
  — Cricket on the hearth; 1846. 343
  — Extra Christmas numbers of "All the Year Round"; 1859-67. 357
  — Extra Christmas numbers of "Household Words"; 1850-58. 347
  — Haunted man and the ghost's bargain; 1848. 346

  THACKERAY. Doctor Birch and his young friends; 1849. 700
  — Kickleburys on the Rhine; 1850. 704
  — Mrs. Perkins's ball; 1847. 696
  — Our street; 1848. 698
  — Rose and the ring; 1855. 711
Christmas tree, A; Dickens; 1850. *in* 347
Chronicle of the "Compleat Angler"; Westwood; 1864. 114
— *same*; Westwood, Thomas, *and* Thomas Satchell; 1888. *in* 66
Chronicle of the drum (autograph manuscript); Thackeray; 1840. 690
— *same*; 1st edition; London, 1841. *in* 694
Chronicles of the Canongate; 1st series; Scott; 1st edition, 1827. 549
— *same*; 2d series; 1st edition, 1828. 550
Churchill, Charles. Poetical works; Aldine edition; London, 1844. *in* 195
Cicero, Marcus Tullius. Treatises on Old age, Friendship, and the Declamation of noblesse; London, 1481. 224
Clarke, William. Three courses and a dessert; 1st edition; London, 1830. 263
Clement Lorimer; Reach; 1849. 293
Cokayne, *Sir* Aston. Small poems of divers sorts; 1st edition; London, 1658. 233
Coleman, Robert W. SABIN. Bibliographical catalogue of the Waltonian library of Robert W. Coleman; 1866. 115
Coleridge, Samuel T., *editor*. BOWLES *and others*. Selected sonnets; 1796. 417
Colin Clouts come home againe; Spenser; 1st edition, 1595. 661

Collier, John. Tim Bobbin's Lancashire dialect, and poems; 2d edition; London, 1833. 307
Collier, John Payne. Punch and Judy; 1st edition; London, 1828. 258
Collins, Wilkie, *and* Charles Dickens. Holly-tree Inn; London, 1855. *in* 347
  No thoroughfare; London, 1867. *in* 357
  Perils of certain English prisoners; London, 1857. *in* 347
  Wreck of The Golden Mary; London, 1856. *in* 347
Collins, William. Poetical works; Aldine edition; London, 1853. *in* 195
Combe, William. Dance of life; 1st edition; London, 1817. 520
  English dance of Death; 1st edition; London, 1815-16. 518
  History of Johnny Quæ Genus; 1st edition; London, 1822. 524
  Life of Napoleon, a Hudibrastic poem; 1st edition; London, 1815. 240
  Tour of Doctor Syntax, in search of the picturesque; 1st edition; London, 1812. 516
  Tour (Second) of Doctor Syntax in search of consolation; 1st edition; London, 1820. 521
  Tour (Third) of Doctor Syntax in search of a wife; 1st edition; London, 1822. 522
Combe, William, *imitated*. Doctor Syntax in Paris; London, 1820. 525
  Tour of Doctor Prosody in search of the antique and picturesque; 1st edition; London, 1821. 527
  Tour of Doctor Syntax through London; 1st edition; London, 1820. 526
Comet, The (a folding plate); Cruikshank; 1854. *in* 297
Comic almanacks; Cruikshank; 19 vols.; 1st editions, 1834-52. 275
Comic alphabet; Cruikshank; 2d edition, 1837. 278
Comic Blackstone; À Beckett; 1st edition, 1844. 1
Comic history of England; À Beckett; 1st edition, 1847-48. 2
Comic history of Rome; À Beckett; 1st edition, 1852. 3
Comic tales and sketches; Thackeray; 1st edition, 1841. 693
Complaints; containing sundrie small poemes; Spenser; 1st edition, 1591. 658
Compleat angler, The. *See* (for numerous editions) Walton, Izaak.
Compleat fisherman; Saunders; 1724. 69
Compleat troller, The; Nobbes; 1st edition, 1682. 68
Comus; a maske presented at Ludlow Castle; Milton; 1st edition, 1637. 486

Vol. I., Nos. 1-416; II., 417-748.

Concise but comprehensive treatise on the art of angling; London, c. 1809.	73
Concise treatise on the art of angling; Best; 1st edition, 1787.	72
Confessions of Con. Cregan; Lever; 1st edition, 1850.	459
Consett, Matthew. Tour through Sweden, Swedish-Lapland, Finland, and Denmark; 1st edition; Stockton, 1789.	143
Copland, William, *printer*. LE FEVRE. Recuile of the histories of Troie; 1553.	226
Cornelius O'Dowd; Lever; 1st edition, 1864.	471
Cornwallis, *Sir* William. Discourses upon Seneca the tragedian; London, 1601.	*in* 235
Essays; 1st edition; London, 1600.	234
— *same*; Second Part; 1st edition; London, 1601.	235
Costello, Dudley. Holidays with hobgoblins; London, 1861.	300
Cotton, Charles. Compleat angler, Part 2; 1st edition, 1676.	*in* 38
— *same*.	*in* 39
See also (for numerous other editions) Walton *and* Cotton; Angling.	
Cotton, Charles. NICOLAS. Memoirs of Izaak Walton and Charles Cotton; 1836.	113
Count Robert of Paris; Scott; 1st edition, 1832.	553
Countess of Pembrokes Arcadia; Sidney; 1st edition, 1590.	647
— *same*; 2d edition, 1593.	648
Cowper, William. John Gilpin; London, 1832.	270
Poems; 1st edition, 1st issue; London, 1782.	236
— *same*; 1st edition, 2d issue; London, 1782.	237
— *same*; Vol. 3; London, 1815.	239
Poetical works; Aldine edition; London, 1830-31.	*in* 195
Task, The; 1st edition; London, 1785.	238
Creccelius, Johannes. Collectanea exhistoriis, De origine omnium fere monasticorum ordinum; Francofurti, 1614.	485
Cricket on the hearth; Dickens; 1st edition, 1846.	343
Cronycle of Englonde; Caxton, *editor*; London, 1515.	225
Crowe, Eyre. With Thackeray in America; N. Y., 1893.	736
Crowe sits upon the wall, The; a prettie new ballad (reprint); Tarlton; n. d.	679
Cruikshank, George. The Betting-book; London, 1852.	295
Comic almanack for 1839; 1st edition; London, 1838.	686
Cruikshank, George (*continued*). Comic almanack for 1840; 1st edition; London, 1839.	689
Comic almanacks for 1835-53; 19 vols.; 1st editions; London, 1834-52.	275
Comic alphabet; 2d edition; London, 1837.	278
Discovery concerning ghosts; London, 1863.	303
George Cruikshank's Fairy Library; London, 1853-64.	296
George Cruikshank's Magazine; London, 1854.	297
George Cruikshank's Omnibus; 1st edition; London, 1842.	284
George Cruikshank's Table-book; 1st edition; London, 1845.	287
Humourist, The; London, 1819-20.	241
Loving ballad of Lord Bateman; 1st issue; London, 1839.	330
My sketch book; London, 1834.	273
Plates; collection of 81 plates, India-paper proofs; 1823-43.	244
Points of humour; London, 1823-24.	246
Scraps and sketches; London, 1828-32.	260
Cruikshank, George, *illustrator*:	
À BECKETT. Comic Blackstone; 1st edition, 1844.	1
AINSWORTH. Guy Fawkes; 1st edition, 1841.	8
— Jack Sheppard; 1st edition, 1839.	6
— Rookwood; 4th edition, 1836.	5
— Saint James's; 1846.	9
— Tower of London; 1st edition, 1840.	7
AKERMAN. Tales of other days; 1st edition, 1830.	262
ANSTEY. New Bath guide; 1832.	269
APEL. Der Freischütz travestie; 1st edition, 1824.	247
BARHAM. Ingoldsby legends; 1st edition, 1840-47.	282
BARKER. Greenwich Hospital; 1826.	254
— Land and sea tales; 1836.	277
— Tough yarns; 1835.	276
BASILE. The Pentamerone; 1st edition, 1848.	289
Bee and the wasp; 1st edition, 1832.	271
BOWRING. Minor morals for young people; 1834-39.	274
BROUGH. Life of Sir John Falstaff; 1st edition, 1858.	298
Catalogue raisonné; London, 1828.	259
Cat's tail; 1831.	266
CERVANTES. Don Quixote; Roscoe's Novelist's Library; 1833.	*in* 267
CHAMISSO. Peter Schlemihl; 1824.	248
Christmas stories; 1st edition; Oxford, 1823.	243
CLARKE. Three courses and a dessert; 1st edition, 1830.	263

Vol. I., Nos. 1-416; II., 417-748.

Cruikshank, George, *illustrator* (*continued*):
  COMBE. Life of Napoleon, a Hudibrastic poem; 1st edition, 1815.   240
  COSTELLO. Holidays with hobgoblins; 1861. 300
  COWPER. John Gilpin; 1832.   270
  DEFOE. Robinson Crusoe; Major's edition; 1831.   268
  DIBDIN, C. Songs, naval and national; 1st edition, 1841.   283
  DICKENS. Oliver Twist; 1st edition, 1st issue, 1838.   327
  — *same*; 1846.   328
  — Pic nic papers; 1st edition, 1841.   335
  — Sketches by Boz; 1st complete edition, 1839.   332
  — Strange gentleman (facsimile reprint); 1871.   325
  FIELDING. Amelia; Roscoe's Novelist's Library; 1832.   in 267
  — Joseph Andrews; Roscoe's Novelist's Library; 1832.   in 267
  — Tom Jones; Roscoe's Novelist's Library; 1831.   in 267
  FRANKUM. Bee and the wasp; 1st edition, 1832.   271
  Freischütz travestie; 1st edition, 1824.   247
  Gentleman in black; 1st edition, 1831.   264
  GLASCOCK. Land sharks and sea gulls; 1838.   281
  GOLDSMITH. Vicar of Wakefield; Roscoe's Novelist's Library; 1832.   in 267
  GORE. Modern chivalry; 1843.   285
  Greenwich Hospital; 1826.   254
  GRIMALDI. Memoirs; edited by "Boz"; 1st edition, 1st issue, 1838.   326
  GRIMM. German popular stories; 1823–26.   245
  HALL. Trial of Sir Jasper; 1874.   305
  Hans of Iceland; 1st edition, 1825.   253
  HOOD. The Epping hunt; 1st edition, 1829.   261
  HUGO. Hans of Iceland; 1st edition, 1825.   253
  HUNT. Popular romances of the west of England; 1865.   304
  INGLIS. Rambles in the footsteps of Don Quixote; 1837.   279
  Ingoldsby legends; 1st edition, 1840-47.   282
  Italian tales; 1st edition, 1824.   249
  Land and sea tales; 1836.   277
  LASCELLES. Scenes from the life of Edward Lascelles, Gent.; 1837.   280
  LE SAGE. Gil Blas; Roscoe's Novelist's Library; 1833.   in 267
  LEVER. Arthur O'Leary; 1st edition, 1844.   452
  Life of Napoleon, a Hudibrastic poem; 1st edition, 1815.   240
  LOWELL. Biglow papers; 2d English edition, 1861.   301

Cruikshank, George, *illustrator* (*continued*):
  MAXWELL. History of the Irish Rebellion in 1798; 1st edition, 1845.   288
  MAYHEW, Henry. The World's show, 1851; or, The Adventures of Mr. and Mrs. Sandboys; 1851.   294
  MAYHEW, Henry *and* A. S. Magic of kindness; 2d issue, 1848.   290
  — Whom to marry and how to get married; 1st edition, 1848.   291
  MAYHEW, Horace. The Tooth-ache; 1849.   292
  MERLE. Odds and ends; 1831.   265
  Modern chivalry; 1843.   285
  MOORE. Age of intellect; 1819.   242
  Novelist's Library, Roscoe's; 1831–33.   267
  Oyster, The; London, 1861.   302
  PARIS. Philosophy in sport made science in earnest; 1st edition, 1827.   256
  PAYNE. Punch and Judy; 1st edition, 1828.   258
  Peter Schlemihl; 1824.   248
  Philosophy in sport made science in earnest; 1st edition, 1827.   256
  Punch and Judy; 1st edition, 1828.   258
  RAYMOND. Memoirs of Robert William Elliston, comedian; 1844.   286
  REACH. Clement Lorimer; 1849.   293
  ROSCOE, *editor*. Novelist's Library; 19 vols.; 1831–33.   267
  ROSCOE, *translator*. Italian tales; 1st edition, 1824.   249
  SCOTT. Letters on demonology and witchcraft; 1830.   552
  SMOLLETT. Humphry Clinker; Roscoe's Novelist's Library; 1831.   in 267
  — Peregrine Pickle; Roscoe's Novelist's Library; 1831.   in 267
  — Roderick Random; Roscoe's Novelist's Library; 1831.   in 267
  — Sir Launcelot Greaves; Roscoe's Novelist's Library; 1832.   in 267
  SOANE. Specimens of German romance; 1826.   255
  SOUTHEY. The Cat's tail; 1831.   266
  Specimens of German romance; 1826.   255
  Stenelaus and Amylda; 1858.   299
  STERNE. Tristram Shandy; Roscoe's Novelist's Library; 1832.   in 267
  Sunday in London; 1833.   272
  Tales of Irish life; 1824.   250
  Tales of other days; 1st edition, 1830.   262
  THACKERAY. Essay on the genius of George Cruikshank; 1840.   691
  Three courses and a dessert; 1st edition, 1830.   263
  Tooth-ache, The; imagined by Horace Mayhew; 1849.   292

Vol. I., Nos. 1-416; II., 417-748.

Cruikshank, George, *illustrator* (*continued*):
Tough yarns; 1835. 276
WHITTY. Tales of Irish life; 1824. 250
WIGHT. Illustrations to Mornings at Bow Street; with short extracts; 1827. 252
— More mornings at Bow Street; 1827. 257
— Mornings at Bow Street; 2d edition, 1824. 251
— Sunday in London; 1833. 272
Cruikshank, Isaac R., *illustrator*. WESTMACOTT. The English spy; 1825-26. 308
Cruikshank, Isaac R. *and* George, *illustrators*:
COLLIER. Tim Bobbin's Lancashire dialect, and poems; 2d edition, 1833. 307
EGAN. Life in London; 1821. 306

DALTONS, The; Lever; 1st edition, 1852. 461
Dance of Death, English; Combe; 1st edition, 1815-16. 518
Dance of life; Combe; 1st edition, 1817. 520
Daniel, George. Elizabethan garland; London, 1856. 309
Daphnaïda; Spenser; 1st edition, 1591. 659
— *same*; 2d edition; 1596. *in* 662
Daulby, Daniel. Descriptive catalogue of the works of Rembrandt; Liverpool, 1796. 510
Davenport Dunn; Lever; 1st edition, 1859. 467
Day, John, *printer*. ASCHAM. The Scholemaster; 3d edition; London, 1573. 120
Days and nights of salmon fishing in the Tweed; Scrope; 1st edition, 1843. 90
Day's ride; Lever; 1st edition, 1863. 470
De imitatione Christi; À Kempis; 1653. 416
Debtor and creditor; Kenney; 1st edition, 1814. 434
Decameron, The; Boccaccio; London, 1886. 189
— *same*; London, 1887. 190
— *same*; Londres, 1757-61. 188
Declamation of noblesse; 1481. *in* 224
Decree of Starre-chamber, concerning printing; London, 1637. 387
Defoe, Daniel. Robinson Crusoe, Adventures of; 1st edition, 1st issue; London, 1719. 310
— *same*; Farther adventures; 1st edition, 2d issue; London, 1719. 311
— *same*; Serious reflections during the life and surprising adventures; 1st edition; London, 1720. 312
Robinson Crusoe; Roscoe's Novelist's Library; London, 1831. *in* 267
— *same*; Major's edition; London, 1831. 268
Demeanour of murderers (autograph manuscript); Dickens; 1856. 352
Democritus Junior, *pseudonym*. *See* Burton, Robert.
Demonology and witchcraft, Letters on; Scott; 1st edition, 1830. 552

Denis Duval; Thackeray; 1st edition, 1867. 729
Dernier abbé, Le; Musset; 1891. 502
Description of more than three hundred animals; London, 1812. 177
Dialogus qui vocatur Scrutinium Scripturarum; Paulus de Sancta Maria; 1475. 506
Diary of C. Jeames de la Pluche; Thackeray; 1856. *in* 715
Dibdin, Charles. Songs, naval and national; 1st edition; London, 1841. 283
Dibdin, Thomas Frognall. Bibliographical Decameron; London, 1817. 314
Bibliographical tour in England and Scotland; London, 1838. 318
Bibliographical tour in France and Germany; London, 1821. 315
Bibliomania; 3d edition; London, 1842. 319
Library companion; 2d edition; London, 1825. 316
Reminiscences of a literary life; London, 1836. 317
Typographical antiquities; 1st edition; London, 1810-19. 313
Dickens, Charles. "All the Year Round," Extra Christmas numbers of; 1859-67. 357
American notes; 1st edition, 1st issue; London, 1842. 336
Barnaby Rudge; 1st edition; London, 1841. *in* 334
Battle of life; 1st edition, 1st issue; London, 1846. 342
Bleak House; 1st edition; London, 1853. 350
Boots at the Holly-tree Inn; 1st reading edition; London, 1858. *in* 354
Child's dream of a star; 1st edition; Boston, 1871. 363
Child's history of England; London, 1852-54. 349
Child's story; London, 1852. *in* 347
Chimes, The; 1st edition, 1st issue; London, 1845. 341
Christmas carol; 1st edition, 1st issue; London, 1843. 337
— *same*; 1st edition, 2d issue, 1843. 338
Christmas stories:
Battle of life; 1846. 342
Chimes, The; 1845. 341
Christmas carol; 1843. 337
Cricket on the hearth; 1846. 343
Extra Christmas numbers of "All the Year Round"; 1859-67. 357
Extra Christmas numbers of "Household Words"; 1850-58. 347
Haunted man and the ghost's bargain; 1848. 346
Christmas tree; London, 1850. *in* 347

Vol. I., Nos. 1-416; II., 417-748.

Dickens, Charles (*continued*). Cricket on the hearth; 1st edition; London, 1846.   343
Demeanour of murderers (autograph manuscript); 1856.   352
Doctor Marigold's prescriptions; London, 1865.   *in* 357
Dombey and son; 1st edition; London, 1848.   345
Extra Christmas numbers of "All the Year Round"; London, 1859-67.   357
Extra Christmas numbers of "Household Words"; London, 1850-58.   347
Hard times; 1st edition; London, 1854.   351
Haunted house; 1st edition; London, 1859. *in* 357
Haunted man; 1st edition, 2d issue; London, 1848.   346
House to let; London, 1858.   *in* 347
Household Words, Extra Christmas numbers of; 1850-58.   347
Hunted down; with some account of Wainewright, the poisoner; 1st edition; London, 1870.   360
Is she his wife; 1st edition; Boston, 1877.   364
Lamplighter, The; 1st edition; London, 1879.   366
Lamplighter's story; London, 1841.   *in* 335
Little Dombey, The Story of; 1st reading edition; London, 1858.   355
Little Dorrit; 1st edition; London, 1857.   353
Loving ballad of Lord Bateman; 1st issue; London, 1839.   330
Martin Chuzzlewit; 1st edition, 1st issue; London, 1844.   339
Master Humphrey's clock; 1st edition; London, 1840-41.   334
Message from the sea; London, 1860.   *in* 357
Mr. Nightingale's diary; 1st edition; Boston, 1877.   365
Mrs. Gamp; 1st reading edition; London, 1858.   *in* 354
Mrs. Gamp with the strolling players; N. Y., 1899.   368
Mrs. Lirriper's legacy; London, 1864.   *in* 357
Mrs. Lirriper's lodgings; London, 1863.   *in* 357
Mugby Junction; London, 1866.   *in* 357
Mystery of Edwin Drood; 1st edition; London, 1870.   361
Nicholas Nickleby; 1st edition; London, 1839.   331
Nobody's story; London, 1853.   *in* 347
Old curiosity shop; London, 1840-41.   *in* 334
Oliver Twist; 1st edition, 1st issue; London, 1838.   327
— *same*; London, 1846.   328
Our mutual friend; London, 1865.   359
Pickwick Club, Posthumous papers of the; 1st edition; London, 1837.   321

Dickens, Charles (*continued*). Pickwick Club, Posthumous papers of the; Victorian edition; London, 1887.   322
Pictures from Italy; 1st edition; London, 1846.   344
Plays and poems; London, 1882.   367
Poor relation's story; London, 1852.   *in* 347
Poor traveller; 1st reading edition; London, 1858.   354
Schoolboy's story; London, 1853.   *in* 347
Seven poor travellers; London, 1854.   *in* 347
Sketches by Boz; 1st complete edition; London, 1839.   332
Sketches of young couples; 1st edition; London, 1840.   333
Sketches of young gentlemen; 1st edition; London, 1838.   329
Somebody's luggage; London, 1862.   *in* 357
Speeches literary and social; 1st edition; London, 1870.   362
Strange gentleman; 1st edition; London, 1837.   324
— *same* (facsimile reprint); London, 1871.   325
Tale of two cities; 1st edition; London, 1859.   356
To be read at dusk; London, 1852.   348
Tom Tiddler's ground; London, 1861.   *in* 357
Uncommercial traveller; 1st edition; London, 1861.   358
Village coquettes; 1st edition; London, 1836.   320
What Christmas is, as we grow older; London, 1851.   *in* 347
Dickens, Charles, *and* Wilkie Collins. Holly-tree Inn; London, 1855.   *in* 347
No thoroughfare; London, 1867.   *in* 357
Perils of certain English prisoners; London, 1857.   *in* 347
Wreck of The Golden Mary; London, 1856.   *in* 347

Dickens, Charles — *Miscellaneous*:
ANDREWS. Stray leaf from the correspondence of Washington Irving and Charles Dickens; 1894.   16
CASWELL. Sketches of young ladies; 1st edition, 1837.   323
GRIMALDI. Memoirs; 1st edition, 1st issue, 1838.   326
OVERS. Evenings of a working man; 1844.   340
Pic nic papers; London, 1841.   335
Discovery concerning ghosts; Cruikshank; 1863.   303
Dives and pauper; Parker; 1st edition, 1493.   505
Doctor Birch and his young friends; Thackeray; 1st edition, 1849.   700
Doctor Marigold's prescriptions; Dickens; 1865.   *in* 357

Doctor Prosody, Tour of, in search of the antique and picturesque; Combe *imitated*; 1st edition, 1821. 527
Doctor Syntax in Paris; Combe *imitated*; 1820. 525
Doctor Syntax, Tour of, in search of the picturesque; Combe; 1st edition, 1812. 516
Doctor Syntax, Second tour of, in search of consolation; Combe; 1st edition, 1820. 521
Doctor Syntax, Third tour of, in search of a wife; Combe; 1st edition, 1822. 522
Doctor Syntax, Tour of, through London; Combe *imitated*; 1st edition, 1820. 526
Dodd family abroad; Lever; 1st edition, 1854. 462
Dombey and son; Dickens; 1st edition, 1848. 345
Don Quixote. *See* Cervantes Saavedra, Miguel de.
Don Quixote, Rambles in the footsteps of; Inglis; 1837. 279
Donne, John:
  WALTON. Lives of Donne, Wotton, Hooker, and Herbert; 1670. 740
  — *same*; 1796. 741
  — *same*; 1825. 742
  — *same*; 1827. 743
Dorat, Claude J. Les Baisers, précédés du Mois de mai; 2d issue; La Haye, 1770. 369
  — *same*; Rouen, 1880. 370
Douglas, Gawin, *translator*. VIRGILIUS. The XIII. bukes of Eneados; 1st edition, 1553. 371
D'Oyly, *Sir* Charles. Tom Raw, the griffin; London, 1828. 529
Drummond, William. Poems; 3d edition; London, 1656. 372
Dryden, John. Poetical works; Aldine edition; London, 1852. *in* 195
Dürer, Albrecht. Apocalipsis cum figuris; 4th edition; Nurnberge, 1511. 376
  Little Passion in copper; Nurnbergæ, 1507-13. 373
  Little Passion on wood; 1st edition; Nurnbergæ, 1509-10. 374
  — *same*; 2d Latin edition; Nurnberge, 1511. 375
  Passio Christi; 2d Latin edition; Nurnberge, 1511. 375
Dyce, Alexander, *editor*. SHAKESPEARE. Works; 3d edition; London, 1875-76. 643

EDWARD the Third, The Raigne of; 1st edition; London, 1596. 623
Egan, Pierce. Life in London; London, 1821. 306
  Real life in London; 1st edition; London, 1821. 528
Eisen, Charles, *illustrator*:
  DORAT. Les Baisers; 2d issue, 1770. 369
  — *same*; Rouen, 1880. 370

Elegy wrote in a country church yard; Gray; 1st edition, 1751. 386
Elia, *pseudonym*. *See* Lamb, Charles.
Elizabethan garland; Daniel; 1856. 309
Elliston, Robert W. RAYMOND. Memoirs of Robert William Elliston; 1844. 286
Emblems of mortality; London, 1789. 133
Englands Parnassus; 1st edition; London, 1600. 10
Englebach, Lewis. Naples and the Campagna Felice; London, 1815. 517
English dance of Death; Combe; 1st edition, 1815-16. 518
English gentleman, The; Brathwait; 1st edition, 1630. 192
English gentlewoman, The; Brathwait; 1st edition, 1631. 193
English humourists of the eighteenth century; Thackeray; 1st edition, 1853. 708
English XIX century sportsman and bibliopole; Andrews; 1906. 28 B
English spy, The; Westmacott; 1825-26. 308
Engravers, American:
  ANDREWS. Fragments of American history; 1898. 21
  — Paul Revere and his engraving; 1901. 27
Engravers, French. ANDREWS. Trio of eighteenth century French engravers of portraits in miniature; 1899. 23
Engravings:
  DAULBY. Descriptive catalogue of the works of Rembrandt; 1796. 510
  WILSON. Catalogue raisonné of the engravings of an amateur; 1828. 259
    See also Bewick; Browne; Cruikshank; Dürer; Leech; Rowlandson.
Epping hunt, The; Hood; 1st edition, 1829. 261
Essays:
  BACON. Essayes; 1st edition, 1597. 121
  — *same*; 2d edition, 1598. 122
  CORNWALLIS. Discourses upon Seneca the tragedian; 1601. *in* 235
  — Essayes; 1st edition, 1600. 234
  — *same*; Second Part; 1st edition, 1601. 235
  JOHNSON. Essaies, or rather imperfect offers; 1601. 415
  LAMB. Elia; essays; 1st edition, 1st issue, 1823. 438
  — *same*; 1828. 439
  — *same*; 2d series, 1828. 440
  — Last essays of Elia; 1st edition, 1833. 443
  MINSHULL. Essayes and characters of a prison and prisoners; 1821. 184
Etching:
  HAMERTON. Etching and etchers; 1st edition, 1868. 388

Vol. I., Nos. 1-416; II., 417-748.

Etching (continued):
  HAMERTON. Etching and etchers; 2d edition, 1876. 389
  — same; 3d edition, 1880. 390
Evenings of a working man; Overs; 1844. 340
Experienc'd angler; Venables; 4th edition, 1676. in 39
Exquisites, The; Thackeray; 1839. 688
Eyton, Thomas C. Catalogue of British birds; London, 1836. 378
  History of the rarer British birds; London, 1836. 377

FABLES:
  ÆSOP. Fables; 1793. 4
  ÆSOP and others. Beauties of Æsop and other fabulists; 1786. 142
  — Bewick's select fables; 1871. 130
  — same; 1879. 131
  — Fables of Æsop, and others; 1st edition, 1818. 179
  — same; 2d edition, 1823. 180
  — Select fables; 2d edition, 2d impression, 1784. 128
  — same; Charnley edition, 1820. 129
  FAERNO. Cent fables en Latin et en François; 1744. 379
  GAY. Fables; 1793. 383
  — same; 4th edition, 1811. 176
  LE GRAND D'AUSSY. Fabliaux or tales; 1st edition, 1796-1800. 134
  — same; 2d edition, 1815. 135
Faerie queene; Spenser; 1st edition, 1st issue, 1590. 655
  — same; 1st edition, 2d issue, 1590. 655 A
  — same; 2d edition, 1596. 656
  — same; Second Part; 1st edition, 1596. 657
Faerno, Gabriello. Cent fables en Latin et en François; Londres, 1744. 379
Fair Em, A Pleasant comedie of; 2d edition; London, 1631. 633
Fair maid of Perth; Scott; 1st edition, 1828. in 550
Fairy library, George Cruikshank's; 1853-64. 296
Falconer, William. Poetical works; Aldine edition; London, 1836. in 195
Falstaff, Sir John. BROUGH. Life of Sir John Falstaff; 1st edition, 1858. 298
Falstaff, Sir John, Original letters, etc., of; White; 1st edition, 1796. 419
Famous historie of the seaven champions of Christendome; London, c. 1620. 414
Farmer, Priscilla, Poems on the death of; Lloyd; 1st edition, 1796. 418
Fatal boots, The; Thackeray; 1838. in 686
  — same; 1850. 687
Favorite flies and their histories; Marbury; 1892. 109

Ficquet, Etienne. ANDREWS. Trio of eighteenth century French engravers; 1899. 23
Fielding, Henry. Amelia; 1st edition; London, 1752. 382
  — same; Roscoe's Novelist's Library; London, 1832. in 267
  Joseph Andrews; 1st edition; London, 1742. 380
  — same; Roscoe's Novelist's Library; London, 1832. in 267
  Tom Jones, a foundling; 1st edition, 1st issue; London, 1749. 381
  — same; Roscoe's Novelist's Library; London, 1831. in 267
Fishes and Fishing. See Angling.
Fitz-Boodle papers; Thackeray; 1857. 718
Fletcher, John, and William Shakespeare. Two noble kinsmen; sole edition; London, 1634. 634
Floating flies and how to dress them; Halford; 1886. 106
Flore et Zephyr; Thackeray; London, 1836. 682
Florence, Italy:
  BRACCIOLINI. Historia Fiorentina; 1st edition, 1476. 191
  BRUNI. Historia Fiorentina; 1476. 197
Fly-fisher's entomology; Ronalds; 5th edition, 1856. 98
Fly making, The Art of; Blacker; 1855. 97
Fly-rods and fly-tackle; Wells; 1885. 105
Forester, Frank, pseudonym. See Herbert, Henry William.
Fortunes of Glencore; Lever; 1st edition, 1857. 466
Fortunes of Nigel; Scott; 1st edition, 1822. 541
Fouqué, Friederich, Baron de La Motte. Peter Schlemihl; London, 1824. 248
Four Georges, The; Thackeray; 1st edition, 1st issue, 1861. 723
Foure letters, and certaine sonnets; Harvey; 1592. 636
Fowre hymnes; Spenser; 1st edition, 1596. 662
Fragments of American history; Andrews; 1898. 21
Frankum, Richard. Bee and the wasp; 1st edition; London, 1832. 271
Freischütz travestie, Der; Apel; 1st edition, 1824. 247
Fresh-water fishes of Great Britain; Bowdich; 1828. 79

GARNIER, Robert. Tragedie of Antonie; doone into English by the Countesse of Pembroke; 2d edition, 1595. 507
Gay, John. Fables; London, 1793. 383
  — same; 4th edition; York, 1811. 176

Vol. I., Nos. 1-416;   II., 417-748.

Gentleman in black; 1st edition; London, 1831. 264
Gerald Fitzgerald; Lever; 1st edition, 1866. 475
German popular stories; Grimm, J. L. C. and W. C.; 1823–26. 245
Gil Blas; Le Sage; 1833. *in* 267
Glascock, William N. Land sharks and sea gulls; London, 1838. 281
Godfrey of Bulloigne; Tasso; 1594. 223
Godwin, *Mrs.* Mary Wollstonecraft. Original stories from real life; 1791. 745
Goldsmith, Oliver. Poems by Goldsmith and Parnell; London, 1804. 138
 Poetical works; Aldine edition; London, 1831. *in* 195
 Vicar of Wakefield; 1st edition; Salisbury, 1766. 384
 — *same*; London, 1817. 385
 — *same*; Roscoe's Novelist's Library; London, 1832. *in* 267
Gore, *Mrs.* Catherine G. F. M. Modern chivalry; London, 1843. 285
Gosden, Thomas:
 ANDREWS. An English XIX. century sportsman and bibliopole; 1906. 28 B
 WALTON *and* COTTON. Compleat angler; Gosden's edition, 1822. 51
Gossip about book collecting; Andrews; 1900. 24
Gownsman, The; Cambridge, 1830. 681
Grammars:
 MILTON. Accedence commenc't grammar; 1st edition, 1669. 497
 STANBRIDGE. Vocabula magistri stanbrigi; 1520. 665
Grand master; or, Adventures of Qui Hi? in Hindostan; Quiz, *pseudonym*; 1816. 519
Grandam, The; Lamb; 1st edition, 1796. *in* 418
Grateloup, Jean-Baptiste de. ANDREWS. Trio of eighteenth century French engravers; 1899. 23
Gray, Thomas. Elegy wrote in a country church yard; 1st edition; London, 1751. 386
 Poetical works; Aldine edition; London, 1836. *in* 195
Greenwich Hospital; by an Old Sailor; London and Dublin, 1826. 254
Grimaldi, Joseph. Memoirs; edited by "Boz"; 1st edition, 1st issue; London, 1838. 326
Grimm, Jacob L. C. *and* Wilhelm C. German popular stories; London, 1823–26. 245
Grolier, Jean. ANDREWS. Jean Grolier; 1892. 12
Grolier, Jean, book-binding of. BEMBO. Gli Asolani; 1515. 124
Gulliver's travels; Swift; 1st edition, 1726. 678
Guy Fawkes; Ainsworth; 1st edition, 1841. 8
Guy Mannering; Scott; 1st edition, 1815. 531

HALFORD, Frederic M. Floating flies and how to dress them; London, 1886. 106
Hall, Joseph. Short answer to the tedious vindication of Smectymnuus; London, 1641. 489
Hall, Samuel C. Trial of Sir Jasper; London, 1874. 305
Halliwell-Phillipps, James O. Shakesperiana; a catalogue of the early editions of Shakespeare's plays; London, 1841. 641
Hamerton, Philip G. Etching and etchers; 1st edition; London, 1868. 388
— *same*; 2d edition; London, 1876. 389
— *same*; 3d edition; London, 1880. 390
Hamilton, Edward. Recollections of fly fishing for salmon, trout, and grayling; London, 1884. 104
Hamlet; Shakespeare; 4th edition, 1611. 600
— *same*; 6th edition, 1637. 601
Handley Cross; or, Mr. Jorrocks's hunt; Surtees; 1st edition, 1854. 670
Hans of Iceland; Hugo; 1st edition, 1825. 253
Hard times; Dickens; 1st edition, 1854. 351
Harry Lorrequer; Lever; 1st edition, 1839. 449
Harvey, Gabriel. Foure letters, and certaine sonnets; London, 1592. 636
Haunted house; Dickens; 1859. *in* 357
Haunted man; Dickens; 1st edition, 2d issue, 1848. 346
Hawbuck Grange; Surtees; 1st edition, 1847. 668
Hawkins, *Sir* John, *editor*:
 WALTON *and* COTTON. Compleat angler; 1st edition, 1760. 42
 — *same* (reprint); 1824. 54
 — *same*; 3d edition, 1775. 44
 — *same*; 4th edition, 1784. 45
 — *same*; 5th edition, 2d issue, 1792. 46
 — *same*; 6th edition, 1797. 47
 — *same* (reprint); 1826. 56
 — *same*; 7th edition (4to), 1808. 48
 — *same* (medium 8vo). 49
 — *same*; 8th edition, 1815. 50
 — *same*; 9th edition, 1822. 51
 — *same*; 11th edition, 1825. 55
 — *same*; Hawkins-Rennie edition, 1836. 59
Heads of the people; Meadows; 1840–41. 692
Heart of Mid-Lothian; Scott; 1st edition, 1818. *in* 535
Henry Esmond; Thackeray; 1st edition, 1852. 707
— *same* (another copy, extra-illustrated). 707 A
Henry the Fourth, Part I.; Shakespeare; 2d edition, 1599. 577
— *same*; 5th edition, 1613. 578
— *same*; 6th edition, 1622. 579
— *same*; 8th edition, 1639. 580

Vol. I., Nos. 1–416; II., 417–748.

[1135]

Henry the Fourth, Part II.; Shakespeare; 1st edition (E, 4 leaves), 1600. 581
— *same*; 2d edition (E, 6 leaves), 1600. 582
Henry the Fifth; Shakespeare; 1st edition, 1600. 583
— *same*; 3d edition, 1608. 584
Henry the Sixth, Part II.; Shakespeare; 3d edition, 1619. *in* 585
Henry the Sixth, Part III.; Shakespeare; 2d edition, 1600. 586
— *same*; 3d edition, 1619. 587
Herbert, George:
   WALTON. Lives of Donne, Wotton, Hooker, and Herbert; 1670. 740
   — *same*; 1796. 741
   — *same*; 1825. 742
   — *same*; 1827. 743
Herbert, Henry W. Frank Forester's fish and fishing; N. Y., 1850. 94
— *same*; new edition; N. Y., 1859. 96
— *same*; Supplement; N. Y., 1850. 95
Herbert, Mary, *Countess of* Pembroke, *translator*.
   GARNIER. Tragedie of Antonie; 1595. 507
Herbert, William, *3d Earl of* Pembroke. Poems; 1st edition, 1660. 508
Hercules furens, translated by Jasper Heywood; Seneca; 1581. *in* 504
Hercules Oetæus, translated by John Studley; Seneca; 1581. *in* 504
Hermit of Warkworth; Percy; 2d edition, 1807. 167
Herodian *the Historian*. History of twenty Roman Cæsars and emperors; London, 1629. 391
Herrick, Robert. Hesperides; or, Works both humane and divine; 1st edition; London, 1648. 392
Hesperides; or, Works of Robert Herrick; 1st edition; London, 1648. 392
Heures de la Sainte Vierge; Paris, *c.* 1508. 411
Heywood, Jasper, *translator*:
   SENECA. Hercules furens; 1581. *in* 504
   — Thyestes; 1581. *in* 504
   — Troas; 1581. *in* 504
Heywood, John. Spider and the flie; London, 1556. 393
   Woorkes; 2d edition; Londini, 1566. 394
   — *same*; 4th edition; London, 1587. 395
Highland widow; Scott; 1st edition, 1827. *in* 549
Hippolytus, translated by John Studley; Seneca; 1581. *in* 504
History and adventures of an atom; Smollett; 1st edition, 1769. 649
History of Johnny Quæ Genus; Combe; 1st edition, 1822. 524
Hive of ancient and modern literature; Hodgson; 4th edition, 1812. 153

Hive of modern literature; Hodgson; 1st edition, 1795. 152
Hodgson, Solomon. Hive of ancient and modern literature; 4th edition; Newcastle, 1812. 153
   Hive of modern literature; 1st edition; Newcastle, 1795. 152
Hofland, Thomas C. British angler's manual; 1st edition; London, 1839. 88
Holidays with hobgoblins; Costello; 1861. 300
Holly-tree Inn; Dickens *and* Collins; 1855. *in* 347
Hood, Thomas. The Epping hunt; 1st edition; London, 1829. 261
Hooker, Richard:
   WALTON. Lives of Donne, Wotton, Hooker, and Herbert; 1670. 740
   — *same*; 1796. 741
   — *same*; 1825. 742
   — *same*; 1827. 743
Horace. *See* Horatius Flaccus, Quintus.
Horace Templeton; Lever; 1st edition, 1848. 458
Horæ beatæ Mariæ Virginis. *See* Hours, Books of.
Horatius Flaccus, Quintus. Poemata omnia; 3d Aldine edition; Venetiis, 1519. 396
   — Works; London, 1849. 397
Hore intemerate Virginis Marie. *See* Hours, Books of.
Horne, Richard H. New spirit of the age; London, 1844. 398
Hotten, John Camden. Thackeray the humourist and man of letters; London, 1864. 728
Hours, Books of — *Manuscript:*
   Heures de la rose; about 1400. 400
   Horæ beatæ Mariæ Virginis; 14th century. 399
   — *another*; 15th century. 401
   — *another*; 2d half of 15th century. 402
   — *another*; 2d half of 15th century. 403
   — *another*; latter part of 15th century. 404
   — *another*; 16th century. 405
   — *another*; 16th century. 406
   — *another*; 16th century. 407
Hours, Books of — *Printed:*
   Heures de la Sainte Vierge; Paris, *c.* 1508. 411
   Horæ beatæ Mariæ Virginis; Renes, *c.* 1502. 410
   Hore intemerate Dei Genitricis Virginis Marie; Parisius, *c.* 1512. 412
   Hore intemerate Virginis Marie; Paris, 1497. 408
   — *same*; Paris, 1501. 409
House to let; Dickens; 1858. *in* 347
Household Words, Extra Christmas numbers of; Dickens; 1850–58. 347
Howard, Henry, *Earl of* Surrey. Poems; Aldine edition; London, 1831. *in* 195
Hudibras. *See* Butler, Samuel.
Hugo, Victor M. Hans of Iceland; 1st edition; London, 1825. 253

Vol. I., Nos. 1–416; II., 417–748.

Humourist, The; Cruikshank; London, 1819-20. 241
Humphry Clinker; Smollett; 1831. in 267
Hunt, James H. Leigh. Lord Byron and some of his contemporaries; London, 1828. 413
Hunt, Robert. Popular romances of the west of England; London, 1865. 304
Hunted down; Dickens; 1st edition, 1870. 360

ICONOGRAPHY of the Battery and Castle Garden; Andrews; 1901. 26
Iconophiles, Journey of the; Andrews; 1897. 19
Imitation of Christ; Thomas à Kempis; 1653. 416
Incompleat angler; Burnand; 1887. 107
Inglis, Henry D. Rambles in the footsteps of Don Quixote; London, 1837. 279
Ingoldsby legends; Barham; 1st edition; 1840-47. 282
Irish Rebellion of 1798. MAXWELL. History of the Irish Rebellion in 1798; 1st edition, 1845. 288
Irish sketch-book; Thackeray; 1st edition, 1843. 695
Irving, Washington. ANDREWS. Stray leaf from the correspondence of Washington Irving and Charles Dickens; 1894. 16
Is she his wife; Dickens; 1st edition, 1877. 364
Italian tales; 1st edition; London, 1824. 249
Italy, a poem; Rogers; 1st issue, 1830. 513
Ivanhoe; Scott; 1st edition, 1820. 538

JACK HINTON, the guardsman; Lever; 1st edition, 1843. in 451
Jack Sheppard; Ainsworth; 1839. 6
Jesse, Edward. Angler's rambles; London, 1836. 84
    Scenes and tales of country life; London, 1844. 91
John Gilpin, Diverting history of; Cowper; 1832. 270
John king of England, Troublesome raigne of; 2d edition, 1611. 572
John Woodvil, a tragedy; Lamb; 1st edition, 1802. 423
Johnny Quæ Genus, History of; Combe; 1st edition, 1822. 524
Johnson, Charles P. Early writings of William Makepeace Thackeray; London, 1888. 734
Johnson, Richard. Famous historie of the seaven champions of Christendome; London, c. 1620. 414
Johnson, Robert. Essaies, or rather imperfect offers; London, 1601. 415
Jolly, Jonathan, *pseudonym*. The Care-killer; 1st edition; London, 1807. 425
Jorrocks's jaunts and jollities; Surtees; 1st edition, 1838. 667

Joseph Andrews; Fielding; 1st edition, 1742. 380
— *same;* Roscoe's Novelist's Library; 1832. in 267
Journal of sentimental travels in the southern provinces of France; London, 1821. 523
Julius Cæsar; Shakespeare; 1st separate edition, 1680. 599

KATZLEBEN, *Baroness de, pseudonym.* The Cat's tail; Edinburgh *and* London, 1831. 266
Kelly, Frances M., *and* Charles Lamb. Autograph letters; July 20, 1819. 436
Kempis, Thomas à. De imitatione Christi; Lugduni, 1653. 416
Kenilworth; Scott; 1st edition, 1821. 540
Kenney, James. Debtor and creditor; a comedy; 1st edition; London, 1814. 434
Kickleburys on the Rhine; Thackeray; 1st edition, 1850. 704
King, Edward. MILTON *and others.* Justa Edouardo King naufrago; 1638. 487
King and queen of hearts; Lamb; 1st edition, 1805. 424
King Glumpus; Thackeray; London, 1837. 683
King Lear; Shakespeare; 2d edition, 1608. 603
— *same;* 3d edition, 1655. 604
King Leir, True chronicle history of; earliest known edition, 1605. 602
Knight of Gwynne; Lever; 1st edition, 1847. 457

LAMB, Charles. Adventures of Ulysses; 1st edition; London, 1808. 427
Album verses; 1st edition; London, 1830. 441
Autograph letters to Miss Kelly; July 20, 1819. 436
Autograph letters to Mr. Moxon; 1821-33. 437
Beauty and the beast; "Surprise" edition; London, 1813. 431
— *same;* "Surprize" edition; London, 1813. 432
Elia; essays; 1st edition, 1st issue; London, 1823. 438
— *same;* Phil., 1828. 439
— *same;* 2d series; Phil., 1828. 440
Epilogue to Debtor and creditor; a comedy; by James Kenney; 1st edition; London, 1814. 434
Epilogue to Time's a tell-tale; by Henry Siddons; 1st edition; London, 1807. 426
Grandam, The; 1st edition; Bristol, 1796. in 418
John Woodvil, a tragedy; 1st edition; London, 1802. 423
King and queen of hearts; 1st edition; London, 1805. 424
Last essays of Elia; 1st edition; London, 1833. 433

Vol. I., Nos. 1-416; II., 417-748.

Lamb, Charles (*continued*). Letters (autograph) to Miss Kelly; July 20, 1819. 436
Letters (autograph) to Mr. Moxon; 1821-33. 437
Mr. H., or, Beware a bad name; 1st edition; Phil., 1813. 433
Prince Dorus; 1st edition, 1st issue; London, 1811. 428
— *same*; 1st edition, 2d issue; London, 1811. 429
— *same*; 2d edition; London, 1818. 430
Prologue to Mr. H.; 1st edition; London, 1807. *in* 425
Satan in search of a wife; 1st edition; London, 1831. 442
Tale of Rosamund Gray; 1st edition; Birmingham, 1798. 420
— *same*; 2d edition; London, 1798. 421
Works; 1st edition; London, 1818. 435
See also Lamb, Charles and Mary.

Lamb, Charles:
BOWLES *and others*. Selected sonnets from various authors; Bristol, 1796. 417
JOLLY, *pseudonym*. The Care-killer; 1st edition, 1807. 425
KENNEY. Debtor and creditor; 1st edition, 1814. 434
SIDDONS. Time's a tell-tale; 1st edition, 1807. 426
WHITE. Original letters, etc., of Sir John Falstaff; 1st edition, 1796. 419

Lamb, Charles *and* Mary. Mrs. Leicester's school; 1st edition; London, 1809. 445
Poetry for children; London, 1809. 446
— *same*; Boston, 1812. 447
Tales from Shakespear; 1st edition; London, 1807. 444

Lamb, Charles, *and* Frances M. Kelly. Autograph letters; July 20, 1819. 436
Lamb, Charles, *and* Charles Lloyd. Blank verse; 1st edition; London, 1798. 422
Lamb, John. Poetical pieces on several occasions; 1st edition; London, 1770. 448
Lamb, Mary Ann. *See* Lamb, Charles *and* Mary.
Lamentable and true tragedy of Master Arden of Feversham; 3d edition, 1633. 621
Lamplighter, The; Dickens; 1st edition, 1879. 366
Lamplighter's story; Dickens; 1841. *in* 335
Land and sea tales; Barker; 1836. 277
Land sharks and sea gulls; Glascock; 1838. 281
Lascelles, Edward. Scenes from his life; Dublin, 1837. 280
Lawes, Henry *and* William. Choice psalmes put into musick, for three voices; London, 1648. 492

Leaf out of a sketch-book; Thackeray; author's edition, 1861. 724
Lecture on heads; Stevens; 1808. 515
Leech, John, *illustrator*:
À BECKETT. Comic history of England; 1st edition, 1847-48. 2
— Comic history of Rome; 1st edition, 1852. 3
BARHAM. Ingoldsby legends; 1st edition, 1840-47. 282
DICKENS. Battle of life; 1st edition, 1st issue, 1846. 342
— Chimes, The; 1st edition, 1st issue, 1845. 341
— Christmas carol; 1st edition, 1st issue, 1843. 337
— *same*; 1st edition, 2d issue; 1843. 338
— Cricket on the hearth; 1st edition, 1846. 343
— Haunted man; 1st edition, 2d issue, 1848. 346
— Pickwick papers; Victorian edition, 1887. 322
Ingoldsby legends; 1st edition, 1840-47. 282
SURTEES. "Ask mamma"; 1st edition, 1858. 671
— Handley Cross; or, Mr. Jorrocks's hunt; 1st edition, 1854. 670
— Mr. Facey Romford's hounds; 1st edition, 1865. 673
— Mr. Sponge's sporting tour; 1st edition, 1853. 669
— Plain or ringlets; 1st edition, 1860. 672

Le Fevre, Raoul. Recuile of the histories of Troie; London, 1553. 226
Legend of Montrose; Scott; 1st edition, 1819. *in* 536
Legend of the Rhine; Thackeray; 1845. *in* 287
— *same*; 1856. *in* 713
Le Grand d'Aussy, Pierre J. B. Fabliaux or tales, abridged from French manuscripts; 1st edition; London, 1796-1800. 134
— *same*; 2d edition; London, 1815. 135
Le Sage, Alain R. Gil Blas; Roscoe's Novelist's Library; London, 1833. *in* 267
Lever, Charles J. Arthur O'Leary; 1st edition; London, 1844. 452
Barrington; 1st edition; London, 1863. 469
Bramleighs of Bishop's Folly; 1st edition; London, 1868. 477
Charles O'Malley; 1st edition; Dublin, 1841. 450
Confessions of Con. Cregan; 1st edition; London, 1850. 459
Cornelius O'Dowd; 1st edition; Edinburgh *and* London, 1864. 471
Daltons, The; 1st edition; London, 1852. 461
Davenport Dunn; 1st edition; London, 1859.

Vol. I., Nos. 1-416; II., 417-748.

Lever, Charles J. (*continued*). Day's ride; 1st edition; London, 1863. 470
Dodd family abroad; 1st edition; London, 1854. 462
Fortunes of Glencore; 1st edition; London, 1857. 466
Gerald Fitzgerald; 1st edition; N. Y., 1866. 475
Harry Lorrequer; 1st edition; Dublin, 1839. 449
Horace Templeton, Diary and notes of; 1st edition; London, 1848. 458
Jack Hinton, the guardsman; 1st edition; Dublin, 1843. *in* 451
Knight of Gwynne; 1st edition; London, 1847. 457
Lord Kilgobbin; 1st edition; London, 1872. 480
Luttrell of Arran; 1st edition; London, 1865. 472
Martins of Cro' Martin; 1st edition; London, 1856. 465
Maurice Tiernay; 1st edition; London, 1855. 463
Nuts and nutcrackers; 1st edition; London, 1845. 453
O'Donoghue, The; 1st edition; Dublin, 1845. 454
One of them; 1st edition; London, 1861. 468
Our mess; 1st edition; Dublin, 1843-44. 451
Paul Gosslett's confessions; 1st edition; London, 1868. 478
Rent in a cloud; 1st edition; London, 1865. 473
Roland Cashel; 1st edition; London, 1850. 460
Saint Patrick's eve; 1st edition; London, 1845. 455
Sir Brook Fossbrooke; 1st edition; Edinburgh *and* London, 1866. 476
Sir Jasper Carew; 1st edition; London, 1855. 464
Tales of the trains; by Tilbury Tramp; 1st edition; London, 1845. 456
That boy of Norcott's; 1st edition; London, 1869. 479
Tom Burke of "Ours"; 1st edition; Dublin, 1844. *in* 451
Tony Butler; 1st edition; Edinburgh *and* London, 1865. 474
Library companion; Dibdin; 2d edition, 1825. 316
Life in London; Egan; 1821. 306
Lilliputian magazine; London, 1783. 141
Little dinner at Timmins's; Thackeray; 1856. *in* 714
Little Dombey, The Story of; Dickens; 1st reading edition, 1858. 355
Little Dorrit; Dickens; 1st edition, 1857. 353

Lloyd, Charles. Poems on the death of Priscilla Farmer; 1st edition; Bristol, 1796. 418
Lloyd, Charles, *and* Charles Lamb. Blank verse; 1st edition; London, 1798. 422
Locrine, The Lamentable tragedie of; sole edition; London, 1595. 622
London angler's book; Baddeley; 1834. 82
London prodigal; sole edition; London, 1605. 627
Long Parliament, Character of the; Milton; 1681. 498
Lord Cobham, The First part of Sir John Oldcastle, the good; 2d edition; London, 1600. 625
Lord Cromwell, The True chronicle historie of Thomas; 2d edition; London, 1613. 626
Lord Kilgobbin; Lever; 1st edition, 1872. 480
Lovel the widower; Thackeray; 1st edition, 1861. 725
Lovelace, Richard. Lucasta; 1st edition; London, 1649. 481
Lucasta: Posthume poems; London, 1659. 482
Love's labour's lost; Shakespeare; 1st edition, 1598. 565
— *same*; 2d edition, 1631. 566
Love's martyr; or, Rosalins complaint; Chester; 1st edition, 1601. 558
Loving ballad of Lord Bateman; Dickens; 1st issue, 1839. 330
Lowell, James Russell. Biglow papers; 2d English edition; London, 1861. 301
Lucasta; Lovelace; 1st edition, 1649. 481
Lucasta: Posthume poems; Lovelace; 1659. 482
Lucrece, Rape of; Shakespeare; 1st edition, 1594. 554
— *same*; 5th edition, 1616. 555
— *same*; 6th edition, 1624. 556
— *same*; 8th edition, 1655. 557
Luttrell of Arran; Lever; 1st edition, 1865. 472
Lycidas; Milton; 1st edition, 1638. *in* 487
Lyne, James. ANDREWS. James Lyne's survey; or, The Bradford map of the city of New York; 1900. 25

Magic of kindness; Henry *and* A. S. Mayhew; 2d issue, 1848. 290
Major, John, *editor*:
   WALTON *and* COTTON. Compleat angler; 1st edition, 1823. 52
   — *same*; 2d edition, 1824. 53
   — *same*; 3d edition (reprint), 1839. 60
   — *same*; 4th edition, 1844. 61
   — *same* (reprint); 1866. 64
Major Gahagan; Thackeray; 1841. *in* 693
Malory, *Sir* Thomas. Most ancient and famous history of the renowned Prince Arthur, King of Britaine; London, 1634.

Vol. I., Nos. 1-416; II., 417-748.

Manuscripts:
  BEWICK. Holograph letter, ordering paper, dated Newcastle, July 26, 1821.   183
  DICKENS. Demeanour of murderers; 1856.   352
  Heures de la rose; about 1400.   400
  Horæ beatæ Mariæ Virginis; 14th century.   399
  — *same;* 15th century.   401
  — *same;* 2d half of 15th century.   402
  — *same;* 2d half of 15th century.   403
  — *same;* latter part of 15th century.   404
  — *same;* 16th century.   405
  — *same;* 16th century.   406
  — *same;* 16th century.   407
  LAMB. Autograph letters to Mr. Moxon; 1821-33.   437
  LAMB *and* KELLY. Autograph letters; July 20, 1819.   436
  MILTON. Autograph signature; October 21, 1633.   *in* 485
  THACKERAY. Chronicle of the drum; 1840.   690
  — Virginians (1 page).   *in* 690
  WALTON. Autograph signature.   *in* 740

Maps:
  ANDREWS. Bradford map of the city of New York; 1893.   14
  — James Lyne's survey; or, The Bradford map of the city of New York; 1900.   25

Marbury, *Mrs.* Mary O. Favorite flies and their histories; Boston *and* N. Y., 1892.   109

Marston, John. Workes; 1st edition, 1st issue; London, 1633.   484

Marston, Robert B., *editor.* WALTON *and* COTTON. Compleat angler; Lea and Dove edition, 1888.   66

Martin Chuzzlewit; Dickens; 1st edition, 1st issue, 1844.   339

Martins of Cro' Martin; Lever; 1st edition, 1856.   465

Marvy, Louis. Sketches after English landscape painters; London, 1850.   706

Maske presented at Ludlow Castle ; Milton ; 1st edition; London, 1637.   486

Master Humphrey's clock; Dickens; 1st edition, 1840-41.   334

Maurice Tiernay; Lever; 1st edition, 1855.   463

Maxims and hints for an angler; Penn; 1st edition, 1833.   81

Maxwell, William H. History of the Irish Rebellion in 1798; 1st edition; London, 1845.   288

Mayer, Alfred M., *editor.* Sport with gun and rod in American woods and waters; N. Y., 1883.   103

Mayhew, Augustus S. *See* Mayhew, Henry *and* Augustus S.

Mayhew, Henry. World's show, 1851; or, The Adventures of Mr. and Mrs. Sandboys; London, 1851.   294

Mayhew, Henry *and* Augustus S. Magic of kindness; 2d issue; London, 1848.   290

  Whom to marry and how to get married; 1st edition; London, 1848.   291

Mayhew, Horace. The Tooth-ache; London, 1849.   292

Meadows, Joseph Kenny. Heads of the people; London, 1840-41.   692

Medea, translated by John Studley; Seneca; 1581.   *in* 504

Memoirs of Mr. Charles J. Yellowplush; Thackeray; 1856.   715

Men's wives; Thackeray; 1857.   718

Merchant of Venice; Shakespeare; 1st edition (Roberts), 1600.   568
  — *same;* 2d edition (Heyes), 1600.   569
  — *same;* 3d edition, 1637.   570

Meres, Francis. Palladis tamia; Wits treasury being the Second Part of Wits common wealth; 1st edition; London, 1598.   637

Merle, William H. Odds and ends; London, 1831.   265

Merry devil of Edmonton; 3d edition; London, 1617.   629
  — *same;* 5th edition; London, 1631.   630

Merry wives of Windsor; Shakespeare; 1st edition, 1602.   562
  — *same;* 2d edition, 1619.   563

Message from the sea; Dickens; 1860.   *in* 357

Midsummer night's dream; Shakespeare; 2d edition, 1600.   567

Milton, John. Accedence commenc't grammar; 1st edition; London, 1669.   497
  Areopagitica; a speech for the liberty of unlicenc'd printing; 1st edition; London, 1644.   490
  Autograph signature; October 21, 1633.   *in* 485
  Character of the Long Parliament; London, 1681.   498
  Comus; A Maske presented at Ludlow Castle; 1st edition; London, 1637.   486
  Lycidas; 1st edition; Cantabrigiæ, 1638.   *in* 487
  Maske presented at Ludlow Castle; 1st edition; London, 1637.   486
  Paradise lost; 1st edition, 1st title-page; London, 1667.   494
  — *same;* 4th title-page; London, 1668.   495
  — *same;* 5th title-page; London, 1669.   496
  Poems, both English and Latin; London, 1645.   491
  Poetical works; Aldine edition; London, 1851.   *in* 195
  Reason of church-governement urg'd against prelaty; London, 1641.   88

Vol. I., Nos. 1-416; II., 417-748.

Milton, John (*continued*). Tenure of kings and magistrates; 1st edition; London, 1649.   493
Milton, John, *and others*. Justa Edouardo King naufrago; Cantabrigiæ, 1638.   487
Milton, John:
  HALL. Short answer to the tedious vindication of Smectymnuus; 1641.   489
  LAWES, H. *and* W. Choice psalmes put into musick; 1648.   492
Minor morals for young people; Bowring; 1834-39.   274
Minshull, Geffray. Essayes and characters of a prison and prisoners; Edinburgh, 1821.   184
Mirror for magistrates; Baldwin; 2d edition, 1563.   499
Miscellanies in prose and verse; Swift; 1st edition, 1711.   676
Modern chivalry; Gore; 1843.   285
Monastery; Scott; 1st edition, 1820.   539
Moore, Francis. Age of intellect; London, 1819.   242
More mornings at Bow Street; Wight; 1827.   257
Mornings at Bow Street; Wight; 2d edition, 1824.   251
— same (illustrations, with short extracts); 1827.   252
Morte d' Arthur. *See* Malory, *Sir* Thomas.
Mother Hubberds tale; Spenser; 1st edition, 1591.   *in* 658
Mourning Muse of Thestylis; Bryskett (only known edition); 1595.   *in* 661
Moxon, Edward. LAMB. Autograph letters to Mr. Moxon; 1821-33.   437
Mr. and Mrs. Sandboys, Adventures of; Henry Mayhew; 1851.   294
Mr. Facey Romford's hounds; Surtees; 1st edition, 1865.   673
Mr. H., or, Beware a bad name; Lamb; 1st edition, 1813.   433
Mr. Nightingale's diary; Dickens; 1st edition, 1877.   365
Mr. Sponge's sporting tour; Surtees; 1st edition, 1853.   669
Mrs. Gamp; Dickens; 1st reading edition, 1858.   *in* 354
Mrs. Gamp with the strolling players; Dickens; 1899.   368
Mrs. Leicester's school; Charles *and* Mary Lamb; 1st edition, 1809.   445
Mrs. Lirriper's legacy; Dickens; 1864.   *in* 357
Mrs. Lirriper's lodgings; Dickens; 1863.   *in* 357
Mrs. Perkins's ball; Thackeray; 1st edition, 1847.   696
Mucedorus, A Most pleasant comedie of; 4th edition; London, 1611.   624
Much ado about nothing; Shakespeare; 1st edition, 1600.   564

Mugby Junction; Dickens; 1866.   *in* 357
Muiopotmos; or, The Fate of the butterflie; Spenser; 1st edition, 1590.   *in* 658
Münchhausen, *Baron* Karl F. H. von:
  RASPE. Baron Munchausen's narrative of his marvellous travels; 2d edition, 1786.   500
  — Surprising adventures of the renowned Baron Munchausen; London, 1811.   501
Musset, Paul E. de. Le Dernier abbé; Paris, 1891.   502
Mynshul, Geffray. *See* Minshull, Geffray.
Myrrour for magistrates; Baldwin; 2d edition, London, 1563.   499
Mystery of Edwin Drood; Dickens; 1st edition, 1870.   361

NAPLES and the Campagna Felice; Englebach; 1815.   517
Napoleon Bonaparte:
  COMBE. Life of Napoleon, a Hudibrastic poem; 1st edition; London, 1815.   240
  THACKERAY. Second funeral of Napoleon; 1841.   694
Nash, Thomas. Nashes Lenten stuffe; London, 1599.   503
Neville, Alexander, *translator*. SENECA. Oedipus; 1581.   *in* 504
New Amsterdam, New Orange, New York; Andrews; 1897.   20
New Bath guide; Anstey; 1832.   269
New lottery book of birds and beasts, for children; Newcastle, 1771.   139
New Robinson Crusoe; Campe; 2d edition, 1789.   132
New spirit of the age; Horne; 1844.   398
New York. ANDREWS. Jacob Steendam; a memoir of the first poet in New Netherland; 1908.   29
New York City:
  ANDREWS. Bradford map of the city of New York; 1893.   14
  — Iconography of the Battery and Castle Garden; 1901.   26
  — James Lyne's survey; or, The Bradford map of the city of New York; 1900.   25
  — Journey of the Iconophiles around New York; 1897.   19
  — New Amsterdam, New Orange, New York; 1897.   20
Newcomes, The; Thackeray; 1st edition, 1854-55.   709
Newton, Thomas, *editor*. SENECA. Seneca his tenne tragedies, translated into Englysh; London, 1581.   504
Newton, Thomas, *translator*. SENECA. Thebais; 1581.   *in* 504

Vol. I., Nos. 1-416; II., 417-748.

Nicholas Nickleby; Dickens; 1st edition, 1839. 331
Nicolas, Sir Nicholas H. Memoirs of Izaak Walton and Charles Cotton; London, 1836. 113
No thoroughfare; Dickens *and* Collins; 1867. in 357
Nobbes, Robert. Compleat troller; 1st edition; London, 1682. 68
Nobody's story; Dickens; 1853. in 347
Noodt, Jan van der. Theatre for worldlings; London, 1569. 650
Notary, Julian, *printer*. Cronycle of Englonde; London, 1515. 225
Novelist's Library, Roscoe's. *See* Roscoe, Thomas.
Novels by eminent hands; Thackeray; 1856. 716
Nuce, Thomas, *translator*. SENECA. Octavia; 1581. in 504
Nuts and nutcrackers; Lever; 1st edition, 1845. 453

OCTAVIA, translated by Thomas Nuce; Seneca; 1581. in 504
Odds and ends; Merle; 1831. 265
O'Donoghue, The; Lever; 1st edition, 1845. 454
Œdipus, translated by Alexander Neville; Seneca; 1581. in 504
Old curiosity shop; Dickens; 1st edition, 1840-41. in 334
Old Mortality; Scott; 1st edition, 1816. in 533
Oliver Twist; Dickens; 1st edition, 1st issue, 1838. 327
— *same*; 1846. 328
Omnibus, George Cruikshank's; 1st edition, 1842. 284
One of them; Lever; 1st edition, 1861. 468
Oppianus. Halieuticks; Oxford, 1722. 31
Oppiani poetæ alieuticon seu de piscibus; Venetiis, 1508. 30
Original letters of Sir John Falstaff; 1st edition; London, 1796. 419
Original stories from real life; Wollstonecraft; 1791. 745
Othello; Shakespeare; 2d edition, 1630. 605
— *same*; 3d edition, 1655. 606
Our mess; Lever; 1st edition, 1843-44. 451
Our mutual friend; Dickens; 1st edition, 1865. 359
Our street; Thackeray; 1st edition, 1848. 698
Overs, John. Evenings of a working man; London, 1844. 340
Oxford sausage; or, Select poetical pieces; London, 1814. 178
Oyster, The; London, 1861. 302

PALLADIS tamia; Meres; 1st edition, 1598. 637
Paradise lost; Milton; 1st edition, 1st title-page, 1667. 494
— *same*; 4th title-page, 1668. 495
— *same*; 5th title-page, 1669. 496
Paris, John A. Philosophy in sport made science in earnest; 1st edition; London, 1827. 256
Parker, Henry. Dives and pauper; 1st edition; London, 1493. 505
Parnell, Thomas. Poems by Goldsmith and Parnell; London, 1804. 138
Poetical works; Aldine edition; London, 1833. in 195
Paul Gosslett's confessions; Lever; 1st edition, 1868. 478
Paulus de Sancta Maria. Dialogus qui vocatur Scrutinium Scripturarum; Mantue, 1475. 506
Payne, John, *translator*:
  BOCCACCIO. The Decameron; 1886. 189
  Book of the thousand nights and one night; 1882-84. 117
  Tales from the Arabic; 1884. 118
Payne, Roger. ANDREWS. Roger Payne and his art; 1892. 13
Pembroke, Mary Herbert, *Countess of, translator*. GARNIER. Tragedie of Antonie; doone into English; 2d edition, 1595. 507
Pembroke, William Herbert, 3d *Earl of*. Poems; 1st edition; London, 1660. 508
Pendennis; Thackeray; 1st edition, 1849-50. 703
Penn, Richard. Maxims and hints for an angler; 1st edition; London, 1833. 81
Pentamerone, The; Basile; 1st edition, 1848. 289
Percy, Thomas. Hermit of Warkworth; 2d edition; Alnwick, 1807. 167
Peregrine Pickle; Smollett; 1831. in 267
Pericles; Shakespeare; 2d or *Eneer* edition, 1609. 607
— *same*; 4th edition, 1619. 608
— *same* (another copy). in 585
— *same*; 7th edition, 1635. 609
Perils of certain English prisoners; Dickens *and* Collins; 1857. in 347
Peter Schlemihl; Chamisso; 1824. 248
Peveril of the Peak; Scott; 1st edition, 1822. 542
Phaer, Thomas, *and* Thomas Twyne, *translators*. VIRGILIUS. The XIII. bookes of Æneidos; 1st edition, 1584. 509
Phillips, Henry. True enjoyment of angling; London, 1843. 89
Philosophy in sport made science in earnest; John Paris; 1st edition, 1827. 256
Phiz, *pseudonym*. *See* Browne, Hablôt K., *illustrator*.
Phœnix and the turtle; Shakespeare; 1st edition, 1601. in 558

Vol. I., Nos. 1-416; II., 417-748.

[1142]

Pic nic papers; Dickens, *editor;* 1841. 335
Pickering, William, *publisher:*
  WALTON *and* COTTON. Compleat angler; 2d edition, 1826. 57
  — *same;* 3d edition, 1836. 58
Pickwick papers; Dickens; 1st edition, 1837. 321
  — *same;* Victorian edition, 1887. 322
Pictures from Italy; Dickens; 1st edition, 1846. 344
Pilgrim's progress, The. *See* Bunyan, John.
Pirate, The; Scott; 1st edition, 1822. 543
Piscatorial reminiscences and gleanings; Boosey; 1835. 83
Plain or ringlets; Surtees; 1st edition, 1860. 672
Pleasures of memory; Rogers; 1803. 512
Poetical pieces on several occasions; John Lamb; 1st edition; London, 1770. 448
Poetry, English. *See* British poets.
Poetry for children; Charles *and* Mary Lamb; 1809. 446
  — *same;* 1812. 447
Poggio Bracciolini. *See* Bracciolini Poggio.
Points of humour; Cruikshank; London, 1823-24. 246
Poor relation's story; Dickens; 1852. *in* 347
Poor traveller; Dickens; 1st reading edition, 1858. 354
Pope, Alexander. Poetical works; Aldine edition; London, 1852. *in* 195
Popular romances of the west of England; Hunt; 1865. 304
Portraits:
  ANDREWS. Essay on the portraiture of the American Revolutionary war; 1896. 18
  — Trio of eighteenth century French engravers of portraits in miniature; 1899. 23
  BOADEN. Inquiry into the authenticity of various pictures of Shakespeare; 1824. 639
  WIVELL. Inquiry into the history, etc., of the Shakspeare portraits; 1827. 640
Preston, Thomas. Lamentable tragedy of Cambises king of Percia; 1st edition; London, 1570. 635
Prettie new ballad, intytuled: The Crowe sits upon the wall; Tarlton (reprint); n. d. 679
Prince Dorus; Lamb; 1st edition, 1st issue, 1811. 428
  — *same;* 1st edition, 2d issue, 1811. 429
  — *same;* 2d edition, 1818. 430
Printing in England:
  Decree of Starre-chamber, concerning printing; 1637. 387
  DIBDIN. Typographical antiquities; 1st edition, 1810-19. 313
  Printing in England and Scotland. DIBDIN. Bibliographical tour in England and Scotland; 1838. 318

Printing in France and Germany. DIBDIN. Bibliographical tour in France and Germany; 1821. 315
Prior, Matthew. Poetical works; Aldine edition; London, 1835. *in* 195
Prisons. MINSHULL. Essayes and characters of a prison and prisoners; 1821. 184
Prologue to Mr. H.; Lamb; 1st edition, 1807. *in* 425
Prosody, Tour of Doctor; Combe *imitated;* 1st edition, 1821. 527
Prosopopoia; or, Mother Hubberds tale; Spenser; 1st edition, 1591. *in* 658
Prothalamion; Spenser; 1st edition, 1596. 663
Proverbs. TRUSLER. Proverbs exemplified, and illustrated by pictures from real life; 1790. 125
Psalms. LAWES, H. *and* W. Choice psalmes put into musick, for three voices; 1648. 492
Punch and Judy; Payne; 1st edition, 1828. 258
Puritan, The; or, The Widow of Watling-street; sole edition; London, 1607. 628
Pynson, Richard, *printer.* PARKER. Dives and pauper; 1st edition, 1493. 505

QUADRUPEDS. *See* Bewick, Thomas, General history of quadrupeds; *also* his Natural history of British quadrupeds.
Quarles, John. Tarquin banished; or, The Reward of lust; London, 1655. *in* 557
Queen Mab; Shelley; 1st published edition, 1821. 646
Quentin Durward; Scott; 1st edition, 1823. 544
Quiz, *pseudonym.* Grand master; or, Adventures of Qui Hi? in Hindostan; London, 1816. 519

RAMBLES in the footsteps of Don Quixote; Inglis; 1837. 279
Rape of Lucrece; Shakespeare; 1st edition, 1594. 554
  — *same;* 5th edition, 1616. 555
  — *same;* 6th edition, 1624. 556
  — *same;* 8th edition, 1655. 557
Raspe, Rudolph E. Baron Munchausen's narrative of his marvellous travels; 2d edition; Oxford, 1786. 500
  Surprising adventures of the renowned Baron Munchausen; London, 1811. 501
Raymond, George. Memoirs of Robert William Elliston, comedian; London, 1844. 286
Reach, Angus B. Clement Lorimer; London, 1849. 293
Reading a poem; Thackeray; 1st edition, 1891. 735
Real life in London; Egan; 1st edition, 1821. 528
Reason of church-governement; Milton; 1641. 488

Vol. I., Nos. 1-416; II., 417-748.

Reay, Henry U. Short treatise on that useful invention called the sportsman's friend; Newcastle, 1801. 165
Rebecca and Rowena; Thackeray; 1st edition, 1850. 705
— *same*; 1856. *in* 713
Recollections of fly fishing for salmon, trout, and grayling; Hamilton; 1884. 104
Recuile of the histories of Troie; Le Fevre; 1553. 226
Redgauntlet; Scott; 1st edition, 1824. 545
Religio medici; Browne; 1st unauthorized edition; 1642. 196
Rembrandt Hermanzoon van Rijn. DAULBY. Descriptive catalogue of the works of Rembrandt; 1796. 510
Rennie, James, *editor*. WALTON *and* COTTON. Compleat angler; 1836. 59
Rent in a cloud; Lever; 1st edition, 1865. 473
Returne from Pernassus; 1st edition; London, 1606. 638
Revere, Paul. ANDREWS. Paul Revere and his engraving; 1901. 27
Revolutionary War. *See* American Revolution.
Richard the Second; Shakespeare; 2d edition, 1598. 573
— *same*; 3d edition, 1608. 574
— *same*; 5th edition, 1615. 575
— *same*; 6th edition, 1634. 576
Richard the Third; Shakespeare; 2d edition, 1598. 588
— *same*; 4th edition, 1605. 589
— *same*; 5th edition, 1612. 590
— *same*; 6th edition, 1622. 591
— *same*; 8th edition, 1634. 592
Ristigouche and its salmon fishing; Sage; 1888. 108
River Dove; Anderdon; 1845. 92
— *same*; 1847. 93
Rob Roy; Scott; 1st edition, 1818. 534
Robinson, Thomas. Anatomie of the English nunnery at Lisbon; 3d edition; London, 1630. 511
Robinson Crusoe; Defoe; 1st edition, 1719. 310
— *same*; Farther adventures; 1st edition, 2d issue, 1719. 311
— *same*; Serious reflections; 1st edition, 1720. 312
Robinson Crusoe; Roscoe's Novelist's Library; 1831. *in* 267
— *same*; Major's edition, 1831. 268
Roderick Random; Smollett; 1831. *in* 267
Rogers, Samuel. Italy, a poem; 1st edition, 1st issue; London, 1830. 513
Pleasures of memory; London, 1803. 512
Poems; London, 1834. 514

Roland Cashel; Lever; 1st edition, 1850. 460
Romeo and Juliet; Shakespeare; 2d edition, 1599. 595
— *same*; 3d edition, 1609. 596
— *same*; 4th edition ("W. Shake-fpeare" on title-page), n. d. 597
— *same*; 5th edition, n. d. 598
Ronalds, Alfred. Fly-fisher's entomology; 5th edition; London, 1856. 98
Rookwood; Ainsworth; 4th edition, 1836. 5
Roscoe, Thomas, *editor*. Novelist's Library; 19 vols.; London, 1831-33. 267
Roscoe, Thomas, *translator*. Italian tales; 1st edition; London, 1824. 249
Rose and the ring; Thackeray; 1st edition, 1855. 711
Rowlandson, Thomas, *illustrator*:
COMBE. Dance of life; 1st edition, 1817. 520
— English dance of Death; 1st edition, 1815-16. 518
— History of Johnny Quæ Genus; 1st edition, 1822. 524
— Tour of Doctor Syntax, in search of the picturesque; 1st edition, 1812. 516
— Second tour of Doctor Syntax, in search of consolation; 1st edition, 1820. 521
— Third tour of Doctor Syntax, in search of a wife; 1st edition, 1822. 522
ENGLEBACH. Naples and the Campagna Felice; 1815. 517
GOLDSMITH. Vicar of Wakefield; 1817. 385
Journal of sentimental travels in the southern provinces of France; 1821. 523
QUIZ, *pseudonym*. Grand master; or, Adventures of Qui Hi? in Hindostan; 1816. 519
RASPE. Surprising adventures of the renowned Baron Munchausen; 1811. 501
STEVENS. Lecture on heads; 1808. 515
Rowlandson, Thomas, *imitated*:
COMBE *imitated*. Doctor Syntax in Paris; 1820. 525
— Tour of Doctor Prosody, in search of the antique and picturesque; 1st edition, 1821. 527
— Tour of Doctor Syntax through London; 1st edition, 1820. 526
D'OYLY. Tom Raw, the griffin; 1828. 529
EGAN. Real life in London; 1st edition, 1821. 528
Roydon, Matthew. An Elegie, or friends passion for his Astrophell; 1595. *in* 661
Ruines of time; Spenser; 1st edition, 1591. *in* 658

SABIN, Joseph. Bibliographical catalogue of the Waltonian library of Robert W. Coleman; N. Y., 1866. 115

Vol. I., Nos. 1-416; II., 417-748.

Sage, Dean. Ristigouche and its salmon fishing; Edinburgh, 1888. 108
Saint James's; Ainsworth; 1846. 9
Saint Patrick's eve; Lever; 1st edition, 1845. 455
Saint Ronan's well; Scott; 1st edition, 1824. 546
Saint Valentine's day; or, The Fair maid of Perth; Scott; 1st edition, 1828. *in* 550
Salter, Thomas F. Angler's guide; 2d edition; London, 1815. 75
— *same*; 3d edition; London, 1815. 76
— *same*; 9th edition; London, 1841. 77
Samuel Titmarsh, History of; Thackeray; 1st edition, 1849. 701
Sand and canvas; Bevan; 1849. 702
Sanderson, Robert:
    WALTON. Life of Dr. Sanderson; 1678. 744
    — Lives of Donne, Wotton, Hooker, Herbert, and Sanderson; 1796. 741
    — *same*; 1825. 742
    — *same*; 1827. 743
Satan in search of a wife; Lamb; 1st edition; London, 1831. 442
Satchell, Thomas, *and* Thomas Westwood. Chronicle of the "Compleat Angler" (reprint); London, 1888. *in* 66
Saunders, James. Compleat fisherman; London, 1724. 69
Savart, Pierre. ANDREWS. Trio of eighteenth century French engravers; 1899. 23
Scenes and tales of country life; Jesse; 1844. 91
Scenes from the life of Edward Lascelles, Gent.; Dublin, 1837. 280
Scholemaster, The; Ascham; 3d edition; 1573. 120
Schoolboy's story; Dickens; 1853. *in* 347
Scott, Genio C. Fishing in American waters; N. Y., 1869. 101
Scott, *Sir* Walter. The Abbot; 1st edition; Edinburgh, 1820. 537
    Anne of Geierstein; 1st edition; Edinburgh, 1829. 551
    Antiquary; 1st edition; Edinburgh, 1816. 532
    Betrothed, The; 1st edition; Edinburgh, 1825. *in* 547
    Black dwarf; 1st edition; Edinburgh, 1816. *in* 533
    Bride of Lammermoor; 1st edition; Edinburgh, 1819. *in* 536
    Castle Dangerous; 1st edition; Edinburgh, 1832. *in* 553
    Chronicles of the Canongate; 1st series; 1st edition; Edinburgh, 1827. 549
    — *same*; 2d series; 1st edition; Edinburgh, 1828. 550
    Count Robert of Paris; 1st edition; Edinburgh, 1832. 553

Scott, *Sir* Walter (*continued*). Fair maid of Perth; 1st edition; Edinburgh, 1828. *in* 550
    Fortunes of Nigel; 1st edition; Edinburgh, 1822. 541
    Guy Mannering; 1st edition; Edinburgh, 1815. 531
    Heart of Mid-Lothian; 1st edition; Edinburgh, 1818. *in* 535
    Highland widow; 1st edition; Edinburgh, 1827. *in* 549
    Ivanhoe; 1st edition; Edinburgh, 1820. 538
    Kenilworth; 1st edition; Edinburgh, 1821. 540
    Legend of Montrose; 1st edition; Edinburgh, 1819. *in* 536
    Letters on demonology and witchcraft; 1st edition; London, 1830. 552
    Monastery, The; 1st edition; Edinburgh, 1820. 539
    Old Mortality; 1st edition; Edinburgh, 1816. *in* 533
    Peveril of the Peak; 1st edition; Edinburgh, 1822. 542
    Pirate, The; 1st edition; Edinburgh, 1822. 543
    Quentin Durward; 1st edition; Edinburgh, 1823. 544
    Redgauntlet; 1st edition; Edinburgh, 1824. 545
    Rob Roy; 1st edition; Edinburgh, 1818. 534
    Saint Ronan's well; 1st edition; Edinburgh, 1824. 546
    Saint Valentine's day; or, The Fair maid of Perth; 1st edition; Edinburgh, 1828. *in* 550
    Surgeon's daughter; 1st edition; Edinburgh, 1827. *in* 549
    Tales of my landlord; 1st series; Edinburgh, 1816. 533
    — *same*; 2d series; 1st edition; Edinburgh, 1818. 535
    — *same*; 3d series; 1st edition; Edinburgh, 1819. 536
    — *same*; 4th series; 1st edition; Edinburgh, 1832. 553
    Tales of the Crusaders; 1st edition; Edinburgh, 1825. 547
    Talisman, The; 1st edition; Edinburgh, 1825. *in* 547
    Two drovers, The; 1st edition; Edinburgh, 1827. *in* 549
    Waverley; or, 'Tis sixty years since; 1st edition; Edinburgh, 1814. 530
    Woodstock; 1st edition; Edinburgh, 1826. 548
Scott, William H. British field sports; London, 1820. 182
Scraps and sketches; Cruikshank; 1828-32. 260

Vol. I., Nos. 1-416; II., 417-748.

Scrope, William. Days and nights of salmon fishing in the Tweed; 1st edition; London, 1843. 90
Scrutinium Scripturarum, Dialogus qui vocatur; Paulus de Sancta Maria; 1475. 506
Seasons, The; Thomson; 1805. 738
Seaven champions of Christendome, Famous historie of the; London, c. 1620. 414
Second funeral of Napoleon; Thackeray; 1841. 694
Seneca, Lucius Annæus. Seneca his tenne tragedies, translated into Englysh; London, 1581. 504

Agamemnon; translated by John Studley; London, 1581. *in* 504
Hercules furens; translated by Jasper Heywood; London, 1581. *in* 504
Hercules Oetæus; translated by John Studley; London, 1581. *in* 504
Hippolytus; translated by John Studley; London, 1581. *in* 504
Medea; translated by John Studley; London, 1581. *in* 504
Octavia; translated by Thomas Nuce; London, 1581. *in* 504
Œdipus; translated by Alexander Neville; London, 1581. *in* 504
Thebais; translated by Thomas Newton; London, 1581. *in* 504
Thyestes; translated by Jasper Heywood; London, 1581. *in* 504
Troas; translated by Jasper Heywood; London, 1581. *in* 504

Seneca, Lucius Annæus. CORNWALLIS. Discourses upon Seneca; 1601. *in* 235
Sentimental journey through France and Italy; Sterne; 1st edition; London, 1768. 666
Seven poor travellers; Dickens; 1854. *in* 347
Sextodecimos et infra; Andrews; 1899. 22
Shabby genteel story; Thackeray; 1857. 719
Shakespeare, William. Comedies, histories, and tragedies; First Folio edition; London, 1623. 610
— *same*; Second Folio, "Coppies" edition; Allot imprint; London, 1632. 611
— *same*; "Copies" edition; Aspley imprint; London, 1632. 612
— *same*; Hawkins imprint; London, 1632. 613
— *same*; Meighen imprint; London, 1632. 614
— *same*; Smethwick imprint; London, 1632. 615
— *same*; Third Folio edition; London, 1663. 616
— *same*; London, 1664. 617
— *same*; Fourth Folio edition; Chiswell imprint; London, 1685. 619
— *same*; Herringman, Brewster, and Bentley imprint; London, 1685. 620

Shakespeare, William (*continued*). Comedies, histories, and tragedies; Fourth Folio edition; Knight and Saunders imprint; London, 1685. 618
Hamlet; 4th edition; London, 1611. 600
— *same*; 6th edition; London, 1637. 601
Henry the Fourth, Part I.; 2d edition; London, 1599. 577
— *same*; 5th edition; London, 1613. 578
— *same*; 6th edition; London, 1622. 579
— *same*; 8th edition; London, 1639. 580
Henry the Fourth, Part II.; 1st edition (E, 4 leaves); London, 1600. 581
— *same*; 2d edition (E, 6 leaves); London, 1600. 582
Henry the Fifth; 1st edition; London, 1600. 583
— *same*; 3d edition; London, 1608. 584
Henry the Sixth, Part II.; 3d edition; London, 1619. *in* 585
Henry the Sixth, Part III.; 2d edition; London, 1600. 586
— *same*; 3d edition; London, 1619. 587
Julius Cæsar; 1st separate edition; London, 1680. 599
King Lear; 2d edition; London, 1608. 603
— *same*; 3d edition; London, 1655. 604
Love's labour's lost; 1st edition; London, 1598. 565
— *same*; 2d edition; London, 1631. 566
Lucrece; 1st edition; London, 1594. 554
— *same*; 5th edition; London, 1616. 555
— *same*; 6th edition; London, 1624. 556
— *same*; 8th edition; London, 1655. 557
Merchant of Venice; 1st edition; London (Roberts), 1600. 568
— *same*; 2d edition; London (Heyes), 1600. 569
— *same*; 3d edition; London, 1637. 570
Merry wives of Windsor; 1st edition; London, 1602. 562
— *same*; 2d edition; London, 1619. 563
Midsummer night's dream; 2d edition; London, 1600. 567
Much ado about nothing; 1st edition; London, 1600. 564
Othello; 2d edition; London, 1630. 605
— *same*; 3d edition; London, 1655. 606
Pericles; 2d or *Eneer* edition; London, 1609. 607
— *same*; 4th edition; London, 1619. 608
— *same* (another copy). *in* 585
— *same*; 7th edition; London, 1635. 609
Phœnix and the turtle; 1st edition; London, 1601. *in* 558
Poems; 1st edition; London, 1640. 560
— *same*; Aldine edition; London, 1853. *in* 195

Vol. I., Nos. 1-416; II., 417-748.

Shakespeare, William (*continued*). Richard the Second; 2d edition; London, 1598. 573
— *same*; 3d edition; London, 1608. 574
— *same*; 5th edition; London, 1615. 575
— *same*; 6th edition; London, 1634. 576
Richard the Third; 2d edition; London, 1598. 588
— *same*; 4th edition; London, 1605. 589
— *same*; 5th edition; London, 1612. 590
— *same*; 6th edition; London, 1622. 591
— *same*; 8th edition; London, 1634. 592
Romeo and Juliet; 2d edition; London, 1599. 595
— *same*; 3d edition; London, 1609. 596
— *same*; 4th edition ("W. Shake-fpeare" on title-page); London, n. d. 597
— *same*; 5th edition; London, n. d. 598
Songs of Shakespeare; London, 1843. 561
Sonnets; 1st edition; London, 1609. 559
Taming of the shrew; 1st separate edition; London, 1631. 571
Threnos; 1st edition; London, 1601. in 558
Titus Andronicus; 3d edition; London, 1611. 594
Troilus and Cressida; 2d edition; London, 1609. 593
True tragedie of Richarde Duke of Yorke; 2d edition; London, 1600. 586
Whole contention betweene the two famous houses, Lancaster and Yorke; 3d edition; London, 1619. 585
Works; edited by Alexander Dyce; 3d edition; London, 1875-76. 643

Shakespeare, William. *Source Plays:*
John king of England, Troublesome raigne of; 2d edition; London, 1611. 572
King Leir, True chronicle history of; earliest known edition; London, 1605. 602

Shakespeare, William. *Supposititious Plays:*
Arden of Feversham; 3d edition; London, 1633. 621
Edward the Third; 1st edition; London, 1596. 623
Fair Em; 2d edition; London, 1631. 633
Locrine; sole edition; London, 1595. 622
London prodigal; sole edition; London, 1605. 627
Merry devil of Edmonton; 3d edition; London, 1617. 629
— *same*; 5th edition; London, 1631. 630
Mucedorus; 4th edition; London, 1611. 624
Puritan, The; or, The Widow of Watling-street; sole edition; London, 1607. 628
Sir John Oldcastle; 2d edition; London, 1600. 625
Thomas Lord Cromwell; 2d edition; London, 1613. 626

Shakespeare, William. *Supposititious Plays (continued):*
Two noble kinsmen; sole edition; London, 1634. 634
Yorkshire tragedy; 1st edition; London, 1608. 631
— *same*; 2d edition; London, 1619. 632

Shakespeariana — *Contemporary:*
Englands Parnassus; 1st edition, 1600. 10
HARVEY. Foure letters, and certaine sonnets; 1592. 636
MERES. Palladis tamia; 1st edition, 1598. 637
PRESTON. Lamentable tragedy of Cambises King of Percia; 1st edition, 1570. 635
Returne from Pernassus; 1st edition, 1606. 638
ROBINSON. Anatomie of the English nunnery at Lisbon; 3d edition, 1630. 511
SPENSER. Colin Clouts come home againe; 1st edition, 1595. 661
— Teares of the Muses; 1st edition, 1591. in 658

Shakespeariana — *Modern:*
BOADEN. Inquiry into the authenticity of various pictures of Shakespeare; 1824. 639
HALLIWELL-PHILLIPPS. Shakesperiana; a catalogue of the early editions of Shakespeare's plays; London, 1841. 641
LAMB, C. *and* M. Tales from Shakespear; 1st edition, 1807. 444
SMIRKE *and others*. Illustrations of Shakespeare's plays; London, n. d. 642
WINSOR. Bibliography of the original quartos and folios of Shakespeare; Boston, 1876. 644
WIVELL. Inquiry into the history, etc., of the Shakspeare portraits; 1827. 640

Shelley, Percy Bysshe. The Cenci; 1st edition; Leghorn, 1819. 645
Queen Mab; 1st published edition; London, 1821. 646
Shepheardes calender; Spenser; 1st edition, 1579. 651
— *same*; 2d edition, 1581. 652
— *same*; 3d edition, 1586. 653
— *same*; 5th edition, 1597. 654
Short answer to the tedious vindication of Smectymnuus; Hall; 1641. 489
Short treatise on that useful invention called the sportsman's friend; Reay; Newcastle, 1801. 165
Siddons, Henry. Time's a tell-tale; 1st edition; London, 1807. 426
Sidney, Mary, *Countess of* Pembroke, *translator.*
GARNIER. Tragedie of Antonie; 2d edition, 1595. 507
Sidney, *Sir* Philip. Countesse of Pembrokes Arcadia; 1st edition; London, 1590. 647
— *same*; 2d edition; London, 1593. 648

Vol. I., Nos. 1-416; II., 417-748.

Sir Brook Fossbrooke; Lever; 1st edition, 1866, 476
Sir Jasper Carew; Lever; 1st edition, 1855. 464
Sir John Oldcastle, the good Lord Cobham, The First part of; 2d edition; London, 1600. 625
Sir Launcelot Greaves; Smollett; 1832. in 267
Sketches and travels in London; Thackeray; 1856. 717
Sketches by Boz; Dickens; 1st complete edition, 1839. 332
Sketches of young couples; Dickens; 1st edition, 1840. 333
Sketches of young gentlemen; Dickens; 1st edition, 1838. 329
Sketches of young ladies; Caswell; 1st edition, 1837. 323
Small poems of divers sorts; Cokayne; 1st edition, 1658. 233
Smectymnuus, Short answer to the tedious vindication of; Hall; 1641. 489
Smirke, *Sir* Robert, *illustrator*. Adventure of Hunch-back, and the stories connected with it; London, 1814. 119
Smirke, *Sir* Robert, *and others*. Illustrations of Shakspeare's plays; London, n. d. 642
Smollett, Tobias G. History and adventures of an atom; 1st edition; London, 1769. 649
   Humphry Clinker; Roscoe's Novelist's Library; London, 1831. in 267
   Peregrine Pickle; Roscoe's Novelist's Library; London, 1831. in 267
   Roderick Random; Roscoe's Novelist's Library; London, 1831. in 267
   Sir Launcelot Greaves; Roscoe's Novelist's Library; London, 1832. in 267
Snob, The; Cambridge, 1829. 680
Soane, George, *translator*. Specimens of German romance; London, 1826. 255
Soltau, G. W. Trout flies of Devon and Cornwall; 2d edition; London *and* Plymouth, 1856. 99
Somebody's luggage; Dickens; 1862. in 357
Somerville, William. The Chase; 1st edition; London, 1796. 136
— *same*; 2d edition; London, 1802. 137
Songs, naval and national; Charles Dibdin; 1st edition; 1841. 283
Sonnets:
   BOWLES *and others*. Selected sonnets; 1796. 417
   HARVEY. Foure letters, and certaine sonnets; 1592. 636
   SHAKESPEARE. Sonnets; 1609. 559
   SPENSER. Epigrams; 1569. in 650
   — *same*; 1591. in 658
Southey, *Mrs.* Caroline A. B. The Cat's tail; Edinburgh *and* London, 1831. 266
Specimens of German romance; Soane; 1826. 255

Spenser, Edmund. Amoretti and Epithalamion; 1st edition; London, 1595. 660
Brittain's Ida; 1st edition; London, 1628. 664
Colin Clouts come home againe; 1st edition; London, 1595. 661
Complaints; containing sundrie small poemes of the worlds vanitie; 1st edition; London, 1591. 658
Daphnaïda; 1st edition; London, 1591. 659
— *same*; 2d edition; London, 1596. in 662
Epigrams; London, 1569. in 650
— *same*; Visions of Petrarch; London, 1591. in 658
Faerie queene; 1st edition, 1st issue; London, 1590. 655
— *same*; 1st edition, 2d issue; London, 1590. 655 A
— *same*; 2d edition; London, 1596. 656
— *same*; Second Part, Books iv.-vi.; 1st edition; London, 1596. 657
Fowre hymnes; 1st edition; London, 1596. 662
Muiopotmos; or, The Fate of the butterflie; 1st edition; London, 1590. in 658
Poetical works; Aldine edition; London, 1839. in 195
Prosopopoia; or, Mother Hubberds tale; 1st edition; London, 1591. in 658
Prothalamion; 1st edition; London, 1596. 663
Ruines of time; 1st edition; London, 1591. in 658
Shepheardes calender; 1st edition; London, 1579. 651
— *same*; 2d edition; London, 1581. 652
— *same*; 3d edition; London, 1586. 653
— *same*; 5th edition; London, 1597. 654
Sonnets; London, 1569. in 650
— *same*; Visions of Bellay; London, 1591. in 658
Teares of the Muses; 1st edition; London, 1591. in 658
Spenser, Edmund. NOODT. Theatre for worldlings; London, 1569. 650
   See *also* Englands Parnassus (10); and Returne from Pernassus (638).
Spider and the flie; Heywood; 1556. 393
Sport with gun and rod in American woods and waters; Mayer; 1883. 103
Sports. SCOTT. British field sports; 1820. 182
Sportsman's friend; Reay; 1801. 165
Stanbridge, John. Vocabula magistri stanbrigi; London, 1520. 665
Steendam, Jacob. ANDREWS. Jacob Steendam; a memoir of the first poet in New Netherland; 1908. 29
Stenelaus and Amylda; London, 1858. 299

Vol. I., Nos. 1–416; II., 417–748.

Sterne, Laurence. Sentimental journey through France and Italy; 1st edition; London, 1768. 666

Tristram Shandy; Roscoe's Novelist's Library; London, 1832. in 267

Stevens, George A. Lecture on heads; London, 1808. 515

Stewart, W. C. Caution to anglers; Edinburgh, 1871. 102

Stothard, Thomas. BRAY. Life of Thomas Stothard; 1851. 194

Strange gentleman; Dickens; 1st edition, 1837. 324
— same (facsimile reprint); 1871. 325

Stubbs's calendar; or, The Fatal boots; Thackeray; 1850. 687
— same; 1838. in 686
— same; 1841. in 693

Students' quarter; Thackeray; 1st edition, 1864. 727

Studley, John, translator:
SENECA. Agamemnon; 1581. in 504
— Hercules Oetæus; 1581. in 504
— Hippolytus; 1581. in 504
— Medea; 1581. in 504

Sunday in London; Wight; 1833. 272

Surgeon's daughter; Scott; 1st edition, 1827. in 549

Surrey, Henry Howard, Earl of. Poems; Aldine edition; London, 1831. in 195

Surtees, Robert S. "Ask mamma"; 1st edition; London, 1858. 671
Handley Cross; or, Mr. Jorrocks's hunt; 1st edition; London, 1854. 670
Hawbuck Grange; 1st edition; London, 1847. 668
Jorrocks's jaunts and jollities; 1st edition; London, 1838. 667
Mr. Facey Romford's hounds; 1st edition; London, 1865. 673
Mr. Sponge's sporting tour; 1st edition; London, 1853. 669
Plain or ringlets; 1st edition; London, 1860. 672

Swift, Jonathan. Battle of the books; 1st edition; London, 1704. in 674
Baucis and Philemon; 1st edition; London, 1709. 675
Cadenus and Vanessa; 1st edition; London, 1726. 677
Gulliver's travels; 1st edition; London, 1726. 678
Miscellanies in prose and verse; 1st edition; London, 1711. 676
Poetical works; Aldine edition; London, 1833-34. in 195
Tale of a tub; 1st edition; London, 1704. 674

Syntax, Tours of Doctor. See Combe, William.

TABLE-BOOK, George Cruikshank's; 1st edition, 1845. 287

Tale of a tub; Swift; 1st edition, 1704. 674

Tale of Rosamund Gray; Lamb; 1st edition; Birmingham, 1798. 420
— same; 2d edition; London, 1798. 421

Tale of two cities; Dickens; 1st edition, 1859. 356

Tales for youth, in thirty poems; Wynne; 1794. 126

Tales from Shakespear; Charles and Mary Lamb; 1st edition 1807. 444

Tales from the Arabic; Payne, translator; 1884. 118

Tales of Irish life; Whitty; 1824. 250

Tales of my landlord; 1st series; Scott; 1st edition, 1816. 533
— same; 2d series; 1st edition, 1818. 535
— same; 3d series; 1st edition, 1819. 536
— same; 4th series; 1st edition, 1832. 553

Tales of other days; Akerman; 1st edition, 1830. 262

Tales of the Crusaders; Scott; 1st edition, 1825. 547

Tales of the trains; Lever; 1st edition, 1845. 456

Talisman, The; Scott; 1st edition, 1825. in 547

Taming of the shrew; Shakespeare; 1st separate edition, 1631. 571

Tarlton, Richard. Prettie new ballad, intytuled: The Crowe sits upon the wall; London, n. d. 679

Tarquin banished; or, The Reward of lust (a sequel to Shakespeare's Lucrece); Quarles; 1st edition, 1655. in 557

Task, The; Cowper; 1st edition, 1785. 238

Tasso, Torquato. Godfrey of Bulloigne; London, 1594. 223

Teares of the Muses; Spenser; 1st edition, 1591. in 658

Tenure of kings and magistrates; Milton; 1st edition, 1649. 493

Thackeray, William M. Adventures of Philip; 1st edition; London, 1862. 726
Ballads; 1st edition; London, 1855. 710
Barber Cox, and the cutting of his comb; 1st edition; London, 1839. in 689
Barry Lyndon; London, 1856. 712
Bedford-Row conspiracy; London, 1841. in 693
— same; London, 1856. in 714
Book of snobs; 1st edition; London, 1848. 697
Burlesques: A Legend of the Rhine and Rebecca and Rowena; London, 1856. 713
Character sketches; London, 1856. in 716
Chronicle of the drum (original manuscript); 1840. 690
— same; 1st edition; London, 1841. in 694
Collection of letters of Thackeray; N. Y., 1887. 733

Vol. I., Nos. 1-416; II., 417-748.

Thackeray, William M. (*continued*). Comic tales and sketches; 1st edition; London, 1841. 693
Denis Duval; 1st edition; London, 1867. 729
Diary of C. Jeames de la Pluche; London, 1856. *in* 715
Doctor Birch and his young friends; 1st edition; London, 1849. 700
English humourists of the eighteenth century; 1st edition; London, 1853. 708
Essay on the genius of George Cruikshank; London, 1840. 691
Etchings; London, 1878. 730
Exquisites, The; London, 1839. 688
Extracts from the writings of Thackeray; London, 1881. 732
Fitz-Boodle papers *and* Men's wives; London, 1857. 718
Flore et Zephyr; London, 1836. 682
Four Georges, The; 1st edition, 1st issue; London, 1861. 723
Henry Esmond; 1st edition; London, 1852. 707
— *same* (another copy, extra-illustrated). 707 A
History of Samuel Titmarsh and the great Hoggarty diamond; 1st edition; London, 1849. 701
Irish sketch-book; 1st edition; London, 1843. 695
Kickleburys on the Rhine; 1st edition; London, 1850. 704
King Glumpus; London, 1837. 683
Leaf out of a sketch-book; author's edition; London, 1861. 724
Legend of the Rhine, 1845. *in* 287
— *same*; London, 1856. *in* 713
Letters, Collection of; N. Y., 1887. 733
Little dinner at Timmins's *and* The Bedford-Row conspiracy; London, 1856. 714
Lovel the widower; 1st edition; London, 1861. 725
Loving ballad of Lord Bateman; 1st issue; London, 1839. 330
Major Gahagan; London, 1841. *in* 693
Memoirs of Mr. Charles J. Yellowplush *and* The Diary of C. Jeames de la Pluche; London, 1856. 715
Men's wives; London, 1857. *in* 718
Mr. Thackeray's writings in "The National Standard," and "Constitutional"; London, 1899. 737
Mrs. Perkins's ball; 1st edition; London, 1847. 696
Newcomes, The; 1st edition; London, 1854-55. 709
Novels by eminent hands *and* Character sketches; London, 1856. 716

Thackeray, William M. (*continued*). Our street; 1st edition; London, 1848. 698
Pendennis; 1st edition; London, 1849-50. 703
Reading a poem; 1st edition; London, 1891. 735
Rebecca and Rowena; 1st edition; London, 1850. 705
— *same*; London, 1856. *in* 713
Rose and the ring; 1st edition; London, 1855. 711
Second funeral of Napoleon *and* The Chronicle of the drum; London, 1841. 694
Shabby genteel story; London, 1857. 719
Sketches and travels in London; London, 1856. 717
Stubbs's calendar; or, The Fatal boots; N. Y., 1850. 687
— *same*; London, 1838. *in* 686
— *same*; London, 1841. *in* 693
Students' quarter; 1st edition; London, 1864. 727
The Three sailors (Little Billee); 1849. *in* 702
Vanity fair; 1st edition, 1st issue; London, 1848. 699
Virginians, The; 1st edition; London, 1858-59. 720
— *same* (one page of the original manuscript). *in* 690
Yellowplush correspondence; 1st edition; Phil., 1838. 684
Yellowplush papers; London, 1841. *in* 693
Thackeray, William M., *contributor*:
BEVAN. Sand and canvas; 1849. 702
CRUIKSHANK. Comic almanack for 1839; 1st edition, 1838. 686
— Comic almanack for 1840; 1st edition, 1839. 689
Gownsman, The; 1830. 681
MARVY. Sketches after English landscape painters; London, 1850. 706
MEADOWS. Heads of the people; 1840-41. 692
Snob, The; 1829. 680
Thackeray, William M., *illustrator*. ADDISON. Damascus and Palmyra; London, 1838. 685
Thackeray, William M. — *Miscellaneous*:
CROWE. With Thackeray in America; 1893. 736
HOTTEN. Thackeray the humourist and man of letters; 1864. 728
JOHNSON. Early writings of Thackeray; 1888. 734
TROLLOPE. Thackeray; 1879. 731
William Makepeace Thackeray at Clevedon Court; Bristol, 1860. 722
YATES. Mr. Thackeray, Mr. Yates, and the Garrick Club; 1859. 721

Vol. I., Nos. 1-416; II., 417-748.

That boy of Norcott's; Lever; 1st edition, 1869. 479
Theatre for worldlings; Noodt; 1569. 650
Thebais, translated by Thomas Newton; Seneca; 1581. *in* 504
Thomas Lord Cromwell, The True chronicle historie of; 2d edition; London, 1613. 626
Thomson, David C. Life and works of Thomas Bewick; London, 1882. 186
Thomson, James. Poetical works; Aldine edition; London, 1830. *in* 195
    The Seasons; London, 1805. 738
Thornton, Robert J. New family herbal; 1st edition; London, 1810. 175
Thoughts on hunting; Beckford; 1820. 181
Three courses and a dessert; Clarke; 1st edition, 1830. 263
Threnos; Shakespeare; 1st edition, 1601. *in* 558
Thyestes, translated by Jasper Heywood; Seneca; 1581. *in* 504
Tilbury Tramp, *pseudonym. See* Lever, Charles J.
Tim Bobbin's Lancashire dialect, and poems; Collier; 2d edition, 1833. 307
Time's a tell-tale; Siddons; 1st edition, 1807. 426
Titmarsh, Michael Angelo, *pseudonym. See* Thackeray, William M.
Titus Andronicus; Shakespeare; 3d edition, 1611. 594
To be read at dusk; Dickens; 1852. 348
Tom Burke of "Ours"; Lever; 1st edition, 1844. *in* 451
Tom Jones; Fielding; 1st edition, 1st issue, 1749. 381
  — *same;* 1831. *in* 267
Tom Raw, the griffin; D'Oyly; 1828. 529
Tom Tiddler's ground; Dickens; 1861. *in* 357
Tommy Trip's history of beasts and birds; Newcastle, 1779. 140
Tony Butler; Lever; 1st edition, 1865. 474
Tooth-ache, The; Horace Mayhew; 1849. 292
Tough yarns; Barker; 1835. 276
Tour of Doctor Prosody, in search of the antique and picturesque; Combe *imitated;* 1st edition, 1821. 527
Tour of Doctor Syntax, in search of the picturesque; Combe; 1st edition, 1812. 520
Tour (Second) of Doctor Syntax in search of consolation; Combe; 1st edition, 1820. 521
Tour (Third) of Doctor Syntax in search of a wife; Combe; 1st edition, 1822. 522
Tour of Doctor Syntax through London; Combe *imitated;* 1st edition, 1820. 526
Tower of London; Ainsworth; 1st edition, 1840. 7
Travels into several remote nations of the world; by Lemuel Gulliver; 1st edition; London, 1726. 678

Treatyse of fysshynge wyth an angle; Berners; 1827. 78
  — *same;* 1903. 28 A
Trial of Sir Jasper; Hall; 1874. 305
Trio of eighteenth century French engravers; Andrews; 1899. 23
Tristram Shandy; Sterne; 1832. *in* 267
Troas, translated by Jasper Heywood; Seneca; 1581. *in* 504
Troilus and Cressida; Shakespeare; 2d edition, 1609. 593
Trollope, Anthony. Thackeray; 1st edition; London, 1879. 731
Troublesome raigne of John king of England; 2d edition); 1611. 572
Trout flies of Devon and Cornwall; Soltau; 2d edition, 1856. 99
True chronicle history of King Leir (earliest known edition); 1605. 602
True enjoyment of angling; Phillips; 1843. 89
True tragedie of Richarde Duke of Yorke; Shakespeare; 2d edition, 1600. 586
Trusler, John. Proverbs exemplified, and illustrated by pictures from real life; London, 1790. 125
Tuckerman, Henry T. Book of the artists; N. Y., 1867. 739
Twenty Roman Cæsars, History of; Herodian; 1629. 391
Two drovers, The; Scott; 1st edition, 1827. *in* 549
Two noble kinsmen; sole edition; London, 1634. 634
Twyne, Thomas, *and* Thomas Phaer, *translators.* VIRGILIUS. The XIII. bookes of Æneidos; 1st edition, 1584. 509

UNCOMMERCIAL traveller; Dickens; 1st edition, 1861. 358
Universal angler; Walton, Cotton, *and* Venables; 1676. 39

VANITY FAIR; Thackeray; 1st edition, 1st issue, 1848. 699
Venables, Robert. Experienc'd angler; 1st edition; London, 1662. 67
  — *same;* 4th edition; London, 1676. *in* 39
Vicar of Wakefield. Goldsmith; 1st edition, 1766. 384
  — *same;* 1817. 385
  — *same;* Roscoe's Novelist's Library; 1832. *in* 267
Village coquettes; Dickens; 1st edition, 1836. 320
Virgilius Maro, Publius. The XIII. bukes of Eneados; translated by Gawin Douglas; 1st edition; London, 1553.

Vol. I., Nos. 1-416; II., 417-748.

VIRGILIUS   *Index*   WHOM

Virgilius Maro, Publius (*continued*). The XIII. bookes of Æneidos; translated by Thomas Phaer *and* Thomas Twyne; 1st edition; London, 1584.   509
Virginians, The; Thackeray; 1st edition, 1858–59.   720

WALTON, Izaak. Compleat angler; 1st edition; London, 1653.   33
— *same* (Bagster's reprint); 1810.   34
— *same*; 2d edition; London, 1655.   35
— *same*; 3d edition; London, 1661.   36
— *same*; 4th edition; London, 1668.   37
— *same*; 5th edition; London, 1676.   38
    See (for later editions) Walton, Izaak, *and* Charles Cotton.
Life of Dr. Sanderson; London, 1678.   744
Lives of Donne, Wotton, Hooker, and Herbert; 1st collected edition; London, 1670.   740
Lives of Donne, Wotton, Hooker, Herbert, and Sanderson; York, 1796.   741
— *same*; London, 1825.   742
— *same*; London, 1827.   743
Walton, Izaak:
    NICOLAS. Memoirs of Izaak Walton and Charles Cotton; 1836.   113
    ZOUCH. Life of Isaac Walton; 1823.   110
— *same*; 1824.   111
— *same*; 1826.   112
Walton, Izaak, *and* Charles Cotton. Compleat angler; Walton's 5th and Cotton's 1st edition; London, 1676.   38
— *same.*   *in* 39
— *same*; Bagster's 1st edition (4to), 1808.   48
— *same* (medium 8vo).   49
— *same*; Bagster's 2d edition, 1815.   50
— *same*; Bethune's 1st edition; N. Y. *and* London, 1847.   62
— *same*; Bethune's 2d edition; N. Y., 1880.   65
— *same*; Browne's 1st edition; London, 1750.   40
— *same*; Browne's 2d edition; London, 1759.   41
— *same*; Browne's 3d edition; London, 1772.   43
— *same*; Causton's edition; London, 1851.   63
— *same*; Gosden's edition, 1822.   51
— *same*; Hawkins' 1st edition; London, 1760.   42
— *same* (reprint); Chiswick, 1824.   54
— *same*; Hawkins' 3d edition; London, 1775.   44
— *same*; Hawkins' 4th edition; London, 1784.   45
— *same*; Hawkins' 5th edition, 2d issue; London, 1792.   46
— *same*; Hawkins' 6th edition; London, 1797.   47
— *same* (reprint); London, 1826.   56

Walton, Izaak, *and* Charles Cotton (*continued*). Compleat angler; Hawkins' 7th and Bagster's 1st edition (4to); London, 1808.   48
— *same* (medium 8vo).   49
— *same*; Hawkins' 8th and Bagster's 2d edition; London, 1815.   50
— *same*; Hawkins' 9th or Gosden's edition; London, 1822.   51
— *same*; Hawkins' 11th edition (reprint); London, 1825.   55
— *same*; Hawkins-Rennie edition; London, 1836.   59
— *same*; Lea and Dove edition; London, 1888.   66
— *same*; Major's 1st edition; London, 1823.   52
— *same*; Major's 2d edition; London, 1824.   53
— *same*; Major's 3d edition (reprint); London, 1839.   60
— *same*; Major's 4th edition; London, 1844.   61
— *same* (reprint); Boston, 1866.   64
— *same*; Marston's Lea and Dove edition; London, 1888.   66
— *same*; Pickering's 2d edition; London, 1826.   57
— *same*; Pickering's 3d edition; London, 1836.   58
— *same*; Rennie's edition, 1836.   59
Walton, Izaak, Charles Cotton, *and* Robert Venables. Universal angler; Walton's 5th, Cotton's 1st, and Venables' 4th edition; London, 1676.   39
Waverley; or, 'Tis sixty years since; Scott; 1st edition, 1814.   530
Wells, Henry P. Fly-rods and fly-tackle; N. Y., 1885.   105
Westmacott, Charles M. The English spy; London, 1825–26.   308
Westwood, Thomas. Chronicle of the "Compleat Angler"; London, 1864.   114
Westwood, Thomas, *and* Thomas Satchell. Chronicle of the "Compleat Angler" (reprint); London, 1888.   *in* 66
What Christmas is, as we grow older; Dickens; 1851.   *in* 347
White, Henry Kirke. Poetical works; Aldine edition; London, 1853.   *in* 195
White, James. Original letters, etc., of Sir John Falstaff; 1st edition; London, 1796.   419
Whitty, Michael J. Tales of Irish life; London, 1824.   250
Whole contention betweene the two famous houses, Lancaster and Yorke; Shakespeare; 3d edition, 1619.   585
Whom to marry and how to get married; Henry *and* A. S. Mayhew; 1st edition, 1848.   291

Vol. I., Nos. 1–416; II., 417–748.

Wight, John. Illustrations to Mornings at Bow Street; with short extracts; London, 1827. 252
— More mornings at Bow Street; London, 1827. 257
— Mornings at Bow Street; 2d edition; London, 1824. 251
— Sunday in London; London, 1833. 272
Wilson, Thomas. Catalogue raisonné of the select collection of engravings of an amateur; London, 1828. 259
Winsor, Justin. Bibliography of the original quartos and folios of Shakespeare; 1876. 644
Wits common wealth, Palladis tamia, Wits treasury, being the Second Part of; Meres; 1st edition, 1598. 637
Wits treasury, Palladis tamia; Meres; 1st edition, 1598. 637
Wivell, Abraham. Inquiry into the history, etc., of the Shakspeare portraits; London, 1827. 640
Wollstonecraft, *Mrs.* Mary. Original stories from real life; London, 1791. 745
Wood, Arnold. Bibliography of "The Complete Angler"; N. Y., 1900. 116
Wood engravings from a pretty book of pictures; Newcastle, 1779. 140
Woodstock; Scott; 1st edition, 1826. 548
Worde, Wynkyn de, *printer.* STANBRIDGE. Vocabula; 1520. 665
World's show, 1851; Henry Mayhew; 1851. 294
Wotton, *Sir* Henry:
  WALTON. Lives of Donne, Wotton, Hooker, and Herbert; 1670. 740
  — *same;* 1796. 741
  — *same;* 1825. 742
  — *same;* 1827. 743

Wreck of the Golden Mary; Dickens *and* Collins; 1856. *in* 347
Wyatt, *Sir* Thomas. Poetical works; Aldine edition; London, 1831. *in* 195
Wynne, John H. Tales for youth, in thirty poems; London, 1794. 126

YARRELL, William. History of British birds; London, 1843. 746
— *same;* Supplement; London, 1845. 747
— *same;* Second Supplement; London, 1856. 748
— History of British fishes; London, 1836. 85
— *same;* Supplement; London, 1839. 86
— *same;* Second Supplement; London, 1860. 87
Yates, Edmund. Mr. Thackeray, Mr. Yates, and the Garrick Club; London, 1859. 721
Yellowplush, Memoirs of Mr. Charles J.; Thackeray; 1856. 715
Yellowplush correspondence; Thackeray; 1st edition, 1838. 684
Yellowplush papers; Thackeray; 1841. *in* 693
Yorick, Mr., *pseudonym.* See Sterne, Laurence.
Yorkshire tragedy; 1st edition; London, 1608. 631
— *same;* 2d edition; London, 1619. 632
Young, Edward. Poetical works; Aldine edition, London, 1852. *in* 195

ZOUCH, Thomas. Life of Isaac Walton; London, 1823. 110
— *same;* London, 1824. 111
— *same;* London, 1826. 112
Zouch, Thomas, *editor.* WALTON. Lives of Donne, Wotton, Hooker, Herbert, and Sanderson; 1796. 741

Vol. I., Nos. 1-416; II., 417-748.

"*To the Christian Reader.* If you are troubled with a pride of accuracy, and would have it completely taken out of you, print a catalogue."— HENRY STEVENS, *My English Library* (1853), p. v.

"*To the Reader.* Who faulteth not, liueth not: who mendeth faults is commended: The Printer hath faulted a little: it may be the Author ouerfighted more. Thy paine (Reader) is the leafte; Then erre not thou moft by mifconftruing or by fharpe cenfuring; left thou be more vncharitable than either of them hath been heedleffe ı God amend and guide vs all." — FOULKE ROBARTES, *Treatife on Tythes* (1613), colophon.